Money,
the Financial System,
and Monetary Policy

Money, the Financial System, and Monetary Policy

FOURTH EDITION

Thomas F. Cargill
University of Nevada, Reno

Prentice-Hall, Inc., Englewood Cliffs, New Jersey   07632

Library of Congress Cataloging-in-Publication Data

Cargill, Thomas F.
    Money, the financial system, and monetary policy / Thomas F.
    Cargill. — 4th ed.
        p.   cm.
    Includes bibliographical references and index.
    ISBN 0-13-601410-0
    1. Finance. 2. Money. 3. Monetary policy. 4. Banks and banking.
    I. Title.
    HG173.C29   1991
    332—dc20   90-20179
                                                                    CIP

Editorial/production supervision: Lind Graphics Inc.
Interior design: Nancy Field
Cover design: Bruce Kenselaar
Prepress buyer: Trudy Pisciotti
Manufacturing buyer: Bob Anderson

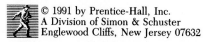

© 1991 by Prentice-Hall, Inc.
A Division of Simon & Schuster
Englewood Cliffs, New Jersey 07632

Printed in the United States of America
10 9 8 7 6 5 4 3 2 1

ISBN 0-13-601410-0

Prentice-Hall International (UK) Limited, *London*
Prentice-Hall of Australia Pty. Limited, *Sydney*
Prentice-Hall Canada Inc., *Toronto*
Prentice-Hall Hispanoamericana, S.A., *Mexico*
Prentice-Hall of India Private Limited, *New Delhi*
Prentice-Hall of Japan, Inc., *Tokyo*
Simon & Schuster Asia Pte. Ltd., *Singapore*
Editora Prentice-Hall do Brasil, Ltda., *Rio de Janeiro*

CONTENTS

ch 1,2,3(4+2-9)
69,15,16

PART I—BASIC COMPONENTS OF THE FINANCIAL AND MONETARY ENVIRONMENT OF THE U.S. ECONOMY, MONEY, THE FINANCE SYSTEM, AND INTEREST RATES

CHAPTER 1
The Student and Monetary Economics   3

Chapter 1 Boxes

CHAPTER 2
The Concept of Money   17

Chapter 2 Boxes

PART II—I.O.U'S IN THE FINANCIAL SYSTEM, BANKS, NONBANK FINANCIAL INSTITUTIONS, AND THE MONEY SUPPLY PROCESS

PART VI—THE FEDERAL RESERVE SYSTEM, INSTRUMENTS OF MONETARY POLICY, AND HOW THE FEDERAL RESERVE CONTROLS THE MONEY SUPPLY

CHAPTER **18**

The Structure of the Federal Reserve System   417

CHAPTER **19**

Depository Institution Reserves, The Reserve Equation, and the Monetary Base   439

CHAPTER **20**

The Instruments of Monetary Policy   461

PART VII—MONETARY POLICY AND MODELS OF THE ECONOMY: CLASSICAL, KEYNESIAN, AND EXTENSIONS

CHAPTER **21**
Framework for Stabilization
Policy   481

CHAPTER **22**
The Pre-Great Depression
Classical or Quantity
Theory View   488

CHAPTER **23**
The Basic Keynesian Model   506

Chapter 29 Boxes

Preface

The fourth edition of *Money, the Financial System, and Monetary Policy* is a complete revision of the third edition. This was necessary to capture the many new and different issues that have changed the content of financial and monetary economics courses. All but a few chapters are either extensively rewritten or new, chapter organization has been changed, and new supplements have been developed to aid the student's comprehension of financial and monetary issues. The book continues to focus on policy issues and theoretical material is developed only to a stage necessary to understand policy issues. Each chapter starts with an overview to help the student gain perspective on the specific material in each chapter. Each chapter ends with a list of key points, key terms, questions, and suggested readings. With the exception of the theory chapters, each chapter contains several items of boxed material relating to points raised in the chapter. Boxed material was omitted from the theory discussion so as not to distract from the flow of the material since students find this material frequently the most difficult.

A variety of supplements have been prepared to accompany the fourth edition. I have prepared a test bank of 1,740 true-false and multiple choice questions available on computer diskette. While not the most exciting job, I felt it necessary to maintain consistency between the book and questions that might be used in the classroom. Merwin Mitchell of the University of Nevada, Reno has prepared a student's guide, Joseph Fuhrig of Golden Gate University, San Francisco has prepared an instructor's manual and Prentice-Hall has prepared 100 transparencies of the most important tables and figures with at least two items selected from each chapter. I have also prepared a book of readings, *Readings on Money, the Financial System, and Monetary Policy*, containing 42 articles. The articles have been selected to correspond closely with the textbook, although the book of readings could be used by itself. The readings are recent and like the textbook, focused on policy issues regarding the financial system and monetary policy.

The Need for a Major Revision

An obvious question is why should I go to such an extent to revise the third edition. The basic reason is simple. I want the book to reflect current policy issues and the dynamic and rapid changes taking place in our financial and monetary environment simply require that any subsequent edition be more than a warmed over version of the previous edition.

As we enter the last decade of the twentieth century a whole new and different set of issues require attention in a monetary and financial economics course.

The following is a short list of important issues affecting the financial system that need to be addressed: growing concern about the stability of the financial system; deposit insurance and its "moral hazard" of risk incentives; the thrift problem and the massive sums of taxpayer money it will require; internationalization of finance and the growing presence of foreign financial institutions in the United States; continued risk exposure of large U.S. banks to third world or LDC debt; and massive external imbalances of the United States, especially with respect to Japan.

New and different issues affecting monetary policy also need to be considered. The theory underlying monetary policy has been extended in the 1980s in ways that differ fundamentally from the 1970s. At one time the monetarist-Keynesian debate occupied a major part of a monetary economics textbook; however, this is no longer necessary. Much of the debate is over and while models can still loosely be classified as either activist or nonactivist, economists and even some policy makers within the Federal Reserve have become less activist oriented compared to a decade ago. Economists have reached a consensus about the most important contribution monetary policy can make to economic stability. It is now widely accepted that price stability and on occasion, being a lender of last resort, represent the most meaningful and long lasting contributions of monetary policy. This is a major departure from not many years ago when economists and policy makers argued that monetary policy could "fine tune" the economy or change the underlying growth path of real GNP.

Economists are now more concerned about constraints which interfere with the central bank's ability to control inflation. Political influence is one problem and as a result, greater attention is now devoted to political business cycle models and to public choice views about how the Federal Reserve formulates monetary policy. Economists have come to recognize an even more difficult problem, referred to as time inconsistency, that generates an inflation bias to monetary policy. As a result a few economists argue discretionary power should be taken away from the central bank and monetary policy conducted according to a rules approach. Others argue that rules are not needed, however; monetary policy should take a less activist role and refrain from trying to offset every shock to the economy and focus more on long-run price stability.

This is dynamic and exciting material and the landscape is in a state of constant flux. A textbook writer must make the effort to incorporate these issues if he wants to provide the students with something that meaningfully contributes to their understanding of the financial and monetary environment. Every effort has been made to have the fourth edition meet this standard.

Organization of the Fourth Edition

Chapters are written to provide continuity of information; however, specific chapters can be omitted without adversely affecting the flow of discussion. The book is organized around 9 sections.

Part I (Chapters 1–5) lays out the basic elements of the financial system. Chapter 1 presents an overview of financial and monetary topics and how they relate to the individual. This introductory chapter is designed to motivate the student's interest in the subject. Chapter 2 discusses the concept of money, its measurement, and its relationship to economic activity. Chapter 3 presents the basic structure of the financial system in terms of flow of funds concepts and an appendix to the chapter presents the official flow of funds matrix for 1988. Chapter 4 discusses basic considerations about interest rates, how they are reported, and the difference between the interest rate and total return of a financial asset. Chapter 5 completes the introductory section on the financial system by reviewing the determinants of the interest rate and the structure of interest rates.

Part II (Chapters 6 through 10) provides detailed information regarding financial markets, instruments, institutions, and the money supply process. Chapter 6 reviews the major types of financial institutions, different types of financial instruments, and the securitization process. Chapters 7 and 8 focus on the individual commercial bank and the banking industry, respectively. The two chapters devoted to commercial banks reflect their major role in the financial system. Chapter 9 discusses a wide variety of nonbank financial institutions and introduces the student to the unique portfolio problems of the thrift industry. Chapter 10 presents a discussion of the money supply process, develops a framework to highlight the determinants of the money supply, and discusses the necessary conditions for Federal Reserve control over the money supply.

Part III (Chapters 11 through 14) focuses on financial regulation, deregulation, and the thrift problem. Chapter 11 discusses the rationale for government regulation of the financial system, the evolution of financial regulation, and the current structure of financial regulation. The role of the banking collapse during the Great Depression is emphasized in the evolution of financial regulation. Chapter 12 outlines the functions of the financial system and develops a taxonomy to illustrate why and how financial reform occurs. The taxonomy is used to highlight the catalysts that arose in the 1970s that induced financial innovation and regulation reform. Chapter 13 focuses on the regulatory responses to the forces for financial change. Specifically, this chapter summarizes major policy events that took place from October 1979 through October 1982 such as the Deregulation and Monetary Control Act of 1980 and how they have changed the structure of the U.S. financial system. Chapter 14 reviews the accomplishments and failures of financial reform and focuses attention on the thrift problem. The thrift problem is presented in historical perspective and the most recent policy event—the Financial Institutions Reform, Recovery, and Enforcement Act of August 1989 or FIRREA—is evaluated in detail.

Part IV (Chapters 15 and 16) focus on international issues. Chapter 15 discusses the statement of international transactions, foreign exchange rates, and exchange rate regimes. Chapter 16 summarizes recent changes in the world financial system that have greatly increased capital mobility, interest rate differentials among countries, external currency markets, and discusses important institutions in the international flow of funds. This chapter also discusses two major international problems that are likely to continue into the 1990s: external imbalances between the United States and the rest of the world and third world or LDC debt.

Part V consists of an introductory chapter (Chapter 17) which illustrates the role of monetary (and other government policies) in efforts to stabilize the economy. The chapter reviews the major goals of economic stabilization, indicators of economic performance, and the evolution of attitudes about the role of government stabilization from the pre-Great Depression classical views to the post-Great Depression activist views associated with the Keynesian model. The chapter ends with recent issues raised about the activist approach.

Part VII (Chapters 18 through 20) discusses the Federal Reserve System and how the Federal Reserve controls the money supply. Chapter 18 presents the basic structure of the Federal Reserve, discusses the nonmonetary policy responsibilities of the Federal Reserve, and reviews the issues regarding the independence of the Federal Reserve from government. Chapter 19 presents the important financial statements of the Federal Reserve that reveal how the Federal Reserve influences reserves available to depository institutions and hence, how the Federal Reserve influences credit, interest rates, and the money supply. Chapter 20 discusses the major policy instruments of the Federal Reserve and evaluates their relative effectiveness.

Part VIII (Chapters 21 through 26) reviews the major models of the economy and their indicated role for stabilization policy in general, and monetary policy in particular. Chapter 21 is a short introduction to develop the concept of an economic model and to briefly review the evolution of monetary policy models. Chapter 22 presents the classical or quantity theory model and the reasons for its downfall during the Great Depression period. Chapter 23 presents the basic outline of the Keynesian model in a partial equilibrium setting with prices and wages held constant while Chapter 24 extends the Keynesian model to the general equilibrium case with *IS* and *LM* functions. This chapter also introduces the concepts of aggregate demand and supply and discusses the implications of relaxing the rigid price and wage assumption. Chapter 25 discusses the reemergence of the classical model in the form of monetarism and summarizes the monetarist-Keynesian debate. Chapter 26 reviews new developments of monetary models organized into three categories: neo-classical which includes monetarism, neo-Keynesian, and political economy models. The chapter also offers reasons to help the student understand why there are so many models used to describe the economy despite the availability of extensive data bases, powerful computers, and high-powered statistical modelling capabilities.

Part IX (Chapters 27 through 29) is the last component of the book and focuses on a variety of issues regarding the formulation and conduct of monetary policy. Chapter 27 discusses Federal Reserve operations, how they have evolved over the past several decades, and issues regarding the use of interest rates or monetary aggregates as intermediate targets. Chapter 28 introduces the rules versus authorities debate, lags in the effect of monetary policy, and time inconsistency. Chapter 29 focuses on the effects of inflation, the relationship between inflation and the money supply, and problems central banks have in maintaining a noninflationary monetary growth rate.

A Note of Appreciation

I owe much gratitude to a number of individuals who have helped with the fourth edition. In particular, I would like to thank Andrea L. DeMaskey, Katrina Dorman, Thomas Gooch, Michael Hutchison, Thomas Mayer, Merwin Mitchell, Linda Nordvig, and C. Daniel Vencill for either reading chapters or discussing issues that permitted me to develop specific points. I would also like to thank those who contributed to the production of the fourth edition: two Prentice-Hall editors—William Webber and Whitney Blake and the production editor—Robert Tebbenhoff. Finally and ultimately most important, I would like to thank my wife, Mary, for support and encouragement during this project.

PART I

Basic Components of the Financial and Monetary Environment of the U.S. Economy: Money, the Financial System, and Interest Rates

CHAPTER 1

The Student and Monetary Economics

Chapter Overview

This chapter offers a rationale to the sometimes reluctant student of money and banking as to why he or she should be interested in monetary economics beyond the obvious reason of eliminating one more requirement placed in the student's path toward graduation.

Few individuals go through life without being touched by the financial and monetary environment. Even when people think that their lives are largely immune to the issues discussed in this book, on close inspection, they find that their lives are often strongly influenced by financial and monetary issues. In fact, our interaction with the monetary environment has become even more important and complicated because of major changes in the structure of the financial system caused by deregulation and financial innovation. We deal with a far more complex set of financial assets and services than in the past. This complexity comes not only from the domestic side, but from an increasingly internationalized financial environment.

At a more general level, we are bombarded with news about interest rates, exchange rates, bank failures, the thrift problem, deposit insurance, the government deficit, the trade deficit, the money supply, the Board of Governors, the Federal Reserve, and a host of other manifestations of the financial and monetary environment.

We need to keep abreast of these financial changes and issues not only because we should remain knowledgeable about the environment surrounding us, but because, from a self-interest perspective, these changes and issues together influence the cost of our borrowing, the return on our deposits, the prices we pay for goods and services, and sometimes even our jobs.

Why Study Monetary Economics?

This question presupposes a working definition of monetary economics. Monetary economics concerns the nature, functions, and influence of money, credit, and the financial system on employment, output, prices, and interactions with the world economy. The subject of monetary economics is vast and encompasses many components. The following lists merely a few:

1. The role of money, financial institutions, and markets in the economy.

2. International finance, exchange rates, and determinants of the flow of goods, services, and financial assets between the United States and the rest of the world.

3. How the financial system influences employment, output, and prices.

4. The changing structure of the financial system, deregulation, financial innovation, and the growing internationalization of finance.

5. The role of the government as a regulator of financial institutions and markets and the type of government regulation that will lead to an efficient, adaptable, and sound financial system.

6. The role of fiscal policy (government spending and taxation) and monetary policy (changes in money, interest rates, and credit) in stabilizing the economy.

7. The various models of economic behavior and whether they view the market system as inherently stable or unstable and what type of government actions will most effectively contribute to the goals of economic stabilization: full employment, price stability, economic growth, and balance in our external relationships with the rest of the world.

8. The structure of the Federal Reserve System and how the Federal Reserve conducts monetary policy to achieve the goals of economic stabilization.

9. The interaction between political institutions and the conduct of stabilization policy. Specifically, is the Federal Reserve and monetary policy independent of government and, if not, what are the consequences?

10. Should monetary policy (and fiscal policy) take an activist or nonactivist role in the economy. Are there inherent limits to the ability of monetary policy to influence the economy?

11. The causes and effects of inflation and the role played by monetary policy to achieve a noninflationary growth path of the economy consistent with the economy's resource base.

12. The impact of government deficits on the financial system and the economy.

These and other topics make up the study of monetary economics. It is designed to provide the student with the institutional and analytical tools necessary to understand monetary economics. The bottom line or basic objective of the book is to make the student a more knowledgeable and critical observer of the financial and monetary environment of the U.S. economy. Specifically, this book is designed to make the student a critical and knowledgeable reader of *The Wall Street Journal* and other prominent business publications as well as a critical and knowledgeable observer of the political discussions about government stabilization policy in general and monetary policy in particular.

The question naturally arises: Why study monetary economics beyond merely getting through another obstacle placed in the path of students by uncaring college administrators? Of the many reasons, four appear especially important.

First, the subject is inherently interesting in its own right. Among other things, we gain insight into the nature and function of financial institutions and markets, the conduct of monetary policy, the impact of government deficits on the financial system, the relationship between exchange rates and interest rates, and other similar issues. These are intellectually interesting issues in their own right, and while knowledge of these issues cannot guarantee financial success, the study of monetary economics will definitely increase our knowledge about a number of important issues and concepts that we encounter every day.

Second, some of the most heated controversies of our time center on the stability of the financial system, bank failures, thrift institutions, interest rates, exchange rates, government deficits, trade deficits, and inflation. A minimal knowledge of monetary economics is a prerequisite for our comprehension of the significant debates of our time. The outcome of these debates will surely influence our jobs, the ability of our income to purchase goods and services, the overall quality of our lives, and the role of the United States in the world economy.

Third, monetary policy has come to be regarded as the most important instrument of government stabilization in the United States as well as in other countries of the world. Monetary policy has profound effects on our lives and, hence, deserves greater understanding by the educated individual. One encounters on an almost daily basis references to the Federal Reserve, the Board of Governors, the discount rate, or open market operations. These are not mere technical issues that have little impact on our lives. The conduct of monetary policy influences how much interest you will pay on the next loan you request, how much the next car will cost, and your employment prospects.

Fourth, monetary economics now plays a more important role in the rhetoric of politicians than ever before. This reflects the growing complexity of the financial system, the increasing internationalization of finance, and the major role that monetary policy plays in the economy. Whether running for office or already in office, politicians concern themselves with issues of monetary economics. They take credit for favorable outcomes, shift the blame to others for unfavorable outcomes, or argue that if their economic policies were being followed, the situation would be more favorable. Sometimes politicians have a good grasp of the issues; more frequently, their views are fundamentally flawed. The limited ability of the voting public to understand economic and monetary issues will ultimately weaken our democratic institutions. A public largely ignorant of important issues regarding government economic policy makes bad public policy possible. Thus, the study of monetary economics will provide a better basis to judge the merits of various positions with respect to the economy. Politicians are frequently criticized for vagueness, double-talk, or just plain stupidity on many issues regarding monetary economics—but in all honesty, it's the lack of understanding about basic monetary economics by the public that permits such behavior.

Monetary Economics in Transition

The subject of monetary economics has undergone much change during the past several decades, but the last decade has witnessed a major acceleration in the rate of change. New issues and concerns have emerged in the past decade that render many previous efforts to survey the field out of date. Financial and monetary economics have become one of the most difficult teaching assignments because of this rapid change in issues and concepts—writing a textbook for the subject has become even more difficult as a result. To gain some insight into the rapid change of monetary economics as a subject, let us consider the transitional features of monetary policy and the financial system.

The Evolution of Monetary Policy

The role of monetary policy reflects our views of money, how money influences economic activity, and whether the market system is inherently stable or unstable. Attitudes toward these issues have evolved over four distinct periods:

1 Pre-1930s Great Depression
2 Great Depression to early 1960s
3 The 1960s to late 1970s
4 Late 1970s to the present

Let us briefly discuss each of the four periods.

Starting from the development of economics in the late 1700s through just prior to the Great Depression, money was regarded as a necessary foundation for understanding the economy. The most widely held view about money and the economy was referred to as the *quantity theory of money*, which itself stood at the center of the *classical model* of the economy.

The quantity theory and classical model regarded the economy as inherently stable and as long as competitive conditions existed, market forces would ensure the economy would operate at full employment and achieve an efficient allocation of resources. Flexible wage and price adjustments would ensure that full employment would be maintained over the long run, and if the economy were pushed away from full employment for any reason, flexible wage and price adjustments would return it to full employment. Since total spending or aggregate demand would always be sufficient to generate full employment, classical economists were concerned with encouraging the greatest supply of goods and services that could be produced from a given resource base; hence, the origin of the term *supply-side economics*. Government played a minimal role in the classical view that was primarily limited to providing a system of laws to protect private property, providing national defense and other goods that the private market was unable to supply, and providing a *stable financial and monetary environment*.

The stable financial and monetary framework was the responsibility of the central bank. Specifically, the central bank was responsible for generating a steady growth of money and credit to meet the needs of trade and economic growth at stable prices and to ensure the soundness of the financial system. Government budgets should be balanced. Thus, there was government stabilization in the classical model, but it was clearly *nonactivist* in the sense that it did not react to the state of the economy since the economy was viewed as inherently stable and needing little direction from government.

The next period—Great Depression to the early 1960s—saw the rejection of the quantity theory of money and the classical model by most economists and policymakers. The Great Depression fundamentally changed attitudes about money, monetary policy, and the economy. The failure of the Federal Reserve to prevent the depression or to reduce its severity after it started suggested that money and monetary policy were not very important for understanding how the economy worked. The depression itself with the collapse of the banking system along with the severest decline in economic activity ever experienced in the United States destroyed faith in the view that the economy was inherently stable and always functioned to generate full employment over the long run.

This set the stage for the *Keynesian revolution* based on ideas expressed by John Maynard Keynes in the *General Theory of Employment, Interest, and Money* in 1936. The Keynesians argued that the economy was inherently unstable and, in fact, could easily reach an equilibrium with substantial amounts of unemployment. Automatic wage and price adjustments could not be relied upon, and even if they did work in the long run, "We are all dead in the long run."

The key to understanding economic activity was in understanding what determined total spending or aggregate demand. While money and monetary policy could influence aggregate demand, other factors were far more important. Private aggregate demand was subject to wide swings and could be insufficient to maintain full employment. In this environment, government had both the responsibility and the ability to influence the pace of economic activity. Aggregate demand could be influenced by monetary policy; however, Keynesians during this period regarded fiscal policy as a far more effective policy instrument.

Hence, Keynesian economics introduced the concept *demand-side economics* and *aggregate demand management.* Keynesian economics was clearly *activist* in the sense that government should take actions in response to the state of the economy. Keynesian views dominated professional thinking until the early 1960s. At that time, a group of economists commonly referred to as *monetarists* challenged the Keynesian view on a number of key points. The term "monetarists," or the concept of monetarism, is far too narrow to classify these individuals; however, the term has come to be widely accepted.

It is important to understand that the monetarist view was essentially a restatement of the quantity theory and the classical model involving a more acceptable theoretical basis and supported by an extensive program of empirical research to test the predictions of the classical and Keynesian models. Much of the discussion that took place in the 1960s and 1970s is referred to as the *monetarist-Keynesian* debate.

The Keynesian view was challenged on two fronts. First, the Keynesian view that money and monetary policy were relatively unimportant was rejected. Even in the Keynesian model monetary policy emerged as the most important policy instrument while at the same time, fiscal policy was regarded as less effective than monetary policy. In this regard, the view that monetary policy did everything it could to stimulate the economy during the Great Depression was rejected. In fact, the monetarist argued that the Federal Reserve had actually conducted *tight* rather than easy *monetary policy, and as a result, much of the decline in the economy could be laid at the feet of the Federal Reserve.* Second, the Keynesian view that the market was inherently unstable and prone to unemployment equilibrium was rejected. The economy had a strong tendency to grow at a rate determined by the economy's resource base referred to as the *natural growth rate of output*. At this rate of output growth, labor markets would be in equilibrium, and unemployment would be at the so-called *natural unemployment rate*.

Monetarists argued that, in large part, economic fluctuations were the result of activist policies that on balance did more harm than good. In particular, they argued that efforts by central banks to manage the economy and the lack of concern with the money supply were primary reasons for observed economic fluctuations and not inherent market instability, as claimed by Keynesians.

The monetarist-Keynesian debate is over and economists have reached a consensus on a number of issues; however, debate still continues over how the economy functions and what role government stabilization policy should play to ensure achievement of the goals of economic stabilization.

The end of the debate brings us to the fourth and current stage of the discussion about money, monetary policy, and the economy, which is essentially a debate over *activist versus nonactivist* government stabilization policy, primarily monetary policy. What are the characteristics of the current period?

First, all sides of the debate regard monetary policy as a powerful, if not the most powerful, instrument of government stabilization. The earlier Keynesian argument that fiscal policy is a flexible and powerful instrument has few advocates today.

Second, all sides of the debate regard the classical model and the Keynesian model as the two polar models for understanding how the economy functions and the proper role for monetary policy and other forms of government stabilization. However, the Keynesian model is now regarded as a long-run full-employment model in the sense that eventually market forces will ensure that output and employment grow at rates determined by the economy's resource base. At the same time, Keynesians continue to emphasize instability, price and wage rigidities, and other forces that interfere with the ability of the economy to return to normal long-run equilibrium smoothly and rapidly. Thus, economists in the classical and Keynesian tradition now have similar long-run views of the equilibrium of the market system; however, they continue to differ over the shorter-run performance of the economy and the role of monetary policy.

Third, the two foundation models have been extended in a number of ways. The neoclassical and neo-Keynesian models are theoretically richer than are the traditional models; however, they retain their respective fundamental views of the economy and the role of government. The most important extensions involve the role of information and how information about future actions of the monetary authority influence current economic decisions. The role of information in modeling has revealed fundamental problems about the conduct of monetary policy irrespective of whether one adopts an activist or nonactivist perspective.

Fourth, economists have turned their attention during this period to understanding the institutional aspects of monetary policy. Specifically, they focus on a wide range of incentives influencing monetary policy that may interfere with the ability of the central bank to contribute to economic stability. Specifically, there is increasing interest in understanding how political institutions influence monetary policy.

Fifth, while economists can still be placed in the activist or nonactivist camp, the distinction has become much less sharp than it was during the monetarist-Keynesian debate period of the 1970s. While the nonactivist are about as nonactivist as they have always been, the activist group has become less activist. This has occurred for a variety of reasons. The majority of economists accept the premise that monetary policy cannot significantly change the long-run performance of the economy and now accept the argument that price stability is the primary responsibility of the central bank. In addition, the role of the central bank as a *lender of last* resort to ensure the stability of the financial system is now recognized as critically important by all economists. And even though an argument can be made for activist monetary policy in the short run, economists now have a greater understanding of the difficulty of achieving effective discretionary monetary policy. Thus, the activist of the 1990s is considerably less activist than even a decade ago.

The Transition of the Financial System or "Deregulation"

The past decade has witnessed major changes in the financial arrangements of the United States referred to as *deregulation*. The transition has been characterized by the removal or relaxation of constraints on the financial system that had previously limited competitive behavior; hence, the term deregulation. Thus, the financial system is in transition from rigidly regulated to a more flexible structure in which the competitive forces play an increasingly important role in allocating credit. The transition has been manifested by the removal of interest rate ceilings on the majority of deposits, increased competition between different financial institutions and markets, and the introduction of a host of new financial services and assets. In addition, the financial transition has required the Federal Reserve to reevaluate the way it conducts monetary policy as well as imposed new responsibilities on the structure and content of government financial regulation to ensure a stable and sound financial government.

The transition of financial and monetary arrangements currently underway reveals several elements:

1. The transition was initiated by a series of conflicts between an economic environment that emerged in the 1970s and the then existing rigidly controlled and regulated financial system. The new economic environment was characterized by inflation, high and uncertain interest rates, discrete shifts in economic growth, discrete shifts in established flow of funds patterns, and increased world trade and financial integration. In particular, the high rates of inflation in the 1970s and early 1980s rendered many financial regulations binding and interfered with the flow of funds between borrowers and lenders. As a result, the financial system failed to satisfy its basic responsibilities of providing an efficient transfer of funds from lenders to borrowers, of being adaptable to the changing needs of the economy, and of being stable and sound.

2. The rapid application of computer technology to financial transactions enhanced the ability of market participants to introduce new financial assets and services, which in turn, played a key role in the market's ability to circumvent binding government regulations on portfolio behavior. This activity is referred to as *financial innovation*.

BOX 1   Importance of the Federal Reserve and monetary policy

The Federal Reserve is the central bank of the United States and has responsibility for monetary policy. This involves providing a sufficient monetary growth rate to support the needs of a growing economy while simultaneously ensuring price stability. In addition, the Federal Reserve plays an important role in maintaining stability and public confidence in the financial system. Two recent examples can be used to emphasize the importance of the Federal Reserve and monetary policy.

Failure and Success of Federal Reserve Policy in Controlling Inflation   Inflation was a serious problem in the 1970s. The inflation rate gradually accelerated from about 5% in the late 1960s to almost 14% in 1980 (Figure 1B). While oil price increases in 1974–75 and 1979–80 played some role in the inflation process, the failure of the Federal Reserve to restrain monetary growth during the 1970s is regarded as the source of the inflationary process. There are many reasons for this failure, some not under the control of the Federal Reserve. Aside from the source of inflation, its impact on the U.S. economy was severe. Fluctuations in the inflation rate around an upward trending core inflation adversely impacted economic growth, reduced productivity growth, induced recessions, and set into motion a set of forces that made the financial system increasingly unstable and inefficient throughout the 1970s. In fact, many of the problems still plaguing the U.S. financial system such as the large number of insolvent thrift institutions had their beginning in the inflationary 1970s.

The inflation and unstable financial conditions reached a crisis situation in 1979. Dramatic action was needed. The Federal Reserve in 1979 under the leadership of the newly appointed chair of the Board of Governors, Paul Volker, changed operating procedures and strategy and launched an all-out effort to bring inflation under control and reestablish itself as a credible central bank that could be counted on to maintain price stability. The inflation rate was lowered from double-digit levels to about 4% in 1982, however, not without cost. To break the inflation psychology, the Federal Reserve induced a short, but sharp, recession that saw the employment rate go above 10%—a level not experienced since the Great Depression of the 1930s.

Monetary policy has done a much better job in the 1980s compared to the previous decade in controlling inflation. Allan Greenspan, the new chairman of the Board in 1987, made it clear that the Federal Reserve would continue to pursue the goal of price stability. The Federal Reserve continues to be the target of criticism from a wide range of economists, however, monetary policy has played a far greater role in stabilizing the U.S. economy in the past decade than it did in the 1970s.

Federal Reserve as Lender of Last Resort   A traditional role of a central bank is to be a lender of last resort when depository institutions are experiencing deposit outflows or other adverse conditions that threaten to involve more than a few institutions. The financial system consists of a complex network of markets and institutions that relies heavily on public confidence to function properly. Failure in one part of the system can spread if liquidity is not made available on short order. Central banks have the ability to create liquidity because they have ultimate control over the money supply.

On at least two occasions in the 1980s the Federal Reserve played an important role in supporting the financial system. In 1984 the Federal Reserve provided over $5 billion in funds in a one-week period to Continental Illinois, the seventh largest bank in the United States, to ensure that it would not collapse and bring down other banks. In October 1987, the stock market crashed. In one day—Black Monday—the Dow Jones industrial average fell 508 points and the value of stocks declined 22%. To ensure that the market decline would not spread and threaten other financial markets and banks, the Federal Reserve publicly announced its willingness to provide whatever funds were needed to ensure financial stability. This action was an important reason why the 1987 stock market crash did not spread and did not generate a recession.

These two examples illustrate the important role played by monetary policy and should offer some motivation to find out more about the Federal Reserve. In fact, the Federal Reserve and monetary policy have even hit the best-sellers list.

William Greider's *Secrets of the Temple: How the Federal Reserve Runs the Country* (New York: Simon & Schuster, 1987) received extensive press coverage and was on the best-seller list for several months in 1987. This 700-plus-page book has nothing to do with the intimate personal lives of those who work at the

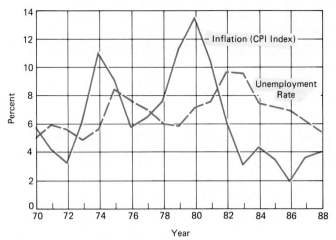

Source: Data from Citicorp Database Services.

FIGURE 1B   Inflation and unemployment in the
United States, 1970–1988

Federal Reserve or is a fictionalized account of the Federal Reserve with heavy doses of sex and violence. Rather, it is a book about monetary policy and those who conducted monetary policy from the late 1970s through the few months after the October 1987 stock market crash.

Greider's book is worth reading for the insights it provides about recent Federal Reserve decision making, even though many economists have criticized the book on a number of accounts. The book was reviewed in *The New York Times*, January 21 1988 (page 21), in *The New York Times Book Review*, January 17, 1988 (page 7), and by Brian Motley, "Temple Secrets," Federal Reserve Bank of San Francisco, *Weekly Letter*, June 17, 1988.

The fact that a book on monetary policy could attract the amount of attention that it has and the fact that the book was a best-seller, right up there with the self-help books, suggests that the subject of monetary economics has come of age!

3. Conflicts between the market and the regulatory authorities have become more frequent and intense. Financial innovations designed to circumvent binding constraints frustrated the regulatory authority's efforts to limit portfolio behavior. As a result, regulatory authorities often redefined the regulatory parameters to limit financial innovation; however, the market frequently reinnovated. The regulatory-market conflict became so intense in the United States that the process has been characterized in terms of a Hegalian regulatory-market dialectic.[1]

4. The new economic environment, market innovations, regulatory-market conflict, and regulatory changes have increased the role of competition in the allocation of credit.

5. Two important feedback relationships have become apparent during the transition. There is a feedback relationship between financial reform and monetary policy. The changing financial structure requires a reevaluation of how monetary policy is

[1] Edward J. Kane, "Accelerating Inflation, Technological Innovation, and the Decreasing Effectiveness of Banking Regulation," *Journal of Finance*, 36 (May 1981), 355–367.

conducted and the ability/willingness of the monetary authority to maintain price stability and determine the environment in which financial reform occurred. There is a feedback relationship between the structure of financial regulation and the reform process. The structure of regulation (multiple or few regulatory authorities and legislatively or administratively enforced regulation) influences the character of the reform process, which in turn, imposes new requirements on the regulatory structure.

6. The transition of finance is neither unique nor novel to the United States. The past decade has witnessed major changes in the financial and monetary arrangements of both developing and developed countries. Despite differences with regard to historical development pattern, social/political/economic institutions, and stages of economic development, a number of countries are experiencing a major transition in their financial systems from rigidly regulated and administratively controlled to more flexible structures in which competitive forces play an increasingly important role in allocating credit. As a result, there has occurred a convergence of different financial systems and a more integrated world financial system.

The financial reform process in the United States has yet to be completed. It is still in progress. The administration, Congress, and regulatory authorities in the 1990s continue to deal with a variety of issues raised by the financial transition. Let us briefly review the major policy events that have been part of the reform process.

Major Policy Events: October 1979, February 1980, March 1980, October 1982, and August 1989

These policy events reflect efforts to deal with structural problems in the financial system and monetary policy that became apparent in the 1970s. While they have significantly changed the financial system and the conduct of monetary policy, they represent a less than complete solution to the problems. They can be categorized in terms of whether they were directed toward restructuring the financial system or directed toward monetary policy issues.

Restructuring the Financial System

In this regard, the most significant of the policy events is the *Depository Institutions Deregulation and Monetary Control Act of 1980 or* the Deregulation and Monetary Control Act. This is the most important piece of financial reform and monetary control legislation since the passage of the financial reform legislation of the 1930s in the wake of the collapse of the banking system during the Great Depression. The act has exerted a fundamental change on the structure of the financial system, the competitive positions of various types of depository institutions, and the types of financial services offered to the public. The 1980 act, however, was not sufficient to deal with the problems of the structurally unsound financial system, and in October 1982, the *Garn-St Germain Depository Institutions Act of 1982*, or Garn-St Germain Act, was passed, which made further changes in the financial system.

The 1980 and 1982 acts were concerned with a wide range of reform issues; however, both acts devoted special attention to the condition of the *thrift* industry, which consists of savings and loan associations (S&Ls) and saving banks. S&Ls and savings banks are similar in that they have traditionally allocated a large part of their loan portfolio to residential mortgages. S&Ls represent both the major part of the thrift industry (83 percent of thrift assets in 1988) and the major source of the thrift problem. Thus, one will encounter references to the problem as a "thrift problem or crisis" and as a "S&L problem or crisis"; however, both refer to the same situation.

In the 1970s the thrift industry was under siege. S&Ls and savings banks were subject to intense periods of disintermediation as funds were withdrawn and transferred to open money markets to earn market-determined returns. Their limited portfolio flexibility in terms of both uses and sources of funds prevented them from competing in an increasingly competitive and flexible financial environment. The 1980 and 1982 acts sought to correct the problem by removing deposit rate ceilings and providing thrifts (as well as other depository institutions) with enhanced diversification powers. Unfortunately, the situation only intensified for the thrifts. The condition of the thrift industry deteriorated steadily, and by 1985, almost 500 of the 3,000 thrifts were insolvent and another 800 were financially weak by any reasonable standard. These some 1,300 thrifts represented about 43 % of the total thrift assets. At the same time, the federal deposit insurance fund for thrifts, the Federal Savings and Loan Insurance Deposit Corporation was *insolvent* itself since it had insufficient reserves to bail out even a small percentage of the insolvent thrifts.

It became apparent that additional changes directed at both thrifts and banks would be required and that efforts to deal with the large number of insolvent thrift institutions would require a massive taxpayer bailout. As a result, the *Financial Institutions Reform, Recovery, and Enforcement Act* (FIRREA) was passed August 1989 to become the most recent policy event influencing the financial system. The 1989 act introduces major changes in how thrifts are regulated and imposes new requirements on banks. To restructure the thrift insurance fund and finance liquidations of insolvent thrifts, the act contemplated a total bill of $166 billion over a ten year period, most of which will be provided by taxpayers.

This is not the last word. The act, for example, mandates a broad study of federal deposit insurance that might become the basis for additional legislation in the early 1990s, and more important, the act has not solved the thrift problem. Less than one year after the 1989 act, the cost of dealing with troubled thrifts has already far exceeded projections, and many critics point out that the act failed to deal with fundamental issues that created the thrift problem in the first place.

Changes in the Conduct of Monetary Policy

In this regard, four major changes have taken place. In October 1979, the Federal Reserve announced a fundamental shift in operating procedures designed to enhance its control over the money supply and improve its ability to bring inflation under

BOX 2   Why you should be concerned about the financial system: deposit insurance and the thrift problem

The financial system and public policy issues related to its regulation were once regarded as dull and largely irrelevant to the daily lives of most people. While there may be disagreement over whether the issues are dull, there can be little debate about their impact on our lives or the interest that the public has recently shown toward these issues.

There has been a major problem in the financial system and efforts to reform this system. The problem relates primarily to banks and other depository institutions and involves a conflict between increasing opportunities to assume risk and government policies and actions that provide incentives to assume risk. Deregulation and financial innovation have greatly expanded the portfolio flexibility of depository institutions and the risks they can assume while at the same time, federal deposit insurance and the manner in which regulatory authorities deal with troubled institutions have provided incentives to assume levels of risk that may be imprudent. This is especially true in the case of thrift institutions—savings and loan associations and savings banks. The thrift problem has been gathering speed since the late 1970s; however, in 1989 it became widely known and accepted that it would take a massive federal bailout to remove insolvent thrifts (numbering 496 mid-1988) and recapitalize the federal deposit system for thrifts.

The thrift industry as a whole was insolvent (primarily savings and loan associations) as was the Federal Savings and Loan Insurance Corporation (FSLIC), which provided federal deposit insurance up to $100,000 per account. The thrift problem is the result of many complex forces; however, economists are generally critical of the unwillingness of regulatory authorities, Congress, and the administration to recognize the magnitude of the problem and to adopt politically difficult solutions. The dimensions of the thrift problem were well known in the early 1980s; however, it was not until 1988 that it started to receive the attention of Congress.

Edward J. Kane's *The Gathering Crisis in Federal Deposit Insurance* (Cambridge, Mass.: MIT Press, 1985), for example, lays the blame primarily at the feet of the politicians, the administration, and the regulatory authorities responsible for deposit insurance. He argues that both the Federal Deposit Insurance Corporation, which insures bank deposits, and the FSLIC have been administered in such a way as to understate grossly the cost of dealing with troubled institutions and encouraging imprudent levels of risk taking by banks and thrifts. His more recent *The S&L Insurance Mess: How Did It Happen?* (Washington, D.C.: The Urban Institute, 1988) focuses more on the special circumstances of the thrift problem.

Again the student may be inclined to push this off as just another policy issue that has little impact on his or her life. Consider the cost of solving the thrift problem in the 1990s, however. The bill for bailing out hundreds of thrift institutions was officially estimated in August 1989 to be $166 billion over a 10 year period and as much as $300 billion over a 30 year period. Since then the official estimates have been raised as events during the remainder of 1989 and 1990 showed that the previous estimates were understated. On April 6, 1990, the General Accounting Office testified to Congress that the plan to salvage insolvent thrifts (about 500 in 1990) will cost at least $325 billion and perhaps as much as $500 over a 30 year period. These estimates include the interest cost on bonds that are being issued to obtain much of the funding needed to close insolvent thrift institutions and thus, from a *present value* perspective overstate the cost. It is not appropriate to consider the undiscounted sum of interest payments as part of the cost of the thrift bailout. Most observers as of late 1990 believe the present value cost of dealing with the thrift problem will be in the range of $125 to $200 billion. Using $150 billion in present value dollars as the estimate, this represents about $1,275 for every working individual. The subject of financial regulation might be dull, but it directly affects your pocket!

control. Then, in February 1980, the Federal Reserve announced new definitions of the money supply that recognized the evolving and continually changing instruments that satisfy the basic functions of the money supply.

The 1980 Deregulation and Monetary Control Act significantly changed the operating environment of the Federal Reserve. The act introduced a new reserve requirement system that extended requirements to all depository institutions (banks, thrifts, and credit unions). Before 1980, only banks were subject to reserve requirements. The monetary control features of the 1980 act were designed to improve the Federal Reserve's ability to control the money supply.

In late 1982 however, the Federal Reserve abandoned the money-focused policy and returned to an interest rate–focused policy similar to the operating procedures employed in the 1970s. While the Federal Reserve has been criticized for de-emphasizing monetary control, monetary policy has done a reasonably good job of keeping the inflation low in the second half of the 1980s.

Further Changes?

These policy events are not the last of the efforts to reform the monetary and financial structure of the economy. Considerable debate continues about the proper conduct of monetary policy and the ability or willingness of the monetary authority to pursue anti-inflation policies through the 1990s. The financial system itself continues to change and present new and perplexing regulatory issues. Further policy events will likely take place in the next few years to deal with such areas as the separation of commercial from investment banking, deposit insurance, and the thrift industry. Most important, no one seriously believes the thrift problem has been solved by the 1989 act.

Key Points

1. Monetary economics deals with the financial system and monetary policy and concerns the nature, functions, and influence of money, credit, and finance on the economy.

2. There are four reasons that rationalize a study of monetary economics: the subject is inherently interesting, major debates about public policy often revolve around monetary economics, our lives are significantly influenced by developments in the financial system and the conduct of monetary policy, and knowledge of monetary economics will help make one a more informed voting member of society.

3. Monetary economics is not static; it is dynamic. There have been at least four different periods in the evolution of our thinking about money, monetary policy, and the economy. In addition, the financial system has been in transition since the early 1970s towards a more flexible and competitive structure.

4. A number of major policy events have taken place in the 1980s that have fundamentally changed the structure of the financial system and the way monetary policy is conducted. Additional policy events are anticipated in the 1990s.

Key Terms

Activist-nonactivist debate

Classical economics

Demand-side economics

Deregulation

Deregulation and Monetary Control Act of 1980

Federal Reserve October 1979 announcement

Financial innovation

Financial Institutions Reform, Recovery, and
  Enforcement Act of 1989 (FIRREA)

Financial reform

Financial system

Garn-St Germain Depository Institutions Act of
  1982

*General Theory of Employment, Interest, and
  Money*

Market-regulatory conflict

Monetary economics

Monetary policy

Quantity theory of money

Supply-side economics

Keynesian economics

Monetarist-Keynesian debate

Questions

1. Look at a recent issue of the newspaper, even a
   local paper, and see how many articles deal
   with some aspect of monetary economics. Do
   the same exercise with the evening news program, though you will have more luck with the
   news on public television.

2. Consider how each of the following events in
   the financial system might influence your life:
   (a) an increase in interest rates, (b) an increase
   in the rate of price inflation, (c) a decline in
   the value of the dollar relative to the Japanese
   yen (that is, it takes more dollars to buy a yen
   than previously).

3. What are the four periods in the evolution of
   attitudes about monetary policy?

4. What is meant by the statement that the financial system is in transition?

5. Explain the meaning of regulatory-market conflict.

Suggested Readings

1. *Business Week, Fortune, The Economist*, and *The
   Wall Street Journal*, to mention a few, provide extensive coverage of issues raised in this introductory
   chapter. In addition, each of the 12 Federal Reserve
   banks publishes a quarterly review, and the Board of
   Governors of the Federal Reserve System publishes
   the *Federal Reserve Bulletin*. These official Federal
   Reserve publications are excellent sources of information on monetary economics.

2. Thomas F. Cargill and Gillian G. Garcia, *Financial
   Reform in the 1980s* (Stanford Calif., Hoover Institution Press, 1985). An overview of financial reform in
   the United States through 1984.

3. Kerry Cooper and Donald R. Fraser, *Banking Deregulation and the New Competition in Financial Services* (Cambridge, Mass.: Ballinger, 1986). Discusses
   the changing environment of banking brought about
   by deregulation and financial innovation.

4. William Greider, *Secrets of the Temple* (New York:
   Simon & Schuster, 1987). An interesting attempt to
   provide a laypersons description of monetary policy
   in the 1970s and 1980s.

5. Edward J. Kane, *The S&L Insurance Mess: How Did
   It Happen?* (Washington, D.C.: The Urban Institute,
   1989). An excellent overview of the thrift problem
   just prior to the 1989 act.

CHAPTER 2

The Concept of Money

Chapter Overview

The concept of money is explored in this chapter to provide a foundation for the more detailed discussion of the financial system and monetary policy in subsequent chapters. Money is one of those concepts about which everyone has an opinion since it's impossible not to have some daily contact with some form of money, and yet, the commonsense view of money falls short of that needed to understand money's role in the economy.

The purpose of this chapter is to provide some basic building blocks to understand the role of money in the financial system and monetary policy. The first step is to get a working definition of money and some related concepts.

Money has both a general and functional definition. The functional definition focuses on the various roles that money plays in the economy and is the basis for the official measures of money known as M1, M2, and M3. In addition, there is a broad measure of liquidity referred to as L and a measure of debt or credit held by non-financial entities. The existence of several measures of money as well as the broad measure of liquidity reflects the difference of opinion that exists as to which is the most appropriate measure of the money supply. The transition of the financial system has been responsible for part of the measurement problem since deregulation and financial innovation have introduced new financial services and assets that fundamentally alter our view of what functions as money.

Once the money supply is defined, we review the historical evolution of monetary systems to understand better the current system in which the Federal Reserve, depository institutions, and the public jointly determine the money supply.

The chapter ends with a discussion of the meaning of the value of money and the role money plays in determining economic activity.

BOX 1   Mathematics of barter

The mathematics of a barter economy clearly indicates the importance of the unit of account function. If we have two goods—apples and oranges—we need only one price ratio to express their relative value, that is, the price of apples in terms of oranges or what amounts to the same, the price of oranges in terms of apples. If we have three goods—apples, oranges, and pears—we need three price ratios: apples in terms of oranges, apples in terms of pears, and oranges in terms of pears.

In general, if we have n goods, we need $n(n - 1)/2$ price ratios. Use this formula to calculate how many price ratios would be required for an economy with 1,000 goods. The answer is 499,500! If we could choose one good to be the unit of account, the number of prices could decline drastically.

In general, an n good economy using one of the goods as the unit of account, requires n-1 price ratios since the good selected as the unit of account has a defined price ratio of 1. Prices of the remaining goods can be expressed in terms of the unit of account. Instead of 499,500 prices, the economy can function with 999 prices using one of the goods as the unit of account.

What Is Money? A General and Functional Definition

Money is anything used to make a payment for a good, a service, or a debt obligation. In a sense, money is whatever people are willing to accept for exchange, and, historically, a variety of items have served the role of money (shells, gold, buttons, teeth, beads, fishhooks, precious metals other than gold, etc.). In fact, during World War II, in Korea, and in Vietnam, cigarettes have functioned as the basic money supply in POW camps.

More specifically, money can be defined in terms of the three general functions it performs:

1. *Money serves as a unit of account.* It represents an item with which we compare all other items to obtain a measure of relative value. The dollar is the basic unit of account in which the value of everything traded in the market can be expressed. Once we express the value of a car in terms of dollars and the value of a house in terms of dollars, we have a measure of the relative value of the car as compared with the house. Even a moderately advanced economic system would be inconceivable without money as a unit of account. Can you imagine a Sears, Roebuck catalog without money as a unit of account? One spark plug would be worth 1/487 of a lawn mower of specific characteristics and on and on!

2. *Money serves as a medium of exchange.* Money makes it possible to separate the decision to buy from the decision to sell. In a barter economy without money as a medium of exchange, trade cannot take place unless there is a *coincidence of wants* between the two traders. Since goods are exchanged for goods in a barter economy, each trader must desire the goods or services offered by the other trader if a transaction is to occur. If one trader has oranges to offer and the other has apples, trade will not occur unless the trader with oranges (apples) desires apples (oranges). If we introduce money as a medium of exchange, trade will take place even though there is no coincidence of wants. Assume that the trader with apples detests oranges.

Without money as a medium of exchange, there is no coincidence of wants, and trade will not occur; however, when money is introduced as a medium of exchange, the coincidence of wants is no longer necessary since goods are exchanged for money and money exchanged for goods. The trader with oranges can sell the oranges for money, which can be used to purchase apples from the trader who dislikes oranges. This trader, in turn, can exchange the money for whatever good or service he or she desires. As with the unit of account function, it is difficult to imagine even moderately advanced economic systems functioning without money as a medium of exchange.

3. *Money serves as a store of wealth.* Wealth is the total stock of real and financial assets owned by an individual. Real wealth consists of the stock of durables—cars, washing machines, houses, and any other material asset. Financial wealth consists of the stock of money, bonds, equities, and any other kind of I.O.U. Financial assets represent a claim on present or future real wealth or a method of storing real wealth. Money is a financial asset to whoever holds it and thus represents a method of storing wealth. Money is frequently the more desirable method of holding wealth as compared with many other commodities; however, money may not represent the most optimal method. Money has a relatively low transaction cost in terms of its command over resources, and the value of money is relatively more stable than other things that could be used to store wealth. First, consider the low transaction cost of money as a store of wealth. Since money is an acceptable medium of exchange, it can be converted easily into other goods and services with little difficulty, whereas some other forms of wealth holding such as a house would entail considerable transaction cost to convert to other goods and services. Second, money has a relatively stable value in terms of other goods and services compared with any particular real asset. Debts are fixed in terms of money, and the prices of goods and services do not change rapidly with regard to money except in times of rapid inflation. Low transaction cost and relative stability of value in terms of other goods and services make money an important way of holding wealth. We often refer to the store of wealth characteristic of money by saying that money has a very high degree of *liquidity* in that money has immediate command over resources in the marketplace. At the same time, some forms of money earn no explicit interest return and may not be the optimal method of storing wealth.

Money is thus defined in terms of these three specific functions. And armed with these functional roles of money, the task of measuring the money supply should be relatively easy—we would only need to identify the items in the economy that satisfied the three basic functions of money. Unfortunately, although there is little controversy over the three functions, controversy does exist as to the relative importance of each: specifically, the dispute relates to the medium of exchange and the store of wealth functions. Those who emphasize the medium of exchange function define money more narrowly than do those who emphasize the store of wealth or liquidity function. To complicate the issue further, the financial system continually introduces new financial instruments and methods of making money transactions that require redefinition of the money supply from time to time.

TABLE 2-1   Measures of the money supply, liquidity and debt, January 1988

Measure	Components	Amount (billions)
M1	Coin, currency, traveler's checks, demand deposits, and other checkable deposits (NOW accounts, ATS accounts, and credit union share drafts)	
	Total	$ 758.8
M2	M1, plus savings deposits, small-denomination time deposits, MMDAs, MMMFs, overnight RPs, and overnight Eurodollar deposits	2,166.2
	Total	$2,925.0
M3	M2, plus large CDs, term RPs, and term Eurodollar deposits	761.8
	Total	$3,686.8
L	M3, plus other liquid assets such as short-term Treasury securities, bankers' acceptances, commercial paper, and U.S. savings bonds	673.9
	Total	$4,360.7
Debt	Debt of domestic nonfinancial sectors consisting of outstanding debt obligations of the federal, state, and local governments, and private nonfinancial sectors	3,892
	Total	$8,352.7

[1] Data seasonally adjusted

Source: Federal Reserve Statistical Release, H.6 (508), August 11, 1988.

(handwritten annotation: monetary Aggregate measures)

Measures of the Money Supply

There is no single measure of the money supply on which all agree, and as a result the Federal Reserve provides three measures of the money supply, one measure of liquidity, L, and one measure of debt. The money supply measures are referred to as *monetary aggregate* measures. These measures were introduced February 1980 to reflect the evolving nature of money in the economy that made the previous measures obsolete. The three measures of the money supply are M1, M2, and M3. The M1 measure is the most narrow; the others increasingly broaden the measure of the money supply. Table 2-1 presents recent data for the three measures as well as the measures of L and debt.

M1, defined as coin, currency, traveler's checks, and transaction deposits at depository institutions, includes the items most widely used as a medium of exchange. While M1 can serve as a store of wealth, it is frequently not a good store of wealth since some components earn zero interest (coin, currency, traveler's checks, and demand deposits) while the others earn a lower interest rate than other financial assets. Coin and currency held by the pubic are obvious components of the money supply; however, together they represent only about 25 percent of M1. Transaction or "checkable" deposits represent the major component of M1. These are deposits subject to transfer, usually by a written check or draft, and referred to as transaction deposits because they are widely used by individuals, business, and governments in their everyday transactions of paying and receiving funds. Transaction deposits are defined by the Federal Reserve as

> all deposits on which the account holder is permitted to make withdrawals by negotiable or transferrable instruments, payment orders of withdrawal, telephone and pre-authorized transfers (in excess of three per month), for the purpose of making payments to third persons or others.[1]

Historically, demand deposits at commercial banks were the most widely used transaction deposit; however, during the 1970s new types of transaction deposits were introduced by nonbank depository institutions (savings and loan associations, savings banks, and credit unions) which were close substitutes for bank demand deposits, and, in addition, paid an explicit interest rate. Banks are prohibited by law from paying explicit interest on demand deposit accounts. The new demand deposit substitutes include NOW (negotiable order of withdrawal) accounts, ATS (automatic transfer service) accounts, and credit union share draft accounts.[2]

NOW accounts are interest-earning savings accounts on which checks can be written; ATS accounts allow for automatic transfer from savings accounts to demand deposit accounts, thus transforming a savings account into a transaction account; and credit union share draft accounts are essentially NOW accounts. The Deregulation and Monetary Control Act of 1980 gave authority to all depository institutions to issue these new types of transaction balances, and, at present, all depository institutions offer some variety of checkable or transaction balance. M1 defines the money supply to include coin, currency, traveler's checks, and transaction balances at *all* depository institutions.

The components of M1 in percentage terms are illustrated in Figure 2-1. There are several important aspects of Figure 2-1 that should be kept in mind. First, demand deposits are primarily issued by commercial banks. Other institutions such as savings and loan associations or savings banks are permitted to offer demand deposits in certain circumstances; however, for all practical purposes, banks dominate the issuance of demand deposits. Second, the terms "transaction balances" or "checkable accounts" refer to the sum of demand deposits and other checkable deposits such as NOW accounts, ATS accounts, and credit union share drafts. Third, the term "depository institution" refers to banks, savings and loan associations, savings banks, and credit unions because their loan and investment operations are supported by funds obtained from offering deposits to the public.

M2 broadens the M1 measure further by including items that have some medium of exchange characteristics but emphasize the store of wealth function to a greater extent. M2 is defined as M1 plus regular savings deposits, small-denomination time deposits, and money market deposit accounts (MMDAs) at *all* depository institutions; money market mutual funds (MMMFs); overnight security repurchase agreements (RPs); and overnight Eurodollar balances. Regular savings

---

[1] Board of Governors of the Federal Reserve System, *Federal Reserve Bulletin* (April 1984), p. 197.

[2] NOW accounts were first issued by depository institutions in the early 1970s in New England. Nationwide NOW accounts were introduced January 1, 1981 by the Deregulation and Monetary Control Act. ATS accounts and credit union share draft accounts were introduced in the 1970s and also now have nationwide authorization.

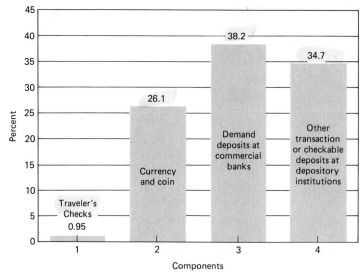

Source: *Federal Reserve Statistical Release*, H.6, August 11, 1988.

FIGURE 2-1 **Components of M1, January 1988. (1). Outstanding amount of U.S. dollar-denominated traveler's checks of nonbank issuers. Traveler's checks issued by depository institutions are included in demand deposits. (2). Currency outside U.S. Treasury, Federal Reserve banks, and the vaults of depository institutions. (3). Demand deposits at commercial banks and foreign-related institutions other than those due to depository institutions, the U.S. government and banks and official institutions, less cash items in the process of collection and Federal Reserve float. (4). Consists of NOW and ATS balances at all depository institutions, credit union share draft balances, and demand deposits at thrift institutions.**

deposits are not subject to transfer by check; however, they can usually be withdrawn on demand, although depository institutions can legally invoke a 7-day waiting period. Computer technology and changes in the regulatory environment have increased the moneyness of savings deposits. Individuals now transfer funds more easily from savings accounts than in the past. Small-denomination time deposits are deposits of less than $100,000, and, despite the interest rate penalties for early withdrawal, time deposits have many characteristics in common with savings deposits. MMDAs were introduced in December 1982 by the Garn-St Germain Act of 1982 so that depository institutions could effectively compete with MMMF shares. MMDAs are interest earning deposits and have limited transactions features in that they provide up to six preauthorized transfers per month of which three can be by check. Unlimited personal withdrawals are permitted. Money market mutual funds accept share deposits (usually in minimum amounts of $1,000) on which shareholders can write checks (usually in minimum accounts of $500). Overnight RPs are mainly offered by banks and represent a sale of securities (usually Treasury securities) to a depositor for a short period of time. The depositor earns interest on the deposited funds overnight, which are then made available for spending the next day when the bank repurchases the securities. Overnight Eurodollars are short-term deposits denominated in dollars in banking offices outside the United States.

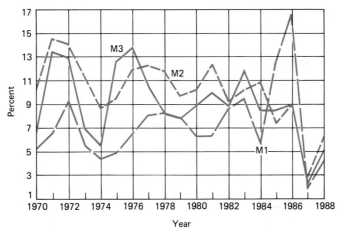

Source: Based on Data in Council of Economic Advisers, *Economic Report of the President* (Washington, D.C.: GPO, January 1988) and August 1989 issue of the *Survey of Current Business.*

FIGURE 2-2 **Percentage changes in annual values of M1, M2, and M3, 1960–1988**

M3 broadens the definition of the money supply even further and is defined as M2 plus large-denomination certificates of deposit (amounts of $100,000 or more), longer-term RPs, and longer-term Eurodollars. Large certificates of deposit, or CDs, differ from regular or small-denomination time deposits by the existence of an active secondary market in which CDs can be traded before maturity.

M1, M2, and M3 are the three basic measures of the money supply that start from the narrow view in which the medium of exchange function is emphasized to measures that give increasing weight to the store of wealth function. The Federal Reserve also publishes a broad measure of liquid assets, L, and total debt of the nonfinancial sectors of the economy.

There would not be a great problem in selecting one of the three measures of the money supply if they all behaved more or less the same over time; however, inspection of the year-to-year percentage changes in the three measures in Figure 2-2 suggests divergent behavior.

Economic theory is of little help in deciding which is the most appropriate measure of the money supply, that is, the measure that best reflects the items that satisfy the basic functions of money in the economic system. The majority of discussion on this issue has focused on the three money measures. Few argue that the measure of liquidity, L, is a useful reflection of the money supply because it is too broad and too far removed from the medium of exchange function. On the other hand, there is little disagreement that coin, currency, traveler's checks, and transaction balances or checkable deposits are the basic money supply in the sense that they are used extensively as a medium of exchange. One approach to measuring the money supply has been to determine how closely the broader elements are related to the basic components of the money supply. Few would disagree with the view that M1 is part of the money supply, but only whether it should be broadened to include other items that may have a high degree of "moneyness" or "liquidity."

A Spectrum of Liquidity

To gain insight to the difficulty of measuring the money supply, consider a *spectrum of liquidity*, with the components of M1 at the most liquid end of the spectrum and real assets such as a car and house at the least liquid end. Liquidity represents the ability to convert an asset (either financial or real) into M1 rapidly and without losing income. M1 can be regarded as the most liquid of the financial assets in that it represents immediate command over goods and services in the marketplace. To regard the components of M1 as completely liquid is only an approximation since there are some differences in the degree of liquidity, for example, between currency and transaction deposits. Currency (and coin) is *legal tender* in the United States, which means that it must be accepted in payment of a debt unless the debt specifies some other type of payment. Transaction deposits are not legal tender. Despite the legal difference, transactions deposits are regarded as a more convenient and useful medium of exchange than currency for a wide range of transactions. Demand deposit accounts at commercial banks have traditionally been the major type of transaction deposit available to the public; however, since the introduction of NOW accounts, ATS accounts, and credit union share drafts, the concept of a transaction deposit is broadened. It should be kept in mind, however, that these new types of transaction deposits are not always perfect substitutes for demand deposits at commercial banks even though they perform much of the same function and earn interest income whereas banks are prohibited from paying interest on demand deposits. As a legal matter, the new types of accounts are not subject to transfer on demand as are demand deposit accounts. In addition, NOW and credit union share draft accounts cannot be held by a profit-making organization.

Even real assets (a car or a house, for example) possess liquidity in that they can be converted into M1, but conversion usually involves delay and inconvenience, and the transaction may result in a loss. Financial assets possess more liquidity than do real assets. Among financial assets, savings deposits, small time deposits, MMDAs, and MMMFs are very close to M1. CDs (negotiable time certificates of $100,000 or larger) are also very liquid, as there is an active *secondary market* in large certificates that allows the holder to sell the certificate for money without much delay and significant cost before maturity. Many other financial assets have liquidity because of the existence of secondary markets.

The secondary market for financial assets is the used-car market of the financial system in which securities can be sold and purchased numerous times before they mature. For example, assume that a bank issues a $100,000 CD with a 30-day maturity. The holder of the CD may need money only 10 days after purchasing the CD and does not wish to wait until the CD matures. By selling the CD in the secondary market, the individual obtains the needed funds. Who buys the CD? Someone with idle funds looking for an interest return. In turn, this individual may very well sell the CD before it matures. Treasury bills (obligations of the federal government with maturities of one year or less) are also very liquid because they have an active secondary market.

Table 2-2 illustrates the basic concept of a spectrum of liquidity by ranking important financial assets in declining order of liquidity along with an indication of the relative ranking of real assets. The ranking should not be regarded as exact or complete, and it is subject to change over time; for example, savings deposits have

TABLE 2-2   Spectrum of assets in terms of liquidity

	Approximate amount of liquidity
Financial assets	100%
Currency and coin held by the public[1]	
Demand deposits[1,2]	
Other transaction deposits at depository institutions[1]	
Money market deposit accounts at depository institutions	
Savings deposits at depository institutions	
Small-denomination time deposits at depository institutions	
Money market mutual funds	
Large certificates of deposit at depository institutions	
U.S. Treasury bills (one year or less)	
U.S. Treasury notes (one to ten years)	
Short-term corporate debt (commercial paper)	
U.S. Treasury bonds (more than ten years)	
Municipal government debt (state and local)	
Long-term corporate debt (bonds)	
Corporate equity	
Real assets	
Car, house, etc.	0%

[1] Component of the money supply measured as M1.

[2] Demand deposits are issued by commercial banks; however, savings banks and savings and loan associations can also issue demand deposits under certain conditions.

increased their degree of liquidity as computer technology has increased their accessibility by the public.

There is another aspect of the spectrum of liquidity that should be mentioned at this point. In general, there is a trade-off in the financial system between liquidity and interest income. Other things held constant, the higher (lower) the degree of liquidity, the lower (higher) the interest rate. Individuals demand a higher rate of interest to hold less liquid assets. Long-term corporate bonds generally pay a greater interest rate than do long-term Treasury obligations because the former have a greater risk of default. An obligation with a higher degree of default risk will have a lower degree of liquidity in that it would not be as easy to convert into money as an obligation with either no or a lesser amount of default risk.

The spectrum of liquidity concept and Table 2-2 illustrate the basic problem of determining a statistical measure of the money supply. There is little debate that M1 satisfies the three major functional roles played by money, even though there are some differences in liquidity among the individual components. Should the measure of the money supply be broadened to include items that are very close in liquidity to M1? Savings and small-denomination time deposits, MMDAs, MMMFs, and large CDs are liquid and close to M1 on the spectrum; however, the important question is: How close? And, if these components have enough liquidity to be regarded as part

BOX 2   Measures of money based on degree of moneyness or liquidity

During the 1980s a number of economists and the Federal Reserve have questioned the traditional measures of money. Their concern is whether the money supply measures are reliable indicators of future changes in the level of economic activity. In 1985, for example, M1 grew at almost 12 percent while nominal GNP rose by only 5.5%. In the past, a 12% increase in the money supply would have produced an increase in nominal GNP much greater than 5.5%. Many argue that deregulation and financial innovation have changed the relationship between money and the economy in such a manner that the traditional measures such as M1, M2, or M3 are no longer reliable guides for the conduct of monetary policy.

This has led some economists to develop alternative measures of the money supply based on the spectrum of liquidity concept discussed in the chapter. Traditionally, M1 is defined as an *unweighted* sum of currency, coin, and transaction balances, M2 is defined as an *unweighted* sum of M1, savings deposits, small time deposits, and so on. Economists question whether this is appropriate. Instead of weighting each component of the money supply equally, they suggest assigning each component different weights based on the degree of moneyness of the component to basic money.

Carl E. Walsh ("Measuring Money," Federal Reserve Bank of San Francisco, *Weekly Letter*, May 30, 1986) discusses two recent approaches to revising the money measures.

In recent years, two alternative monetary aggregates have been developed using differential weighting. Both try to measure monetary services by adding together the services produced by different monetary assets. Since not all assets yield the same level of transaction services, different assets receive different weights. The two approaches differ in the method used to estimate the monetary service flows produced by particular assets. One approach uses the economic theory of index numbers and the resulting measures are called Monetary Services Indexes. The second approach attempts to measure directly the transaction services yielded by different assets by focusing on how frequently various deposits are used in making transactions, i.e., their turnover

Despite the theoretical advantage of weighted versus unweighted measures of the money supply, a number of practical problems are encountered in determining the weights. As a result, the new measures of the money supply have failed to provide more meaningful information than the traditional measures. The basic problem is one of determining a reliable set of weights and given the fact that the financial system is in transition, it is unlikely that a reliable measure of money can be devised based on weights determined by the degree of moneyness or liquidity of each asset component.

of the money supply, what about other liquid assets such as Treasury bills? In fact, the basic problem with expanding the definition beyond M1 is that there is no logical point to stop including financial assets in the money supply; however, few argue that financial assets beyond those included in M2 should be part of the measure of the money supply. The main argument is focused on the components of M1 and M2.

Availability of Money Supply Statistics

The official measures of the money supply known as the *monetary aggregates* as well as measures of liquidity and debt are compiled by the Board of Governors of the Federal Reserve System. The data are currently released each Thursday at 4:30 P.M. EST and reported in a variety of formats in a number of easily accessible places. Measures of the monetary aggregates are published in *The Wall Street Journal* usually on the day following the Federal Reserve release. Other sources of monetary aggregate data are the *Federal Reserve Bulletin* (Board of Governors), *Survey of Current Business* (Commerce Department), and *Economic Report of the President* (Council of Economic Advisors). In addition, several of the Federal Reserve Banks made monetary aggregate and related data available.

There are four considerations to keep in mind when examining the published money supply data aside from the conceptual problems already discussed. First, the monetary aggregates are published as both levels and annual percentage changes. The annual percentage changes are the most meaningful because they abstract from the strong upward trend in the levels of the money supply over time.

Second, the money supply levels (and percentage growth rates based on the levels) are reported in both seasonably adjusted and not seasonally adjusted forms. The seasonal adjustment procedure attempts to eliminate the influence of periodic events; for example, currency in circulation exhibits a well-defined seasonal pattern over the year that repeats itself year after year. The seasonally adjusted money supply measures are the most useful for many purposes; however, the seasonal adjustment procedure itself can contaminate the data—either by taking more from the data than just the seasonal influence or adding some variation to the data that did not previously exist. This is not a trivial issue because there is no perfect seasonal adjustment procedure and the differences in results between different seasonal adjustments can be large. Annual growth rates of M1 using three approaches to seasonal adjustment are presented in Table 2-3 for a 15-month period.

Third, the monetary aggregates are available for as short an interval as a week. Unfortunately, the financial press and news media in general frequently refer to these week-to-week changes in the money supply as containing meaningful information. Even the Federal Reserve cautions against this and states: "Special caution should be taken in interpreting week-to-week changes in money supply data, which are highly volatile and subject to revision."[3] Even the month-to-month changes should be cautiously interpreted, though they are more reliable than the weekly figures.

Fourth, there is an immense amount of effort required to calculate the nation's money supply and as such, previously published values are frequently revised as new information becomes available or statistical procedures are altered. Table 2-4 compares the "revised" and "old" or previously reported annual growth rates for M1 on a monthly, quarterly, semiannual, and annual basis for a recent period. The difference between revised and old is fairly large for monthly values; however, the differences appear to decline as the measurement interval gets larger.

What's the Bottom Line on the Money Supply Measures?

The money supply can be defined in a functional sense without too much trouble; however, there are two general problems to defining a specific group of financial assets as a measure of the money supply. First, there are numerous statistical prob-

---

[3] *Federal Reserve Statistical Release*, H.6 (508), August 11, 1988, p. 3.

TABLE 2-3   Levels and annual growth rates of M1 using standard,[1] concurrent,[2] and experimental alternative[3] seasonal adjustment procedures, monthly average, 1987–1988

	Levels (in billions of dollars)			Annual growth rates (in percent)		
	Standard	Concurrent	Experi-mental alternative	Standard	Concurrent	Experi-mental alternative
1987—May	746.5	747.0	745.5	2.9	4.8	9.9
June	742.1	742.3	743.0	−7.1	−7.6	−4.0
July	743.6	744.0	742.7	2.4	2.7	−0.5
August	746.5	747.0	747.4	4.7	4.8	7.6
September	747.5	747.9	746.1	1.6	1.4	−2.1
October	756.2.	756.4	755.0	14.0	13.6	14.3
November	752.7	753.1	751.8	−5.6	−5.2	−5.1
December	750.8	750.8	749.6	−3.0	−3.7	−3.5
1988—January	758.8	757.5	756.3	12.8	10.7	10.7
February	759.5	758.9	757.4	1.1	2.2	1.7
March	762.9	762.7	759.4	5.4	6.0	3.2
April	770.1	769.1	765.8	11.3	10.1	10.1
May	770.2	770.8	769.6	0.2	2.7	6.0
June	776.5	776.9	775.8	9.8	9.5	9.7
July	782.4	783.1	783.0	9.1	9.6	11.1

[1] Standard monthly seasonal factors are derived at the beginning of each year by applying an X-11/ARIMA–based procedure to the data through the end of the previous year.

[2] Concurrent monthly seasonal factors are derived each by applying an X-11/ARIMA–based procedure to data through that month.

[3] Alternative monthly seasonal factors are derived using an experimental model–based procedure. This procedure uses a combination of statistical regression and time series modeling techniques to construct seasonal factors that are more sensitive than standard factors to unique characteristics of each series. These characteristics include fixed and evolving seasonal patterns, trading day effects, within-month seasonal variations, holiday effects, outlier adjustments, special events adjustments, and serially correlated noise components.

Source: Federal Reserve Statistical Release, H.6 (508), August 11, 1988.

lems with current monetary aggregate measures that will never be completely solved, and there are frequent revisions in previously reported measures. This should be enough to warn the individual: "Handle with care—the use of money supply measures can be dangerous to your economic health." Second, the transition of the financial system and the new financial innovations of the past decade have and will likely further complicate the definition of the money supply. New financial services and assets that substitute for the traditional forms of money (currency and deposits) make it increasingly difficult to define a meaningful measure of the money supply.

So what's the bottom line? The student should view weekly and even monthly measures of the money supply with a respectable amount of caution. Quarterly growth rates in the money supply over a period of several years will reveal far more meaningful information about the money supply and its impact on the economy.

TABLE 2-4 Comparison of revised and old M2 growth rates (percentage changes at annual rates)

	Revised (1)	Old (2)	Difference (1) − (2) (3)
Monthly			
1986—October	9.8	10.8	−1.0
November	7.2	6.5	0.7
December	10.8	10.8	0.0
1987—January	8.5	9.6	−1.1
February	0.6	−0.2	0.8
March	2.1	1.5	0.6
April	5.5	5.7	−0.2
May	0.7	0.2	0.5
June	1.0	0.5	0.5
July	2.7	2.7	0.0
August	4.8	6.2	−1.4
September	4.7	5.4	−0.7
October	6.0	6.8	−0.8
November	1.0	−0.5	1.5
December	2.0	1.6	0.4
1988—January	9.8	10.8	−1.0
Quarterly			
1986—QIV	9.0	9.3	−0.3
1987—QI	6.5	6.4	0.1
QII	2.6	2.3	0.3
QIII	2.8	3.0	−0.2
QIV	4.0	4.2	−0.2
Semiannual			
1987—QIV 1986 to			
QII 1987	4.6	4.4	0.2
QII 1987 to			
QIV 1987	3.4	3.7	−0.3
Annual (QIV to QIV)			
1986	9.4	9.0	0.4
1987	4.0	4.1	−0.1

Source: Federal Reserved Statistical Release, H.6 (508), February 18, 1988.

Even here, however, the transition of the financial system renders these longer-run money supply movements more difficult to interpret than they may have been in the past. Thus, the money supply measures are still useful as long as one focuses on longer-run movements (at least quarterly changes) and keeps in mind that the financial system and, hence, the concept of money are in transition.

Now that we have a working knowledge of money supply measures, the natural question to ask is how is the money supply determined at any point in time. The detailed answer to this question will have to wait until later; however, we can start to think about an answer by considering the historical evolution of money and monetary systems.

Monetary Systems: Commodity and Credit Money

To understand the determinants of the money supply, we must first consider the major types of monetary systems or types of money that have been used. The major types are *commodity money* (either full bodied or token), *representative commodity money*, and *credit money*. Each type has had a long history both in the United States and in other countries. An economy that uses commodities (usually gold, silver, or copper) as money is a commodity money system. If the commodity has equal value as a commodity and as a medium of exchange, the system is a full-bodied commodity system, whereas, if the commodity has greater value as a medium of exchange than as a commodity, the system is then a token commodity system. A token copper penny, for example, would be composed of less than a penny's worth of copper. Full-bodied commodity systems have historically been inefficient and not very responsive to the needs of a growing economy for a smooth expansion of the money supply over time.

Representative full-bodied commodity systems exist when paper money circulates rather than commodities but the paper money can be redeemed in full value for a specific commodity; for example, a $100 gold certificate would be used as a medium of exchange and could be redeemed for $100 of gold (or whatever commodity is used to back the paper currency).

Commodity monetary systems by their nature were dependent either partially or wholly on the supply of the commodity used as money or as a reserve behind whatever circulated as a medium of exchange. As such they limited the ability of the central bank to manage money and in the final analysis often failed to provide the proper amount of money to meet the needs of the ecomony over time in a consistent and stable manner. The inherent problems of a commodity system led to the widespread use of credit or fiat based systems.

Credit or fiat money exists when money does not have value as a commodity and cannot be redeemed for a commodity such as gold or silver. Credit money is essentially a promise to pay without any explicit commodity reserve to back up the promise. The supply of credit money is thus not tied to the supply of some commodity and is susceptible to control by the central bank for purposes of economic stabilization.

There is a rich history to the evolution of money in the United States as it has developed toward a form that accomplishes three objectives. First, money should be convenient to use as a medium of exchange and not subject to easy counterfeiting or debasement of its value. Second, the money supply should be responsive to the growing needs of the economy. As the economic system expands over time in response to the growth of population, capital, and technology, the money supply must also grow in a smooth fashion to meet the transaction needs of an expanding economy. Third, the money supply should be of a form that can be influenced by the central bank as part of the overall policy to achieve long-run and short-run goals of economic stabilization.

The money system presently in use in the United States and other countries has been simplified and modified over time to meet the three objectives. Money in the United States is composed of essentially two types: token coins and credit money. Coins are issued by the U.S. Treasury and have greater value as a medium of exchange than as a commodity. Currency consists primarily of Federal Reserve notes issued by the Federal Reserve System. The Treasury also has outstanding certain currency issues that are in the process of retirement. Currency issued by the government is credit money and is not backed by any commodity. About the only backing one gets with currency is the statement "In God We Trust." Coin and currency represent a relatively small part of the total money supply (about 25%). Checkable deposits offered by depository institutions are the major part of the money supply and, like currency, are credit money. Traveler's checks are also credit money.

Now that we have a working measure of the money supply (M1) and understand that the money supply is not backed by any particular commodity such as gold or silver, there are two issues that need to be considered. First, since money is not backed by any type of commodity that has value in the marketplace, why is money valuable and how do we measure its value? Second, since money is not tied to the supply of any particular commodity, what determines the money supply?

What Is Meant by the Value of Money?

Money has value because people are willing to accept it in exchange for goods and services and payment of debts. Thus, despite the fact that money has no value as a commodity, money has value simply because others are willing to use it as a medium of exchange and store of value. Money also becomes a suitable store of wealth because of its widespread acceptability. Credit money economizes on scarce resources since commodities that have value in other uses are not utilized as part of the money supply and the cost of manufacturing credit money is minimal compared with the cost of manufacturing and maintaining a commodity money system.

Everyone says that a dollar is not worth a dollar anymore and that money has lost value. This has nothing to do with the amount of gold in Fort Knox. The phrase "value of money" refers to the ability of money to command resources in the market: a dollar is still a dollar, but the dollar simply does not command as many resources in the market as it did in the past. The value of money has nothing to do with the amount of gold or any other commodity that stands behind currency. The value of money is determined by the prices of the goods and services that it can command in the market. As prices increase (decrease), the value of a given amount of money decreases (increases).

Credit money has been found to be more efficient than other forms of money, more responsive to the needs of a growing economy, and more susceptible to influence by the central bank to achieve goals of economic stabilization. At the same time, credit money requires considerable sophistication on the part of government to maintain its ultimate value, which is the willingness of individuals to accept money in exchange for goods and services. Inflation will result if government allows the money supply to grow more rapidly than is required to support real economic growth. Extremely rapid inflation such as hyperinflation can destroy the value of credit

---

BOX 3   Mathematics of real versus nominal and rates of change

The concept of the value of money in terms of its purchasing power is a good point to reacquaint the student with an important concept—the difference between real and nominal magnitudes. We can use the difference between real GNP and nominal GNP to illustrate this point.

Nominal GNP is the market value of the final output of goods and services produced during the year. Consider a simple economy in 1990 that produces a final output of 1 apple and 1 orange, each selling for $1.00. The nominal GNP will then be $2.00. If in the next year, 1991, the economy continues to produce 1 apple and 1 orange, but the price of each increases to $2.00, then the nominal GNP will be $4.00. The 1991 nominal GNP thus gives misleading information about the real productive performance of the economy. In some way, we need to factor out the price increase from one year to the next to obtain a measure of real GNP. The GNP Price Deflator is used for such a purpose.

Set the price index equal to 100 for 1990 and 200 for 1991 to reflect that fact that prices have doubled in one year. The 1991 real GNP evaluated in 1990 dollars is calculated as

$$\text{Real GNP in 1991} = \frac{\text{Nominal GNP in 1991}}{\text{Price index in 1991}}$$

or

$$\text{Real GNP in 1991} = \frac{\$4.00}{(2.00)} = \$2.00$$

Thus, the real GNP in 1991 is unchanged from the value in 1990 despite a 100 percent increase in the value of nominal GNP. The higher value of nominal GNP is due entirely to inflation and not an increase in the real production of the economy.

The principle of converting from nominal to real (or from real to nominal) is general. Any price index such as those illustrated in Table 2-5 can be used to convert any nominal value into a real value. For example, the nominal M1 money supply for 1987 is $753.2 billion. Using the GNP Deflator of 117.4 for 1987, the real M1 money supply in terms of 1982 prices is calculated as ($753.2/1.174) = $641.6. It is obvious that the higher the price level, the lower the real value of money.

This is a good point to reacquaint the student with another concept. We have frequently referred to percentage changes or growth rates and though the student may already be aware of how to calculate rates of change, a few words to remind us of the calculation would be useful at this point.

The growth rate of, say, M1, from period $t - 1$ to period t is calculated as

$$\text{Growth rate of M1 from period } t - 1 \text{ to } t = \left[\frac{M1(t)}{M1(t - 1)} - 1 \right] * 100$$

We prefer to annualize rates of growth in monetary economics and depending on the data interval, the foregoing formula may need to be modified. First the annual growth rate for annual observations of the variable is obtained from the above formula with no need for modification. Second, if M1 is measured on a monthly basis, then the formula is modified to ($\{[M1(t)/M1(t - 1)] **12\} - 1) * 100$ to calculate the annual growth rate based on a monthly interval. Third, if M1 is measured on a quarterly basis, then the formula is modified to ($\{[M1(t)/M1(t - 1)] **4\} - 1) * 100$ to calculate the annual growth rate based on a quarterly interval. These are not the only way to annualize monthly and quarterly rates of change; however, they are commonly employed.

---

money. If prices are increasing at rapid rates, the public will refuse to hold credit money, because it will lose value continually and become unacceptable as a medium of exchange. In fact, in countries that do have extreme hyperinflationary experiences, monetary transactions are replaced with barter exchange because money loses its most important determinant of value—the willingness of others to accept money in exchange for goods and services.

Three methods are widely used to represent changes in value of money: the consumer price index (CPI), the producer price index (PPI), and the implicit GNP

TABLE 2-5   The Consumer Price Index (1982–84 = 100), Producer Price Index (1982–84 = 100), and the GNP Deflator (1982 = 100), 1965–1988

	CPI		PPI		GNP Deflator	
	Index	*% Change*	*Index*	*% Change*	*Index*	*% Change*
1965	31.5	1.6%	32.3	2.0%	33.8	2.7%
1966	32.5	3.1	33.3	3.2	35.0	3.6
1967	33.4	2.7	33.4	0.3	36.0	2.8
1968	34.8	4.2	34.2	2.5	37.8	5.0
1969	36.7	5.4	35.6	4.0	39.8	5.4
1970	38.8	5.9	36.9	3.7	42.0	5.6
1971	40.5	4.2	38.1	3.3	44.4	5.7
1972	41.8	3.3	39.8	4.4	46.5	4.7
1973	44.4	6.3	45.0	13.2	49.6	6.6
1974	49.3	11.0	53.5	18.8	54.0	9.0
1975	53.8	9.1	58.4	9.2	59.3	9.8
1976	56.9	5.8	61.1	4.7	63.0	6.3
1977	60.6	6.5	64.9	6.1	67.3	6.7
1978	65.2	7.6	69.9	7.8	72.2	7.3
1979	72.6	11.3	78.7	12.6	78.6	8.8
1980	82.4	13.5	89.8	14.1	85.7	9.1
1981	90.9	10.4	98.0	9.2	93.9	9.6
1982	96.5	6.2	100.0	2.0	100.0	6.5
1983	99.6	3.2	101.3	1.2	103.9	3.8
1984	103.9	4.4	103.7	2.4	107.8	3.8
1985	107.6	3.6	103.2	−0.5	110.9	3.0
1986	109.7	1.9	100.2	−2.9	113.8	2.6
1987	113.7	3.7	102.8	2.6	117.4	3.1
1988	118.3	4.1	106.9	4.0	121.2	3.3

Source: Citicorp Database Services. Data can also be found in the latest issue of the *Economic Report of the President*.

Deflator. These are comprehensive price indexes estimated by the federal government. A price index is a method of measuring the average behavior of a number of prices over time with reference to a base period.

Table 2-5 illustrates the CPI, PPI, and the GNP Deflator for the years 1965 through 1988. Each index is expressed as a relative number compared to a base period set equal to 100; for example, the GNP Deflator has a 1982 base. Prices measured by the GNP Deflator in other years are either higher (lower) than prices in the base year depending on whether the index is higher (lower) than 100. The 1988 value of 121.2 means that prices in 1988 were 21.2% higher than they were in 1982 in terms of the GNP Deflator.

The CPI, a widely used price index, represents the average prices of goods and services typically consumed by the household. It is estimated and published on a monthly basis. The PPI represents the average price behavior of commodities and materials used by business to produce goods and services. Like the CPI, it is estimated and published every month.

The CPI and PPI are less comprehensive in coverage than the GNP Deflator. The GNP Deflator is a price index that represents the prices of all the goods and services included in GNP which is an estimate of the final production of goods and services in the economy during a period of time. The GNP Deflator thus represents prices over a much broader class of goods and services than do either the CPI or the PPI; however, it is available only on a quarterly basis, when the GNP estimates are made by the U.S. Department of Commerce.

These three price indexes tend to move together, though not always at the same rate, and provide information on changes in the value of a given amount of money. They are also of importance in providing information on how well the economy is doing with respect to the goal of price stability.

The Supply of Money

What determines the amount of money in the economy? The amount of money is determined by a complicated process involving the public, depository financial institutions, and the Federal Reserve System. This will be a separate topic for later discussion (Chapter 10); however, a few brief remarks can be offered here.

Checkable deposits or transaction balances are the major component of the money supply and are issued by commercial banks, savings and loan associations, savings banks, and credit unions as part of their lending and investment activities. These depository institutions operate on the basis of a *fractional reserve system* in which they are required to maintain only a fraction of their deposit liabilities as a reserve. Assume that the reserve requirement for depository institutions is 10%, which means that, for every $100 of checkable deposit liabilities, the depository institution is required to maintain a reserve equal to $10. What is the source of reserves? As will be explained more fully in Chapters 18–20, the Federal Reserve has the ability to create and destroy reserves available to the depository institutions. If the Federal Reserve expands reserves by $10 million, then depository institutions can expand deposit liabilities by $100 million, assuming the 10% reserve requirement. Deposit liabilities can be expanded by making loans and investments; for example, when an individual borrows from a depository institution, the institution does not hand over cash for the amount of the loan but, rather, creates a deposit account in the borrower's name. The borrower can then write checks on the deposit account, and these checks will be accepted by others since they are considered part of the money supply.

Although this example overlooks a number of important parts of the money supply process, it illustrates the important role played by the Federal Reserve (changing reserves), depository institutions (their willingness to create checkable deposits in the act of making loans), and the public (their willingness to borrow and hold checkable deposit accounts). The Federal Reserve has considerable control over the process and can offset or reinforce other forces that are changing the money supply.

money. By demand for money, we mean the amount of money the public desires and is willing to hold at any point in time.

There are a number of reasons why the public decides to hold a certain amount of money. First, there are *transactions* reasons. Economic units receive receipts only at discrete points in time, though they must generally make expenditures on a more continuous basis. Thus, at any point in time, the economic unit must keep a certain amount of money to finance economic activity. This is similar to a "petty" cash fund of a business firm. Generally, the higher the income, the greater the demand for money for transactions purposes. Second, economic units are uncertain about the future and will desire to hold money for *precautionary* reasons. Third, there are *opportunity cost* reasons. Individuals will hold a certain amount of money depending on current interest rates. When interest rates are high, the quantity of money held by the public tends to be low. Because money earns little or no interest income, there is an *opportunity cost* to holding money. This opportunity is represented by the interest income that could be earned from a higher-yielding savings or time deposit account or debt or equity obligation in the financial market.

The forces determining the public's demand for money are many and complex, but a great deal of theoretical and empirical work has shown that the public does have a demand for money. Changes in economic activity occur when the demand for and supply of money differ and the public attempts to establish equilibrium by changes in spending, lending, and borrowing actions.

Let us consider a simple form of the public's demand for money that will show why the demand for money is important in the conduct of monetary policy. Assume that the demand for money can be expressed as

$$DM = 0.50 \text{ GNP} \tag{1}$$

where DM represents the amount of money in dollar terms that the public wishes to hold relative to the level of dollar GNP. This is a simple function that assumes money demand depends only on the level of nominal GNP. A more realistic function would include the interest rate and other variables; however, for purposes of this discussion, it will suffice. According to the expression, for every dollar of GNP, the public wishes to hold $0.50 in money. The demand for money can also be expressed in terms of the *velocity* of money or how rapidly money changes hands to support a given level of GNP. Velocity is measured by the ratio of GNP to the money supply. According to the expression, the velocity of money must be equal to 2.00 in order for the public to achieve its desired money holdings relative to GNP. If the public desires to hold $0.50 for each dollar of GNP, then $0.50 in money can support $1.00 of GNP. Since velocity is defined as the ratio of GNP to money supply, velocity is then equal to 2.00. The demand for money and velocity are inversely related to each other. An increase (decrease) in the amount of money held relative to GNP implies that the numerical value of velocity decreases (increases), other things held constant.

Now let us see how we can use the concept of the demand for money and velocity to understand the problem of monetary policy. Assume that the current level of GNP is $1,000 and that the demand and supply for money are equal. That is, the public's demand for money equals $500 and the Federal Reserve has supplied $500 in money. Based on current short- and long-run economic forces, GNP is expected to increase to $1,500, and at this level, the economy is fully employed and growing at a desired rate.

There are two important issues for the Federal Reserve. First, it must determine the demand for money at a GNP level of $1,500 and supply enough money to meet the demand. According to the expression, the public's demand for money at the higher level of GNP will be $750. If the Federal Reserve allows the money supply to increase above $750, there will be a condition of "excess supply of money," and if the money supply increases to a level below $750, there will be a condition of "excess demand for money." In either case, the public will alter its spending, lending, and borrowing activities to establish equilibrium. There is considerable controversy over how the public adjusts to excess supply of or demand for money; however, it will be useful to consider two possible adjustments assuming the public is reacting to an excess money supply. (1) The excess supply of money can be used to purchase financial assets closely related to money such as short-term securities. A change in the demand for securities will change interest rates, and, hence, business investment spending, consumer spending, and even some types of government spending at the state and local level will be affected by changes in the interest rate. (2) The excess money supply may also be used to purchase goods and services directly such as cars, houses, services of psychiatrists, and so on, in addition to purchasing financial assets closely related to money. The real world is a combination of (1) and (2).

Second, if the Federal Reserve provides a money supply of $750, it may still be too high or too low if the demand for money relationship given by (1) changes. For example, assume that the demand for money increases as a proportion of GNP or, what is the same thing, that the velocity of money declines. The money supply of $750 will not be sufficient to support a GNP of $1,500. As a result, there will exist a condition of excess demand for money and the public will reduce spending. On the other hand, if the demand for money declines or velocity increases, the $750 money supply will generate a condition of excess money supply.

Thus, the Federal Reserve must supply the required amount of money, assuming an accurate money demand estimate, and further, the Federal Reserve must accurately estimate money demand. If the Federal Reserve makes an error in supplying money or determining money demand, either a condition of excess money demand or excess money supply will occur. In this event, the public will change spending, and hence economic activity, to adjust to the imbalance between the supply and demand for money.

Much of the focus of monetary policy is directed toward the demand function for money as well as is much of the debate among economists about the proper conduct of monetary policy. While this example is highly stylized and neglects important issues, it does underline why the demand function for money is important in the conduct of monetary policy. The more (less) stable and predictable the demand function for money, the less (more) difficult the job of monetary policy in satisfying the short- and long-run needs of the economy for money.

Key Points

1. Money is defined in terms of the three basic functions performed in an economic system: as a unit of account, as a medium of exchange, and as a store of wealth. Money can be measured reasonably as coin, currency, traveler's checks, and checkable deposits at depository institutions (M1).

2. Money represents immediate command over resources in the marketplace and can be regarded as 100% liquid. Other financial and real assets have varying degrees of liquidity according to the ease with which they can be converted into money. There is an inverse relationship between the liquidity of a financial asset and the interest earned on holding the asset.

3. The money supply is determined by the interaction of the public, the depository institutions (banks, savings and loan associations, savings banks, and credit unions), and the Federal Reserve. The Federal Reserve has the ability to either increase or decrease the money supply.

4. The value of money has nothing to do with the gold stock; rather, the value of money is inversely related to the general price level. The value of money expresses the command of a given amount of money over resources in the marketplace. The CPI, PPI, and GNP Deflator are the three most widely used measures of the price level.

5. The role of money in monetary policy and money's importance in the economy depends on the ability of the Federal Reserve to control the money supply and the existence of a relationship between money and economic activity.

6. The demand for money plays a critical role in the relationship between changes in the money supply and economic activity. The amount of money desired to be held by the public determines whether too much or too little money has been created by the Federal Reserve. If the money supply exceeds the public's demand for the money, the excess supply will be spent and there will be an increase in the level of economic activity. If money demand exceeds the money supply, individuals will cut back on spending and there will be a decrease in the level of economic activity. The specific process of adjustment to an imbalance between demand and supply for money is a subject of considerable debate in the economics profession.

Key Terms

Coincidence of wants

Commodity money

Credit or fiat money

Debt

Demand deposits

Demand for money

Depository institutions

Inflation

Liquidity (spectrum of liquidity)

M1, M2, and M3

Money

Monetary aggregates

Monetary policy

Medium of exchange

Nominal or dollar GNP

Price index (CPI, PPI, and GNP Deflator)

Real or constant dollar GNP

Representative commodity money

Seasonal adjustment

Supply of money

Transaction balances or deposits (checkable deposits)

Unit of account

Store of wealth

Value of money

Questions

1. Calculate the number of separate price ratios that would be needed to compare the values of 100 goods without the use of money as a unit of account. Now consider money as a unit of account—how many prices are needed to compare the values of the 100 goods?

2. The absence of money as a medium of exchange is generally considered a serious limitation on economic activity; however, a number of transactions are conducted on a barter basis in the United States. Despite the sophisticated financial system, some argue that barter-type transactions have actually increased in the past few decades. Why does barter continue to exist in a sophisticated financial system?

3. Electronic Funds Transfer Systems in which transactions are made without currency, coin, or checks have been slow to develop in the United States despite the tremendous advance in computer technology. Why?

4. Go to the library and obtain a recent issue of the *Federal Reserve Bulletin* and look up recent values for M1, M2, and M3. How have they behaved during the past year?

5. Why does a business firm hold demand deposits when interest-earning NOW accounts are offered by depository institutions? Does this mean that banks have a privileged position in the financial system since nonbank depository institutions are greatly limited in their ability to offer demand deposits?

6. Why do individuals hold coin, currency, or traveler's checks when they earn no interest income?

7. Refer to a recent issue of *The Wall Street Journal* and turn to the section labeled "Federal Reserve Data." This is usually in the Friday edition, though it infrequently appears in the Monday edition. How are the money supply measures reported? How would you interpret the weekly changes in any of the money supply measures?

8. Why would one want to distinguish between seasonally adjusted and not seasonally adjusted money supply? Is the distinction important for other measures of economic activity?

9. Why do revisions in the official money supply measures appear to be smaller for longer-run movements in the money supply?

10. If the CPI for January 1990 is 400 and 402 for February 1990, what is the monthly rate of growth of the CPI? What is the annualized growth rate and what is one assuming in calculating the annualized growth rate based on the monthly data?

Suggested Readings

1. James N. Duprey, "How the Fed Defines and Measures Money," Federal Reserve Bank of Minneapolis, *Quarterly Review* (Spring–Summer 1982), 10–19. Discusses the official measures of money.

2. Milton Friedman and Anna J. Schwartz, *A Monetary History of the United States, 1867–1960* (Princeton, N.J.: Princeton University Press, 1963), and *Monetary Statistics of the United States* (New York: Columbia University Press, 1970). Classical studies of the role of money in the U.S. economy.

3. John Judd and Bharat Trehan, "Portfolio Substitution and the Reliability of M1, M2, and M3," *Economic Review*, Federal Reserve Bank of San Francisco (Summer 1987), 5–31. The influence of deregulation and financial innovation on the use of M1 as a guide to monetary policy.

4. Thomas Mayer, "Federal Reserve Policy Since October 1979: A Justified Response to Financial Innovations?" In Stephen Frowen (ed.), *Monetary Policy and Financial Innovations in Five Leading Industrial Countries* (London: Macmillan, 1988). Discusses how innovation has changed the usefulness of money as a guide to Federal Reserve policy.

5. R. A. Radford, "The Economic Organization of a P.O.W. Camp," *Economica*, 12 (November 1945), 189–201. An interesting discussion of the role of money in a POW camp.

6. Howard L. Roth, "Has Deregulation Ruined M1 as a Policy Guide?" *Economic Review*, Federal Reserve Bank of Kansas City (June 1987), 24–37. The influence of deregulation and financial innovation on the use of M1 as a guide to monetary policy.

7. Richard G. Sheehan, "Weekly Money Announcements: New Information and Its Effects," *Review*, Federal Reserve Bank of St. Louis (August–September 1985), 25–34. Analyzes how the market responds to weekly money supply announcements.

8. Thomas D. Simpson, "The Redefined Monetary Aggregates," *Federal Reserve Bulletin* (February 1980), 97–113. Discusses the reasons for new money measures in 1980.

9. John R. Walter. "Monetary Aggregates: A User's Guide," *Economic Review*, Federal Reserve Bank of Richmond (January/February 1989), 20–28. Provides useful information on the monetary aggregates.

10. Lawrence H. White, "Competitive Payments Systems and the Unit of Account," *American Economic Review*, 74 (September 1988), 699–712. A short but excellent review of how money evolved from commodity to credit based forms.

CHAPTER 3

Basic Elements of the Financial System

Chapter Overview

Comprehending the structure and purpose of the financial system is difficult for two reasons. First, the sheer complexity and number of institutional components makes it difficult to see the underlying structure. The large number of institutions, markets, services, and assets offered by the financial system appears to defy definition. Second, the financial system is dynamic rather than static and, especially in the past decade, has experienced major structural changes. Competition among all components of the financial system, both domestically and internationally, has increased since the mid-1970s. Changes in government regulation have played an important part in the transition; however, financial innovation has played a far more important role than government deregulation efforts. In fact, financial innovation reveals the weakness of previous financial structures and provides government regulators with a guide for regulatory reform.

Despite the apparent complexity of the financial system in static terms and the transition of the financial system toward a more competitive and flexible structure, its basic elements are straightforward. In fact, the basic elements of the financial system discussed in this chapter apply to financial systems of other countries and provide a framework to track better the changing structure of finance.

This chapter lays out the basic elements of the financial system in terms of the two basic channels it provides for the transfer of funds from ultimate lenders to ultimate borrowers. All the financial complexity merely reflects different variations of the two ways of transferring funds. The chapter also introduces the interest rate as the basic indicator of financial conditions. The interest rate can be viewed as either the reward for lending or the cost of borrowing.

Thus, this chapter develops the basic foundation of the financial system and defines key terms used to describe the financial system. The next several chapters provide the institutional detail of the U.S. financial system to fit over the basic foundation. Later chapters will focus on the dynamic aspect of the financial system in terms of why it is in transition and what likely direction it will take in the 1990s.

General Definition of the Financial System

The financial system does not exist in a definite geographic place or as a definite institution with an address; rather, it is an "area" in which funds are traded between borrowers and lenders. The interest rate is the price of funds in the financial system. The interest rate from the perspective of the borrower is what he or she is required to pay in order to obtain funds while from the perspective of the lender, it is the reward for providing funds.

The nature of the financial system is illustrated by considering the economy as composed of economic units. Each unit is placed in one of the following groups:

Households

Nonfinancial businesses

Government (local, state, and federal)

Each group and the units within each group are examined in terms of a budget framework, that is, in terms of the relationship between total expenditures and total receipts. The particular grouping of households, nonfinancial businesses, and government reflects the different receipt and expenditure characteristics of each group. Notice that only real or nonfinancial economic units are considered at this point. Banks and other financial institutions will be considered shortly.

Households receive receipts primarily in the form of wage and salary payments, and expenditures are made for durable and nondurable consumer goods and services and housing. Nonfinancial businesses receive receipts from selling goods to households, governments, and other nonfinancial business firms, and their expenditures represent payments for the cost of production and additions to capital stock in the form of new buildings and equipment. Governmental units obtain receipts from taxes and fees, and expenditures represent the cost of providing governmental services as well as capital expenditures for roads, buildings, and the like.

The budget position of any unit within a group as well as the entire group itself has three possible positions: a *balanced* budget position, in which receipts and expenditures are equal; a *surplus* position, in which receipts exceed expenditures; and a *deficit* position, in which expenditures exceed receipts.

The financial system is concerned with *surplus units (SUs)* and *deficit units (DUs)*. SUs are economic units with surplus budgets; DUs are economic units with deficit budgets. The SU is faced with a problem. By definition, the SU does not desire to spend all receipts and has funds left over. In terms of the spectrum of liquidity, the SU is at the most liquid position, but there is a trade-off between liquidity and interest return. The higher the degree of liquidity, the higher the opportunity cost associated with being liquid. Opportunity cost represents the interest income an individual forgoes by holding assets with high liquidity; for example, in the case of currency and/or demand deposits, the individual earns no explicit interest return and thus incurs a high opportunity cost to being completely liquid. The SU is thus in a position to lend funds and accept an I.O.U. from a DU, who by definition, desires to spend more than he or she receives. We can think of an I.O.U. as a promise to pay a specific sum (the principal) plus an interest rate over a period of time (maturity of the loan). From the point of view of the SU, the I.O.U. is a financial asset that can either be a debt or equity claim on the DU. From the point of view of the DU, the I.O.U. is a financial obligation that represents a claim on the real resources of the DU if the obligations stated by the I.O.U. are not fulfilled.

Two important considerations are involved in the relationship between the SU and DU. First the SU has excess funds and as such does not desire to engage in further expenditures; however, there is an opportunity cost to holding highly liquid funds. The SU would be willing to move down the spectrum of liquidity if compensated for the smaller degree of liquidity and increased risk. Second, the DU has a different problem in that it wants to spend more than is received in the current period. If a household unit, the DU will obtain extra satisfaction from purchasing in the current period. If a nonfinancial business, the DU expects to earn additional profit by making a new addition to equipment or building.

Thus there is a quid pro quo between the SU and DU. A financial system is essentially an "area" that allows the two units to engage in a transfer of I.O.U.s for funds.

Saving, Investment, Surplus Units, and Deficit Units

An SU is defined as an economic unit (household, nonfinancial businesses, governmental unit) with total receipts exceeding total expenditures during a given period of time; a DU is an economic unit with total expenditures exceeding total receipts during a given period of time. It is obvious that the plans of the DU cannot be fulfilled unless there is some mechanism that allows for the transfer of funds from the SU to the DU.

Let us take a closer look at the SU and DU and see if we cannot develop a more precise definition of what these terms mean. This can be done by considering each sector's real and financial transactions in the framework of a current receipts–expenditures statement and balance sheet statement.[1] We can think of the current receipts–expenditures statement as an income statement.

Total receipts, or sources of funds, represent the sum of all nonfinancial sources of funds over a given period of time. Nonfinancial sources of funds are obtained by selling goods or services in the market; financial sources of funds are obtained by selling I.O.U.s in the financial system (borrowing). Total expenditures, or uses of funds, for any given sector are for current expenditures and expenditures on capital account. Current expenditures represent expenditures for items with a life expectancy of one year or less; expenditures on capital account are made for items with a life expectancy of more than one year.

The income statement summarizes the total receipts, current expenditures, and a general balancing term called *saving*. Saving is defined as the difference between total receipts and current expenditures and thus serves as the balancing item and is

---

[1] The development of a flow of funds expression based on general income and balance sheet information follows the excellent presentation by Lawrence S. Ritter, "An Exposition of the Flow-of-Funds Accounts," *Journal of Finance*, 18 (May 1963), 219–230. Also see Ritter's "The Flow of Funds Accounts: A Framework of Financial Analysis," *New York University Bulletin* (August 1968), 52.

TABLE 3-1 Typical income statement

Expenditures (uses)		*Receipts (sources)*	
Current expenditures	$3,000	Receipts	$5,000
Saving	2,000		
	$5,000		$5,000

analogous to the use of profits as a balancing item in the typical income statement for a business firm. Table 3-1 presents a general income statement for a sector or economic unit within a sector. Receipts are considered sources of funds and current expenditures are considered uses of funds. Saving or receipts not spent on current expenditures are also recorded as a use of funds.

There are three important things to consider about a sector's income statement. First, the amount of saving that is found on the income statement is defined as total receipts less *current* expenditures; we are not subtracting total expenditures from receipts to obtain saving but only current expenditures from receipts. Second, the items on the income statement are recorded on a *flow* basis; that is, each item indicates the change during the year. Third, saving is the residual that is available for other purposes after current expenditures. Saving as the balancing item ensures that uses of funds will equal total sources of funds. Saving appears on the uses side of the statement because it represents something that is done with receipts. To determine how saving is distributed for any given sector, we turn to the sector's balance sheet statement.

Before the balance sheet can be related to the income statement, however, the balance sheet must be transformed from a *stock* basis to a flow basis, as balance sheets record assets, liabilities, and net worth at a point in time such as December 31, 1990. To convert the balance sheet to a flow basis, simply take the difference between the balance sheet items between December 31, 1989 and December 31, 1990 and determine the change in assets, liabilities, and net worth over the year. (Change in a stock is indicated by placing the symbol Δ in front of the item.) By definition, the change in assets equals the sum of the change in liabilities and net worth. Table 3-2 illustrates a typical balance sheet on a flow basis. The change in real assets is also referred to as investment.

In this example, the saving from the income statement and the change in net worth on the balance sheet are equal. This is not a coincidence. In fact, saving and change in net worth have to be equal because they really represent the same quan-

TABLE 3-2 Typical balance sheet on a flow basis

Δ *Assets (uses)*		Δ *Liabilities* + Δ *net worth (sources)*	
Δ Real Assets (investment)	+$ 500	Δ Liabilities	−$1,000
Δ Financial assets	+ 500	Δ Net worth (saving)	+ 2,000
	$1,000		$1,000

tity. The difference between receipts and current expenditures, whether positive or negative, must be reflected in changes in assets and/or changes in liabilities on the balance sheet. Thus, saving is both a use (income statement) and a source (balance sheet) of funds.

Positive saving is available to reduce liabilities, increase real assets (goods with a life expectancy of over one year), or increase financial assets (e.g., holdings of money and savings and time deposits). Negative saving occurs when current expenditures exceed receipts and can be accommodated by a decrease in real assets (selling a house or piece of capital equipment), decrease in financial assets (drawing down money holdings or selling off Treasury securities), or an increase in liabilities. There are an infinite number of ways in which changes in assets and changes in liabilities can reflect a given amount of saving from the income statement. For example, Table 3-2 is only one of many adjustments in the balance sheet consistent with the income information in Table 3-1. The sector receives $5,000 in the form of money, allocates $3,000 for current expenditures, and, hence, saves $2,000. What does the sector do with the surplus of $2,000? The changes in the balance sheet in Table 3-2 indicate that real assets increased by $500, perhaps the sector is a household and the $500 represents the purchase of a stereo. Financial assets increased by $500, reflecting increased holdings of money, savings, and time deposits, or some other financial asset. Part of the $2,000 of saving is used to pay off liabilities as liabilities declined by $1,000. The combined changes in assets and liabilities equal $2,000, the amount of saving from the income statement.

That a given sector has positive saving does not mean that the sector is an SU. Likewise, that investment is undertaken does not mean that the sector is a DU. Whether a sector is an SU or DU depends on the relationship between saving and investment or lending and borrowing. This can be seen by the following expressions derived from Tables 3-1 and 3-2. From the income statement, we have

$$\text{Current expenditures} + \text{saving (change in net worth)} = \text{receipts} \qquad (1)$$

From the balance sheet, we have

$$\text{Change in real assets (investment)} + \text{change in financial assets} \\ = \text{change in liabilities} + \text{change in net worth (saving)} \qquad (2)$$

Then by combining, we obtain

$$\text{Investment} = \text{saving} + (\text{change in liabilities} - \text{change in financial assets}) \qquad (3)$$

The change in real assets represents the amount of investment made during the year by the particular sector. Investment or change in real assets represents the change in the stock of goods that have a life expectancy greater than one year.[2]

One more adjustment is needed to derive a *fundamental flow of funds equation.* The change in liabilities in expression (3) really represents borrowing activity. Whenever an individual increases borrowing, this will show up as an increase in the individual's liabilities; likewise, decreased borrowing occurs when previous debts are paid thus reducing liabilities. The change in financial assets in expression (3) really

[2] Change in real assets can also include the change in inventories for the business sector.

represents lending activity. Increased lending shows up as increased holding of financial assets and decreased lending shows up as decreased holding of financial assets. Thus expression (3) can be written as

$$\text{Investment} = \text{saving} + (\text{borrowing} - \text{lending}) \tag{4}$$

Expression (4) must hold for any given economic unit since it is based on accounting definitions. This expression can be viewed as the fundamental flow of funds equation for any given economic unit since it summarizes the real and financial transactions as they are reflected on income and balance sheet statements.

The SU and DU can now be defined in terms of either the relationship between receipts and expenditures or between investment and saving. The following relationships characterize the SU:

$$\text{Total receipts} > \text{total expenditures (current expenditures} + \text{investment)} \tag{5}$$
$$\text{Total receipts} - \text{current expenditures} > \text{investment} \tag{6}$$
$$\text{Saving} > \text{investment} \tag{7}$$

and, because expression (3) must hold for every sector since the expression is obtained from income and balance sheet definitional relationships, the only way in which saving can exceed investment is for

$$\text{Change in financial assets (lending)} > \text{change in liabilities (borrowing)} \tag{8}$$

or

$$\text{Lending} > \text{borrowing} \tag{9}$$

Even if the SU decides merely to hold onto the saving in the form of money, this represents lending activity during the year, since coin and currency are regarded as I.O.U.s of the Treasury and Federal Reserve, respectively, and demand deposits and other checkable deposits are I.O.U.s owed by commercial banks and depository institutions, respectively.

The following relationships characterize the DU:

$$\text{Total receipts} < \text{total expenditures (current expenditures} + \text{investment)} \tag{10}$$
$$\text{Total receipts} - \text{current expenditures} < \text{investment} \tag{11}$$
$$\text{Saving} < \text{investment} \tag{12}$$
$$\text{Change in financial assets (lending)} < \text{change in liabilities (borrowing)} \tag{13}$$

or

$$\text{Lending} < \text{borrowing} \tag{14}$$

Thus, a DU must borrow more funds during the year than it lends to achieve the desire of investing more than is saved. Expression (4) can be considered a fundamental flow of funds equation for any given economic unit or sector in the economy. It summarizes the spending and financial transactions and indicates whether a sector is a net lender or net borrower in the financial system depending on the relationship between saving and investment.

The financial system is thus concerned with transferring funds from those sectors of the economy that are SUs to those that are DUs. SUs are those units whose receipts exceeded their total expenditures or saving exceeds their investment; DUs are those units whose total expenditures exceed their receipts or their investment exceeds their saving.

Transferring Funds from Surplus Units to Deficit Units

The SU has funds left over after completing current consumption and real asset expenditures. These funds have complete liquidity but have a high opportunity cost in terms of the trade-off between liquidity and interest income. On the other hand, the DU spends more than was received, and, unless the DU wishes to reduce expenditures, it must obtain the funds from the SU. Presumably, the DU will be willing to pay interest for the funds.

There are essentially two methods for transferring the funds from the SU to the DU, and these two methods constitute the basic foundation of the financial system. The two methods are *direct* and *indirect* finance.

Direct Finance

Direct finance exists when the DU and SU exchange money and I.O.U.s directly. The SU and DU deal directly with each other either "eyeball to eyeball" or, as is often the case, through the services of specialized brokers and agents. The brokers and agents merely act as "matchmakers" between the SU and DU and charge a commission fee for their services. They do not take a position in the I.O.U.s being traded or assume the risk of the DU. In direct financial relationships between an SU and a DU, the SU assumes the risk of lending to the DU. Examples of direct finance include

1. A household (SU) that purchases a newly issued share of IBM (DU) stock through a stockbroker
2. An employee (SU) of IBM who purchases a newly issued share directly from IBM (DU)
3. A local governmental unit with a surplus budget (SU) that purchases newly issued federal securities (DU)
4. A household (SU) that purchases commercial paper issued by GM (DU)

Direct Finance and Economic Activity

The relationship between direct finance and general economic activity is illustrated in Figure 3-1. The top portion of the figure illustrates the flow of economic activity based on the division of activity into consuming and producing functions, *C* and *P*,

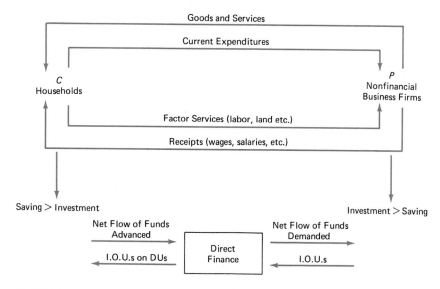

FIGURE 3-1   General economic activity and direct finance

respectively. To engage in consuming activity, households sell their factor services to the producing sector for which they receive income payments in the form of money. Saving is defined as current income (receipts) less current expenditures, and, assuming that their saving exceeds their investment, the household sector is an SU. Household investment refers to the purchase of any real asset with a life expectancy in excess of one year, such as a car or house. The household sector has traditionally been an SU. The producing sector has traditionally been a DU, as current receipts are seldom sufficient to cover current expenditures and expenditures for new capital equipment and additional buildings.

The SU has income left over after all spending decisions have been completed and would be willing to exchange the excess funds for a promise to pay (I.O.U.) in the future at an appropriate interest rate. The DU is willing to pay the interest cost, on the grounds that the expenditure to be supported by the borrowed funds will increase profits sufficiently over the period of the loan to repay both the principal and interest cost.

Indirect Finance

Direct finance has historically provided an efficient method of transferring funds from SUs to DUs for a wide range of lending-borrowing purposes. At the same time, direct finance imposes a number of conditions that limit participation in the financial system, especially for smaller SUs and DUs.

Specifically, three conditions are necessary before direct finance between SU and DU can occur. First, the amount of the transfer must be consistent with the spending plans of both SU and DU. In many cases this is not accomplished easily. The typical household unit generally has a surplus budget of small magnitude, whereas the DU often requires large sums of funds. Second, the time horizon of both

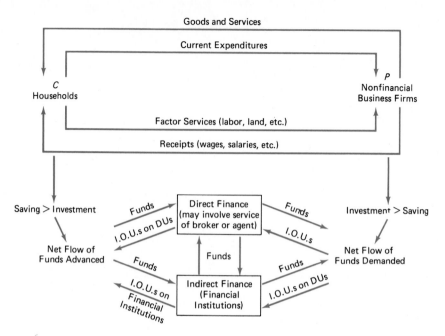

FIGURE 3-2   General economic activity with direct and indirect finance

SU and DU must be the same. Again, the time horizon of the household unit is typically shorter than that of the DU. The SU may only wish to lend funds for one year, whereas the DU is looking for a loan with a maturity of at least several years. Third, the degree of risk associated with the DU's I.O.U. must be compatible with the SU's degree of risk aversion. In direct finance, the SU must assume all the risk of the DU, and the SU generally does not have the time, expertise, or funds to spread that risk over several loans. Thus, although direct finance was the first form of financial relationship to evolve historically in market-oriented economic systems, its limitations provided the opportunity for the emergence of indirect finance.

Indirect finance involves the introduction of a financial intermediary between the SU and DU that assumes the risk of the DU and relaxes the requirements of a successful transfer of funds between SU and DU. Indirect finance separates the SU and DU to such an extent that neither one is aware of the other's existence. Figure 3-2 illustrates the process of indirect finance and the relationship of indirect to direct finance and economic activity in general. The figure also indicates that direct and indirect channels interact with each other. More on this later.

The SU exchanges the surplus funds for an I.O.U. drawn on the financial institution that can be tailored more appropriately to the liquidity needs of the SU. At the same time, the financial institution deals with a large number of SUs and can accumulate large sums of funds to lend to many DUs. The accumulated fund allows large loans—loans with long-term maturities—and spreads the risk over a number of DUs. Indirect finance has a number of significant advantages for both the SU and the DU.

Benefits to the Surplus Unit   SUs can purchase I.O.U.s from financial institutions in small or large amounts and for very short or long holding periods. Financial institutions can diversify to a greater extent than can any single SU as well as achieve other economies of scale (e.g., determining the creditworthiness of the DU). As a result, the I.O.U. of a financial institution that pays the same interest return as an I.O.U. drawn directly on a DU will generally involve a smaller degree of risk for the SU.

Benefits to the Deficit Unit   The large accumulation of funds from numerous small SUs allows the DU to borrow large amounts over long periods of time. The existence of the financial institution reduces the search costs of the DU in finding a suitable lender compared with a regime of direct finance. Moreover, the financial institution can offer other services to the DU such as investment and market analysis.

Thus, for a large number of financial transactions, indirect finance offers significant improvements for all concerned compared with direct finance.

Will the Real Surplus and Deficit Unit Please Stand Up!

The concept of an SU and a DU is an analytical method of defining the basic nature of the financial system. In practice, one does not observe an SU and a DU on opposite ends of a given financial transaction. Instead, one observes a lender and a borrower at opposite ends of the transaction exchanging funds for I.O.U.s. Focusing on one or even several financial transactions provides little information as to whether the lender is an SU or the borrower is a DU. Whether an economic unit is an SU (DU) or net supplier (demander) of funds to (from) the financial system depends on their net lending and borrowing activities aggregated over all transactions during a given period of time.

This is an important point since analytically, the financial system is defined in terms of SU and DU concepts; however, it is usually discussed in terms of lending and borrowing. Figure 3-3 illustrates the flow of funds in terms of lenders and borrowers with a little more institutional detail added than in Figure 3-2. The Federal Reserve has been added since it can influence the amount of funds depository institutions have available for lending. Also, Figure 3-3 separates financial institutions into depository and nondepository types.

Funds are advanced or supplied to the financial system through either direct or indirect channels by nonfinancial lenders: nonfinancial businesses, households, government, and foreigners. Funds are demanded or borrowed in the financial system by the same set of nonfinancial entities. Thus, a given sector or unit within a sector can operate on both sides of the financial system at the same time.

Whether any individual or sector is an SU or DU depends on the total amount of lending and borrowing. An SU is a *net* lender or supplier of funds to the financial system while a DU is a *net* borrower or demander of funds. This is clearly reflected by the definition of the SU and the DU in terms of investment, saving, lending, and borrowing. The SU is characterized by

$$\text{Saving} > \text{investment} \quad \text{and} \quad \text{Lending} > \text{borrowing} \tag{15}$$

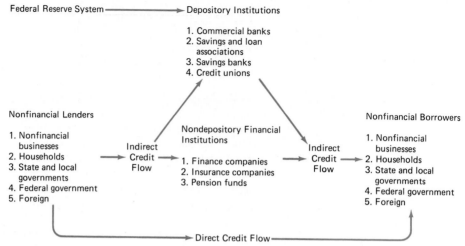

Source: Diagram based on William N. Cox III, "Impairment in Credit Flows: Fact or Fiction?" *Review*, Federal Reserve Bank of Atlanta (February 1970), p. 25.

FIGURE 3-3   Flow of funds through the financial system

and the DU is characterized by

$$\text{Investment} > \text{saving} \qquad \text{and} \qquad \text{Borrowing} > \text{lending} \qquad (16)$$

In the case of direct finance between SU and DU, the excess of lending over borrowing for the SU will show up as an increase in holding of I.O.U.s owed by the DU. The surplus unit assumes the direct risk of the DU. The excess of borrowing over lending for the DU will be represented by an increase in outstanding I.O.U.s owed to SUs.

In the case of indirect finance, the excess lending over borrowing of the SU will be represented by increases in I.O.U.s owed by financial institutions, and the excess of borrowing over lending of the DU will be represented by an increase in outstanding I.O.U.s held by financial institutions. The financial institution assumes the direct risk of the DU.

Relative Roles of Direct and Indirect Finance

Over the years indirect finance has accounted for a significant percentage of the funds channeled through the financial system. We can approximate the importance of indirect finance by expressing the total funds advanced through private financial institutions as a percentage of the total funds advanced in a given year. Figure 3-4 presents such an index for the years 1960–1987.

During this period indirect finance accounted for the major flow of funds in the U.S. economy—about three-fourths of the total; however, note the declines in the

BOX 1 A flow of funds matrix for the economy

The fundamental flow of funds equation can be constructed for any economic unit or group of units in the economy. It is merely a way of summarizing real and financial uses and sources of funds. So far we have constructed the equation for the major nonfinancial sections—business, household, and government. We can just as easily construct an equation for the financial sector, though this sector will have characteristics different from those of the nonfinancial sectors. In fact, a complete set of equations for all sectors provides an overview of the financial system in terms of inter- and intrasector flow of funds.

The Federal Reserve constructs a complete set of flow of fund accounts for the U.S. economy based on the basic equation discussed in this chapter. While the appendix presents the actual flow of fund matrix for 1988, the following example will help provide an overview of the financial system.

Table 1B illustrates a simple economy with three nonfinancial sectors (household, business, and government) and one financial sector (financial institutions). Keep in mind that saving is both a use of funds (income account) and a source of funds (balance sheet account) and is placed in the source column. Let us examine in detail the household flow of funds equation.

Investment = saving + (borrowing or sources of funds − lending or uses of funds)

or

$$\$200 = \$2,400 + (-\$100 - \$2,100)$$

Remember that all the terms are flows. Investment of $200 means that real assets increased by $200 during the period, saving of $2,400 means that the excess of current expenditures over receipts increased by $2,400 during the period, borrowing of −$100 means that outstanding I.O.U.s declined by $100 during the period, and lending of $2,100 means that financial assets increased by $2,100 during the period.

There is one minor point that needs to be cleared up before proceeding. The flow of funds views all sectors except government engaged in both saving and investment. The lack of an investment entry for the government sector reflects the convention that all government spending is regarded as current consumption; hence, a government deficit (surplus) is recorded as negative (positive) saving.

Several important aspects of the financial system are revealed by Table 1B. First, total uses and sources are equal for each sector, but saving and investment are not equal for each sector. Households have surplus budgets (saving exceeds investment), whereas business and government have deficit budgets (investment exceeds saving). Second, the accounts illustrate the manner in which a deficit is financed and how a surplus is distributed. For example, households have excess funds of $2,200 of which $1,400 is put on deposit as a savings and time deposit in a financial institution, $700 is used to purchase government securities from the government sector, and $100 is used to repay a loan at the financial institution. Third, total borrowing and total lending are equal for all sectors combined. For every debt, there must be a credit, and, because aggregate borrowing and lending cancel out, saving equals investment for the entire economy. Fourth, the account illustrates both direct and indirect finance. For example, households' purchase of Treasury securities (an increase in financial assets for the household sector) from the government (an increase in liabilities for the government sector) represents direct finance between SU and DU. The business sector borrows $1,500 from the financial institution (an increase in liabilities for the business sector), and the financial institutions obtained the funds, originally from household SUs. Fifth, the account illustrates the basic intermediary function performed by financial institutions. Activity in the financial sector is concentrated in the financial uses and sources part rather than in the saving and investment part.

TABLE 1B Flow of funds for a four-sector economy

	Household U	Household S	Business U	Business S	Government U	Government S	Financial institutions U	Financial institutions S	Total U	Total S
Saving Investment	$200	$2,400	$2,000	$500		–$700	$10	$10	$2,210	$2,210
Net changes in financial assets										
(1) Savings and time deposits	1,400						$1500		1,400	
(2) Treasury securities	700								700	
(3) Loans							–100		1,400	
Net changes in liabilities										
(1) Savings and time deposits								$1,400		1,400
(2) Treasury securities						700				700
(3) Loans		–100		1,500						1,400
	$2,300	$2,300	$2,000	$2,000	0	0	$1,400	$1,400	$5,700	$5,700
Surplus (deficit)		$2,200		($1,500)	0	($700)	—		—	

Handwritten annotations:

- Increase Saving For Period
- Indicat increal asset increase during Period
- INCOME acct
- Fixed assets increase by $100 during period
- Balance sheet acct
- outstanding loans decrease by 100 eg 100
- household surplus shown as 1400 in savings, 700 T.S, 100 to repay loans

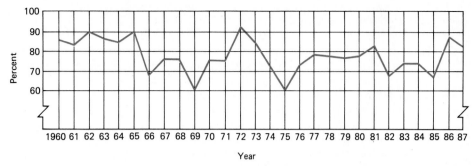

Source: Based on data in Board of Governors of the Federal Reserve System, *Flow of Funds Accounts, 1946–1975* (December 1976), various issues of the *Federal Reserve Bulletin*, and *Flow of Funds Accounts* (Third Quarter 1989).

FIGURE 3-4 Percentage of funds advanced
by private financial institutions, 1960–1987

intermediation index in 1966, 1969, 1975, and 1982. These periods are generally known as "credit crunches" and reflect fundamental problems in the financial system.

The indirect part of the financial system that accounts for a major portion of the flow of funds at any point in time is composed of two categories of financial institutions: depository and nondepository financial institutions. Depository institutions accept some form of deposit as the main source of funds from SUs. Many of these deposits are used as transaction accounts and represent the major form of money in the United States. Commercial banks, savings and loan associations, savings banks, and credit unions are the major depository institutions. Savings and loan associations, savings banks, and credit unions are collectively referred to as *savings institutions*. Savings and loan associations and savings banks are collectively referred to as *thrifts*. Nondepository institutions differ from depository institutions in that the former's funds come from sources other than deposits.

Don't get the impression that indirect and direct finance are separate since each is based on a different relationship between SUs and DUs. They are very closely related in two important respects. First, many financial institutions purchase I.O.U.s (financial assets) in direct financial markets as well as obtain funds in direct markets (sell I.O.U.s or liabilities). Direct market participants use the services of financial institutions in a variety of ways including borrowing from financial institutions to conduct direct market activities. Second, all financial markets and institutions respond to the same set of economic forces that either restrain or expand credit and these economic forces ensure that the operations of both indirect and direct finance are in balance with each other.

The interaction between direct and indirect finance is illustrated in Figure 3-2, which indicates that funds flow back and forth between direct and indirect finance.

BOX 2   Indirect finance in the United States and Japan

The basic elements discussed in this chapter can be used to examine the financial structure of other countries. Japan in particular has become an interesting economy in this regard. Once regarded as a developing economy in the 1960s, Japan has emerged like a Phoenix from the ashes of World War II to the world's second largest democracy in terms of GNP. Japan's financial system has also come to play an important part of the world's financial system, especially since Japan in 1985 became the world's largest creditor nation. The growing role of Japanese banking in the world reflects the financial responsibilities being increasingly assumed by Japan. In 1988 the largest 10 banks in the world were Japanese and 17 of the largest 25 banks in the world were Japanese (*American Banker*, July 19, 1988). Thus, interest in Japan's financial system is based on more than passing intellectual curiosity.

The Bank of Japan (Japan's central bank and similar in function to the Federal Reserve) also constructs flow of fund accounts based on the fundamental flow of funds equation discussed in the chapter. Some modifications of the U.S. and Japanese accounts are required to directly compare Japan and the United States because of measurement differences and different financial structures. Once this is accomplished, the modified flows provide interesting comparisons, especially in regard to the relative role of indirect finance in the two countries.

Thomas F. Cargill and Shoichi Royama, in *The Transition of Finance in Japan and the United States: A*

Comparative Perspective (Stanford, Calif.: Hoover Institution Press, 1988), report the following indirect finance ratios:

Year	Japan	United States
1960–1965	84.0	90.0
1965–1970	91.7	82.0
1970–1975	91.6	76.3
1975–1980	90.0	73.1
1980–1985	84.5	63.5

The ratios show that indirect finance plays a larger role in the financial system in Japan than in the United States. Much of the indirect finance in Japan is provided by banks and government financial institutions. In contrast, banks and government financial institutions play a smaller role in the United States than in Japan.

The more important role of indirect finance in Japan reflects the close and long-term relationships that exist between Japanese financial institutions and their business customers than has been the case in the United States. In general, long-term customer relationships are more important in Japan's economy than in the United States while market-type transactions are more important in the United States than in Japan.

Common Terms Used to Describe the Financial System

There are numerous terms used to describe the specific aspects of the financial system. The following is certainly not an exhaustive list; however, these are among the most frequently used financial terminology.

The Primary Market   The primary market represents the point at which the I.O.U. is created. All I.O.U.s have primary markets. When someone borrows from a commercial bank and the bank creates a demand deposit account in the process, the financial claim (demand deposit account) has been created in the primary market. Likewise, when IBM issues new stock purchased by individuals, the stock has emerged in the primary market.

The Secondary Market The secondary market is the used-car market of the financial system, in which certain I.O.U.s can be sold one or more times before maturity. All I.O.U.s have a primary market, but only I.O.U.s with widely recognized characteristics and legal negotiability have a secondary market. Treasury securities (especially short-term securities), bankers' acceptances, and large-denomination time certificates or CDs have very active secondary markets.

Intermediation Market The intermediation market refers to the creation of I.O.U.s in the process of indirect finance. Checkable deposits, time and savings deposits, and life insurance policies are I.O.U.s created in the intermediation market. If the I.O.U.s are not created in the intermediation market, then they are the result of direct finance. Financial intermediaries or institutions that transfer funds between the SU and DU include commercial banks, savings and loan associations, savings banks, credit unions, finance companies, insurance companies, money market mutual funds, and others.

Money Market I.O.U.s with maturities of one year or less are regarded as money market instruments. These are also referred to as short-term financial instruments.

Capital Market I.O.U.s with maturities of more than one year are regarded as capital market instruments. These are also referred to as long-term financial instruments.

Debt Market The debt market is differentiated from the equity market. In the debt market, the borrower issues a debt instrument or I.O.U. (commercial paper, corporate bond, mortgage, or consumer loan) and promises to pay the holder of the instrument in some specified manner or over a given period of time. Debt instruments can be either short term or long term. The issuer of the debt instrument has a legal obligation to honor the interest payments and principal payment of the instrument. Failure to meet the conditions of the debt instrument provides the grounds for the holder of the debt to take legal action to secure payment.

Equity Market Corporations can issue equity instruments instead of debt instruments to obtain funds. Equity instruments are fundamentally different from debt instruments. Equity instruments represent a residual claim on the profits of the corporation and the corporation is under no legal obligation to pay dividends to holders of equity. In fact, equity instruments have no maturity. Equity instruments are classified as long-term or capital market instruments.

Foreign Exchange Market This is an international market in which the currency of one country is exchanged for the currency of another at the exchange rate. The foreign exchange market is critical to the functioning of international trade and finance. Actual currencies are not traded in the foreign exchange market; rather, financial assets (short and long term) denominated in foreign currencies are traded.

Key Points

1. The basic function of the financial system is to facilitate and encourage the transfer of funds from SUs to DUs.

2. SUs are economic units whose total receipts exceed total expenditures or, what amounts to the same thing, whose saving exceeds investment. This can only occur when lending exceeds borrowing in the financial system.

3. DUs are economic units whose total expenditures exceed their total receipts or whose investment exceeds saving. This can occur only when borrowing exceeds lending in the financial system.

4. Direct and indirect finance are the basic methods used by the financial system to transfer funds from SUs to DUs. Direct financial relationships exist when the SU assumes the risk of the DU by exchanging funds for an I.O.U. Indirect financial relationships involve a financial intermediary or institution, whereby the financial institution directly assumes the risk of the DU and the SU only assumes the risk of the

I.O.U. issued by the financial institution. Because financial institutions can achieve economies of scale and greater diversification, the risk to a small SU is generally less than that associated with direct finance.

5. The fundamental flow of funds equation for any sector in the economy can be expressed as

$$\text{Investment} = \text{savings} + (\text{borrowing} - \text{lending})$$

This indicates that an SU that is saving more than it invests must be a net lender (lending exceeds borrowing) in the financial system. A DU that invests more than it saves must be a net borrower (borrowing exceeds lending) in the financial system.

6. Many of the financial assets, or I.O.U.s, used in the financial system can be defined in terms of the market in which they are traded. The most important are the primary, the secondary, the intermediation, the money, the capital, the debt, the equity, and the foreign exchange markets.

Key Terms

Balance sheet

Capital market

Current expenditure

Deficit unit (DU)

Direct finance

Flow measurement

Financial asset

Financial system

Flow of funds

Foreign exchange market

Fundamental flow of funds equation

Income statement

Indirect finance

Intermediation market

Investment

I.O.U.

Liability

Money market

Net worth and saving

Primary market

Real asset

Saving and net worth

Secondary market

Stock measurement

Surplus unit (SU)

Questions

1. How can an individual borrow in the financial system and still be classified as an SU? How can an individual lend in the financial system and still be classified as a DU?

2. Intermediation is often defined as the process of shifting the lending and borrowing activity from the direct to the indirect part of the financial system. What is "disintermediation" and under what conditions might it occur?

3. Assume that you have $1,000 of positive saving from your income statement. Develop several different combinations of balance sheet changes consistent with positive saving of $1,000. What about negative saving of $1,000?

4. Explain the meaning of the statement, "A financial obligation always has two sides: it is an asset to one entity and a liability to another."

5. If we computed the values of the fundamental flow of funds equation for every sector in the economy and totaled them, what would happen to the term (borrowing-lending) in the equation?

6. List the advantages of indirect finance from the perspective of an average household.

7. Indicate how the existence of a secondary market in, say, Treasury bills, increases their liquidity.

8. If you owned a business, what considerations would be relevant to whether you issued debt or equity instruments as a source of funds.

9. Why is the nonfinancial business sector traditionally a DU?

10. Given the following incomplete balance sheet information;

	December 31, 1989	December 31, 1990
Assets	$500	$600
Liabilities	400	
Net worth		350

   a. Determine the missing information for both years.
   b. Determine whether saving is positive or negative during the year.
   c. Is there sufficient information to determine the level of receipts and current expenditures during the year?
   d. Show that the balance sheet in flow terms satisfies the basic accounting definition that assets = liabilities + net worth.

Suggested Readings

1. Board of Governors of the Federal Reserve System. *Introduction to the Flow of Funds* (Washington, D.C.: The Board of Governors, 1980). Explains the flow of funds statistics.

2. Thomas F. Cargill and Shoichi Royama, *The Transition of Finance in Japan and the United States: A Comparative Perspective* (Stanford, Calif.: Hoover Institution Press, 1988). Uses flow of funds framework to compare the financial systems of Japan and the United States.

3. Jacob Cohen, "Copeland's Money-Flows After Twenty-five years: A Survey," *Journal of Economic Literature*, 10 (March 1972), 1–25. Reviews the development of flow of funds.

4. Raymond W. Goldsmith, *Capital Market Analysis and the Financial Accounts of the Nation* (Morristown, N.J.: General Learning Press, 1982). How an economy can be characterized by the flow of funds.

5. John G. Gurley and Edward S. Shaw, "Financial Aspects of Economic Development," *American Economic Review*, 45 (September 1954), 515–538.

6. John G. Gurley and Edward S. Shaw, "Financial Intermediaries and the Saving-Investment Process," *Journal of Finance*, 11 (May 1956), 257–276. Both Gurley and Shaw papers develop the concept of the financial system in terms of deficit and surplus units.

7. Lawrence S. Ritter, "An Exposition of the Flow-of- Funds Accounts," *Journal of Finance*, 18 (May 1963), 219–230.

8. Lawrence S. Ritter, *The Flow of Funds Accounts: A Framework for Financial Analysis* (New York: New York University Bulletin, August 1968). Both papers by Ritter are excellent sources for understanding the flow of funds framework.

APPENDIX

Flow of Funds

Measures of Economic Activity

There are many measures of real and financial economic activity for the U.S. economy. There are measures to reflect specific types of economic activity and performance such as various types of price indexes (CPI, PPI, and the GNP Deflator), unemployment rates, manufacturing output indexes, money supply estimates, interest rates, amounts of credit, and so on. The list is extremely long, and the student should skim recent issues of the *Federal Reserve Bulletin*, published monthly by the Board of Governors of the Federal Reserve System; *Survey of Current Business*, published monthly by the U.S. Department of Commerce; and the *Economic Report of the President*, published annually by the Council of Economic Advisors. These three sources provide a wealth of statistical information about the economy.

In addition to the large number of measures of specific types of economic activity and performance, there are three broader measures that provide an overall impression of the performance of the economy and together form a fairly complete economic accounting system: (1) the gross national product (GNP) and national income (NY) accounts, (2) the flow of funds accounts (FOF), and (3) the balance-of-payments accounts or statement of international transactions. The GNP and NY accounts measure the final output of goods and services produced during a given period, usually in a quarter or a year, and the total income earned by factors of production in producing the output of goods and services. GNP provides information on the total amount of investment spending for capital goods during a given period, whereas NY provides information on the amount of saving during a given period. The FOF accounts measure the financial flows between SUs and DUs and indicate the way in which the saving in the economy was transferred to those economic units that undertook the investment. The statement of international transactions summarizes the real and financial relationships between the United States and the rest of the world.

The FOF accounts will be outlined in this appendix since the accounts provide extensive information about flows in the financial system as discussed in Chapter 3 while the international statement and GNP will be discussed in Chapters 15 and 17 respectively.

The Flow of Funds Accounts

The FOF accounts are derived as follows:

1. The economy is divided up into sectors (e.g., households, nonfinancial businesses, and government).

2. A balance sheet and income statement for each sector is constructed, and, from these two statements, a uses and sources of funds statement is derived for a given time period, usually a quarter or a year. (This is done on the same basis as that followed in Chapter 3.)

3. The uses and sources statements are then combined to provide the FOF accounts for the entire economy, which presents the information on the transfer of funds both intra- and intersectorally.

The uses and sources statement for any given sector summarizes all the sources and uses of funds on a flow basis. The information for this statement is based on the income statement, which is constructed on a flow basis, and comparison of one balance sheet with a previous balance sheet to convert the balance sheet items from a stock to a flow basis. By definition, the uses and sources of funds for each sector are equal. The distinction between sources and uses for a given sector is not always readily apparent; however, a useful method of determining whether a transaction represents a use or source is the following. If the transaction increases assets or reduces liabilities, the transaction is regarded as a use; if the transaction reduces assets or increases liabilities, the transaction is regarded as a source. In addition, keep in mind that a source can be recorded as a negative entry in the use category and a use can be recorded as a negative entry in the source category.

Components of a general uses and sources statement can be listed as follows:

Uses of Funds

1. Current expenditures (e.g., expenditures for services and goods with a life expectancy of one year or less)

2. Decreases in a liability item on the balance sheet (e.g., repayment of a loan)

3. Increases in a real asset item on the balance sheet (e.g., buying a house, new capital equipment): investment

4. Increases in a financial asset item on the balance sheet (e.g., buying securities, increasing bank balances): lending

Sources of Funds

1. Receipts from any source (e.g., wage payments, interest income, sales revenue, tax revenue)

2. Increases in a liability item on the balance sheet: borrowing

3. Decreases in a real asset item on the balance sheet (e.g., selling off a car, house, capital equipment): disinvestment
4. Decreases in a financial asset item on the balance sheet (e.g., selling off Treasury securities, reducing a demand deposit account at the bank, reducing time and savings deposits)

Let us take a closer look at some of the items. Current expenditures are an obvious item to include in the uses of funds. Likewise, any expenditures that increase real assets (spending on goods that have a life expectancy in excess of one year) also represent a use of funds. An increase in any financial asset also represents a use of funds. For example, if the household unit increases deposits at the commercial bank during the current period or purchases time certificates or commercial paper, the transaction will show up as an increase in financial assets and constitute a use of funds. If the household unit pays off a loan at the bank (or any other I.O.U. created in previous periods), the decrease in liabilities constitutes a use of funds.

Defining receipts from all sources as part of a sector's source of funds is obvious; however, the reason for including increases in liability terms and decreases in asset items as sources of funds may not be so obvious. Consider the household sector. If the household sector borrows funds from a bank, savings and loan association, or any other financial institution, the increase in liabilities represents a source of funds for the current period. Likewise, if the household unit draws down some of its deposit balance at the bank, or sells Treasury securities, or sells real assets, the decreases in assets serve to increase the funds available to the household sector. The same reasoning can be used for any given sector in the economy.

The uses and sources statement for any sector can be simplified by the following manipulations: given that uses equal sources of funds by definition, we can write

$$\begin{aligned} &\text{Current expenditures + decreases in liabilities + increases in real assets} \\ &\quad + \text{increases in financial assets} \\ &= \text{receipts + increases in liabilities + decreases in real assets} \\ &\quad + \text{decreases in financial assets} \end{aligned} \quad (1)$$

Saving for any sector is defined as receipts less current expenditures, and we can combine the increases and decreases in assets and liabilities into one general term to obtain

$$\Delta \text{ Real assets } + \Delta \text{ financial assets } = \text{saving } + \Delta \text{ liabilities} \quad (2)$$

To express (2) another way,

$$\begin{aligned} \text{Investment or real uses of funds} &= \text{saving or real sources of funds}[1] \\ &+ (\text{borrowing or financial sources of funds} \\ &- \text{lending or financial uses of funds}) \end{aligned} \quad (3)$$

[1] Saving is regarded as a source of funds in the FOF accounts. Even though we introduced saving as a use of funds in the income statement on page 45, saving is also a source of funds in the balance sheet on page 45.

where changes in liabilities are represented by borrowing, changes in financial assets are represented by lending, and changes in real assets are represented by investment. An increase (decrease) in liabilities will show up as an increase (decrease) in borrowing, whereas an increase (decrease) in financial assets will show up as an increase (decrease) in lending. Expressions (2) and (3) must hold by definition for each sector of the economy; however, there is no inherent reason for saving and investment to be identical. If a sector wishes to invest more than it saves (act as a DU), then borrowing must exceed lending. If a sector wishes to save more than it invests (act as an SU) in a given period, it can only accomplish this if lending exceeds borrowing.

Because expressions (2) or (3) must hold for each sector, they will hold for all sectors combined. But, for all sectors combined, borrowing will equal lending, because, for every act of borrowing in the economy, there is an act of lending somewhere else in the economy. Thus, total borrowing must equal total lending for all sectors combined, although borrowing and lending do not necessarily have to be equal for any given sector in the economy. Because borrowing equals lending for all sectors combined, then saving equals investment for all sectors combined.

The Flow of Funds for 1988

Table A-1 presents the summary FOF account for 1988 according to nine sectors of the economy: households, business, state and local government, the foreign sector, the U.S. government, federally sponsored credit agencies, monetary authorities (the Federal Reserve and certain monetary transactions of the Treasury), commercial banks, and private nonbank financial institutions (savings and loan associations, life insurance companies, etc.). Very detailed uses and sources of funds for each sector (and divisions within each sector) are also available.

A direct comparison can be made between the FOF matrix in Box 1 and the actual FOF matrix for 1988 in Table A-1. There are two ways in which to examine the FOF matrix. First, we can take a given sector and examine the entries row by row to determine whether or not that sector was an SU or a DU and how the excess or deficit funds are distributed or obtained over various types of financial uses and sources. Looking at the rows for a given sector column provides detailed information on the intrasector movement of funds. Second, we can take an item in a given row and examine the interaction between the various sectors to gain information on intersector transfers of funds.

The gross saving row (1) corresponds to saving in Table 1B; the gross investment row (4), however, does not correspond to investment, as the item gross investment includes both real and financial transactions. Private capital expenditures (5) corresponds to investment or change in real assets in the example. By comparing row 1 with row 5, you can determine whether the sector is an SU or a DU. The basic equation for each sector is

$$\text{Investment} = \text{saving} + (\text{borrowing or financial sources} - \text{lending or financial uses}) \quad (4)$$

In the actual FOF account in Table A-1, the equation is

$$\begin{aligned}\text{Private capital expenditures (5)} &= \text{gross saving (1)} \\ &+ [\text{financial sources (13)} - \text{financial uses (12)}]\end{aligned} \quad (5)$$

Two ways to look at FOF

TABLE A-1 Summary of flow of funds accounts for the year 1988 (millions of dollars)

	Private domestic nonfinancial sectors								Foreign sector		U.S. government		Total	
	Households		Business		State and local governments		Total							
	U	S	U	S	U	S	U	S	U	S	U	S	U	S
1 Gross saving		775,021		471,831		−9,752		1237,100		136,151		−162,282		20,905
2 Capital consumption		412,092		394,281				806,373						31,725
3 Net saving (1−2)		362,929		77,550		−9,752		430,727		136,151		−162,282		−10,820
4 Gross investment (5+11)	824,963		452,705		−9,045		1268,623		116,513		−185,047		10,951	
5 Pvt. capital expenditures	690,236		483,878				1174,114				−3,307		46,793	
6 Consumer durables	451,125						451,125							
7 Residential construction	220,142		9,329				229,471						228	
8 Plant and equipment	18,969		422,867				441,836						46,565	
9 Inventory change			48,375				48,375							
10 Mineral rights			3,307				3,307				−3,307			
11 Net financial investment	134,727		−31,173		−9,045		94,509		116,513		−181,740		−35,842	
12 Financial uses	420,306		84,384		25,230		529,920		163,412		−2,707		857,236	
13 Financial sources		285,579		115,557		34,275		435,411		46,899		179,033		893,078
14 Gold & off. fgn. exchange									473	4,041	1,045		2,523	
15 Treas. currency and SDR ctfs.												511		622
16 Checkable deposits & curr.	15,691		10,199		2,221		28,111		−582		8,996		5,872	42,877
17 U.S. government											8,996			10,627
18 Foreign									−582					−582
19 Private domestic	15,691		10,199		2,221		28,111							32,832
20 Small time & savings dep.	113,470				7,125		120,595				−247			119,022

No.		Col A	Col B	Col C	Col D	Col E	Col F	Col G	Col H	Col I	Col J	Col K	Col L	Col M
21	Money market fund shares	20,655	3,147			23,802						−1,944	21,858	
22	Large time deposits	28,566	12,166	−8,440		32,292		3,022			18,181	53,495		
23	Fed. funds & security RP's		8,209	1,268		9,477	1,098				17,477	41,483		
24	Foreign deposits	−7,257			−7,257		826			8,083				
25	Life insurance reserves	12,862			12,862			326		12,536				
26	Pension fund reserves	244,572			244,572			19,631		224,941				
27	Interbank claims					6,837			−904	4,135				
28	Mutual fund shares	−6,366	3,736		−2,630				2,207	−423				
29	Other corporate equities	−113,993		−130,500	−113,993	−130,500	−3,105		746	2,555	15,211			
30	Credit mkt. instruments	148,458	276,376	7,610	275,589	19,477	32,013	175,545	583,978	104,676	5,888	−7,301	157,457	254,887 729,290
31	U.S. treasury securities	54,277	−1,462	13,515	66,330			68,311		140,028	12,109			
32	Federal agency securities	79,851	−67	370	80,154			—	17,434	68,031	137,473			
33	Tax-exempt securities	18,158	507	247	1,642	32,501	20,047	33,092			13,045			
34	Corporate & foreign bonds	−12,722		84	−12,722	97,187	22,914	6,728		144,419	50,696			
35	Mortgages	−3,641	221,537	97,187	3,950	3,637	295,802		−1,052		293,130	−82	−5	
36	Consumer credit		51,066	74,265	3,207	51,066				47,859				
37	Bank loans N.E.C.	−2,891	50,388		47,497	14,109	−1,844	39,092	−6,561					
38	Open-market paper	12,535	2,357	11,596	14,892	11,596	−658	9,634	60,634	53,638				
39	Other loans	6,157	42,069	−488	47,738	−8,630	−6,249	50,971	19,723					
40	Security credit	3,579	2,568		3,579	2,568	—		691	1,702				
41	Trade credit	21,406	21,406	−403	2,262	21,406	5,137	3,072	7,144	−1,962	−6,534	3,407	3,779	
42	Taxes payable			964	3,579	964				−5,446	641			
43	Equity in noncorp. bus.	−75,425		−79,660	−75,425	−79,660					4,235			
44	Miscellaneous	28,237	3,357	25,168	49,567	53,405	52,924	47,921	28,254	2,208	7,642	70,502	92,699	
45	Sector discrepancies (1–4)	−49,942	19,126	−707	−31,523	19,638		22,765			9,954			

TABLE A-1 Continued

		Financial Sectors											
		Spons. Ag. & Mtg. Pools		Monetary Authority		Commercial Banking		Pvt. Nonbank Finance		All Sectors		Distr.	Natl. Svg. & Inv.
		U	S	U	S	U	S	U	S	U	S		
1	Gross saving		1,033		−1,778		19,762		1,888		1,231,874		1,095,723
2	Capital Consumption						21,124		10,601		830,023		830,023
3	Net saving (1–2)		1,033		−1,778		6,713		−8,713		401,851		265,700
4	Gross investment (5+11)	1,128		−1,778		−1,373		12,974		1,211,040		20,834	1,101,087
5	Pvt. capital expenditures					22,007		8,799		1,217,600		14,274	1,217,600
6	Consumer durables									451,125			451,125
7	Residential construction							228		229,699			229,699
8	Plant and equipment					22,007				488,401			488,401
9	Inventory change							24,558		48,375			48,375
10	Mineral rights												
11	Net financial investment	1,128		−1,778		−23,380		−11,812		−6,560		6,560	−116,513
12	Financial uses	139,717		18,478		177,473		521,568		1,547,861		6,560	46,899
13	Financial sources		138,589		20,256		200,853		533,380		1,554,421		163,412
14	Gold & off. fgn. exchange			2,523						4,041	4,041		
15	Treas. currency and SDR ctfs.			622						622	511	−111	
16	Checkable deposits & curr.	−31			18,086	200	16,530	5,703	8,261	42,397	42,877	480	
17	U.S. government				3,292		7,335			8,996	10,627	1,631	
18	Foreign				61		−643			−582	−552		
19	Private domestic	−31					9,838	5,703	8,261	33,983	32,832	−1,151	
20	Small time & savings dep.				14,733	200	73,349	−1,326	45,673	119,022	119,022		

#	Item											
21	Money market fund shares							−1,944		21,858	21,858	21,858
22	Large time deposits					42,107		18,181	11,388	53,495	53,495	53,495
23	Fed. funds & security RP's	6,593		5,545		19,639	5,339	21,844	28,052	41,483	41,483	13,431
24	Foreign deposits					8,083				826	826	
25	Life insurance reserves							12,536		12,862	12,862	
26	Pension fund reserves							224,941		244,572	244,572	
27	Interbank claims			−1,170	266	266	3,869		5,933		4,135	−1,798
28	Mutual fund shares							2,207	−423	−423	−423	
29	Other corporate equities					−1	1,666	2,556	13,545	−114,543	−114,543	
30	Credit mkt. instruments	131,149	137,473	10,524		156,003	−2,487	431,614	119,901	1002,210	1002,210	
31	U.S. treasury securities	5,754		11,111		−9,330		4,574		140,028	140,028	
32	Federal agency securities	192	137,473	−587		30,326		38,100		154,907	154,907	
33	Tax-exempt securities					−22,498		35,543		33,092	33,092	
34	Corporate & foreign bonds					12,172	1,347	132,247	49,349	154,611	154,611	
35	Mortgages	101,491				77,684		113,955	−82	295,715	295,715	
36	Consumer credit					33,608		14,251		51,066	51,066	
37	Bank loans N.E.C.			—		39,092		39,092	−6,561	39,092	39,092	
38	Open-market paper	355				−1,628	−3,834	61,907	57,472	74,868	74,868	
39	Other loans	23,357		—		−3,423		31,037	19,723	58,831	58,831	
40	Security credit					−478		1,169	1,702	4,270	4,270	
41	Trade credit							3,407	3,779	25,923	9,526	−16,397
42	Taxes payable						186		455	−1,867	1,605	3,472
43	Equity in noncorp. bus.								4,235	−75,425	−75,425	−75,425
44	Miscellaneous	2,006	1,116	434	1,904	21,483	45,994	46,579	43,685	174,036	181,519	7,483
45	Sector discrepancies (1–4)	−95		—		21,135		−11,086	20,834	20,834	20,834	−5,364

Rows 14–44 provide detailed information on the financial uses and sources of funds for each sector. Row 45 is an intrasector discrepancy adjustment. By definition the accounts are constructed on the basis that expression (5) holds for every sector; however, errors in data collection require an adjustment to obtain expression (5). Using the estimate provided by the 1988 FOF matrix, expression (5) for the household sector (in billions) is

$$\$690.2 = \$775.0 + [\$285.6 - (\$420.3 \text{ plus sector discrepancies of} - \$49.9)] \tag{6}$$

keeping in mind that totals may not add due to rounding.

Rows 14 through 44 reveal how the household sector allocated the excess funds of \$84.8 billion. Households increased their holdings of checking deposits, time and savings deposits, life insurance, and pension reserves. These actions can be regarded as lending to commercial banks and various nonbank financial institutions. Households also increased their holdings of Treasury securities. Even though the household sector was an SU overall, the household sector borrowed, primarily for home mortgages and consumer credit.

Thus, looking at a particular sector heading and the rows under that heading reveals whether the sector is an SU or a DU and how the excess funds were dispersed or the deficit funds obtained.

A column-by-column examination of the FOF account provides detailed information on the interaction of the various sectors. For example, the household sector increased its holdings of time and savings deposits by \$113.5 billion, part of which shows up as the source of funds for commercial banks.

The foreign sector is essentially a summary measure of the U.S. balance-of-payments position. It indicates whether or not the United States had any outstanding claims against itself or against other countries. The column marked for national saving and investment represents the domestic saving and investment components of the GNP and NY accounts. There is also a column for statistical discrepancies between sectors.

CHAPTER 4

Some Basics About Interest Rates in the Financial System

Chapter Overview

The financial system consists of many direct and indirect markets for I.O.U.s. In any given market, borrowers sell I.O.U.s (liabilities or claims on themselves) to lenders in order to obtain funds. The I.O.U.s from the lenders' perspective represent financial assets. The interest rate is the cost of funds to the borrower and the return to the lender. There are many different types of interest rates in the financial system; however, they respond to the same economic forces and share the same conceptual framework.

Interest rates influence the individual more than ever as a result of deregulation and innovation which have removed most interest rate ceilings and now provide a whole array of new financial assets with market-sensitive interest rates. The cost of consumer and mortgage credit is now more market sensitive than it once was. In particular, homeowners have become especially concerned about interest rate changes because of the widespread use of adjustable rate mortgages or ARMs. Prior to 1980, homeowners cared little about interest rate movements once mortgage financing had been secured because virtually all mortgage interest rates were fixed over the term of the mortgage. Deregulation and innovation have been responsible for the widespread use of ARMs, which provided over 50 percent of new mortgage financing in the late 1980s. Aside from influencing the cost of consumer and mortgage credit, interest rate changes influence the return on deposits. Deregulation and innovation have also made interest received on deposits more sensitive to market forces than previously.

At a more general level, interest rates influence the overall level of economic activity as well as the flow of goods, services, and financial assets between the United States and the rest of the world.

This chapter discusses several basic concepts related to interest rates. In this regard, we review the concept of present value, yield to maturity, types of interest rates found in both indirect and direct financial markets, and where one can find interest rate information.

The next chapter focuses on what determines the level of interest rates and what determines the relationship between different interest rates.

Present Value

The interest rate relates the present to the future and vice versa. The most instructive way to understand the interest rate in this regard is to consider the concept of *present value*. Present value can be illustrated by considering a *simple loan* transaction.

Joe Hickenlupper loans $100 on December 31, 1989 to Martha Murgatroyd for one year, the maturity of the loan. Martha promises to repay the principal of $100 plus an interest rate of 5% on December 31, 1991. The rate of interest relates the initial amount of A_0 or $100 at time t (December 31, 1989) to the expected cash flow of A_1, or $105 receivable at time $t + 1$ (December 31, 1991). Let r represent the rate of interest

$$A_1 = A_0 + rA_0 \tag{1}$$
$$A_1 = A_0(1 + r) \tag{2}$$

A_1 is the future value of A_0 if A_0 accumulates at the rate r over the one-year period. The student should note that in this and the following examples in this chapter, calculations are for a one-year period, and thus all interest rates are annualized. In actual practice, interest payments occur at intervals of less than a year and the formulas need to be modified to calculate annualized interest rates; however, this refinement is not necessary to understand the basic nature of the interest rate in the financial system.

In terms of the simple loan example then, expression (2) provides the amount owed by Martha on December 31, 1991

$$\$105 = \$100 (1 + 0.05) \tag{3}$$

Expression (2) also expresses the interest rate as a measure of the *yield to maturity* of the loan from the perspective of the lender, Hickenlupper. It represents the expected cash flow to the lender over the maturity of the loan.

The concept of present value will help us better understand yield to maturity, the most frequently used interest rate measure in the financial system. The relationship between A_0 and A_1 in expression (2) can be reversed as

$$A_0 = \frac{A_1}{(1 + r)} \tag{4}$$
$$\$100 = \frac{\$105}{(1 + 0.05)} \tag{5}$$

In this case, A_0 represents the *discounted present value* of A_1 received one year from time t discounted at the rate r. In this respect, Hickenlupper is indifferent between receiving $105 one year from now or $100 today. The present value of $105 receivable one year from now is the same as $100 received today if discounted at the rate of 5%.

The yield to maturity of the loan is thus the interest rate that equates the discounted value of the expected future stream of payments over the maturity of the loan to the initial amount of the loan. The yield to maturity assumes that the I.O.U. is held to maturity and relates the entire expected stream of future payments to the initial amount.

Expressions (1), (2), and (4) can be expanded for a simple loan transaction of two years:

$$A_2 = A_0 + \underbrace{rA_0}_{\substack{\text{Interest for} \\ \text{first year}}} + \underbrace{r(A_0 + rA_0)}_{\substack{\text{Interest for} \\ \text{second year}}} \tag{6}$$

$$A_2 = A_0 + rA_0 + rA_0 + r^2A_0 \tag{7}$$
$$A_2 = A_0(1 + r)^2 \tag{8}$$
$$A_0 = \frac{A_2}{(1 + r)^2} \tag{9}$$

If $A_0 = \$100$ is loaned for two years at a rate of 5.0%, then A_0 will accumulate to $110.25 ($A_2$), or $110.25 two years from today has a present value of $100 if discounted at the rate of 5.0%. Again, the interest rate, r, is the yield to maturity because it equates the discounted expected payment stream ($110.25 payable in two years) to the initial amount paid for the I.O.U.

These expressions can be generalized for a loan with a maturity of n periods in the future.

$$A_n = A_0 + rA_0 + r(A_0 + rA_0) + \cdots + r(A_0 + r^{n-1}A_0) \tag{10}$$
$$A_n = A_0(1 + r)^n \tag{11}$$
$$A_0 = \frac{A_n}{(1 + r)^n} \tag{12}$$

The rate of interest can thus be used in each of two ways: we can calculate how much a given sum of money loaned at time t will accumulate in $t + n$ periods, and we can calculate the present value of any sum of money receivable in the future at a given rate of interest.

Interest Rates in the Indirect and Direct Markets

The financial system is composed of indirect and direct markets. The interest rate on any given I.O.U. traded in a market is nothing more than a way of relating the present to the future and vice versa. At the same time, there are important differences between interest rates in various markets that should be kept in mind.

Interest Rates in Indirect Markets

Individuals encounter interest rates in indirect markets in one of two ways: as a return on deposits or as a cost of borrowing.

As a result of deregulation, deposit interest rates with one exception have not been subject to legal ceilings (known as Regulation Q deposit rate ceilings) since March 31, 1986. Demand deposits represent the major exception since they continue to be subject to a zero interest rate ceiling. Expression (11) can be used to calculate the interest earned on a simple time deposit account.

Assume Hickenlupper purchases a $1,000 time deposits paying an 8 percent interest rate compounded annually with a five-year maturity. Setting A_0 = $1,000, r = 0.08, and n = 5, Hickenlupper will receive $1,469.33 at the end of five years

$$\$1,469.33 = \$1,000 \, (1 + 0.08)^5 \tag{13}$$

Assuming the time deposit is held to maturity, the interest rate is also the yield to maturity from Hickenlupper's perspective since he has effectively loaned $1,000 to the depository institution for a five-year period.

The interest rate as a cost of borrowing can be illustrated by considering two types of loans in indirect markets: *simple loans* and *fixed payment loans*. Simple loans are often made to businesses in which the borrower pays the principal and interest at the time the loan matures. The example on page 70 illustrates a simple loan transaction.

Consumer and mortgage loans as well as many business loans, however, are of the fixed payment type. The borrower receives a given sum of funds and is then required to make periodic and equal payments over the maturity of the loan. Each payment contributes toward repaying the principal and the interest on the loan. This is referred to as *amortization* of the loan. In general, the fixed yearly payment (FYP) for a loan of n years is determined by

$$\text{Amount borrowed} = \frac{\text{FYP}}{(1 + r)} + \frac{\text{FYP}}{(1 + r)^2} + \cdots + \frac{\text{FYP}}{(1 + r)^n} \tag{14}$$

Given the amount borrowed, the interest rate, and maturity, solution of FYP requires a pocket calculator or, more commonly, the use of books that provide numerous tables for different interest rates, payment schedules, and amounts borrowed that make it easy to determine the fixed payment.

To illustrate the use of expression (14), assume Hickenlupper borrows $1,000 for five years at 8% on a fixed payment basis.

$$\$1,000 = \frac{\text{FYP}}{(1.08)} + \frac{\text{FYP}}{(1.08)^2} + \frac{\text{FYP}}{(1.08)^3} + \frac{\text{FYP}}{(1.08)^4} + \frac{\text{FYP}}{(1.08)^5} \tag{15}$$

Using a standard book of tables (*Realty Bluebook*, Professional Publishing Corporation, San Rafael, California, 1980), the FYP is $250.46. The 8% is also the yield to

---

BOX 1   Truth in lending and saving—interest rate disclosure

Participants in direct financial markets tend to be more sophisticated about interest rates, if for no other reason than that these markets move so fast and are so competitive that limited understanding of the basic mechanics of the market is dangerous to your economic health in very short order. Participants in indirect markets (depositors and borrowers, in particular) also need to understand the basics; however, they tend to have fewer financial transactions and indirect markets don't move as quickly as direct markets. As a result, indirect market participants tend to be less sophisticated about interest rates and the like.

As a result, government financial regulation has made an extensive effort to better inform the consumer of financial services about certain interest rate basics. The best known of the disclosure laws regarding the cost of borrowing is the Truth in Lending Act. It was part of the 1968 Consumer Credit Protection Act and is currently implemented by the Board of Governors as Federal Reserve Regulation Z. Creditors that regularly extend consumer credit for personal or household purposes are covered by Regulation Z. The major focus of Regulation Z is to ensure that the financial charges and annual percentage interest rate are clearly represented in a uniform and consistent manner. The regulation is explicit about how interest rates are to be calculated.

In 1987 Congress became concerned about the apparent lack of proper disclosure about interest rates on deposits. Prior to the start of deregulation, this was not a major issue because interest rates were regulated on almost all savings and time deposits offered by depository institutions. The deposit rate ceilings were administered by the Federal Reserve's Regulation Q. An important part of the deregulation process has been to remove deposit rate ceilings, and at present, only demand deposits are subject to a zero rate ceiling. In addition, depository institutions have been permitted to offer a much wider range of deposits than previously.

As a result, there have been several efforts in the past few years to establish a Truth in Saving regulation similar to the Truth in Lending regulation. Specifically, it would require greater disclosure about deposit interest rates and prohibit misleading impressions. One of the problems that frequently was brought to the Congress's attention was the wide variation in interest payments associated with the same advertised interest rate and time period because of different compounding, crediting, and other conventions used by the depository institution.

To date, no specific Truth in Saving regulation has been established.

---

maturity from the perspective of the lender since the discounted expected payment stream equals the initial amount of $1,000 allowing for slight round-off:

$$\$1,000 = \frac{\$250.46}{(1.08)} + \frac{\$250.46}{(1.08)^2} + \frac{\$250.46}{(1.08)^3} + \frac{\$250.46}{(1.08)^4} + \frac{\$250.46}{(1.08)^5} \tag{16}$$

Interest Rates in Direct Markets

Interest rates in direct markets differ from those commonly found in indirect finance for two reasons. First, direct market interest rates are determined in open and highly competitive markets with numerous sellers and buyers of specific types of I.O.U.s. As a result, direct market rates are the most sensitive indicators of demand and supply for funds in the financial system. While deregulation and innovation have rendered interest rates in indirect markets more market sensitive, these interest rates do not respond as rapidly to general market forces as direct interest rates. For example, ARMs usually provide for an interest rate adjustment every six months or so, and rates on NOW accounts are adjusted only, say, every month or so. Interest rates in direct markets are the pivotal interest rates in the economy. Second, most direct market I.O.U.s have secondary markets that fundamentally change the nature of the direct market I.O.U. compared to the indirect market I.O.U. As a result, we need to distinguish between interest rates in primary and secondary markets since an I.O.U. may be traded in secondary markets for amounts different than the original primary market.

There are three types of interest rates in the direct market related to certain characteristics of the I.O.U. requiring discussion. Most frequently, these are expressed as yield to maturity.

I.O.U.s Without Interest Payments   Short-term I.O.U.s of one year or less in maturity do not pay an explicit interest payment to the holder of the I.O.U. These instruments are sold at discount from the face value, and the difference between the discounted price and the face value adjusted for maturity determines the interest rate. The yield to maturity of a discount I.O.U. is

$$r = \left(\frac{MV - MP}{MP}\right) \cdot \left(\frac{365}{n}\right) \tag{17}$$

where

$$r = \text{the yield to maturity}$$
$$MV = \text{maturity value, par or face value of the I.O.U.}$$
$$MP = \text{market price of the I.O.U.}$$
$$n = \text{maturity in days}$$

Of the numerous types of discount I.O.U.s, Treasury bills are the most important. Treasury bills are I.O.U.s of the U.S. Treasury of one year or less in maturity issued to finance the spending activities of the federal government. The Treasury bill market is large and active and plays an extremely important role in the financial system and the conduct of monetary policy.

Dealers in Treasury bills, have traditionally quoted interest rates on a *discount basis* rather than the more appropriate yield to maturity basis as given in expression (17). Despite the sophistication of the financial system and use of high technology of every type to facilitate financial transactions, some elements remain traditional and unchanged. Quoting Treasury bill rates on a discount basis is one of these unchanging elements. The discount yield is

$$\text{Discount yield} = \left(\frac{MV - MP}{MV}\right) \cdot \left(\frac{360}{n}\right) \tag{18}$$

To illustrate the difference between expression (17) and (18), assume Hickenlupper purchases a 91-day \$10,000 Treasury bill for \$9,750. The yield on a discount basis is

$$9.89 = \frac{\$10,000 - \$9,750}{\$10,000} \cdot \frac{360}{91}$$

while the yield to maturity is

$$10.28 = \frac{\$10,000 - \$9,750}{\$9,750} \cdot \frac{365}{91}$$

The discounted yield *understates* the yield to maturity because the formula uses the face amount as a denominator rather than the market price. The magnitude of the understatement increases the longer the maturity and the larger the difference between market price and face value. The discounted yield also understates the yield to maturity because it is based on a 360- rather than a 365-day year.

The discount yield is not a true yield since it relates the expected cash flow to the face value and not the amount actually paid for the Treasury bill.

The use of discount yields on Treasury bills is not a serious problem, however. Yield to maturity can easily be calculated on the basis of the same information, yield to maturity is always greater than discount yield, and yields on a discount and maturity basis move together in response to economic forces.

There is an important relationship between the market price and the yield on I.O.U.s revealed by expressions (17) and (18). *The price of the I.O.U. and the yield are inversely related.* In the example, if the market price of the Treasury bill *decreases* to $9,650, the discount yield will *increase* from 9.89% to 13.85% and the yield to maturity will *increase* from 10.28% to 14.55%.

I.O.U.s with Interest Payments or Coupon Bonds I.O.U.s with maturity longer than one year frequently pay the holder a fixed interest payment at periodic points in time before the I.O.U. matures. The interest payment is known as a coupon payment. The coupon payment expressed as a percentage of the face or par value of the security is referred to as the coupon interest rate and should not be confused with the market rate of interest or yield to maturity of the security. Treasury notes and bonds, municipal bonds, and corporate bonds are long-term I.O.U.s that have coupon payment provisions. In these cases, the I.O.U. is characterized by five pieces of information:

1. C, the coupon payment, usually expressed as a percentage of the par value of the bond (I.O.U.). This payment is made to the holder of the bond for as long as the bond is outstanding. C remains constant throughout the life of the bond. The coupon interest rate is also constant throughout the life of the bond since the coupon payment, C, and the face or par value of the bond remain constant over the life of the bond.

2. MV, the maturity value, face amount, or par value. This is the amount paid when the bond matures and is not influenced by the market price of the bond at any point in time.

3. MP, the market price of the bond, which varies over the life of the bond, depending on the forces of demand and supply in the financial system.

4. r, the yield to maturity, which varies over the life of the bond, depending on the forces of demand and supply in the financial system.

5. n, the term to maturity of the bond or the number of years the bond will remain outstanding.

TABLE 4-1   Sample page from a standard bond table book

Coupon payment (C) = $6, Maturity value (MV) = $100, Coupon rate (C/MV × 100) = 6%

Yield (r)	10–6	11–0	11–6	12–0	12–6	13–0	13–6	14–0
8.00	85.97	85.55	85.14	84.75	84.38	84.02	83.67	83.34
8.10	85.34	84.90	84.48	84.07	83.68	83.31	82.95	82.60
8.20	84.71	84.25	83.82	83.40	83.00	82.61	82.24	81.88
8.30	84.09	83.62	83.17	82.73	82.32	81.92	81.53	81.16
8.40	83.47	82.99	82.52	82.07	81.64	81.23	80.84	80.46
8.50	82.86	82.36	81.88	81.42	80.98	80.55	80.15	79.76
8.60	82.26	81.74	81.25	80.77	80.32	79.89	79.47	79.07
8.70	81.66	81.13	80.62	80.13	79.67	79.22	78.80	78.39
8.80	81.06	80.52	80.00	79.50	79.03	78.57	78.13	77.71
8.90	80.48	79.92	79.39	78.88	78.39	77.92	77.47	77.04
9.00	79.89	79.32	78.78	78.26	77.76	77.28	76.82	76.39
9.10	79.32	78.73	78.18	77.64	77.13	76.65	76.18	75.73
9.20	78.74	78.15	77.58	77.04	76.52	76.02	75.55	75.09
9.30	78.18	77.57	76.99	76.44	75.91	75.40	74.92	74.45
9.40	77.62	77.00	76.41	75.84	75.30	74.79	74.30	73.83
9.50	77.06	76.43	75.83	75.25	74.71	74.18	73.68	73.20
9.60	76.51	75.87	75.26	74.67	74.11	73.58	73.07	72.59
9.70	75.96	75.31	74.69	74.10	73.53	72.99	72.47	71.98
9.80	75.42	74.76	74.13	73.53	72.95	72.40	71.88	71.38
9.90	74.89	74.21	73.57	72.96	72.38	71.82	71.29	70.79
10.00	74.36	73.67	73.02	72.40	71.81	71.25	70.71	70.20

Source: Expanded Bond Values Tables (Boston: Financial Publishing Company, 1970), p. 590.

The following expression illustrates the relationship among the five items for any long-term bond:

$$MP = \frac{C_1}{1+r} + \frac{C_2}{(1+r)^2} + \cdots + \frac{C_n}{(1+r)^n} + \frac{MV}{(1+r)^n} \tag{19}$$

The market price of the bond is thus equal to the discounted present value of the expected stream of coupon payments each year and the maturity value of the bond. The interest rate, r, is the yield to maturity because it equates the discounted expected future stream of payments to the initial amount paid for the I.O.U.

As in the case of fixed payment loans, bond tables have been prepared for easy solution of expressions similar to (19) for a variety of values of C, MV, and n. According to the excerpt from a standard bond book (Table 4-1), a $100 bond ($MV = 100) with a 6% coupon rate ($C = 6) and a 12-year maturity ($n = 12$) that sells for $81.42 in the bond market yields a rate of interest of 8.50% ($r = 0.085$).

That is, if you paid $81.42 for a 12-year bond with a 6% coupon payment provision and held the bond to maturity, you would have earned 8.50% on the original $81.42.

The reader should take note again of an important relationship between price and yield. There is an *inverse* relationship between the market price and the rate of interest or yield. For the specific example considered, a bond selling for $81.42 per $100 of face value provides a yield to maturity of 8.5%. If the market price *increases* to $84.75, the yield *decreases* to 8%.

Equity I.O.U.s Unlike coupon bonds, equities make no promise to pay, have no specified maturity, and represent a residual claim on assets should the business declare bankruptcy. On the other hand, equities provide the holder with an ownership interest and the potential to influence management decisions.

To determine the yield on equities, we need to consider a *consol*, a special type of debt I.O.U. used in England. The consol is a debt I.O.U. that has no maturity date (i.e., $n = \infty$). The consol promises to pay the holder a coupon payment, C, every year for as long as the consol is held.

The market price of the consol can be determined by using expression (19) and allowing $n \to \infty$.

$$MP = \frac{C_1}{1 + r} + \frac{C_2}{(1 + r)^2} + \frac{C_3}{(1 + r)^3} + \cdots \tag{20}$$

The coupon payment, C, in each year is the same, and, defining $d = 1/(1 + r)$, expression (19) can be written as

$$\begin{aligned} MP &= Cd + Cd^2 + Cd^3 + \cdots \\ &= Cd(1 + d + d^2 + \cdots) \end{aligned} \tag{21}$$

Since d is less than the value of 1.00, the infinite geometric progression contained in the parentheses is equal to $1/(1 - d)$; thus (21) can be written as

$$\begin{aligned} MP &= \frac{Cd}{1 - d} \\ &= \frac{C/(1 + r)}{(1 + r - 1)/(1 + r)} = \frac{C}{r} \end{aligned} \tag{22}$$

The market price of a consol is simply the coupon payment divided by the rate of interest. A $10,000 consol with a $500 coupon payment selling at $9,900 yields a rate of interest of 5.05%.

The concept of a consol can be used to express the yield on equities by considering the equity to have an indefinite maturity, with the current annual dividend continuing indefinitely into the future. Under these assumptions, the yield on an equity is

$$MP = \frac{D}{r} \tag{23}$$

$$r = \frac{D}{MP} \tag{24}$$

where

$$D = \text{annual dividend}$$
$$MP = \text{market price of the equity}$$
$$r = \text{implied rate of interest or yield on the equity}$$

Notice again from expression (24) that the price of the security and the interest rate vary inversely.

Expression (24) is only an approximation of the yield implied on an equity instrument. More complicated formulas can be developed to allow for more realistic assumptions about expected dividend performance.

This expression can also be used to approximate the yield to maturity for a coupon bond. Rather than solve the yield from expression (19), the yield can be approximated by dividing the coupon payment, CP, by the market price, MP. This is referred to as the *current yield* on a coupon bond.

$$\text{Current yield on coupon bond} = \frac{CP}{MP} \qquad (25)$$

The yield to maturity of the coupon bond example on page 76 was 8.5%. Using the approximation formula, the current yield of the same bond is \$6.00/\$81.42, or 7.37%.

Price and Yield Once More

The inverse relationship between the price and yield of an I.O.U. traded in an open market is fundamental; thus, we should pause and be sure we understand the relationship.

Let us assume that the going interest rate in the government bond market is 8.5%. If the Treasury is considering to sell a 12-year, 6% coupon bond, what price is the market willing to pay? The market expects a future cash flow from holding the bond—the coupon payments each year and the final principal payment when the bond matures. For a coupon bond to earn a yield to maturity of 8.5%, the bond tables indicate that the price must be \$81.42 for a \$100 bond. That is, anyone who purchases the coupon bond for \$81.42 and keeps the bond until it matures will obtain an 8.5% yield on the initial amount paid for the bond.

Let us assume that the Treasury offers this bond for \$84.75. Any buyers? Not in a competitive financial market where everyone knows that the going rate is 8.5%. At a market price of \$84.75, the coupon bond yields 8.00%—less than the market interest rate. In order to sell the bonds, the Treasury will be required to lower the price until the bond yields 8.5%. If the Treasury had priced the bond at \$79.50, there would have been an intense demand for these bonds because the bond would then be yielding 8.80%—a rate higher than the market. The Treasury would have then raised the price.

The price and the yield of the Treasury bond are thus adjusted until they reflect market conditions, and in this adjustment, the yield and the price vary *inversely* with

---

BOX 2   Where to find interest rates

Interest rates in intermediation markets are not as readily accessible as interest rates in the direct money and capital markets. Information about intermediation interest rates are generally available in local newspapers, billboards, or other forms of local advertisement; however, it's difficult to get information on these rates across different institutions on a uniform and consistent basis. *The Wall Street Journal* publishes some limited information on deposit rates.

Interest rates in direct markets are readily available to the market participant. The most up-to-date and complete source of information is *The Wall Street Journal*. Interest rates for virtually every organized direct market (and some indirect markets) are available in the *Journal*. Without going into a lengthy discussion, it will be instructive to look at two reports published in the *Journal:* key money market interest rates and interest rates on Treasury securities. These are important interest rates from a variety of perspectives, especially the conduct of monetary policy.

Figure 1B illustrates a part of one page from *The Wall Street Journal* and provides only a small indication of the type of interest rate information available in the *Journal*. The money rates section reports key interest rates on important money market I.O.U.s, discount rates of the Federal Reserve and central banks of selected countries, and some interest rates for intermediation finance (the prime interest rate and savings rates).

Interest rates on the entire range of Treasure securities are available in the *Journal*. Treasury bills, or TBs, are issued regularly in three-month, six-month, and one-year maturities. Treasury notes are issued in maturities ranging from one to ten years, while bonds are issued in maturities greater than ten years.

Treasury bonds and notes are coupon bonds unlike Treasury bills which provide no coupon payment. Figure 1B presents only part of the Treasury bonds and notes section. Column (1) lists the coupon interest rate for a specific issue while column (2) provides the maturity date. Market prices (columns (3) and (4)) are in terms of thirty-seconds; for example, the bid price of the May 2018 Treasury bond is 97-27, which means that for each $100, the bid price is $97 plus 27/32nds, or $97.84. The bid price is what the dealer will pay to someone selling the bond while the asked price is what the dealer will sell to someone purchasing the bond. Since bond dealers want to make a profit, the asked price is above the bid price. Column (5) is the change in the bid price from the previous trading day. Column (6) lists the yield to maturity based on the asked price; for example, the May 2018 bond has a yield to maturity of 9.32 percent. The yield will move inversely with the market price and change from day to day.

Treasury bills are reported somewhat differently. Column (7) provides the maturity; however, there is no coupon interest payment since these are discount I.O.U.s that pay no coupon interest payment. The bid and asked yields are calculated on a *discount* basis (columns (8) and (9)). That is, the discount rate is calculated according to expression (18) in the chapter, which uses the face amount of the Treasury bills as the denominator and bases the rate on a 360-day year. The yield to maturity based on expression (17) in the chapter is provided by column (10). The yield to maturity is based on the asked price.

---

respect to each other. The inverse relationship between price and yield is general and applies to any financial asset or I.O.U. traded in the financial system.

The relationship between price and yield is significantly influenced by the maturity of the I.O.U. For any given change in yield, the amount of the change in the price of the I.O.U. is directly related to the maturity of the I.O.U., other things held constant. The greater the maturity—the greater the relative price change in response to a change in the interest rate. To illustrate, consider the price of two coupon bonds from Table 4-1 at 8.00 percent.

11 year maturity:	price of I.O.U. = $85.55
14 year maturity:	price of I.O.U. = $83.34

Tuesday, August 30, 1988

Representative Over-the-Counter quotations based on transactions of $1 million or more as of 4 P.M. Eastern time.

Hyphens in bid-and-asked and bid changes represent 32nds; 101–01 means 101 1/32. a-Plus 1/64. b-Yield to call date. d-Minus 1/64. k-Nonresident aliens exempt from withholding taxes. n-Treasury notes. p-Treasury note; nonresident aliens exempt from withholding taxes.

Source: Bloomberg Financial Markets

Treasury Bonds and Notes

(1)	(2)	(3)	(4)	(5) Bid	(6)
Rate	Mat. Date	Bid	Asked	Chg.	Yld.
6⅛ 1988 Aug p		99–30	100 –01		0.36
6⅜ 1988 Sep p		99–26	99 –29		7.33
11⅜ 1988 Sep p		100–07	100 –10		7.20
15⅜ 1988 Oct n		100–25	100 –28	–01	7.74
6⅜ 1988 Oct p		99–22	99 –25		7.55
6¼ 1988 Nov p		99–17	99 –20		7.67
8¾ 1988 Nov n		100–03	100 –06		7.63
8⅝ 1988 Nov p		100–02	100 –05	+01	7.66
11¾ 1988 Nov n		100–21	100 –24	–01	7.79
10⅝ 1988 Dec p		100–20	100 –24	–01	8.16
6¼ 1988 Dec p		99–10	99 –14	+01	7.91
6⅛ 1989 Jan p		99–05	99 –09	+01	7.87
14⅝ 1989 Jan n		102–10	102 –14		7.74
8 1989 Feb p		99–28	100		7.97
6¼ 1989 Feb p		99–02	99 –06	+01	7.94
11⅜ 1989 Feb n		101–11	101 –15		8.00
11¼ 1989 Mar p		101–19	101 –23	–01	8.14
6⅜ 1989 Mar p		98–30	99 –02		8.04
7⅛ 1989 Apr p		99–05	99 –09		8.23
14⅜ 1989 Apr n		103–20	103 –24		8.04
6⅞ 1989 May p		98–30	99 –02		8.24
9¼ 1989 May n		100–17	100 –23		8.15
8 1989 May p		99–21	99 –25		8.28
10⅜ 2004–09 Nov		106–24	106 –30	+01	9.52
11¾ 2005–10 Feb		118–01	118 –07	–01	9.53
10 2005–10 May		103–25	103 –31	–02	9.52
12¾ 2005–10 Nov		126–30	127 –04	+04	9.51
13⅞ 2006–11 May		136–22	136 –28	+12	9.52
14 2006–11 Nov		138–02	138 –08	+09	9.53
10⅜ 2007–12 Nov		107–05	107 –11	+03	9.53
12 2008–13 Aug		121–24	121 –30	+08	9.52

(1)	(2)	(3)	(4)	(5) Bid	(6)
Rate	Mat. Date	Bid	Asked	Chg.	Yld.
13¼ 2009–14 May		133–07	133 –13	+12	9.52
12½ 2009–14 Aug k		126–22	126 –28	+11	9.52
11¾ 2009–14 Nov k		120–24	120 –30	+10	9.44
11¼ 2015 Feb k		117–15	117 –21	+10	9.43
10⅝ 2015 Aug k		111–19	111 –25	+08	9.41
9⅞ 2015 Nov		104–05	104 –11	+03	9.43
9¼ 2016 Feb k		98–09	98 –15	+04	9.41
7¼ 2016 May k		78–26	79	+01	9.39
7½ 2016 Nov k		81–08	81 –14	+04	9.38
8¾ 2017 May k		93–16	93 –22	+03	9.39
8⅞ 2017 Aug k		94–24	94 –30	+03	9.39
9⅛ 2018 May k		97–27	98 –01	+03	9.32

U.S. Treas. Bills

Mat. date	Bid	Asked Discount	Yield
(7)	(8)	(9)	(10)
-1988-			
9–1	8.01	7.49	7.60
9–8	7.76	7.24	7.35
9–15	6.64	6.37	6.48
9–22	7.99	7.82	7.97
9–29	7.35	7.08	7.22
10–6	7.14	7.10	7.25
10–13	7.22	7.18	7.34
10–20	7.23	7.17	7.34
10–27	7.27	7.20	7.38
11–3	7.23	7.16	7.35
11–10	7.26	7.19	7.39
11–17	7.28	7.21	7.43
11–25	7.34	7.30	7.53
12–1	7.31	7.27	7.51
12–8	7.31	7.25	7.50
12–15	7.30	7.24	7.50
12–22	7.34	7.30	7.57
12–29	7.19	7.15	7.43
-1989-			
1–5	7.31	7.25	7.54
1–12	7.44	7.38	7.69
1–19	7.48	7.42	7.75
1–26	7.47	7.41	7.75
2–2	7.49	7.43	7.78

FIGURE 1B Yields in the financial press

Mat. date	Bid	Asked	Yield
		Discount	
(7)	*(8)*	*(9)*	*(10)*
2–9	7.52	7.46	7.83
2–16	7.56	7.50	7.88
2–23	7.48	7.44	7.83
3–16	7.62	7.56	7.97
4–13	7.67	7.61	8.04
4–20	7.77	7.71	8.15
5–11	7.73	7.67	8.13
6–8	7.71	7.65	8.13
7–6	7.74	7.68	8.20
8–3	7.74	7.68	8.23
8–31	7.71	7.67	8.26

MONEY RATES
Tuesday, August 30, 1988

The key U.S. and foreign annual interest rates below are a guide to general levels but don't always represent actual transactions.

PRIME RATE: 10%. The base rate on corporate loans at large U.S. money center commercial banks.

FEDERAL FUNDS: 8$\frac{3}{16}$% high, 8% low, 8% near closing bid, 8$\frac{1}{8}$% offered. Reserves traded among commercial banks for overnight use in amounts of $1 million or more. Source: Fulton Prebon (U.S.A.) Inc.

DISCOUNT RATE: 6$\frac{1}{2}$%. The charge on loans to depository institutions by the New York Federal Reserve Bank.

CALL MONEY: 9$\frac{1}{8}$% to 9$\frac{1}{4}$%. The charge on loans to brokers on stock exchange collateral.

COMMERCIAL PAPER placed directly by General Motors Acceptance Corp.: 8% 30 to 34 days; 8.175% 35 to 62 days; 8$\frac{1}{4}$% 63 to 89 days; 8.15% 90 to 119 days; 8.10% 120 to 149 days; 8.05% 150 to 179 days; 7.90% 180 to 270 days.

COMMERCIAL PAPER: High-grade unsecured notes sold through dealers by major corporations in multiples of $1,000: 8.15% 30 days; 8.20% 60 days; 8.25% 90 days.

CERTIFICATES OF DEPOSIT: 7.69% one month; 7.85% two months; 7.91% three months; 8.26% six months; 8.46% one year. Average of top rates paid by major New York banks on primary new issues of negotiable C.D.s usually on amounts of $1 million and more. The minimum unit is $100,000. Typical rates in the secondary market: 8.15% one month; 8.40% three months; 8.85% six months.

BANKERS ACCEPTANCES: 8.08% 30 days; 8.17% 60 days; 8.27% 90 days; 8.27% 120 days; 8.40% 150 days; 8.42% 180 days. Negotiable, bank-backed business credit instruments typically financing an import order.

LONDON LATE EURODOLLARS: 8$\frac{1}{2}$% to 8$\frac{3}{8}$% one month; 8$\frac{9}{16}$% to 8$\frac{7}{16}$% two months; 8$\frac{11}{16}$% to 8$\frac{9}{16}$% three months; 8$\frac{15}{16}$% to 8$\frac{13}{16}$% four months; 9% to 8$\frac{7}{8}$% five months; 9% to 8$\frac{7}{8}$% six months.

LONDON INTERBANK OFFERED RATES (LIBOR): 8$\frac{1}{2}$% one month; 8$\frac{11}{16}$% three months; 9$\frac{1}{16}$% six months; 9$\frac{15}{16}$% one year. The average of interbank offered rates for dollar deposits in the London market based on quotations at five major banks.

FOREIGN PRIME RATES: Canada 11.25%; Germany 6%; Japan 3.375%; Switzerland 6%; Britain 12%. These rate indications aren't directly comparable; lending practices vary widely by location.

TREASURY BILLS: Results of the Monday, August 29, 1988, auction of short-term U.S. government bills, sold at a discount from face value in units of $10,000 to $1 million; 7.26% 13 weeks; 7.50% 26 weeks.

FEDERAL HOME LOAN MORTGAGE CORP. (Freddie Mac): Posted yields on 30-year mortgage commitments for delivery within 30 days. 10.48%, standard conventional fixed-rate mortgages; 8.125%, 2% rate capped one-year adjustable rate mortgages. Source: Telerate Systems Inc.

FEDERAL NATIONAL MORTGAGE ASSOCIATION (Fannie Mae): Posted yields on 30 year mortgage commitments for delivery within 30 days (priced at par). 10.51%, standard conventional fixed rate mortgages; 9.75%, 6/2 rate capped one-year adjustable rate mortgages. Source: Telerate Systems Inc.

MERRILL LYNCH READY ASSETS TRUST: 7.25%. Annualized average rate of return after expenses for the past 30 days; not a forecast of future returns.

Source: The Wall Street Journal, August 31, 1988, p. 35.

BOX 3   Financial markets and the 1989 San Francisco/Oakland earthquake

Financial markets, especially direct markets, are competitive by any measure. They react quickly to new information. Opportunities to purchase I.O.U.s at prices different than equilibrium prices don't last long. As an illustration of the speed with which financial markets react to new information, consider what happened on Wall Street, Wednesday, October 17, the day after a major earthquake rocked the San Francisco Bay Area.[1]

Insurers, Builders Stock Rose in Wake Of Earthquake
BY LINDA SANDLER *Staff Reporter of* THE WALL STREET JOURNAL

NEW YORK—On Wall Street yesterday, northern California's killer earthquake was just another chance to make a buck.

At the opening bell, investors quickly began singling out shares of companies expected to profit or suffer in some way from the California disaster, including insurers, construction-related companies, refiners and housing lenders. Brokerage houses jumped in, touting "post-quake demand" stocks, and Kidder, Peabody & Co. set up a toll-free hot line for San Franciscans who might need emergency investment advice and help in transferring funds.

"Wall Street thinks of everything in terms of money," says Tom Gallagher, a senior Oppenheimer & Co. trader. However, he added, such event-driven trading moves typically last only a few hours and are often made without full information.

The most popular plays of the day were insurance companies such as **General Re** Corp., which rose $2.75 to $86.50, **Nac Re** Corp., up $2 to $37.75, **American International Group** Inc., up. $3.25 to $102.625, and **Cigna** Corp., up. 87.5 cents to $62.50. Yesterday, the brokerage firm Conning & Co. said insurers will use the earthquake as an excuse to raise insurance rates, ending their long price wars.

Before this bullish theory surfaced, some insurance stocks initially fell, indicating that investors thought the quake might cost insurers a lot of money. In fact, **Fireman's Fund** Corp., which ended the day off 50

cents to $36.50, said earthquake damage would slightly hurt fourth-quarter profit.

On the prospect for rebuilding northern California, investors bid up cement-makers **Calmat** Co., up $2.75 to $28.75, and **Lone Star Industries** Inc., up $1.75 to $29.25. Bridge and road builders had a field day, including **Kasler** Corp., up. $2.125 to $9.875, **Guy F. Atkinson** Co., up 87.5 cents to $61.875, and **Morrison Knudsen** Corp., which reported higher third-quarter earnings yesterday, up $2.25 to $44.125. **Fluor** Corp., a construction engineering firm, gained 75 cents to $33.375. But home-building stocks were a mixed bag.

Timber stocks got a big boost. **Georgia-Pacific** Corp., up $1.25 to $58, and **Maxxam** Inc., up $3 to $43.75, both reported strong profits. Merrill Lynch & Co. touted **Georgia-Pacific**, **Louisiana Pacific** Corp. and **Willamette Industries** Inc. as the best postquake plywood plays.

Other gainers were companies with one or more undamaged California refineries. **Tosco** Corp. jumped $1.125 to $20.125 and **Chevron** Corp., despite a temporary pipeline shutdown, rose $1 to $65.

Meanwhile, shares of some big housing lenders got hit, on the likelihood that the lenders' collateral—people's homes—suffered physical damage and perhaps a loss in value. **Well's Fargo** & Co. fell 50 cents to $81.50, **BankAmerica** Corp. fell 50 cents to $31.875. Some California thrift stocks also fell, including **Golden West Financial** Corp. and **H.F. Ahmanson** & Co., which reported lower earnings yesterday.

"Property values didn't go up in California yesterday," says one money manager.

Pacific Gas & Electric Co. fell 37.5 cents to $19.625. One of its power generators was damaged, though the company said there won't be any financial impact. **Pacific Telesis Group** lost 62.5 cents to $44.625. A computer failure delayed its earnings announcement, and some investors think it might have extra costs to repair damaged telephone lines.

[1] *The Wall Street Journal*, October 19, 1989, p. A13.

Assume the yield increases to 10.00 percent. The new prices are

			Percentage Fall in Price
11 year maturity:	price of I.O.U. = 73.67		−13.9%
14 year maturity:	price of I.O.U. = 70.20		−15.8%

Interest Rates and Total Return on Financial Assets

The inverse relationship between the interest rate or yield and price introduces another concept—the *realized rate of return* on a financial asset. In some cases, the interest rate and the realized rate of return are the same; however, the existence of secondary markets means that they can differ if the I.O.U. is sold prior to maturity at a different price than originally paid for the I.O.U.

The relationship between the rate of return and the interest rate can easily be illustrated for the case of a consol. The rate of return from holding a consol for a given period of time consists of two parts: the yield (coupon payment as a percentage of the market price) and the capital gain (positive or negative) when the consol is sold in the secondary market. The rate of return, RR, on the consol held for one year and then sold at time t is

$$RR \text{ on consol}_t = (CP/MP)_{t-1} + \frac{(MP_t - MP_{t-1})}{MP_{t-1}} \qquad (26)$$

where $(CP/MP)_{t-1}$ is the yield based on the initial purchase price at time $t-1$ and $(MP_t - MP_{t-1})/MP_{t-1}$ is the capital gain or loss depending on the market price at time t when the consol is sold relative to the initial purchase price at time $t-1$. If the consol is sold at a price higher than that paid initially, the gain will be positive, and if the consol is sold at a price lower than that paid initially, there will be a loss or negative gain. Expression (26) can then be restated more generally as

$$RR \text{ on consol} = \text{current yield} + \text{capital gain} \qquad (27)$$

Thus, the yield may have been, say, 8%, when the consol was purchased, but if the consol is sold at a price lower than originally paid (negative capital gain or depreciation in price), RR will be less than the yield. On the other hand, if the consol is sold at a higher price than originally paid, the RR will exceed the yield. In the case of a consol, the yield and the rate of return will be the same only when the consol is sold at the same price originally paid—that is, the capital gain is zero.

The consol provides a convenient example for illustrating the relationship between yield and rate of return even though consols are not traded in the United States. In general, there exist only two situations in which the interest rate or yield and the rate of return are the same:

BOX 4   The crash of October 1987—A lesson in the difference between yield and rate of return

The October 1987 stock market crash or "meltdown," as market participants called it, was spectacular by any reasonable standard. On October 19, stock values declined by almost 22 percent! The decline brought back memories of the October 1929 decline and some forecasts that the economy was headed for a serious recession, if not depression. As it turned out, the October 1987 (see Figure 2B) crash became the "big nonevent of 1987." The economy continued its advance through the next several years without any adverse effects.

The crash clearly illustrated, however, the difference between yield and rate of return. If you had purchased $100,000 worth of stock one year earlier and, at that time, the dividend to price ratio was 10% and the anticipated dividend performance was realized, the stock would have provided an interest return of 10% over the year. If you chose to sell the stock in a declining market such as October 19, the rate of return would have to reflect the capital loss ($78,000 − $100,000)/$100,000, or −22%. While the initial interest return was 10%, the capital loss would have generated a rate of return of −12%. If you did not sell the stock but chose to ride it out and continued to receive a 10% dividend, the yield would remain at 10% despite the stock market crash.

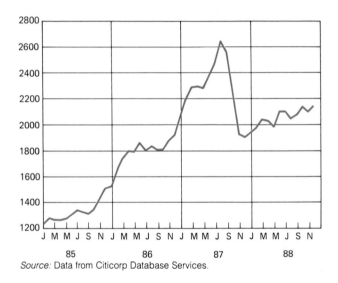

Source: Data from Citicorp Database Services.

FIGURE 2B   Monthly values of the Dow Jones industrial average of common stock prices, January 1985–December 1988.

1. If the I.O.U. is held to maturity
2. If the I.O.U. is sold in the secondary market before it matures at the same price originally paid (zero capital gain)

Let us illustrate the difference between yield and rate of return for the coupon bond example developed page 76. By purchasing the bond for $81.42, the yield to maturity is 8.5%. If Hickenlupper holds the bond until it matures in 12 years, then the holding period yield or rate of return will be 8.5%—the initial yield to maturity. If, on the other hand, Hickenlupper sells the bond in the secondary market one year after the purchase, then the yield and the rate of return may differ depending on the market price of the bond when sold.

TABLE 4-2 Rate of return and yield on a coupon bond originally purchased at $81.42

Case	Secondary Market Price of Bond After One Year	Current Yield Based on Original Purchase Price	Capital Gain Over the Year	Rate of Return (RR)
I	$85.00	7.37%	$\left(\dfrac{\$85.00 - \$81.42}{\$81.42}\right) = 4.40\%$	11.77%
II	$81.42	7.37%	$\left(\dfrac{\$81.42 - \$81.42}{\$81.42}\right) = 0.00\%$	7.37%
III	$75.00	7.37%	$\left(\dfrac{\$75.00 - \$81.42}{\$81.42}\right) = -7.89\%$	-0.52%

Table 4-2 illustrates the three possible cases. In all three cases the relevant interest rate from Hickenlupper's perspective is the current yield, that is, the coupon payment as a percentage of the original market price of the bond. Hickenlupper paid $81.42 for the $100 bond and at the end of the year when the bond was sold, he had received $6 in coupon payments and thus, the current yield is 7.37 percent. The current yield, like the yield to maturity, is a measure of the interest rate on the bond. Case I indicates that Hickenlupper realizes a capital gain over the year because the bond sells for a higher price than originally paid. The rate of return exceeds the initial yield. Case III indicates that Hickenlupper realizes a capital loss over the year because the bond sells for a lower price and the rate of return is lower than the yield. Only in case II, when the bond sells for the same price, is the rate of return and the yield identical.

Key Points

1. The interest rate connects the present to the future and vice versa. The interest rate expresses how much a given sum will accumulate to at some given point in the future, or equivalently, the interest rate expresses how much a given sum in the future is worth in the present.

2. Yield to maturity expresses the yield on a financial asset in terms of the total expected cash flow relative to the market price of the asset.

3. Interest rates in direct financial markets are determined in a highly competitive environ-

ment. While interest rates in indirect markets are more market sensitive than previously because of deregulation and innovation, they are not generally as market sensitive as direct market interest rates.

4. There are three basic types of interest rates in direct markets corresponding to characteristics of the I.O.U.: I.O.U.s without coupon payments, I.O.U.s with coupon payments, and I.O.U.s or equities without a maturity date.

5. Consols are a type of bond without a maturity date traded in England.

6. There is an inverse relationship between yield and price of an I.O.U. Price increases (decreases) are accompanied by yield decreases (increases).

7. Treasury bills are quoted on both a discount and yield-to-maturity basis, though the yield to maturity basis is the most appropriate interest rate measure.

8. The interest rate and the total return are not necessarily the same since total return consists of yield plus capital gain. They are the same only if the I.O.U. is sold prior to maturity at the price at which it was purchased or if the I.O.U. is held to maturity. If the I.O.U. is sold at a higher (lower) price, the return will be greater (smaller) than the yield.

Key Terms

Consol

Coupon bonds

Coupon yield

Current yield

Equities

Fixed payment loan

Interest rate

Market price

Maturity

Present value

Rate of return

Simple loan

Yield on a discount basis

Yield to maturity

Questions

1. Explain how the present and the future are connected to each other by the interest rate.

2. What is the present value of $1,000 receivable ten years from today using a rate of interest of 10%?

3. Use the example of a Treasury bill ($10,000 face value and a market price of $9,750) and calculate the yield to maturity and the discount yield for two maturities: 91 and 182 days. Discuss the difference between the two yields in terms of the two maturities.

4. Assuming the going rate of interest is 8.5%, explain why you would not purchase the bond on page 76 at a price higher than $81.42. Why would we rush to buy the bond if it were offered at $75.00?

5. What is the relationship between yield and price for any I.O.U.?

6. What are the two conditions that will permit you to earn a total rate of return on a financial asset equal to the yield to maturity when you purchased the financial asset?

7. If you purchase a bond for $100 with a current yield of 10% and sold the bond in the secondary market for $99 one year later, what would be your rate of return?

8. If you purchase a bond for $100 with a current yield of 10% and sold the bond in the secondary market for $101 one year later, what would be your rate of return?

9. If interest rates increase after you purchased a bond, what would happen to your realized rate of return if you sold the bond in the secondary market?

10. Using the excerpt from the bond table book in Table 4-1 and assume the market yield increases from 8.0% to 8.5%. How does maturity influence the bond's price response to the change in yield?

Suggested Readings

1. Richard Brealey and Stewart Myers, *Principles of Corporate Finance* (New York: McGraw-Hill, 1984). This and the Van Horne book provide extensive detail on all aspects of interest rates on different financial instruments and interest rate formulas.

2. James C. Van Horne. *Financial Management and Policy* (Englewood Cliffs, N.J.: Prentice-Hall, 1983).

3. Richard D. Trainer, *The Arithmetic of Interest Rates,* Federal Reserve Bank of New York (1983).

4. *The Wall Street Journal*, any issue. An important source of up-to-date information on the broad spectrum of interest rates in direct financial markets.

5. *Wall Street Journal Educational Edition, 1988/89— How to Read Between the Lines.* Special guide to reading the regular issue of *The Wall Street Journal.*

CHAPTER 5

The Level and Structure of Interest Rates

Chapter Overview

The last two chapters have provided the basic elements of the financial system. In Chapter 3 we saw that the financial system is a collection of markets in which suppliers of funds purchase I.O.U.s from demanders of funds. The I.O.U. becomes a financial asset to the lender and an obligation to the borrower. Financial markets can be classified as either direct or indirect markets depending on the role of financial institutions.

The I.O.U. or financial asset itself is characterized by either an interest rate or price. From the perspective of the lender, the interest rate is part of the total return from holding financial assets, and from the perspective of the borrower, the interest rate is the cost of funds. Interest rates (and prices of I.O.U.s) play an important role in the economy. Chapter 4 presented several important interest rate definitions and discussed the ways in which interest rates are reported in the financial system. The inverse relationship between interest rates and prices of I.O.U.s was an important relationship emphasized in that discussion.

This chapter is concerned with two general questions that logically follow the discussion of the previous two chapters.

Question 1: What determines the rate of interest in the financial system? Specifically, we are concerned with the determinants of the rate of interest in direct financial markets since these are the most competitive markets in the financial system. In this regard, we discuss the determinates of the interest rate in a *partial equilibrium* setting that holds constant the level of employment, output, and other variables determined in the nonfinancial sector of the economy. There are two approaches to understanding interest rates: liquidity preference and loanable funds. In addition, the role of price anticipations is emphasized since price anticipations have been recognized as important determinants of interest rates in the past few decades. As part of our discussion of what determines the level of interest rates, we review past trends in interest rates in general and, in particular, focus on interest rate movements in the 1970s and 1980s.

Question 2: What determines the relationship among interest rates in different direct markets at any point in time? That is, why are some interest rates higher or lower than other interest rates? Differences between interest rates across financial markets is referred to as the structure of interest rates. In addition to accounting for the structure of interest rates at a point in time, how does the structure change over time?

The Level of Interest Rates

Assume that all the interest rates in the financial system can be averaged together and represented by one rate of interest, r. What determines the level of r at any particular point in time? We can provide only a partial answer to this question now, because the level of the interest rate depends on interactions between the financial system and the real system, and we have yet to develop a model of the real system that will provide information on the determinants of income and employment levels.

Economists distinguish between the real sector of the economy and the monetary or financial sector based on their different types of activity. The term "real" refers to the flow of spending on goods and services and the resulting income that is generated. Real economic activity is summarized by the gross national product (GNP) and national income (NY) accounts. The financial sector is in no sense any less "real," but it represents the associated financial flows by changes in financial assets and liabilities. Both sectors of the economy are highly interrelated. In fact, the basic flow of funds equation summarizes both real and financial activity and illustrates their close relationship.

$$\text{Investment} = \text{saving} + (\text{borrowing} - \text{lending}) \tag{1}$$

The investment and saving activities emerge primarily in the real sector of the economy. The relationship between investment and saving is reflected in the relationship between borrowing and lending, both of which represent the financial or monetary system. Figure 5-1 illustrates the relationship between the real and financial components of the economy. The rate of interest is determined primarily in the financial system, but it is also influenced by the real system because the saving and investment decisions of households, businesses, government, and other sectors influence the flow of funds.

Figure 5-1 indicates the forces that determine the rate of interest. In the real sector, economic units make decisions to spend and save. The income statement indicates the surplus (or saving) that remains after spending for current consumption items has occurred. The balance sheet indicates the addition (or subtraction) from real assets that we term investment. Spending on current consumption items, saving, and investment occur in the real sector of the economy.

From the flow of funds equation, however, we know that lending and borrowing relate to decisions to save and invest. Decisions by the economic unit to save and invest must involve decisions to lend and borrow in the financial system. If saving

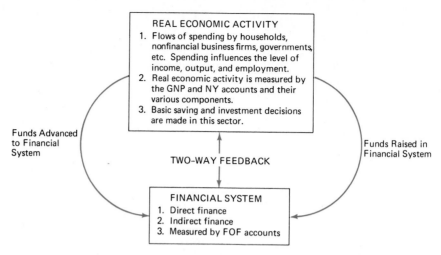

FIGURE 5-1   **Relationship between the real and financial sectors of the economy**

exceeds investment, lending must exceed borrowing, and the unit is then a surplus unit (SU). If investment exceeds saving, borrowing must exceed lending, and the unit is then a deficit unit (DU). Figure 5-1 illustrates the flow of funds to the financial system from the lending activity (increases in financial assets on the balance sheet) and the demand for funds (increases in liabilities on the balance sheet). These flows determine the interest rate in a demand-supply framework; however, the interest rate and the flows themselves determine decisions to save and invest. This is why we have drawn an arrow indicating a feedback relationship between the real and financial sectors.

In the following sections, we adopt a *partial equilibrium* approach to see what determines the rate of interest in the sense that the real sector of the economy is held constant at a given level of income, employment, and spending. Or another way of saying the same thing—changes in the real sector can influence the interest rate but not the reverse. We will turn our attention to the forces in the financial system that determine the rate of interest holding constant the real sector. Of course, this is not a complete theory of interest rate determination, because changes in the real sector influence the financial sector and change the rate of interest, which in turn, influence the real sector. But it will be a useful starting point.

Two Approaches to Determining the Level of Interest Rates: Liquidity Preference and Loanable Funds

There are two approaches to determine the rate of interest in the financial system: the *loanable funds* and *liquidity preference* approaches. Both assume that the level

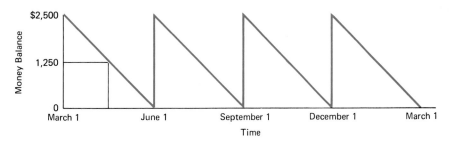

FIGURE 5-2   Demand for money and velocity

of income and employment determined in the real sector of the economy is constant, and both focus primarily on the forces in the financial sector as determinants of the rate of interest. In addition, both approaches assume that market participants in the financial system have zero anticipations of price changes. That is, they anticipate a zero rate of inflation.

The Liquidity Preference Approach

The liquidity preference approach views the interest rate as determined by the stock of money demanded and supplied in the financial system. The liquidity preference approach expresses the demand for money balances as a function of the level of income and the rate of interest,

$$DM = DM(r, Y); \quad \frac{\Delta DM}{\Delta r} < 0, \quad \frac{\Delta DM}{\Delta Y} > 0 \qquad (2)$$

where DM is the demand for money, r is the rate of interest, and Y is the level of income. There are a number of reasonable arguments for the public's having a demand for money—those related to the level of income and those related to the rate of interest.

Income-related reasons are generally referred to as *transaction* reasons for the demand of money. The incomplete synchronization between receipts and expenditures, the frequency of receipts and expenditures, and other factors that form the payments mechanism give rise to a demand for money by the public. Money balances are required to bridge the gap between expenditures and receipts. To illustrate this concept, consider the situation in Figure 5-2. Joe Hickenlupper is paid every three months and receives $2,500 per pay period or $10,000 per year. On March 1, for example, Hickenlupper is paid $2,500 and adds it to his money balance. The next payment is three months in the future; however expenditures must be made on a daily basis. Assuming that funds are spent so that the money balance becomes zero the day before the next payment, Figure 5-2 then illustrates the behavior of Hickenlupper's money balance over the year. On average he holds $1,250 or 12.5% of annual income as a money balance. If income increases to $20,000 per year and the payment period and expenditure pattern remain the same as in Figure 5-2, then his average money balance will be $2,500. That is, as income expands, the transaction need for money to finance expenditures also increases. Figure 5-2 can also be used to show how the transaction demand for money is influenced by how frequently individuals are paid. If Hickenlupper is paid an annual salary of $10,000 in 12 payments and funds are exhausted by the end of the month, then the average money balance or transaction demand for money would be $417 or 4.17 percent of annual income.

Figure 5-2 illustrates the transaction demand for money from the point of view of an individual; however, the same type of argument can be extended to the public in general. As a result of the incomplete synchronization of receipts and expenditures, the public demands a certain stock of money with which to finance transactions. Because the level of income represents a good proxy for the level of transactions in the economy, we can assume that there is a direct and positive relationship between the demand for money and the level of income.

Interest rate–related reasons for holding money take a variety of forms, but all hypothesize that the demand for money is inversely or negatively related to the rate of interest. A number of rationalizations support an inverse relationship between the rate of interest and the demand for money. Perhaps the most obvious is to realize that the interest rate is the *opportunity cost* of holding money. Money is the most liquid asset in the spectrum of liquidity introduced in Chapter 2, yet it yields either no interest income (currency and demand deposits) or less interest income (NOW accounts, etc.) than do other financial assets.

As we move down the scale and encounter financial assets of decreasing degrees of liquidity, interest income tends to increase. In this sense, the interest rate is the opportunity cost of holding money balances. The individual always faces the problem of holding money that has perfect liquidity but yields little or no interest income or holding less liquid assets that yield higher interest income.

At low rates of interest, the opportunity cost of holding money is relatively low, so the public tends to hold larger money balances. At high rates of interest the opportunity cost of holding money is high so the public tries to economize as much as possible on its money balances, transferring excess money balances to interest-yielding financial assets, such as bonds.

The opportunity cost concept of holding money is only one way in which to explain the inverse relationship between the demand for money and the interest rate. Other factors are also important; for example, the relative risk of money versus other financial assets can explain the basic relationship. Money is simply less risky than other assets. Individuals are likely to hold more (less) money the lower (higher) the level of interest for a given level of risk. At higher interest rates, individuals are willing to hold smaller money balances because they have a higher expected return from holding other financial assets and are willing to shift to riskier assets.

In 1936, Keynes advanced another explanation. He suggested that individuals formulated, either via "seat of the pants" or sophisticated methods, an expected or *normal* rate of interest that they believed would prevail in the market. If current rates were lower (higher) than the normal rate, then individuals expected rates to increase (decrease) over time. Remember from Chapter 4 that there is an inverse relationship between the price of an I.O.U. and the interest rate; therefore, if individuals expect interest rates to increase (decrease), they likewise expect the prices of I.O.U.s to decrease (increase). Assume that, for a large number of individuals, current rates are lower than their expected or normal interest rate. They would be inclined to hold larger money balances and smaller amounts of financial assets since they expected the price of I.O.U.s to decline. On the other hand, if the current rate

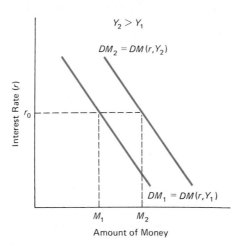

FIGURE 5-3 The demand function for money

is higher than the normal rate, individuals expect interest rates to fall and would be inclined to hold smaller money balances and larger amounts of financial assets since they expect the price of I.O.U.s to increase as interest rates decline.

There are thus several rationalizations to explain the inverse relationship between the demand for money and the interest rate; however, they all stress essentially the same point. Once the transaction needs of the public are determined, the equilibrium level of money held by the public is influenced by the prevailing interest rate. In reality, we cannot separate the different components of the public's money balance into income-related and interest rate–related components. Each dollar supplies services to the public, and the amount of money held is influenced simultaneously by the level of income and the interest rate.

Figure 5-3 illustrates the demand for money function assuming that the level of income is constant at Y_1. The amount of money balances desired by the public is inversely related to the rate of interest. Figure 5-3 also illustrates a shift in the demand function as a result of an increase in income to Y_2. At any given rate of interest, the public desires to hold larger money balances because transaction needs will be higher at a higher level of income.

The theoretical argument has found support from an extensive body of empirical work. Estimates of the demand function for money over a wide variation of the basic relationship expressed in (2) suggest overwhelming empirical evidence that the demand for money is related *significantly* and *positively* to income and *significantly* and *inversely* to the interest rate.

The supply of money is determined by the interaction of depository institutions, the public, and the Federal Reserve. As will be shown in Chapter 10, the Federal Reserve has the ultimate power to change the money supply in one direction or another. Figure 5-4 illustrates the supply function for money assuming it is determined exogenously by the Federal Reserve.

There is reason to believe that the supply of money should actually be drawn with a positive slope; that is, holding the influence of the Federal Reserve constant, the supply of money is positively related to the interest rate. This point will be discussed further in Chapter 10, but at this point, we will leave the money supply

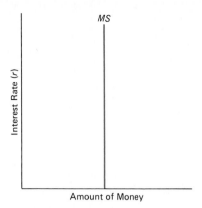

FIGURE 5-4   Interest-insensitive money supply function

function as illustrated in Figure 5-4. Even if we drew the money supply function so that the money supply were positively related to the interest rate to some degree, it would not alter the basic view of how interest rates are determined in the liquidity preference framework.

Figure 5-5 illustrates the equilibrium interest rate according to the liquidity preference approach. What would happen if the rate of interest were at any other level?

At an interest rate above the equilibrium rate, there is an excess supply of money. The liquidity preference theory views individuals as always choosing between holding money and interest-bearing financial assets. Money has perfect liquidity but earns relatively less or no interest, whereas other financial assets are less liquid but earn higher interest income. Thus, an excess supply of money will be used to purchase financial assets. As the demand for financial assets increases, their price increases, and this will lower the rate of interest. Likewise, if the rate of interest is below the equilibrium point, there is an excess demand for money, so individuals will

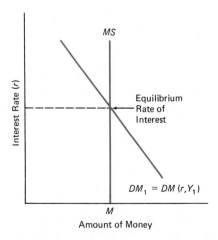

**FIGURE 5-5   Interest rate determination according
to the liquidity preference approach**

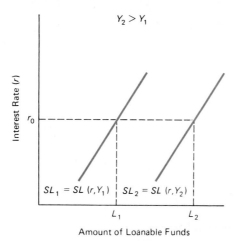

FIGURE 5-6 The supply function for loanable funds

sell off their financial assets to obtain a larger money balance, and this will cause the interest rate to increase.

The Loanable Funds Approach

The loanable funds approach to interest rate determination views the financial system as an "area" in which loanable funds are traded on both primary and secondary markets and the interest rate equates the supply and demand of loanable funds. The supply of loanable funds can be represented by

$$SL = SL(r, Y); \qquad \frac{\Delta SL}{\Delta r} > 0, \quad \frac{\Delta SL}{\Delta Y} > 0 \qquad (3)$$

where SL is the supply of loanable funds.

There is a positive relationship between the quantity of loanable funds supplied in the financial system and the rate of interest as indicated in Figure 5-6. Holding Y constant at Y_1, the quantity of funds supplied varies directly with the rate of interest. At higher rates of interest, there is a greater willingness to postpone current spending and supply funds to the credit market. Changes in the level of income will shift the supply of loanable funds function. For example, if the level of income increases to Y_2, the supply function will shift to the right, indicating that at any rate of interest the quantity of loanable funds supplied will be larger.

The major components of the supply of loanable funds include retained earnings and depreciation by the business sector, household savings, government surpluses, and increases in the supply of money.

The total demand for loanable funds can be represented by

$$DL = DL(r); \qquad \frac{\Delta DL}{\Delta r} < 0 \qquad (4)$$

where DL is the demand for loanable funds. There is an inverse or negative relationship between the quantity of loanable funds demanded and the rate of interest holding

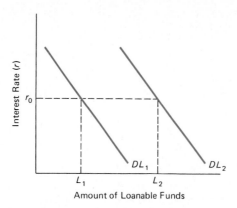

FIGURE 5-7   The demand function for loanable funds

other factors constant as illustrated in Figure 5-7. The interest rate represents the cost of borrowing. As the interest rate increases, the cost of borrowing also increases, leading to a decrease in the quantity of funds demanded in the financial system.

Figure 5-7 also illustrates how a rightward shift will increase the quantity of loanable funds demanded at any rate of interest. The demand for loanable funds represents the demand for consumer credit and residential mortgages by the household sector, the demand for loans to finance inventories and plant and equipment expenditures by the nonfinancial business sector, and government deficits. Combining the demand and supply functions together in Figure 5-8, we can see that the rate of interest is the rate that achieves equilibrium in the financial system between the quantity of loanable funds demanded and supplied.

The interest rate that equates SL and DL functions is an equilibrium rate, and, as long as competitive forces are allowed to operate in the financial system, there is a natural mechanism to bring the interest rate to this point. For example, if the rate of interest is higher than the equilibrium rate, then a condition of excess supply of

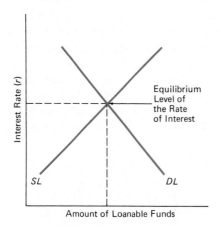

FIGURE 5-8   The equilibrium rate of interest determined by the demand and supply of loanable funds

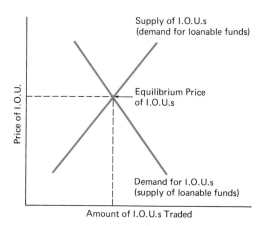

FIGURE 5-9   The equilibrium price of an I.O.U.
determined by the supply and demand for I.O.U.s

funds would exist in the financial system. Lenders will lower the asking rate to lend their funds, and borrowers aware of the excess funds will bargain for lower rates. On the other hand, if the rate happened to be lower than the equilibrium rate, competitive forces would increase the rate to the intersection point.

The formulation of the loanable funds determination of interest rates is based on the supply and demand for loanable funds as functions of the interest rate. But we can also express the loanable funds theory another way. The supply of loanable funds is the same as the demand for I.O.U.s or financial claims by lenders. If someone is willing to supply $100 in loanable funds, this is the same as saying that the individual is willing to demand an I.O.U. worth $100. Likewise, the demand for loanable funds is equivalent to the supply of I.O.U.s or financial obligations by borrowers. The demand and supply of I.O.U.s will determine the price of the I.O.U. rather than the interest rate. However, there is a definite relationship between the price of an I.O.U. and the rate of interest as discussed in Chapter 4. Figure 5-9 illustrates the equilibrium price of I.O.U.s as determined by the supply of I.O.U.s (demand for loanable funds) and the demand for I.O.U.s (supply of loanable funds).

Which One Is Best?

The loanable funds and liquidity preference approaches are partial explanations of the interest rate, as both assume that the level of activity in the real sector of the economy is constant. Changes in the level of income or any other variable in the real sector that influences the supply and demand functions in the financial system will alter the rate of interest but changes in the interest rate are assumed to have no influence on the real sector. In both Figures 5-5 and 5-8, we necessarily assumed that the level of income and other variables remained constant to determine the equilibrium rate of interest. Thus, both approaches highlight only the partial determinants of the rate of interest. So which one is best as a partial approach to determining interest rates in the financial system? Several considerations need to be made in response to this question.

BOX 1   Liquidity preference and loanable funds—half a dozen or six?

Liquidity preference and loanable funds yield the same interest rate in a general equilibrium setting. This can be illustrated by considering a three-market model of the economy: a commodity market concerned with the demand and supply for goods, a bond market concerned with the demand and supply for bonds, and a money market concerned with the demand and supply for money. There is some level of economic activity (including the level of the interest rate) that will ensure overall equilibrium in the three markets and, hence, the general equilibrium of the economy. Think of demand and supply in each market as depending on the level of income and the interest rate and express the equilibrium in each market as

Demand for goods (Y, r) = supply of goods (Y, r)
Demand for bonds (Y, r) = supply of bonds (Y, r)
Demand for money (Y, r) = supply of money (Y, r)

The solution of general equilibrium models relies on a procedure suggested by Leon Walras in his 1871 *Elements of Pure Economics*, where he developed a mathematical approach to solving the general equilibrium of a multimarket economy. Now referred to as Walras's law, the principle states that if you have three interrelated markets and equilibrium is achieved in any two markets, the third market must by mathematical necessity be in equilibrium. This is equivalent to saying that the third market is redundant.

Thus using Walras's law, if we have equilibrium in the real sector (demand for goods = supply of goods at Y and r) and in the loanable funds market (demand for bonds = supply of bonds at Y and r), then by necessity, the demand for money will equal the supply of money at Y and r. It does not make a real difference which of the three markets is considered redundant. Making the money market redundant elevates the loanable funds market as the determinant of the interest rate given the overall equilibrium of the economy. Making the bond market redundant, on the other hand, elevates the money market as the determinant of the interest rate.

In general equilibrium, both liquidity preference and loanable funds provide the same equilibrium interest rate. It took several decades of intense debate in the economics profession to finally recognize this point.[1]

[1] Don Patinkin, "Liquidity Preference and Loanable Funds: Stock and Flow Analysis," *Economica*, 25 (November 1958), 300–318, provides one of the best known reconciliations of the two approaches.

First, both approaches can be shown to yield the same equilibrium rate of interest in a general equilibrium context. At one time, considerable discussion was devoted to whether the liquidity preference and loanable funds approaches yielded different results. It is now accepted that, in a general sense, both lead to the same rate of interest; however, the chief difference between the two resides in their methodology.

The liquidity preference model is based on the demand and supply for a *stock* of money and regards all financial decisions as focusing on the money end of the spectrum of liquidity. The loanable funds approach is based on the *flow* of funds to and from the financial system and considers financial decisions as being made along a much wider range on the liquidity spectrum.

Second, both approaches are partial equilibrium theories because they determine the rate of interest without regard to changes in the real sector of the economy. They do this by holding constant those variables determined in the real sector that influence the flow of funds or demand for money. Thus both suffer the same theoretical disadvantages in this regard.

Third, the loanable funds approach has found wider acceptance among those interested in the financial institutions and markets of the economy. The loanable funds approach has a more institutional orientation than does the liquidity preference approach. In addition, the loanable funds approach underlies the flow of funds framework discussed in earlier chapters. Thus, for those wishing to emphasize the institutional makeup of the financial system, the loanable funds approach is generally preferred over the liquidity preference approach. On the other hand, for those interested in model building and caring not to emphasize institutions, the liquidity preference approach is often preferred.

Real and Nominal Interest Rates

The loanable funds and liquidity preference approaches to the interest rate assume that individuals regard the price level as constant over the maturity of securities traded in the financial system. In the real world, however, individuals anticipate future price changes, and these expectations are part of the process that determines the rate of interest. We distinguish between the *real* and *nominal* or market rate of interest to illustrate the role played by price anticipations. The real rate is the equilibrium rate determined by either loanable funds or liquidity preference, where market participants assume that there will be no price changes in the future. The nominal rate is the actual observed rate in the financial system and is equal to the real rate plus an adjustment to account for the fact that market participants have anticipations about future price changes. The relationship between the nominal and real rate of interest can be expressed as

$$nr(t) = rr(t) + p_a(t) \tag{5}$$

where $nr(t)$ represents the nominal rate of interest at time t, $rr(t)$ is the real, or equilibrium, rate of interest in the absence of anticipated price changes, and $p_a(t)$ is the anticipated percentage change in the price level.[1] The nominal rate of interest is the rate actually observed in financial markets, and only in the special case where market participants have no anticipations of price changes, $p_a(t) = 0$, will the real and nominal rates be the same. The fact that nominal interest rates incorporate anticipated inflation is often referred to as the *Fisher effect* in honor of Irving Fisher, the first to clearly spell out the relationship between nominal rates, real rates, and anticipated inflation.

Expression (5) assumes that the nominal interest rate adjusts fully to the anticipated rate of price change. If the real rate of interest is 5% and market participants anticipate an inflation rate of 3% over the period of the loan, then the nominal rate will be 8%. However, this is based on two assumptions: (1) both the supplier and demander of funds in the financial system have the same anticipations about price behavior, and (2) the adjustment is complete. To see how anticipated inflation influences interest rates, let us consider a simple example.

Suppose that two individuals, an SU and a DU, agree to exchange money and an I.O.U. for one year in the amount of $100. At the end of the year, the DU agrees to

---

[1] Expression (5) technically includes an interactive term, $rr(t) \cdot p_a(t)$, on the right-hand side of the equation, so that the market rate is high enough to maintain the real value of the interest payment on the I.O.U. This term is usually ignored because that product term is very small for the range of anticipated inflation rates observed in the United States.

pay back the principal of $100 plus a 5% interest return. In a sense we can think of the 5% as the real rate of interest determined between the SU and DU if both had no anticipation of price changes over the year. However, let us assume that both anticipate that prices in general will increase 3% over the coming year. Obviously, the SU would not lend the $100 at 5% because a 5% return is expected in terms of the real resources that can be purchased, but, at the end of the year, these resources will cost 3% more than they do at the time of the loan. If the loan is to be made, the SU will demand 8%, that is, 5% plus an additional 3% inflation premium. The DU will be willing to pay the additional 3% if he or she also has the same anticipations about price changes over the year. If the DU anticipates that prices will increase by 3%, then the DU also anticipates that his or her wages, if a worker, or profits, if a businessperson, will increase by 3%.

Theoretically, there is no limit to how much anticipated inflation the nominal rate will incorporate. Any anticipated inflation will become incorporated into nominal interest rates, whether small or large; however, there is a lower bound to the nominal rate in the case of anticipated deflation. With a real rate of interest of 5% and an anticipated inflation rate of -10% or deflation of 10%, expression (5) implies that the nominal rate is 0%. SUs will never lend funds at a negative rate when they always have the option of holding onto their funds. This would be preferable even if they earned no interest income.

The relationship between real rates, nominal rates, and anticipated inflation was suggested by Fisher almost a century ago; however, the issue received increasing attention during the 1970s. In an effort to understand why interest rates were high and variable during the 1970s, economists resurrected Fisher and argued that high interest rates were due largely to inflationary anticipations. Economists now recognize that the interest rate changes observed in the financial system are significantly influenced by inflationary anticipations as well as the underlying forces that determine the real rate of interest. In fact, many studies suggest that the real rate of interest varies within the range of 2 to 4% over time and that in the late 1970s, when interest rates reached double-digit levels, most of the increase in nominal rates was due to increasing inflationary anticipations.

Thus, economists have devoted major effort to understanding the relationship between interest rates and anticipated inflation; however, the literature on the subject has encountered several difficult issues in attempting to determine to what extent expression (5) holds in practice. First, there is disagreement over how best to measure anticipated price changes. All measures of this variable are subject to criticism. Second, the real rate is assumed constant in expression (5); however, the real rate itself will vary with changes in the demand and supply for loanable funds. For example, oil price increases in the 1970s lowered the productivity of capital, which in turn, shifted the demand for loanable funds to the left. Oil price declines in the second half of the 1980s increased the productivity of capital, which in turn, shifted the demand for loanable funds to the right. In the 1980s, large federal deficits shifted the demand for loanable funds to the right while the decline in the nation's saving rate shifted the supply of funds to the left. Each of these nonfinancial forces change the real rate of interest so that expression (5) should be regarded as a very simple relationship between inflationary anticipations and nominal interest rates. Third, there is considerable discussion regarding the completeness of the adjustment of nominal rates to anticipated inflation. According to expression (5), there should be a one-to-one relationship between nominal rates and anticipated inflation; however,

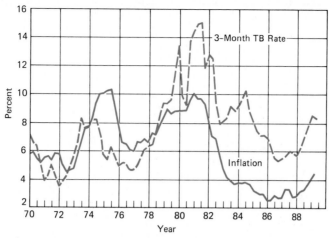

Source: Data based on Citicorp Database Services.

FIGURE 5-10   **Three-month Treasury bill rate and five-quarter moving average of annualized rates of change of the GNP deflator, first quarter 1970–second quarter 1989**

most empirical research has found a less than one-to-one relationship, more on the order of 0.80. That is, an increase in anticipated inflation by 1% will cause the nominal rate to increase by 0.8%. In fact, the debate is even more confusing because many argue that the relationship should be greater than one to one since interest income is subject to progressive federal income taxation. SUs are interested in maintaining the real after-tax rate of return so that the nominal rate must not only adjust to incorporate anticipated inflation but also to maintain the real after-tax return as higher interest rates are subject to higher marginal tax brackets. Expression (5) can be modified to incorporate taxation effects by

$$nr(t) = \frac{rr^*(t) + Pa^{(t)}}{(1 - \tau)} \tag{6}$$

where $rr^*(t)$ is defined as the real after-tax interest rate and τ is the relevant marginal tax rate. Thus with a marginal tax rate of 25%, nominal rates must increase by 1.33 percentage points for each percentage point increase in anticipated inflation to maintain a constant real after-tax rate of return.

These and other issues have been the subject of much debate during the past; however, there is no question that interest rates have been influenced significantly by anticipated inflation. Anticipated inflation itself, while difficult to measure, is associated closely with current and past actual inflation rates. Figure 5-10 illustrates the behavior of the nominal or market rate on Treasury bills and the actual inflation rate measured by the GNP deflator for the 1970s and 1980s. The association is obvious.

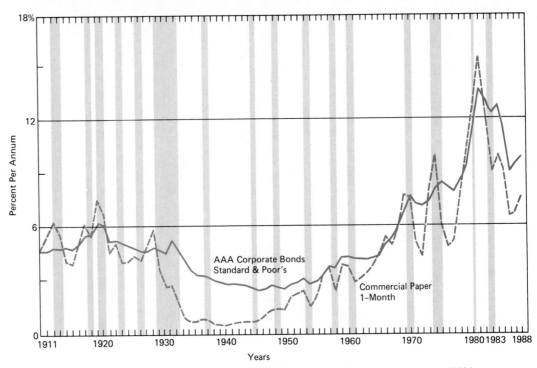

Source: Board of Governors of the Federal Reserve System, 1988 *Historical Chart Book*, p. 96. Updated to 1988 by author. Shaded areas represent recessions. The long-term interest rates through 1983 are Standard & Poor's AAA corporate bond rate. Moody's corporate AAA bond rate is used to update the figure.

FIGURE 5-11   Long- and short-term interest rates, 1911–1988

Interest Rates Over Time

The level of interest rates at a point in time or over time is the result of a complex set of forces occurring both in the financial and real sectors of the economy. Interest rates reflect anticipated inflation along with either demand and supply for money or demand and supply for loanable funds, depending on whether one emphasizes liquidity preference or loanable funds, respectively. The level of interest rates has been a subject of considerable concern during the past as interest rates have reached high levels and have imposed severe problems on intermediation markets. Figure 5-11 illustrates the behavior of short- and long-term interest rates from 1911 through 1988. There are two noticeable characteristics of the behavior of interest rates over time. First, interest rates have exhibited a long-run upward trend over much of the period, especially after 1965. Second, while the trend has been upward, there is a cyclical pattern to interest rate movements. Interest rates tend to increase during periods of business expansion and decrease during business contraction (the shaded areas of Figure 5-11).

It will be useful to focus on a specific period to highlight the variety of factors that influence the interest rate. In particular, the second half of the 1970s and the first half of the 1980s have been a period of unprecedented interest rate behavior that will illustrate the variety of forces that determine interest rates.

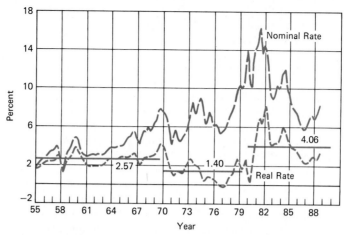

Source: Anticipated inflation series provided by the Federal Reserve Bank of Philadelphia and represents the 12-month CPI forecasts from the Livingston Survey. Nominal interest rates are represented by the 1-year constant maturity U.S. Treasury rate obtained from Citicorp Database Services.

FIGURE 5-12   Nominal and real one-year Treasury interest rates, first quarter 1955–fourth quarter 1988

Figure 5-12 illustrates the nominal and real one-year Treasury bill rate from 1955 through 1988. The nominal or market rate equals the real rate of interest, *rr*, and the anticipated rate of inflation, *Pa*

$$nr = rr + p_a \tag{7}$$

The expected real rate of interest can then be expressed as

$$rr = nr - p_a \tag{8}$$

once we agree on some measure of anticipated inflation.

The nominal interest rate illustrated in Figure 5-12 is directly observable while the expected real interest rate is based on a measure of anticipated inflation. Figure 5-12 illustrates several interesting aspects of interest rate movement in recent years.

First, the real interest rate was relatively constant in the 1955–1965 period and only slightly lower than the nominal rate. The nominal rate gradually began to raise above the real rate in the mid-1960s as inflation and inflationary anticipations increased. Inflation increased throughout the 1970s and finally reached almost a 20% inflation rate in early 1980.

Second, while the nominal rate continued to increase in the 1970s along with inflation, the real rate declined during the decade. Many observers[2] attribute the decrease in the real rate in the 1970s to the effects of oil price increases in 1974–75 when they increased almost 400 percent. Increased oil prices lowered the rate of

[2] For example, see James Wilcox "Why Real Interest Rates Were So Low in the 1970s," *American Economic Review* (March 1983), 44–53.

BOX 2   Measuring anticipated inflation

The most relevant concept of the real rate of interest is the anticipated real interest rate because it is the anticipated value that influences lending and saving decisions. The actual or realized real rate measured as the nominal rate minus the actual inflation rate is less meaningful for determining future changes in economic activity. Thus, we need some estimate of anticipated inflation to calculate anticipated real rates of interest.

There have been two general approaches. The first involves applying some simple or sophisticated time series technique to the actual inflation rate and then decomposing the actual inflation rate into two components: anticipated and unanticipated. These measures, while being based on sometimes very sophisticated statistical techniques, are in the end nothing more than curve-fitting exercises. A problem with statistical methods of generating inflationary anticipations is that these techniques tend to be "backward looking" since they rely on past behavior in the actual rate of inflation or other related variables. To get a more "forward-looking" measure of anticipated inflation economists have thus looked for other ways to measure anticipated inflation and have increasingly relied on survey methods.

The most well known measure of anticipated inflation is based on a survey first established by Joseph Livingston of the *Philadelphia Inquirer.* Starting in 1947 Livingston conducted a survey of business, government, and labor representatives and reported their forecasts of the CPI 6 and 12 months ahead. These combined with the actual CPI values at the time of the survey then permits the calculation of anticipated inflation rates 6 and 12 months into the future. The Livingston data have been extensively used in the economics literature and carefully analyzed as to their construction by John A. Carlson.[1] The Livingston data are currently maintained by the Federal Reserve Bank of Philadelphia. The real interest rate in Figure 5-12 is based on the Livingston data.

Another short-run survey of inflationary anticipations is the NBER-ASA survey for the period from 1968 on. The NBER-ASA survey refers to the GNP Deflator while the Livingston survey refers to the CPI; however, both are short-run measures of anticipated inflation. The NBER-ASA survey is published by the Survey Research Center of the University of Michigan in their *Economic Outlook USA* and complete data tapes are maintained by the National Bureau of Economic Research.

There was also a long-run (ten years ahead) survey of anticipated CPI inflation that had been provided by Richard Hoey of Drexel Burnham Lambert, which was based on the opinions of institutional portfolio managers.

Figure 2B illustrates a short-run (two quarters ahead) forecast of inflation based on the Livingston and NBER-ASA surveys and a long-run (ten-year ahead) forecast based on the Hoey survey. A detailed analysis of the accuracy of the survey methods as well as selected statistical methods is provided by Adrian W. Throop of the Federal Reserve Bank of San Francisco.[2]

[1] "A Study of Price Forecasts," *Annals of Economic and Social Measurement* (Winter 1977), 27–56.

[2] "An Evaluation of Alternative Measures of Expected Inflation," *Economic Review*, Federal Reserve Bank of San Francisco (Summer 1988), 27–43.

return on capital investment and, hence, shifted the demand for loanable funds to the left, thereby lowering the real rate of interest.

Anticipated inflation itself contributed to lowering the real rate even though expression (5) indicates the two elements are independent influences on the market rate. Anticipated inflation induces individuals to shift from financial assets to real capital thereby depressing the marginal productivity of capital and lowering its rate of return. The lower rate of return on capital, in turn, shifts the demand for loanable funds to the left. Anticipated inflation also drives up the replacement cost of real capital while tax law bases depreciation on historical cost of capital—again, lowering the expected return from capital investment.

Thus, nominal rates rose in the 1970s because of anticipated inflation while real

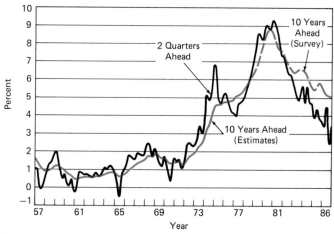

Source: Adrian W. Throop, "An Evaluation of Alternative Measures of Expected Inflation," *Economic Review,* Federal Reserve Bank of San Francisco (Summer 1988), p. 35.

FIGURE 2B   **Survey measures of anticipated inflation**

rates fell because of the effect of oil price increases and anticipated inflation on the demand for funds.

Third, the nominal rate fell after 1980 but remained at historically high levels despite declining inflation and inflationary anticipations. At the same time, the real rate rose in the early 1980s and continued to remain high throughout the rest of the 1980s.

Why has the nominal interest rate remained high in the 1980s despite a significant reduction in the inflation rate? The answer lies in those forces that determine the real rate of interest, but before discussing these, we need to dispense with the possibility that nominal rates remained high because of high anticipated inflation. Anticipated inflation is not likely the main cause of high rates because the actual inflation rate declined considerably after 1981 and has remained relatively low through most of the 1980s. In addition, if anticipated inflation were the main factor, the real rate should have either remained steady as in the 1960s or declined as in the 1970s. In fact, the real rate increased in the early 1980s and remained high throughout the decade.

Thus nominal interest rates remained at historically high levels in the 1980s, not because of inflationary anticipations but because of high real rates. Why have real rates been high?

Monetary Policy   The effects of monetary policy on the nominal and real rate of interest are complex. To see the issues, let us consider the effects of an increase in money supply growth. The initial effects of an expansionary monetary policy lowers the real rate (and nominal rate) because it increases the supply of loanable funds. The lower real rate, in turn, stimulates investment, spending, and income. The increase in income increases the demand for money balances, which in turn, increases the interest rate as depicted by the liquidity preference view of the interest rate. At the same time that the expansionary monetary policy stimulates the economy, inflation and inflationary anticipations increase and cause the nominal rate to raise to a level higher than it was originally while the real rate returns to its previous level.

Figure 5-13 illustrates these effects. Start at time *t* and assume anticipated

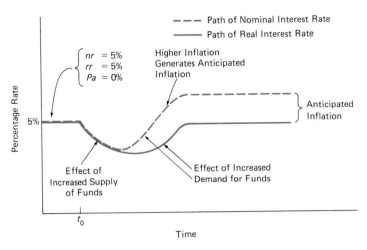

FIGURE 5-13   Response of nominal and real
interest rate to increased monetary growth

inflation is zero so that the nominal and real rates are the same. At time t_o, the money
supply growth rate increases. The real and nominal rate both decline because of
increased liquidity in the financial system. Lower real rates stimulate spending which
in turn shifts the demand for money to the right. Real and nominal interest rates thus
start to increase. The real rate returns to the original level, but the nominal rate
continues to increase because of higher inflation resulting from the expanded money
supply and increased spending.

   The scenario in Figure 5-13 has found considerable empirical support and suggests that monetary policy is not capable of changing the real rate over long periods
of time. However, expansionary (restrictive) monetary policy can lower (increase)
the real rate for a short period of time. Thus, part of the explanation for the high real
rate in the early 1980s revolves around the very tight monetary policy imposed by the
Federal Reserve in 1980 and 1981; however, this cannot explain high real rates
beyond 1982. Monetary policy became less restrictive after 1982, and in any event,
monetary policy cannot influence real rates over a long period of time.

Business Investment and Taxation   The Tax Act of 1981 significantly changed the
rules for business depreciation that increased the profitability of investment at least
until the Tax Reform Act of 1986. As a result, there occurred a major increase in
business investment during the first half of the 1980s, which increased the demand
for loanable funds and, hence, generated higher nominal and real interest rates.

Declines in Oil Prices   After two major oil price increases in 1973–74 and 1979–80,
oil prices began to decline slowly and then declined significantly starting in 1986. To
the extent high oil prices reduced the real rate in the 1970s, lower oil prices may have
contributed to a higher real rate in the 1980s. Lower oil prices would contribute to
shifting the demand for loanable funds to the right.

Government Budget Deficits and Low Saving Rates   Many observers view large
federal budget deficits combined with a low national saving rate as the major cause

TABLE 5-1 Selected interest rates in the financial system to illustrate the structure of interest rate for January 1989

Federal funds	9.12%
Bankers' acceptances, 90 days	8.93
Commercial paper, 6 month	9.14
Large CDs, 1 month	9.06
Eurodollar deposit rate, London, 6 months	9.40
Prime interest rate charged by banks	10.50
Treasury bills, 1 year	8.37
Treasury notes, constant maturities, 7 year	9.14
Treasury bonds, constant maturities, 30 year	8.93
Moody's AAA corporate bond	9.62
Moody's BAA corporate bond	10.65
Moody's AAA municipal bond	7.23
Bond Buyer's municipal 20-bond average	7.53
Moody's average public utility	10.02
Standard & Poor's common stock dividend yield	3.54
Conventional home mortgage, fixed rate	10.60
Conventional home mortgage, adjustable rate	8.80

Source: Citicorp Database Services.

of high real and nominal interest rates for much of the 1980s. Increased budget deficits shift the demand for funds to the right and decreased saving shifts the supply of funds to the left. The effect of both shifts is to increase nominal and real rates.

The Structure of Interest Rates

The previous discussion focused on the determinants of the rate of interest, the rate of interest taken to be the average rate in short-term, long-term, private, public, primary, and secondary markets. At any point in time, however, there is a range of interest rates observable in the financial system. Table 5-1 illustrates rates of interest on various types of financial claims for January 1989 and underscores the diversity of rates of interest at any one point in time. We now turn our attention to reviewing the determinants of the *structure of interest rates* in the financial system.

The structure of rates is determined primarily by

1. Maturity of the financial claim
2. Taxation characteristics of the financial claim
3. Degree of default risk of the financial claim
4. Marketability of the financial claim and other factors

At any point, these four factors interact to determine the structure of interest rates. Of the four determinants, maturity differences among financial claims is the one most often emphasized. The relationship between maturity and the interest rate is referred to as the *term structure of interest rates*. The other factors—tax treatment, default risk, and marketability—are important determinants of the structure of interest rates, but it is often easier to determine how they influence the structure of interest rates. Most of the remaining discussion will focus on the term structure of interest rates.

Term Structure of Interest Rates

The term structure of interest rates refers to the relationship between the rate of interest on various financial claims that are similar in all characteristics but differ in maturity. Government securities are the best example of a financial claim to see the effect of maturity on the structure of interest rates as maturity is the major difference among Treasury bills, notes, and bonds. All these government securities have zero default risk, all generally have the same tax treatment in that interest income and capital gains are subject to federal income taxation, and all have more or less similar degrees of marketability. Thus, the major cause for differences in the rate of interest on short- and long-term government securities is maturity.

The yield curve is the most widely used method for presenting the relationship between the interest rate and maturity of comparable financial claims. The yield curve approximates the relationship between the yield and the maturity of obligations traded in the financial system at a point in time. Figure 5-14 illustrates the yield curve for Treasury securities as of March 1989 and shows that the yield or interest rate on Treasury obligations tends to increase as the maturity gets longer. Care must be exercised in constructing yield curves, and a variety of methods are employed. One must be especially careful not to include the yields of obligations with special features associated with them that sharply differentiate those obligations from others.

Four possible patterns to the yield curve have been observed in the United States. An *ascending* yield curve shows interest rates increasing as the maturity increases; a *descending* yield curve shows interest rates declining as the maturity increases; a *flat* yield curve shows interest rates constant across different maturities; a *humped* yield curve shows interest rates at first increasing as maturity increases up to about two years' duration and then declining as maturity increases. The humped yield curve has only been observed with any regularity starting in the late 1960s and seems to be characteristic of periods of rapidly increasing interest rates. Figure 5-15 illustrates the four possible yield curve shapes.

What Determines the Shape
of the Yield Curve?

Considerable effort has been devoted to determining the forces behind the shape of the yield curve. Despite extensive empirical and theoretical work in this area, however, no definite conclusions have been drawn, and three theories compete for explaining the term structure of interest rates: the expectations theory, the liquidity premium theory, and the segmented market theory.

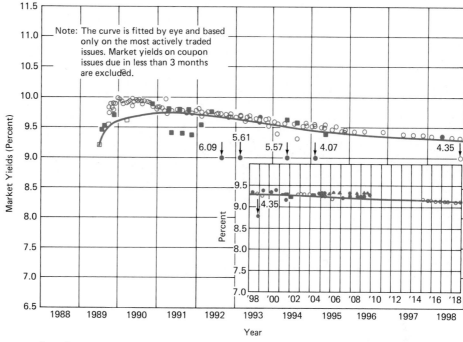

Legend

○ Fixed maturity coupon issues under 12%.
■ Fixed maturity coupon issues of 12% or more.
● Callable coupon issues under 12%.
□ Bills. Coupon equivalent yield of the latest
   13–week, 26–week, and 52–week bills.

▲ Callable coupon issues of 12% or more.
   Note: Callable issues are plotted to the earliest
   call date when prices are above par and to
   maturity when prices are at par or below.

Source: U.S. Treasury, *Treasury Bulletin* (June 1989), p. 55.

FIGURE 5-14   **Yield curve of Treasury securities, March 31, 1989. (The curve is fitted by eye and based only on the most actively traded issues. Market yields on coupon issues due in less than three months are excluded.)**

Expectations Theory   The expectations theory views the term structure of interest rates as determined by expectations of future interest rate movements. The market participants are assumed to buy and sell securities with the objective of maximizing profits with available funds. In addition, the expectations theory assumes that market participants have no preference between holding a long-term security or a series of short-term securities. They are concerned only with maximizing profit. This necessarily implies that the transaction costs of shifting between short- and long-term securities are not relevant.

The expectations theory says that the long rate of interest is equal to the mean of the current short-term rate of interest plus the short-term rates of interest that market participants expect to prevail over the maturity of the long-term security. For example, the interest rate on a ten-year bond should equal the sum of the current short-term rate (rate on a one-year bond) plus the short-term rates of interest anticipated to prevail over the long-term obligation divided by the maturity of the long-term obligation. To illustrate, assume that two types of obligations are available to market participants: a one-year bond and a two-year bond. Market participants have funds available to use over a two-year period and desire to allocate those funds in

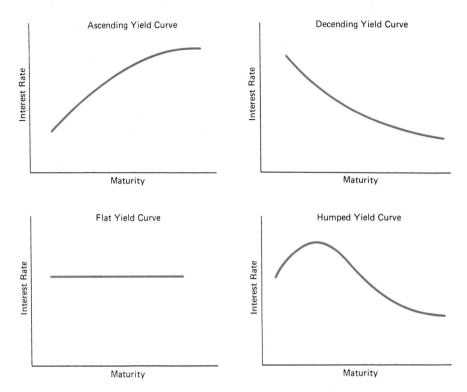

FIGURE 5-15   Four possible patterns of the yield curve

such a manner as to maximize profits. If the current rate of interest on the one-year obligation is 5.0% and market participants expect interest rates on a one-year obligation for the second year to be 10.0%, the actual rate of interest on the two-year obligations is approximately 7.5%. The long-term rate (two-year bond rate) is the average of the current short-term rate and the expected short-term rates over the maturity of the long-term bond:[3]

$$1.075 = \frac{1.05 + 1.10}{2} \tag{9}$$

[3] The discussion and expression (9) exclude the compounding effect to highlight the logic behind the pure expectations approach. Compounding, though, should be considered in a complete discussion of the expectations mechanism. Instead of the arithmetic mean of the short rate and the expected short rates, we should really be talking about the geometrically weighted mean. The relationship between the current long-term rate of n periods (R_n) and the expected short-term rates is given by

$$1 + R_n = [(1 + r_1) \cdot (1 + r_2) \cdots (1 + r_n)]^{1/n}$$

where r_1 is the current short-term rate and $r_2, r_3, \ldots$ are the short-term rates expected to prevail over n periods at the present time. Using this expression for the example just given, we have

$$1 + R_2 = [(1 + 0.05) \cdot (1 + 0.10)]^{1/2} = 1.0747$$

Thus, R_2 equals 7.47%, which differs from the arithmetic mean in expression (9). The longer the maturity of the obligation, the more important the compounding effect.

The important point emphasized in the expectations theory is that market participants have definite expectations about the short-term rate in the second year at the beginning of the first year; however, this does not imply that the expectations have to be realized.

According to expression (9), the long-term rate should be 1.075 or 7.5%. Why must this be? If market participants really anticipate a 10.0% short-term rate on one-year loans in the second year and the current short-term rate is 5.0%, then the long-term or two-year rate must be 7.5%. If it were higher, say, at 8.0%, then market participants could earn more profit by holding the two-year obligation instead of buying two one-year obligations in consecutive years. The increased relative attractiveness of long-term over short-term obligations would increase demand and thereby increase long-term prices and lower long-term interest rates until they were approximately 7.5%. If long-term rates were lower than 7.5%, the opposite sequence would occur.

The yield curve depends on the short-term rates of interest expected to prevail over the life of the long-term obligation. If market participants expect short-term interest rates to increase, the yield curve will be of the ascending type. Each long-term rate equals the current short-term rate plus the expected short-term rates over the life of the long-term maturity, and, because longer-term bonds will have a greater number of expected short-term interest rates included in their average, long-term interest rates will be higher than short-term interest rates.

Likewise, if market participants expect short-term interest rates to decline in the future, the yield curve will be of the descending type. If no changes in short-term interest rates are anticipated, the yield curve will be flat. A humped yield curve can be generated by the expectations theory if market participants expect interest rates to increase first and then fall.

Liquidity Premium Theory   The liquidity premium theory is based on the expectations theory but rejects the assumption that market participants are indifferent to short-term versus long-term obligations. Because of their greater liquidity due to a more active secondary market and the small price fluctuations for any given change in interest rates, short-term securities are more desirable. The interest rate on the long-term obligation must include a liquidity premium to compensate for the smaller degree of liquidity that it affords. According to the liquidity premium theory, the long-term rate is equal to the mean of the current short-term rate, the expected short-term rates, *and* a liquidity premium.

All four shapes of the yield curve are consistent with the liquidity premium theory; however, because the liquidity premium added to the long-term rate is positive, the upward-sloping yield curve is the most common shape predicted by the liquidity premium theory. Even if no changes in short-term rates are anticipated, the yield curve will still be upward sloping, because the liquidity premium is positive; that is, long-term rates of interest will exceed short-term rates of interest by the amount of the liquidity premium. A descending yield curve could arise if market participants expected short-term rates to decline significantly below long-term rates so as to more than offset the liquidity premium.

The Segmented Market Theory   This approach differs sharply from the expectation and liquidity premium theories. It regards the short- and long-term rates of interest as being determined in relatively separate markets. These markets are separated for institutional reasons. For example, many purchasers of securities have specific needs in mind usually related to the nature of their liabilities and thus restrict their purchases to segments of the maturity spectrum. Many sellers of securities also have specific maturity objectives, usually related to the nature of their assets. Given the institutional factors that determine the segment of the maturity spectrum in which buyers and sellers of securities will operate, we then have restrictions on the degree of substitutability among securities of differing maturities. The segmented market theory in its most extreme form would require no substitution, but few would rule out some degree of substitution.

According to the segmented market theory, the term structure is determined by the relative supply and demand functions in each segment of the maturity spectrum. The theory is consistent with any particular shape of the yield curve.

Which Is Right?

In the past, much has been published on the term structure. Although some of the simpler versions have been rejected, there is still considerable controversy over which theory best explains the term structure. The basic problem is that all these theories, especially in their more expanded form, can account for any particular shape of the yield curve. Thus, economists have found that the same set of data on interest rates can be consistent with several theories of the term structure. Unfortunately, this is a common problem in the empirical testing of theoretical models.

Although there is still controversy over which theory is correct, there is widespread acceptance of the role of expectations of interest rates as being an important component of any interpretation of the term structure. The problem has been in determining how these expectations are formed by market participants and how these expectations shape the term structure.

What Difference Does It Make Anyway?

There is a tendency to dismiss much of the discussion on the term structure of interest rates as not being very relevant; however, the term structure is significant to our understanding of the financial system and the conduct of monetary policy.

A knowledge of the many forces that connect short- and long-term rates of interest provides us with a better understanding of the various markets within the financial system. The expectations theory emphasizes the high degree of substitutability among obligations of varying maturities and implies that market participants can move with ease up and down the spectrum of liquidity in their quest for profit. However, the segmented market theory emphasizes basic fundamental differences among financial markets and implies greater rigidity in moving up and down the spectrum of liquidity. Not only does knowledge of the term structure provide greater understanding of the financial system, but it is useful in making bond-financing decisions for corporations and portfolio management for financial institutions, especially for depository institutions. In corporate bond financing, the corporation should issue a maturity structure of debt that minimizes the expected cost over the time horizon of the loan requirement. Long-term borrowing needs should not always be satisfied with issuing long-term debt obligations. Depending on the term structure and the changes likely in the term structure over the horizon of the loan requirement, it may be less costly to issue short-term debt and roll it over for a period of time.

In the case of depository institutions, the term structure of interest rates is critically important for profitable operations. Institutions that borrow short and lend long, such as savings and loan associations, have been faced with increasing problems of *interest rate* risk. This refers to unexpected changes in the yield curve, especially if the yield curve becomes unexpectedly flat or downward sloping. To deal with interest rate risk, depository institutions that make long-term real estate loans are increasingly adopting adjustable rate mortgages (ARMs), which allow the mortgage rate to vary on a short-term basis with the cost of funds. As long as interest rate risk remains important, ARMs will remain an important mortgage instrument. Conventional fixed rate mortgages will not be displaced completely; however, they will be attainable only at a premium. Thus, knowledge of the term structure is critically important for any lender that lends longer than it borrows.

An understanding of the term structure provides information on the strength and magnitude of the relationship between short- and long-term rates of interest. Monetary policy, according to many observers, operates first by altering short-term rates of interest, which in turn influence long-term rates of interest. Changes in long-term rates then influence spending decisions for fixed investments by business, residential purchases by households, and capital-spending decisions by governmental units. An understanding of monetary policy requires knowledge of the response of long rates to changes in short rates.

Other Determinants of the Structure of Interest Rates

Differences in maturity are the most important factor leading to differences in interest rates at any given point in time and have received most of the attention. This is not to say that other factors such as tax treatment, degree of default risk, and degree of marketability do not play a role in the structure of interest rates; rather, their influence on the structure is often easier to understand. In addition, with a few exceptions, these factors are not as significant in determining the yield structure as are differences in maturities.

Tax Treatment   There are three levels of government in the United States, all of which can and do impose taxes on income. The federal government taxes income, many state governments tax income, and even a few large municipal governments tax income. And the interest income from some types of securities is treated differently than is interest income from other types of securities. Securities with favorable tax treatment have lower rates of interest. Municipals—debt obligations of state and local governments—are the most important recipients of preferential tax treatment. Unlike the interest income earned on federal and private securities, the interest income on municipals is not subject to federal income tax, although capital gains are subject to the same capital gains tax as other securities. The favorable treatment of interest income from municipals constitutes an indirect subsidy from the federal to state and local government units, to provide a more active and receptive market for municipals.

In addition, most state and local governments that impose income taxes do not tax the interest income from municipals issued by themselves or their political subdivisions.

The importance of the tax exemption feature of municipals depends on the marginal tax rate of the holder. The higher the marginal tax rate the more important the tax exemption. To convert the interest rate on a municipal to the rate that would be earned on a fully taxable I.O.U., multiply the municipal rate by $1/(1 - \tau)$, where τ is the marginal tax rate. Thus a 5.0% rate on a municipal is equivalent to a fully taxable rate of 8.33%, assuming a 40% marginal tax rate. Municipal rates are significantly lower than are interest rates on government and private securities. The difference is determined approximately by the marginal tax rates of those who hold municipals.

The effect of different tax treatment between two I.O.U.s can be approximated by

$$\text{Tax effect} = \text{I.O.U.}_1 - \text{I.O.U.}_2 \tag{10}$$

where I.O.U._1 is an obligation subject to full taxation and I.O.U._2 is an obligation subject to some type of favorable tax treatment. Expression (10) assumes that all other characteristics of the I.O.U.s such as maturity, default risk, and marketability are the same. To illustrate, the interest rates in Table 5-1 for AAA corporate bonds and AAA municipals were 9.62% and 7.23%, respectively. The tax effect due to the exemption of interest income from federal taxation for municipals was 2.39 percentage points.

Default Risk   Default risk refers to the possibility that the interest and/or principal of the security will not be paid. Federal government securities have no default risk because the government always has the ability to print money to pay off the bonds. No other issuer can guarantee payment of interest and principal as well as the federal government, and hence all other securities bear some degree of default risk. Table 5-2 illustrates two systems that rate the degree of default risk of municipals and private securities.

The higher the degree of default risk associated with a given security, other things being equal, the higher the interest rate. For example, Treasury bills and commercial paper have the same maturity except that commercial paper has a higher degree of default risk. As a result, commercial paper has a higher interest rate than a comparable Treasury bill.

The default risk effect between two I.O.U.s can be approximated by

$$\text{Default risk effect} = \text{I.O.U.}_1 - \text{I.O.U.}_2 \tag{11}$$

where the two I.O.U.s differ only in default risk and other characteristics such as tax treatment, maturity, and marketability are approximately the same. I.O.U._1 is the obligation with the higher-level default risk and I.O.U._2 has either no or less default risk. To illustrate, the interest rates in Table 5-1 for BAA and AAA corporate bonds

TABLE 5-2	Ratings by Moody's and Standard & Poor's investor rating service		
	Moody's		*Standard & Poor's*
Aaa	Best quality	AAA	Highest grade
Aa	High quality	AA	High grade
A	Higher-medium grade	A	Upper-medium grade
Baa	Lower-medium grade	BBB	Medium grade
Ba	Possess speculative elements	BB	Lower-medium grade
B	Generally lack characteristics of desirable investment	B	Speculative
Caa	Poor standing; may be in default	CCC-CC	Outright speculation
Ca	Speculative in a high degree; often in default	C	Reserve for income bonds
C	Lowest grade	DDD-D	In default; rating indicates relative salvage value

Source: James C. Van Horne, *Function and Analysis of Capital Market Rates* (Englewood Cliffs, N.J.: Prentice-Hall, 1970), p. 110.

were 10.65% and 9.62%, respectively. The difference of 1.03 percentage points represents the higher default premium incorporated in the BAA rate compared with the AAA rate.

Marketability and Other Factors The degree of marketability and the existence and extent of secondary markets increases the liquidity of any obligation. Securities that differ only in the degree of marketability will still have interest rate differences. The obligation with the most active and accessible secondary market will have a lower interest rate at any point in time than will the obligation with the less active secondary market.

The maturity, default risk, tax treatment, and degree of marketability are the four major determinants of the structure of interest rates. Other special features of obligations also explain differences across obligations at any point in time such as call provisions and convertibility provisions, but these are considered minor compared with the four factors just discussed.

Key Points

1. Interest rates are influenced by actions in both the real and financial sectors of the economy; however, most discussions of the determinants of the interest rate level use a *partial equilibrium* framework and hold the real sector constant. The focus, then, is on the forces in the

financial part of the economy that determine the interest rate.

2. There are two approaches to determining the level of interest rates. First, the liquidity preference approach regards the interest rate as the equilibrium force balancing the demand and supply for money; second, the loanable funds approach regards the interest rate as the equilibrium force balancing the supply and demand for funds. Both approaches provide the same interest rate in a general equilibrium sense and differ primarily in their methodology and institutional detail.

3. Assuming the financial market anticipates a zero inflation rate, liquidity preference or loanable funds determine the real rate of interest. If inflation anticipations are zero, the nominal or market rate of interest is the same as the real rate of interest. In general, the nominal rate equals the real rate plus anticipated inflation.

4. In the 1970s anticipated inflation accounted for most of the increase in the nominal interest rate; however, it has played a smaller role in the 1980s because the actual inflation rate was considerably lower in the 1980s compared to the 1970s. Nominal interest rates have re-

mained relatively high in the 1980s despite lower anticipated inflation because real interest rates have increased since the 1970s. Real interest rates have increased because of tight monetary policy in the early 1980s, reduced oil prices, increased federal budget deficits, and lower saving.

5. The response of interest rates to changes in monetary growth is complex. An increase in monetary growth first lowers nominal and real interest rates. Increased spending and income reverse the movement and increase real and nominal rates. Inflation and inflationary anticipations increase the nominal rate to a level higher than existed before the increased monetary growth.

6. The structure of interest rates deals with factors that explain why interest rates on one set of obligations are higher or lower than they are on another set of obligations. The existing structure of interest rates at any point in time can be accounted for by four general factors: (a) differences in maturity, (b) differences in the degree of default risk, (c) differences in the tax treatment of interest income, and (d) differences in marketability and other factors.

Key Terms

After-tax interest rate
Anticipated inflation
Before-tax interest rate
Default premium
Demand for loanable funds
Demand for money
Fisher effect
Liquidity preference
Loanable funds
Marketability premium

Nominal interest rate
Partial versus general equilibrium
Real interest rate
Response of interest rate to changes in monetary growth
Structure of interest rates
Supply of loanable funds
Supply of money
Term structure of interest rates

Questions

1. Explain why anticipated inflation influences the nominal or market interest rate.

2. Explain how real and nominal interest rates respond to an increase in monetary growth. Recognizing that real investment depends on the real rate of interest, can monetary policy permanently stimulate investment?

3. How would the existence of a secondary market for some I.O.U.s and not others influence the structure of interest rates?

4. Explain how an upward-sloping yield curve might be a signal that the market anticipates inflation in the future.

5. Consider your own demand for money. Why do you hold part of your wealth in the form of coin, currency, and checking accounts, and how do these reasons fit in with the general discussion of income-related and interest rate–related reasons for holding money?

6. What type of I.O.U. would you compare with an AAA corporate bond to estimate the default risk premium contained in the AAA interest rate?

7. Explain nominal and real interest rate movements in the 1970s and 1980s.

8. If the nominal interest rate is 10% and the marginal tax rate is 20%, calculate the required nominal interest rate for a 5% anticipated inflation rate needed to maintain a constant after-tax real rate of interest?

9. Is there an upper bound on how high the nominal interest rate can go in response to anticipated inflation?

10. If the anticipated inflation rate was -10% and the real interest rate was 5%, explain why the nominal rate of interest would not be -5%. What would the nominal interest rate be in this situation?

Suggested Readings

1. James S. Ang and Kirithumar A. Patel, "Bond Rating Methods: Comparison and Validation," *Journal of Finance*, 30 (May 1975), 631–640. Study on the prediction ability of bond ratings.

2. Thomas F. Cargill and Robert A. Meyer, "The Intertemporal Stability of the Relationship Between Interest Rates and Price Changes," *Journal of Finance*, 32 (September 1977), 1001–1015. Empirical study of the relationship between anticipated inflation and interest rates covering over 100 years for the United States.

3. Stephen G. Cecchetti, "High Real Interest Rates: Can They Be Explained?" Federal Reserve Bank of Kansas City, *Economic Review* (September–October 1986), 31–41. Discusses why real interest rates increased after 1980.

4. M. R. Darby, "The Financial and Tax Effects of Monetary Policy on Interest Rates," *Economic Inquiry*, 13 (June 1975), 266–276.

5. Martin Feldstein, "Inflation, Income Taxes, and the Rate of Interest: A Theoretical Analysis," *American Economic Review* (December 1976), 809–820. Theoretical discussion of the relationship between anticipated inflation, taxes, and interest rates.

6. Martin Feldstein and Lawrence Summers, "Inflation, Tax Rules, and the Long-Term Interest Rate," *Brookings Papers on Economic Activity*, 1 (1978), 61–99.

7. Irving Fisher, *Appreciation and Interest* (1896), reprints of Economic Classics (Augustus M. Kelley, Bookseller, 1965). The original source of the distinction between nominal and real interest rates.

8. C. Alan Garner, "The Yield Curve and Inflation Expectations," *Economic Review* (September–October 1987), 3–15. Analyzes how yield curves can be utilized and what they might imply about future inflation.

9. A. Steven Holland, "Real Interest Rates: What Accounts for Their Recent Rise? *Economic Review*, Federal Reserve Bank of St. Louis (December 1984, 18–29. Good discussion of interest rate movements in the 1970s and first half of the 1980s.

10. Burton Gordon Malkiel, *The Term Structure of Interest Rates* (Princeton, N.J.: Princeton University Press, 1966). A classic study of the term structure of interest rates.

11. James C. Van Horne, *Financial Market Rates and Flows*. (Englewood Cliffs, N.J.: Prentice-Hall, 1984). Detailed discussion of determinants of the level and structure of interest rates.

12. James Wilcox, "Why Real Interest Rates Were So Low in the 1970s," *American Economic Review* (March 1983), 44–53. Discusses the importance of oil price increases for understanding why real rates increased in the 1970s.

13. William P. Yohe and Dennis S. Karnosky, "Interest Rates and Price Level Changes: 1952–69," *Review*, Federal Reserve Bank of St. Louis (December 1969), 18–93. An early study of the importance of anticipated inflation as a cause of increasing interest rates in the 1960s.

PART II

I.O.U.s in the Financial System, Banks, Nonbank Financial Institutions, and the Money Supply Process

Institutions and I.O.U.s in the Financial System, Interest Rate Ceilings, and Securitization

Chapter Overview

This and the next four chapters review the basic institutional components of the financial system as they exist today.

These chapters will provide sufficient information to make sense out of the institutional complexity of the financial system. The U.S. financial system is the most diverse and the broadest in the world. It is impossible to describe accurately its institutional detail at any point in time. First, the institutional characteristics are too varied to attempt full coverage, and such an effort would go far beyond the needs of the business and economics student. Second and more important, the financial system is in transition, and any attempt to provide a time-invariant institutional picture would be futile. Regulatory and legislative changes along with financial innovation have and will continue to change fundamentally the structure of finance.

This chapter begins the discussion by considering four general aspects of the financial system. First, we review the major types of financial institutions that make up indirect finance; second, we review the major types of I.O.U.s or financial assets used in both indirect and direct financial markets; third, we discuss the role interest rate ceilings have played in the U.S. financial system; and fourth, we discuss the implications of the so-called *securitization* process that is likely to generate major change in U.S. financial institutions during the 1990s.

Securitization involves the packaging and selling of loans on the books of financial institutions in the open market. It has exhibited phenomenal growth during the

1980s, and while largely confined to mortgage loans to date, other types of loans are increasingly being securitized. This will have a profound impact on the financial system since it represents a type of financial innovation that is diminishing the roles played by traditional financial institutions such as banks and thrifts and traditional financial instruments.

The next two chapters (Chapters 7 and 8) focus specifically on commercial banks since they are the largest and most diversified of the financial institutions while the third chapter (Chapter 9) focuses on nonbank financial institutions with special attention to thrift institutions and the thrift problem. The fourth chapter (Chapter 10) explains how depository institutions along with the public and the Federal Reserve determine the nation's money supply.

Major Types of Financial Institutions

Financial institutions serve as an intermediary between SUs and DUs for indirect finance, which accounts for around 75% of the total flow of funds in any given year. That is, 75% of the financial assets purchased by nonfinancial lenders (I.O.U.s issued by nonfinancial borrowers) flow through indirect financial markets.

There are two categories of financial institutions depending on their primary source of funds: depository institutions and nondepository institutions. Depository institutions accept some form of deposit as the main source of funds. Many of these deposits are used as transaction accounts and represent the major form of money. Commercial banks, savings and loan associations, savings banks, and credit unions are the major depository institutions. Savings and loan associations, savings banks, and credit unions are collectively referred to as *savings institutions*. Savings and loan associations and savings banks are collectively referred to as *thrifts*. Nondepository institutions differ from depository institutions in that their funds come from sources other than deposits. Table 6-1 indicates the most important financial institutions classified as to whether they accept deposits or whether some other type of I.O.U. is issued to obtain funds. Table 6-2 presents the financial assets of major financial institutions in 1975 and 1988 ranked according to share of total assets in 1988 along with their relative annual growth rates between 1975 and 1988. Commercial banks are the largest of the institutions, but other institutions have demonstrated more rapid growth.

The components of the direct part of the financial system are more difficult to identify since a direct transfer of funds takes place at any point in time and place when the SU accepts the I.O.U. of the DU. The money and capital markets represent the direct components of the financial system; however, they are not defined in terms of a specific institutional or geographic place but, rather, in terms of the types of I.O.U.s traded in various organized and unorganized markets. Obligations with one year or less in maturity are traded on the money market, whereas obligations with maturities greater than one year are traded on the capital market.

The student should keep in mind that the distinction between direct and indirect components of the financial system is an analytical distinction and that there is considerable overlap in these two components; for example, financial institutions are involved heavily in both money and capital market transactions. In addition, partic-

TABLE 6-1 Major financial institutions in the United States

	Financial institutions
Depository	Commercial banks
	Savings and loan associations
	Savings banks
	Credit unions
Nondepository	Life insurance companies
	Private pension funds
	State and local government employee retirement funds
	Finance companies
	Other insurance companies
	Money market mutual funds
	Open-end investment companies
	Security brokers and agents

TABLE 6-2 Financial assets held by major financial institutions, Year-end 1975 and 1988[1]

Institution	1975 Amount (billions)	1975 % Share	1988 Amount (billions)	1988 % Share	1975–1988 Annual growth rate
Commercial banks	$ 885.9	39.8%	$2,938.2	30.9%	9.7%
Savings and loan associations	328.2	14.7	1,359.9	14.3	11.6
Life insurance companies	279.7	12.6	1,113.3	11.7	11.2
Private pension funds	225.0	10.1	1,139.9	12.0	13.3
State and local retirement funds	104.8	4.7	610.1	6.4	14.5
Open-end investment companies (mutual funds)	43.0	1.9	478.3	5.0	20.4
Finance companies	99.1	4.5	489.3	5.1	13.1
Other insurance companies	77.3	3.5	434.4	4.6	14.2
Money market mutual funds	3.7	0.2	338.0	3.6	41.5
Savings banks	121.1	5.4	280.0	2.9	6.7
Credit unions	36.9	1.7	196.2	2.1	13.7
Security brokers and dealers	21.5	1.0	140.5	1.5	15.5
Total	$2,226.2	100.0%	$9,518.1	100.0%	11.8%

[1] Totals may not add due to rounding.

Source: Based on data in Board of Governors of the Federal Reserve System, *Flow of Funds Financial Assets and Liabilities, Year-End 1965–1988* (September 1989).

ipants in the direct transfer of funds use the services of financial institutions to a considerable extent.

Types of I.O.U.s Used in the Financial System

The financial system provides for the transfer of funds from SUs to DUs by the use of financial obligations or I.O.U.s. In the case of direct finance, the SU accepts the I.O.U. of the DU as well as the default risk incorporated in the I.O.U. In the case of indirect finance, the SU accepts the I.O.U. of the financial institution, and the financial institution in turn accepts the I.O.U. (and, hence, default risk) of the DU. In both direct and indirect finance, the I.O.U. and funds travel in opposite directions.

At this point we should consider the more important I.O.U.s used in the financial system. While certain obligations are used primarily to transfer funds between SUs and DUs in the direct component and others are used primarily to transfer funds in the indirect component of the financial system, most I.O.U.s are actually used in all parts of the financial system at any point in time.

I.O.U.s Issued by Depository Financial Institutions

Depository institutions issue a variety of obligations to obtain funds to lend. A number of these I.O.U.s serve as money.

Demand Deposits   Demand deposits are referred to as "third-party" payment accounts since the holder of the demand deposit can write a check ordering the depository institution to transfer funds to a third party on "demand." At present, commercial banks have a dominant position in the issuance of demand deposits. Savings banks have limited authority to issue demand deposits, and savings and loan associations received limited authority to offer demand deposits by the Garn-St Germain Act of 1982.

Demand deposit accounts do not earn an *explicit* interest rate. There has been a legal zero interest rate ceiling since 1933 on all demand deposit accounts; however, the student should keep in mind that the prohibition against paying interest applies only to explicit interest payments. Banks have evolved methods to evade the legal prohibition against paying interest by paying *implicit* interest to the demand deposit account holder in response to the general increase in interest rates. Implicit interest payments occur in a variety of forms: minimum or no-deposit checking, free checks, financial services offered at below cost or no cost, greater convenience in the form of extensive branching networks, 24-hour banking through computer terminals, and so on. The magnitude of these implicit interest payments on demand deposits has been significant. One economist[1] estimated the amount of implicit interest paid on demand deposits over the period from 1960 through 1975 and found that the implicit interest rate on demand deposits had increased over time. Implicit interest averaged 1.09% and 1.85%, respectively, over the two periods 1954–1964 and 1965–1975. In comparison, explicit savings deposit rates over the same periods ranged from 3 to 5%.

Demand deposits are only one form of "checkable deposit" or "transaction account"; however, they differ from the other types of checkable deposits (NOW accounts and credit union share drafts) in four ways. First, banks are prohibited from paying interest on demand deposit accounts while there are no legal restrictions on interest payments offered on the other types of checkable accounts. Second, demand deposits are subject to transfer on demand whereas other types of checkable deposits may be subject to an advance notice of transfer (usually seven days). This distinction has become less meaningful over time, however, as the other types of checkable deposits have gained widespread use as a transaction account. For all practical purposes, they are treated as transferable on demand even though from a legal perspective, they are not. Third, for all practical purposes, banks dominate the issuance of demand deposit accounts whereas the other types of checkable deposits can be issued by any depository institution. Fourth, commercial or for-profit entities are generally prohibited from holding NOW accounts or credit union share drafts and, thus, are confined to using demand deposits at banks as their primary transaction account.

NOW Accounts Negotiable order of withdrawal accounts are interest-earning savings deposits that can be transferred by a check and hence serve as third-party payment or transaction account in the same manner as demand deposits. NOW accounts are issued by banks and thrifts.

Credit Union Share Draft Accounts Credit union share drafts for all practical purposes are NOW accounts. That is, they are a savings deposit subject to transfer by a check or draft. Credit union share accounts are issued only by credit unions.

ATS Accounts Automatic transfer service accounts are a type of sweep account that permits funds to be transferred from one account (high-interest-paying account) to another account (low- or zero-interest-paying account). Banks offer ATS accounts that permit funds to be automatically transferred to or from a savings account from a demand deposit account whenever the demand deposit account is at a certain level and, thus, effectively circumvent the zero ceiling on demand deposits. Banks also offer sweep services from demand deposit accounts into repurchase agreements, which again circumvents the zero ceiling on demand deposits. Keep in mind in both cases that the interest is not being paid on the demand deposit account (that would be illegal); rather, the interest is being paid on the savings deposit or repurchase agreement. Nonbank depository institutions also offer ATS accounts in a variety of forms.

Savings Deposits Savings or passbook accounts, which are offered by all depository institutions, typically allow the account holder to withdraw funds on demand, although institutions can require advance notice. Businesses were not allowed to hold

[1] R. Startz, "Implicit Interest on Demand Deposits," *Journal of Monetary Economics*, 5 (October 1979), 515–534.

savings deposits prior to 1975; however, business savings deposits are now permitted up to $150,000.

Small-Denomination Time Deposits   Depository institutions offer a variety of small-denomination time certificate accounts. Time deposits of less than $100,000 are essentially savings deposits with a maturity date. Early withdrawal is permitted, albeit at a substantial loss of interest income.

MMDAs   Money market deposit accounts are issued by all depository institutions. They were authorized by the Garn-St Germain Act of 1982 to provide depository institutions with a deposit directly competitive with the rapidly growing money market mutual fund shares. They earn a market rate of interest, have no maturity date, and provide six preauthorized transfers per month, of which three can be made by check.

Other Sources of Funds   The items listed in the preceding paragraphs represent the most important types of I.O.U.s issued by depository institutions in terms of total dollar value; however, several other types of I.O.U.s have become important during the past decade, but, because of their denomination, liquidity, and role played in the financial system, they are classified as money market instruments and so will be discussed in the paragraphs that follow.

Insurance of I.O.U.s Issued by Depository Financial Institutions

The majority of deposits held by depository institutions are federally insured up to $100,000. Insured deposits include demand deposits, NOW accounts, credit union share drafts, savings deposits (including ATS accounts), time deposits, and MMDAs. The Federal Deposit Insurance Corporation (FDIC) insures deposits of commercial banks and savings banks, the Federal Savings and Loan Insurance Corporation (FSLIC) up to 1989 insured deposits of savings and loan associations and the deposits of some savings banks, and the National Credit Union Administration (NCUA) insures the deposits of credit unions. Federal insurance thus eliminates the default risk of holding deposits in these institutions, at least up to the amount of $100,000 per account holder.

Federal deposit insurance became a major policy issue in the late 1980s as the number of bank failures increased from less than 10 per year in the 1970s to as many as 203 in 1987 and the thrift industry as a whole was declared insolvent. The FDIC's reserves declined in the 1980s and in 1988, the FDIC lost income for the first time since first established in 1934. The situation was more drastic at FSLIC, which was insolvent with a negative net worth estimated to be $11.6 billion in 1988.

FSLIC was reorganized and recapitalized in late 1989 by the Financial Institutions Reform, Recovery, and Enforcement Act of 1989. Renamed the Savings Association Insurance Fund (SAIF) and made an agency of the FDIC, the insurance fund now insures the deposits of savings and loan associations.

BOX 1 How sound is deposit insurance?

The deregulation and financial innovation process has significantly changed the way funds flow from SUs to DUs. The majority of interest rate ceilings on deposits and loans have either been removed or relaxed, market participants now have increased portfolio flexibility, and there is considerably more competition among financial institutions and markets than in the past. This has had many effects on the economy and the conduct of monetary policy; however, one of the most significant impacts that became apparent by the mid-1980s was the impact on deposit insurance.

Federal deposit insurance was once one of those subjects that was buried in the basement of monetary economics. Established in 1934, deposit insurance for banks, savings banks, and savings and loan associations appeared to work well. Bank failures numbered only a few each year up until the mid-1970s and as a result, the FDIC accumulated so many reserves that it regularly lowered the yearly premium. The other major deposit insurer established in 1934, the FSLIC, also appeared to be highly successful. Almost no savings and loan failures and reserves grew. Federal deposit insurance for credit unions was not established until 1971.

In the 1980s increasing concern about the health of federal deposit insurance was voiced and the subject occupied more and more attention of economists and policymakers. Why the sudden change?

In 1985, two state-sponsored insurance programs for state chartered savings and loan associations failed in Ohio and Maryland. While there was no serious concern that the effects of these failures would contaminate the financial system, the failure of large numbers of depository institutions brought back memories of the banking collapse of the 1930s and questioned whether deposit insurance could protect depositors in the future.

There is a fundamental difference between state-sponsored deposit insurance systems such as existed in Ohio or Maryland and federal deposit insurance, and while one cannot generalize from the experiences of the state systems, the publicity given their failure raised questions about federal deposit insurance.

The FDIC during the 1980s experienced a continuing decline in the ratio of its reserve fund to insured deposits (Table 1B), and in 1988, the FDIC experienced its first operating loss since it was established in 1934. While the FDIC's reserve fund stood at about $18 billion in 1988 and appeared adequate for the near future, the trend in the ratio of reserves to insured deposits was of great concern.

In the case of the FSLIC the concern was far more serious. The FSLIC insured thrift institutions (mainly savings and loan associations), and as of late 1989, almost 500 institutions were insolvent and a large number considered financially weak. FSLIC reserves of about $4 billion in 1988 were insufficient to close even a small percentage of the insolvent institutions. FSLIC itself was thus insolvent with net worth estimated to be a negative $11.6 billion in 1988!

The Financial Institutions Reform, Recovery, and Enforcement Act of 1989 initiated a program to recapitalize FSLIC, changed its name to the Savings Association Insurance Fund, and made it an agency of the FDIC. FSLIC had previously been part of the Federal Home Loan Bank Board.

What's the bottom line—Is your insured deposit at risk? Not really because the FDIC as well as the credit union insurance fund have the full faith and credit of the federal government. Even if the insurance fund is not adequate, the government will in one form or another make up the difference. The federal government and the Federal Reserve are simply not going to permit the type and number of failures that occurred during the Great Depression when almost 10,000 banks failed from 1929 to 1933. However, there is no free lunch, and someone will have to pay the bill; for example, the thrift bailout bill was officially estimated in late 1989 to cost $166 billion over a ten-year period. Most observers regarded this as conservative. Events in 1990 showed that they were right.

The 1989 act requires a broad study of federal deposit insurance which will likely generate additional legislation in the early 1990s.

TABLE 1B Ratio of FDIC deposit fund to insured commercial bank deposits	
Year	*Ratio of fund to insured deposits*
1980	1.16
1981	1.24
1982	1.21
1983	1.22
1984	1.19
1985	1.19
1986	1.12
1987	1.10
1988	0.80

Source: Federal Deposit Insurance Corporation, *1988 Annual Report*, p. 74.

I.O.U.s Issued by Nondepository Financial Institutions

Depository financial institutions constitute a major portion of indirect finance. Depository institutions account for about three quarters of the indirect flow of funds. At the same time, nondepository financial institutions also represent a significant portion of the flow of funds advanced through the financial system. There are two major differences between the I.O.U.s issued by depository and nondepository financial institutions: degree of liquidity and the services provided by the I.O.U. Demand deposits, NOW accounts, ATS accounts, and credit union share drafts serve as part of the money supply and are thus highly liquid. Many of the other I.O.U.s issued by depository institutions are also liquid even though they are not considered part of the money supply. The major services provided by I.O.U.s issued by depository institutions are in the form of high liquidity in that they provide medium of exchange and store of wealth functions. A major portion of the I.O.U.s issued by nondepository institutions, however, possess a smaller degree of liquidity and most frequently provide a specific service to the holder such as insurance and pension services.

There are essentially three categories of nondepository financial institutions that differ from each other in terms of the types of I.O.U.s offered: insurance companies, investment or mutual fund companies, and others.

Insurance companies sell I.O.U.s in the form of insurance policies to cover the financial losses associated with death, fire, accidents, and the like. These I.O.U.s are not particularly liquid, but they offer a stream of services in the form of protection against financial losses arising from the occurrence of a particular event.

Investment or mutual fund companies grew rapidly during the 1960s by selling I.O.U.s (called mutual fund shares) and pooling the funds to purchase long-term debt and equity instruments in the capital market. Mutual fund shares are claims against the asset portfolio of the investment company and thus permit small SUs to participate in purchasing capital market instruments. Fund shares have an active secondary market. The mutual fund is concerned primarily with purchasing capital

---

BOX 2 MMMFs—A major financial innovation

Financial innovation refers to the creation of new financial assets and services by market participants designed to circumvent regulations that limit profit or to take advantage of profit opportunities created by regulation. Financial innovation has been a major driving force for change in the U.S. financial system and throughout the world.

MMMFs represent a good example of financial innovation in terms of how they circumvented binding regulation and how they forced major regulatory changes. MMMFs emerged in the early 1970s as a result of the increasing spread between the Regulation Q deposit rate ceilings applied to savings and time deposits at depository institutions and interest rates in the open money markets. The Regulation Q ceiling was set at about 5% throughout the 1970s and early 1980s while interest rates in direct money markets were significantly higher.

MMMFs emerged as a way to take advantage of the profit opportunities created by deposit rate regulation. Depository institutions found it difficult to circumvent the regulated deposit ceilings; however, securities companies that were not subject to a Regulation Q type ceiling and as such introduced MMMFs as a way to take advantage of the limited ability of depository institutions to pay a market determined interest rate on deposits. MMMFs were close substitutes for savings and time deposits as well as possessing some transactions features. Most important, MMMFs made it possible for even small depositors to have access to interest rates paid by money market instruments (MMMFs could be purchased in minimum amounts of $500)

MMMFs first showed up in the Federal Reserve's flow of funds accounts in 1974 and remained relatively small until 1976. At that time money market interest rates rose significantly above the Q ceilings. As the spread between the Q ceilings and money market rates (like the Treasury bill rate) increased, MMMFs grew rapidly. In 1982, the Garn-St Germain Depository Institutions Act provided depository institutions with the power to issue MMMDs which were close substitutes for MMMFs and, in addition, were federally insured up to $100,000. At this point, MMMFs declined—however, by 1984, they had reestablished themselves and continued to grow. Despite the introduction of MMMDs, money market funds have continued to grow because securities companies have offered increased services to accompany MMMFs such as case management accounts—another example of financial innovation.

Figure 2B illustrates the level of MMMFs from 1977 through 1986, the spread (measured in basis points) between the three-month Treasury bill rate (unregulated money market rate) and the Regulation Q deposit ceiling rate and the level of MMDAs from 1982 through 1985. The figure ends in 1985 because Regulation Q ceilings were officially removed March 31, 1986. The 1977–1982 period covers the most dramatic growth of MMMFs. The positive association between the growth of MMMFs and the unregulated-regulated interest rate spread is obvious. Also note the sharp drop in MMMFs after 1982 when MMDAs were introduced in October 1982; however, also note that MMMFs had reestablished a growth trend after 1983.

---

market instruments; however, in the early 1970s, a new type of mutual fund emerged that specialized in money market instruments. Money market mutual funds (MMMFs) grew rapidly during the 1970s as a result of high interest rates and the fact that money market fund shares were not subject to interest rate ceilings. The first MMMF was established in 1972, and total assets of market funds increased to $207 billion by year-end 1982. MMMFs sell shares and invest the pooled funds in short-term money market instruments such as Treasury bills, large CDs, commercial paper, and the like. MMMFs compete for funds with depository institutions and were very successful in this competition until MMDAs were authorized by the Garn-St Germain Act in December 1982. MMDAs are close substitutes for MMMF shares since they earn a market rate of interest and have limited transaction features. Unlike fund shares, however, MMDAs are federally insured. Since their introduc-

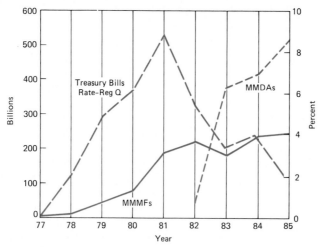

Source: Data obtained from *Economic Report of the President* (Washington, D.C.: GPO, 1988); annual reports of the Board of Governors of the Federal Reserve System; and Citicorp Database Services.

FIGURE 2B   Performance of MMMFs, 1977–1986, and MMDAs, 1982–1985.

tion, they have grown rapidly. By year-end 1988, they totaled $503 billion compared with $338 billion for fund shares.

The third, or other, category of nondepository institutions includes private pension funds, state and local pension funds, finance companies, and nonfinancial businesses. Pension funds sell I.O.U.s to individuals to provide financial benefits at the time of retirement. Pensions are purchased by periodic payments, usually contributed by both employee and employer; however, pension funds, called Keogh accounts, also exist for self-employed individuals. Pension I.O.U.s are not particularly liquid. Finance companies do not deal directly with SUs in terms of selling I.O.U.s; rather, finance companies obtain their funds by selling finance paper in the money market (discussed subsequently) and offer specialized credit to DUs usually to purchase consumer durables. Nonfinancial business firms in recent years, such as American Express and Sears, have made inroads into the financial system by offering a variety of financial services in the form of bill-paying services, credit card services, and traveler's checks.

I.O.U.s Issued in the Money and Capital Markets

There is a variety of instruments used in money and capital markets. Instruments differ from each other in terms of maturity (money market or capital market instruments), liquidity, existence of a secondary market, type of risk (default and interest rate risk), type of interest payment, collateral, and their status as debt or equity.

Money Market Instruments

Treasury Bills   Treasury bills are short-term obligations of the U.S. Treasury with maturities of up to one year. Treasury bills are issued to finance the short-term spending activities of the federal government. They are sold at discount (the interest rate is determined by the difference between the market price and face value of the Treasury bill) and have a broad and active secondary market. Treasury bills are not subject to default risk, but do have interest rate risk. Since the government can always issue more debt or create money, there is no effective risk that either the interest and/or principal will not be paid. Interest rate risk refers to the risk that the holder of the Treasury bill assumes in the event that it is sold on the secondary market before it matures. In this case, there is a risk that the selling price will be lower than the original purchase price because of higher interest rates.

Large CDs   Large certificates of deposits are negotiable time deposits in amounts of $100,000 or greater. Negotiable CDs can be sold before maturity in the secondary market. Introduced in the early 1960s, large CDs have become an important source of funds for banks as well as an important asset for investors since the existence of an active secondary market makes them highly liquid. Some nonbank depository institutions, primarily savings and loan associations, also issue negotiable CDs. These are referred to as thrift CDs; however, CDs issued by banks are the most important.

Repurchase Agreements or RPs   RPs are issued primarily by banks and can be either "overnight" or "term" RPs, depending on their maturity. An RP represents the purchase of a demand deposit account of a large deposit holder (often overnight) with Treasury bills usually used as collateral. Essentially, the bank obtains control of the demand deposit account by selling Treasury bills to the account holder. The bank then returns the funds the next morning by repurchasing the Treasury bills at a higher price than originally sold. The funds thus earn an interest income overnight and become available for spending the following morning. The bank will often sell the borrowed funds in the Federal funds market (discussed shortly). The large deposit holder is thus able to receive interest on demand deposits despite the legal prohibition against paying interest.

Eurodollars   Eurodollars are dollar-denominated deposits, usually time deposits, at commercial banks outside of the United States. The term "Eurodollar" arose because banks that first offered these types of deposits were located in Europe; however, Eurodollars presently represent deposits in banks throughout much of the world. Eurodollars are interest-bearing time deposits with maturities of one day up to several years. In addition, there is an active secondary market for Eurodollar CDs. Eurodollar transactions and deposits can occur in a variety of forms, but let us consider a typical example of how the Eurodollar account can be used as a source of funds for a bank located in the United States.

Assume that a German citizen receives a dollar-denominated check in the amount of $100,000 for selling goods to the United States. The German citizen transfers the dollar deposit to his own German bank in the form of a time deposit. The German bank now has the $100,000 deposit at the U.S. bank on which the check was written as an asset and the $100,000 time deposit as a liability. The Eurodollar bank in

Germany can now lend the funds to anyone requiring dollars, including the U.S. bank, which can then use the Eurodollar deposit as a source of funds. Eurodollar deposits grew rapidly in the 1970s since Eurodollar deposits were not subject to interest rate ceilings. In addition, Eurodollar CDs have an active secondary market, thus enhancing their liquidity.

Commercial Paper   Commercial paper is an unsecured short-term obligation issued in bearer form by large and well-known business firms. Maturities range from a few days to nine months or 270 days. There are two types of commercial paper depending on how it is sold: direct and dealer paper. Direct paper accounts for over 70% of outstanding commercial paper and is issued directly by large business firms to investors. Direct paper is issued by firms with continuing borrowing needs who find it practical to maintain their own sales force rather than place their paper through the services of a dealer. Dealer paper is placed through one of a number of commercial paper dealers. Both direct and dealer commercial paper are sold on a discount basis. There is only a very weak secondary market for commercial paper.

Finance Paper   Finance paper is essentially a special type of commercial paper placed directly by finance companies.

Bankers' Acceptances   Bankers' acceptances are used primarily to finance international trade on a short-term basis. An acceptance is a draft or order to pay drawn by a seller of goods on the purchaser of goods to pay a specified sum at a specified date. When the purchaser formally accepts the draft, usually by stamping "Accepted" on the face of the draft, it then becomes an acceptance. When a bank accepts a draft, it then becomes a bankers' acceptance and payment is guaranteed by the bank. Banks offer this service to their customers; for example, an importer who purchases foreign goods can have the bank accept the draft calling for payment. The acceptance can then be held by the seller, sold to the accepting bank to receive funds, or sold in the secondary market, which is fairly broad.

Federal Funds   Federal funds, or Fed funds, are reserve balances maintained by banks and other depository institutions at the Federal Reserve above required levels that are available to lend on a short-term basis to other banks and institutions. Federal funds are sold usually on a one-day basis, although they can be turned over several times to increase maturity. Fed fund transactions are accomplished through the facilities of the Federal Reserve. The transaction can be initiated by a funds lender or funds borrower either directly with each other or through the services of a specialized funds broker. The Federal funds rate of interest is considered to be a sensitive indicator of money market pressures and is watched closely by market participants and the Federal Reserve.

Capital Market Instruments

Treasury Notes and Bonds   Treasury notes and bonds are long-term obligations of the U.S. Treasury used to finance long-term spending activities. Notes have maturities between 1 and 10 years; bonds can have maturities up to 30 or more years.

Notes and bonds carry a coupon interest payment provision in which regular coupon interest payments are made to the holder. There is a fairly broad secondary market for notes and bonds, although it is not as broad as the secondary market for Treasury bills. Notes and bonds, like Treasury bills, do not have default risk but do possess interest rate risk.

Agency Securities These are long-term securities issued by agencies established by the government to pursue various types of social policies through the financial system. These agencies can be either part of the federal government or sponsored, but under private ownership. Most agency securities are issued by sponsored agencies. Several of the more important issuers are Federal National Mortgage Association (Fannie Mae), Federal Home Loan Mortgage Association (Freddie Mac), Small Business Administration, Federal Land Banks, Federal Intermediate Credit Banks, Government National Mortgage Association (Ginnie Mae), Federal Housing Authority (FHA), and the Export-Import Bank. Each of these agencies sells long-term obligations to obtain funds to provide credit to selective sectors of the economy at subsidized interest rates. Many of these agencies are concerned with increasing the flow of credit into residential housing as well as supporting a national secondary market in residential mortgages. The agencies also issue short-term debt. Short-term agency issues are regarded as money market instruments.

Agency issues are secured only by the agency and, as such, possess default risk. As a practical matter, the federal government is not likely to permit default, and thus agency debt should be regarded as essentially default free. The existence of a secondary market makes them still subject to interest rate risk.

Municipal Bonds Municipal bonds, which are issued by local and state governmental units, differ considerably from other obligations in the financial system since interest income earned on municipals is subject neither to federal income tax nor generally to income taxes levied by local and state governments. Municipals are generally long term, pay an interest coupon, and have a fairly active secondary market. Unlike Treasury securities, municipal bonds have both default and interest rate risk. Default risk varies considerably depending on the political unit issuing the bonds and can range from very low to very high.

Corporate Bonds and Equity Corporate bonds represent a debt obligation of a business firm and are issued by large business firms either publicly or privately (private placement). They carry both default and interest rate risk, have a secondary market, and pay interest coupons to the bondholder. Unlike bonds, corporate equity or stock has no maturity date or fixed value and no contractual interest payment. Equity obligations represent ownership of the corporation, and holders are entitled to a claim on profits only after all other obligations are satisfied.

Interest Rate Ceilings in the Financial System

Interest rate ceilings on deposits and selected types of loans offered by depository institutions were a prominent feature of the U.S. financial system from the 1930s when they were first established until the 1980 Deregulation and Monetary Control Act initiated their removal or relaxation. These ceilings, especially on deposits, have played a major role in the financial system and were a source of instability in the 1970s that forced a restructuring of finance. Thus, it is important to review the role of interest rate ceilings to understand why our financial system is in transition.

Interest rate regulations were not the subject of much debate until the late 1960s when inflation and high interest rates in money and capital markets rendered deposit and loan ceilings increasingly binding. Interest rates in the money and capital markets had not been subjected to interest rate ceilings and thus were free to reflect the forces of supply and demand. By the late 1970s most observers regarded interest rate ceilings in the indirect component of the financial system as destabilizing and producing results far different from those originally intended. As a result, the deregulation process focused on removing or relaxing these interest rate constraints. The deregulation process has focused on two sets of interest rate ceilings: Regulation Q deposit rate ceilings and a wide variety of loan rate ceilings.

The Deregulation and Monetary Control Act of 1980 officially declared a phase-out of Regulation Q ceilings which had for all practical purposes started with the 1978 introduction of money market certifications or MMCs ($10,000 time deposits not subject to an interest rate ceiling). MMCs were the death knell of Regulation Q since they made it impossible to effectively enforce Regulation Q ceilings on savings and time deposits. Table 6-3 lists the steps in the phase-out of Regulation Q, which was completed March 31, 1986. At this time, demand deposits are the only deposit offered by depository institutions subject to an interest rate ceiling. Banks are not permitted to pay an explicit interest on demand deposits—in effect, the interest rate ceiling is zero.

The deregulation process has also focused on removing or relaxing interest rate ceilings applied to consumer and mortgage loans. These ceilings are enforced by *usury laws* many of which were established at the state level. As part of the deregulation process, federal overrides to state-imposed usury ceilings were made, and in other cases, states themselves on their own initiative removed or relaxed usury limits. While some types of loan ceilings continue (government-insured mortgages and some types of consumer credit in several states), the overwhelming number of loan transactions in indirect finance are no longer influenced by government-imposed ceilings.

Deposit Interest Rate Ceilings and Disintermediation

Interest rate ceilings on deposits and various types of loans imposed severe difficulties on the financial system during periods of high interest rates in the late 1970s and early 1980s.

High interest rates in the presence of constraints on what depository institutions

TABLE 6-3   **Steps in the phase-out of regulation Q**

Effective date of change	*Nature of change*
June 1, 1978	MMCs established, with minimum denomination of $10,000 and maturities of 26 weeks. The floating ceiling rates for each week were set at the discount yield on 6-month Treasury bills at S&Ls and MSBs, 25 basis points less at CBs.
November 1, 1978	CBs authorized to offer ATS accounts, allowing funds to be transferred automatically from savings to checking accounts as needed to avoid overdrafts. The ceiling rate on ATS accounts was set at 5.25%, the same as the ceiling rate on regular savings accounts at CBs.
July 1, 1979	SSCs established with no minimum denomination, maturity of 30 months or more and floating ceiling rates based on the yield on 2½-year Treasury securities, but 25 basis points higher at S&Ls and MSBs. Maximums of 11.75% at CBs and 12% at S&Ls and MSBs.
June 2, 1980	The floating ceiling rates on SSCs raised 50 basis points relative to the yield on 2½-year Treasury securities at S&Ls and MSBs and at CBs. The maximum ceiling rates set in June 1979 were retained.
June 5, 1980	New floating ceiling rates on MMCs. All depository institutions may pay the discount yield on 6-month Treasury bills plus 25 basis points when the bill rate is 8.75% or higher. The ceiling rate will be no lower than 7.75%. A rate differential of up to 25 basis points favors S&Ls and MSBs if the bill rate is between 7.75% and 8.75%.
December 31, 1980	NOW accounts permitted nationwide at all depository institutions. Ceiling rates on NOW and ATS accounts set at 5.25%.
August 1, 1981	Caps on SSCs of 11.75% at CBs and 12% at S&Ls and MSBs eliminated. Ceiling rates float with the yield on 2½-year Treasury securities.
October 1, 1981	Adopted rules for the All Savers Certificates specified in the Economic Recovery Act of 1981.
November 1, 1981	Floating ceiling rates on MMCs each week changed to the higher of the 6-month Treasury bill rate in the previous week or the average over the previous 4 weeks.
December 1, 1981	New category of IRA/Keough accounts created with minimum maturity of 1½ years, no regulated interest rate ceiling and no minimum denomination.
May 1, 1982	New time deposit created with no interest rate ceiling, no minimum denomination and an initial minimum maturity of 3½ years.
	New short-term deposit instrument created with $7,500 minimum denomination and 91-day maturity. The floating ceiling rate is equal to the discount yield on 91-day Treasury bills for S&Ls and MSBs, 25 basis points less for CBs.
	Maturity range of SSCs adjusted to 30–42 months.
September 1, 1982	New deposit account created with a minimum denomination of $20,000 and maturity of 7 to 31 days. The floating ceiling rate is equal to the discount yield on 91-day Treasury bills for S&Ls and MSBs, 25 basis points less for CBs. These ceiling rates are suspended if the 91-day Treasury bill rate falls below 9 percent for four consecutive Treasury bill auctions.
December 14, 1982	MMDAs authorized with minimum balance of not less than $2,500, no interest ceiling, no minimum maturity, up to six transfers per month (no more than three by draft), and unlimited withdrawals by mail, messenger or in person.
January 5, 1983	Super NOW accounts authorized with same features as the MMDAs, except that unlimited transfers are permitted.
	Interest rate ceiling eliminated and minimum denomination reduced to $2,500 on 7- to 31-day accounts.
	Minimum denomination reduced to $2,500 on 91-day accounts and MMCs of less than $100,000.

TABLE 6-3   Steps in the phase-out of regulation Q (*cont.*)

Effective date of change	Nature of change
April 1, 1983	Minimum maturity on SSCs reduced to 18 months.
October 1, 1983	All interest rate ceilings eliminated except those on passbook savings and regular NOW accounts. Minimum denomination of $2,500 established for time deposits with maturities of 31 days or less (below this minimum, passbook savings rates apply).
January 1, 1984	Rate differential between commercial banks and thrifts on passbook savings accounts and 7- to 31-day time deposits of less than $2,500 eliminated. All depository institutions may pay a maximum of 5.50%.
January 1, 1985	Minimum denominations on MMDAs, Super NOWs, and 7- to 31-day ceiling-free time deposits reduced to $1,000.
January 1, 1986	Minimum denominations on MMDAs, Super NOWs, and 7- to 31-day ceiling-free time deposits eliminated.
March 31, 1986	All interest rate ceilings eliminated, except for the requirement that no interest be paid on demand deposits.

Terms:

S&Ls—savings and loan associations	SSCs—small saver certificates
MSBs—mutual savings banks	ATS accounts—automatic transfer service accounts
CBs—commercial banks	NOW accounts—negotiable order of withdrawal accounts
MMCs—money market certificates	MMDAs—money market deposit accounts

Note: Mutual savings banks and savings banks can be considered as the same institution.
Source: R. Alton Gilbert, "Requiem for Regulation *Q:* What It Did and Why It Passed Away," *Review*, Federal Reserve Bank of St. Louis (February, 1981); p. 31.

could pay and the absence of constraints on interest rates in the direct component of the financial system set the stage for *disintermediation*. Disintermediation represents the transfer of funds from depository financial institutions to direct financial markets. Interest rate ceilings prevented institutions from paying higher rates when interest rates in general were increasing. Interest rates were not constrained in money and capital markets, so that deposits were withdrawn and used to purchase higher-yielding direct I.O.U.s. Disintermediation was made easier by the rapid growth of MMMFs during the 1970s. These made it possible for a greater number of small deposit holders to transfer funds to money market instruments by purchasing MMMF shares (usually in minimum amounts of $500 or $1,000). The MMMF used the pooled funds to purchase Treasury bills, CDs, commercial paper, Eurodollars, and other market assets in amounts that would have been uneconomical for most share-holders. To the extent that MMMFs purchased CDs, the funds were returned to the intermediation market; however, there was still a serious problem because the funds would return only to those large money market banks that issued CDs.

As funds were disintermediated out of financial institutions into direct markets, the flow of consumer and mortgage credit was reduced sharply. Depository institutions are the major suppliers of consumer and mortgage credit, and, during periods of intensive disintermediation, the availability of credit from depository institutions was reduced drastically; these periods are thus referred to as periods of "credit crunch." The most significant periods of disintermediation and credit crunch have been 1966, 1969, 1974–1975, 1979–1980, and 1982.

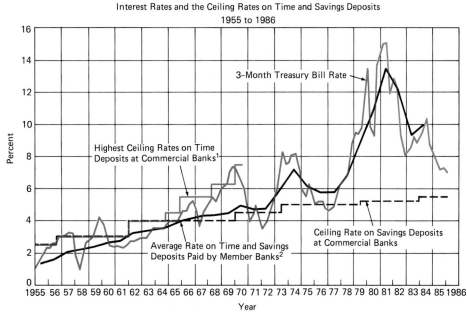

Interest Rates and the Ceiling Rates on Time and Savings Deposits
1955 to 1986

Source: R. Alton Gilbert, "Requiem for Regulation Q: What It Did and Why It Passed Away," *Requiem,* Federal Reserve Bank of St. Louis (February 1986), p. 29.

FIGURE 6-1   **Interest rates and the ceiling rates on time and savings deposits**

Figure 6-1 illustrates the comparison between Regulation Q interest rate ceilings, average rates paid on time and savings deposits, and the three-month Treasury bill rate. Notice that the "credit crunch" periods were associated with a wide spread between the Treasury bill rate and the Regulation Q rate. In addition, you might notice that the average rate paid on time and savings deposits slightly exceeded the Regulation Q rates after 1970. This is because some categories of time deposits in excess of $100,000 were exempted from the Regulation Q ceilings after June 1970.

Impact of Usury Laws on the Flow of Funds

Usury laws, another type of interest rate ceiling, also interfered with the flow of funds. Usury laws limit the amount of interest that can be charged on a specific type of credit. Most usury limits are imposed at the state level, although significant federal usury limits are also important. Figure 6-2 illustrates the general economic impact on the flow of funds of a typical usury limit. If the equilibrium rate of interest established in the market is 12% and the legal ceiling is 14%, the ceiling has no economic impact on the market. The flow of funds between the lenders and borrowers is unaffected by the legal ceiling. On the other hand, if the legal ceiling is established at 10%, then

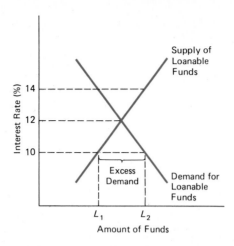

FIGURE 6-2   Effect of interest rate ceiling

the flow of funds will be influenced. An excess demand for funds will exist at the legal ceiling of 10% in that lenders are only willing to loan L_1 dollars at 10%, given all the factors that determine the cost of making the loan, whereas the quantity of loanable funds demanded is L_2. The excess demand, L_1L_2, will be handled in one of two ways. First, the lender will use some nonprice method to allocate the credit. In most cases this means that the high-risk, and usually low-income, borrower will be eliminated. Thus, the interest rate ceiling ends up hurting the very group in society that the ceiling was designed to protect. Other nonprice methods include the size of the borrower, previous business with the borrower, and other services currently provided to the borrower. Second, the lender will find methods to increase the effective interest rate above the ceiling; for example, by requiring points in the case of mortgage loans, compensating balances, or loan application fees, the lender can effectively raise the interest rate beyond the ceiling.

Thus when interest rate ceilings are effective or binding in the sense that the market rate of interest is higher than the ceiling, the ceilings interfere with the flow of funds and end up having an adverse impact on those groups in society that the ceilings were designed to protect—the low-income borrower who will, most likely, be the high-risk borrower.

Almost Complete Elimination of Interest Rate Ceilings

The Deregulation and Monetary Control Act, the Garn-St Germain Act, and other reforms have achieved considerable success in eliminating the type of disintermediation experienced during the 1970s and early 1980s and the adverse effects of certain usury ceilings. Depository institutions now have greater ability than ever to offer deposits that earn market interest rates, and borrowing and lending activities are much less affected by usury limits than in the past. At the same time, interest rate ceilings in the form of the zero ceiling on demand deposits still impact the financial system.

Securitization

At one time there existed a fairly sharp distinction between direct and indirect finance. The conditions required for direct financial transactions discussed in Chapter 3 made it unlikely that small SUs and DUs would participate in direct financial markets. In response, financial intermediaries emerged to provide services that would overcome the limitations of direct finance for small SUs and DUs. The growth in number and variety of financial institutions in the United States during the post–World War II period has been dramatic. There now exists a multitude of financial institutions that tailor their operations to the specific needs of a wide variety of SUs and DUs, many of which would not participate in the financial system in the absence of financial intermediaries. Financial institutions obtain funds by offering I.O.U.s drawn on themselves and lend out the pooled funds. Because financial institutions can specialize and achieve economies of scale, can diversify their loan portfolios to reduce risk, and can be efficient information processors, they are able to tailor the sources and uses of funds to the specific needs of individual SUs and DUs, respectively. They can offer the SU a higher rate of return and lower risk than if the SU tried to participate in direct markets while at the same time offer the DU a lower overall cost of funds compared to direct financial markets. These services of intermediation are unique to financial institutions. At the same time, keep in mind that some of the existing specialization among different financial institutions has also been influenced by government regulation restricting portfolio activities to certain types of deposits and loans. For example, the dominant role played by thrifts in providing mortgage credit has been largely a result of government policy designed to implement a national housing policy whose goal is to provide home ownership to every American.

In the early 1970s a new innovation called *securitization* emerged with profound effects on the flow of funds by blurring the distinction between direct and indirect finance, reducing the uniqueness of financial institutions as special processors of information, increasing competition between all financial institutions and markets, and making it possible for traditionally nonfinancial oriented firms to offer financial services. This innovation is rapidly changing the structure of the financial system and bypassing traditional financial institutions and instruments. Three questions need to be addressed: What is securitization? What forces have been responsible for securitization? What are the implications of securitization with regard to the structure of the financial system and government financial regulation? Let us consider each question in turn.

What Is Securitization?

Securitization involves the packaging of loans (financial assets to the intermediary or I.O.U.s drawn on individual borrowers) in a composite security or I.O.U. that is then sold in the open money and capital market. In a broad sense, securitization shifts the funding of loans from the intermediary to the open market. Securitization occurs in

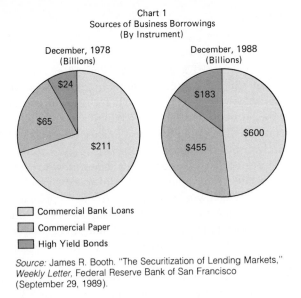

Chart 1
Sources of Business Borrowings
(By Instrument)

December, 1978
(Billions)

December, 1988
(Billions)

$24

$65

$211

$183

$600

$455

☐ Commercial Bank Loans
☐ Commercial Paper
■ High Yield Bonds

Source: James R. Booth. "The Securitization of Lending Markets,"
Weekly Letter, Federal Reserve Bank of San Francisco
(September 29, 1989).

FIGURE 6-3   Sources of business borrowings (by instrument)

a number of ways; however, important examples are (1) bypassing traditional markets, (2) asset securitization, and (3) resecuritizing securities.[2]

Bypassing Traditional Markets

Computers and enhanced access to information have made it possible for businesses that in the past would have borrowed from banks to issue I.O.U.s in the direct money and capital markets. In terms of short-term borrowing, businesses have increased reliance of issuing commercial paper and reduced their dependence on bank loans (Figure 6-3). From 1978 to 1988, commercial paper borrowing increased 600% while bank borrowing increased by only 284%. In terms of long-term borrowing, businesses have increasingly resorted to issuing bonds. In the past, only businesses with high and visible credit standing issued bonds in the capital market; others were forced to rely on loans made by financial institutions, primarily banks, as a source of funds. In the past decade increasing numbers of business with less credit standing are issuing so-called "high-yield" or "junk" bonds. From 1978 to 1988, businesses increased the issue of high-yield bonds by 579%.

While this form of securitization bypasses bank lending, banks have been able to play a facilitating role; for example, a bank can provide a letter of credit that promises to pay an obligation if the business fails to pay. Recently the Federal Reserve has permitted bank holding companies to establish subsidiaries that purchase commercial paper so banks can now provide some of the funding for securitized borrowing.

---

[2] James R. Booth, "The Securitization of Lending Markets," *Weekly Letter*, Federal Reserve Bank of San Francisco (September 29, 1989).

Asset Securitization

Banks, thrifts, and other financial institutions have been active participants in the securitization process by a packaged security of traditional loans and then selling the security in the direct markets. The cash flows from the individual loans are dedicated to the security. While any type of loan is theoretically capable of being securitized, mortgage loans have been the most extensively securitized. To a lesser degree, consumer credit, auto leases, credit card loans, and Small Business Administration loans are also being securitized.

There are several minimum requirements that loans should meet before they can be securitized. The loans need to be generally similar in terms of purpose, collateral, default risk, and maturity, and the loans must generate a predictable cash flow that can be used to pay interest to security holders. As a result, adjustable rate mortgages have not been successfully securitized on a large scale compared to fixed rate mortgages to the time of this writing. At the same time, even these requirements are becoming less important as computer technology and innovation have devised ingenious methods for combining loans for resale as a single security.

The first asset securitization efforts were made by government or government-sponsored agencies to facilitate a broader market for single-family residential mortgages. The first effort occurred in 1971 when the Government National Mortgage Association (GNMA) developed and offered the "Ginnie Mae" pass-through backed by Federal Housing Administration (FHA)–guaranteed and Veterans Administration (VA)–insured residential mortgages. Ginnie Maes found a receptive market because these mortgages have essentially no default risk. In 1971, the Federal Home Loan Mortgage Corporation, or Freddie Mac, developed a similar type of security referred to as a participation certificate (PC) and in 1981, the Federal National Mortgage Association or Fannie Mae introduced the mortgage-backed security (MBS). Unlike Ginnie Maes, PCs and MBSs are backed by uninsured and privately insured mortgages.

Ginnie Maes, PCs, and MBSs are *pass-through* securities in which the purchaser of the security has ownership of the mortgages and the asset does not appear as part of the bank or thrifts' assets; however, the institution retains the servicing component and continues to earn service income. Since the cash flow of the pass-through security is based on the underlying mortgages, the pass-through security has the same prepayment risk as the underlying mortgages. Thus, the size and time of interest/principal payments on pass-through securities are uncertain.

Mortgage-backed bonds (MBBs) are issued by securities companies and thrift institutions to obtain funds and were designed to overcome the uncertainty of the cash flow of pass-through securities. In the case of MBBs, the underlying loans remain part of the issuer's balance sheet, and the bonds show up as a debt liability. Unlike the pass-through securities, the income generated by the mortgages that collateralize the security are not dedicated to paying principal and interest; thus, the expected cash flow to the purchaser of MBBs is certain and not subject to prepayment risk. The limitation of the MBB, however, is that there is no guarantee to the cash flow since the MBB cash flow is not legally related to the cash flow of the underlying mortgage loans. As a result, MBBs are overcollateralized to enhance their marketability. *Pay-through bonds* combine features of pass-through securities and MBBs chiefly by dedicating income from the collateral to the payment of interest and

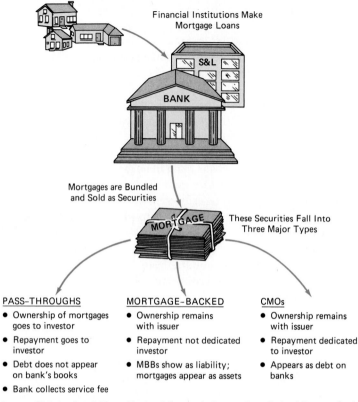

Financial Institutions Make
Mortgage Loans

S&L

BANK

Mortgages are Bundled
and Sold as Securities

MORTGAGE

These Securities Fall Into
Three Major Types

PASS–THROUGHS	MORTGAGE–BACKED	CMOs
• Ownership of mortgages goes to investor	• Ownership remains with issuer	• Ownership remains with issuer
• Repayment goes to investor	• Repayment not dedicated investor	• Repayment dedicated to investor
• Debt does not appear on bank's books	• MBBs show as liability; mortgages appear as assets	• Appears as debt on banks
• Bank collects service fee		

Source: Christine Pavel, "Securitization," *Economic Perspectives,* Federal Reserve Bank of Chicago (July–August 1988), p. 20. The figure has been slightly modified from the original: Pavel referred to CMOs as "pay-throughs."

FIGURE 6-4   **Turning mortgages into securities**

principal (like the pass-through) while the issuer of the security retains ownership of the collateral (like the MBB).

Collateralized mortgage obligations or CMOs combine features of both pass-through securities and MBBs. Like a pass-through, CMOs are collateralized by mortgages whose cash flows are dedicated to the CMO security. Thus, there is no need for overcollateralization. Like MBBs, CMOs are treated as debt by the issuer and show up as a debt liability.

The object of CMOs is to create a broad class of bonds each tailored in such a manner as to offer alternative cash flow options. To illustrate each CMO issue can be divided into two maturity classes: (1) Class 1 holders receive scheduled interest payments, principal payments, and prepayments until Class 1 holders are paid off, and (2), Class 2 holders receive only interest payments until Class 1 holders are paid off. Thus, the first class is paid off within, say, five years while the second in ten years.

CMOs have grown rapidly in the past few years and are now offered in a wide variety of forms.

Figure 6-4 illustrates the securitization of mortgage loans via the three main tyes of securities. In 1980 they represented 12.8% of 1- to 4-family residential mortgages. By the end of the 1980s, securitized mortgage loans account for over 30% of the outstanding mortgages. Pass-through securities have been the most important of the three in terms of total outstanding amounts; however, CMOs are growing rapidly.

Mortgages have been the most intensively securitized loans; however, other types of loans have also been securitized in recent years. The 1990s should see even greater efforts to securitize a wide variety of loans held as assets by banks, thrifts, credit unions, and other financial institutions.

Resecuritizing Securities

Resecuritization involves packaging the cash flows of already existing direct market instruments in ways to tailor characteristics of the underlying securities to specific sectors of the financial market. An important example of resecuritization are the CMOs discussed earlier. The majority of CMOs are backed by mortgaged-backed securities created by GNMA, FNMA, and FHLMC.

What Is Behind Securitization?

There are two explanations both of which offer important insights into why securitization is expanding.

Government Regulation   Financial institutions are one of the most heavily regulated and supervised sectors of the U.S. economy. Even in the so-called deregulation period, financial institutions remain subject to much government regulation. Reserve requirements on deposits, portfolio restrictions, capital-asset requirements, and deposit insurance regulations are major regulatory forces that influence portfolio decisions. The impact of these are often summarized as imposing a *regulatory tax* on the financial institution, and as a result, financial institutions have an incentive to innovate toward activities that reduced the impact of the regulatory tax.

In recent years, regulators have raised minimum capital requirements that induce institutions to sell assets (securitize loans) rather than retain ownership of the assets. In this way, the institution is required to hold less capital and be more leveraged. The Financial Institutions Reform, Recovery, and Enforcement Act of 1989, for example, requires depository institutions to hold capital related to the risk level of their assets. Thus, securitized mortgages would be subject to either a no capital or less capital reserve compared to nonsecuritized mortgages. Reserve requirements on deposits provide an incentive to seek sources of funds not subject to reserve requirements such as selling a debt instrument that represents a package of loans on the asset side of the balance sheet.

Thus, regulatory taxes in the form of capital and reserve requirements provide an incentive to securitize.

Economic Forces   Government regulation is only part of the story, however, since many of the new innovations—securitization, in particular—would have occurred in

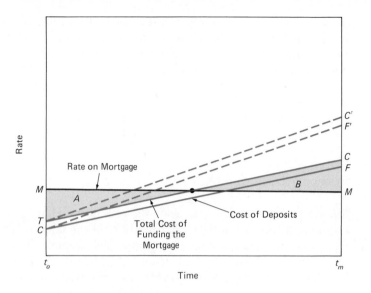

FIGURE 6-5 Illustration of interest rate risk in
pricing a long-term fixed rate mortgage

a less regulated environment. There are significant economic motives to securitization. Some of the more important include the following: (1) it increases the liquidity
of the loans used as collateral, (2) it increases the ability of the institution to diversify
and thus reduce risk, (3) it increases the ability of the institution to attract long-term
sources of funds rather than rely on short-term deposits, and (4) most important in
the case of mortgage loans, it allows the institution to manage *interest rate risk* more
effectively.

Interest rate risk in general arises from the nonzero probability that an asset may
be sold at a different price than the original purchase price. In regard to fixed rate
mortgages (or adjustable rate mortgages with caps), interest rate risk refers to the fact
that the actual cost of funds will differ from the forecasted cost of funds at the time
the mortgage loan was funded. In general, the rate of interest on a mortgage loan is

$$\begin{aligned}
\text{Fixed rate on mortgage loan} =& \\
\text{current cost of funds}& \\
+ \text{ forecasted cost of funds over the expected maturity of the mortgage}& \\
+ \text{ administrative cost of servicing the loan}& \\
+ \text{ profit}&
\end{aligned}$$

(1)

If the actual cost of funds was forecasted with a reasonable degree of accuracy, then
the loan will yield a positive profit to the institution. If the actual cost of funds
exceeded the forecasted cost, as it frequently did in the 1970s and early 1980s, a
mortgage loan that appeared to be profitable at the time it was made ends up being
unprofitable.

Figure 6-5 illustrates the concept of interest rate risk. Line *MM* represents the
rate of interest for a fixed rate mortgage loan with an expected maturity of t_m made
at time t_0. Line *CF* represents the actual cost of deposits at time t_0 and the forecasted

cost of deposits over the expected maturity of the mortgage loan. Line *TC* presents the total cost of funding the mortgage consisting of (1) cost of deposits, (2) administrative costs, and (3) profit. Administrative costs and profit are assumed to be fixed over the expected maturity of the loan.

The fact that the total cost of funding the loan increases over time does not render the mortgage loan unprofitable. Lines *MM*, *CF*, and *TC* are drawn so that the area marked *A* is equal to the area marked *B*. This is merely an illustration of the pricing formula given by expression (1). If *CF* ends up being the actual cost of funds, the mortgage will yield a positive profit; however, if the cost of funds in the future were under forecasted as was common in the 1970s and *CF'* and hence *TC'* represented the actual cost of funds, the mortgage would yield a negative return.

There are several ways in which securitization can help in the management of interest rate risk. First, securitization provides a way to obtain long-term funds that is not possible with deposits. In this manner, the institution can match the maturity of the fund source with the maturity of the asset (mortgage) and thus reduce interest rate risk. Second, securitization removes the asset from the balance sheet and transfers the interest rate risk to another party that may be in a better position to manage the risk. Third, securitization diversifies the sources of funds and thus enables an institution to function in a more flexible and competitive environment.

Banks and thrifts have pursued other types of activities to manage interest rate risk for mortgage loans such as adjustable rate mortgages; however, the rapid growth of securitized mortgages during the late 1980s reflects the considerable advantages they provide in managing interest rate risk.

Implications for Regulatory Policy and the Future of Financial Intermediation

There are two major implications of the securitization process: financial regulation and the role of financial intermediation.

In terms of financial regulation, securitization has raised a variety of new issues regarding reserve and capital requirements. Should the sale of securitized assets be subject to reserve requirements as deposits? How should capital requirements be adjusted to the mix of securitized and nonsecuritized assets? These and other issues have not been decided on, but one thing is for certain, securitization will continue and will generate new regulatory concerns.

Implications for the financial system are profound and, as of yet, undetermined. Securitization suggests that financial institutions no longer have an exclusive comparative advantage of funding and holding loans. As nonmortgage loans become increasingly securitized, major changes can be forecasted for the indirect component of the financial system. Christine Pavel of the Federal Reserve Bank of Chicago offered two scenarios for the banking industry.[3]

First, banks continue to accept deposits and make loans with the intent of securitizing the majority of loans. In this scenario, the assets on the balance sheet are

---

[3] "Securitization," *Economic Perspectives*, Federal Reserve Bank of Chicago (July–August 1988), 16–31.

ephemeral and in transition to be securitized. Banks earn the major portion of the income by the initial credit evaluation and loan service. Deposits then become a less critical part of running a bank, and the bank becomes more like an agent or broker. There will be a considerable blurring of the roles of indirect and direct finance in this scenario.

Second, banks may specialize in either loan making or deposit taking but not both. The future bank would then be quite different than the bank of today.

These are only two of many possible scenarios. When one considers the different scenarios for banks as well as other financial institutions, the outcome of the securitization process for the structure of the financial system is difficult to predict. At this point, the only definite outcome is a blurring of the roles of indirect and direct finance, greater competition among institutions and markets, and greater assets and services available to the consumer of financial services whether it be households, businesses, government, or the international sector.

Key Points

1. Financial institutions are classified as either depository or nondepository depending on the sources of their funds.

2. Indirect and direct financial markets can be characterized by the types of I.O.U.s traded. An important aspect of direct financial markets is the existence of secondary markets where I.O.U.s can be sold before they mature.

3. The financial system is in transition. Many of the institutions and I.O.U.s play fundamentally different roles from those of even a decade ago. We can anticipate further change as regulatory reforms and financial innovation continue to change the institutional structure of the financial system.

4. As one illustration of that change, interest rate ceilings were pervasive in intermediation markets through the early 1980s. They imposed severe problems and threatened the stability of the financial system. Regulatory reforms en-

acted by the 1980 Deregulation and Monetary Control Act and the 1982 Garn St Germain Depository Institution Act effectively removed or significantly relaxed interest rate ceilings in the United States. At present, demand deposits are the only form of deposit subject to an interest rate ceiling. Some states have reimposed usury limits on selected types of loans and government guaranteed mortgage loans continue to be subject to ceilings. Despite these exceptions, however, the financial system after 1986 was free of the most binding and troublesome of the interest rate ceilings.

5. Securitization involves the packaging and selling of loans by financial institutions in the open market. In principle, any loan can be securitized. This innovation has grown at a phenomenal rate and will change the structure of the financial system in the 1990s. Securitization raises new regulatory issues and blurs the distinction between direct and indirect finance.

Key Terms

Agency securities

ATS accounts (automatic transfer service accounts)

Bankers' acceptances

Collateralized mortgage obligations (CMOs)

Commercial paper

Credit union share drafts

Demand deposits

Deposit insurance

Depository institution

Eurodollar deposits

Federal funds

Finance paper

Ginnie Mae

Interest rate ceiling

Interest rate risk

Large CDs

MMDAs (money market deposit accounts)

MMMFs (money market mutual funds)

Mortgage-backed bonds (MBBs)

Municipal securities

Nondepository institution

NOW accounts (negotiable order of withdraw)

Pass-through securities

Usury laws

Regulation Q

Repurchase agreements

Savings deposits

Securitization

Thrift institution or thrifts

Treasury bills, notes, and bonds

Questions

1. The financial system plays an important role in a market-oriented economy such as that in the United States. Does the financial system play the same or different role in less-market oriented economies such as the Soviet Union?

2. How does the existence of a secondary market improve the ability of financial institutions to better meet the needs of SUs and DUs?

3. Consider a bank in which a demand deposit account is held by a business. Make a list of the ways in which the bank pays implicit interest. Would a bank ever pay implicit interest on an account that earns explicit interest?

4. If transaction deposits (accounts subject to transfer either by check or some other type of authorization) are being offered by several different depository institutions, how does this influence the type of competition between these institutions? Have commercial banks lost their dominant position in the financial system?

5. When interest rates rose above the Q ceilings such as in the late 1970s (Figure 6-1), what effect did this have on the viability of depository institutions?

6. Did the gap between interest rates in direct markets and Regulation Q raise equity issues with regard to the size of deposits held at depository institutions?

7. Remembering that interest rates represent the combined influence of demand for funds, supply of funds, and anticipated inflation, did the failure of the Federal Reserve to prevent inflation in the 1970s have anything to do with the gap between direct market rates and Regulation Q as illustrated in Figure 6-1?

8. Discuss the concept of interest rate risk for a thrift institution that allocates a major portion of funds to mortgages. Do adjustable rate mortgages eliminate interest rate risk if they have caps? How does securitization help manage interest rate risk?

Suggested Readings

1. Herbert L. Baer and Christine A. Pavel, "Does Regulation Drive Innovation," *Economic Perspectives*, Federal Reserve Bank of Chicago (March–April 1988), 3–15. Discusses how regulation imposes regulatory taxes on portfolio activities and thus provides incentives to innovate around the regulation.

2. George J. Benston, "Interest Payments on Demand Deposits and Bank Investment Behavior," *Journal of Political Economy* (October 1964), 431–449. A well-known study on the effects of paying interest on demand deposits.

3. Lawrence Benvensite and Allen N. Berger, "Securitization with Recourse: An Instrument That Offers Uninsured Bank Deposits Sequential Claims," *Journal of Banking and Finance*, 11 (September 1987), 402–424. More on securitization.

4. James R. Booth, "The Securitization Revolution in Lending Markets," *Focus*, Center for Financial System Research, Arizona State University (Spring 1988), 3–4. Brief survey of securitization.

5. James R. Booth, "The Securitization of Lending Markets," *Weekly Letter*, Federal Reserve Bank of San Francisco (September 29, 1989). More on securitization.

6. Norman N. Bowsher, "Repurchase Agreements," *Review*, Federal Reserve Bank of San Francisco (September 1979), 17–22.

7. Thomas F. Cargill and Gillian Garcia, *Financial Reform in the 1980s* (Stanford, Calif.: Hoover Institution Press, 1985). Discusses disintermediation and other problems in the financial system during the 1970s and early 1980s.

8. Timothy Q. Cook and Ruce J. Summers (eds.), *Instruments of the Money Market*, Federal Reserve Bank of Richmond, 1981. Reviews all the major money market instruments.

9. R. Alton Gilbert, "Requiem for Regulation Q: What It Did and Why It Passed Away," *Review*, Federal Reserve Bank of St. Louis (February 1986), 22–37. A good overview of the history of Regulation Q, its effects, and final burial in March 31, 1986. Extensive reference list.

10. Edward C. Lawrence and Gregory E. Elliehausen, "The Impact of Federal Interest Rate Regulations on the Small Saver: Further Evidence," *Journal of Finance* (June 1971), 677–684. Shows how Regulation Q discriminated against the small depositor.

11. Charles M. Lucas, Marcos T. Jones, and Thom B. Thurston, "Federal Funds and Repurchase Agreements," *Quarterly Review*, Federal Reserve Bank of New York (Summer 1977), 33–48.

12. Christine Pavel, "Securitization," *Economic Perspectives*, Federal Reserve Bank of Chicago (July–August 1988), 16–31. More on securitization.

13. David H. Resler and Richard W. Lang, "Federal Agency Debt: Another Side of Federal Borrowing," *Review*, Federal Reserve Bank of St. Louis (November 1979), 10–19.

14. Gordon H. Sellon, Jr., and Deana VanNahmen, "The Securitization of Housing Finance," *Economic Review*, Federal Reserve Bank of Kansas City (July–August 1988), 3–20.

15. Donna C. Vandenbrink, "Usury Ceilings and DIDMCA," *Economic Perspectives*, Federal Reserve Bank of Chicago (September–October 1985), 25–30. The impacct of the 1980 Deregulation and Monetary Control Act on state-imposed loan ceilings.

16. Donna C. Vandenbrink, "The Effects of Usury Ceilings," *Economic Perspectives*, Federal Reserve Bank of Chicago (Midyear 1982), 44–55. Economic analysis of usury ceilings.

CHAPTER 7

The Commercial Bank

Chapter Overview

We begin discussion of the most important financial institution in the United States—the commercial bank. While commercial banks have lost some market share to other financial institutions (Table 6-2 in Chapter 6), they remain the largest in terms of financial assets, the most diversified, the most numerous, and the major player in international financial transactions. Most important, banks have aggressively pursued new markets and types of activities that may very well increase their future role in the financial system.

This chapter focuses on the individual bank while the next chapter focuses on the banking industry. In this chapter, we discuss the sources and uses of bank funds, considerations that are important to running a profitable bank, and the unique liquidity problem faced by a bank or any depository institution that makes running a bank (any depository institution) a challenging occupation. In this latter respect, the role of bank reserve requirements is explained along with the form of the current reserve requirement system. Finally, we explore the new and more competitive environment faced by banks and bank innovations that have fundamentally changed the nature of running a bank in the past decade.

Thus, while banks have lost market share measured in the traditional way, other considerations suggest that banks will remain the major financial institution and may very well increase their relative role in the 1990s.

Banks and the Financial System

Commercial banks are profit-making financial institutions that have many characteristics in common with other financial institutions; however, six distinguishing features require separate consideration of banks. First, banks are, by any reasonable standard, the largest financial institution. Table 6-2, which listed the major financial institutions according to total financial assets in 1975 and 1988, indicated that banks are by far the largest of the financial institutions, though they have not exhibited the most rapid rate of growth. Second, banks are the most diversified of the financial institutions to the extent that they deal with the broadest spectrum of SUs and DUs. Third, banks dominate the issuance of demand deposits. Demand deposits are a major type of transaction account. As of January 1988, demand deposits represented 38.2% of the M1 money supply measure compared with 34.7% for other checkable deposits. Fourth, the check-clearing mechanism established by banks along with the check-clearing facilities of the Federal Reserve System essentially constitutes our national payments mechanism. Some estimates indicate that as many as 90% of the total economic transactions occurring in the United States during any year are conducted by checks, and those checks are cleared through the bank check-clearing process.

Fifth, banks play an important role in international finance and this role is rapidly increasing as the world financial system becomes more integrated. Funds flow between countries in search of higher returns more freely than ever before and a major part of the international flow of funds pass through banks. Sixth, banks are a major focal point of the conduct of monetary policy. Although the actions of the Federal Reserve impact the entire financial system, banks are generally the first to be affected by changes in monetary policy, and their dominance in the financial system ensures that the initial impact will spread throughout the entire system.

At the same time, one should not overemphasize the unique position of banks in the financial system for two reasons. First, regulatory reforms such as the Deregulation and Monetary Control Act of 1980, the Garn-St Germain Depository Institutions Act of 1982, and to a much lesser extent the 1989 Financial Institutions Reform, Recovery, and Enforcement Act have permitted nonbank depository institutions to compete more directly with banks. Prior to 1980 for example, bank demand deposits were the only form of transaction account available to the public. After 1980, nonbank depository institutions were permitted to offer transaction accounts to households and even to businesses on a limited basis. Consumer credit and credit cards can now be obtained as easily from a nonbank depository institution as a bank. Prior to 1980 thrift institutions did not offer these services. While regulatory changes need to be pushed much further to reduce the remaining differences between banks and nonbank institutions, the trend is clear. Deregulation and financial reform have narrowed the differences among all depository institutions in the past decade and will likely narrow them further in the 1990s.

Second, financial innovations on the part of nonbank depository institutions will continue to blur the uniqueness of banks. There is a strong incentive to provide innovations that take advantage of the zero interest rate ceiling on demand deposits. Since other transaction balances (not generally available to businesses) offer a market-determined interest rate, demand deposit holders have a strong incentive to seek substitutes for demand deposits that earn interest. There is a strong incentive to provide financial services to satisfy this demand. The advance of computer technology increasingly makes it easier to create new forms of money that circumvent to zero interest ceiling on demand deposits.

Another innovation that could increase the role of nonbank financial institutions is *securitization*. While banks have played a major role in the securitization process, there is no reason why nonbank institutions cannot aggressively take part in the process.

Despite these two factors, however, one must be careful about predicting the further decline of banks in the financial system. First, banks have been a major player in the securitization of loan markets—an innovation that is rapidly changing the traditional role of the financial institution as a lender. While nonbank institutions have been part of the process, banks have aggressively moved into this area to a much greater degree. These and other *off–balance sheet* operations based on the ability to unbundle loans is a major development that will change the nature of banking in the United States. Second, banks remain the major financial institution involved in international finance. The growing internationalization of the U.S. financial system and greater world financial integration provides an environment for which banks have a comparative advantage over other institutions. Third, Congress is considering a major restructuring of banking powers that would permit banks to engage in securities underwriting as well as other related services that have been off limits to banks in the past. In this regard, the most significant and controversial issue regarding expanded bank powers involves the repeal or modification of a part of the 1933 Banking Act referred to as Glass-Steagall. The Glass-Steagall act placed a regulatory wall between investment and commercial banks. Investment banks underwrite and trade in securities while commercial banks since 1933 have been confined to making loans and accepting deposits. Congress appeared ready in late 1988 to grant banks expanded security powers by removing or relaxing the 1933 Glass-Steagall Act restrictions; however, Congress's attention was diverted to the thrift problem. While Congress has not repealed Glass-Steagall at this time, the past decade has seen an increasingly looser interpretation of the Glass-Steagall act by bank regulators permitting banks to expand into securities markets. Banks themselves have aggressively pushed the limits of Glass-Steagall.

Banks Are a Business

A bank is a business that has a revenue and cost function like any other business. This point can be illustrated by the following expression:

$$\text{Profit} = R(Q) - C(Q) \tag{1}$$

where

Q = output of the bank
R = revenue to the bank from selling the output
C = cost to the bank of producing and selling the output

Revenue is a function of output. The amount of revenue earned by the bank depends on the amount of output produced and sold. Lending activities are the primary output of a bank and range from making consumer loans to purchasing various types of financial claims or I.O.U.s in the financial market. Costs are also a function of the level of output. Bank costs consist of interest and other expenses used to attract deposits as well as the costs of making and administrating loans.

Profit is the difference between revenue and cost, and the bank's objective is to make profit. No matter how public spirited the advertising campaign of the bank, no

TABLE 7-1   **Real and financial transactions for selected sectors based on the 1988 flow of funds accounts[1] (billions of dollars)**

Sector	Investment	=	Saving	+	(Borrowing	−	Lending)
Households	$690.2	=	775.0	+	285.6	−	370.4
Business	483.9	=	471.8	+	115.6	−	103.5
Commercial banks	22.1	=	19.8	+	200.9	−	198.6

[1] The statistical discrepancy for each sector is included in the lending component.

matter how many public activities the bank supports, the basic objective of the bank is to make a profit.

Banks (as well as financial institutions in general) differ from other business firms in two important respects, however. First, banks deal in financial transactions, whereas nonfinancial businesses deal in both financial and real transactions, with the latter dominating. This can be illustrated by using the FOF accounting data for 1988 and the fundamental flow of funds equation derived in Chapter 3.

The flow of funds equation summarizes the real and financial transactions of any economic unit for a given period of time. Table 7-1 summarizes the real and financial transactions for households, businesses, and banks. Notice the saving and investment (real transactions) for banks represent only about 10% of the magnitude of their financial sources and uses of funds. Real transactions for the household and business sectors greatly exceed financial transactions. This underlines the fact that banks, like other financial institutions, are intermediaries that obtain funds from SUs (financial sources) and lend these funds to DUs (financial uses).

Second, banks and other depository institutions differ from nonfinancial businesses because of a unique liquidity problem. Banks rely on deposits as a source of funds, many of which are very short term and subject to transfer. Deregulation and innovation have made deposits even more short term than in the past in that depositors will shift funds whenever they can earn higher interest rates from other institutions on the same or similar type of deposit. As a result, banks must be careful in the maturity structure of the uses of funds and make an effort to match the maturity of the uses with the source of funds. In fact, part of the thrift problem is due to a mismatch that was common throughout the thrift industry in the 1970s—making long-term fixed rate mortgage loans based on short-term deposits.

Flow of Funds Through a Bank, or What Does a Bank Do For a Living?

Table 7-2 presents the major balance sheet items of all insured commercial banks for December 31, 1988. These components provide important information on the uses and sources of funds to gain insight into bank operations.

TABLE 7-2 Basic balance sheet for commercial banks, December 1988

	Amount (billions)	As a % of assets
Total cash assets	$ 246.3	8.1%
Reserves with Federal Reserve banks	34.5	1.1
Cash in vault	30.3	1.0
Cash items in process of collection	92.3	3.0
Demand balances at U.S. depository institutions	34.4	1.1
Other cash assets	54.8	1.8
Loans and securities	2,601.6	85.4
Investment securities	533.5	17.5
U.S. government securities	345.3	11.3
Other	188.2	6.2
Trading account assets	19.2	0.6
Total loans	2,048.9	67.2
Interbank loans	165.7	5.4
Loans excluding interbank	1,883.2	61.8
Commercial and industrial	608.8	20.0
Real Estate	676.3	22.2
Individual	361.4	11.9
All other	236.6	7.8
Other assets	200.0	6.6
Total assets/total liabilities and capital	3,047.9	100.0
Deposits	2,145.7	70.4
Transaction deposits	642.7	21.1
Savings deposits	535.6	17.6
Time deposits	967.5	31.7
Borrowings	473.1	15.5
Other liabilities	233.7	7.7
Residual (assets less liabilities)	195.3	6.4

Source: Federal Reserve Bulletin, (September 1989).

Source of Funds

Banks obtain funds from four sources: (1) transaction deposits, (2) nontransaction deposits, (3) nondeposit sources, and (4) changes in the capital account or net worth.

Transaction Deposits While all depository institutions are permitted to offer some type of transaction deposit, banks have the unique distinction of being the only institution able to offer demand deposits as part of their general service to depositors. Demand deposits are subject to immediate transfer upon receipt of a written notice of withdrawal in the form of a check. At one time, demand deposits represented the major source of funds for banks; however, they have become increasingly less important for two reasons. First, high interest rates in the past increased the opportunity cost of using a transaction deposit that did not earn an explicit interest rate. As a result, holders of demand deposits economized on the size of their deposits as much as possible. Second, deregulation and innovation have provided several forms of checkable deposits (NOW and ATS accounts) that nonbusiness entities can substitute for demand deposit accounts.

While demand deposits as a source of funds have declined in importance, the fact that businesses are generally prohibited from holding other forms of transaction accounts continues to make demand deposits an important source of funds for banks. Demand deposits at year-end 1988 represented 20% of total transaction deposits held by banks.

Nontransaction Deposits   Nontransaction deposits consist of passbook savings deposits, time deposits, and money market deposit accounts, or MMDAs. Passbook savings deposits have no maturity date and can be withdrawn at any time, although banks can impose a seven-day advance notice requirement before the funds can be transferred. Time deposits include regular time deposits in amounts less than $100,000 that are like savings deposits except that they carry a maturity date. They can be withdrawn before maturity; however, substantial interest rate penalites are imposed on early withdrawal. Large CDs are time certificates in amounts of $100,000, or more, negotiable, and possess a high degree of liquidity because they can be sold in an active secondary market; however, they are regarded as a nondeposit source of funds since they share characteristics more in common with money market instruments than they do with other deposits. MMDAs have no maturity date and are classified as savings deposits; however, unlike other nontransaction deposits, MMDAs possess some limited transactions features. Banks and other depository institutions are permitted to allow six preauthorized transfers per month from an MMDA, of which three can be by check.

Nontransaction deposits have become an important source of deposit funds for banks since they pay higher interest rates than transaction deposits and, in the case of MMDAs, offer limited transactions features.

Nondeposit Sources of Funds   Nondeposit sources of funds grew rapidly during the 1970s because they were not subject to interest rate ceilings (Regulation Q), often had a secondary market, and were either subject to a zero reserve requirement or to a smaller reserve requirement compared with deposits. The nondeposit sources of funds are frequently referred to as *managed liabilities* because the bank manages their amount in accordance with their need for funds. Let us consider the more important forms of nondeposit sources of funds.

Large CDs are negotiable time certificates in amounts of $100,000 or more with maturities ranging from two weeks to one year. The average maturity is three months. While technically a time deposit, they are regarded as a money market instrument since they possess default risk (for amounts above $100,000) and an active secondary market.

Federal funds purchased (borrowed) from other depository institutions are excess reserve balances of banks and other depository institutions that are loaned to other depository institutions for short periods of time, usually for only a few days. The Federal funds market emerged in the 1920s and up until the mid-1960s was used mainly by banks that needed funds to meet their legal reserve requirement; however, in recent years Federal funds have become regarded more as a source of funds for bank lending.

BOX 1   Repurchase agreements—A financial innovation to circumvent the zero ceiling on demand deposits

The repurchase agreement (RP) or "repo" has become a major money market instrument because it offers a financial service that permits banks to "pay interest on demand deposits" as well as satisfying the credit needs of short-term borrowers. A repo might occur in the following way. The cash manager of FlimFlam Corporation determines that the bank deposit account has $1 million in funds not needed for a day. The bank offers to sell FlimFlam Treasury securities and repurchase them the next day. The repo is thus a security or I.O.U. sold by the bank to FlimFlam to obtain funds. The phrase "reverse repurchase agreement" is the transaction from the lender's point of view—FlimFlam buys the security and sells it back at maturity. The transaction in T-account form would appear as

Bank Sells RP to FlimFlam Corp.

Bank		FlimFlam Corp.	
A	L	A	L
	Deposits − $1 million RP + $1 million	Deposits − $1 million RP + $1 million	

The RP is secured by Treasury securities held by the bank.

Bank Purchases Back RP from FlimFlam Corp.

Bank		FlimFlam Corp.	
A	L	A	L
	Deposits + $1 Million RP − 1 Million	Deposits + $1 Million RP − $1 Million	

The T-accounts omit the difference in selling and purchase price to simplify the transaction example. FlimFlam will thus earn interest on funds not needed for a day or so and the bank now has funds available to lend elsewhere in the financial system. Since repos are frequently collateralized by default-free Treasury securities, they have low risk, since most transactions occur between institutions with high reputations in the financial system.

Large banks and government security dealers are major borrowers in the RP market, while large businesses and municipal and state governments are major suppliers of funds.

Repurchase agreements or RPs represent an agreement to sell securities, usually Treasury securities, to the holder of a large demand deposit and repurchase the same securities the next day. The bank then has access to the funds "overnight," and the deposit holder will receive an interest return as well as having the funds available for spending the next day when the securities are repurchased. RPs can have maturities of more than one day, in which case they are referred to as "term" RPs.

Eurodollars represent dollar-denominated deposits, usually time deposits, in banks outside of the United States. By encouraging large deposit holders to transfer deposits to Eurobanks, banks in the United States were able to use Eurodollar deposits as a source of funds that were not subject to deposit rate ceilings in the 1970s. As a result, Eurodollars grew rapidly during the 1970s.

Borrowing from the Federal Reserve System is also a source of funds. Any bank, be it a member or nonmember of the Federal Reserve, has the privilege of requesting a loan from the Federal Reserve. The purpose of these loans, however, is not to serve as a continuous source of funds but, rather, to help a bank through a difficult period. Borrowing from the Federal Reserve by any single bank fluctuates considerably year to year due to the state of the economy, financial markets, monetary and fiscal policy, as well as regional conditions. The Federal Reserve tries to discourage long-term indebtedness by banks, but it is not always successful.

Changes in the Capital Account   Transaction and nontransaction deposits as well as CDs, RPs, Eurodollars, Federal funds purchased, and borrowings from the Federal Reserve constitute the major sources of finds listed under liabilities. The change in the capital account is also regarded as a source of funds. The capital account generally provides less than 10% of the total flow of funds. Increases in the capital account over time result from increased earnings and additional issues of bank stock.

The sources of funds are the input to the bank, and the cost incurred by banks in attracting and maintaining these funds constitutes the most important part of the cost of operations in the profit equation. The income statement in Table 7-3 for all banks in 1988 illustrates the cost incurred by banks in attracting funds from the various sources.

In 1988 banks had gross revenues of $317 billion, of which 52% was used to obtain funds from deposits and other sources such as borrowings from other banks (Federal funds and Eurodollars) and the Federal Reserve. Of this, interest on transactions deposits, savings deposits (including MMDAs), and time deposits (including large CDs) required 32% of revenue. This understates the costs of attracting and maintaining deposits since demand deposits are subject to a zero rate ceiling; however, an important part of noninterest expense is required to administration demand deposit accounts.

Use of Funds

Banks are diversified in their uses of funds. The uses of funds can be grouped in the following categories: (1) cash assets, (2) loans, (3) financial investments or securities, and (4) other assets.

Loans and investments provide the primary source of revenue to the bank. In 1988, interest income represented almost 86% of total operating income. Cash assets do not earn interest income for the bank but provide bank liquidity and satisfy legal reserve requirements.

Cash Assets   Banks operate with very-short-term liabilities as sources of funds. Transactions deposits can be withdrawn immediately in the case of demand deposits and, for all practical purposes, immediately in the case of other checkable deposits. Nontransactions deposits are also very short term as are most nondeposit sources of funds. Cash assets provide the liquidity that short-term liabilities require.

Cash assets consist of (1) deposits held at the Federal Reserve to satisfy the legal reserve requirement and to facilitate the check-clearing process; (2) vault cash (currency and coin) held on the premises of the bank to satisfy part of the legal reserve requirement and to meet the currency requirements of the banks' customers; (3) correspondent balances with other banks, that is, checking accounts at other banks maintained for check clearing and to "compensate" correspondent banks for services provided; and (4) cash items in process of collection, checks deposited at the bank but not yet collected on from the drawn bank.

Legal reserve requirements prior to 1980 differed significantly from the current reserve requirement system established by the 1980 Deregulation and Monetary Control Act. The current system illustrated in Table 7-4 applies to all depository institutions. Prior to 1980, reserve requirements applied only to banks and were

TABLE 7-3 Basic income statement for all insured commercial banks, 1988

Interest Income	
Interest and fees on Loans	$ 62.37
Interest on balances due from depository institutions	4.31
Interest of municipal securities	2.62
All other securities	10.63
Interest on Federal funds sold and security purchases	3.24
Other	2.64
Noninterest income	
Service charges on deposit accounts	2.97
Other	11.12
Gains on securities not held in trading account	0.09
Total Additions to Revenue	100.00
Interest Expenses	
Interest on transaction accounts	2.86
Interest on MMDAs	6.29
Interest on other savings accounts	3.08
Interest on CDs $100,000 or more	7.44
Interest on regular time deposits	12.19
Federal funds purchased and securities sold	5.88
Other	14.28
Noninterest expense	
Salaries & employee benefits	14.67
Premises and fixed assets	4.97
Other	12.26
Provision for loan & lease losses and other adjustments	5.32
Total Subtractions from Revenue	89.24
Net Income before taxes and other adjustments	10.76

Note 1: Each item expressed in amounts per $100 of total additions to revenue
Source: Federal Deposit Insurance Corporation

considerably more complex than those illustrated in Table 7-4. The 1980 act simplified reserve requirements and extended them to all federally insured depository institutions. The Garn-St Germain Act of 1982 further modified the new reserve requirement system to ease the burden of meeting reserve requirements for small depository institutions.

Reserve requirements are imposed on two categories of accounts: transaction and certain nontransaction deposits. All other deposits such as regular time deposits and nonbusiness savings deposits are not subject to a legal reserve requirement.

TABLE 7-4   **Reserve requirements of depository institutions (percent of deposits)**[1]

Type of deposit, and deposit interval[2]	Depository institution requirements after implementation of the Monetary Control Act	
	Percent of deposits	Effective date
Transaction Deposits		
Net transaction accounts[3,4]		
$0 million–$40.5 million	3	12/15/87
More than $40.5 million	12	12/15/87
Nontransaction Deposits		
Nonpersonal time deposits[5]		
By original maturity		
Less than 1½ years	3	10/6/86
1½ years or more	0	10/6/83
Eurocurrency liabilities		
All types	3	11/13/80

[1] Reserve requirements in effect on December 31, 1987. Required reserves must be held in the form of deposits with Federal Reserve banks or vault cash. Nonmembers may maintain reserve balances with a Federal Reserve bank indirectly on a pass-through basis with certain approved institutions. For previous reserve requirements, see earlier editions of the *Annual Report* and of the *Federal Reserve Bulletin*. Under provisions of the Monetary Control Act, depository institutions include commercial banks, mutual savings banks, savings and loan associations, credit unions, agencies and branches of foreign banks, and Edge corporation.

[2] The Garn–St Germain Depository Institutions Act of 1982 (Public Law 97–320) requires that $2 million of reservable liabilities (transaction accounts, nonpersonal time deposits, and Eurocurrency liabilities) of each depository institution be subject to a zero percent reserve requirement. The Board is to adjust the amount of reservable liabilities subject to this 0% reserve requirement each year for the succeeding calendar year by 80% of the percentage increase in the total reservable liabilities of all depository institutions, measured on an annual basis as of June 30. No corresponding adjustment is to be made in the event of a decrease. On December 15, 1987, the exemption was raised from $2.9 million to $3.2 million. In determining the reserve requirements of depository institutions, the exemption shall apply in the following order: (1) net NOW accounts (NOW accounts less allowable deductions), (2) net other transaction accounts, and (3) nonpersonal time deposits or Eurocurrency liabilities starting with those with the highest reserve ratio. With respect to NOW accounts and other transaction accounts, the exemption applies only to such accounts that would be subject to a 3% reserve requirement.

[3] Transaction accounts include all deposits on which the account holder is permitted to make withdrawals by negotiable or transferable instruments, payment orders of withdrawal, and telephone and preauthorized transfers in excess of three per month for the purpose of making payments to third persons or others. However, MMDAs and similar accounts subject to the rules that permit no more than three can be checks, are not transaction accounts (such accounts are savings deposits subject to time deposit reserve requirements).

[4] The Monetary Control Act of 1980 requires that the amount of transaction accounts against which the 3% reserve requirement applies be modified annually by 80% of the percentage increase in transaction accounts held by all depository institutions, determined as of June 30 each year. Effective December 15, 1987 for institutions reporting quarterly and December 29, 1987 for institutions reporting weekly, the amount was increased from $36.7 million to $40.5 million.

[5] In general, nonpersonal time deposits are time deposits, including savings deposits, that are not transaction accounts and in which a beneficial interest is held by a depositor that is not a natural person. Also included are certain transferable time deposits held by natural persons and certain obligations issued to depository institution offices located outside the United States. For details, see section 204.2 of Regulation D.

Source: Board of Governors of the Federal Reserve System, *Federal Reserve Bulletin* (April 1988), p. A8.

Transaction deposits are any type of account subject to transfer either by written or other means. At present, these consist of demand deposits, NOW accounts, ATS accounts, and in the case of credit unions, credit union share draft accounts. Transaction deposits are subject to a two-tiered reserve requirement. First, transaction deposits up to $40.5 million (as of 1988) are subject to a 3% reserve requirement while deposits above $40.5 million are subject to a 12% requirement. The reserve requirement for the second tier can be adjusted by the Board of Governors of the Federal Reserve System within the range of 8 to 14%. The break point of $40.5 million is adjusted yearly to reflect deposit growth.

Nontransaction deposits subject to reserve requirements at present consists of two items: nonpersonal time deposits that consist mainly of large CDs and Eurodollar deposits. These deposits are subject to a 3% reserve requirement that can be varied by the Board of Governors from 0 to 9%.

To reduce the burden of reserve requirements on small depository institutions, the first $3.2 million (in 1988 and adjusted yearly) of total reservable deposits is subject to a zero reserve requirement.

There are only two acceptable ways in which a bank or nonbank depository institution can satisfy the legal reserve requirement: (1) reserve balances at the Federal Reserve and/or (2) vault cash. Banks typically meet most of their reserve requirement with reserve balances at the Federal Reserve. Vault cash or reserves balances, however, earn no interest income.

The existence of legal reserve requirements has often been interpreted to mean that banks are forced to hold reserves. Without legal reserve requirements banks would operate with little or no liquidity. This is not accurate and represents a misconception of the bank as a business.

Banks deal in very-short-term liabilities as sources of funds and will always experience the loss of some of these funds as bank customers make withdrawals, write checks deposited in other banks, and so on. Thus, a bank that operates without cash reserves of some type to meet these everyday withdrawals is a bank that will not be in business for long. Even without legal reserve requirements, banks would hold reserves to meet everyday turnover of their deposits. Not to hold some reserves would be economic suicide, although banks would probably not hold as large a reserve as is presently imposed by law and they would likely hold more reserves in short-term securities (referred to as "secondary reserves" as opposed to cash assets or "primary reserves").

Loans Commercial banks allocate the largest percentage of their funds to *business loans*. In fact, the term "commercial bank" reflects a time when banks only made loans to commercial establishments. Business loans are generally short term, with maturities of less than one year, although banks have been increasing the number of term loans that carry maturities of up to ten years. The most attractive business loan from the bank's point of view is the self-liquidating short-term loan. The maturity of the loan is short, usually only a few months, the purpose of the loan being to generate revenues to repay the principal and interest. A loan to finance additional inventory during the Christmas season would be in this category. The interest charged the largest and most creditworthy borrowers is called the *prime rate*. The prime rate of interest is not a free market rate; rather, it is established by one or more well-known banks in a region, with the remainder of the banks following the administered prime rate. There is usually a New York prime, a Chicago prime, and a San Francisco prime.

Real estate loans are long-term loans (10–30 years) to individuals for the purchase of residential structures as well as commercial structures. Banks have become important competitors in this type of lending activity and are the second most important supplier of real estate loans. Savings and loan associations and savings banks together are the largest suppliers of real estate credit.

Loans to individuals are consumer loans that can be either installment or single-payment loans. Installment loans are amortized and repaid in a number of installments; single-payment loans are repaid in one payment. Installment loans are the most common type of consumer credit. Banks are the largest supplier of installment credit, with finance companies and credit unions the second and third largest, respectively. Consumer credit also includes credit generated by the use of credit cards.

Financial institution loans consist primarily of loans to finance companies. Finance companies differ from other financial institutions in that they do not deal directly with the SU but obtain their funds by selling finance paper to individuals, banks, and other financial institutions.

Security loans are made to individuals, brokers, or agents to purchase various types of I.O.U.s in the financial market, usually equities and bonds. Banks cannot purchase equities for their own portfolios, although they are allowed to make loans to others to make such purchases. The securities purchased by the proceeds of a security loan are used as collateral. Security loans for equities or for bonds that are convertible into equities are subject to margin requirements established by the Federal Reserve. The margin requirement prescribes the maximum loan value, which is a specified percentage of the market value of the collateral. Margin requirements are the difference between the market value (100%) and the maximum loan value. Thus a margin requirement of 60% means that only $40,000 could be borrowed to purchase stock with a market value of $100,000. Margin requirements, which had been unchanged since 1974, have been set at 50%.

Federal funds sold represent reserve balances sold to other depository institutions on a short-term basis. Federal funds have come to play an important role in bank operations, especially for large banks. The difference between Federal funds sold (asset item) and Federal funds purchased (liability item) represents the net funds position of the bank and indicates whether the bank is a net supplier or demander of Federal funds in the money market.

Securities   By law, banks cannot hold equities for their own account and are strictly limited in the types and amounts of corporate debt that they can hold. The two major types of financial investments made by banks are *government securities* and *municipals*.

Government securities consist of Treasury bills (maturities of one year or less, sold on a discount basis), Treasury notes (maturities of one to ten years, with coupon payments), and Treasury bonds (maturities of longer than ten years, with coupon payments). Government securities are desirable investments for banks because they have no default risk and have an active secondary market. The absence of default risk does not mean that government securities have no risk. There is still the chance that the holder may experience a capital loss if the security is sold before it matures.

Municipals are debt obligations of local and state governmental units. Banks hold significant amounts of their funds in these securities, in part, because of the growth in local and state expenditures but, more important, because the interest income from municipals is not subject to federal taxation. At a marginal tax rate of 30%, for example, the after-tax yield of a 7.00% municipal is 7.00%, whereas the after-tax yield on a 7.00% Treasury bond is 4.90%.

To Be or Not To Be Liquid

Running a bank is to be constantly on the "horns of a dilemma." The short-term nature of the bank's sources of funds requires the bank to be liquid. The bank must maintain adequate liquidity to meet deposit withdrawals when considering the various uses of funds. However, the more liquid the financial assets, the less interest income generated. Remember the spectrum of liquidity concept: the closer one moves to the highest degree of liquidity on the asset scale, the more the interest return declines.

Vault cash, reserve deposits at the Federal Reserve, and other cash assets are the most liquid, but they earn no interest. Interest income is the source of revenue in the profit function for a bank. Thus the bank is presented with a difficult problem: it must maintain a certain amount of liquidity to meet deposit withdrawals, but, at the same time, if it maintains too much liquidity, it loses interest income.

Three general approaches have emerged to deal with the liquidity problem of a bank. They differ as to how the sources side of the flow of funds is viewed.

Asset Management

Asset management, the traditional and oldest approach, makes certain assumptions about the flow of funds through a bank. It regards the sources side of the flow of funds to be determined outside the bank's control and, as such, must be taken as given. Specifically, the bank regards the composition of its deposit liabilities and their rate of turnover as fixed. The objective of asset management is to maintain a level of liquidity consistent with the nature of the deposits. For example, a bank in a large metropolitan area with a large percentage of deposits subject to rapid turnover has a higher liquidity requirement than does a bank in a rural community with a large percentage of time and savings deposits.

The problem, then, is to establish a level and degree of liquidity consistent with the nature of the sources of funds. Liquidity depends on the amount of funds devoted to primary and secondary reserves. The higher the ratio of primary and secondary reserves to total assets, the greater the liquidity of the bank.

Primary reserves—the bank's most liquid financial asset—consist of (1) vault cash, (2) reserves held as a deposit at the Federal Reserve, (3) correspondent demand deposits in other banks, and (4) cash items in process of collection. The first three items are available immediately to meet deposit withdrawals. Cash items in process of collection represent checks drawn on another bank that have not cleared through the check-clearing process, but, because checks clear almost always within a few days, cash items are regarded as part of primary reserves. Primary reserves represent immediate liquidity that yields no interest income.

Secondary reserves consist of financial assets that possess a high degree of liquidity either because they have active secondary markets or very short-term maturities while, at the same time, provide interest income. Assets that meet the standards of secondary reserves include Federal funds sold to other banks, Treasury securities with maturities of one year or less, prime bankers' acceptances, and other assets with an active secondary market.

According to the asset management approach, the amount and composition of the sources side of the flow of funds then determines the allocation of the uses side to primary and secondary reserves. The higher the proportion of primary and secondary reserves in the total uses of funds, the greater the liquidity of the bank. Asset management is a fairly passive approach to running the bank, whereby the bank adapts to the particular amount and composition of its sources of funds.

Liability Management

Liability management emerged in the 1960s as a then new and aggressive approach to running a bank. Unlike asset management, liability management explicitly recognized that the bank can influence the source of funds by competing aggressively for demand deposits, time and savings deposits, and borrowings in the Federal funds and Eurodollar markets. Even borrowing from the Federal Reserve can be considered a source of funds. Banks aggressively sought funds by issuing time certificates with higher interest rates than savings accounts, as time deposits had higher Regulation Q ceilings. Banks were given greater freedom in issuing large CDs in 1970, when interest rate ceilings were eliminated for short maturities, and in 1973, when interest rate ceilings were eliminated for all large-denomination certificates. Banks also made expanded use of the Federal funds market, RPs, and Euordollars as sources of funds. The expansion of one-bank holding companies provided another source of funds. The holding company could issue commercial paper in the open market with no interest rate restrictions and then deposit the funds in the bank subsidiary.

Liability management views the sources of funds as subject to bank manipulation. By increasing the source of funds through aggressive advertising, interest rate competition, "free dishes," and so forth, banks can then expand the uses side and overall size and profitability of the bank.

What about liquidity? Liability management still viewed primary and secondary reserves to be an important part of the bank's liquidity but also viewed the sources of funds as a source of liquidity. If a bank experienced deposit withdrawals, it could borrow funds from the Eurodollar or Federal funds market as well as use its primary and secondary reserves. In a sense, liability management says that, if a bank needs liquidity, it can purchase liquidity somewhere in the financial system.

Asset/Liability Management: Bank Management in the 1990s

The banking environment has changed drastically during the past decade. Running a bank, maintaining an adequate level of liquidity, and earning a profit have become more difficult than ever. As a result of deregulation, new financial services made possible by computer technology, and new forms of competition, all depository institutions have found it more difficult to operate at a profitable level.

Asset or liability management by themselves are no longer adequate for running a bank in the competitive and deregulated environment. New approaches have emerged that combine both sides of the balance sheet and incorporate elements of each approach as well as incorporate new elements. To illustrate, banks now face greater risks when the maturity of their assets is not matched with the maturity of their liabilities. In the past, when interest rates were relatively stable and bank deposits were subject to interest rate ceilings, uneven maturity of the uses and sources of funds was not a major problem. Interest rates have been more volatile, and banks have had to pay market interest rates to keep and maintain deposits. Even demand deposits effectively earn interest income despite the zero ceiling because of the widespread use of RPs for large commercial accounts.

Since banks make a large number of loans at fixed rates, volatile interest rates increase the risk that the bank will be forced to pay higher rates to maintain deposits than they earn on their assets if the maturity of liabilities is shorter than the maturity of assets. The greater the imbalance between maturity of the uses and sources of funds, the greater the risk.

The End of 3-6-3 Banking

The new approaches to running a bank and the new competitive environment have together changed the nature of banking, once referred to as "3-6-3" banking. Its origin is unclear, but the 3-6-3 view has been repeated in many places. In the days before deregulation and financial innovation, as the saying goes, bankers paid 3% on deposits, loaned funds at 6%, and headed for the golf course by 3 P.M.! While this overstates the actual competitive environment of banking even before deregulation and innovation become important characteristics of the financial system, it does offer some insight into the differences between the old way of running a bank and the new breed of bankers in the 1990s.

Banks have lost competitive advantages once held from two sources: regulatory reforms such as the Deregulation and Monetary Control Act of 1980 and the Garn-St Germain Depository Institutions Act of 1982 and financial innovations of a wide variety have provided substitutes for services previously supplied by banks. Regulatory reforms and financial innovation have continually blurred the distinction between banks and nonbank financial institutions and, as a result, have increased the competitive environment of the typical bank.

Regulatory changes have permitted nonbank depository institutions to offer transaction deposits and even limited authority to offer demand deposit accounts. Prior to 1980, banks were the main suppliers of checking account services. Regulatory changes have permitted other institutions to compete with banks more aggressively for consumer and business loans, credit card services, and fiduciary services. In the past, banks dominated these markets.

Banks have responded in a variety of ways to the new competitive environment, and while securites companies, thrifts, insurance companies, and nonfinancial businesses such American Express are now offering banking services, banks have responded by redesigning their traditional opertions and pursuing new markets. This is most evident in the dramatic growth of *off–balance sheet* banking.

Off—Balance Sheet Banking

Traditionally, whenever the bank intermediated between the lender and the borrower, the balance sheet reflected the entire transaction. When the funds were obtained, bank liabilities increased, and when the loan was funded, bank assets increased and the new asset generally remained with the bank. Off–balance sheet operations depend on the ability of the bank to unbundle the various parts of the loan transaction and while retaining some parts, transferring the other parts to others in such a manner that they are not reflected on the balance sheet. Unbundling of the traditional loan transaction is not unique to banks, but banks have aggressively pursued these activities as a competitive response to regulatory changes and financial innovations.

There are three important examples of off–balance sheet banking: securitized loans, commercial loan sales, and stand by letters of credit or SRCs.

Securitized Loans

Chapter 6 introduced the concept of *securitization*—the process of pooling loans and then using them as collateral for debt instruments placed in the direct financial markets. Securitization is one of the most significant innovations of the 1980s, and almost all financial institutions have been involved in the process. While banks probably have a comparative advantage in the process, almost any type of loan made by any type of financial intermediary can be securitized. While securitization has exposed banks to new competitive pressures, banks themselves have aggressively been securitizing mortgage loans as well as automobile and credit card loans.

Commercial Loan Sales

Commercial loan sales are usually without recourse (the bank does not guarantee payment) because then the proceeds of the sold loan are not subject to a reserve requirement. Loans sold to others with recourse (bank guarantee's payment) are subject to a reserve requirement. The 1980s witnessed a major increase in loan sales as a percentage of total commercial and industrial loans made by banks (Figure 7-1). By 1986, commercial loan sales represented almost 25% of total commercial and inductrial loans and have grown faster than commercial and industrial loans. Commercial loan sales can also be a form of securitization if pools of loan are sold.

In a commercial loan sale the bank unbundles the loan by retaining some aspects of the loan and selling other aspects to one or more parties. The bank keeps the servicing component and other related aspects of the loan and retains some of the credit risk because commercial loan sales often involve less than the entire loan. This is because the loan is sold without recourse, and the bank is usually required to assume some of the credit risk in order to make the loan marketable. At the same time, the bank transfers part of the funding component to another party.

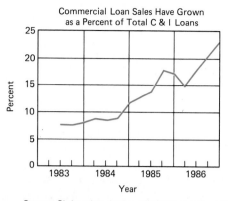

Commercial Loan Sales Have Grown
as a Percent of Total C & I Loans

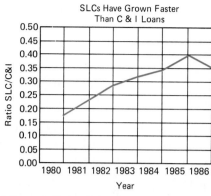

SLCs Have Grown Faster
Than C & I Loans

Source: Christopher James, "Off–Balance Sheet Banking." *Economic Review,* Federal Reserve Bank of San Francisco (Fall 1987), p. 23.

FIGURE 7-1 Growth of selected types of off–balance sheet banking in the 1980s

Standby Letters of Credit or SLCs

An SLC is a guarantee by the issuing bank to cover the obligations of the bank's customer if the customer fails to perform the obligation in question such as repaying a loan. The bank evaluates the credit risk of the holder of the SLC and assumes the credit risk, but transfers the funding obligation to another party. Again, the bank has unbundled the traditional loan arrangement. Figure 7-1 illustrates the growth of SLCs in the 1980s relative to commercial and industrial loans, and like commercial loan sales, SLCs have become a major banking activity.

BOX 2 **Does government regulation drive bank innovation and does innovation increase bank risk? Off–balance sheet banking**

The dramatic increase in off–balance sheet banking operations has raised two questions: What accounts for their growth? and Do they increase bank risk? Both questions have to do with the role of bank regulation in the financial system.

With regard to the first question, economists have argued that financial innovation in general is a market response to government regulation that limits profit making. Government regulation is essentially a "regulatory tax" that induces financial institutions to shift from regulated to less or unregulated activities. These regulatory taxes are imposed by reserve requirements, capital-asset requirements, deposit insurance premiums, interest rate ceilings on demand deposits, and prior to 1986, interest rate ceilings on time and savings deposits. Thus, the most important innovations of the past decades—RPs, CDs, Eurodollars, and most recent, off–balance sheet operations—reflect the bank's

desire to shift to activities less subject to the regulatory tax. The rapid advance of computer technology and the increasing ease with which finanical transactions can be handled via computers significantly increases the ability of the market to innovate around regulations. Other explanations suggest that these innovations would have occurred in some form or other even in a deregulated environment. There are economic and technological forces at work independent of government regulation that induce banks to innovate.

Christopher James of the University of Florida,[1] for example, has argued that SLCs and commercial loan sales are as much a response to economic forces as they are to government regulation and regulatory taxes. The important economic or nonregulatory motives include: increased ability to manage interest rate risk, increased diversification, lower cost of funds, and ability to make a wider range of loans in terms of risk. These motives are largely independent of the taxes imposed by government regulation. While one would have difficulty rejecting the argument that nonregulatory factors have played a role, most observers regard the major innovations since the 1970s as a response to regulations that limited profit making. We will return to this issue in Chapters 11 and 12 when we discuss the financial reform process.

The relationship between these innovations and government regulation and the fact that they are not just a response to government regulation, suggests the second question. Do these innovations increase bank risk and thus ultimately weaken the financial system? This is a difficult question to answer, either from a theoretical or an empirical point of view.

Two recent studies, for example, suggest that com-

mercial loan sales have no measurable impact on bank risk. Christopher James mentioned above and Christine A. Pavel of the Federal Reserve Bank of Chicago[2] found that two different measures of bank risk were not sensitive to loan sales. In addition, James included the influence of SLCs in his analysis and also found that these had no meaningful impact on bank risk.

These and similar studies are certainly not definitive; however, they suggest that bank innovations have not increased bank risk.

[1] "Off-Balance Sheet Banking," *Economic Review*, Federal Reserve Bank of San Francisco (Fall 1987), 21–36.
[2] "Loan Sales Have Little Effect on Bank Risk," *Economic Perspectives*, Federal Reserve Bank of Chicago (March–April 1988), 23–37.

Key Points

1. Banks are similar to other financial intermediaries in the sense that they facilitate the flow of funds from SUs to DUs; however, banks play a special role in the financial system.

2. Regulatory reforms and financial innovation have blurred the distinction between banks and other financial institutions and thus reduced the role of banks in the financial system. Other forces such as increased internationalization of finance, new powers granted to banks, and new bank innovations suggest that banks will remain and perhaps increase their role in the 1990s.

3. The bank has a profit function and manages the sources and uses of funds to generate a positive profit. In this regard, bank sources of funds are very short term, and the bank must manage its liquidity. Too much liquidity and the bank

loses money—too little liquidity and the bank fails.

4. Banks are subject to legal reserve requirements; however, banks would still find it necessary to hold a reserve balance even in the absence of legal reserve requirements.

5. Banks have always been innovators—RPs, CDs, and Eurodollar deposits—and banks have continued to innovate to maintain their role in the financial system: securitized loans, commercial loan sales, and SLCs. This chapter has focused on the traditional role of a bank in terms of balance sheet measures, and while still accurate for the typical bank, banks are moving into new areas that depart from their traditional role and change the way in which a bank operates.

Key Terms

Asset management
Asset/liability management
Borrowing from the Federal Reserve
Cash assets

Large CDs
Commercial loan sales
Eurodollars
Federal funds purchased or sold

Liability management

Managed liabilities

Margin requirements

Off–balance sheet banking

Repurchase agreements (RPs or repos)

Reserve requirements

Standby letters of credit or SLCs

Securitization

3-6-3 banking

Vault cash

Questions

1. List the forces that have increased and those that have decreased the role of banks in the financial system.

2. Do you think banks will be able to retain their dominant position in the issuance of demand deposit accounts during the next decade?

3. Banks frequently borrow funds in the Federal funds market at rates above the Federal Reserve discount rate. Does this make any sense? If you were a bank, why would you be willing to pay more for funds than they might be available at the Federal Reserve?

4. Banks hold small levels of reserves above the legal reserve requirement even though reserves earn zero interest. How would each of the following influence a bank's willingness to hold excess reserves: (a) ratio of checkable to total deposits, (b) ratio of large CDs to total deposits, and (c) ratio of demand deposits to checkable deposits.

5. How would anticipated interest rates influence the bank's decision to hold reserves above the legal minimum?

6. How would lower tax rates influence the bank's decision to hold municipals? Are there noneconomic reasons why a bank might hold municipal securities, especially those issued by the governmental entity in the region the bank operates?

7. How does the existence of a secondary market influence the liquidity of secondary reserves?

8. Liability management argues that a bank can always purchase liquidity in the money market. What happens if all banks desire liquidity at the same time? Who would then provide the liquidity?

Suggested Readings

1. Federal Reserve Bank of Chicago. Each year the Federal Reserve Bank of Chicago holds a conference on banking and the papers are published in a volume entitled *Structure and Competition Conference.* Each annual volume contains the views and research results of leading experts on banking drawn from the financial services industry, government, and academics. An excellent source of information of recent changes in the banking industry.

2. R. Alton Gilbert, "A Comparison of Proposals to Restructure the U.S. Financial System," *Review,* Federal Reserve Bank of St. Louis (July–August 1988), 58–73. Surveys recent proposals to restructure the banking industry.

3. Beverly Hirtle, "The Growth of the Financial Guarantee Market," *Quarterly Review,* Federal Reserve Bank of New York, (1987), 12. Off–balance sheet banking is discussed.

4. Christopher James, "Off–Balance Sheet Banking," *Economic Review,* Federal Reserve Bank of San

Francisco (Fall 1987), 21–36. Analyzes the effect of two types of off–balance sheet banking on overall bank risk.

5. Jean M. Lovati, "The Changing Competition Between Commercial Banks and Thrift Institutions for Deposits," *Review*, Federal Reserve Bank of St. Louis (July 1975), 2–8. Even before the start of deregulation, banks were under increasing competitive pressure.

6. Christine Pavel and David Phillis, "Why Commercial Banks Sell Loans: An Empirical Analysis," *Economic Perspectives*, Federal Reserve Bank of Chicago (May–June 1987), 3–14. More on off–balance sheet banking.

7. Christine A. Pavel, "Financial Services in the Year 2000," *Economic Perspectives*, Federal Reserve

Bank of Chicago (September–October 1988), 13–16. A view of what banks will be like in the future.

8. Havey Rosenblum, John Di Clemente, and Kit O'Brien, "The Product Market in Commercial Banking: Cluster's Last Stand?" *Economic Perspectives*, Federal Reserve Bank of Chicago (January–February 1985), 21–34. Banks under siege.

9. George Salem, "Selling Commercial Loans: A Significant New Activity for Money Center Banks," *Journal of Commercial Bank Lending* (1986). Off–balance sheet banking is discussed.

10. Gordon H. Sellon, Jr., "Restructuring the Financial System: Summary of the Bank's 1987 Symposium," *Economic Review*, Federal Reserve Bank of San Francisco (January 1988), 17–28. Summary of a conference on the financial system and banks sponsored by the Federal Reserve Bank of San Francisco.

CHAPTER 8

The Banking Industry

Chapter Overview

The previous chapter focused on banking from the perspective of the individual bank. This chapter considers banking from the perspective of the industry. Specifically, this chapter presents information on the number of banks, size distribution of banks, institutional features of the U.S. banking industry, and the relationship between banks and regulatory agencies. The U.S. banking system is unique among banking systems in the world because of the large number of banks (over 13,000) and the *dualistic* system of supervision and regulation.

After reviewing the major institutional features of the U.S. banking industry, the chapter ends with a general discussion of whether banking has become less or more competitive over the years.

How Many Banks?

There were 13,139 individual banks in operation as of December 31, 1988, ranging from very small to virtual giants in terms of asset or deposit size. Table 8-1 indicates the size distribution of banks according to their assets as of year-end 1988.

Two important implications can be drawn from the distribution of banks in Table 8-1. First, a large number of small banks hold a small portion of the total assets. At the end of 1988, 78.5% of the banks had assets of less than $100 million and, in the aggregate, held 12.1% of the total assets. Second, at the other end of the spectrum are 364 banks, each with more than $1 billion in assets. This small number of very large banks held 69.0% of the total bank assets. In terms of deposits, the five largest banks in the United States as of December 31, 1988, were Citibank, Bank of America, Chase Manhattan, Morgan Guaranty Trust Co., and Manufacturers Hanover Trust Co. Of these, Citibank held deposits of $105 billion, while Manufacturers Hanover Trust Co. held deposits of $43 billion.

The number of banks has been relatively constant since the 1930s. Prior to the

TABLE 8-1 Distribution of banks in the United States based on asset size December 31, 1988

	Banks			Assets		
Asset Size	Number	% of Total[1]	Cumu-lative	Amount (millions)	% of Total[1]	Cumu-lative
$ 0–24.9 million	4,141	31.5%	31.5%	$62,487	2.0%	2.0%
$ 25.0–49.9 million	3,384	25.8	57.3	122,186	3.9	5.9
$ 50.0–99.9 million	2,783	21.2	78.5	194,037	6.2	12.1
$100.0–249.9 million	1,746	13.3	91.7	264,699	8.5	20.6
$250.0–499.9 million	503	3.8	95.6	175,547	5.6	26.2
$500.0–1 billion	218	1.7	97.2	151,680	4.8	31.0
$ 1.0 billion or more	364	2.8	100.0	2,160,153	69.0	100.0
Total	13,139	100.0%		$3,130,789	100.0%	

[1] Totals may not add due to rounding.
Source: Federal Deposit Insurance Corporation.

Great Depression, there were almost 30,000 banks; however, during the period from 1929 through 1933, many banks failed. Since the 1930s, government regulation has limited the expansion of individual banks by imposing a variety of entry restrictions. Despite the relatively constant number of individual banks, bank offices or branches have increased significantly. Figure 8-1 illustrates the number of banks and bank branches since 1915.

State and National Banks: Concept of Dual Banking

Banks operate under either a state or a federal charter. Banks were first chartered by states; national banks chartered by the federal government came into existence with the National Bank Act of 1864. The presence of both state and national banks reflects the federal structure of our political system and is referred to as the *dual* banking system. A bank that operates under a national charter has the word "national" contained somewhere in the official title of the bank.

   The National Bank Act of 1864 is responsible for the dual banking system in the United States, though a dual banking system was not the intent of the 1864 act. Prior to the 1864 act, banks operated under various types of charters granted by state governments. There was considerable variety in the standards used to grant these charters as well as considerable abuse of banking powers. The decades prior to the National Bank Act were characterized by confusion and disarray in the banking industry, and, as a result, the act sought to bring order to the banking system by creating a new type of bank charter and establishing the Comptroller of the Currency as part of the U.S. Treasury to administer all national banks. To convert all banks to

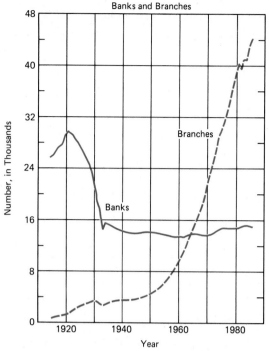

FIGURE 8-1 Banks and branches, 1915–1987

national banks, legislation was passed to drive state-chartered banks out of existence by imposing a 10% tax on state bank–issued bank notes. Bank notes circulated in the economy as part of the money supply and were the major source of funds for banks as deposit accounts had not yet been introduced on a large-scale basis. A bank note represented a bank I.O.U. that circulated like currency, whereas a checking deposit represents an I.O.U. on which the depositor can write checks to transfer funds to a third party. The effort to eliminate state-chartered banks was unsuccessful since they shifted to deposits as a source of funds. Another example of financial innovation. Demand deposits were accepted as a superior substitute for bank notes and quickly replaced bank notes as part of the money supply.

Thus the National Bank Act sought to achieve a unified banking system, with each bank operating under a national charter; however, the end result was a dual banking system. The dual concept has also been extended to other depository institutions. Savings and loan associations, savings banks, and credit unions operate under either a national (usually called federal) charter or state charter. It should be obvious that the dual approach to the chartering of depository institutions reflects the philosophy of separate state-federal government activity that permeates our political system.

Table 8-2 presents the distribution of federally insured banks and deposits according to charter and membership in the Federal Reserve System. All national banks must be members of the Federal Reserve System; state banks can apply and

TABLE 8-2 Classification of insured banks and deposits according to type of charter and membership in the Federal Reserve System, June 30, 1988

All Commercial Banks: Distribution of Total Numbers and Deposits by	*Banks*		*Deposits*	
	Number	*% of Total*	*Amount (billions)*	*% of Total*
	13,274	100%	$1,987	100%
Charter				
National Banks	4,459	34	1,159	58
State banks	8,815	66	828	42
	13,274	100%	$1,987	100%
Membership in Federal Reserve System				
National Banks	4,459	34	1,159	58
State banks	1,071	8	284	14
	5,530	42%	$1,443	72%

Source: Board of Governors of the Federal Reserve System, *Annual Report*, 1988.

receive membership status if they meet Federal Reserve requirements on capital adequacy, lending restrictions, and so on. Members of the Federal Reserve must belong to the Federal Deposit Insurance Corporation (FDIC), while nonmember banks may apply for FDIC membership. Virtually all banks in the United States operate under FDIC insurance. There are a very small number of banks, about 250, that operate without federal insurance; however, they hold an insignificant amount of bank assets.

What determines whether a bank operates under a state or national charter? The answer to this question has been influenced significantly by the Deregulation and Monetary Control Act of 1980. Prior to the act, there were two considerations that determined a bank's choice of charter. First, historical factors generally accounted for a bank's choice of a state charter over a national charter in states where the federal and state banking regulations were similar, especially with respect to reserve requirements. A state bank could perform all the functions and avail itself of all the opportunities available to national banks such as federal deposit insurance. A state bank could become a member of the Federal Reserve, and, even if it decided not to become a member, it could still obtain many of the same advantages by correspondent relationships with banks that were members.

Second, the differences between national and state banking regulations often varied considerably, and, in those states in which there were major differences, banks preferred to operate under the less restrictive charter. The most significant element influencing the choice of charter type was the type of reserve requirement imposed on banks by state banking agencies and the Federal Reserve. In some states nonmember banks could hold part of their reserve requirement in the form of interest-earning assets or in other forms not permitted to member banks. In addition, the actual reserve ratio imposed by some states was lower than that imposed by the Federal Reserve. In those states in which the reserve requirement was less restric-

BOX 1   U.S. banks no longer world's largest

During the first few decades after the end of World War II, U.S. banks dominated international finance. They were among the largest in the world and reflected the fact that the U.S. economy was truly the only economic superpower.

The past decade has witnessed major changes in the world economy and the role that U.S. banks occupy in international finance. The dominant position the United States once held in international trade and finance has been gradually eroded over the years as other industrial economies (Japan and Germany, for example) and even developing economies (South Korea, for example) have experienced major increases in economic activity both domestically and internationally. Japan, in particular, has exhibited astonishing growth in the past few decades and has truly become the phoenix that has arisen from the ashes of war. As a reflection of the shift in relative roles between Japan and the United States, the United States in 1985 became the largest debtor nation in the world while Japan has become the major creditor nation and Tokyo has emerged as a major world financial center.

The relative decline of U.S. influence in the world economy has been reflected by a relative decline in the role of U.S. banks in world banking. The *American Banker* on July 24, 1989 published a survey of the largest banks in the world ranked by deposits with the somewhat astounding result that U.S. banks have become second to Japanese banks (Table 1B) and other foreign banks. U.S. banks were not even included in the top 25 banks and only 2 U.S. banks made the top 50 list. While part of this ranking was the result of the decline in the value of the U.S. dollar that started in 1985, there is little doubt that U.S. banks were no longer the largest and most influential banks in the world.

The largest bank in the world is Dai-Ichi Kangyo Bank. At the exchange rate in effect July 1989, Dai-Ichi Kangyo Bank held deposits of $312 billion! This is more than the combined deposits of the top five U.S. banks mentioned on page 169.

TABLE 1B   The dominance of Japanese banks in the world as of December 31, 1988

Rank	Japanese Banks	Percent
Top 10	10	100%
Top 25	17	68
Top 50	25	50
Top 100	33	33

Source: American Banker, July 24, 1989, p. 26.

tive, banks would often prefer to operate under a state charter and forego membership in the Federal Reserve.

These two considerations—historical factors and differences in reserve requirements—strongly influenced the choice of charter type; however, the second consideration is no longer relevant since the Deregulation and Monetary Control Act. Historical considerations will undoubtedly continue to play a role in the selection of charter type, but the act replaced the wide variety of state-imposed reserve requirements with a unified system administered by the Federal Reserve. All banks, despite location or charter type as well as other depository institutions, now operate under a uniform reserve requirement structure.

The current reserve requirement system introduced in 1980 was a radical change, and since it placed all depository institutions irrespective of charter type under Fed-imposed reserve requirements, it was contrary to the dual system. Why was the unified reserve requirement system established? This involves understanding the declining membership problem faced by the Federal Reserve in the 1970s.

TABLE 8-3   Percentage of all banks and bank deposits held by members of the Federal Reserve System, selected years 1941–1979

Year	Member Banks	Member Bank Deposits
1941	46.4%	86.6%
1947	48.8	85.0
1960	45.8	84.0
1970	42.1	80.0
1971	41.6	79.1
1972	41.0	78.3
1973	40.5	77.3
1974	40.0	77.0
1975	40.0	75.1
1976	39.2	73.6
1977	38.5	72.5
1978	37.7	71.2
1979	36.8	70.9

Source: Board of Governors of the Federal Reserve System, *Federal Reserve Bulletin* (June 1976), and Federal Deposit Insurance Corporation, *Annual Report*, 1979.

The Declining Membership Issue and the 1980 Act

Table 8-3 presents information on the percentage of banks belonging to the Federal Reserve and their deposits over the period from 1941 through 1979. Member banks did not represent a majority in terms of numbers, but they did account for the overwhelming majority of total deposits. However, the percentage of member banks and member bank deposits declined steadily over much of the period, especially in the 1970s. Many factors accounted for this trend, but high interest rates and different reserve requirement structures at the national and state level were the most significant. The Federal Reserve's requirements were frequently more restrictive than were those imposed on state nonmember banks. While membership conferred a number of benefits, the cost of membership exceeded the benefits for a large number of banks as interest rates rose in the 1970s.

The Federal Reserve continually proposed legislation to require membership of all banks or require all banks to meet uniform reserve requirements. Legislation of this type, however, found an unreceptive Congress and administration since there was considerable political support for the dual banking system.

Despite the political opposition, the situation became drastic by late 1979, and, as part of the Deregulation and Monetary Control Act, the entire reserve requirement structure was altered. The current reserve requirement system is characterized by the following: First, all insured banks are subject to the same reserve requirement despite charter type. Second, the same reserve requirement is imposed on insured nonbank depository institutions (savings and loan associations, savings banks, and credit unions). Third, the reserve requirement is imposed and enforced by the Federal Reserve. Fourth, banks and other depository institutions can satisfy the reserve requirement only in two ways: vault cash and/or reserve balances at the Federal Reserve. Fifth, reserve balances at the Federal Reserve earn no interest. Sixth, all insured banks and depository institutions have access to a variety of Federal Reserve services on a nondiscriminatory fee basis. These services include check clearing, currency shipments, wire transfers, and other services offered by the Federal Reserve.

Thus the reserve requirement feature of the 1980 act has, for all practical purposes, eliminated the membership problem. There is no longer an incentive to shift from national to state charter to operate under less restrictive reserve requirements. There is no longer a significant difference between being an official member of the Federal Reserve or not an official member. In terms of operating a bank, the Deregulation and Monetary Control Act has made all banks and nonbank depository institutions de facto members of the Federal Reserve. This was a considerable weakening of the dual character of U.S. banking.

Unit and Branch Banking

One of the more heated controversies in banking concerns the issue of unit versus branch banking. There are two aspects of the controversy. First, should banks be allowed to operate full-service branches within the state in which the head office is located? And, second, should banks be allowed to operate full-service branches outside the state? The first issue refers to *intrastate* branching and the second to *interstate* branching.

In regard to intrastate branching, the federal government leaves the decision to states to determine whether they will allow unlimited, limited, or no branching. If a national bank is located in a unit banking state, it is not allowed to establish branches.

Figure 8-2 provides a visual impression of the interstate banking restrictions for the United States. Two implications are clear. First, there has been a fairly stable regional distribution of the rules governing branching within a state. Western states generally allow statewide branching, the Midwestern states largely favor unit banking, and the Eastern and Southern states permit various degrees of branching. The concentration of unit banking in the Midwest reflects the resistance of farmers in the late nineteenth century to penetration by large Eastern banks. Second, branching laws have been relaxed to some extent over the past decades. Table 8-3 indicates that 15 states as of 1985 had relaxed their branching restrictions since 1960. This is also reflected by Figure 8-2.

In regard to interstate branching, the federal government has taken a more aggressive role compared with intrastate banking. Branching beyond state boundaries was effectively prohibited by the McFadden Act of 1927 and the Banking Act of 1933. This legislation established state boundaries as the ultimate limit for branching and gave states the right to determine their own regulations regarding branching.

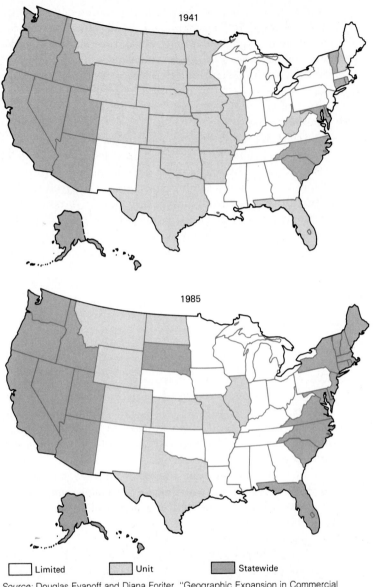

Limited ☐   Unit ☐   Statewide ■

Source: Douglas Evanoff and Diana Foriter, "Geographic Expansion in Commercial Banking: Inferences from Intrastate Activity," in Herbert Baer and Sue F. Gregorash (eds.), *Toward Nationwide Banking,* Federal Reserve Bank of Chicago (1986), p. 43

FIGURE 8-2   Regional distribution of branching regulations in the United States, 1941 and 1985

Until recent years, states have prohibited out-of-state banks from establishing full-service branches within the state.

Thus, there continues to exist restrictions against both intra- and interstate branching. This situation suggests two questions. First, what are the arguments for and against branching? And, second, given that innovation and regulatory reform have been a prominent feature of the U.S. financial system in the past decade, what have been the major developments in relaxing restrictions against branching?

TABLE 8-3 States changing branching regulations, 1960 to 1984[1]

State and status (1960)		Changes in status	Status (1984)	Number of years at status (1985)
Massachusetts	(L)	1984 (S)	(S)	1
New Hampshire	(L)	1980 (S)	(S)	2
New Jersey	(L)	1973 (S)	(S)	12
New York	(L)	1975 (S)	(S)	10
Arkansas	(U)	1976 (L)	(L)	9
Florida	(U)	1977 (L)	(S)	5
		1980 (S)		
Iowa	(U)	1976 (L)	(L)	9
Minnesota	(U)	1980 (L)	(L)	5
Nebraska	(U)	1984 (L)	(L)	1
Oklahoma	(U)	1984 (L)	(L)	1
West Virginia	(U)	1984 (L)	(L)	1
Wisconsin	(U)	1968 (L)	(L)	18
Maine	(L)	1968 (S)	(S)	18
South Dakota	(U)	1968 (S)	(S)	18
Virginia	(L)	1963 (S)	(S)	23

Note: L = limited branching, U = unit banking, and S = statewide branching.

[1] These states did not change branching status from 1941 to 1960. Thus, this list also refers to states changing branching status over the past 43 years (1941–1984).

Source: Douglas Evanoff and Diana Foriter, "Geographic Expansion in Commercial Banking: Inferences from Intrastate Activity," in Herbert Baer and Sue F. Gregorash (eds.), *Toward Nationwide Banking*, Federal Reserve Bank of Chicago (1986), p. 42.

Debate over Unit and Branch Banking

Large banks generally argue in favor of branching on the grounds that it offers important advantages to the general public. Banks with many branches can operate at a substantially lower unit cost of operation. The branch bank then can pass on increased operating efficiency in the form of higher interest payments on deposits and lower interest charges and more services to the borrower. Also, large banks with many branches can better mobilize the bank's financial resources to those geographic areas needing particular types of credit and services.

Small banks, which generally oppose branching, argue that branch banking leads to higher concentration ratios in banking and various types of monopoly pricing behavior as branch banks drive out small-unit banks. In addition, because the small-unit bank has a close association with the community it serves, it is thus better able to meet the needs of the community than the branch office of some large and distant bank.

There are many aspects to the debate. Although much of the debate is emotional, both sides recognize that an important consideration concerns the possible existence of *economies of scale* in banking, and how branching influences the ability of the bank to realize those economies.

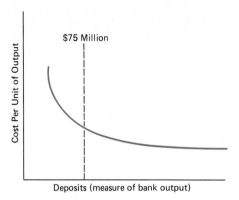

FIGURE 8-3 Cost per unit at
various levels of bank output for a unit bank

One would think that this question would have an easy empirical answer; however, the question of economies of scale in banking is complex for two reasons. First, to draw implications about the relationship between cost and output, we need to define bank output—not an easy task. Even abstracting from the transition of the financial system and the changing activities of banks such as off–balance sheet banking, any measure of bank output—loans, assets, deposits, and so on—is plagued with problems. Even in static terms, the bank is a multidimensional institution producing a complex set of services. Second, the financial system is in transition, and technology has made it increasingly easy to set up branches. For example, computer technology has allowed banks to establish ATMs (automatic teller machines) that free the bank from relying exclusively on a stand-alone "brick and mortar" office as a branching operation.

Despite these problems a number of investigators have attempted to determine whether branching contributes to lower operating costs. The studies suggest that a large-unit bank is more efficient than a small-unit bank such as that illustrated by Figure 8-3, which measures bank output in terms of deposits. There exist substantial economies up to, say, $75 million in deposits while the economies become much smaller after that amount. In fact, there is evidence that very large banks may encounter decreasing economies of scale in that the cost function begins to rise. The result that a large-unit bank is more efficient in terms of average cost than is a small-unit bank is important; however, it does not directly answer the question of whether branching is more efficient holding other factors constant.

The relevant question is whether a $100 million deposit bank with four branches is more efficient than four $25 million deposit unit banks. We already know that a $100 million deposit unit bank (or a $100 million deposit four-branch bank) is more efficient than is a $25 million deposit bank (or a $25 million four-branch bank). Studies have attempted to hold other factors constant and isolate the impact of branching on the cost function. The results are difficult to interpret; however, they fail to show that branching in and of itself generates major economies of scale.

This does not mean that it is a toss of the coin over whether the public would benefit from relaxed geographic constraints on bank operations. A number of advantages to branching have been documented. Branch banks tend to be large and thus able to realize economies of scale more easily than unit banks. Branch banks have greater diversification opportunities because their operations are spread over a wider geographic area and, hence, are better able to manage risk. Branch banking makes it easier to establish offices and compete with existing banks and thus increase the level of overall bank competition. Branch banking is more likely to provide banking services to small communities that could not support a unit bank. This is an important point because it offsets the criticism that branch banks are less likely to identify with the community.

Sometimes the critics of branch banking portray the debate in terms of small versus large banks and that branch banking is likely to drive small banks out of existence. However, the evidence for this claim is not easy to establish. In California, for example, where some of the country's larger banks operate with extensive branching networks, small banks continue to remain viable. In 1984, about 40% of the banks in California maintained only one office despite the existence of extensive branching networks of competing banks as well as very large banks.

The Federal Reserve Bank of Chicago in 1986 published an extensive study on the issue of branching.[1] The study provided a comprehensive look at many of the issues regarding intra- and interstate branching and concluded that

> The evidence to date suggests that lifting of legislation restricting intrastate branching and interstate banking would improve the efficiency of the banking system. Liberalization of restrictions on intrastate branching would improve convenience, increase lending activity, and create a more competitive banking system. Removal of restrictions on interstate banking would increase the number of banking alternatives, particularly in urban markets.[2]

Recent Changes in Branching Regulations

The continuation of restrictions on inter- and intrastate branching are in conflict with efforts to achieve a more flexible and competitive financial environment. As a result, pressures have accumulated and forced regulatory authorities to relax the restrictions. In addition, the market has found ways to circumvent the restrictions. This section will consider the changes that have occurred at the official level, while the next section will consider several innovations that have circumvented the geographic restrictions.

There have been many proposals calling for a national branching regulation that would override any state-imposed restrictions on branching—either inter- and intrastate. The obvious political problems of such an effort and the states' rights issues involved in such a bold action at the federal level have effectively prevented nationwide branching.

There have been three types of official actions in the past decade that have weakened geographic constraints on banking: (1) regulators have reduced restrictions on cross-state acquisitions in order to find buyers for failing banks and thrifts, (2)

---

[1] Herbert Baer and Sue F. Gregorash, *Toward Nationwide Banking*, Federal Reserve Bank of Chicago (1986).

[2] Karl A. Scheld and Herbert Baer, "Interstate Banking and Intrastate Branching: Summing Up," in ibid., p. 82.

some states have relaxed restrictions on intrastate branching, and (3) a number of states have entered into regional interstate branching agreements with other states. Let us briefly consider each in turn.

Deregulation and financial innovation have increased the competitiveness of the financial system, and as a result, a number of banks and thrifts have not been able to remain profitable. In order to increase the number of potential buyers of failing institutions, the Garn-St. Germain Depository Institutions Act of 1982 and more recently, the Financial Institutions Reform, Recovery, and Enforcement Act of 1989 have made it easier for banks to purchase failing banks and thrifts, even across state lines. Once an out-of-state bank purchases a failed thrift, for example, it can then have the thrift charter changed to a bank charter in some states.

Second, 15 states have relaxed their restrictions on intrastate branching (Figure 8-2 and Table 8-3). Unit states have shifted to limited branching status while limited branching states have shifted to unlimited states.

Third, in the absence of federal action on interstate branching, states again have taken the lead. In 1985, there were 24 states plus Washington, D.C., that had permitted some form of interstate branching. At the time of this writing, a few more states have initiated interstate branching proposals. The most frequent approach to removing restrictions on interstate branching at the state level is *reciprocity*. The principle of reciprocity requires that banking laws governing out-of-state banks seeking entry into the home state be the same as those governing home banks seeking entry into another state. Within the reciprocal arrangement among various states, considerable variation exists. Some agreements permit de novo or new entry; that is, an out-of-state bank can set up a new bank in another state belonging to the reciprocal agreement. Many states prohibit de novo entry and require that the entering institution purchase an already operating home state bank.

There is no doubt that efforts at the federal level to deal with troubled institutions and by some states to relax restrictions on inter- and intrabranching have increased the ease with which existing banks can branch. At the same time, geographic restrictions on banking are still an important feature of the U.S. banking industry. This naturally suggests the question: What type of innovations have been used by the market to circumvent regulations that limit branching? In many cases, the innovations that have been used to circumvent restrictions on geographic operation have also been designed to circumvent restrictions on product line activities. Three important innovations in this respect are bank holding companies, trust activities, and nonbank banks.

Bank Holding Companies

Bank holding companies or BHCs have expanded rapidly since the 1950s and represent an innovation designed to circumvent restrictions over geographic and product line activities. Prior to 1956, the federal government did not regulate BHCs, and as a result, *multibank holding companies*, or *MBHCs*, expanded rapidly as a means of extending the bank's product line into other areas such as leasing, management consulting, finance companies, loan servicing, data processing services, and to circumvent restrictions on inter- and intrastate branching. The MBHC consists of at

TABLE 8-4 BHCs, banks, and deposits, December 31, 1987

	Number of BHCs	Number of banks	Deposits (billions)
MBHCs	985	4,393	$1,387
SBHCs	4,919	4,929	400
Total	5,904	9,322	$1,787
All banks	—	13,634	1,980
% in BHC	—	64.4%	70.1%

Source: Board of Governors of the Federal Reserve System, *Annual Statistics*, (1988).

least two banks and related affiliate operations. Congress became alarmed at the rapid growth of holding companies and saw it as a direct innovation to expand operations intra- and interstate as well as move into other types of activities that might provide banks with the ability to control the market for financial services.

The 1956 Bank Holding Company Act sought to bring BHCs under federal regulation to be administered by the Board of Governors of the Federal Reserve System. The 1956 act defined a BHC as an organization of at least two banks and thus established a "loophole" since it provided an incentive to establish *single bank holding companies* or *SBHCs*. While the number of MBHCs remained fairly steady after 1956 for several years and represented less than 10% of total bank deposits, SBHCs grew rapidly in the 1960s. The SBHC innovation again alarmed Congress and regulators because it permitted nonfinancial firms to take over banks and a single bank to take over nonfinancial firms.

The 1970 amendment to the 1956 act or the so-called Douglas Amendment sought to bring SBHCs under federal regulation, again to be administered by the Board of Governors. The amendment further reinforced the restrictions on interstate banking established by the McFadden Act of 1927 and the Banking Act of 1933 by limiting the ability of BHCs to acquire bank subsidiaries outside of the home state. The amendment allows such out-of-state acquisitions only if the state permits such acquisitions. While the amendment extended federal regulation, it clarified the non-bank activities that would be permitted by the Federal Reserve and those that would be denied. In addition, it liberalized some of the nonbank activities permitted BHCs. As a result, BHCs have continued to expand and have become a major feature of U.S. banking. Table 8-4 indicates that there is a larger number of SBHCs than MBHCs; however, the MBHCs have only slightly less the number of banks but three times the deposits of SBHCs. Overall, BHCs account for 70% of deposits held by 65% of the total number of banks in the United States.

The Banking Holding Company Act and the 1970 amendment have limited the ability of BHCs to operate full service banks across state lines; however, affiliates of BHCs can be operated in many states in which the activity is permitted. BHCs have been permitted to conduct mortgage banking, consumer finance, and credit card operations across state lines. BHCs are putting constant pressure on states to liberalize the activities that can be made part of the BHC structure.

One of the most aggressive moves in using the BHC to circumvent restrictions against interstate banking occurred in the early 1980s with the establishment of "nonbank banks."

When Is a Bank Not a Bank? The Innovation of the Nonbank

Banks have frequently innovated around restrictive financial regulation limiting their activities. BHCs emerged to circumvent restrictions on geographic and product line activities. Securitization and other off–balance sheet activities have provided ways in which banks can become more involved in the securities markets. Trust activities are another effort to innovate around the Glass-Steagall restrictions on securities activities.

Another innovation—the nonbank bank—emerged in the 1980s as another circumvention. Banks found a "loophole" in the Bank Holding Company Act that defined a bank as an entity that accepts demand deposits *and* engages in commercial lending. An entity that does not fit this technical definition is not subject to the Bank Holding Company Act. As a result, a number of nonbank banks were established that engaged in banking activities but did not accept demand deposits *and* make commercial loans; for example, they provided consumer credit and accepted federally insured deposits.

Nonbank banks thus avoided many of the product and geographic limits, and, as a result, there was much interest in establishing nonbank banks. Nonbank banks were chartered by the Comptroller of the Currency as a national bank; however, the applicant agreed not to accept demand deposits or make commercial loans.

Nonbanks raised concern in 1983 when the Comptroller and chair of the Board of Governors called for a moratorium on the establishment of nonbank banks. Congress was urged to address what product and geographic lines are appropriate for a "bank" and to reevaluate the legal definition of a bank.

Congress took a step in this direction with the Competitive Equality Banking Act of 1987. This act failed to deal with the broader issues of Glass-Steagall and other new powers banks desired; however, it did put a stop to the nonbank bank innovation. It grandfathered some 55 nonbank banks established before March 1987, although the act imposed new constraints on their activities. More important, the act prohibited nonbank banks by requiring companies that acquired a nonbank bank after March 1987 to comply with the Bank Holding Company Act or divest their bank subsidiary.

BHCs and Glass-Steagall

Over the years, the Board of Governors has restricted the range of activities that BHC affiliates can conduct. Even though a broad range of activities falls under the heading "closely related to banking," the Board has tended to adopt a narrow definition of what is closely related and what is not. One activity that has definitely been restricted to BHCs is the power to underwrite debt and equity I.O.U.s issued by businesses.

The Glass-Steagall Act of 1933 (part of the 1933 Banking Act) prohibited banks from underwriting and distributing debt or equity I.O.U.s with the exception of federal securities, municipal bonds, and deposit-type I.O.U.s such as large CDs. These restrictions extend to the affiliates of BHCs.

There have been some official efforts to relax the restrictions against underwriting and dealing in securities, most notably at the state level. BHCs can hold both state and national banks, and more than half the banks in the United States are not official members of the Federal Reserve. Even though these nonmembers must still meet Federal Reserve–imposed reserve requirements because they are federally insured, most of the regulation and supervision of state nonmember banks is left to the state government. While Congress debated the issue of whether banks through their BHC affiliates could assume security powers in the late 1980s, a number of states moved to relax the Glass-Steagall restrictions on state nonmember banks. Since a BHC can include a state nonmember bank, BHCs are finding that they can enter the securities underwriting business via a state bank subsidiary.

As a result, Congress in 1988 turned its attention to repeal of the Glass-Steagall restrictions that prohibited the affiliates of BHCs to assume securities powers. There was increasing concern that the relaxation occurring at the state level in the absence of any overall direction only served to confuse financial regulation. In 1988 a variety of proposals were considered in the Senate and the House; however, no legislation was passed. The proposals differed in regard to three issues:

1. *The extent of the securities powers that could be assumed by the BHC.* Some would permit a wide range of powers, while others would restrict security powers to only high-grade corporate debt and prohibit the underwriting of equities.

2. *The form and extent of the "firewall" between the bank and the BHC affiliate that would assume the new security powers.* The firewall concept is intended to prevent the insured deposits of the bank being used in any fashion to support the security operations of the BHC or its security affiliates.

3. *The extent of regulatory oversight and supervision.* Some proposals would require the Federal Reserve to assume the responsibility while other proposals would establish a new regulatory agency.

Despite the restrictions currently imposed by Glass-Steagall and the failure of Congress to repeal Glass-Steagall, banks have found several ways to circumvent the restrictions on security market operations. We have already mentioned how state regulatory authorities provided a loophole for expanded securities powers. In the same vain, the Federal Reserve has taken an aggressive role in permitting expanded securities powers to banks. In 1987, the Board of Governors permitted bank holding company subsidiaries to underwrite limited amounts of mortgage-backed securities, municipal bonds tied to revenue from specific projects (banks have always been permitted to hold general municipal obligations), commercial paper, and corporate debt. The underwriting activity must be conducted by a separate subsidiary and cannot generate more than 5% of the subsidiary's total gross revenue. The majority of revenue from the subsidiary must come from the considerably less risky underwriting of federal, state, and municipal debt. In 1989, the Federal Reserve indicated that it was seriously considering allowing subsidiaries to underwrite corporate equities; however, the quantity limitation would likely apply to this activity also.

Not only have regulatory authorities permitted limited bank extension into the securities business, but banks have increasingly resorted to securitization and other off–balance sheet activities to increase their role in the securities markets. Trust banking has been another bank innovation in this regard.

Thus, despite the limitations of Glass-Steagall, banks have made some inroads into the securities business; however, there continues to exist a regulatory separation between investment and commercial banking in the United States.

Trust Activities

The 1933 Glass-Steagall Act removed banks from the investment banking business; however, banks still play an important role in equity markets through their trust activities in which a portfolio of debt and equity I.O.U.s is managed, rather than owned, by the bank.

Personal and employee benefit (pension) trusts are the most important type of trust account maintained by banks. The assets acquired by banks for their trust accounts range from Treasury obligations to common and preferred stocks. Equities represent a major form of trust investment and often constitute anywhere from 30 to 60% of the trust, depending on the type of trust. In fact, bank trust departments have held as much as 25% of the outstanding equities and a slightly smaller percentage of the outstanding corporation debt in the United States. There has been much discussion about the bank trust activity, as the concern is that the already concentrated banking industry is increasing its influence in the stock and bond markets through the trust function. Many banks operate trust departments; however, the trust activities are more concentrated than are the regular banking activities.

Correspondent Banking

Correspondent banking relationships between banks, usually a small bank and larger bank, are another important characteristic of the banking industry. A correspondent relationship is established between banks when one bank maintains a deposit account with another bank. The smaller bank benefits in several ways from the correspondent relationship with a large bank. The large correspondent bank can often provide services such as trust functions and loan evaluation, which the small bank would find more expensive to provide itself.

The larger banks benefit from the correspondent relationship because the demand deposits of the smaller banks represent an important source of funds. Unlike most demand deposit accounts, the bank has more knowledge about the stability of the correspondent deposit account, which makes it a more suitable source of funds than normal demand deposit accounts.

Before the passage of the Deregulation and Monetary Control Act, nonmember banks often established correspondent relationships with member banks to have indirect access to various Federal Reserve services such as wire transfer facilities, currency shipments, and check-clearing facilities. In addition, states often permitted nonmember banks to use correspondent deposits to satisfy reserve requirements. However, the 1980 act eliminated the major difference between nonmember and member banks regarding Federal Reserve services. All banks are now required to meet the same set of reserve requirements and, all banks have equal access to the services of the Federal Reserve on an equal fee basis. While the differential treatment between member and nonmember banks will no longer influence the growth of correspondent banking, correspondent banking is still likely to continue growing given the other benefits it provides to both sides of the relationship.

International Banking

Banks play a major role in international finance and the rapid growth of international banking reflects the growing interdependence of the world economies. International banking has increased even more in the past decade as deregulation and innovation in many countries have removed or relaxed restrictions of flows of funds between countries and made it easier for foreign financial institutions to operate in a large number of countries.

There are three aspects to international banking from the U.S. perspective. First, there has been a major expansion in the number of banking facilities operated by U.S. banks in foreign countries; second, there has been a major expansion in the number of banking facilities operated by foreign banks in the United States; and, third, the federal government established *international banking facilities* or IBFs in 1981 to increase U.S. competitiveness to attract international banking activity. U.S. banks have expanded their foreign operations by *branching*, forming *Edge Act corporations*, and obtaining interests in *foreign subsidiaries* that specialize in various types of financial services. Branch offices are located throughout the world, although London is the most important location in terms of number of branches. Edge Act corporations are special facilities of U.S. banks that accept deposits and nondeposit funds and specialize in financing international trade. U.S. banks have also expanded their foreign operations by obtaining interests in foreign financial subsidiaries.

U.S. banks have significantly increased their financial influence in foreign markets since the 1960s. For example, in 1960 only 8 U.S. banks operated 128 branch offices abroad; however, by late 1987, 153 banks operated almost 900 branch offices.

Foreign banking institutions have likewise grown rapidly in the United States. In late 1972 there were 101 foreign banking facilities. In mid-1987 the number had increased to 658—a sixfold increase. There are three major types of foreign banking facilities operated in the United States: *branch* of a foreign bank, *agency* of a foreign bank, and *subsidiary bank*. Branch offices are the most important. The overwhelming majority of foreign operations in the United States are concentrated in New York and California.

Branch offices of a foreign bank have full banking powers, and prior to 1978, branch offices had considerable advantages over U.S. banks. For example, foreign banks could set up branches in several states despite the prohibition against interstate banking. The 1978 International Banking Act ended many of the advantages of foreign banks. In regard to branching, the foreign bank must indicate the "home state" and branching beyond the home state is limited to the same extent it is for domestic banks. In general, branch offices of foreign banks are subject to most of the same regulations as imposed on domestic banks.

Agencies of a foreign bank offer limited banking services and cannot accept deposits. Most agencies concentrate on trade financing and services related to money market transactions.

Subsidiary banks are incorporated as a separate entity from the foreign parent bank and offer the full range of banking services. Like branches of foreign banks, subsidiary banks are subject to the same regulations as U.S. banks.

Foreign bank operations in the United States have grown rapidly in the past two decades and recently have become a source of controversy. More specifically, concern has grown over the presence of Japanese banks. In California, for example, Japanese banks held 11% of California's bank assets in 1982. In 1988 they held 25% of California's bank assets and accounted for over 30% of bank loans made in California.[3]

The growth of Japanese banking presence in the United States as well as in Europe is due to four factors: (1) increasing world financial integration, (2) financial liberalization in Japan, which has permitted Japanese banks to operate abroad more freely; (3) the large trade surpluses experienced by Japan, which has provided the Japanese with funds to invest abroad, and (4) the appreciation of the yen in the 1980s, which has increased the value of their dollar holdings and thus further increased their purchasing power to invest in the United States.

Another manifestation of international banking in the United States is some 550 *international banking facilities* or *IBFs*. Domestic and foreign banks in 1981 were given permission to establish IBFs, most located in New York. An IBF is like an overseas branch of a bank. It accepts time deposits from and makes loans to foreigners; however, it is located in the United States. There is a regulatory wall between IBFs and domestic banking since IBFs are not subject to the same requirements. Most important, IBF deposits are not subject to reserve requirements.

Banks and Regulatory Agencies

Banks are among the most heavily regulated businesses in the United States because of their role in the financial system as the largest and most diversified financial institution, their role in the national payments mechanism, and the fact that bank transaction deposits constitute a significant part of the money supply. There are four bank regulatory agencies with considerable overlapping jurisdiction between them.

State Banking Agencies   Every state has a banking agency that charters and regulates state banks under its jurisdiction. State-chartered banks are the oldest and date back to the late 1700s.

Comptroller of the Currency   The Comptroller is part of the U.S. Treasury and was established by the National Bank Act of 1864. This act established the first national banks as well as the concept of *dualism* in U.S. banking.

---

[3] Gary C. Zimmerman, "The Growing Presence of Japanese Banks in California," *Economic Review*, Federal Reserve Bank of San Francisco (Summer 1989), 3–17.

TABLE 8-5 Division of authority among bank regulatory agencies

Agency	Chartering[1]	Branching	Mergers
Comptroller of the Currency	National banks	National banks	Resulting bank a national bank
Federal Reserve Board	State member banks	State member banks	Resulting bank a state member bank
Federal Deposit Insurance Corporation	Nonmember insured state banks	Nonmember insured state banks	Resulting bank a nonmember insured bank
State banking agencies	All state banks	All state banks	Resulting bank a state bank

[1] Charters for national banks are issued by the Comptroller of the Currency; state bank charters are issued by state banking agencies. The Federal Reserve Board reviews charter applications when acting on applications of state banks for membership in the Federal Reserve System. The FDIC reviews charter applications when acting on applications of state nonmember banks for deposit insurance.

Source: Gerald P. Dwyer, Jr., and William C. Niblack, "Branching, Holding Companies, and Banking Concentration in the Eighth District," *Review*, Federal Reserve Bank of St. Louis, (July 1974), p. 19.

Federal Deposit Insurance Corporation The FDIC was established by the Banking Act of 1933 to provide insurance for bank deposits. The FDIC presently insures bank deposits up to $100,000 per account holder and maintains its insurance fund by a fixed percentage fee applied to deposits.

Board of Governors The Board of Governors of the Federal Reserve is the major decision-making body for the Federal Reserve. Although much of its operation is directed toward the formation and execution of monetary policy, the Board has considerable regulatory and supervisory responsibilities over banks in a number of areas.

Table 8-5 summarizes the division of authority among the four bank regulatory agencies. The Comptroller is concerned primarily with national banks, the Federal Reserve with state member banks, the FDIC with nonmember insured banks, and the state agencies with ensuring that both state and national banks, whether members of the Federal Reserve or not, adhere to the particular state banking laws in effect. In general, national banks are required to follow state banking laws.

The regulatory agencies undertake a large number of activities with regard to the banking industry, though their most important regulatory functions concern entry, branching, acquisitions by bank holding companies, and capital adequacy.

Entry Banks must operate under a state or a federal charter, and entry into the banking community is regulated. There are five general standards applied to an application for either a state or federal charter: (1) the characteristics of the individuals making application for the charter, (2) the amount of initial capital, (3) the profit prospects of the bank if a charter is granted, (4) the "convenience and needs" of the community, and (5) the possible "adverse" effects of the new banks on existing banks.

Entry considerations ensure that existing banks will not be subject to significant competitive forces as the consideration of profit prospects, convenience and needs, and adverse effects ensure that no prospective bank will be given a charter unless the new bank and the existing banks can maintain adequate growth and profit performance.

Mergers   Mergers, the combination of two or more banks into one bank under one management, have contributed significantly to the increasing concentration of banking over the last two decades. In effecting a merger, insured banks must obtain permission from a federal banking agency; if it involves a state bank, the state banking agency must also be consulted. All insured banks come under the jurisdiction of the Bank Merger Act of 1960.

The Bank Merger Act is explicit about several factors similar to those used to grant a new charter that must be considered: (1) effect of the merger on competition, (2) earnings prospects of the merged bank, (3) convenience and needs of the community, (4) other considerations.

Branching   Each state has laws on branching, and all banks, whether state or national, are subject to those laws. The same considerations as used in granting a charter or allowing a merger are employed in making a branching decision.

Bank Holding Companies   The Bank Holding Company Act of 1956 brought multiple-bank holding companies under the control of the Federal Reserve. The approval of the Federal Reserve was required for any purchase of 5% of a bank by a company made up of two or more banks. The 1956 Bank Holding Company Act did not apply to single-bank holding companies; however, the 1970 amendment to the Bank Holding Company Act brought single-bank holding companies under the jurisdiction of the Federal Reserve as well. Any nonbank acquisition by a single-bank holding company is closely supervised by the Board of Governors.

The Evolving Competitive Structure of the Banking Industry

The sheer size of banks and their major role in the financial system have led many observers to argue that banking is not competitive and society suffers as a result. Size itself implies little about competition, however. There is no doubt that the banking industry has a number of noncompetitive characteristics, and there is some evidence that the quantity of bank services would be higher and their price lower if banking were more competitive. At the same time, there are unique aspects of banking and finance that suggest caution in permitting the full range of competitive forces. This is a complex issue; however, we need to consider several aspects of bank competition.

1. *Regulation and supervision have been designed to establish a noncompetitive banking structure.* Banking is one of the most heavily regulated industries in the United States, certainly on a par with the type of regulation imposed on public utilities and the transportation industry. The focus of bank regulation has been to restrict competition among banks and between banks and other financial institutions.

As a necessary result, some banks earn profits significantly above competitive levels and the anticompetitive focus of bank regulation allows inefficient banks to remain viable.

Three basic forms of regulation have restricted competition in the banking industry: restrictions over entry (and exit), restrictions on portfolios or product lines, and interest rate ceilings. A charter is required to open a bank, and a charter will not be granted unless the applicant has demonstrated that the community can support an additional institution such that the new bank will earn an adequate rate of return and will not adversely impact the profits of existing institutions. The same criteria are used to authorize new branches in those states that allow branch banking. In addition, the restrictions on entry differ from state to state. Entry into banking is further restricted by the prohibition against interstate branching.

The banking industry is subject to a variety of portfolio restrictions that limit loan size and regulate the quality of assets. Banks are thus constrained in their use of funds. Constraints are also imposed on their sources of funds since demand deposits remain subject to a zero interest rate ceiling.

2. *Concentration in the banking industry depends on the market being serviced.* Concentration is an important aspect of the competitiveness or noncompetitiveness of the banking industry. The higher the degree of concentration (the smaller the number of banks in a given market), the greater the likelihood of collusion and monopoly behavior. The market for any given bank is difficult to identify since it depends on the particular type of banking service being offered. Banks compete on a national basis for large borrowers and large deposits. In these markets collusion is difficult to achieve given the large number of banks competing on the national level; however, the smaller the bank market and in view of the restrictions on entry, the more likely are noncompetitive elements to play a large role in the delivery of financial services. On the national level, concentration does not appear to be excessive and has actually declined slowly since 1940. In 1978, for example, the ten largest banks in the United States held 18.2% of the total deposits, whereas in 1960 the ten largest banks held 21.2% of the total deposits. Compared with other industries such as the steel and automobile industries, this national concentration is not out of line. At the state and local levels, however, concentration is much higher. In 1978, the five largest banks in Standard Metropolitan Statistical Areas (SMSAs) throughout the United States held at least 60.0% of the deposits in their SMSAs.[4]

3. *Studies of the bank cost function fail to find the conditions necessary for a natural monopoly.* Competition will degenerate into monopoly if the production and cost functions are subject to economies of scale so that per unit costs continue to decline as output size is increased. Even if one started with a large number of banks, none of which dominated the market, a natural monopoly would result. If one bank could realize the economies of scale and become larger than the other banks, that bank would be able to produce and price on the basis of a lower per unit cost of production. Each time the bank expanded its size, further economies would enhance its ability to drive the others out of the market, and, once the bank became the single monopoly, further competition could easily be prevented since no new firm could achieve the necessary economies of scale. The existence of significant economies of scale in the

---

[4] These concentration ratios are from Donald T. Savage and Elinor H. Solomon, "Branch Banking: The Competitive Issues," *Journal of Bank Research*, 11 (Summer 1980), 112, 114.

production function has been the primary rationale for regulation of utilities. Society should have the benefits of low per unit costs of production made possible by economies of scale but, at the same time, not be subject to the pricing and output decisions of one or a few firms. Thus, in the case of a public utility, society allows one producer to operate so as to obtain the economies of scale, but it regulates the price and rate of return of the public utility.

Are there significant economies of scale in banking? Despite the difficulties of estimating production and cost functions for banks, evidence indicates that there are significant economies of scale for small banks (per unit costs decline) but that economies of scale are not very significant for medium and large banks (per unit costs decline much more slowly or not at all.)

4. *Competition within the banking industry and between the banking industry and other financial institutions has been influenced by the Deregulation and Monetary Control and Garn-St Germain Acts.* These acts have expanded the sources of funds for all banks, removed Regulation Q ceilings, and generally made the banking industry more competitive. At the same time, the acts have expanded the sources and uses of funds for savings and loan associations, savings banks, and credit unions, which in many ways, have increased the degree of competition between the banking industry and nonbank depository institutions. Thus the banking industry is more competitive both within and without as a result of regulatory changes.

Despite these changes, banks still dominate the issuance of demand deposit accounts. NOW accounts and other similar new instruments are close substitutes for demand deposit accounts and have the added advantage that they pay interest income; however, technically they are not subject to transfer on demand, and, what is more important, they can be held only by individuals or nonprofit-making organizations. Thus, for a large part of the transaction account market, banks retain a considerable advantage. Savings and loan associations and savings banks received limited authority to issue demand deposits by the Garn-St Germain Act and state chartered savings banks had previously offered demand deposit accounts. In spite of this, banks will dominate the issuance of demand deposits for some time to come.

5. *Regulation and supervision have been designed to prevent bank failures.* The banking industry was much more competitive in the 1920s than today. The current anticompetitive focus of regulation and supervision emerged from the experience of the 1930s. The banking collapse started in 1930 and ended in March 1933 when a national bank holiday was called to prevent further deposit withdrawals. The accepted interpretation of the events argued that the collapse of the banking system resulted from too much competition among banks. Prior to the 1930s, banks were permitted to pay interest on demand deposits, were not subject to Regulation Q ceilings, and were not subject to many portfolio restrictions. As a result, banks competed aggressively with each other to attract funds, and higher interest costs necessitated a higher-yielding but riskier asset portfolio. When the decline in economic activity occurred in 1929, the banking system was structurally weak and, as a result, collapsed. Thus the focus of the financial reform of the 1930s sought to restrict the range of competition among banks to restore public confidence and prevent bank failures.

6. *Competition within the banking industry and between the banking industry and other financial institutions has been influenced by the general process of financial*

BOX 2 Why banks are subject to so much regulation even in an era of "deregulation"[1]

Despite the frequent reference to the term "deregulation," used to describe the financial regulatory reforms and innovations of the past decade, the current reforms are not designed to remove all types of government regulation. In fact, many depository institutions are now subject to more of some types of regulation than before.

Traditionally, banking has been viewed as inherently unstable in the absence of extensive government regulation. The most well-known period in our financial history used to support this view is the collapse of the banking system from about 1930 to 1933 when almost 10,000 banks failed (Figure 11-1).

To determine whether banking is inherently unstable, one must distinguish between economywide and local shocks. Large numbers of bank failures spread over a wide geographic area as a result of an economywide shock is not proof that the banking system is inherently unstable since by definition such a shock would affect the majority of banks. Inherent instability is characteristic of a banking system in which local shocks, which affect only a few banks, threaten the continued operation of other banks. Contagion is thus a necessary condition for the concept of inherent instability in banking.

Unregulated banking has traditionally been viewed as subject to contagion effects, and hence, inherently unstable, for four reasons. First, banks operate under a fractional reserve system in which only a small percentage of reserves are available to meet deposit withdrawals. Thus, banks are unable to convert large amounts of outstanding deposits into currency should depositors wish to withdraw funds on short notice. Second, depositors have incomplete information about the ability of banks not affected by a local shock to remain in operation. Hence, they are not sure whether the other banks will be able to convert deposits into currency at par. Lack of knowledge induces depositors to withdraw funds from the unaffected banks and thereby possibly force them to close.

Third, competition among banks presumably forces each bank to accept riskier portfolios of assets and liabilities than is prudent for institutions whose liabilities (deposits) constitute part of the nation's money supply. Fourth, competitive unregulated banks may resort to fraud and deliberately misinform the public about their operations. They thus generate public distrust of banking and raise the probability that banks will fail.

There have been some challenges to the view that banking is inherently unstable in the absence of government regulation; however, the traditional view continues to permeate much of the current policy toward banking. Thus, even in an era of deregulation and increased competition banks will continue to be subject to extensive government regulation and supervision.

[1] This material has been taken from Thomas F. Cargill, "Is Competitive Banking Stable?," *Weekly Letter*, Federal Reserve Bank of San Francisco (April 18, 1986).

innovation. Financial innovation makes it possible to exploit profit opportunities in the financial system. Thus if banks are able to earn excessive profits because of limited competition, it is more likely than ever that these profits will attract competition. Innovation and computer technology make it increasingly easier to introduce new financial assets and services that are close substitutes for bank services. NOW accounts and credit union share drafts were market innovations in the 1970s introduced to compete more directly for checking accounts. The securitization process that has attracted considerable attention from banks can just as easily be conducted by nonbank financial institutions.

7. *Is banking competitive?* There are three parts to this complex question. First, should banking be competitive without constraints on bank activities? Few want to go this far. Banks and other depository institutions should be subject to some degree of regulation and supervision, which in turn, has the effect of limiting competition. How far this regulation should go is an entirely different question. Second, recognizing that the banking system has noncompetitive elements, has banking become more competitive? Few would argue against the view that banking is now more

competitive than even a decade ago. Deregulation and innovation have greatly increased competition both within the banking industry and between banks and other financial institutions. Third, should there be even more competition in the banking industry? Strong arguments could be made to end the banking industry's virtual regulatory monopoly over demand deposits and permit any depository institution to issue any type of deposit. At the same time, banks correctly argue that regulatory advantages offered other institutions should then be made available to banks.

This entire discussion can be summed up in the following: banking is not a competitive industry by usual definitions of competitive markets; however, banking is far more competitive than even a decade ago because of deregulation and innovations.

Key Points

1. A little over 13,000 banks in the United States operate over 38,000 banking offices. The large number of individual banks conceals the degree of concentration in banking.

2. Banks are subject to regulation by four government regulatory agencies: a state chartering agency, the Comptroller of the Currency, the Federal Reserve, and the FDIC. Almost all banks belong to the FDIC; however, fewer than one-half are members of the Federal Reserve. National banks must become members, whereas state banks have the privilege of applying for membership.

3. Prior to the Deregulation and Monetary Control Act, there were significant costs to Federal Reserve membership in those states imposing less restrictive reserve requirements. This contributed to a declining membership problem for the Federal Reserve during the 1970s as high interest rates increased the opportunity cost of membership. The banking system now operates under a uniform reserve requirement structure maintained by the Federal Reserve.

4. Empirical evidence indicates that branching may be more efficient than unit systems, but this is a tentative conclusion. There are severe problems in measuring and estimating the relationship between costs and output for banks.

Banks are complex firms that offer a heterogeneous mix of products and services. The restrictions on branching, however, have been relaxed over the past decade as regulators need to find buyers for financially weak banks and thrifts, and a number of states have relaxed restrictions on intrastate branching and interstate branching. Despite these efforts, however, geographic restrictions continue to characterize U.S. banking.

5. Banks have innovated around restrictions in various ways. BHCs, trust departments, and nonbank banks represent efforts to get around restrictions that limit profit either by limiting the bank's product line or geographic market.

6. Banks are heavily regulated. The Comptroller of the Currency, the Federal Reserve, the FDIC, and various state banking agencies regulate and supervise banks with respect to entry into the banking industry, mergers between banks, branching activities, and bank holding activities.

7. The banking system is not competitive in many respects; however, regulatory changes and financial innovation have increased the degree of competition both within the banking industry and between banks and other sectors of the financial system.

Key Terms

Bank holding companies (BHCs)

Bank Holding Company Act of 1956 and 1970 Amendments

Comptroller of the Currency

Correspondent banking

Declining membership issue and the 1980 Deregulation and Monetary Control Act

Dual banking system

Economies of scale in banking

Federal Deposit Insurance Corporation (FDIC)

Glass-Steagall Act of 1933

International banking

Interstate branching

Intrastate branching

Multibank holding companies (MBHCs)

National Bank Act of 1864

National banks

Nonbank banks

Reciprocity at the state level

State banking agencies

Single-bank holding companies (SBHCs)

Size distribution of banks

State banks

Trust banking activities

Questions

1. Comment on the following: "The size distribution information in Table 8-1 obviously suggests too much concentration in U.S. banking."

2. Comment on the following: "The size distribution information in Table 8-1 obviously suggests that there are too many small banks in the United States."

3. Why should banks continue to have a regulatory monopoly over the issuance of demand deposits?

4. Is it consistent with efforts to deregulate the financial system by removing interest rate ceilings on almost all deposits and, yet, retain the zero interest rate ceiling on demand deposits?

5. Why are banks (and other depository institutions) regulated and supervised so closely?

6. Does it make any difference to depositors whether their bank is a member or nonmember bank? What about membership in the FDIC?

7. There are valid arguments to some regulation over the activities of banks; however, is regulation of banking always in the public interest?

Suggested Readings

1. George J. Benston, "Interest on Deposits and the Survival of Chartered Depository Institutions, " *Economic Review*, Federal Reserve Bank of Atlanta (October 1984), 42–56. Discusses interest rate ceilings on bank deposits.

2. Kerry Cooper and Donald R. Fraser, *Banking Deregulation and the New Competition in Financial Services*. Cambridge, Mass.: Ballinger, 1986. Discusses the impact of deregulation and innovation on bank competition.

3. Federal Deposit Insurance Corporation, *FDIC Banking Review*. Publication of the FDIC containing articles on bank regulation and summaries of recent regulatory changes.

4. Federal Reserve Bank of Chicago, *Bank Structure*

and Competition, various issues. Each year the Federal Reserve Bank of Chicago sponsors a conference on banking whose reports are published in an annual proceedings volume. Excellent source of information on the banking industry. The Bank also publishes a quarterly *Economic Perspectives*, which contains many articles on banks and the banking industry.

5. Carter H. Golembe and Davis S. Holland, *Federal Regulation of Banking, 1986–87* (Washington, D.C.: Golembe Associates, 1986). A comprehensive summary of bank regulation.

6. James V. Houpt, *International Trends for U.S. Banks and Banking Markets*, Board of Governors of the Federal Reserve System, Staff Study 156 (May 1988).

7. David B. Humphrey, "Cost Dispersion and the Measurement of Economies in Banking," *Economic Review*. Federal Reserve Bank of Richmond (May–June 1987), 24–38. Evidence on economies of scale in banking.

8. George Kaufman, *Banking Structures* (Norwell, Mass.: Kluwer Academic, 1991). Reviews banking structures in a number of countries.

9. Peter S. Rose, *The Changing Structure of American Banking* (New York: Columbia University Press, 1987).

10. Kenneth Spong, *Banking Regulation*, Federal Reserve Bank of Kansas City (1985). Reviews a wide variety of bank regulations.

11. Gary C. Zimmerman, "The Growing Presence of Japanese Banks in California," *Economic Review*, Federal Reserve Bank of San Francisco (Summer 1989), 3–17.

CHAPTER 9

Nonbank Financial Institutions

Chapter Overview

Financial institutions of all types play essentially the same role. They provide a conduit to transfer funds from surplus units (SUs) to deficit units (DUs). In this general sense, there are no "unique" financial institutions only differences in the types of I.O.U.s issued to SUs to obtain funds and the types of I.O.U.s purchased from borrowers.

This view is correct in a general sense, but it fails to recognize the unique role played by banks and the other three depository institutions—savings and loan associations, savings banks, and credit unions. These four depository institutions are different than other financial institutions because of the important role they play in the money supply process. The transaction deposits issued by these institutions together represented about three-fourths of the M1 money supply. The last two chapters have focused on banks—the largest and most diversified of the depository institutions—and now we need to discuss the other three depository institutions as well as other financial institutions.

This chapter has three objectives. First, we review the three nonbank depository institutions: savings and loan associations, savings banks, and credit unions. Together with banks, these depository institutions are "unique" because their transaction deposits represent the major part of the nation's money supply, and as a result, they play an important role in the conduct of monetary policy.

Second, we review some major changes in the savings and loan industry and to a lesser extent, the savings bank industry. Savings and loan associations and savings banks are collectively called *thrifts*. The Financial Institutions Reform, Recovery, and Enforcement Act of 1989 (FIRREA) has made fundamental structural changes in the thrift industry.

Third, we review a number of important financial institutions that obtain funds primarily from sources other than deposits. These are called nondepository financial institutions, and while they don't play the same role in the money supply process as depository institutions, they nonetheless are a major part of the flow of funds in the United States.

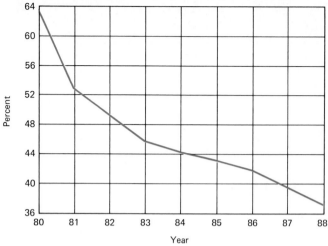

Source: U.S. Department of Commerce, *Survey of Current Business*, various issues.

FIGURE 9-1   Bank demand deposits as a percentage of M1, 1980–1988.

Financial Institutions and the Money Supply

Financial institutions can be placed into three categories in terms of their role in the money supply process. First, banks dominate the issuance of demand deposits, which represented 38.4% of the M1 money supply in January 1988. Thus, aside from the size and extent of diversification of banks vis-à-vis other financial institutions, banks at this point in time remain more "unequal" than other institutions. In addition, banks account for 24.1% of the nondemand deposit checkable accounts (NOW accounts and ATS accounts) in the January 1988 M1 money supply.

Second, nonbank depository institutions—savings and loan associations, savings banks, and credit unions—have become less "unequal" to banks in the past decade. The 1980 Deregulation and Monetary Control Act authorized these institutions to issue transaction deposits: NOW accounts, ATS (automatic transfer service) accounts, and credit union share drafts. The 1982 Garn-St Germain Depository Institutions Act permitted thrifts (savings and loan associations and savings banks) to issue demand deposit accounts if the account is part of a business loan relationship. While nonbank depository institutions are not presently able to compete with banks for commercial transaction deposits as a normal course of business, demand deposits have become a smaller part of the money supply as businesses innovate around the zero interest ceiling on demand deposits and find other substitutes (Figure 9-1). Nonbank depository institutions have thus become a major element in the money supply process— checkable deposits at these institutions in January 1988 represented 27.4% of the M1 money supply. In addition, nonbank depository institutions have significantly increased their role relative to banks in terms of their share of total financial assets relative to the banking system. Table 6-2 illustrated the declining role of banks relative to nonbank depository institutions from 1975 through 1988 measured in terms of financial assets.

Third, there is a wide range of financial institutions referred to as nondepository financial institutions that are very important in the financial system in terms of assets, but play a decidedly less important role in the money supply process compared to depository institutions. This is because the I.O.U.s they issue as a source of funds are not very good money substitutes, or in terms of the spectrum of liquidity discussed in Chapter 2, they are decidedly less liquid than M1.

Nonbank Depository Institutions

Savings and Loan Associations

Savings and loan associations (S&Ls) are the second largest type of financial institution in the United States, numbering about 3,000. S&Ls were established originally to provide a source of mortgage credit to households. About 60% of the S&Ls are state chartered and the remaining 40% are federally chartered. S&Ls can be organized on either a mutual or stock basis. Mutual S&Ls are legally owned by the depositors who receive dividends based on their deposit levels. Stock S&Ls issue stock so that stockholders are the legal owners and depositors are creditors of the S&L. The majority of S&Ls are organized on a stock basis.

The Financial Institutions Reform, Recovery, and Enforcement Act of 1989 (FIRREA) has made significant changes in the S&L industry. This act was designed to bail out the S&L industry, which for all practical purposes had become insolvent by the mid-1980s, and to restructure the industry to prevent reoccurrence of the same problem. While the issues surrounding the 1989 act are commonly referred to in conjunction with the thrift industry, it is the S&L component of the thrift industry that was the focal point of concern.

Prior to 1989 S&Ls were regulated by the Federal Home Loan Bank System consisting of the Federal Home Loan Bank Board (FHLBB), the Federal Savings and Loan Insurance Corporation (FSLIC), and 12 Federal Home Loan District Banks. Federally chartered S&Ls had to be members while state-chartered S&Ls could apply for membership in the System. About 80% of all S&Ls were members of the System and over 90% of the S&Ls were members of FSLIC, which insured deposits of up to $100,000 per deposit.

FIRREA changed all this. The Federal Home Loan Bank System was divided into three separate parts: First, the independent FHLBB was abolished. Most of its functions were transferred to the new Office of Thrift Supervision (OTS). The OTS, like the Comptroller of the Currency, is under the general guidance of the U.S. Treasury. Second, FSLIC was reorganized into the Savings Association Insurance Fund (SAIF) and transferred into the Federal Deposit Insurance Corporation (FDIC) as a separate insurance fund. The FDIC now has two insurance funds: the Bank Insurance Fund and the SAIF. Third, the Federal Housing Finance Board was established to oversee the credit advance activities of the 12 district Home Loan Banks. The 12 district banks sell agency securities in the open market and make these funds available to S&Ls to support their role as major suppliers of residential mortgage credit.

We will return to consider some of the other aspects of FIRREA when we discuss the thrift problem. First, we need to finish discussing the general features of S&Ls, savings banks, and credit unions.

In addition to regulatory agencies specifically designed to deal with S&Ls, S&Ls also interact with the Federal Reserve. The 1980 Deregulation and Monetary Control act made all federally insured S&Ls subject to Federal Reserve reserve requirements. At the same time, S&Ls have access to Federal Reserve services on a nondiscriminatory fee basis, including borrowing from the Federal Reserve. However, few S&Ls borrow from the Federal Reserve since S&Ls, savings banks, and credit unions must first exhaust their normal governmental sources of liquidity. The Federal Home Loan District Banks are the normal sources of liquidity for S&Ls and are an important source of funds (10% at year-end 1988).

Transactions deposits (NOW and ATS accounts), MMDAs, along with savings and time deposits represent the major source of S&L funds. In 1988, deposits accounted for 73 percent of S&L fund sources (Table 9-1) followed by advances from Federal Home Loan District Banks.

S&L uses of funds have changed significantly during the past two decades. In the 1970s residential mortgages represented about 85% of S&L assets, with the remainder being held in the form of government and municipal securities. Deregulation has brought about two major changes in S&L uses of funds.

First, mortgages have steadily declined in overall importance so that by 1988 they represented only 57% of financial assets. In addition, mortgages are no longer confined to the fixed rate variety. To deal with flexible and uncertain deposit rates, S&Ls (and other mortgage lenders) offer adjustable rate mortgages or ARMs. One can still obtain a fixed rate mortgage, but one has to be willing to pay a premium. The majority of new mortgages (60 to 70%) are of the ARM variety.

Second, the increase in nonmortgage lending activity has been reflected by consumer and business loans, high-yielding corporate debt or "junk" bonds, and a wide variety of real estate development loans.

S&L deposits are insured up to $100,000 by SAIF, and all federal S&Ls must enroll in SAIF, while state-chartered S&Ls may apply for federal insurance. The majority of S&Ls operate with federal insurance; however, unlike bank deposit insurance, state-sponsored insurance systems had been offered in some states as an alternative to federal deposit insurance. Most noteworthy, state-sponsored insurance funds were established in Massachusetts, Maryland, North Carolina, Ohio, and Pennsylvania. While these state-sponsored insurance funds covered only a small percentage of S&L deposits (less than 2% of total S&L deposits), they have become even less important after 1985 with the failure of the Ohio and Maryland insurance funds.

S&Ls are subject to less restrictive rules regarding intrastate branching than are banks, and recent regulatory actions have in effect permitted some interstate branching. In 1980, the FHLBB permitted federally chartered S&Ls to branch in any state as long as it is not prohibited by state law. The 1982 Garn-St Germain Act permitted S&Ls to purchase troubled S&Ls in other states, and as the problems in the S&L industry intensified by the end of the 1980s, banks and other institutions were permitted to purchase troubled S&Ls in other states.

TABLE 9-1   Financial assets and liabilities of savings and loan associations as of December 31, 1988

	Amount (billions)	*% of Total*
Financial assets		
Mortgages	$ 777.0	57.1%
Consumer credit	54.5	4.0
Government securities	253.0	18.6
Other	275.5	20.3
	$1,360.0	100.0%
Liabilities		
Deposits	$ 972.3	73.3%
Fed funds and RPs	98.4	7.4
FHLB loans	134.1	10.1
Other	120.8	9.1
	$1,325.6	100.0%
Residual (net worth − real assets)	34.4	
	$1,360.0	

Source: Board of Governors of the Federal Reserve System, Flow of Funds Accounts, *Financial Assets and Liabilities, Year-End, 1965–1988* (September 1989).

Savings Banks

Savings banks were established originally to provide a safe savings outlet for the small household and, over the years, have been conservatively managed. In fact, during the 1930s only a few savings banks suspended operations while most other financial institutions experienced widespread closings. There are about 370 savings banks today.

Savings banks have much in common with S&Ls. First, they obtain their funds from NOW and ATS accounts, MMDAs, passbook savings accounts, and time deposits. Savings banks have not, however, relied on nondeposit sources of funds to the same extent as S&Ls have in recent years. Deposits represent 84% of the total sources of funds (Table 9-2). Second, savings banks allocate a major portion of their funds to mortgages though they have more flexibility to hold corporate debt and equity than S&Ls. Third, savings banks are subject to Federal Reserve–imposed reserve requirements on transaction and other reservable deposits. Fourth, savings banks and S&Ls are collectively referred to as *thrifts* given their similarities in the uses and sources of funds.

The similarity of savings banks to S&Ls has exposed them to many of the same problems experienced by S&Ls. In general, regulatory changes to improve the condition of S&Ls have been applied equally to savings banks; hence, this is the reason why the term "thrift problem" or "thrift reforms" is frequently used even though savings banks represent a small part of the thrift industry, either in terms of the number of institutions or total assets.

TABLE 9-2   Financial assets and liabilities of savings banks as of December 31, 1988

	Amount (billions)	% of Total
Financial assets		
Mortgages	$161.9	57.8%
Consumer credit	12.3	4.4
Corporate bonds and equities	21.7	7.8
Government securities	38.8	13.9
Other	45.3	16.2
	$280.0	100.0%
Liabilities		
Deposits	$214.7	83.7
Other	41.8	16.3
	$256.5	100.0%
Residual (net worth—real assets)	23.5	
	$280.0	

Source: Board of Governors of the Federal Reserve System, Flow of Funds Accounts, *Financial Assets and Liabilities, Year-End 1965–1988* (September 1989).

At the same time, there are differences between savings banks and S&Ls. First, savings banks were all state chartered prior to 1980. There was no dual system in the savings bank industry; however, federal charters have been available since 1980. Second, with few exceptions, savings banks are concentrated in the Atlantic seaboard region, whereas S&Ls have a fairly broad geographic distribution. Third, state-chartered savings banks have had greater authority to issue demand deposits; however, savings bank demand deposits represent a small portion of total deposits. Federally chartered savings banks received limited authority to issue demand deposits as did federally chartered S&Ls by the Garn-St Germain Act. Fourth, savings banks have not experienced the rapid growth during the past decades as exhibited by S&Ls. According to Table 6-2, S&Ls have grown more rapidly than have savings banks; in fact, savings banks had the lowest growth rate of financial assets over the period 1975–1988 than the other financial institutions.

Savings banks are federally insured by the FDIC or SAIF, with a small number operating under state insurance programs.

Credit Unions

Credit unions have been one of the fastest-growing financial institutions in the United States, with financial asset growth of about 15% per year over the last two decades. There are some 17,000 state- and federally chartered credit unions established on a cooperative basis—the membership must have a *common bond* of association, which is usually occupational. Transaction deposits (credit union share drafts) along with

BOX 1 Credit unions and deregulation

Credit unions remain a small part of the flow of funds in terms of their contribution to total financial assets held by intermediaries. In another respect, however, credit unions play an important role in providing consumer credit. During the past decade, approximately 10% of household consumer credit has been provided by credit unions. Credit unions have also benefited from the deregulation process and now offer checking accounts or share drafts and have diversified their uses of funds into RPs and Federal funds. As a reflection of this, the share of credit union assets to total financial assets held by all private financial institutions increased from 1.7% in 1975 to 2.1% in 1988.

This has raised an important issue in the deregulation process. Credit unions have been provided with new diversification powers, and the credit union regulators (National Credit Union Administration and state credit union agencies) have increasingly provided them with more flexibility to expand their operations. In the past, most credit unions have been organized around an occupation common bond, which limited their growth. In recent years, credit unions have increasingly relied on a looser common bond such as residential area. That is, it's not required that you work at a given place to join a credit union—merely living in a given area is sufficient.

The debate over credit unions is based on the fact that credit unions have a major advantage over other suppliers of consumer credit. They are tax exempt.

Many observers argue that credit unions should be placed on a similar tax basis as other financial institutions, especially since they have been recipients of the new powers provided by deregulation and innovation. Several administrations in the past have introduced legislation that would tax credit unions, but the influence of 17,000 credit unions spread throughout the country has simply been too powerful to change their tax status.

Credit unions remain one of the fastest-growing financial institution in the United States. They grew at an annual rate of 13.7% from 1975 through 1988, while all financial institutions grew at 11.8% over the same period. At these comparative growth rates, credit unions will increasingly constitute a hindrance in the deregulation process.

savings and time deposit shares represent the major source of credit union funds while short-term consumer lending represents the major use of funds (Table 9-3), although real estate loans have increased in importance. Despite their small size on average and the fact that all credit unions combined hold only a fraction of the total financial assets of financial institutions, credit unions are the third largest supplier of short-term consumer credit in the United States, after banks and finance companies. Credit unions accounted for 13% of total consumer installment credit as of year-end 1988.

Credit union share draft accounts are subject to reserve requirements imposed by the Federal Reserve. However, the Garn-St Germain Act modified the reserve requirement structure to exempt most credit unions and other small depository institutions. The first $3.2 million (in 1988) in reservable deposits is subject to a zero reserve requirement.

Credit union deposits are insured up to $100,000 by the National Credit Union Administration, which regulates the approximately 9,000 nationally chartered credit unions and provides a source of liquidity to credit unions. State-chartered credit unions can enroll in the federal insurance program and a number of states have their own insurance program.

Credit unions differ significantly from all other financial institutions in that their cooperative organizational structure makes them exempt from federal taxation. Their large share of the consumer loan market and rapid growth has brought criticism from banks and finance companies regarding their tax-free status.

TABLE 9-3	Financial assets and liabilities of credit unions as of December 31, 1988	
	Amount (billions)	% of Total
Financial assets		
Consumer credit	$ 87.1	44.3%
Home mortgages	39.3	20.0
Government securities	20.8	10.6
Time deposits	24.0	12.2
Other	25.0	12.7
	$196.2	100.0%
Liabilities		
Shares/checkable	19.2	10.8
Shares/time and saving	159.2	89.2
	$178.4	100.0%
Residual (net worth − real assets)	17.8	
	$196.2	

Source: Board of Governors of the Federal Reserve System, Flow of Funds Accounts, *Financial Assets and Liabilities, Year-End 1965–1988* (September 1989).

Nonbank Nondepository Institutions

Life Insurance Companies

Life insurance companies do not normally come to mind as financial institutions because they do not obtain funds by accepting deposits as do banks, S&Ls, savings banks, and credit unions. Nevertheless, they are the second or third largest financial institutions in the United States, depending on the year being examined. Life insurance companies are regulated by the state insurance agency in the state in which they conduct business. Life insurance companies have not experienced very rapid growth over the last two decades compared with other financial institutions.

Life insurance funds come primarily from the sale of insurance policies that have a savings feature as part of the insurance contract. The source of funds is composed primarily of two types of liabilities: (1) life insurance reserves, which are related to the life insurance policies outstanding, and (2) pension reserves, which are related to insured pension plans offered by life insurance companies to various nonfinancial business firms. The predictability of withdrawals on the life insurance liabilities provides them with considerable latitude in their use of these funds (Table 9-4). Funds are allocated primarily for the longer term, with corporate bonds, equities, home mortgages, and other mortgages being the most important uses.

TABLE 9-4 Financial assets and liabilities of life insurance companies as of December 31, 1988

	Amount (billions)	% of Total
Financial assets		
Corporate bonds	$ 437.0	39.3%
Mortgages	232.6	20.9
Corporate equities	108.1	9.7
Policy loans	53.1	4.8
Other	282.5	25.4
	$1,113.3	100.0%
Liabilities		
Life insurance reserves	$ 302.5	28.7
Pension fund reserves	634.7	60.3
Other	115.1	10.9
	$1,052.3	100.0%
Residual (net worth − real assets)	61.0	
	$1,113.3	

Source: Board of Governors of the Federal Reserve System, Flow of Funds Accounts, *Financial Assets and Liabilities, Year-End 1965–1988* (September 1989).

Private and Government Pension Funds

Private pension funds obtain their funds from employer and employee contributions and have grown rapidly during the last two decades. Their sources of funds are long term, which permits considerable flexibility in the uses of their funds. Pension funds generally invest in corporate equities and bonds.

State and local government employee retirement funds are similar to their private counterpart (Table 9-5). Funds are obtained from employee and governmental contributions and, like private funds, are used to purchase corporate equities and bonds, although a smaller percentage of funds is allocated to equities.

Social Security is a pension fund for individuals; however, it is regarded as a pay-as-you-go system and is generally excluded from the list of financial institutions. The financial position of the Social Security program, however, had grown increasingly weaker over the years because benefits increased to levels that could not be supported from past and current taxes. In addition, the age distribution of the population has been such that more persons were becoming eligible for benefits than were entering the work force. A major overhaul of Social Security was accomplished in 1983 primarily by increasing the contribution rate. At the end of the 1980s, a substantial surplus had been established intended to honor commitments after the year 2000.

TABLE 9-5   Financial assets of private pension funds and state and local pension funds as of December 31, 1988

	Amount (billions)	% of Total
Financial assets		
Corporate equities	$ 542.4	47.6%
Corporate bonds	180.5	15.8
Mortgages	5.7	1.0
Government securities	139.7	12.3
Other	271.6	23.8
	$1,139.9	100.0%

Source: Board of Governors of the Federal Reserve System, Flow of Funds Accounts, *Financial Assets and Liabilities, Year-End 1965–1988* (September 1989).

Nonlife or Casualty Insurance Companies

Casualty insurance companies insure against all events other than the loss of life that have some reasonably predictable outcome. They obtain funds by selling insurance policies of various types. The uses of funds are for bonds, equities, municipals, and government securities as well as for providing trade credit.

Finance Companies

Finance companies take a variety of forms. Some deal directly with individuals; others deal with business firms. They obtain their funds by selling debt, short-term finance paper, and borrowing from banks (Table 9-6). Their primary use of funds is for consumer and business loans.

Investment Companies, Money Market Mutual Funds, and Security Dealers and Agents

Investment companies or mutual funds deal in equities on both the sources and uses of funds. They obtain their funds by selling equities to small investors and offer the advantage of diversification by using these funds to purchase the equity securities of other businesses. There are two types of investment companies: closed end and open end. Closed-end companies have a fixed number of shares; open-end companies have no fixed number of shares but will sell shares and redeem them continually according to investor preference.

Investment companies or mutual funds have grown rapidly and represented a method by which small SUs could invest directly in bond and stock markets and obtain the benefits of diversification and expert market knowledge. Investment companies allocated the majority of their funds to the capital market; however, starting

TABLE 9-6 Financial assets and liabilities of finance companies as of December 31, 1988

	Amount (billions)	% of Total
Financial assets		
Consumer credit	$ 174.3	35.6%
Loans to business	236.5	48.3
Other	78.5	16.0
	$ 489.3	100.0%
Liabilities		
Corporate bonds	$ 149.1	26.6
Bank loans	26.6	4.7
Open market paper	270.2	48.2
Other	48.8	20.5
	$ 494.7	100.0%
Residual (net worth − real assets)	−5.4	
	$ 489.3	

Note: The negative residual item raises from anomalies in the sampling method used to obtain estimates of financial assets.
Source: Board of Governors of the Federal Reserve System, *Financial Assets and Liabilities, Year-End 1965–1988* (September 1989).

in 1972 a new form of mutual investment company emerged that allocated funds to the money market. The money market mutual fund (MMMF) obtained funds by selling shares and using the pooled funds to purchase money market instruments. MMMFs grew rapidly during the 1970s. MMMF assets increased from $2.4 billion in 1974 to $219.8 billion by the end of 1982—an average annual growth rate of 75.9%! This dramatic growth record has been reversed as a result of competition from MMDAs offered by depository institutions. Authorized by the Garn-St Germain Act, MMDAs are designed to compete directly with MMMF shares and have the added advantage of being federally insured up to $100,000. MMMF shares are not federally insured and, thus, are subject to default risk. MMMF assets declined sharply after MMDAs were introduced at the end of 1982. In 1983, MMMF assets declined by 18.4% to $179.4 billion. From 1983, however, MMMF assets have continued to grow at a rapid rate, reaching $338.0 billion at year-end 1988 (Table 9-7).

The dramatic growth of MMMFs through 1982 was the result of Regulation Q ceilings on savings and time deposits at depository institutions in an environment of high interest rates. As market rates of interest increased over the 1970s, increasing numbers of depositors transferred their funds to the direct component of the financial system; however, in the absence of MMMFs, the ability to disintermediate was only available to fairly large deposit holders. Commissions and other transaction costs made it uneconomical to transfer funds in small denominations ($50,000 or less) to the money and capital markets. The emergence of MMMFs occurred for the same reason that mutual fund companies expanded: they provided a method for small SUs

TABLE 9-7 Financial assets and liabilities of money market mutual funds as of December 31, 1988

	Amount (billions)	% of Total
Financial assets		
Time and foreign deposits, RPs	$104.2	30.8%
Government securities (includes tax-exempt)	95.6	28.3
Open market paper	129.1	38.2
Other	9.1	2.7
	$338.0	100.0%
Liabilities		
Shares outstanding	$338.0	100.0%

Source: Board of Governors of the Federal Reserve System, Flow of Funds Accounts, *Financial Assets and Liabilities, Year-End 1965–1988* (September 1989).

to invest directly in markets that required large denominations and considerable expertise to reduce risk. They required small minimum amounts of $500 or $1,000 to purchase shares, and they provided transaction account services on the share accounts by allowing individuals to write checks or drafts on their share account, usually in minimum amounts of $500. MMMF shares are included in the M2 measure of the money supply. MMDAs are likewise included in M2.

Security dealers and brokers are normally regarded as part of the direct component of the financial system in merely serving as the go-between for SUs and DUs, charging a fee for bringing the two together to exchange funds. In direct finance, the dealer or broker does not take a position in the I.O.U.s of the DU. However, to the extent that security brokers and dealers maintain inventories of corporate equities, bonds, and other I.O.U.s of borrowers and thereby assume the risk, we regard them as part of the indirect component of the financial system.

Federal Agencies as Financial Institutions

Direct and indirect financial relationships between lenders and borrowers are established primarily by privately owned financial institutions, although governmental agencies also make up part of the financial system. We have already mentioned state and local retirement systems as special types of financial institutions that perform much the same function as private pension plans. There are two other types of involvement by government in the financial system that deserve special consideration.

Mortgage Credit   There is a strong commitment to provide the means for every household to own its own home. The purchase of a home results in a substantial expenditure of funds; consequently, the household must borrow a large amount over long periods of time to purchase a home. In line with the social commitment, the federal government has established several agencies to facilitate the flow of funds into the residential real estate market.

The Federal Housing Administration (FHA) was established in 1934 and guarantees mortgages against loss to the lender and establishes interest rate ceilings. The Veterans Administration (VA) was established in 1944 to help ex-servicemen obtain funds to purchase residential and business real estate; the VA insures real estate loans and establishes favorable loan terms by imposing interest rate ceilings generally below the market rate of interest and requiring smaller down payments. Mortgage loans that are not FHA insured or VA guaranteed are referred to as conventional mortgage loans.

S&Ls, banks, savings banks, life insurance companies, and individuals and other institutions are the major suppliers of total mortgage credit. At the end of 1988, these suppliers held over 75% of the total mortgage credit outstanding. The remaining percentage of mortgage credit was supplied via the services of various federal and federally sponsored agencies. The primary function of these agencies is to create an active secondary market for residential mortgages. The most important are the Federal National Mortgage Association (FNMA), the Government National Mortgage Association (GNMA), and the Federal Home Loan Mortgage Company (FHLMC). FNMA purchases FHA-insured, VA-guaranteed, and conventional mortgages from banks and other lenders with funds obtained by selling securities in the capital market. FNMA also makes advance commitments to buy mortgages from 3 to 12 months in the future. GNMA and FHLMC put together packages of mortgages and then sell participations in these packages. The activities of FNMA, GNMA, and FHLMC have contributed significantly to the establishment of a national secondary market for mortgages as well as increasing the flow of funds into housing.

Agricultural Credit   The agricultural sector of the economy has traditionally been the recipient of governmental loan programs. Like housing, there is a political commitment to the agricultural sector of the economy. The three most important governmental suppliers of credit to the agricultural sector are the Federal Land Bank System, the Federal Intermediate Credit Banks, and the Cooperative Farm Credit System. Each of these agencies is composed of 12 regional banks that obtain funds by selling I.O.U.s in the money and capital markets. They do not lend directly to farmers but provide funds to various types of farmer cooperatives and associations at the regional level that, in turn, lend the funds directly to farmers.

Key Points

1. Depository institutions play a key role in the financial system and the economy because their I.O.U.s serve as the money supply. While banks still dominate the money supply process, nonbank depository institutions have significantly increased their role in the process during the 1980s.

2. The thrift industry plays a key role in the U.S. financial system as the major supplier of mortgage credit. The past two decades have witnessed a deterioration in the condition of the thrift industry that reached massive dimensions by the mid-1980s.

3. The Financial Institutions Reform, Recovery, and Enforcement Act of 1989 was designed to deal with the thrift problem. The act reorganized thrift regulatory agencies and made a number of other important changes that will be discussed in Chapter 14.

4. Nonbank nondepository financial institutions play a relatively minor role in the money supply process; however, they represent a major conduit for the transfer of funds from SUs to DUs.

5. Government agencies also play a role in the financial system. They are primarily concerned with encouraging the flow of mortgage and agricultural credit.

Key Terms

Bank Insurance Fund

Credit union

Disintermediation

Explicit versus implicit interest payments

Federal agencies and the financial system

Federal Home Loan Bank Board (FHLBB)

Federal Savings and Loan Insurance Corporation (FSLIC)

Finance companies

Financial Institutions Reform, Recovery and Enforcement Act of 1989 (FIRREA)

Insurance companies

Money market mutual funds (MMMFs)

National Credit Union Administration

Nonbank nondepository financial institutions

Office of Thrift Supervision (OTS)

Savings and loan association (S&L)

Savings Association Insurance Fund (SAIF)

Savings bank

Questions

1. Make a list of the types of financial institutions you come in contact with during the year.

2. Why did money market mutual funds decline in 1983 and why have they reestablished some of their pre–October 1982 growth?

3. Virtually all financial institutions hold some government securities in their asset portfolio. Why?

4. What are the major differences between banks and nonbank depository institutions?

5. How did FIRREA change the S&L regulatory structure?

6. How do credit unions differ from the other nonbank depository institutions? How do credit unions differ from banks?

7. Do thrifts and credit unions have the same access to the Federal Reserve's discount window as do banks?

Suggested Readings

1. American Council of Life Insurance, *Life Insurance Fact Book* (Washington, D.C., published annually). Source of information on life insurance companies.

2. Andrew S. Carron, *The Plight of the Thrift Institutions* and *The Rescue of the Thrift Industry* (Washington, D.C.: Brookings Institution, 1982 and 1983, respectively). Discusses problems faced by the thrift industry in the 1970s and early 1980s.

3. Timothy Q. Cook and Jermy G. Duffield, "Money Market Mutual Funds," *Economic Review*, Federal Reserve Bank of Richmond (July–August 1979), 15–31. The evolution of money market mutual funds.

4. Alice H. Munnel, *The Economies of Private Pensions* (Washington, D.C.: Brookings Institution, 1982).

5. Douglas K. Pearce, "Recent Developments in the Credit Union Industry," *Economic Review*, Federal Reserve Bank of Kansas City (June 1984), 3–19.

6. Harvey Rosenblum and Christine Pavel, "Financial Services in Transition: The Effects of Nonbank Competition," in Richard C. Aspinwall and Robert A. Eisenbeis (eds.), *Handbook for Banking Strategy* (New York: John Wiley, 1985).

CHAPTER 10

The Money Supply Process

Chapter Overview

Changes in the money supply play an important role in determining the state of the economy in both the short and long run. In the short run, changes in the money supply influence both prices and real output while in the long run, changes in the money supply have the greatest impact on the price level. Monetary policy is ultimately concerned with the level and changes in the level of the money supply irrespective of whatever operating procedure the central bank chooses to conduct monetary policy.

There has been much discussion during the past decade about the suitability of the money supply as a focus of monetary policy or as an indicator of monetary policy. Some observers argue that deregulation and financial innovation have made it more difficult to pursue a money-focused monetary policy. They claim that it is becoming more difficult to define a set of financial assets as money (unit of account, medium of exchange, and store of value) or to control this set of assets in a deregulated environment constantly subject to financial innovation.

It is premature to argue that the money supply is no longer important in the conduct of monetary policy. While it may be more difficult to focus on a specific money supply measure, evidence from the experiences of the United States and a number of other countries strongly suggests that the behavior of the money supply remains important to the performance of the economy. Central banks that achieve a low variation and noninflationary monetary growth have a more stable macroeconomic environment than countries that permit wide variations in money supply growth or permit inflationary money supply growth to persist over long periods of time.

This chapter lays out the basic elements of the money supply process. The money supply is the outcome of the actions of three groups: the public, the depository institutions, and the Federal Reserve. Of the three, the Federal Reserve plays the most critical role because it has the power to offset or reinforce the actions of the public and/or depository institutions to determine a given growth path of the money supply. The Federal Reserve cannot achieve accurate control of the money supply on a week-to-week basis or even a month-to-month basis, but as the period of time lengthens, the ability of the Federal Reserve to control money increases.

The chapter first approaches the money supply process in the most simplistic form possible to motivate the basic idea and then progressively makes the framework more realistic.

Depository Institutions and the Money Supply Process

Depository institutions play a unique role in the financial system. First, they represent a significant part of the flow of funds in the financial system. Second they play a major role in the money supply process. The liabilities of depository institutions classified as transaction deposits represent the major part of the money supply.

Transaction deposits include demand deposits and "other checkable deposits" (NOW accounts, ATS accounts, and share draft accounts). The various types of transaction deposits are not perfect substitutes for each other; however, as far as reserve requirements are concerned, the Federal Reserve regards all transaction accounts as subject to the same fractional reserve requirement.

Depository institutions have the ability to destroy and create money because their transaction deposits are subject to a *fractional* reserve requirement. This means that, for every dollar of reserves, depository institutions can support several dollars of transaction deposits; for example, if depository institutions held $1 million in reserves and the reserve requirement equaled 20% of total transaction deposits, depository institutions collectively could support $5 million in transaction deposits. Conversely, if for some reason the depository institutions lost $1 million in reserves, the depository institutions collectively would have to destroy $5 million of deposits.

Transaction deposits are created or destroyed during the lending-investment activities of depository institutions. To illustrate, assume that a bank makes a $1,000 loan. The transfer of funds to the borrower can occur in many forms; however, they can all be represented by the establishment of a $1,000 transaction deposit in the borrower's name with permission to use the funds for the specific purposes of the loan. Thus the $1,000 loan is represented by the creation of a $1,000 transaction deposit, and, given that the banking system operates on a fractional reserve system, one dollar of reserves will support several dollars of loans and, hence, transaction deposits. The outcome is the same if the bank purchased a security, that is, made a financial investment. A $1,000 security purchase by the bank is paid for by setting up a $1,000 transaction deposit in the name of the seller. Again, one dollar of reserves will allow the purchase of several dollars of securities and hence transaction deposit creation.

The reverse process of destroying transaction deposits during the lending and investment process can also be illustrated with the bank example. Assume that the individual who originally borrowed the $1,000 pays off the loan by drawing down the transaction deposit (at the same bank, other bank, or nonbank depository institution). If the bank does not make a new loan to replace the paid-off loan, then transaction deposits have been lowered permanently by $1,000. Likewise, in the case of financial investment activity, if the bank sells a security for $1,000 and holds onto the funds, transaction deposits are destroyed in the process.

Basic Outline and Assumptions
of the Process

The multiple expansion and contraction of transaction deposits by depository institutions is based on three interacting components: (1) the depository institutions and the fractional reserve requirement system; (2) the Federal Reserve, as the determinant of the *monetary base,* which starts or stops the money supply process; and (3) the public's decision to hold transaction deposits, currency, and nonpersonal deposits.

The monetary base is defined as reserves held by depository institutions (reserve balances as the Federal Reserve and vault cash) and currency held by the public. Every dollar of the monetary base held by depository institutions (reserve deposits at the Federal Reserve and vault cash) is capable of supporting several dollars of transaction deposits because of the fractional reserve system. In addition, every dollar of the monetary base held by the public as currency is capable of supporting several dollars of deposits if that currency is deposited into institutions. The monetary base is also referred to as *high-powered money* because every dollar of the monetary base can support several dollars of transaction deposits and, hence, the money supply.

The ability of depository institutions to expand and contract money depends on the level of the monetary base provided by the Federal Reserve and reserve requirements. Increases (decreases) in the monetary base generate lending and investment decisions on the part of depository institutions that will increase (decrease) the money supply.

We describe the process first by taking the most restrictive and unrealistic set of assumptions to highlight the nature of the expansion and contraction process. Then we will relax the restrictions one by one to obtain an increasingly realistic view of how the money supply is determined today. The discussion will also deal with increases in the money supply, although the analysis can be used just as easily to deal with decreases in the money supply.

The following restrictions are imposed for a clear understanding of the expansion process:

1. There is only one depository institution, with all the individual entities controlled by one management and ownership; that is, there is one monopoly depository institution in the United States.[1]

2. The public does not change its holdings of currency during the expansion process; that is, the public does not withdraw deposits from the depository institutions in the form of currency.

3. The public does not change its holdings of nonpersonal deposits and other nontransaction deposits subject to a reserve requirement during the expansion process.

4. The depository institutions do not change their desire to hold excess reserves during the process. In other words, depository institutions loan out all available funds during the expansion process and thus desire to be "loaned up."

---

[1] There are about 33,000 depository institutions in the United States counting banks, S&Ls, savings banks, and credit unions.

These restrictive assumptions will be relaxed to obtain a full view of how the money supply is determined; however, they eliminate some of the complexities while providing a view of the basic nature of the expansion of transaction deposits and the money supply.

Case 1: Monopoly Depository Institution, No Changes in Currency in Circulation, No Changes in Nonpersonal Deposits, Depository Institutions Desire to Be Loaned Up

Let us assume that the Federal Reserve purchases a $1,000 bond from Joe Hickenluper by writing out a check payable to Joe Hickenluper for $1000. Do not be too concerned at this point about how the Federal Reserve got the $1,000. Joe Hickenluper deposits the check in the depository institution, referred to as the Monopoly Bank.

The uses and sources statement for the depository institution would appear as

Monopoly Bank

Assets	Liabilities

Cash items in process of collection
    + $1,000
	Transaction deposits
	    + $1,000

The depository institution adds the $1,000 to the account of Joe Hickenluper and increases its "cash items in process of collection." When the check is presented to the Federal Reserve, the Federal Reserve simply makes a bookkeeping entry to indicate that the depository institution now has an additional $1,000 of reserves. The change in the depository institution's reserves will be indicated on the uses and sources statement as

Monopoly Bank

Assets	Liabilities

Reserves
    + $1,000
Cash items in process of collection
    + $1,000
    − $1,000
	Transaction deposits
	    + $1,000

The depository institution has $1,000 of reserves that earn no interest income but is required only to maintain a fractional reserve of, say, 20%. Thus, of the $1,000 of reserves, $200 represent required reserves and $800 represent excess reserves. Depository institutions are in the business to make money. They do not make money by holding large sums of reserves that earn no interest income, so keeping large reserve balances above the legal reserve requirement is not a profitable use of funds.

The depository institution can do one of two things with its excess reserves. It can purchase a debt I.O.U. in the financial market such as a Treasury bill. Or, what is more likely, it can use the excess funds to make a business or consumer loan. It makes no difference in terms of the ultimate expansion process if the depository institution expands its financial investments or its loans. Assuming that the depository institution makes consumer loans, it has to decide on the form of the loan granted and how much should be loaned. Any expansion of credit by the depository institution can be represented as the creation of transaction deposit accounts. That is, if a depository institution makes a loan of $1,000 to a customer, the depository institution does not hand over the $1,000 in the form of currency; rather, it sets up a transaction deposit account for the customer in the amount of $1,000. In effect, the depository institution says to the customer, "You now have a checking account of $1,000 that can be used for the specific purpose of the loan."

How much can the depository institution expand loans and transaction deposit accounts? Initially, one would say that the depository institution can lend out the $800 in excess reserve, in which case, the uses and sources statement would appear as

Monopoly Bank

Assets		Liabilities	
Reserves	+ $1,000	Transaction deposits	+ $1,000
Loans	+ $800		+ $800

But the depository institution still has excess reserves in the amount of $640, as total deposit liabilities have increased only to $1,800 and the reserve requirement is 20%: required reserves = $1,800(0.20) = $360.

To determine the total amount of loans the depository institution can create, we would have to know how much total transaction deposits would have to be for the entire $1,000 in the reserve account to become required reserves. If the reserve requirement is 20%, the largest possible level of total transaction deposits would be $5,000. This includes the original increase in the transaction deposits when Hickenluper deposited the $1,000 check drawn on the Federal Reserve. This could be accomplished by making loans totaling $4,000.

Monopoly Bank

Assets		Liabilities	
Reserves	+ $1,000	Transaction deposits	+ $1,000
Loans	+ $4,000		+ $4,000

The depository institution is fully "loaned up"; that is, excess reserves are zero since the institution has no desire to hold any excess reserves. Is there any chance that the transaction deposits will be withdrawn in the form of currency? No. We assumed that there are no changes in currency in circulation as a result of the expansion process. What about transaction deposits being transferred from one depository institution to another as the proceeds of the loan are spent by the borrower? By assuming a monopoly depository institution with many branches, there is no change in the total uses and sources statement as the deposits will stay within the depository institution even though they may change ownership among its customers.

TABLE 10-1 Symbols used to explain the expansion and contraction of the money supply

Symbol	Definition
1. B	Monetary base determined essentially by the Federal Reserve
2. T	Transaction deposits
3. C	Currency in circulation held by the public
4. M	M1 money supply, defined as $C + T$
5. E	Desired excess reserves held by depository institutions in the form of vault cash or reserve deposits at the Federal Reserve
6. N	Nonpersonal or nontransaction deposits
7. rt	Reserve requirement for transaction deposits
8. rn	Reserve requirement for nonpersonal or nontransaction deposits
9. KT	Ultimate change in T as a result of a change in B or the transaction deposit multiplier: $(KT = \Delta T/\Delta B$ or $\Delta T = KT \cdot \Delta B)$
10. KC	Ultimate change in C as a result of a change in B or the currency multiplier: $(KC = \Delta C/\Delta B$ or $\Delta C = KC \cdot \Delta B)$
11. KM	Ultimate change in M as a result of a change in B or the money multiplier: $(KM = \Delta M/\Delta B$ or $\Delta M = KM \cdot \Delta B)$
12. k	Change in C as a result of a change in T: $(k = \Delta C/\Delta T$ or $\Delta C = k \cdot \Delta T)$
13. n	Change in N as a result of a change in T: $(n = \Delta N/\Delta T$ or $\Delta N = n \cdot \Delta T)$
14. e	Change in E as a result of a change in T: $(e = \Delta E/\Delta T$ or $\Delta E = e \cdot \Delta T)$

What is important about this example is the original change in the monetary base by $1,000 and the ultimate multiple expansion in transaction deposits. The base can change in many ways, but, once the base changes, the depository institution finds itself with too much liquidity. As a result, the depository institution expands lending until the entire increase in the base is required as a reserve behind transaction deposits. A multiple expansion in the money supply has occurred. The original $1,000 increase in the monetary base resulted in a $5,000 increase in transaction deposits and, hence, the money supply.

T-accounts can be used to illustrate the expansion process for simple cases with restrictive assumptions; however, as we relax the restrictions and come close to reality, the T-accounts become too cumbersome and impractical. Thus we are forced to use symbols. Table 10-1 summarizes the most important symbols we will be using.

To develop a framework for understanding the expansion process, we ask two questions, the answers to which will aid in developing expressions that tell us the total effect of changes in the monetary base on the total money supply and various components of the money supply: What starts the multiple expansion process? and What stops the multiple expansion process? The answer to the first question is always the same regardless of the set of restrictive assumptions: the change in the monetary base always starts the process, although the base can change for a number of reasons. The answer to the second question depends on the set of respective assumptions made about the money supply process.

Case I: In Symbols

What starts the process? The change in the base, ΔB, of \$1,000. Why the base changed makes no difference to the analysis. What will stop the expansion of lending and transaction deposits by the depository institution? When the base is no longer available to support any further expansion in depository institution lending. Under the set of restrictive assumptions for this case, the only item that will absorb the base is the increase in required reserves as transaction deposits expand.

To determine the ultimate change in transaction deposits as a result of the change in the base, we solve the following, which defines the ending point of the process by setting the base equal to the factors that absorb the base:

$$\Delta B = rt \cdot \Delta T$$

$$\Delta T = \frac{1}{rt} \cdot \Delta B \tag{1}$$

$$\frac{\Delta T}{\Delta B} = \frac{1}{rt}$$

$$KT = \frac{\Delta T}{\Delta B} = \frac{1}{rt}$$

(The dot between two terms means that the first term is multiplied by the second; that is, $rt \cdot \Delta T$ means that rt is multiplied by ΔT.)

We thus have a special expression for determining the total change in transaction deposits as a result of any change in the base for any given reserve requirement. KT, the transaction deposit multiplier, is a number that indicates the ultimate change in transaction deposits as a result of a change in the base given the reserve requirement. For example, in the case of the monopoly depository institution, the reserve requirement on transaction deposits is 20%; thus $KT = 1/0.20 = 5.0$. That is, transaction deposits will change by 5 times the amount of the change in the base, $\Delta T = KT \cdot \Delta B = 5(\$1,000)$. If the base is increased by \$1,000, transaction deposits would eventually expand by \$5,000. The expression for KT is general and can be used for any assumed reserve requirement or change in the base. There are no changes in currency in circulation, so the change in transaction deposits results in the same change in the money supply.

We can also obtain an expression to show how much the money supply will change as a result of a change in the base. The money supply is defined as currency and transaction deposits, so changes in the money supply equal the sum of the changes in currency in circulation and transaction deposits.

$$\Delta M = \Delta T + \Delta C \tag{2}$$

We can express the money multiplier, KM, as the total change in the money supply due to a change in the base.

$$
\begin{aligned}
KM = \frac{\Delta M}{\Delta B} &= \frac{\Delta T}{\Delta B} + \frac{\Delta C}{\Delta B} \\
&= KT + KC \\
&= KT + 0 \\
&= \frac{1}{rt}
\end{aligned} \tag{3}
$$

The money multiplier is equal to the transaction deposit multiplier, as we have assumed that changes in currency in circulation do not occur during the process; that is, we assume $\Delta C = 0$, so $KC = 0$. The currency multiplier, defines the ultimate change in currency in circulation due to a change in the base. Both KM and KT depend on the reserve requirement behind transaction deposits. Once we know rt, we can calculate the ultimate change in the money supply and transaction deposits for any change in the base.

Case II: Multiple Depository Institutions, No Changes in Currency in Circulation, No Changes in Nonpersonal Deposits, Depository Institutions Desire to Be Loaned Up

Case I assumed a monopoly system in which all depository institutions were under the same ownership and management. Now we drop this restrictive assumption and deal with the present situation in the United States. The depository institutions are separate from each other, operating under different ownerships and management. We are now dealing with a multiple system, but we will retain the other restrictive assumptions for this case.

Joe Hickenluper has just sold a $1,000 bond to the Federal Reserve and deposits the check in his depository institution, Bank A. The uses and sources statement for Bank A after the Federal Reserve credits Bank A's reserve account will appear as

Bank A

Assets	Liabilities
Reserves +$1,000	Transaction deposits +$1,000

Bank A finds that it now has $800 of excess reserves and must determine the amount of loans that can be expanded while still meeting the reserve requirement. In the monopoly case, loans and transaction deposits could expand by $4,000, at which point the depository institution would be fully loaned up; however, in the case of a single depository institution in a multiple system, this would not be advisable.

If Bank A made loans amounting to $4,000 and created a like amount of transaction deposits, the uses and sources statement would appear as

Bank A

Assets	Liabilities
Reserves +$1,000	Transaction deposits +$1,000
Loans +$4,000	+$4,000

It would appear that Bank A has achieved a profitable position. Loans have expanded by $4,000, and Bank A's reserves of $1,000 meet the legal reserve requirement: $(0.20)\$5,000 = \$1,000$.

However, individuals do not borrow and pay interest simply to keep the money on deposit. The money was borrowed for some specific expenditure purpose such as paying for a car, house, or a new piece of capital equipment. That is, the individual borrowing the $4,000 will write a check and clear out his or her account, and the probability is very high that the check will ultimately be deposited in another depository institution such as Bank B. At that time, Bank B will return the check to Bank A and request that the $4,000 be transferred to the reserve account at Bank B. Unfortunately, Bank A has only $1,000 in reserves and cannot honor the request for funds. Had Bank A lent out the $4,000 originally, then it would have only met its reserve requirement for a short period of time. It would have lost the deposit to another depository institution and then be required to transfer $4,000, which it does not possess. In the monopoly case, it could loan out the $4,000 because the newly created transaction deposit would not leave the depository institution; it would only circulate among different branches of the same institution. In a multiple system, a single depository institution must assume that it will lose newly created transaction deposits to another depository institution.

We come back to the question: In what amount of lending can Bank A safely engage? *A single depository institution in a multiple system can safely lend out no more than the amount of excess reserves because it can lose these excess reserves in the check-clearing process and still meet the legal reserve requirement.* Bank A's excess reserves are $800. If it makes a loan for $800 and creates a transaction deposit in the same amount, the uses and sources statement will appear as

Bank A

Assets		Liabilities	
Reserves	+ $1,000	Transaction deposits	+ $1,000
Loans	+ $800		+ $800

Martha Murgatroyd who borrowed from Bank A uses the transaction deposit of $800 to buy a stereo outfit from a firm that has a deposit account at Bank B. Bank B receives the $800 check, sends the check back to Bank A, which transfers $800 in reserves to Bank B.

Bank B

Assets		Liabilities	
Reserves	+ $800	Transaction deposits	+ $800

Bank A

Assets		Liabilities	
Reserves	+ $1,000	Transaction deposits	+ $1,000
	− $800		+ $800
	+ $200		− $800
			+ $1,000
Loans	+ $800		

Bank A's statement shows that loans had been expanded by $800, but, when the proceeds of the loan have been spent, Bank A's deposit liabilities will decline by $800. In addition, Bank A will need to transfer $800 from its reserve account to Bank B. Bank A's remaining reserves of $200 satisfy the legal reserve requirement.

Bank B now has excess reserves of $640, and, because these reserves yield no income, the bank will desire to lend the excess reserves out as quickly as possible. After Bank B creates a transaction deposit of $640, the funds will be transferred eventually to another depository institution, say, Bank C. Bank C will then have excess reserves of $512 that can be lent out by creating transaction deposits. In fact, the process will continue on to institutions D, E, F, and so on until no more excess reserves are available to lend. Each depository institution through its lending and transaction deposit expansion will contribute to the expansion process:

Depository Institution	Net Change in Transaction Deposits
A	+ $1,000
B	800
C	640
D	512
.	.
.	.
.	+ $5,000

When we total the contributions of each depository institution to the expansion process, we still obtain a total increase in transaction deposits and, hence, the money supply of $5,000 when the reserve requirement is 20%. The only difference between case I and case II is in the process of the expansion. In a multiple system (case II), the process must work through individual depository institutions as each institution creates transaction deposits and loses transaction deposits. But the end result is exactly the same in both cases.

What about the expressions for calculating *KT* and *KM* for case I and case II? The expressions are designed to indicate the change in transaction deposits and money supply that result from a change in the base, and, because the only difference between case I and case II is the process, not the end result, the expressions are the same in both cases.

Case III: Multiple Depository Institutions, No Changes in Nonpersonal Deposits, Depository Institutions Desire to Be Loaned Up, but Changes in Currency in Circulation Are Allowed

As depository institutions expand lending and transaction deposits, a certain amount of currency will be withdrawn from the system. Currency represents about 25% of the total money supply at any point in time, and the withdrawal of a dollar of reserves in the form of currency reduces the system's ability to expand transaction deposits and, hence, the money supply. Assuming that a certain amount of currency will be withdrawn, how do we determine the response of transaction deposits to changes in the monetary base? Again, we start with the same two questions: What starts the process? A change in the base, ΔB. What ends the process? When the base is no longer available to support an expansion in lending. There are now two factors that absorb the base during the process and reduce its availability to support lending. As transaction deposits expand, required reserves expand. And, as transaction deposits expand, some of these deposits will be withdrawn in the form of currency. The base will be absorbed by the change in required reserves for transaction deposits, $rt \cdot \Delta T$, and the change in currency in circulation, ΔC. The process ends when the change in the base that started the process equals the sum of the factors absorbing the base:

$$\Delta B = rt \cdot \Delta T + \Delta C \tag{4}$$

Let us assume that the change in currency in circulation is related directly to the change in transaction deposits, that is, $\Delta C = k \cdot \Delta T$. The symbol k indicates the change in the amount of currency in circulation in response to a change in transaction deposits, or $k = \Delta C / \Delta T$. The k ratio depends on a variety of factors that influence the public's demand for currency. A value of 0.25 for k means that we can expect currency in circulation to increase by $0.25 for every $1.00 increase in transaction deposits. Changes in the total money supply now include the change in transaction deposits and the change in the currency in circulation.

How much will transaction deposits expand as a result of a change in the base? Using the expression for k and substituting into (4), we can write

$$\begin{aligned}
\Delta B &= rt \cdot \Delta T + k \cdot \Delta T \\
\Delta B &= (rt + k) \cdot \Delta T \\
\Delta T &= \frac{1}{rt + k} \cdot \Delta B \\
KT &= \frac{\Delta T}{\Delta B} = \frac{1}{rt + k}
\end{aligned} \tag{5}$$

Thus the value of KT is $1/(rt + k)$. Assuming that $rt = 0.20$ and $k = 0.25$, the value of KT will be 2.22 rather than 5.00 as in cases I and II. Currency withdrawals during the expansion process sharply limit the amount of transaction deposits that depository institutions can support with a given change in the monetary base.

We can determine the ultimate change in currency in circulation and combine this with the ultimate change in transaction deposits to obtain the ultimate change in the money supply as a result of a change in the monetary base. The change in currency in circulation can be found by the following:

$$\begin{aligned}
KC &= \frac{\Delta C}{\Delta B} \\
&= \frac{k \cdot \Delta T}{\Delta B} \\
&= \frac{k}{rt + k}
\end{aligned} \tag{6}$$

The money multiplier is defined as

$$
\begin{aligned}
KM = \frac{\Delta M}{\Delta B} &= \frac{\Delta T}{\Delta B} + \frac{\Delta C}{\Delta B} \\
&= KT + KC \\
&= \frac{1}{rt + k} + \frac{k}{rt + k} \\
&= \frac{1 + k}{rt + k}
\end{aligned}
\tag{7}
$$

We now have expressions for the transaction deposit multiplier, the currency multiplier, and the money supply multiplier, each of which is a number that indicates the total change in transaction deposits, currency in circulation, and the money supply as a result of a change in the monetary base. The multipliers can be calculated once we know the reserve requirement for transaction deposits and the ratio k. For example, with $rt = 0.20$ and $k = 0.25$, the multipliers would be calculated as follows:

$$
KT = \frac{1}{rt + k} = \frac{1}{0.20 + 0.25} = \frac{1}{0.45} = 2.22 \tag{8}
$$

$$
KC = \frac{k}{rt + k} = \frac{0.25}{0.45} = 0.56 \tag{9}
$$

$$
KM = KT + KC = 2.22 + 0.56 = 2.78 \tag{10}
$$

Once we have the values of the multipliers, we can use them to determine the total impact of a change in the base on transaction deposits, currency in circulation, and the money supply:

$$
\Delta T = KT \cdot \Delta B \tag{11}
$$
$$
\Delta C = KC \cdot \Delta B \tag{12}
$$
$$
\Delta M = \Delta T + \Delta C = KM \cdot \Delta B \tag{13}
$$

Case IV: Multiple Depository Institutions, Depository Institutions Desire to Be Loaned Up, but Changes in Currency in Circulation and Nonpersonal Deposits Are Allowed

As depository institutions expand loans and transaction deposits, some individuals will change their holdings of certain managed liabilities that are subject to reserve requirements such as nonpersonal time deposits and Eurodollar deposits. Changes in the public's holding of these managed liabilities will influence the expansion process, because the reserve requirement for these deposits, rn, is less than the reserve requirement for transaction deposits. At present, nonpersonal time deposits and Eurodollars have the same requirement, 3%; however, they may have different requirements in the future. If the two types of managed liabilities have different reserve requirements, then the money supply framework would have to treat each separately. At this time they are equal and we gain simplicity by combining the two separate deposits into one category called nonpersonal or nontransaction reservable deposits, N.

How do nonpersonal deposits behave during the expansion process? We can assume that the public maintains a proportional relationship between its holdings of nonpersonal and transaction deposits. The n ratio can summarize this relationship, where $n = \Delta N/\Delta T$ or $\Delta N = n \cdot \Delta T$. A value of 1.2, for example, means that, if transaction deposits increase by \$1.00, the public's holding of nonpersonal deposits will increase by \$1.20.

How do we calculate the multipliers when nonpersonal deposit holdings change during the expansion process? What starts the process? The process always starts from a change in the base, ΔB. What ends the process? The process ends when the base is no longer available to support lending and transaction deposit creation. In case IV, three factors absorb the base: (1) the change in required reserves behind transaction deposits, (2) the change in currency in circulation, and (3) the change in required reserves behind nonpersonal deposits. When the sum of these factors equals the original change in the base, the expansion process must come to an end. That is, the process stops when

$$\Delta B = rt \cdot \Delta T + k \cdot \Delta T + rn \cdot \Delta N \tag{14}$$

The last term, $rn \cdot \Delta N$, which indicates the change in required reserves behind nonpersonal deposits, can be simplified further by remembering that $\Delta N = n \cdot \Delta T$, so that

$$\Delta B = rt \cdot \Delta T + k \cdot \Delta T + rn \cdot n \cdot \Delta T \tag{15}$$

Expression (15) can be used to solve for the ultimate change in transaction deposits and the value of KT.

$$\Delta B = (rt + k + rn \cdot n) \cdot \Delta T$$
$$\Delta T = \frac{1}{rt + k + rn \cdot n} \cdot \Delta B \tag{16}$$
$$KT = \frac{\Delta T}{\Delta B} = \frac{1}{rt + k + rn \cdot n}$$

Once we have the transaction deposit multiplier, the currency multiplier and money supply multiplier can be derived with ease.

$$KC = \frac{\Delta C}{\Delta B} = \frac{k \cdot T}{\Delta B} = \frac{k}{rt + k + rn \cdot n} \tag{17}$$

$$KM = \frac{\Delta M}{\Delta B} = \frac{\Delta T}{\Delta B} + \frac{\Delta C}{\Delta B} = KT + KC = \frac{1 + k}{rt + k + rn \cdot n} \tag{18}$$

Assuming that $rt = 0.20$, $k = 0.25$, $n = 1.0$, and $rn = 0.05$, we can calculate the values of KT, KC, and KM as follows:

$$KT = \frac{1}{rt + k + rn \cdot n} = \frac{1}{0.20 + 0.25 + (0.05)(1.00)} = \frac{1}{0.50} = 2.00 \tag{19}$$

$$KC = \frac{k}{rt + k + rn \cdot n} = \frac{0.25}{0.50} = 0.50 \tag{20}$$

$$KM = KT + KC = 2.00 + 0.50 = 2.50 \tag{21}$$

Each of these multipliers indicates the total change in transaction deposits, currency, and money supply resulting from a change in the base.

Case V: Multiple Depository Institutions, Changes in Currency in Circulation Allowed, Changes in Nonpersonal Deposits Allowed, and Depository Institutions Change Their Demand for Excess Reserves

This is the most realistic case as it recognizes the ability of depository institutions to make portfolio decisions regarding the amount of liquidity (reserves) they wish to maintain. Of course, institutions must hold reserves behind transaction and other deposits at least equal to the legal requirement, but a depository institution may wish to hold reserves above those required for a period of time.

How can we express the willingness to hold excess reserves? Assume that the willingness of institutions to hold excess reserves is a proportion of its total transaction deposit liabilities. This can be summarized by an e ratio defined as $e = \Delta E/\Delta T$ or $\Delta E = e \cdot \Delta T$. The e ratio will be sensitive to a number of factors and conditions in the financial system, but especially to the going rate of interest. During periods of high rates of interest, depository institutions would like to get as much of their excess reserves as possible out into the financial system in the form of loans and investments, thus lowering the e ratio. During periods of low interest rates, depository institutions may be less willing to loan out all available reserves either because the interest return does not justify the cost of setting up and administering the loan or because depository institutions expect interest rates to increase in the near future. In any case, during periods of low interest rates, the e ratio will be higher than during periods of high interest rates.

To determine how the money supply and its components will respond to a change in the base, we again ask and answer the same two questions: What starts the process? The process always starts from a change in the base. What ends the process? The process ends when the base is no longer available to support lending and transaction deposit creation.

There are now four factors that absorb the base and reduce its availability to support lending: (1) the increase in required reserves for transaction deposits, (2) the increase in currency in circulation, (3) the increase in required reserves for nonpersonal deposits, and (4) the increase in desired excess reserves held by depository institutions. When the sum of these four absorbing factors equals the original change in the base, the expansion process must stop. That is, the process stops when

$$\Delta B = rt \cdot \Delta T + k \cdot \Delta T + rn \cdot n \cdot \Delta T + e \cdot \Delta T \tag{22}$$

and we can determine the ultimate change in transaction deposits, currency, and the money supply.

$$\Delta B = (rt + k + rn \cdot n + e) \cdot \Delta T$$

$$\Delta T = \frac{1}{rt + k + rn \cdot n + e} \cdot \Delta B$$

$$KT = \frac{\Delta T}{\Delta B} = \frac{1}{rt + k + rn \cdot n + e} \tag{23}$$

$$KC = \frac{\Delta C}{\Delta B} = \frac{k \cdot \Delta T}{\Delta B} = \frac{k}{rt + k + rn \cdot n + e} \tag{24}$$

$$KM = KT + KC = \frac{1 + k}{rt + k + rn \cdot n + e} \tag{25}$$

The Multipliers in Summary

The fractional reserve requirement system ensures that a change in the monetary base will lead to changes in lending and transaction deposits that will be a multiple amount of the original change in the base. The ability of the system to expand or contract transaction deposits and, hence, the money supply depends on the assumptions made about the public's desire to hold nonpersonal deposits relative to transaction deposits, the public's desire to hold currency relative to transaction deposits, and the willingness of depository institutions to hold excess reserves.

The transaction deposit, currency, and money multipliers summarize the response of transaction deposits, currency, and money to a change in the base given specific assumptions about the public and depository institutions. The multipliers for the general case allow for currency changes, nonpersonal deposit changes, and the willingness of depository institutions to hold excess reserves. These can be used to determine the total change in transaction deposits, currency in circulation, and the money supply in response to any change in the base.

Let us assume that the base increases by \$1,000 and that the reserve requirements for transaction and nonpersonal deposits are 0.10 and 0.08, respectively. The k, n, and e ratios are 0.20, 0.50, and 0.06, respectively. The three multipliers will then be

$$KT = \frac{1}{rt + k + rn \cdot n + e}$$

$$= \frac{1}{0.10 + 0.20 + (0.08)(0.50) + 0.06} = \frac{1}{0.40} = 2.5 \tag{26}$$

$$KC = \frac{k}{rt + k + rn \cdot n + e} = \frac{0.20}{0.40} = 0.5 \tag{27}$$

$$KM = KT + KC = 2.5 + 0.5 = 3.0 \tag{28}$$

and the change in transaction deposits, currency in circulation, and money can be determined by

$$\Delta T = 2.5 \cdot \Delta B = 2.5(1,000) = \$2,500 \tag{29}$$

$$\Delta C = 0.5 \cdot \Delta B = 0.5(1,000) = 500 \tag{30}$$

$$\Delta M = 3.0 \cdot \Delta B = 3.0(1,000) = 3,000 \tag{31}$$

These are the ultimate changes that will result from the \$1,000 increase in the base, so we should be able to show that the factors absorbing the base total \$1,000 because this is what determines the stopping point of the process. The four absorbing factors are

Change in required reserves for transaction deposits, 0.10(\$2,500)	=	\$ 250
Change in required reserves for nonpersonal deposits, 0.08(0.50)(\$2,500)	=	100
Change in currency in circulation, 0.20(\$2,500)	=	500
Change in excess reserves held by depository institutions, 0.06(\$2,500)	=	150
		\$1,000

Changes in the money supply can be now seen as the result of two factors: (1) the change in the base, ΔB, and (2) the value of the money multiplier, KM. The same relationship can be used to determine the level of the money supply at any point. That is, instead of

$$\Delta M = KM \cdot \Delta B \tag{32}$$

we can just as easily write

$$M = KM \cdot B \tag{33}$$

The level of the base at any point in time along with the value of the money multiplier determines the level of the money supply.

The relationship between the monetary base, the money multiplier, and the money supply reflect the interaction of the three groups that determine the money supply.

1. The Federal Reserve influences the money supply by being able to alter the monetary base and change reserve requirements for transaction and nonpersonal deposits.

2. Depository institutions influence the money supply by lending and investing and in deciding the level of excess reserves they want to maintain.

3. The public influences the money supply by borrowing from depository institutions and deciding on the amount of currency and nonpersonal deposits they wish to hold relative to the transaction deposits.

Although these groups interact together to determine the money supply, the Federal Reserve is the most important of the three. First, the Federal Reserve has considerable control over the level and changes in the level of the monetary base since the Federal Reserve has the ability to offset or reinforce changes in the base independent of Federal Reserve actions. Second, control over the base would be of little importance if the money multiplier were unstable and changed radically over time. The Federal Reserve does not control the values of k, n, or e, which significantly influence the value of KM. Actual estimates of the multiplier, however, indicate that it is stable enough for the Federal Reserve to achieve monetary control if it so desires. Figures 10-1, 10-2, and 10-3 provide information on the Federal Reserve's ability to control the M1 money supply.

Figure 10-1 presents the quarterly values of the M1 money supply and a measure of the monetary base. There appears to be a reasonably close relationship between the level of M1 and the monetary base over the period from 1980 through 1988. Figure 10-2 presents M1 and the monetary base in terms of annualized quarterly growth rates, and again, there appears to be a fairly close relationship between the two variable. In this case, however, the relationship is not as close as is suggested by Figure 10-1. This is because the levels of the variables in Figure 10-1 are dominated by trend movements whereas the growth rates abstract from the trend and reveal greater period-to-period movements.

Figure 10-3 presents the estimated value of the M1 money multiplier and suggests that it is less than completely stable. The average value for the 1980–1988

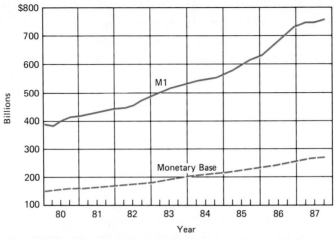

Source: Based on data from Citicorp Database Services. The monetary base illustrated has been adjusted for changes in reserve requirements and, thus, is not exactly the same as the monetary base discussed in the chapter. At the same time, the reserve requirement adjustment is relatively small.

FIGURE 10-1 **The Ml money supply and the monetary base, first quarter 1980–fourth quarter 1988.**

period was 2.68; however, the multiplier ranged from a low of 2.55 to a high of 2.88. Even small changes in *KM*, however, can generate large changes in the money supply.

What does all this mean in terms of the Federal Reserve's ability to control money? The Federal Reserve's ability to determine the monetary base, the fact that movements in the monetary base dominate movements in the money supply, and the

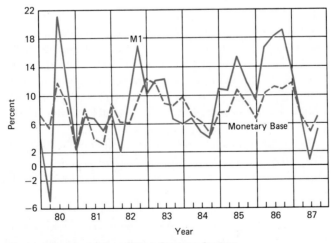

Source: Based on data from Citicorp Database Services.

FIGURE 10-2 **Annualized growth of Ml and the monetary base, first quarter 1980–fourth quarter 1988.**

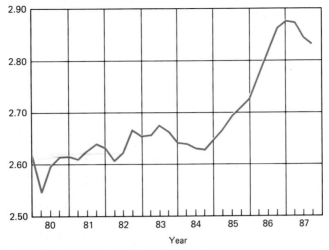

Source: Based on data from Citicorp Database Services.

FIGURE 10-3 The M1 multiplier, first quarter 1980–fourth quarter 1987

ability to predict values of the multiplier with a reasonable degree of error all suggest that the Federal Reserve can control the money supply. The Federal Reserve's control, however, is weakest for weekly and monthly changes in the money supply, but, for longer periods such as quarterly or biannually, the Federal Reserve has considerable control over the money supply if it so chooses.

Decreases in Money as Opposed to Increases, and Investments as Opposed to Loans

The multipliers have been discussed in the context of expansions in the monetary base and corresponding expansion in transaction deposits, currency, and the money supply. In addition, we have assumed that depository institutions adjust to changes in the monetary base by expanding loans. The multiplier expressions derived above are in no way dependent on either of these conditions.

A decrease in the monetary base will lead to a decrease in transaction deposits, currency, and the money supply according to the value of the multipliers. For example, if the base declined by $1,000 in the example on page 224, transaction deposits, currency and the money supply would have ultimately declined by $2,500, $500, and $3,000, respectively. Depository institutions contract deposits by reducing outstanding loans.

Likewise, it makes no difference to the ultimate change in transaction deposits, currency, and the money supply whether the depository institutions change their

BOX 1   The *k*, *n*, and *e* ratios in reality

The chapter has adopted a simple approach to incorporate the behavior of currency, nonpersonal deposits, and desired excess reserves by making them dependent on transaction deposits. This permits us to focus on the essential foundation of the money supply process and keeps the algebra straightforward. At the same time, the behavior of these variables is the outcome of a complex set of economic forces that cannot be so easily represented. In fact, it is the difficulty of predicting the behavior of *k*, *n*, and *e* that makes it difficult to determine the value of the money multiplier for monetary policy purposes. Let us consider some of the economic forces that influence these ratios.

Currency held by the public   The amount of currency held by the public relative to checkable deposits will depend on such things as interest rates, use of credit cards, development of electronic banking, perceived risk to one's person, and considerations related to concealing transactions from governmental authorities.

Other things held constant, higher interest rates will provide incentives to the public to hold a smaller amount of currency since currency earns no interest while transaction deposits earn interest with the exception of demand deposits.

The greater the use of credit cards in financing every-day transactions, the smaller the amount of currency relative to deposits. Likewise, the expanded use and acceptability of electronic banking such as ATMs provides incentives for the public to hold a smaller amount of currency relative to transaction deposits.

Currency is a risky way to hold monetary wealth since it is difficult to insure against loss or theft. Thus, as crime becomes a more important concern to individuals and as the perceived risk to one's person increases, there exists a greater incentive to hold less currency relative to deposits.

Given these forces one would expect the amount of currency relative to checkable deposits to decline over time; however, the opposite has been the case. Figure 1B presents the ratio of currency to checkable deposits over the period from 1961 through 1988 along with the three-month Treasury bill rate. The figure suggests that currency relative to deposits has increased despite higher interest rates and other changes occurring in the economy that would tend to reduce the incentive for holding currency.

This persistent increase in the relative role of currency suggests to many observers that it reflects the growth of the *underground economy* relative to reported transactions.

In the late 1970s a number of investigators used the currency-deposit ratio to estimate the size of the underground economy based on the reasonable hypothesis that currency is a preferable medium of exchange for those interested in concealing their legal transac-

tions from the Internal Revenue Services and to those concealing their illegal transactions from the IRS and the police. The tax evasion incentive became particularly strong in the 1970s as inflation pushed households and businesses into higher tax brackets since the tax brackets were not adjusted to the inflation rate. Several investigators suggested that the underground economy ranged from 10% to 20% of GNP in any given year and that the underground economy had steadily grown during the post–World War II period. Others criticized the methodology of these studies and argued that the currency-deposit ratio could not be so easily interpreted nor was the underground economy nearly as large.

The debate is conveniently summarized by Norman N. Bowsher.[1] Bowsher concluded that all the studies were subject to problems and that while the currency-deposit ratio could not easily be used to derive an indirect estimate of the size of the underground economy, "the persistent expansion in currency outstanding at a time of strong incentives to avoid reporting could indicate that unreported activities have been expanding faster than economic activity generally."

The decline in the currency-deposit ratio after 1980 is consistent with the slowdown in the inflation rate; the lower personal tax rates resulting from the Tax Reform Act of 1981 and the introduction of indexing the tax brackets after 1985.

Nonpersonal Deposits   Nonpersonal deposits relative to checkable deposits have generally increased over time as a result of higher interest rates. Figure 2B, for example, presents the ratio of the sum of overnight RPs, Eurodollar deposits, and large CDs to checkable deposits over the 1961–1988 period. This is a close approximation to the *n* ratio used in the chapter and shows that nonpersonal deposits vary with the interest rate. The ratio has tended to increase over time with interest rates.

Desired Excess Reserves   Depository institutions have a demand for excess reserves. Even though excess reserves are based on the legal distinction between total and required reserves, depository institutions possess a well-defined demand for excess reserves. The level of the interest rate and anticipated movements in future interest rates play a role in determining the level of desired excess reserves. Figure 3B, for example, presents the excess reserve–transaction deposit ratio and the Treasury bill rate over the 1961–1988 period and suggests an inverse relationship. The higher the interest rate, the lower the level of excess reserves held by depository institutions.

[1] Norman N. Bowsher, "The Demand for Currency: Is the Underground Economy Undermining Monetary Policy?" *Review*, Federal Reserve Bank of St. Louis (January 1980), 11–17.

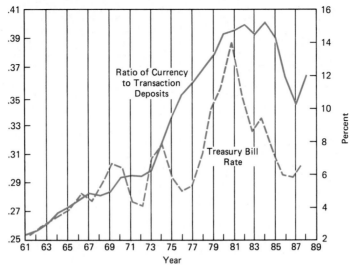

Source: Business Statistics, 1986, and *Survey of Current Business*, Department of Commerce, and Citibase Data Services.

FIGURE 1B   Ratio of currency to transaction deposits and the three-month Treasury bill rate, 1961–1988

loans or financial investments. If a depository institution uses the monetary base to purchase financial assets in the money and capital markets, transaction deposits will be created in the process. For example, when a depository institution purchases a bond for $1,000 with a check drawn on itself, a transaction deposit account would be established when the seller of the bond deposits the check in their depository institution.

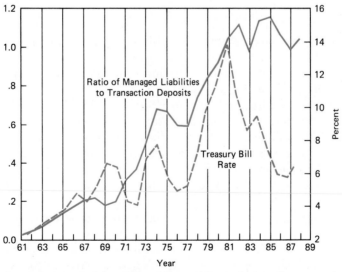

Source: Business Statistics, 1986, and *Survey of Current Business*, Department of Commerce, and Citibase Data Services.

FIGURE 2B   Ratio of nontransaction deposits (Eurodollar deposits and large CDs) to transaction deposits and the three-month Treasury bill rate, 1961–1988

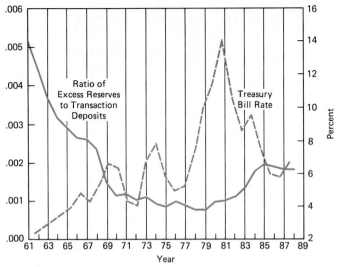

Source: *Business Statistics, 1986*, and *Survey of Current Business*, Department of Commerce, and Citicorp Database Services.

FIGURE 3B   Ratio of excess reserves held by depository institutions to transaction deposits and the three-month Treasury bill rate, 1961–1988

The Money Multiplier for Broader Measures of Money

So far we have focused the entire discussion on the money supply defined as M1 since we defined $M = C + T$, where T represented transaction deposits. What about the multiplier for a broader definition of the money supply? No problem—a little algebra is all that is needed. The basic concept of the money multiplier remains intact. The money supply, no matter how defined in a fractional reserve system, will be a multiple of the monetary base. In addition, the money supply no matter how defined will be the outcome of the actions of the public, the depository institutions, and the Federal Reserve with the Federal Reserve being the ultimate determinant.

To illustrate, let us derive the money multiplier for a broader measure of money. Define changes in a broader measure of money as

$$\Delta M' = \Delta C + \Delta T + \Delta N \tag{34}$$

where we now consider nonpersonal accounts as part of the money supply and we denote money as M' to distinguish from the M1 measure used in the chapter. The broader money multiplier is now defined as

$$KM' = KC + KT + KN \tag{35}$$

The values for *KC* and *KT* have already been derived for the most general case, and the value for *KN* can likewise be determined.

$$KN = \frac{\Delta N}{\Delta B} \qquad (36)$$

Remembering that $N = n \cdot \Delta T$, *KN* is then

$$KN = \frac{n}{(rt + k + rn \cdot n + e)} \qquad (37)$$

Thus, the broader money multiplier is

$$KM' = \frac{1 + k + n}{(rt + k + rn \cdot n + e)} \qquad (38)$$

KM' is obviously larger than *KM* derived above since the money supply is more broadly defined.

We could derive a multiplier for an even broader measure of the money supply for such as the following:

$$\Delta M'' = \Delta C + \Delta T + \Delta N + \Delta S + \Delta MMDA + \Delta MMMF \qquad (39)$$

where ΔS represents changes in regular time and savings deposits, $\Delta MMDA$ represents changes in money market deposit accounts, and $\Delta MMMF$ represents changes in money market mutual funds. Under the present reserve requirement system, there are no reserve requirements for *S*, *MMDA*, or *MMMF*. To incorporate them into the money multiplier framework, however, we need to assume some type of relationship to explain their behavior as we did for *C*, *N*, and *E*. We can assume that changes in *S*, *MMDA*, and *MMMF* are related to changes in transaction deposits by the following:

$$\Delta S = s \cdot \Delta T \qquad (40)$$

$$\Delta MMDA = md \cdot \Delta T \qquad (41)$$

$$\Delta MMMF = mf \cdot \Delta T \qquad (42)$$

Using these ratios, we can derive the money multiplier, *KM''*, for the broader measure of the money supply

$$KM'' = \frac{(1 + k + n + s + md + mf)}{(rt + k + rn \cdot n + e)}$$

Key Points

1. Depository institutions can create and destroy money because (a) transaction deposits represent about three-fourths of the money supply and (b) institutions operate on a fractional reserve system so that changes in the monetary base lead to multiple changes in transaction deposits and, hence, the money supply.

2. The multiple expansion and contraction process of the money supply is summarized by the expressions for *KT*, *KC*, and *KM*. Although we developed these expressions for various assumptions, the most important set of expressions are those for case V. Case V allows for realistic complications in how money, transaction deposits, and currency respond to changes in the monetary base.

3. The money multiplier and the monetary base reflect the role played by depository institu-

tions, the Federal Reserve, and the public in determining the level and changes in the level of the money supply. The Federal Reserve, however, should be considered the most important determinant of the money supply.

4. The expressions for *KT*, *KC*, and *KM* were developed in terms of the monetary base. The monetary base is equal to the sum of reserves held by depository institutions and currency held by the public and is considered to be a useful reserve measure for purposes of monetary policy. The Federal Reserve has considerable control over the monetary base.

5. The various multipliers were derived for the M1 measure of the money supply as currency plus transactions deposits. Multipliers can also be derived from broader measures of the money supply.

Key Terms

Currency multiplier, *KC*

Desired excess reserves, *E*

e ratio

Fractional reserve system

High-powered money, *B*

k ratio

Monetary base, *B*

Money multiplier, *KM*

Money multipliers for broader measures of the money supply, *KM'* and *KM''*

n ratio

Nonpersonal deposit multiplier, *KN*

Reserve requirement for transaction deposits, *rt*

Reserve requirement for nonpersonal or nontransaction deposits, *rn*

Transactions deposit multiplier, *KT*

Questions

1. We have developed money supply expressions assuming that depository institutions and the public react to an increase in the base. Outline what will happen if there is a decrease in the base.

2. If the government decided tomorrow to allow all depository institutions to hold and accept demand deposits, what effect would this have on the money multiplier?

3. We have made simple assumptions about the k, n, and e ratios and assumed that currency, nonpersonal deposits, and desired excess reserves are proportional to transaction deposits. What more realistic assumptions could be made about the determinants of k, n, and e?

4. Why is it important for purposes of monetary policy to derive a money multiplier expression in terms of a base that the Federal Reserve can control with some degree of accuracy?

5. Bankers and others often argue that they do not create or destroy money, they merely lend out the funds that have been deposited with them by their customers. We know that this is not true for the entire system. To what extent is it true for an individual depository institution in a multiple system?

6. Given the following information—10% reserve requirement on transactions deposits, 4% reserve requirement on nonpersonal deposits, desired excess reserves increase $0.03 for each $1.00, nontransaction deposits increase $0.50 for each $1.00 increase in transactions deposits, currency in circulation increases $0.10 cents for each $1.00 increase in transactions deposits— calculate the value of the M1 money multiplier.

7. Given the information in question 6, calculate the change in desired excess reserves resulting from a change in the monetary base of $1 million.

8. Given the information in question 6, calculate the change in transaction deposits resulting from a change in the monetary base of $1 million.

9. Given the information in question 6, calculate the change in required reserves for nontransaction deposits resulting from a change in the monetary base of $1 million.

Suggested Readings

1. N. N. Bowsher, "The Demand for Currency: Is the Underground Economy Undermining Monetary Policy?" *Review*, Federal Reserve Bank of St. Louis (January 1980), 11–17. Discusses factors related to the underground economy that influence the k ratio.

2. Albert E. Burger, *The Money Supply Process* (Belmont, Calif.: Wadsworth, 1971). Detailed derivation of the money multipliers.

3. Phillip Cagan, *Determinants and Effects of Changes in the Stock of Money, 1875–1960* (New York: Columbia University Press, 1965). Studies the various components of the money stock from a historical perspective.

4. R. W. Hafer, Scott E. Hein, and Clemens J. M. Kool, "Forecasting the Money Multiplier: Implications for Money Stock Control and Economic Activity," *Review*, Federal Reserve Bank of St. Louis (October 1983), 22–33. Problems in forecasting money multipliers after the start of deregulation.

5. Michelle R. Garfinkel and Daniel L. Thornton. "The Link Between M1 and the Monetary Base in the 1980s," *Review*, Federal Reserve Bank of St. Louis (September/October 1989), 35-52. Discusses the impact of deregulation and innovation on the relationship between M1 and the monetary base.

PART III

Financial Regulation, the Transition of Finance, Major Changes in Financial Regulation in 1979 and the 1980s, and Evaluation of the Regulatory Changes

The Regulation of Financial Markets and Institutions: General Principles and Historical Perspective

Chapter Overview

This chapter discusses the rationale for government financial regulation, the evolution of government regulation, the influence of the Great Depression of the 1930s on the development of regulation, and the main regulatory agencies and the forms of government regulation. As in previous chapters, we are more concerned with an overview than with a detailed presentation. The material in this chapter serves as a starting point for our discussion of deregulation and recent changes in the financial system.

The complexity of the financial system is matched by the complexity of financial regulation. The extensive amount of financial regulation in the United States is a relatively recent event having emerged from the financial reforms passed in the wake of the banking collapse in the 1930s. Financial regulation itself was not extensive or complex compared to current standards for most of the U.S. financial history prior to the Great Depression of the 1930s. The Great Depression, however, was a major turning point in the evolution of government involvement in the financial system in particular and the economy in general.

The Basic Rationale of Government Regulation

The rationale for government regulation of the financial system is fundamentally related to the natural evolution of monetary systems over time. This does not explain all aspects of government regulation or account for all rationales, especially in a complex financial system such as in the United States; however, it does provide the foundation rationale.

The first monetary systems to evolve were *commodity based*; that is, some commodity such as gold or silver circulated as the medium of exchange and served as a unit of account and store of wealth. These types of monetary standards required no government intervention in principle, though governments often assumed the role of minting and guaranteeing weight of the commodity money. Commodity-based systems, however, had a number of disadvantages. They were resource using in the sense that the commodity used as money had an opportunity cost since its use as money precluded its use in other forms. Additionally, society devoted considerable resources to supplying the commodity money, which themselves had an opportunity cost. Most important, there was no reliable mechanism for ensuring that an adequate supply of the commodity money would be available over time to meet the needs of a growing economy. In the case of a gold standard, for example, the supply of the commodity money depended as much on random change as it did on determined human effort.

Monetary systems next evolved to *representative commodity* standards in which individuals found it advantageous to store their commodity money with specialized warehouse-type institutions. The receipts or *promises to pay* issued by these institutions were backed 100% by the commodity money. As the public began to regard the promises to pay as redeemable at any time into commodity money, the public found it more advantageous to use the promises to pay rather than the actual commodity as money—the promises to pay required less effort to use than actual gold or silver and were not subject to the same wear and tear from exchange as commodities. A typical warehouse institution's balance sheet might appear as

Hickenlupper's Warehouse

Assets	Liabilities

Commodity money
    + $1 million
	Promises to pay
	    + $1 million

The institution earned income chiefly by providing storage services for the commodity money, and the more its I.O.U.s circulated, the more likely it would receive additional deposits of commodity money for safekeeping. The representative standard offered a few advantages over the commodity standard; however, it was essentially a commodity standard.

At this point in the evolution of the monetary system, a fundamentally important innovation occurred. The longer the institution remained in business, an important fact became clear. Only a small percentage of the promises to pay were actually presented for redemption into commodity money—as long as the institution was able to redeem those I.O.U.s that were presented, the public was willing to keep using the promises to pay as a medium of exchange. The warehouse institution at this point embarked on an innovation that would have profound implications for the monetary and financial system.

The institution realized that a *fractional reserve* of the commodity money would be sufficient to meet requests for conversion of the outstanding promises to pay at any point in time. The institution could then issue additional promises to pay and distribute these in the process of making loans. In this manner, the institution would enhance profit, and as long as it made conservative loans and maintained an adequate commodity money reserve, it could continue to operate with a fractional reserve. The warehouse then started to look like a modern bank. The institution's balance sheet might appear as

Hickenlupper's Bank

Assets	Liabilities
Commodity money $1 million	Promises to pay $10 million
Loans $9 million	

In this case, $1 million in commodity money (reserve) supported the original $1 million in promises to pay as well as an additional $9 million. The promises to pay were issued whenever the bank made a loan and their general acceptability ensured that they would circulate in the community as money. The institution illustrated in the T-account has a fractional reserve of 10% behind its promises to pay, which would be sufficient to redeem those promises to pay that were presented for redemption.

This was a fundamental change in the nature of the monetary system because it introduced *fiat* or *fiduciary* elements into the money supply process in the sense that the total amount of outstanding promises to pay were backed by a fractional rather than a 100% reserve of commodity money. The willingness of the public to use the promises to pay as money depended on the credit and reputation of the issuing institution. A fiduciary system was far more efficient than the commodity-based system. It was less resource using because a given amount of commodity money could support a much larger amount of money in the form of promises to pay. It was more responsive to the needs of trade since economic growth would be matched by increased demand for credit, and this would be translated into increased supply of promises to pay as banks expanded credit.

It is important to realize that this evolution of the monetary system to incorporate fiduciary elements was a *market innovation*. It emerged independently of government regulation; however, ironically, the evolution toward fiduciary monetary systems provides the basic rationale for government regulation.

It was at this stage of the evolution of the monetary system that government regulation became important because the fiat-based system raised two problems because of the existence of *third-party* effects or *externalities*.

First, by its very nature, a fractional reserve system cannot support the conversion of large amounts of promises to pay into reserve money in a short period of time. This raised the potential of *contagion* in that the failure of even a small number of banks could generate a widespread run on other banks and, ultimately, bring the entire system to collapse if the public doubted the general acceptability of the prom-

BOX 1 Is competitive and unregulated banking unstable?

The view that competitive and unregulated banking is unstable seems intuitively obvious given the fractional reserve nature of banking and given the numerous periods of banking instability in the United States during the past two centuries. At the same time, the view that unregulated competitive banking is inherently unstable has been difficult to test empirically because there have been few periods in recent history when banks functioned in an unregulated environment. At a minimum, the following conditions must hold to define such an environment: banks must be subject to little or no government regulation that restricts their portfolio opportunities, there must be a large number of banks, and entry into and exit from the banking industry must be relatively easy.

The banking conditions of the Great Depression do not qualify because banks were then subject to government regulation. In addition, the banking system experienced a series of economy-wide shocks that make it difficult to isolate contagion effects. We must turn to earlier historical periods for examples of unregulated competitive banking.

Two interesting periods appear to satisfy the institutional requirements of unregulated competitive banking: the "Free Banking Eras" in the United States from 1837 to 1863 and in Scotland from 1800 to 1845.

The Free Banking Era in the United States has traditionally been regarded as strong evidence that competitive banking in the absence of extensive regulation is unstable. High rates of inflation in the late 1830s and a sharp recession in the early 1840s, which has been compared to the first few years of the Great Depression in its intensity, were regarded as the outcome of unstable banking. Accounts of the period emphasized the high number of bank failures, bank panics, and the large number of bank notes that circulated at various rates of discount as evidence of unstable banking that destabilized the economy.

Perhaps the most oft-cited facet of unstable banking during this period consists of the so-called "wildcat banks," which many observers claimed dominated the banking scene. Wildcat banks were established in remote areas (where only wildcats roamed) and issued bank notes in excess of the value of their assets. The remote locations made it difficult to convert notes into specie.

This traditional view has been challenged by economists Arthur J. Rolnick and Warren E. Weber (1983) in their detailed study of state auditor reports for New York, Indiana, Wisconsin, and Minnesota. They found evidence that local failures were not contagious, that many banks did not fail, that failed banks frequently redeemed notes at par, that total losses to noteholders resulting from bank failures were much smaller than originally thought, and that wildcat banking was not a major part of the banking scene.

Rolnick and Weber have not, however, demonstrated unambiguously that banking in the absence of any regulation was stable. While there was no federal regulation during this period, banks were subject to varying degrees of regulation at the state level. State regulation was minimal, but its existence leaves us uncertain as to whether a competitive and completely unregulated banking system would be stable or not.

The Free Banking Era in Scotland offers stronger support for the hypothesis that competitive banking can be stable. During the first half of the nineteenth century, Scotland had no central bank, bank entry and exit were unrestricted, and note issuance was universal and unregulated. Unlike U.S. banks, which were subject to some government regulation, Scottish banks were free of government regulation for all practical purposes.

Lawrence White (1984), economist, has presented convincing evidence that unregulated banking in Scotland was stable, competitive, and supported significant economic growth. He found that local shocks and local bank failures did not spread, banks held adequate reserves, bank notes circulated at par, banks that failed frequently compensated the majority of note-holders fully, and the widespread use of extended liability provision for bank shareholders ensured that banks were conservatively operated. In addition, Scotland experienced no problem with the kind of wildcat banking that played a role in the U.S. experience.

Together, these two studies challenge the traditional view that competitive banking in the presence of minimal or no government regulation is inherently unstable. Both studies suggest that contagion was not a characteristic of the banking system, that individual banks had strong economic incentives not to "overissue" bank notes or deposits, and that the public had adequate information on which to judge the quality of individual banks.

Implications for the 1980s and 1990s

The reinterpretation of the U.S. experience and the new evidence regarding Scotland appear to refute the instability hypothesis. However, the evidence must be regarded as only suggestive at this time. The data are not detailed enough in either case to provide strong empirical tests of the instability hypothesis. Furthermore, both situations lacked highly integrated inter-bank and financial markets that might have increased the degree of actual contagion. Both banking systems used a commodity-based, rather than a fiat-based, monetary standard that may have been responsible for the apparent stability.

Historical reevaluations of the two periods will surely generate debate and further research. Assuming that these recent historical studies are correct, what lessons can we draw?

First, efforts to remove constraints on competitive behavior should not be held back by fears that increased competition will generate instability in the banking system. While some individual banks will cease to exist in a more competitive environment, their passing will not destabilize the banking system. Competitive banking is not necessarily unstable and contagion is not necessarily characteristic of competitive banking.

Second, while the studies are consistent with the view that competitive banking was stable over 100 years ago, this does not mean that government regulation cannot improve the performance of a competitive banking system. Deposit insurance, audits, and financial disclosure requirements are ways in which regulation could improve the performance of a competitive banking system.

Arthur J. Rolnick and Warren E. Weber, "New Evidence on the Free Banking Era," *American Economic Review*, 73 (December 1983), 1080–1091.

Lawrence H. White, *Free Banking in Britain* (Cambridge: Cambridge University Press, 1984).

Source: Thomas F. Cargill, "Is Competitive Banking Stable?" *Weekly Letter*, Federal Reserve Bank of San Francisco (April 18, 1986).

ises to pay. In an environment without government regulation, there was no guarantee that institutions would make prudent loans or maintain a prudent level of risk. If an institution failed because it had assumed too much risk, its failure could contaminate otherwise financially sound institutions. Even if institutions adopted prudent loan and investment strategies, a local shock might cause their failure and, again, create doubt about the ability to convert promises to pay into commodity money.

Second, there was no mechanism to ensure that the total amount of promises to pay would generate stable prices. Either too many or too few promises to pay would be issued in the aggregate and, thus, generate inflation or deflation over time. Between these two outcomes, it was more likely that an unregulated banking system with fractional reserves would overissue the promises to pay in the aggregate and thus generate inflation. Individual institutions would have an incentive to issue promises to pay without regard to what other institutions were doing in order to make more profit.

The fact that individual banks would assume levels of risk without taking into account the potential for contagion and the fact that individual banks would expand loans without regard to the effect on the inflation rate were both consistent with profit seeking activity. These individual actions, however, had adverse impacts (externalities or third-party effects) on the rest of the economy that were not considered in the individual bank's decision making process. Thus, the market system in the absence of government, had no mechanism to limit individual bank risk or limit money expansion.

It was at this point that government regulation and supervision became necessary for a stable financial and monetary environment that would permit the economy to grow at a noninflationary rate consistent with its resource base. Government regulation of some degree was needed to ensure that individual institutions maintained prudent levels of risk given that their promises to pay circulated as money and to protect the holders of these promises to pay from loss. Only in this way would the public willingly use the promises to pay as money. It also became apparent that some type of government monetary authority would be required to serve as a *lender of last resort* for individual institutions in the event that they were unable to meet demands for conversion of their promises to pay. In this manner, the monetary authority could provide liquidity and prevent the failure of a small number of institutions from contaminating the entire financial system. The monetary authority would also be responsible for ensuring that the total amount of promises to pay was sufficient to meet the noninflationary needs of trade.

As the monetary system naturally evolved to incorporate fractional reserves, it was likely that an unregulated financial system would operate with high levels of risk, would be subject to contagion, and would generate aggregate levels of credit and money that produced inflation. Government financial regulation and involvement was increasingly recognized as a necessity for ensuring the soundness of the financial system and a stable value of money. This recognition, however, still left considerable room for debate. There are a variety of approaches that government involvement may take to fulfill this responsibility, and the past several decades have seen broad changes in attitudes about the type of government involvement that will ensure a stable financial and monetary environment.

In terms of financial regulation, for example, the 1930s and 1980s present very different approaches. In the 1930s, government reforms sought to constrain competitive forces as a way to limit risk taking, while in the 1980s, the deregulation effort is designed to increase the role of competitive forces. In terms of monetary policy, there are those who argue for an activist-oriented monetary policy in which the Federal Reserve is in constant motion to keep the economy growing smoothly, and there are those who argue for a more nonactivist approach. An extreme view of the nonactivist approach is offered by some monetarists who would replace the Federal Reserve with a PC; that is, the Federal Reserve should adopt a constant growth rate of money and forget about changing monetary policy from quarter to quarter.

But this is getting ahead of the story. At this point, we now move toward getting an historical perspective of the evolution of government regulation of the financial system.

Development of Regulatory Policy Through the Great Depression

There are five distinct periods to the development of financial regulation in the United States: (1) from the earliest days of the republic to 1863 when the National Currency Act was passed (amended in 1864 as the National Bank Act); (2) from the beginning of the national banking system to the establishment of the Federal Reserve System in 1913; (3) from the beginning of the Federal Reserve to the start of the Great Depression of the 1930s; (4) from the financial reform legislation of the 1930s to the start of deregulation and financial reform in the mid-1970s.

The deregulation process (5) represents the last and current stage of the evolution of government involvement and will be discussed in greater deal in later chapters. So let us start at the beginning.

Regulation Prior to the National Banking System

This period covers about seven decades of the early financial history of the United States and is a period largely devoid of federal government involvement in the financial system. State government took the leading role in chartering banks for the purpose of accepting deposits, issuing bank notes, and making loans. Prior to 1837, a state bank charter required a special legislative act, and as a result, chartering a bank was subject to considerable abuse and special privilege. Those banks that were chartered had minimal state regulation and none at the federal level. By 1837 a number of states introduced "free banking" regulations, making it much easier to obtain a bank charter. These free banking regulations frequently involved some state government regulation usually in the form of minimum capital requirements and the form in which capital must be held, but overall, American banking was essentially unregulated and competitive, and as a result, the period from 1837 through 1863 is referred to as the *Free Banking Era*.

There were two exceptions to the absence of federal government influence: the First (1791–1811) and the Second (1816–1836) Bank of the United States. Both were private banks in which the federal government owned 20% of the capital, and each bank functioned as the government's fiscal agent—receiving and disbursing funds. Otherwise, each bank operated as a private bank, though on a much larger scale than most state banks. There was considerable controversy over each bank despite the fact that each was well managed and functioned as an effective fiscal agent for the federal government. Many saw the federal government's role in each bank as a conflict with states' rights and there was concern that the banks were subject to foreign influence because part of the capital was foreign held. The state banks resented the presence of the two banks because they increased competition, had the advantage of size and being fiscal agents for the government, and tended to be more conservatively managed.

The debate surrounding each bank was intense. The First Bank's charter was not renewed by the lack of one vote in Congress while the charter of the Second Bank was a victim of the famous "Bank War" between President Andrew Jackson and Nicholas Biddle, the Second Bank's president, over how the Second Bank should function. The failure to recharter the Second Bank ended the federal government's involvement in the financial system until passage of the National Currency Act of 1863.

The National Banking System

The Free Banking Era represented the period from the end of the Second Bank of the United States to the establishment of the National Banking System in 1863. It was a competitive environment for banks and one that lacked extensive government regulation and none at the federal level. Traditionally, the era is regarded as strong evidence that competitive banking in the absence of extensive government regulation is unstable. Accounts of the period emphasized the high number of bank failures, fraud, and disarray in the nation's money supply that had adverse effects on the nation's economy. Nor was the system efficient. The large number of separate bank notes in existence (as many as 10,000 by 1860) that circulated at various rates of discount was regarded as evidence that the free banking system had failed to provide an efficient money supply.

The most frequently cited example of the instability of the free banking system were the so-called *wildcat banks*. Wildcat banks were established in remote areas of the country (where only wildcats lived) and issued bank notes far in excess of the value of their assets. Because of their remote location, however, it was difficult to redeem bank notes for commodity money.

By the early 1860s the federal government decided that the U.S. banking system needed to be unified and a national currency system was established in order to provide a stable and efficient financial structure. The National Bank Act of 1864 was previously mentioned in Chapter 6 as the starting point of the dual system of finance in the United States, though that was not the design of the federal legislation.

The act sought to establish a more efficient and sound banking system:

1. National charters would be provided to private banks through a new office of the U.S. Treasury, the Comptroller of the Currency.
2. Only national banks were permitted to issue national bank notes.
3. National banks were subject to minimum capital and reserve requirements to limit risk and reporting requirements were imposed to monitor bank activity.
4. State banks were induced to shift to national charters by imposing a 10% tax on state bank note issues.

The act had other purposes, however. A major objective of the national banking system was to help finance federal government expenditures. The financing needs of the government were partly met by requiring every national bank note to be backed by a 90% reserve of U.S. government bonds deposited with the Comptroller.

The 10% tax on state bank note issues had an immediate effect in reducing the number of state banks; however, state banks reestablished their role in the United States by the early 1870s and came to surpass national banks in number and total assets by 1900. This was accomplished by changing the type of promise to pay from the bank note to deposits, which were not subject to the 10% tax. Deposit money was more convenient in general than bank notes and rapidly became an important part of the nation's money supply.

The period from the start of the national banking system until the Federal Reserve was established in 1913 is notable for several reasons: first, it represents an extension of government regulation over banks; second, it represents a shift in regulatory responsibility from the state to the federal level; and third, it illustrates the fact that regulation is often imposed for other reasons than to ensure the efficiency and soundness of the financial system. In particular, the National Bank Act of 1864 had as much to do with financing the needs of the federal government as it did with improving the efficiency of the private banking system.

The Establishment of a Central Bank

The national banking system made some improvements over the earlier system; however, much was left to be desired. Bank failures, bank runs, and general financial instability were not uncommon features of the United States during this period.

Figure 11-1 (panel A) indicates the bank instability as measured by the number of bank failures did not disappear with the establishment of the national banking system.

There were four fundamental problems with the national banking system that eventually required a major regulatory change in the U.S. financial system in 1913 that further expanded Federal government involvement.

First, while the national bank note represented a more unified currency than the large number of state bank–issued notes, there was no mechanism to provide and absorb currency over time. Second, the national banking system had grossly underestimated the growth of deposits relative to bank notes as the preferred form of promise to pay. As a result, no nationwide mechanism for check clearing was established. Third, the reserve requirement system established by the 1864 act was based on a pyramiding principle in which smaller banks could maintain part of their reserve as a deposit with a larger bank. Unfortunately, this imposed strains on the financial system whenever the smaller banks needed to transfer funds back to meet seasonal demand for credit. The larger banks would be required to search for liquidity, and at times, this resulted in high interest rates and bank failures. Fourth, the 1864 act failed to establish a central bank to provide overall monetary policy guidance and to function as a *lender of last resort*.

In addition to these limitations, the national banking system was a dismal failure in terms of unifying the banking system under federal regulation. It generated a dual system of finance, and while one can point to some advantages of such a system, on balance the dual system has been a source of many problems and interferes with an efficient financial system.

The deficiencies of the national banking system became clearly evident with the financial panic of 1907, which was attributed directly to the inherent weaknesses of the national banking system. A National Monetary Commission was established and, after several years of study, recommended the creation of a central bank. Specifically, a central bank could regulate the supply of currency, provide lender of last resort services, provide a national check-clearing mechanism, and bring additional federal regulation and supervision over the banking system. After much debate the Federal Reserve System was established in 1913.

The institutional structure of the Federal Reserve will be discussed in a later chapter; however, in terms of the evolution of government regulation three points should be noted: the Federal Reserve represented a further extension of federal relative to state government regulation; the Federal Reserve made it possible to influence the economy by influencing the overall supply of credit and money; and unfortunately, the Federal Reserve had barely begun to function as a central bank when the most intense breakdown in the economy and financial system occurred—the Great Depression.

By the time we reach the late 1920s just prior to the start of the Great Depression, there were three definite features of government financial regulation in the United States:

1. Overall government financial regulation was not extensive. Banks had to operate according to the conditions of their charter and, if organized as a national bank, were likely to be subjected to more regulation and supervision because it would then be an official member of the Federal Reserve. Banks were subject to restrictions on intrastate branching depending on the state in which they were located, and the 1927

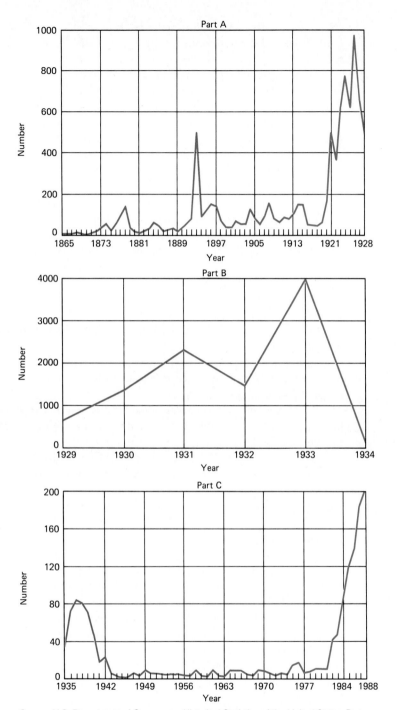

Source: U.S. Department of Commerce, *Historical Statistics of the United States*, Part II, and Federal Deposit Insurance Corporation, *1988 Annual Report.*

FIGURE 11-1   Bank failures, 1865–1988

McFadden Act essentially prohibited interstate branching. At the same time, banks had considerable freedom to manage their portfolios, set interest rates, and deal in corporate debt and equity I.O.U.s. Entry into banking was relatively easy. Government regulation was even less important for the emerging direct markets in corporate debt and equity I.O.U.s

2. A shift had occurred in regulatory responsibility from the state to the federal government.

3. Government involvement in the financial system was more focused on regulation and supervision of individual banks, while considerations of aggregate monetary policy played a lesser role prior to the Great Depression.

The Great Depression had a fundamental impact on the role of government regulation and stabilization policy in terms of the extent of government regulation, the dominance of federal over state regulation, and the role of monetary policy. The Great Depression had profound effects on the type of government regulation and supervision that would dominate the U.S. economy through today. In fact, one cannot completely comprehend the major issues of the 1990s and attitudes of policymakers without some understanding of the financial reforms that were undertaken in the wake of the worst financial and economic collapse experienced by the United States in its entire history.

The Great Depression

The financial system, which consisted primarily of banks, evolved from the end of the Revolutionary War to the start of the Great Depression without an extensive amount of government regulation. Government regulation did gradually become more important over time, but compared to today, banking was competitive and subject to little binding regulation throughout most of the period. The emerging direct markets were subject to even less regulation and supervision. In addition, there had existed no central bank to provide overall guidance to money and credit until 1913, and even then, it was not until the 1920s that the Federal Reserve was fully established and freed from the needs of financing World War I.

The Great Depression more than any other period in our economic history demonstrated the problems that result from a malfunctioning financial system and a failure to provide sufficient credit and money.

The Great Depression started in August 1929, reached the lowest point in March 1933, and continued until the late 1930s. The collapse of the economic system was intensified and prolonged by the collapse of the financial system represented by the large number of bank failures and the closing of all banks by the Roosevelt administration in March 1933. Figure 11-2 reports the number of bank failures in historical perspective and dramatically highlights the experience of the 1930s.

The Great Depression also dramatically revealed what happens when the central bank fails to provide sufficient overall credit and money growth and fails to act as a lender of last resort. During the period from 1929 to March 1933, the Federal Reserve allowed the money supply to decline by 25%. This was the most prolonged

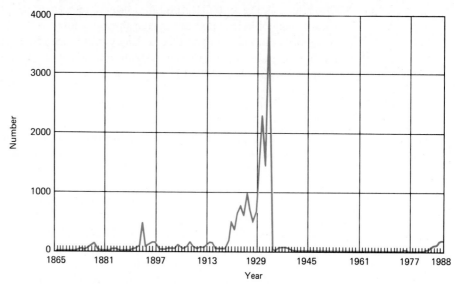

Source: U.S. Department of Commerce, *Historical Statistics of the United States,* Part II, and Federal Deposit Insurance Corporation, *1988 Annual Report.*

FIGURE 11-2 **Bank failures during the great depression in historical perspective, 1865–1988.**

decline in the money supply experienced in the Untied States and has led some economists to conclude that the Federal Reserve was responsible for the Great Depression. This thesis was advanced by Milton Friedman and Anna J. Schwartz in a well-known history of money in the Untied States from 1867 through 1960.[1]

Notwithstanding whether the Federal Reserve bears some or most of the blame for the Great Depression, there is little disagreement among economists that monetary policies pursued by the Federal Reserve during the 1930s were incorrect and contributed to the depressed conditions. The Federal Reserve had the power to prevent the dramatic decline in the money supply over the period 1929–1933 and should have done so. There is even less debate over the Federal Reserve's record as a lender of last resort—the Federal Reserve failed dismally in this regard. Had the central bank prevented the money supply from declining and, most important, had the central bank provided lender of last resort services, the decade of the 1930s might not have been called the decade of the Great Depression.

The Great Depression marked a major turning point in the role of government regulation over money and credit. In the space of a few years, government regulation of the financial system became pervasive, and it became widely accepted that government stabilization policy (monetary and fiscal policy) should play an active role in managing the economy. Let us now turn to some of the major changes brought about by the Great Depression.

---

[1] Milton Friedman and Anna Jacobson Schwartz, *A Monetary History of the United States, 1867–1960* (Princeton, N.J.: Princeton University Press, 1963), pp. 299–545.

Financial Reforms of the 1930s

To understand the current deregulation process, we must understand the main focus of the reforms introduced during the Great Depression. These reforms came in the wake of the most serious disruption of financial and real economic activity ever experienced in the United States. They also illustrate two important characteristics of financial reform in the United States. Reform is both *crisis* oriented and concerned with enhancing the *soundness* of the financial system. These two themes were clearly present during the financial reform process of the 1930s. In many ways, they are also reflected in the current reforms.

The most significant changes in the financial system were introduced by the Banking Acts of 1933 and 1935, the Securities Act of 1933, the Securities Exchange Act of 1934, and various revisions to the Federal Reserve Act.

The package of financial reform legislation sought to achieve a stable financial system by placing a variety of competitive constraints on bank operations and significantly extending federal supervision and regulation to banks as well as other financial institutions and markets. The reform legislation focused on commercial banks since they dominated the financial system; however, similar types of competitive constraints were extended to nonbank institutions as they came into prominence after World War II. In line with the emphasis on preventing competition between financial institutions of a given type, each major type of institution was treated as separate and distinct from other categories. This created a situation of *artificial heterogeneity* among financial institutions that ignored their similar economic and functional operations. Stability of the financial system was also to be achieved by expanding the supervisory and regulatory powers of the Federal Reserve and other federal agencies, providing the Federal Reserve with new tools of monetary policy, and concentrating and centralizing the decision making in a newly restructured Board of Governors (formerly known as the Federal Reserve Board).

Reform of the Financial System

There were five main components of the effort to establish a more stable financial system. First, Regulation Q interest rate ceilings on savings and time deposits and the zero ceiling on demand deposits limited the ability of banks to compete for funds. Regulation Q, set by the Board of Governors, was designed to prevent banks from bidding against each other to obtain funds and thereby necessitating risky uses of funds. In addition, it was thought that keeping low interest rates on deposits would, in turn, help to keep low interest rates on loans. Regulation Q did not apply to nonbank depository institutions when first instituted during the 1930s. Regulation Q ceilings were extended to savings banks and savings and loan associations (S&Ls) in 1966.

Second, limits were placed on the asset acquisition powers of banks. The quality of assets held by banks was to be monitored closely, and banks were not permitted to hold securities of a speculative nature in their portfolios. Security loans by commercial banks to finance the purchase of equities were to be subject to margin requirements established by the Board of Governors. Nonbank financial institutions were subject to even greater limits of their asset acquisition powers compared with banks.

Third, the newly formed Federal Deposit Insurance Corporation (FDIC) insured deposits of banks and savings banks as a move to restore public confidence in the banking industry. Federal deposit insurance was to be available to both national and state chartered banks. FDIC insurance prevented runs on banks because depositors no longer feared the loss of their deposits even if the bank failed. Figure 11-1 (panel C) illustrates the dramatic impact of FDIC insurance on the number of bank failures after 1933. The FDIC insured deposits initially up to $2,500 for banks and savings banks, and the amount has steadily increased to $100,000 as of today. Other depository institutions were also provided with federal deposit insurance. The Federal Savings and Loan Insurance Corporation (FSLIC) was established in 1934 to insure deposits of S&Ls. In 1971, the National Credit Union Administration established an insurance program for credit unions.

Fourth, the FDIC, the Board, and the Comptroller of the Currency were provided with expanded powers to regulate and supervise banks to ensure that they were being managed prudently. These agencies exercised greater control over entry, and they adopted many policies that were designed to limit competition. Again, the same type of regulation and supervision was extended to nonbanks.

Fifth, while most of the reforms were directed toward the banking system in particular and intermediation finance in general, two significant reforms were directed toward the direct money and capital markets. (1) The Securities and Exchange Act established an elaborate financial disclosure framework that required issuers of debt or equity I.O.U.s sold on organized markets to file and publicly report their financial condition in standardized form. These requirements provided the foundation for an entire industry of credit evaluators—Standard & Poors, Moody's, etcetera—who rate securities as to default risk. Financial disclosure was designed to provide reliable information to the participants in direct markets and greater government supervision over the markets. There was a major difference in the regulatory approach to the direct markets compared to intermediation finance, however. There was no attempt to control interest rates or limit portfolio flexibility. In fact, the reforms were designed to increase the role of competition in these markets by increasing the amount of reliable information. (2) Prior to the Great Depression, there existed a complete overlap between commercial banking and investment banking. A large percentage of the corporate debt and equity—as much as 60%—in the 1920s was underwritten and placed by commercial banks. There had been a few attempts to restrict banks from securities markets, but these were not very binding and were relatively easy to innovate around. The collapse of the banking system was partly attributed to the fact that banks were too heavily involved in speculative bond and equity markets, and thus a major objective of the reform legislation was to establish a legal barrier between commercial and investment banking. The Glass-Steagall act of 1933 prohibited commercial banks from underwriting and placing corporate debt and equity.

Reform of the Federal Reserve

The reforms of the 1930s also focused on the conduct of monetary policy by the Federal Reserve. The then current view of the Federal Reserve's role in the Great Depression recognized the failure of the monetary authority to prevent or reverse the decline in economic activity after 1929; however, the failure of monetary policy was viewed as being beyond the Federal Reserve's control. To improve the Federal

Reserve's performance in the future, however, the reforms of the 1930s sought to provide new or expanded instruments of monetary policy. In addition, the reforms changed the structure of the Federal Reserve by reorganizing the Board of Governors and providing the Board with greater power to oversee the formulation and conduct of monetary policy. Even with expanded instruments and a reorganized Board, however, monetary policy was not regarded as a very effective method of combatting depression and unemployment.

The emergence of fiscal policy as the most important method of stabilizing the economy to the neglect of monetary policy was one of the distinctive characteristics of the Keynesian revolution. This continued until the 1960s when the issue of monetary policy reemerged in the form of the monetarist-Keynesian debate. This debate reestablished monetary policy as the most important approach to stabilization policy.

The Emphasis on Competitive Constraints

To understand the anticompetitive focus of the 1930s financial reforms, one must consider the then popular interpretation of the collapse of the banking system and the economy.

The collapse was viewed essentially as the result of a structurally unsound banking system that was unable to withstand the pressures of a declining economy. It was thought that the unsound structure resulted from excessive competition by banks during the late 1920s. Banks had competed vigorously for funds in an institutional setting without interest rate ceilings and had been pressured increasingly to seek higher-yielding and necessarily higher-risk uses of funds to compensate for the higher cost of these funds. They became involved directly in equity, bond, and real estate markets to a degree far in excess of that prudent for institutions whose demand deposit liabilities constituted the major medium of exchange for the nation.

The collapse in the 1930s of the equity, bond, and real estate markets created severe liquidity problems for banks when they found that their loan portfolios were drastically overvalued. In the absence of deposit insurance, failure of a few banks precipitated bank runs as depositors attempted to convert deposits into currency.

The reform legislation was based on the notion that banks played too important a role in the economic system to remain unregulated, as bank demand deposits constitute the major part of the nation's money supply. The free play of competitive forces encouraged banks and financial markets to engage in activities ultimately unsound for the financial system and, hence, the economy. Competitive forces should, therefore, be constrained.

The shift in attitude toward regulated financial markets and institutions was only part of a much broader shift in attitude and philosophy about the market system that occurred as a result of the Great Depression. Prior to the depression, the competitive market system was expected to yield both an efficient allocation of resources and provide an institutional environment that encouraged economic growth along a full-employment path. Departures from full employment or business cycles were possible; however, any departure set up market adjustments in prices, wages, and interest rates that, in time, would return the economy to full employment. This view still allowed government to play a role in the economy; however, government would play a nonactivist role. Fiscal policy should be conducted in such a way as to achieve a balanced budget, and government expenditures should be confined to areas in which the private system failed to produce certain socially necessary outcomes. Monetary policy was responsible for providing a stable financial environment to support the continued growth in real output resulting from the expanding resource base, productivity increases, and capital accumulation.

The Great Depression dramatically altered attitudes about the market system and the proper role of government. The system was no longer expected automatically to achieve an efficient allocation of resources and full-employment economic growth. The social and political attitude changed from one of faith in the market system to one of skepticism about market solutions.

The shift in attitude was reflected in two areas of government activity. At the microeconomic level, government regulation and supervision of potentially unstable and/or socially important markets was deemed acceptable. Regulation was encouraged in those markets in which the free play of competitive forces produced results perceived to have adverse effects on the rest of the economy system. Financial institutions and markets were the focal point of this shift in attitude.

The role of government was also expanded at the macroeconomic level. Government now had the right and responsibility to engage in actions to stabilize the economy and achieve full employment. The emergence and dominance of the Keynesian paradigm provided the framework for the expanded role of government stabilization policy as well as a formal rationalization of the potential instability of an unregulated market system.

Evolution of Additional Regulatory Objectives

Not only did the Great Depression result in an extensive expansion of government regulation designed to limit risk in intermediation markets and provide a financial disclosure framework for direct markets, it also provided a basis for broadening the objectives of financial regulation. In the decades since the Great Depression financial regulation has adopted objectives in addition to the three primary objectives of financial regulation: ensuring the safety and soundness of the financial system, providing lender of last resort services, and providing for stable credit and money growth.

Specifically, regulation has adopted the following additional concerns: (1) consumer protection, (2) limiting the degree of economic power held by any entity, and (3) supporting favored sections of the economy via subsidized credit flows. Let us consider each of these briefly.

Consumer Protection

This type of financial regulation started with the Truth in Lending Act of 1968 (Federal Reserve Regulation Z), which was intended to provide financial disclosure

---

TABLE 11-1   Consumer protectionist laws

Fair Housing Act of 1968
Fair Credit Reporting Act of 1970
Equal Credit Opportunity Act of 1974 (Federal Reserve Regulation   B)
Real Estate Settlement Procedures Act of 1974
Home Mortgage Disclosure Act of 1975 (Federal Reserve Equation   C)
Consumer Leasing Act of 1976 (Federal Reserve Regulation M)
Fair Debt Collection Practices Act of 1977
Right to Financial Privacy Act of 1978
Electronic Fund Transfer Act of 1978 (Federal Reserve Regulation   E)
Expedited Funds Availability Act of 1987

---

to perspective borrowers of consumer credit. Since 1968 there has been considerable consumer protectionist legislation designed to provide financial disclosure for other types of financial services or to protect the civil rights of consumers. There are listed in Table 11-1.

The Expedited Funds Availability Act of 1987 is one of the more recent consumer protectionist legislation. This act fixes the number of days after which deposited funds can be used and in what form they can be used when deposited in checking, share draft, or NOW accounts at banks, thrifts, and credit unions. Congress has also considered Truth in Saving legislation which would be similar to the Truth in Lending Act but applied to interest on deposits. The Truth in Saving legislation would require more complete disclosure on the terms and conditions of deposit interest. Since deposit interest rates now reflect market conditions and depository institutions have greater authority to design new types of deposits, the variety of deposits has grown rapidly, and it is frequently difficult for the potential depositor to make meaningful comparisons of interest rates. There is also more potential for depository institutions to make misleading claims about interest earned on specific deposits, either intentionally or unintentionally.

The foundation of consumer protection legislation is based on the view that consumers of financial services often lack the proper information to evaluate fully the terms and conditions of a loan or other financial service, especially as the financial system increases in sophistication. In many respects, this type of legislation has the same intended effect as reporting requirements for issuers of securities in organized financial markets—greater information for the participants in these markets to prevent fraud and abuse and to enhance the responsiveness of the financial system to the wishes of the consumer.

Consumer protection legislation is likely to become even more important in the future as the deregulation and innovation process continues to expand the range of financial services available to the economy and simple survival in the financial system requires greater information.

Limit Concentration of Power

Financial services of all types are critically important to all but a few sectors of the economy, and as such, a large concentration of power in the financial system is open

---

BOX 2   Is government regulation always in the public interest?

The emergence of the national banking system in 1863 was in part an effort to help fund the federal government's conflict with the Confederacy as well as to improve the efficiency and stability of the banking system. Thus, even at this early date government regulation had concerns other than improving the operation of the financial system. The multidimensional rationale of government regulation has become even more apparent in modern times. This seems to conflict with the view that government regulates only to offset the third-party effects of fractional reserve banking and to limit contagion. There is no real conflict, however, once one recognizes that basic rationales of government regulation derive from the theoretical models of the economist while actual government regulation is influenced by the political institutions of the country.

There are at least four explanations for government regulation in the current environment:

Public Interest View   Regulation is in the public interest and represents a response to some type of market failure and is pursued to improve the "general welfare" by correcting market failures. In terms of bank regulation, the evolution of the monetary system to incorporate fractional reserves creates a need for government regulation to limit contagion and ensure financial stability, while at the same time, retaining the efficiency of a fiat-based monetary system. This is the traditional rationale for government regulation and the one explained in the chapter.

Special Interest View   This view suggests that regulation is a response to a powerful special interest that benefits from regulation because it protects their market and limits competition. Many observers have ar-

gued that bank regulators are far more responsive to the wishes of the banking industry than the general public. Regulators are "captured" by the regulated entities. William Greider's *Secrets of the Temple* mentioned in Chapter 1, for example, argues that the Federal Reserve is strongly influenced by the financial community, especially the large banks.

Many Interest View   This view is an extension of the special interest view and suggests that regulatory authorities are responsive to two or more special interest groups. For example, since Federal Reserve reserve requirements have been extended to all depository institutions after 1980, the Federal Reserve will be more responsive to nonbank depository institutions than in the past.

Public Choice View   This view argues that government regulators have their own independent existence and their own preference function, which places heavy weight on enhancing regulator power by extending the range of their regulatory influence and preventing other regulatory authorities from infringing on their regulatory spheres of influence.

There has been considerable discussion about which approach best describes government regulation of the financial system and while considerable debate exists regarding the special or many interest view and the public choice view, there is growing recognition that the traditional market failure view does not account for all the current financial regulation. The market failure view certainly provides the basic rationale for government regulation, but regulation has taken on new dimensions that sometimes conflict with the general welfare of the public.

---

to abuse. Traditionally in the United States, there has been a negative attitude about any concentrations of power. The debate over branching is rooted in the fear that the removal of geographic restrictions will permit "big banks" to dominate the supply of financial services. The Federal Reserve's list of nonacceptable types of activities for a bank holding company is designed to limit the concentration of power in the financial system and to limit the extension of power to nonfinancial sectors of the economy. The Glass-Steagall Act restrictions were designed in part to limit the economic power of banks as much as they were designed to limit bank risk.

Attitudes toward concentration of power in the financial system have changed significantly in the past two decades as a result of deregulation and innovation. First, the financial system is simply more competitive than previously. There has been a significant increase in competition among different financial institutions, especially depository institutions, and between indirect and direct financial markets as a result of deregulation and innovation. Second, financial innovation has elevated the importance of the concept of *potential competition* and *contestable markets*, which suggests that actual concentrations of power in the financial system are not as likely to control financial services as may have been possible in the past. Financial innovation has dramatically increased the ease with which new financial assets and services can be substituted for existing assets and services. If, say, one institution has been able to dominate a particular market and earn excess profits, this will only provide an incentive for other market participants to offer a substitute service at a lower price. Thus, even though it may appear that a specific financial market is dominated by a few institutions, the fact that new financial assets and services can be easily created, makes it possible to contest any market whenever excessive profits are being earned. Potential competition will then have the same benefit to society as actual competition—increased quantity at a lower price.

Favored Sectors of the Economy

Financial regulation has been increasingly used in the past to influence the amount and cost of credit for politically favored sectors of the economy such as agriculture, small businesses, low-income groups or areas, and especially housing. Let us consider the last two types of support for favored sectors.

A major objective of financial regulation in the post–World War II period has been to encourage a flow of funds into residential housing at favorable terms. The thrift industry was regulated and provided with tax incentives to be primary mortgage lenders, and as a result, about 85% of their assets were in mortgage loans prior to 1978. Deregulation has weakened the social commitment to housing to some extent in the sense that thrifts now have more diversified asset portfolios and offer adjustable rate mortgages as well as fixed rate mortgages. In addition, there is no enthusiasm on the part of Congress to try to regulate the cost of funds to keep mortgage interest rates low as there was in the past. Despite the weakened commitment, however, there is still a consensus in Congress that mortgage credit has a special place in the flow of funds and, as such, will continue to receive some type of incentives.

The Community Reinvestment Act of 1977 expressed the culmination of political forces designed to encourage banks and other depository institutions to provide funds for local housing and economic development. The act is based on the view that institutions should be willing to provide help to their local communities even if this may not be the most profitable use of funds. The act has been controversial since passed in 1977, partly because it lacks clear guidelines and enforcement procedures; however, it generates considerable interest in Congress and is frequently brought up whenever regulation of banks and other depository institutions are discussed.

Shift in the Focus of Financial Regulation in the 1980s

Through the 1970s financial regulation limited competitive forces in a variety of ways; however, in the 1970s a new economic environment emerged characterized by inflation, high and uncertain interest rates, internationalization of finance, along with advances in computer and communications technology. This new environment rendered many of the regulatory constraints binding for a large number of financial institutions. The conflict between an environment that demanded portfolio flexibility and a regulatory system that limited flexibility exposed the U.S. financial system to many problems in the 1970s and 1980s. The conflict led to a series of innovations by the market as it attempted to circumvent regulations that limited profit and a series of regulatory changes frequently referred to as *deregulation*.

The next three chapters will focus on the U.S. financial system in transition and the major changes in financial regulation; before leaving this discussion, however, we need to consider one more aspect of financial regulation in the United States.

The Structure of Financial Regulation

The current regulatory structure is a direct outcome of the reform legislation of the 1930s. It has already been noted that the United States is unique in terms of the dualistic structure of intermediation finance. Depository institutions in particular operate according to either a state or national (federal) charter. As a result, the structure of regulation is also dualistic. The regulatory structure can be most easily discussed in terms of a four-part decomposition of financial markets: (1) banks, (2) nonbank depository institutions, (3) nonbank nondepository financial institutions, and (4) direct money and capital markets.

Banks

The primary regulatory agencies for commercial banks are the Comptroller of the Currency, the FDIC, the Federal Reserve, and state banking agencies. The Comptroller of the Currency is the oldest regulatory agency at the federal level. It was created in 1863 as part of the effort to establish a national banking system. The Comptroller charters national banks; reviews applications for branching, acquisitions, and mergers; and conducts off-site and on-site examinations.

The FDIC was established in 1934 to provide federal deposit insurance to banks and savings banks. At present, virtually all commercial banks and the majority of savings banks are members of the FDIC. The FDIC has considerable influence over the chartering of new banks even though that is officially the responsibility of the Comptroller in the case of national banks or the state banking agencies in the case of state banks. This results from the fact that virtually all banks operate with FDIC insurance and as such must make an application to the FDIC for deposit insurance

BOX 3   On-site examinations and the camel rating system

On-site and unannounced examination is regarded as the foundation of bank regulation and supervision designed to control bank risk and limit contagion. On-site examination focuses on bank assets, liabilities, capital, management, and anything else that might influence bank performance. At present, banks are subject to more on-site examination than other depository institutions, though thrift institutions are increasingly being targeted for increased on-site examination.

Federal regulatory authorities that examine banks (Comptroller of the Currency, FDIC, and the Federal Reserve) have devised a summary rating system called the CAMEL rating system. Each on-site examination is summarized by an integer from 1 to 5 for each of six aspects of the bank's operation, with 1 being the best and 5 being the worst rating for a given attribute. The acronym CAMEL comes from the separate assignment of a rating for capital, asset quality, management and administration, earnings, and liquidity. An overall or composite rating is also assigned; however, the composite rating is not a specific function of the five individual CAMEL ratings but rather represents the examiners' overall impression of the bank's condition.

The composite CAMEL rating assumed major importance and public attention in the 1980s because it determines whether a bank will be placed on the "problem list" and the number of problem banks increased dramatically during the 1980s. In the 1970s, the list contained 20–50 banks, while in the second half of the 1980s, the list contained over 1,000 banks each year. The problem list includes banks with a composite CAMEL rating of 4 or 5. While the number of banks placed on the problem list is published regularly by the FDIC and the Comptroller, the individual bank names and the CAMEL ratings are strictly confidential.

There has been considerable discussion about the CAMEL ratings and the list of problem banks on which they are based. Many observers argue that they should be made public, especially in light of the effort to make the financial system more competitive and the need to impose market discipline on banks. One argument for public disclosure is that there is good reason to believe that the market is already aware of whether banks are in trouble or not and that there is a high correlation between examiners' opinion of the risk of a bank (as summarized by the CAMEL rating) and the market's evaluation of the bank because both are using a similar information set.[1]

To illustrate this argument, on January 22, 1976, *The New York Times* published an unauthorized list of 35 problem banks. Since the problem list had been confidential, one would expect the market to react in some way if, in fact, the examiners had information not possessed by the market regarding the condition of each bank on the list. James M. Johnson and Paul G. Weber[2] studied the effect of the public release on bank stock prices and found no evidence that the market reacted, that is, the list of problem banks provided no new information to the market.

In another study[3], CAMEL ratings were found to provide no additional information about the risk of a bank than was already available from publicly available sources.

[1] Eric Hirschhorn, "The Information Content of Bank Examination Ratings," *Banking and Economic Review*, Federal Deposit Insurance Corporation, 5 (July–August 1987), 6–11.

[2] James M. Johnson and Paul G. Weber, "The Impact of the Problem Bank Disclosure on Bank Share Prices," *Journal of Bank Research*, 8 (Autumn 1977), 179–182.

[3] Thomas F. Cargill, "CAMEL Ratings and the CD Market," *Journal of Financial Services Research* (1989), 363–374.

at the same time they submit an application for a bank charter. In addition, FDIC insurance has provided an important loophole that allows federal regulation to impact even state-chartered banks. An FDIC-insured state bank is subject to review and examination by a federal agency despite the fact that the state agency is the primary regulatory authority.

The FDIC conducts on-site examinations for state-insured nonmember banks while the Comptroller examines all national banks. State banks that are official members of the Federal Reserve System are examined by the Federal Reserve.

A major rationale for establishing the Federal Reserve System in 1913 was to provide for "a more effective supervision of banking." Before 1980, member banks consisted of national banks that were required to be members of the Federal Reserve System and those few state banks that elected to apply for membership. In addition, prior to 1980, there existed a significant difference between nonmember and member banks with regard to reserve requirements and other regulations; however, the Deregulation and Monetary Control Act established a new reserve requirement that effectively removed any real distinction. All banks must now meet Federal Reserve–imposed reserve requirements as must other depository institutions. The Federal Reserve does not charter banks, but it does yield considerable regulatory influence over banks. In addition, the Federal Reserve regulates bank mergers and bank holding companies.

Every state maintains a state agency responsible for regulating and supervising banks as well as other types of financial institutions. While there is considerable overlap between state and federal agencies, there is a high degree of cooperation and sharing of responsibilities. Over the years, however, federal regulation has tended to dominate. All banks are now subject to reserve requirements established at the federal level, and any state bank applying for FDIC insurance then becomes subject to certain federal regulations even if state regulations are more lax.

The earlier-mentioned agencies—Comptroller, FDIC, Federal Reserve, and state agencies—are the primary regulators of banks in the United States; however, other agencies have responsibility at various times and for various types of bank operations. The more important include the Department of Justice to ensure that federal antitrust laws are respected, the Securities and Exchange Commission to regulate any securities-type activities of banks or bank holding companies, and the Federal Trade Commission to investigate deceptive or unfair business practices.

Nonbank Depository Institutions

The Federal Home Loan Bank System was established in 1932 to encourage mortgage credit and support thrift institutions by providing liquidity to thrifts and encouraging secondary markets for mortgages. The System was until August 1989 composed of the Federal Home Loan Bank Board (FHLBB), Federal Savings and Loan Insurance Corporation (FSLIC), and 12 Federal Home Loan district banks. The system regulated and supervised savings and loan associations in the same way banks are regulated and supervised: chartering, examinations, branching approval, holding company acquisitions and activities, etcetera. The Financial Institutions Reform, Recovery, and Enforcement Act of 1989 changed this structure. The FHLBB and FSLIC no longer exist. The functions of the FHLBB have been largely transferred to a new federal agency—the Office of Thrift Supervision—which is part of the U.S. Treasury. The FDIC now manages a separate savings insurance fund that replaced FSLIC. The District Banks continue to function as before.

The National Credit Union Administration (NCUA) was established in 1970 and is responsible for regulating and supervising federally chartered credit unions. About half of the 17,000 credit unions in 1988 operated under federal charters. Prior to 1970, regulation of federal credit unions had been housed in several other federal agencies. NCUA also provides deposit insurance available to state credit unions and a facility for lending to credit unions. At present almost 90% of the credit union deposits are federally insured.

Each state agency responsible for financial regulation and supervision deals with state-chartered thrifts and credit unions.

Nonbank Nondepository Institutions

There are so many different types of nonbank nondepository institutions that it would be difficult to describe even briefly those agencies responsible for their regulation and supervision. State agencies tend to play a major role in the regulation of several of these institutions such as finance companies, life insurance companies, casualty insurance companies, and state pension programs. Federal regulation ranging from the Federal Reserve's Truth in Lending regulations to supervisory responsibilities of the Securities and Exchange Commission is also applied to these institutions.

Direct Money and Capital Markets

Unlike intermediation markets, state regulatory agencies play a relatively minor role in the regulation and supervision of open money and capital markets. The most important regulatory authority in this regard is the Securities and Exchange Commission established in 1934 to regulate practices in the securities industry and to enforce a comprehensive financial disclosure framework for issuers of securities in organized direct markets.

Uniqueness of the U.S. Regulatory Structure

There are two characteristics unique to the regulatory structure in the United States compared to other countries. First, there exists a *multiplicity* of regulators at the federal level. There exist different regulators for different classes of financial institutions each with similar responsibilities. In addition, the same set of financial institutions might be subject to several federal regulatory agencies. This is especially true in the case of bank regulation.

Second, the multiplicity of regulatory authorities is compounded even further with the other major characteristic of U.S. regulatory structure—a dual system of regulation. The state layer of regulation must be added to the regulatory structure. Table 11-2 attempts to convey the multidualistic regulatory structure of the United States for just that part that focuses on depository institutions. Regulation and supervision of direct financial markets (as well as nonbank nondepository financial institutions) add more layers of regulation. In addition, should Congress repeal Glass-Steagall, there will likely occur another layer of regulation designed to deal with the interrelationships between banks and securities markets.

LEGEND

FDIC	Federal Deposit Insurance Corporation
FTC	Federal Trade Commission
Federal Reserve	Board of Governors of the Federal Reserve System Federal Reserve Banks
IBF	International Banking Facility
NCUAB	National Credit Union Association Board
Member	Member of the Federal Reserve System
N/A	Not applicable
OCC	Office of the Comptroller of Currency
OTS	Office of Thrift Supervision

TABLE 11-2 Depository institutions and their regulators

	1. Chartering & Licensing	Branching 2. Intra-state	3. Inter-state	Mergers, Acquisitions & Consolidations 4. Intra-state	5. Inter-state	6. Reserve Requirements
A. National Banks	Comptroller	Comptroller	(7)	Comptroller (11)	(19)	Federal Reserve (21)
B. State Member Banks	State authority	Federal Reserve & state authority	(7)	Federal Reserve & state authority (12)	(19)	Federal Reserve (21) authority (12)
C. State Non-member Banks Insured	State authority	FDIC & state authority	(8)	FDIC & state authority (13)	FDIC & state authority	Federal Reserve (21) authority (13)
D. Non-insured State Banks	State authority	State authority	(8)	State authority (14)	State authority (14)	Federal Reserve (21)
E. Insured Savings Associations Federal (1)	OTS	OTS	OTS (9)	OTS	OTS (9)	Federal Reserve (21)
Insured Savings Associations State (2)	State authority	OTS & state authority	OTS & state authority	OTS & state authority (15)	OTS & state authority	Federal Reserve (21)
F. Uninsured Savings Associations State	State authority	State authority	State authority	State authority	State authority	Federal Reserve (21)
G. Credit Unions Federal	NCUAB	(5)	(5)	NCUAB	NCUAB	Federal Reserve (21)
Credit Unions State	State authority	State authority	State authority	NCUAB & state authority (16)	NCUAB & state authority (16)	Federal Reserve (21)

H. Bank Holding Companies	Federal Reserve & state authority	Federal Reserve & state authority	Federal Reserve & state authority	Federal Reserve & state authority	Federal Reserve & state authority (20)	N/A
I. Savings & Loan Holding Companies	OTS & state authority (3)	OTS & state authority	OTS & state authority	OTS & state authority	OTS & state authority	N/A
J. Foreign Branches of U.S. Banks National & State Members	Federal Reserve & state authority	N/A	N/A	N/A	N/A	(22)
Foreign Branches of U.S. Banks Insured State Nonmembers	FDIC & state authority	N/A	N/A	N/A	N/A	(22)
K. Edge Act Corporations	Federal Reserve	Federal Reserve	Federal Reserve	Federal Reserve (17)	Federal Reserve (17)	Federal Reserve (21)
Agreement Corporations	State authority (4)	Federal Reserve	Federal Reserve	Federal Reserve (17)	Federal Reserve (17)	Federal Reserve (21)
L. U.S. Branches & Agencies of Foreign Banks—Federal	Comptroller	Comptroller & FDIC (6)	Comptroller & Federal Reserve (10)	Comptroller & Federal Reserve (18)	(18)	Federal Reserve (21)
U.S. Branches & Agencies of Foreign Banks—State	State authority	State authority & FDIC (6)	State authority & Federal Reserve (10)	FDIC or Federal Reserve and state authority (18)	(18)	Federal Reserve (21)

7. Access to the Discount Window	8. Deposit Insurance	9. Supervision & Examination	10. Prudential Limits, Safety & Soundness	Consumer Protection 11. Rulemaking	12. Enforcement
Federal Reserve (23)	FDIC	Comptroller (27)	Comptroller	Federal Reserve	Comptroller
Federal Reserve (23)	FDIC	Federal Reserve & state authority (27)	Federal Reserve & state authority	Federal Reserve & state authority	Federal Reserve & state authority
Federal Reserve (23)	FDIC	FDIC & state authority	FDIC & state authority	Federal Reserve & state authority	FDIC & state authority
Federal Reserve (23)	None or state insurance fund (24)	State authority	State authority	Federal Reserve & state authority	State authority & FTC (31)
Federal Home Loan Bank & Federal Reserve (23	FDIC	OTS (27)	OTS & FDIC	Federal Reserve & OTS	OTS
Federal Home Loan Bank & Federal Reserve (23)	FDIC	OTS & state authority (27)	OTS FDIC & state authority	Federal Reserve, OTS & state authority	OTS & State authority
Federal Home Loan Bank & Federal Reserve (23)	State insurance fund	State authority (28)	State authority	Federal Reserve & state authority	State authority & FTC (31)
Central Liquidity Facility & Federal Reserve (23)	Credit Union Share (25)	NCUAB	NCUAB	Federal Reserve & state authority	NCUAB
Central Liquidity Facility & Federal Reserve (23)	Credit Union Share or state insurance fund (25)	State authority	State authority	Federal Reserve & state authority	State authority & FTC (31)
N/A	N/A	Federal Reserve	Federal Reserve	Federal Reserve & state authority	FTC (31)
N/A	N/A	OTS	OTS	Federal Reserve & state authority	FTC (31)
N/A	N/A	Comptroller or Federal Reserve (29)	Comptroller & Federal Reserve	N/A	N/A
N/A	N/A	FDIC or state authority (29)	FDIC & state authority	N/A	N/A
N/A	N/A	Federal Reserve	Federal Reserve	N/A	N/A
N/A	N/A	Federal Reserve & state authority	Federal Reserve	N/A	N/A
Federal Reserve (23)	FDIC (26)	Comptroller & Federal Reserve (27,30)	Comptroller	Federal Reserve & state authority	FDIC or FTC
Federal Reserve (23)	FDIC (26)	FDIC, state authority & Federal Reserve (27,30)	Federal Reserve or FDIC & state authority	Federal Reserve & state authority	FDIC or FTC & state authority

The Matrix provides an overview of primary regulators of depository institutions as of April 1990. It is not intended to cover each area of regulatory responsibility in detail. Further, the Matrix and accompanying footnotes should not be considered either a substitute for or an interpretation of the regulations. Regulatory agencies should be consulted for answers to specific questions.

(1) Federal savings associations include any thrift institution such as federal savings banks, federally chartered under Section 5 of the Home Owners' Act.

(2) State savings associations include any state chartered savings and loan association, building and loan association, homestead association, or cooperative bank.

(3) Savings and loan holding companies are required to register with the OTS.

(4) Agreement Corporations are subject to the restrictions on powers established by the Federal Reserve for Edge Act Corporations.

(5) Federal credit unions are not required to receive NCUAB approval before opening a branch.

(6) The establishment of federal branches and agencies is subject to the within-state branching restrictions of the McFadden Act. The establishment of state branches or agencies is regulated by state banking law. A foreign bank may not relocate any insured branch within the state without the prior written consent of the FDIC.

(7) While the McFadden Act prevents interstate branching by national and state member banks, banks can provide certain services on an interstate basis.

(8) While the McFadden Act's interstate branching restrictions are not applicable to insured state non-member and non-insured state banks, state laws generally prohibit branching by out-of-state banks.

(9) Federal savings associations are prohibited from out-of-state branching unless they qualify as domestic building and loan associations

under the tax laws or meet certain other requirements.

(10) Foreign banks with state or federal branches or agencies (or commercial lending companies or bank subsidiaries) are not permitted to establish either a federal or state branch or agency outside their home state unless: (a) it is permitted by law in the state in which it will operate and (b) in the case of a branch, an agreement with the Federal Reserve has been entered that will limit deposits at the non-home state branch to those permitted to Edge Act Corporations.

(11) The Comptroller must approve the merger or acquisition if the resulting bank is a national bank. However, if a non-insured bank merges into a national bank, the FDIC must approve the merger.

(12) The Federal Reserve must approve the merger or acquisition if the resulting bank is a state member bank. However, if a non-insured bank merges into a state member bank, the FDIC must approve the merger or acquisition if the resulting bank is an insured state non-member bank or if a non-insured bank merges into an insured state non-member bank.

(13) The FDIC must approve the merger or acquisition if the resulting bank is an insured state non-member bank or if a non-insured bank merges into an insured state non-member bank.

(14) In addition to state authority, the FDIC must approve mergers or acquisitions between insured depository institutions and non-insured institutions.

(15) The OTS must approve the merger or acquisition if the resulting institution is an insured savings association. However, if a non-insured institution merges into an insured savings association, the FDIC must approve the merger.

(16) The NCUAB must approve the merger or acquisition if the resulting credit union is federally insured.

(17) The Federal Reserve supervises acquisitions made by Edge Act Corporations and Agreement Corporations. Agreement Corpo

rations may merge as permitted by state authority.

(18) The International Banking Act of 1978 makes foreign banks that have branches or agencies in the U.S. subject to the provisions of the Bank Holding Company Act of 1956 with respect to non-bank acquisitions. Acquisitions of banks are subject to the Bank Holding Company Act and the home state limitations imposed by the International Banking Act.

(19) The McFadden Act prevents interstate branching by national and state member banks.

(20) The Douglas Amendment to the Bank Holding Company Act allows bank holding companies to acquire banks in other states if the state of the acquired bank specifically allows out-of-state holding companies to acquire in-state banks.

(21) Under the Depository Institutions Deregulation and Monetary Control Act of 1980, the Federal Reserve is required to set a uniform system of reserve requirements (Regulation D) for virtually all depository institutions. Non-insured state banks eligible for deposit insurance may be subject to reserve requirements. Regulation D provides that IBF deposits satisfying the requirements of that Regulation are exempt from reserve requirements.

(22) Deposits at foreign branches of U.S. banks payable only outside the U.S. are generally not subject to reserve requirements.

(23) Nearly all depository institutions in the U.S., including branches and agencies of foreign banks, have access to the discount window. These depository institutions are expected to make reasonable use of their usual sources of funds before requesting loans from Federal Reserve Banks. For example, savings associations and credit unions should first go to the Federal Home Loan Banks and the Central Liquidity Facility, respectively, for loans.

(24) Deposits which are not insured by the FDIC may be insured by states or state authorized insurance funds.

(25) Shares in all federal credit unions and many state credit unions are insured by the National Credit Union Share Insurance Fund, which is administered by the NCUAB. Shares in some state credit unions may be insured by state or state-authorized insurance funds.

(26) Federal branches of foreign banks which accept retail deposits generally must obtain FDIC insurance. State branches of foreign banks which accept retail deposits generally must also obtain FDIC insurance if they are located in a state in which a state bank is required to have deposit insurance.

(27) The FDIC has some residual examination authority over all FDIC-insured depository institutions.

(28) Federally insured S&Ls are supervised and examined by the OTS; non-federally insured state S&Ls by state authority.

(29) Foreign branches of national banks are supervised and examined by the OCC; foreign branches of state member banks by the Federal Reserve; foreign branches of insured state non-member banks by the FDIC; and foreign branches of non-insured state non-member banks by state authority.

(30) Federal branches and agencies are examined by the OCC; state branches insured by the FDIC are examined by the FDIC and state authority; and state non-insured branches and agencies are examined by state authority. The Federal Reserve has residual examining authority over all banking activities of foreign banks.

(31) Enforcement of federal consumer regulations is generally left to the FTC where the institution is not otherwise a federally insured depository institution.

Source: Federal Reserve Bank of New York, April 1990.

Key Points

1. Financial regulation results from the natural evolution of monetary system to become fiat based. The fractional reserve system requires government to limit risk at the individual bank level, provide lender of last resort services, and provide for a noninflationary growth of money and credit.

2. Financial regulation was not extensive prior to the Great Depression. The role of the federal government became permanent in 1863 with the passage of the National Currency Act and has steadily increased over time.

3. The Great Depression and the collapse of the banking system brought about a dramatic increase in the role of government regulation. Financial regulation was designed to limit risk taking and restrain competitive forces based on the then widely held view that the col-

   lapse of the banking system had occurred because of too little regulation and too much competition.

4. Other objectives of financial regulation also became important in the post–World War II period.

5. In the 1970s the structure of regulation that had emerged from the Great Depression became increasingly incompatible with the new economic and technological environment. Financial innovations and regulatory changes in the 1970s and early 1980s brought about a fundamental change in the focus of regulation frequently termed deregulation.

6. The regulatory structure of the United States is unique. It is characterized by a multiplicity of regulators on top of a dualistic system of regulation.

Key Terms

Bank failures

Commodity-based monetary system

Comptroller of the Currency

Consumer protectionist laws

Contagion

Contestable markets

Dual structure of regulation

Externalities or third-party effects

Federal Deposit Insurance Corporation (FDIC)

Federal Home Loan Bank System

Federal Home Loan Bank Board (FHLBB)

Federal Home Loan district banks

Federal Reserve System

Federal Savings and Loan Insurance Corporation (FSLIC)

Fiduciary or fiat-based monetary system

Financial Institutions Reform, Recovery and Enforcement Act of 1989 (FIERRA)

Fractional reserve system

Free Banking Era, 1837–1863

Glass-Steagall Act of 1933

Great Depression of the 1930s

Lender of last resort

Multiplicity of regulatory authorities

National Credit Union Administration (NCUA)

National banking system

Office of Thrift Supervision (OTS)

Potential competition

Representative commodity–based monetary system

Savings Association Insurance Fund

Securities and Exchange Commission

Questions

1. Explain why government regulation is required when monetary systems reach the stage of fractional reserves.

2. Why is regulation concerned with limiting the risk of depository institutions?

3. What are lender of last resort responsibilities of the central bank? Why can they help prevent contagion?

4. What is meant by the view that unregulated and competitive banking is inherently unstable? Why is the collapse of the banking system during the Great Depression not necessarily proof of the instability hypothesis?

5. Why does the United States possess a multiplicity of regulatory authorities at the federal level? Has the dual system of regulation always been a part of U.S. regulation?

6. What is the CAMEL rating system? Why would regulators want to maintain confidentiality about CAMEL ratings?

7. The term "deregulation" is frequently used to describe the transition of finance toward a more flexible and competitive structure. Why might this term be misleading? Is there less regulation?

8. What role does deposit insurance play in limiting contagion? Compare the rate of bank failures before and after 1934. Is this evidence that deposit insurance has been successful?

Suggestion Readings

1. Edward I. Altman and Arnold Sametz (eds.), *Financial Crisis: Institutions and Markets in a Fragile Environment* (New York: Wiley-Interscience, 1977). The role of government regulation for insuring a sound and stable financial environment.

2. Elizabeth Bailey and John C. Panzar, "The Contestability of Airline Markets During the Transition to Deregulation," *Law and Contemporary Problems,* 44 (December 1980), 125–146. Concept of contestable markets and potential competition applied to the airline industry.

3. George Benston, Robert A. Eisenbeis, Paul M. Horvitz, Edward J. Kane, and George Kaufman, *Perspectives on Safe and Sound Banking* (Cambridge, Mass.: MIT Press, 1986). A variety of views about government regulation in the 1930s to the present.

4. Thomas F. Cargill and Gillian G. Garcia, *Financial Reform in the 1980s* (Stanford, Calif.: Hoover Institution Press, 1985). Provides a short review of the evolution of government financial regulation from the end of the Revolutionary War to the reforms of the 1980s.

5. Robert J. Mackay and Joseph D. Reid, Jr., "On Understanding the Birth and Evolution of the Securities and Exchange Commission: Where Are We in the Theory of Regulation?" in Gary M. Walton (ed.), *Regulatory Change in an Atmosphere of Crisis: Current Implications of the Roosevelt Years,* (New York: Academic Press, 1977), pp. 101–121. This is a good summary of various theories of government regulation, and the entire Walton volume includes a number of interesting studies on the emergence of regulation in the 1930s.

6. Milton Friedman, *A Program for Monetary Stability* (New York: Fordham University Press, 1959). An excellent illustration of how even a conservative economist advocates some government regulation of the financial system when monetary systems reach the fiat stage.

7. Milton Friedman and Anna J. Schwartz, *A Monetary History of the United States, 1867–1960* (Princeton, N.J.: Princeton University Press, 1963). A classic work on the role of government in the U.S. monetary system, with special attention focused on the 1930s.

8. Carter H. Golembe and Davis S. Holland, *Federal Regulation in Banking, 1986–87* (Washington, D.C.: Golembe Associates, 1986). A comprehensive review of bank regulation.

9. Ward F. McCarthy, "The Evolution of the Bank Regulatory Structure: A Reappraisal," *Economic Review*, Federal Reserve Bank of Richmond (March–April 1984), 3–21. This study reviews the evolution of federal government regulation from a perspective other than efforts to ensure financial stability, provides an excellent illustration that the motives of government regulation are not always in the public interest and provides a good discussion of how we have reached such a complex regulatory structure as illustrated in Table 11-2.

10. Kenneth E. Scott, "The Patchwork Quilt: State and Federal Roles in Bank Regulation," *Stanford Law Review* (April 1980), 687–742. Discusses the role of dualism in financial regulation.

11. Kenneth Spong, *Banking Regulation: Its Purposes, Implementation, and Effects*, Federal Reserve Bank of Kansas City, (1985). Good overview of current federal bank regulation.

CHAPTER 12

The U.S. Financial System in Transition: The Catalysts for Change in the 1970s

Chapter Overview

Up to this point we have considered the financial system from a *static* perspective. That is, we have developed a general framework to see how funds flow from SUs to DUs and augmented this flow of funds framework with the various institutions involved in the flow of funds through the financial system. It is now time to shift to a *dynamic* perspective and discuss the financial system as an evolving entity that is fundamentally different from its composition as recently as a decade ago.

This chapter outlines a general framework to conceptualize the entire financial reform process and then uses this framework to analyze the forces that emerged in the late 1960s and the 1970s and eventually resulted in a major restructuring of the financial system.

Financial reform occurs when the general economic environment conflicts with the existing structure of the financial system. In the 1970s, inflation and high interest rates exposed depository institutions to new risks because they were functioning under a variety of portfolio constraints that had been previously imposed to limit risk and competition. Most important, the increasing gap between unregulated interest rates such as the Treasury bill rate and the Regulation Q ceilings exposed depository institutions to disintermediation risk. The wider the gap, the greater the incentives for market participants to introduce new financial assets and services that were less regulated; for example, the rapid growth of money market mutual funds or MMMFs in the late 1970s was the direct result of the gap between regulated and unregulated interest rates. The financial innovation process was thus the direct result of increasingly binding constraints that limited portfolio behavior. The basic conflict in the financial system resulted from a new economic environment that demanded greater portfolio flexibility and the inability of financial institutions to adjust portfolios because of prior regulation designed to limit risk and competition.

By the end of the 1970s, it was clear that there existed a complex feedback relationship between the failures of the Federal Reserve to maintain price stability and the failure of the financial system to meet its basic responsibilities. Inflation and high interest rates in money and capital markets induced financial innovations that made it more difficult for the Federal Reserve to control money and credit. In addition, efforts by the Federal Reserve to restrain the growth of money would cause interest rates in the short run to increase, thus exacerbating the problems created by Regulation Q. The declining membership problem further restrained the Federal Reserve from a more aggressive noninflationary monetary policy.

Thus, a major restructuring of the financial system and the conduct of monetary policy was in order. Prior proposals had not resulted in structural changes because the situation was not perceived as one of crisis. This attitude changed in late 1979.

Functions of the Financial System

There are four functions performed by the financial system in a developed economy. First, the system should provide for an efficient flow of funds between SUs and DUs. An efficient flow of funds means that the flow of funds between SUs and DUs is accomplished at the lowest cost possible and that SUs and DUs have a wide range of institutions and instruments from which to choose in making their lending and borrowing decisions. Second, the system should provide a reasonable degree of soundness among financial institutions and markets during adverse economic events. Soundness of the financial system does not have a clear-cut interpretation; however, we regard a sound financial system as one in which institutions and markets maintain an efficient flow of funds even in the presence of adverse economic events such as recessionary or inflationary periods. The failure of individual institutions, though not on a scale like that in the 1930s, is compatible with a sound financial system.

Third, the system should be able to adapt smoothly to new conditions—either external or internal to the financial system. That is, the financial system should be able to adapt to changes in the sources of economic growth, changes in the flow of funds between SUs and DUs, and changes in the degree of world economic integration. Fourth, the system should make it possible to conduct monetary policy in an efficient and equitable manner. Monetary policy is concerned with the overall level of credit and money and has the specific responsibility for maintaining price stability over time. The structure of the financial system should not conflict with the conduct and ultimate responsibility of the monetary authority, but rather, should provide an environment that permits the central bank to control credit and money smoothly without disproportional and uneven impacts on the various sectors of the economy.

A financial system that meets these requirements provides a *stable financial framework* for the economy that is necessary for sustained economic growth at stable prices. There is considerable debate among economists as to the relative importance of each of the four objectives and to what degree a stable financial framework is necessary for economic growth; however, financial history demonstrates the problems that occur when the financial system seriously malfunctions. Perhaps no other period in our history illustrates the importance of a stable financial framework than the period of the Great Depression. The Great Depression started in August 1929, reached the lowest point in March 1933, and continued until the late 1930s. The collapse of the economic system was intensified and prolonged by the collapse of the financial system represented by the large number of bank failures (Figure 11-2) and the closing of all banks by the Roosevelt administration in March 1933.

A stable financial framework cannot hope to contribute effectively to economic growth unless it is accompanied by a *stable monetary framework*. The central bank has two responsibilities in this regard. First, the central bank must provide sufficient growth in money to meet the public's demand for money over time. Excessive monetary growth generates inflation, while insufficient monetary growth generates recession. Second, the central bank must provide effective *lender of last resort* services to prevent contagion among depository institutions.

The Great Depression illustrates the outcome of a central bank's failure to provide adequate monetary growth and effective lender of last resort services. The Federal Reserve permitted the money supply to decline by 25% from 1929 to March 1933 and failed to be a lender of last resort to the large numbers of banks experiencing deposit withdrawals. As a result, the United States thus experienced the most significant and prolonged decline in economic activity in its entire history compounded by a complete collapse of the banking and financial system.

It is obvious that failure to provide either a stable financial and/or stable monetary framework has serious implications for the overall level of economic activity. At the same time, a stable financial and monetary framework is not sufficient to support noninflationary and sustained economic growth. They are merely necessary.

When Does Financial Reform Occur?

The phrase *financial reform* describes the actions of market participants and regulatory authorities to address issues raised by the failure to achieve a stable financial and monetary framework. The actions of market participants are referred to as *financial innovation*, while those of the regulatory authorities are referred to as *regulatory innovation*, which are most frequently reflected by changes in financial legislation. Thus, financial reform is designed to change the structure of the financial system and/or the structure of monetary policy in order to achieve a stable financial and monetary framework. While regulatory innovation represents the most visible part of the reform process since it defines the legal parameters of the financial system and the conduct of monetary policy, the market plays a fundamentally important role. The market in its efforts to circumvent existing constraints that limit profit frequently serves as the leading indicator that regulatory change is required and, just as important, frequently indicates the direction that regulatory change should follow. In the past few decades, regulatory authorities have been passive and reactive while the market has been the major driving force for financial reform.

Financial reform in the United States in the most recent period involves a complex interaction between the market and the regulatory authorities, sometimes working at cross-purposes. We now turn to a detailed taxonomy of the cause of financial reform.

Real sector forces:
- Price and output shocks
- Shift in economic growth
- Shift in composition of economic growth
- Change in degree of world economic integration
- Shift in financial transactions production function
- Change in relative rates of return on real and financial assets

Monetary sector forces:
- Unstable money and credit growth
- Inflation
- High and fluctuating interest rates
- Shift in flow of funds patterns
- Shift in international finance structure
- Change in degree of world financial integration

Noneconomic forces:
- Pressure from special interest groups to maintain market share
- Government pressure
- Revaluation and reinterpretation of past financial and monetary policies
- Revaluation and reinterpretation of past historical episodes
- Revaluation and reinterpretation of the determinants of economic activity

FIGURE 12-1   Catalysts for financial reform

Taxonomy of the Causes of Financial Reform

Figure 12-1 provides a schematic outline of the initiating forces of financial reform.[1] The taxonomy is based on the ability to categorize each catalyst according to whether it emanates from the real sector or the financial sector, or whether it is noneconomic in character. Each catalyst, by implication, represents an exogenous stimulus to the financial reform process. Although important interrelationships exist between items within a category and items between categories, the taxonomy is meant to isolate the specific catalysts for reform based on the historical experience of the United States. As a result, the taxonomy is inductive rather than deductive. Further classifications are possible; for example, a distinction could be made as to whether an item was primarily domestic or international in origin.

[1] This section is taken from Thomas F. Cargill and Shoichi Royama, *The Transition of Finance in Japan and the United States: A Comparative Perspective* (Stanford, Calif: Hoover Institution Press, 1988), Chapter 4. With the permission of the Hoover Institution.

Catalysts
↓
Catalysts conflict with existing financial
and monetary environment
↓
Initiation of financial reform first by market innovations
and then followed by regulatory innovations or reforms
↓
Financial reform forces a reconsideration
of monetary policy
↓
Financial reform forces a reconsideration of
a number of regulatory issues

FIGURE 12-2   Process of financial reform

Real sector catalysts include discrete changes in relative prices due to price shocks such as the oil-price shock of 1973–74, discrete changes in the rate of economic growth as well as the composition of growth, changes in relative rates of return between real and financial assets, changes in the technology of making financial transactions, and changes in the degree of world economic integration in terms of production, consumption, and investment.

Monetary sector catalysts include unstable monetary and credit growth, inflation, high and fluctuating interest rates, change in the international exchange rate environment, and changes in the degree of world financial integration in terms of capital flows.

Noneconomic forces are manifested in a variety of forms and are the least independent of the three categories. Real and monetary catalysts are conceptually and historically independent of each other; however, the noneconomic catalysts frequently emerge as a result of events in the real and monetary sector of the economy. They can, however, exert an independent and reinforcing influence on the financial reform process and thus should be regarded as separate from real or financial sector influences.

Examples of noneconomic forces are pressure brought by special interest groups for reform to maintain their prior claim on the flow of funds; governments that pressure other governments to change their financial and monetary environment to achieve greater coordination of financial policies among countries or for other reasons; and a variety of intellectual influences involving evaluations of past financial and monetary policies, reinterpretations of past historical periods, and new theoretical concepts about the basic nature of the economy and government involvement in the economy.

The initiation of the financial reform process and its process are illustrated by Figure 12-2. The catalysts themselves establish a new environment that conflicts with the existing structure of financial and monetary arrangements; this structure, in turn, has increasing difficulty satisfying its basic responsibilities. As a result, market and regulatory innovations are introduced to change the financial and monetary environment. At that point, the financial reform process attains its own momentum and becomes an ongoing process.

The changing structure of the financial system raises a number of new issues for the conduct of monetary policy. Experience has shown that new financial assets and services will disrupt previously established relationships between monetary policy and the economy and this requires a reconsideration of how monetary policy is conducted. The new structure of finance also raises a number of issues with regard to financial regulation and the role of the government regulator in ensuring the safety and soundness of the financial system.

While the foregoing taxonomy is general and omits a number of complications, it does serve as a convenient framework to understand the transition of finance in the United States. We now will utilize this conceptualization to begin the description of the major changes that have taken place in the financial and monetary framework of the United States during the past two decades.

Summary of the Causes of Financial Change

The taxonomy in Figure 12-1 starts with catalysts that initiate the financial reform process by creating conflicts between the new environment and the existing structure of financial regulation. The major catalyst in the United States emerged from the monetary side. The Federal Reserve failed to achieve price stability from the mid-1960s to the early 1980s. The inflation rate accelerated slowly over time, reaching a rate of almost 20% per year in early 1980. While many nonmonetary factors played a role, the excessive monetary growth permitted by the Federal Reserve is regarded as the primary cause of U.S. inflation. The excessive monetary growth rate occurred because of the technical operating procedures of the Federal Reserve that focused on short-term interest rate movements, pressure on the Federal Reserve to reduce the impact of large federal deficits on the financial system and other political influences, and a mistaken belief that interest rates could be kept at low levels over long periods of time.

Inflation generated anticipated inflation, which in turn, increased interest rates in the money and capital markets. Financial regulation had taken an asymmetrical approach to interest rate ceilings in the 1930s. Direct market rates were free to adjust to market forces while Regulation Q deposit rate ceilings limited the ability of banks to set market-determined rates on savings and time deposits.

As market rates rose above the Regulation Q ceilings (Figure 6-1) in the mid-1960s, thrift institutions were exposed to increased interest rate risk as they were forced to raise deposit rates to maintain and attract funds. Pressure from the thrift industry induced Congress to enact the Interest Rate Control Act of 1966. The 1966 act extended Regulation Q ceilings to thrift institutions. Thus, after 1966 Regulation Q ceilings were imposed on federally insured time and savings deposits held by banks, savings and loan associations, and savings banks. The ceilings were set at a slightly higher level (0.25 to 0.50 basis points) for thrift deposits because thrift institutions were the major suppliers of mortgage credit and because they were prohibited from offering checking accounts. Credit unions were also subject to ceilings imposed by the

National Credit Union Administration, although these deposit ceilings were not tied to the Regulation Q ceilings administered by the Federal Reserve.

The extension of Regulation Q to virtually all deposits set the stage for a major conflict between inflation and the existing regulatory structure. Depository institutions, especially thrifts, were now exposed to disintermediation risks and found that every time market rates rose above Regulation Q ceilings, deposits would flow to the direct money markets. As the 1970s progressed and inflation increased, the gap between market interest rates and the Regulation Q ceilings widened (Figure 6-1). Disintermediation threatened the viability of depository institutions, especially thrifts. Regulation Q and disintermediation also imposed serious distributional effects on the population. Since small deposits could not easily be transferred to the direct markets, small savers were forced to earn an interest rate considerably lower than potentially available to larger depositors.

Interest rate ceilings on loans or usury laws also became binding in the high interest rate environment. Various states, for example, imposed ceilings on consumer credit; however, they found that lenders were unwilling to provide credit at rates considerably lower than could be earned in alternative uses of funds, such as holding money market instruments.

The market responded to the conflict between high interest rates and restrictive regulations by a series of financial innovations. Depository institutions resorted to sources of funds that were subject to less or no regulation: NOW accounts, repurchase agreements, ATS accounts, Eurodollar deposits, credit union share drafts, cash management accounts, and so on. Depository institutions resorted to premium campaigns ("free dishes," etc.) to induce depositors, and thrifts in particular expanded their branching network to attract depositors. Depository institutions also engaged in "loophole mining" to expand their activities beyond the product line and geographic limits imposed by regulation; for example, banks made aggressive use of holding companies to expand activities.

The innovations, however, were not available to all institutions and all depositors and exposed institutions to new risks that threatened their continued viability. For example, thrifts resorted to extensive branching efforts to retain and attract deposits, which raised their cost of operations and made them less able to compete in the 1980s when interest rate ceilings were removed. Banks that resorted to unregulated sources of funds (repurchase agreements, Eurodollar deposits, large CDs, etc.) found that these short-term and market-sensitive sources of funds exposed them to much higher interest rate risks than previously experienced.

Money market mutual funds represented a major innovation of the 1970s that greatly intensified the problem of Regulation Q ceilings. MMMFs made it much easier for depositors to withdraw funds from depository institutions and transfer them to the direct money markets.

By the end of the 1970s, the market innovations made it apparent to regulatory authorities that the existing constraints on intermediation finance were becoming increasingly easy to circumvent. The advances in computer and communications technology made it easier and easier over time to introduce new financial services and assets subject to no or less regulation. The circumvention, however, was less than efficient, since it was not available to all participants and it increased risk.

A crisis was in the making as the 1970s ended, and in 1980 when interest rates had reached a historical high and disintermediation threatened the viability of thrifts

BOX 1 Internationalization of the financial reform process

The type of financial transition taking place in the United States is also occurring in a large number of countries throughout the world that is slowly producing an integrated world financial system.

Despite differences with regard to historical development pattern, social/political/economic institutions, and stage of economic development, a number of countries are experiencing a major transition in their financial system from rigidly regulated and administratively controlled to more flexible structures in which competitive forces play an increasingly important role in allocating credit. In addition, the financial transition has required central banks to reevaluate the tactics and strategy of monetary policy as well as imposed new requirements on the structure and content of financial regulation to ensure a stable and sound financial environment.

The transition of financial and monetary arrangements currently underway reveals several elements of commonality:

1. The transition was initiated by a series of conflicts between an economic environment that emerged in the 1970s and the then-existing rigidly controlled and regulated financial systems. The new economic environment was characterized by inflation, high and uncertain interest rates, discrete shifts in economic growth, discrete shifts in established flow of funds patterns, and increased world trade and financial integration.

2. The rapid application of computer technology to financial transactions has produced a discrete upward shift in the financial services production function. This has enhanced the ability of market participants to introduce new financial assets and services that, in turn, have played a key role in the market's ability to circumvent binding regulations that limit profit. Just as important, the enhanced productivity of the financial services production function reduced the differential between unregulated and regulated interest rates that would generate market innovations.

3. Conflicts between the market and the regulatory authorities have become more frequent and intense. Financial innovations designed to circumvent binding constraints frustrated the regulatory authority's efforts to limit portfolio behavior. As a result, regulatory authorities often redefined the regulatory parameters to limit financial innovation; however, the market frequently reinnovated.

4. The new economic environment, market innovations, and the regulatory-market conflicts led to major changes in the regulation of the financial structure. Regulatory innovations have been designed to remove or relax constraints on portfolio behavior and thereby increase the role of competition in the allocation of credit. The regulatory process has been referred to as "deregulation," "liberalization," or "financial reform."

5. Two important feedback relationships have become apparent during the transition. There is a feedback relationship between financial reform and monetary policy. The changing financial structure required a reevaluation of how monetary policy was conducted and the ability/willingness of the monetary authority to maintain price stability determined the environment in which financial reform occurred. There is a feedback relationship between the structure of financial regulation and the reform process. The structure of regulation (multiple or few regulatory authorities and legislatively or administratively enforced regulation) influenced the character of the reform process, which in turn, imposed new requirements on the regulatory structure.

These and other common elements experienced by many countries suggest that the financial reform process is an international phenomenon. This was clearly made apparent by conferences that focused on the experiences of a wide range of countries sponsored by the Bank for International Settlements,[1] Federal Reserve Bank of San Francisco,[2] and the Institute for Monetary and Economic Studies of the Bank of Japan.[3] The commonality of experiences, however, frequently mask the considerable differences that exist among the financial reform experiences of various countries.

[1] Bank for International Settlements, *Financial Innovation and Monetary Policy* (Basle: BIS, 1984).

[2] Hang-Sheng Cheng (ed.), *Financial Policy and Reform in Pacific Basin Countries* (Lexington, Mass.: D. C. Heath, 1986).

[3] Yosiho Suzuki and Hiroshi Yomo, *Financial Innovation and Monetary Policy: Asia and the West* (Tokyo: Tokyo University Press, 1986).

and other institutions, regulators seriously worried that "it" could happen again, the "it" referring to the collapse of the financial system in the 1930s.

According to the taxonomy in Figure 12-2, the conflict between the new environment and financial regulation also impacted monetary policy. The Federal Reserve acknowledged by the end of the 1970s that lower monetary growth would be required to bring inflation under control; however, the Federal Reserve and many others argued that control over the money supply had become considerably more difficult in the new financial environment. Nonbank financial institutions were increasingly offering financial assets that functioned as transactions accounts. Aside from this issue, the Federal Reserve became increasingly concerned about the "membership problem." As interest rates increased after 1965, the cost of Federal Reserve membership in the form of lost interest income on reserves rose and induced a growing exodus of banks from the Federal Reserve to operate under less restrictive state-imposed reserve requirements. The Federal Reserve became especially alarmed about this declining membership problem in the second half of the 1970s. Not only did the exodus raise tactical problems for monetary control at any point in time, but more important, an aggressive tight monetary policy might induce an even greater exodus of banks in the short run.

Thus the financial and monetary instability in the United States by the end of the 1970s resulted from a complex interaction between the intermediation sector of the financial system and the conduct of monetary policy. The conflicts in the financial system reflected by the large gap between market rates and Regulation Q ceilings and conflicts in the conduct of monetary policy together generated a clear need for regulatory reform of the financial and monetary environment.

The next chapter discusses the specific regulatory responses to the catalysts for financial reform; however, there is one question that needs to be addressed. Almost 15 years elapsed before meaningful reforms were introduced in 1980, and during this period the conflicts in the financial and monetary system were becoming clear to everyone. Why was nothing done at the official level? In fact, the few regulatory actions that were taken actually increased the problems; for example, regulators in 1973 removed interest rate ceilings on large CDs to make it easier for banks to attract funds. However, large CDs attracted funds from nonbank depository institutions and small banks. The most notable regulatory action that set the stage for conflict was the decision in 1966 to extend Regulation Q ceilings to thrifts.

Why Regulatory Change Waited So Long

There were several extensive studies of the U.S. financial environment in the 1970s that recommended the removal of many of the regulatory constraints and an overall emphasis on enhancing the role of competition in the financial system rather than restricting competition. The most notable were the 1971 Hunt Report (*President's Commission on Financial Structure and Regulation*) and the 1975 FINE study (*Financial Institutions and the Nation's Economy*).

The two studies focused primarily on problems in the financial system rather than monetary policy issues. The overall focus of their recommendations is best summarized by the Hunt Report.

BOX 2 A Tale of two financial reforms: Japan and the United States

The financial reform process in the United States is not unique. As Box 1 already indicated, a large number of countries are experiencing changes in the structure of their financial and monetary systems toward more flexible and competitive structures. Of the many countries experiencing financial reform, however, the United States and Japan are among the most important. They are the two largest economies of the world in terms of GNP, and there exist important relationships between the two countries that have major implications for the conduct of international trade and finance.

The experiences of Japan and the United States can be compared by considering the characteristics of each country's financial system prior to financial reform and the catalysts for financial reform in each country.

Financial systems prior to current reforms The U.S. and Japanese financial systems both before and during the current reform efforts differ in terms of the structure of markets and institutions, the extent of open securities markets, the extent of government-supplied credit in the total flow of intermediation finance, and the structure and objectives of financial regulation. Yet despite these differences, both systems shared a common characteristic prior to the current financial reform period.

In both systems, a variety of regulations restricted the portfolio choices of institutions and other market participants, imposed interest rate ceilings on deposits and loans, and attempted to allocate credit by explicit and implicit controls. In Japan's case, financial regulations also restricted international capital movements and isolated the domestic financial system from international forces. These restrictions limited competition and the role of market forces in transferring funds between lenders and borrowers.

Among the differences between the two systems, two stand out. First, financial regulation in Japan restricted market forces to a greater extent than in the United States. For example, almost all interest rates in Japan were regulated whereas in the United States, interest rate restrictions applied only to deposits and selected types of lending.

Second, financial regulation in each country did not always share the same set of objectives. In the United States, much of the financial regulation emerged from the Great Depression period and was designed to limit what were perceived at the time to be unsound banking practices thought to encourage the adoption of risky loan and investment strategies. In the view of many analysts, the effect of these restrictions was to limit competition and the influence of market forces. In addition, regulation was also used as an instrument to encourage a greater flow of credit into housing in the hope of making homeownership possible for all American households. In Japan, financial regulation was designed to encourage industrialization, export-led economic growth, international isolation of domestic finance, and a high household savings rate.

During much of the post-World War II period, both financial systems appeared to function in a satisfactory manner and accommodated rapid economic growth. Starting in the late 1960s and early 1970s, however, the economic environment changed in each country and rendered existing financial arrangements inefficient. The basic problem emerged from a conflict between a financial structure that limited flexibility and a changing economic environment that demanded greater flexibility. The new environment was characterized by oil price shocks, inflation, high and unstable interest rates, changes in established flow of funds patterns, advances in computer and telecommunications technology, and a shift from a fixed to a floating exchange rate system.

In response, both the market system and the regulators in the United States and Japan embarked on a process of reform designed to give market forces more freedom in allocating funds between lenders and borrowers. The private market in the two countries played an important role in this process by innovating to circumvent the more binding constraints, thereby pressuring the regulators to change the structure of the system and often indicating the type of financial reform that would most benefit the public.

Catalyst for financial reform In the United States, financial reform emerged as a result of the conflict between the existing structure of financial regulation and the failure to contain inflationary pressures during the 1970s and especially after 1978. Overly expansionary monetary policy produced successively more serious bursts of inflation as the decade progressed. Interest rates increased to historically high levels as a result and made much of the existing financial regulation, especially Regulation Q deposit ceilings, increasingly burdensome. At the same time, high and volatile interest rates exposed depository institutions, especially thrifts, to new and unexpected risks that had not been present in the low-inflation period.

By the late 1970s, the Federal Reserve had recognized the need to restrain monetary growth to bring inflation under control. Its task, however, was complicated by the growth of money market mutual funds and the new financial instruments and services introduced by depository institutions to circumvent binding regulation. These tensions in the monetary sector of the economy constituted the catalyst for financial reform in the United States.

In Japan, the situation was quite different. The primary catalyst for financial reform emerged in the "real" sector of the economy. The sudden end of fast economic growth in 1973 with the first oil price shocks and the effect this had on the market for credit were the principal causes. In particular, the public sector began to run large deficits after 1975. The ensuing large volume of government debt caused mounting market resistance to the policy of requiring financial institutions to absorb the debt at below-market yields. As a result the government was forced to make a number of concessions, and, increasingly, government debt practices came to reflect market forces.

At the same time, Japanese banks became advocates of new powers to restore their market share in the financial system lost when corporations—which had relied almost exclusively on banks for funding—began to borrow less than before. In addition, corporations urged that new types of financial assets be created to provide them with profit opportunities to replace those lost because of slower economic growth. Similarly, households, which continued to provide a large volume of savings, no longer were willing to invest those savings in a limited set of financial assets at below-market regulated interest rates. Unlike the past, fast real income growth no longer compensated for the limited choice of financial assets and services.

The Commission's objective, then, is to move as far as possible toward freedom of financial markets and equip all institutions with the powers necessary to compete in such markets. Once these powers and services have been authorized, and a suitable time allowed for implementation, each institution will be free to determine its own course. The public will be better served by such competition. Markets will work more efficiently in the allocation of funds and total savings will expand to meet private and public needs.[2]

The Hunt Report also stressed the need for a general restructuring of the financial system rather than a piecemeal approach.

The recommendations are interrelated and the Commission urges that they be considered as a package, even though some of the proposed changes, if enacted separately, would improve the financial system. The commission believes that piecemeal adoption of the recommendations raised the danger of creating new and greater imbalances.[3]

In fact, the philosophy and many of the specific recommendations of the Hunt and FINE studies became the foundation for the 1980 Deregulation and Monetary Control Act.

Why, then, did meaningful regulatory reform fail to occur prior to 1980. Three reasons can be cited. First, the package of proposals was offered in total, and, with so many significant changes, at least some segments of the financial community were likely to disagree over a particular aspect of the legislation, thus preventing enactment of the entire package.

Second, the belief that government could regulate the flows of credit by interest rate ceilings and other means was more powerful than was the belief that a freer

---

[2] *Report of the President's Commission on Financial Structure and Regulation* (Washington, D.C.: GPO, December 1971), p. 9.

[3] Ibid.

competitive environment would provide for a more efficient flow of funds between lenders and borrowers.

Third, and in some respects most important, financial legislation tends to be crisis oriented. It takes a severe malfunction in the financial system before significant structural change is considered seriously. Despite the seriousness of disintermediation, the problems of the financial system had not reached dramatic enough proportions for Congress and the public to raise their voices in favor of change; however, by 1979 and early 1980, the situation changed dramatically to one of crisis proportions.

Key Points

1. A stable financial and monetary framework is an important prerequisite for noninflationary economic growth. When the financial system and/or the monetary authority no longer provide a stable framework, market and regulatory innovations are initiated to change the structure of the financial system and/or the conduct of monetary policy. This initiates a transition in the financial and monetary system referred to as financial reform.

2. The financial reform process itself raises new issues for the conduct of monetary policy and the regulation of the financial system.

3. The financial reform process in the United States started because of the conflict between inflation and the existing structure of regulation that limited portfolio flexibility of depository institutions, especially deposit rate ceilings. These regulations were rooted in the view that the collapse of the banking system in the 1930s was the result of too much portfolio flexibility and too much competition.

4. The lack of a stable financial and monetary environment in the 1970s resulted from a failure on the part of the Federal Reserve to control inflation and the conflicts between inflation and high interest rates with the existing structure of financial regulation, especially Regulation Q deposit rate ceilings.

5. While a number of proposals to deal with many of the problems were offered as early as 1971, there was no broad-based regulatory effort to correct the structural problems until late 1979.

Key Terms

Disintermediation

Dynamic versus static perspective of the financial system

Financial innovation

Financial Institutions and the Nation's Economy (FINE) Study

Financial reform

Hunt Report

Regulation Q

Regulatory innovation

Stable financial framework

Stable monetary framework

Taxonomy of financial reform

Questions

1. Explain how inflation in the 1970s exposed depository institutions to disintermediation risk.

2. Thrift institutions were not subject to Regulation Q prior to 1966 while interest rates in money and capital markets had been increasing since 1964. Did this expose thrifts to disintermediation or interest rate risk? How did the limited diversification of thrift assets limit their ability to manage the resulting risk?

3. Thrifts brought pressure on Congress to extend the Regulation Q ceilings to thrift deposits in 1966. Did this reduce the risk of operating a thrift?

4. How did the advance of computer and telecommunications technology influence the financial innovation process?

5. Why were depository institutions subject to so many portfolio constraints in the 1960s and 1970s?

6. What were the distribution effects of Regulation Q in the 1970s? That is, did it impose different costs on different depositors?

7. Why would the Federal Reserve be concerned about the declining membership base experienced in the late 1970s? Even if the Federal Reserve were technically capable of controlling money and credit with a smaller membership base, why would the Federal Reserve be concerned about the membership base?

8. If financial institutions can innovate and introduce new assets and services to circumvent existing financial regulation, does this mean that the ability of regulatory authorities to limit portfolio flexibility is not as effective as it once was?

9. With regard to question 8, how has computer and telecommunications technology influenced the conflict between regulation and the desire of financial institutions to seek profit?

Suggestion Readings

This chapter is the first of a three-chapter discussion of the transition of the U.S. financial system, and as a result, the suggested reading list will be provided at the end of Chapter 14.

Regulatory Response to the Failure to Achieve a Stable Financial and Monetary Environment

Chapter Overview

It was apparent as early as the second half of the 1960s that serious structural problems were emerging in the financial system. Regulation Q deposit rate ceilings became increasingly binding as market rates rose above the ceilings and exposed depository institutions to disintermediation risk. In 1966, the financial system experienced its first of many "credit crunches" in which funds flowed out of depository institutions in search of higher yields in the money and capital markets, and as a result, consumer and mortgage credit became either unavailable or available only at high rates of interest. Thrift institutions were the most adversely affected by the high interest rates in money and capital markets because a major part of their portfolios consisted of long-term fixed rate mortgages while their sources of funds were becoming increasing interest rate sensitive. The decision to extend Regulation Q ceilings to thrifts in 1966 only exacerbated the thrift problem because it exposed them to serious disintermediation risk.

Problems with the conduct of monetary policy and the Federal Reserve's inability or unwillingness to control inflation did not emerge until the mid-1970s. By the end of the 1970s, however, it became evident that structural problems in the financial system and the intensity of market innovations made monetary control more difficult. At the same time, the failure of the Federal Reserve to restrain inflation increased the severity of the problems in the financial system as unregulated interest rates rose above regulated interest rates as market participants incorporated higher anticipated inflation rates into nominal interest rates.

By late 1979 a crisis situation existed. In response, the Federal Reserve and other regulatory authorities initiated a series of policy events that dramatically changed the structure of the financial system and the way monetary policy was conducted. Not since the Great Depression of the 1930s had the U.S. financial and monetary system been subjected to so many regulatory reforms.

This chapter focuses on the events of the late 1970s that preceded the major regulatory events, outlines the major features of the regulatory changes brought about by several important policy events, and indicates the direction of future regulatory changes. The next chapter assesses several aspects of the regulatory efforts to reform the financial system and provides a detailed discussion of the thrift problem.

Financial Reform in 1979 and 1980:
An Environment of Crisis

The structural problems of the financial system as well as the monetary control problems of the Federal Reserve had been recognized throughout the 1970s. The Hunt Report of 1971 and the FINE study of 1975 both correctly identified the major structural problems. There also occurred a lively discussion in the professional journals regarding the inability of the Federal Reserve to achieve noninflationary monetary growth. Yet, despite these observations and calls for reform, nothing was done in any significant manner. There were a few attempts to patch up some of the more serious problems; however, these half-hearted efforts were only partially successful, often created other problems because of existing restraints on the uses and sources of funds by depository institutions, and were not available to all market participants.

The structural problems of the financial system and the monetary control problems of the Federal Reserve reached serious proportions by late 1979. As a result and in the space of six months, three policy events occurred that set the stage for financial reform in the 1980s. The reform process has yet to be completed and will continue in the 1990s. In October 1979, the Federal Reserve announced new operating procedures that would provide it with more effective monetary control to combat inflation. In February 1980, the Federal Reserve announced new money supply measures that incorporated the extensive financial innovations of the 1970s. In March 1980, the Deregulation and Monetary Control Act was passed. This was the most significant piece of reform legislation since the reforms of the Great Depression period. The question must be asked: What was different in late 1979 that made reform on such a broad scale possible? Four conditions can be identified that combined to create a receptive environment for meaningful reform.

First, the rate of inflation in late 1979 and early 1980 became alarming. Inflation as measured by the CPI was almost 20% per year in early 1980. The correspondingly high interest rates reached levels that few could predict. By April 1980, the prime rate of interest reached 20%. Depository institutions found it increasingly difficult to operate in an environment of Regulation Q ceilings as well as being constrained by regulation to borrow short and lend long at fixed rates. Chrysler and First Pennsylvania Bank were calling for large federal bailouts to avoid bankruptcy, and the speculative increase in the price of gold and silver astounded most observers. In addition, the Hunt Brothers, who owned large amounts of silver, were being forced to sell their holdings of silver to meet demands of creditors. This threatened the collapse of the silver market, and policymakers were concerned that panic could spread to the financial system. Last but not least, the fiftieth anniversary of the Great Depression (which started in August 1929) did not comfort one's view of the soundness of the financial structure.

Second, the financial system found it increasingly easy to introduce financial innovations that circumvented existing regulations, especially interest rate ceilings. Other circumventions were regulator induced; however, they were only partially successful, and they imposed penalties on small savers.

Third, the financial reform legislation of the 1930s was based on the view that banking had been too competitive in the late 1920s. Considerable professional research on this subject, however, provided evidence that the banking collapse of the 1930s was due to forces other than excessive competition. Research provided convincing evidence that the Federal Reserve had failed to provide one of the most basic functions of a central bank during the collapse. The Federal Reserve should have been a lender of last resort, as the Federal Reserve could have increased the monetary base and supplied banks with the necessary funds to meet deposit withdrawals. This is not to deny that the banking system was in need of reform and that deposit insurance significantly improved the stability of the financial system; however, the Federal Reserve's unwillingness to supply reserves to the banking system in the face of deposit withdrawals is now regarded as a primary factor in the collapse.

Fourth, reinterpretation of the causes of the Great Depression has had a considerable bearing on the attitude that competition and freer markets are in society's best interest. The traditional view of the Great Depression placed emphasis on the instability of an unregulated and uncontrolled economy as the major cause of the decline. An unstable system required government involvement and control. Thus, an interventionist view dominated the profession and government policymaking from the 1930s through the mid-1960s. At that time, views that emphasized more free market competition emerged, stressing the benefits of competitive forces and the misallocation of resources likely to result from imposing constraints on competitive behavior.

These forces, together, produced the necessary environment for passage of the Deregulation and Monetary Control Act and related policy events. There are important similarities and differences between the current reforms and those of the 1930s. First, both sets of reforms represent a response to a crisis situation. The reforms of the earlier period were established in response to an actual crisis, whereas the present reforms came in reaction to a potential collapse. Second, both reforms deal with the conduct of monetary policy as well as with the financial system. Third, both reforms focus on the soundness of financial institutions. In the approach toward achieving soundness, however, the current reforms differentiate themselves sharply from the earlier reforms. In the 1930s, reformers interpreted a sound financial system to be one in which competitive forces were restrained, whereas deregulation of many of the constraints introduced in the 1930s is the primary emphasis of the present reforms.

The Main Features of the 1980 Act

The Deregulation and Monetary Control Act has two main components: one dealing with deregulation and the other with monetary control.

Deregulation Features

The overall objective of the deregulation component of the act was to increase the degree of competition in the financial system, primarily among depository institutions. This objective was to be achieved by changing the structure of the intermediation market in three ways: (1) removing or modifying existing interest rate ceilings, (2) expanding the source of funds for depository institutions, and (3) expanding the use of funds and other powers for depository institutions.

Interest Rate Ceilings   Regulation Q ceilings on savings and time deposits were to be phased out over a period ending March 31, 1986. The phase-out process was to be conducted by the Depository Institutions Deregulations Committee, composed of the secretary of the Treasury; chairs of the Board of Governors, FDIC, Federal Home Bank Board, the National Credit Union Administration; and the Comptroller of the Currency (a nonvoting member).

State-imposed usury limits in some cases were subject to a federal override. Usury ceilings on mortgage loans were eliminated, business and agricultural loans above $25,000 could be made at rates five percentage points above the Federal Reserve discount rate (plus any surcharge), and other loans by insured depository institutions could be made at rates one percentage point above the discount rate. The act provided a loophole for states to reimpose affected usury limits if they specifically rejected the federal override by mid-1983.

Credit unions had previously been subject to a 12% ceiling on loans; however, the act increased this to 15%. Under certain conditions, the ceiling could be raised above 15%.

Expanded Sources of Funds   Depository institutions were authorized to issue several types of interest-earning demand deposit substitutes. The most important substitutes in this regard were NOW accounts. ATS accounts, and credit union share draft accounts. Federal insurance was increased from $40,000 to $100,000 per deposit.

Expanded Uses of Funds and Other Powers   The most important beneficiaries in this regard were federal thrift institutions. Thrifts received increased flexibility to make mortgage loans and were provided with the opportunity to develop a more diversified loan portfolio. In this regard they were permitted to make consumer loans (up to 20% of assets), offer credit cards and associated credit, and provide other services such as trust and fiduciary services.

Monetary Control features

The overall objective of the monetary control component of the act was to improve the Federal Reserve's control over the money supply and eliminate the declining membership problem. This objective was achieved in two ways: (1) introducing a new structure of reserve requirements and (2) extending Federal Reserve influence to all depository institutions.

New Reserve Requirements   Reserve requirements have been discussed in previous chapters; however, in addition to the regular reserve requirements placed on transaction deposits and certain types of managed liabilities, the Federal Reserve also received the authority to impose supplemental reserve requirements for limited periods to achieve monetary control objectives.

Federal Reserve Influence to All Depository Institutions   The major distinctions between member and nonmember banks were eliminated, and, hence, the declining membership issue was eliminated. All federally insured depository institutions that issue transaction deposits or other deposits subject to reserve requirements must meet the same requirement regardless of the type of depository institution, charter type, location, or size. On the benefit side, depository institutions were given access to Federal Reserve services on an equal fee basis. These services include borrowing from the Federal Reserve, use of the check-clearing facilities, and other such services provided only to member banks prior to the 1980 act.

Optimism Crashes Against the Rocks of Reality

By March 1980, the financial system and the Federal Reserve entered a period of significant change and redirection. The financial system, primarily the intermediate component, was to become more competitive and, by the frequent use of the term *deregulation*, less regulated. The Federal Reserve was to focus more on stable growth of the money supply, reduce efforts to control interest rates, and thereby lower inflation and eventually lower interest rates. There was considerable optimism at the time that the benefits of the policy events would be realized in the short run. At the same time, the landslide victory of Ronald Reagan over Jimmy Carter in November 1980 and the new economic policies of the Reagan administration were touted as bringing in a new era for the U.S. economy. The focus would be less on activist stabilization policy, greater attention to balancing the federal budget, alteration of the tax structure to reward work effort and increase productivity, and reduced government regulation and supervision of the economy to encourage competition and efficiency. These policies were packaged under the label of *supply-side economics*.

The performance of the economy and the financial system in the early 1980s, however, did not support this optimism. Federal deficits, high interest rates, unstable money supply growth, recession, trade deficits, foreign debt problems of large U.S. banks, the growing size of the thrift problem, and increasing numbers of bank failures suggested that the goals of financial and economic stability were not easily achieved. This does not imply the complete lack of accomplishments. The inflation rate was reduced from double-digit levels in 1980 to 3.2% by 1983, and several major structural defects of the financial systems were being addressed.

Interest rates remained both high and volatile by historical standards during this

BOX 1 Deregulation—the correct phrase?

The phrase "deregulation" has become part of the American vocabulary. It is universally used to describe the transformation of the financial system from one that limited competition to one that encourages competition and portfolio flexibility. What's interesting about the characterization of the transformation in the United States is that the phrase provides a less than complete description of the process but, more important, is misleading.

The phrase fails to convey the idea that monetary policy issues have been an important part of the reform process. By the end of the 1970s, the structural problems in the financial system and the difficulty of achieving a noninflationary monetary policy were linked to each other. Regulatory reforms would be required to deal with both issues simultaneously; hence, the title of the March 1980 act recognizes this fact. Unfortunately, the phrase "deregulation" focuses attention only on the reform of the financial system and neglects the monetary policy issues that are directly related to the transition of the financial system.

On a more significant note, the phrase is misleading in the sense that it suggests a reduction in the regulation over the financial system. In fact, the opposite has occurred. Regulatory authorities have extended their oversight and supervision of financial institutions and imposed new regulations on institutions. A number of cynical observers in 1980 remarked, for example, that the Deregulation and Monetary Control Act should be referred to as the "re-regulation" act since it extended Federal Reserve reserve requirements to virtually all federally insured depository institutions. Other cynics point out that the last activity regulators want to cease is regulation and hence, the concept of deregulation within the context of an extensive regulatory structure is difficult to accept at face value.

These two points thus suggest that the phrase deregulation should be used with caution. Best yet, some other phrase might be more appropriate. Unfortunately, however, it has become entrenched in the discussion, and we will simply have to live with the phrase. What's also interesting is that the transitions of other financial systems in the world are seldom characterized in similar terms. Japan and Korea, for example, use the phrase "financial liberalization" to describe their transformation of finance and money as do many other countries.

period (refer to Figure 6-1) which prevented the aggressive phase-out of Regulation Q since this would expose depository institutions to a sudden increase in the cost of funds and threaten their viability. At the same time, high interest rates encouraged continued disintermediation, especially from thrift institutions to money market mutual funds (MMMFs). Table 13-1 presents deposit levels and growth rates for banks, thrift institutions, (S&Ls, and savings banks) and MMMFs over the period from 1980 to 1982. The dramatic growth of MMMF shares (144% in 1981) occurred at the expense of slower growth of deposits at depository institutions, especially thrift institutions.

The condition of the thrift industry deteriorated rapidly in 1981 and 1982. The industry as a whole lost money and an increasing number of thrifts were becoming insolvent. Regulators also found that other regulatory constraints in the financial system made it difficult to deal with troubled institutions. Restrictions on cross-industry and cross-state mergers and acquisitions made it difficult for regulators to find a willing purchaser of a failing thrift institution. For example, a failing thrift in California would not likely be purchased by another California thrift since all thrifts were experiencing difficulty; thus, the failing thrift could only realistically be sold to a California bank or an out-of-state thrift or bank.

By mid-1982, the increasing failure rate of thrifts, their inability to function in a high interest rate environment with a backlog of low-yielding mortgages, and the

TABLE 13-1   Deposit or share levels and growth rates for banks, thrift institutions, and money market mutual funds, 1980–1982

Year	Banks Deposits (in billions)	Banks Growth Rate (%)	Thrift Institutions Deposits (in billions)	Thrift Institutions Growth Rate (%)	Money Market Mutual Funds Shares (in billions)	Money Market Mutual Funds Growth Rate (%)
1980	$815.6	7.2%	$665.3	8.0%	$ 76.4	69.0%
1981	864.3	6.0	688.3	3.5	186.2	143.7
1982	982.2	13.6	739.0	7.4	219.8	18.0

Source: Board of Governors of the Federal Reserve System, Flow of Funds Accounts, *Assets and Liabilities Outstanding. 1965–1988* (September 1989).

continued growth of MMMFs convinced a number of observers that a crisis was occurring in the thrift industry. As a result, the Garn-St Germain Depository Institutions Act was passed in October 1982 to deal with these problems. While the 1982 act contributed to the overall goals of deregulation, it must be understood as a reaction to the plight of the thrift industry.

The Main Features of the 1982 Act

The 1982 act focused on the thrift industry; however, it did contribute to a more competitive environment for all depository institutions. Unlike the 1980 act, the 1982 act had little to say about monetary control issues. This was not a result of successful monetary control by the Federal Reserve, but more the lack of a crisis situation in monetary policy.

The Deregulation Components

The Garn-St Germain Act contained three major sections that deal with deregulation of depository institutions: (1) expanded sources of funds for depository institutions, (2) expanded uses of funds for depository institutions with particular focus on the thrift industry, and (3) expanded but temporary powers for regulators to deal with the increased failure rates of institutions in a more competitive and deregulated environment.

Expanded Uses of Funds   The 1982 act authorized the money market deposit account (MMDA) to be directly competitive with MMMF shares. The MMDA has been immensely successful in competing with MMMFs. It is federally insured, pays market interest rates, has limited transactions features, and has no maturity. In addition, it can be held by profit-oriented organizations. Personal MMDAs are treated like savings and regular time deposits for reserve requirement purposes; that is they are not subject to reserve requirements, while nonpersonal MMDAs carry a 3% reserve requirement.

The act led to the introduction of another new account called the Super-NOW account. The Super-NOW account had all of the features of the regular NOW account, which would still be subject to a deposit ceiling until 1986; however, it was not subject to Regulation Q ceilings. The distinction between NOW and Super-NOW accounts is no longer relevant since the removal of Regulation Q ceilings in 1986.

The act authorized an expanded clientele for the NOW accounts. Federal, state, and local governmental bodies were given permission to hold NOW accounts; however, they still could not be held by profit-oriented organizations.

Federally chartered S&Ls and savings banks were authorized to issue demand deposit accounts to persons or organizations that had a business loan relationship with the thrift or that wished to receive payment due from business customers.

Expanded Uses of Funds for S&Ls and Savings Banks   The 1982 act enhanced the powers of all depository institutions; however, the most significant changes were directed toward the thrift industry. Specifically, thrifts were authorized to diversify the uses of funds in three areas: First, they could allocate up to 60% of their assets to *commercial loans:* loans secured by commercial real estate (up to 40%), loans related to leasing operations (up to 10%), and general secured or unsecured commercial loans (up to 10%). Second, they received increased authority to make *consumer loans* (up to 30% of assets). Third, they received expanded authority to invest in *municipals*. Overall, these expanded diversification powers allowed thrifts to be less dependent on residential mortgage lending.

Other provisions of the 1982 act enhanced the ability of thrifts to offer variable rate mortgages, expanded the ability of banks to establish service corporations that the Board of Governors found to be closely "related to banking," and expanded the type of transactions that can occur between sister banks of a holding company.

Emergency Powers to Regulators   The 1982 act enhanced for three years the powers of the FDIC and FSLIC to aid troubled banks and thrifts. Institutions could be aided in a variety of ways ranging from purchasing an insured institution's assets or liabilities to organizing charter conversions, mergers, and acquisitions that crossed industry and/or state boundaries. In 1982, the Federal Home Loan Bank Board authorized Citicorp's acquisition of Fidelity Federal Savings and Loan Association located in California—an example of a cross-industry and cross-state acquisition. The act established a set of priorities that had to be followed in these cases. These "temporary" powers have been expanded through the 1980s.

The Monetary Control Components

Unlike the policy events of 1979 and 1980 that dealt with monetary control issues as well as with deregulation of depository institutions, the Garn-St Germain Act dealt almost exclusively with deregulation and the structure of the financial system. There was only one issue related to monetary control worth mentioning. The reserve requirement system established by the Deregulation and Monetary Control Act applied equally to all depository institutions; however, small institutions like credit unions found it difficult to meet reserve requirements. At the same time, these institutions played an insignificant role in the money supply process. As a result, the 1982 act authorized that the first several millions in reservable deposits were subject to a zero reserve requirement. The break point is adjusted annually according to deposit growth. Refer to Table 7-4 for greater detail on the reserve requirement system.

Regulatory Response After October 1982

Just as the 1980 act failed to achieve a stable and efficient financial environment, the 1982 act also failed to achieve the same goals. While both acts made significant progress, the U.S. financial system was still in need of major reform. Regulatory responses and concerns during the remainder of the 1980s fall into two categories: (1) efforts to deal with a wide variety of issues such as, geographic constraints, product line constraints, capital requirements, deposit insurance, consumer protection, structure of financial regulation, and the social contract to support the housing sector, and (2) two legislative efforts designed to deal with the thrift problem, the Competitive Equality Banking Act (CEBA) of 1987 and the Financial Institutions Reform, Recovery, and Enforcement Act (FIRREA) of 1989.

The CEBA and FIRREA will be discussed in the following chapter. The remainder of this chapter focuses on a number of specific issues faced by financial regulators in the 1980s, many of which have not yet been resolved.

Aside from deregulation issues, monetary policy experienced further changes during the remainder of the 1980s. This discussion will have to wait, however, until we learn more about how monetary policy works.

Geographic Constraints

Depository institutions, especially banks, are limited to specific geographic areas of operation by a general restriction on *interstate* branching and by various state restrictions on *intrastate* branching. Many argue that the existence of geographic constraints on bank operations is inconsistent with the current efforts to deregulate the U.S. financial system and increase the role of competitive forces in the flow of funds. Despite these arguments and a volume of evidence that reduced geographic constraints would improve the efficiency of the financial system, most geographic constraints on branching remain in place.

Regulatory changes, however, have taken place at both the federal and state level. As discussed in Chapter 9, a number of states have relaxed restrictions on intrastate branching in recent years, and groups of states have joined regional compacts that permit interstate branching within the compact. While short of permitting nationwide branching, these efforts at the state level have muted efforts at the federal level to enact nationwide branching legislation officially.

At the federal level, constraints on geographic expansion have been weakened as a way of dealing with the large number of troubled institutions, especially thrifts. Regulators found in the early 1980s that the geographic restraints made it difficult to deal with troubled depository institutions. Frequently, the only purchasers of a troubled institution were outside the state boundaries. The 1982 act authorized regulatory authorities to arrange mergers and acquisitions across state boundaries if a suitable purchaser for the troubled institution could not be found within the state. Under the 1982 act, for example, Citicorp headquartered in New York was permitted to acquire two thrift institutions in Illinois and Florida. The 1982 act had intended these powers as temporary; however, federal regulatory authorities have continued to permit interstate mergers and acquisitions in dealing with troubled banks and thrifts. The 1987 CEBA and, more notably, the 1989 FIRREA expanded the ability to arrange cross-industry and cross-state mergers and acquisitions. In this regard, FIRREA permitted any bank holding company (BHC) to purchase a failed or healthy thrift. Once acquired, the thrift charter could potentially be converted into a bank charter.

Aside from regulatory actions that have weakened geographic constraints, financial innovations have continued to weaken the geographic constraints on bank operations. BHCs have aggressively acquired subsidiaries away from the home office that may not be defined as banks but offer a variety of banklike services. The Board of Governors, which regulates the activities of BHCs, has been more willing to permit the expansion of BHCs into other geographic markets. *Electronic banking* has been another recent innovation designed to circumvent regulations against inter- and intrastate branching. Automatic teller machines (ATMs) expanded rapidly in the 1970s, and even more dramatic growth occurred in the 1980s because of reduced cost and increased reliability. ATMs belonging to different banks have been linked statewide and nationally. Banks have also entered into agreements with nonbank depository institutions to link ATM facilities. Other forms of electronic banking include debit cards, point-of-sale (POS) terminals, and home banking arrangements through personal computer facilities.

Regulatory authorities have been willing to view electronic banking facilities differently from a full-service branch. Most states now permit fewer restrictions on electronic banking facilities and permit outside bank access to ATMs within their boundaries because they represent a smaller investment and provide less complete service than does a traditional branch operation. Some states, however, continue to regard ATMs as branches and restrict out-of-state access.

Despite the regulatory reforms and the various financial innovations designed to circumvent geographic restrictions depository institutions remain restricted in many ways to specific geographic markets. Those advocating removal of the geographic restricts raise five issues:

1. The geographic constraints limit competition and efficiency and thus reduce the benefits of the deregulation process to the consumer of financial services.

2. The constraints are imposed unfairly because banks are restricted to a greater degree than other financial institutions.

3. The constraints increase the risk of banking because they limit the bank's deposit base and encourage the bank to rely more on shorter-term and volatile sources of funds (large CDs, Eurodollars, Federal funds, etc.).

4. The restrictions differ from state to state and thus encourage "shopping" for the most favorable set of geographic constraints by market participants.

5. The differing restrictions among states confuse the structure of regulation and expose different institutions to different regulations.

Others argue that the geographic constraints do not impose serious costs on society and, in fact, limit concentration of economic and political power by banks. In addition, they argue that the issue is essentially one of states' rights and involves principles and issues far beyond the efficiency of the banking system.

Product Line Constraints

Depository institutions, especially banks, are limited in the products they can offer. As a result of deregulation and the policy events of 1979–82, depository institutions have been permitted to diversify their assets and liabilities to a far greater degree than previously. Depository institutions can offer a wide variety of checking accounts and other types of deposits; however, banks continue to dominate the issuance of demand deposit accounts. On the asset side, depository institutions, especially thrift institutions, have been permitted to offer a much wider array of financial assets. Thrifts have significantly reduced the percentage of assets allocated to mortgage loans in the past decade (from about 85% to about 55%) and now make consumer and business loans.

Nonbank depository institutions, however, have been the primary beneficiaries of expanded uses and sources of funds while banks have not been afforded the same relative increase in new products. In addition, banks have declined in importance to other financial institutions as judged by the growth of financial assets. Banks have increasingly pressured the regulatory authorities for expanded product lines to meet the new competition from nonbank financial institutions. Banks have also experienced increased competition from the securities industries as securities companies have increased the variety and number of banklike services. For example, in 1977 Merrill Lynch introduced the first cash management account (CMA) that competes directly with banks. The CMA is based on a minimum holding of securities known as the *margin account* against which the customer can obtain credit to purchase other securities. In addition, the customer is provided with a bank credit card, an MMMF account, and a checking account through a bank associated with Merrill Lynch. Funds are deposited in the MMMF account and any checks that reduce the balance below zero are covered by a loan from the investment company secured by the margin account. Thus, the customer earns interest on the checking account and has automatic access to credit.

As a result of increased competition from other financial institutions and securities companies, banks have pressured the regulatory authorities for enhanced product line powers. At the end of the 1980s, a variety of proposals were being considered to change radically the structure of U.S. banking. There are three key issues in recent proposals to restructure the banking system. (1) Each proposal would permit increased product lines through corporate entities (affiliates or subsidiaries) rather than banks themselves, most specifically, permitting banks to underwrite corporate and equity I.O.U.s and to underwrite insurance. This is referred to as the "firewall" approach to minimize the risk to bank depositors that might occur as banks extend their activities in a broader range than presently allowed. (2) Each proposal recognizes the issue of whether nonfinancial entities can purchase banks; however, no clear consensus had emerged by 1990 as to whether nonfinancial entities can own banks. In fact, the 1987 CEBA limited the ability of nonfinancial entities to enter the banking business by prohibiting nonbank banks. (3) Each proposal recognizes that increased product lines may expose banks to new risks, and thus each proposal offers various ways in which risk can be monitored and limited. In this regard, proposals restrict the lending that can occur between the banks and their nonbank activities.

In 1988 the Senate passed a bill called the *Financial Modernization Act of 1988* that would have significantly changed the structure of banking by repealing the 1933 Glass-Steagall restrictions against banks or their affiliates underwriting corporate equity or debt. The House failed to pass its version of repeal in 1988; however, there was high expectation at that time among banks and others that the repeal of Glass-Steagall would occur in some fashion in the near future. However, this was not to be. The thrift problem and FIRREA occupied the attention of Congress in 1989, and as required by FIRREA, deposit insurance will need to be reevaluated in 1991. Thus, it did not appear likely that Glass-Steagall would be repealed or revised by Congress by 1991.

In the absence of congressional action, the Federal Reserve has been willing to provide subsidiaries of bank holding companies with limited securities powers. In 1987 the Board of Governors permitted a bank subsidiary to underwrite commercial paper and most recently in 1989, permitted a subsidiary to underwrite corporate debt. At the time of the ruling, the Board indicated it was considering extending securities powers to include the underwriting of equities. At the same time, the Board has placed fairly tight limits on the amount of securities underwriting. Securities underwriting can be no more than 5% of the subsidiary's total gross revenue and the balance must come from less risky underwriting of federal, state, and municipal debt.

Capital Requirements

Bank capital has traditionally been a major concern to regulators because the capital-asset percentage determines the extent to which assets can fall in value before the bank fails. A 10% capital ratio, for example, means that asset values can fall by 10% before net worth becomes negative. At the same time, the bank wants to avoid holding too much capital because this lowers the rate of return on equity capital, and hence, banks have traditionally wanted to operate with much smaller capital ratios than could be justified from society's point of view.

In fact, one of the first forms of government regulation over the banking system in the United States focused on capital requirements. As the financial system has become more competitive and banks and other institutions have increased opportunities to assume risk, capital requirements have been a major concern of the regulatory authorities, especially since 1984 when Continental Illinois Bank failed (a top-ten bank in 1984) and an increasing number of banks were placed on the "problem list." In 1981, there were 196 problem banks (composite CAMEL ratings of 4 or 5). By 1987, the number had increased to 1,557—the highest number of problem banks over the 1949-1989 period.

Four major regulatory changes have taken place in response to concern over capital requirements. First, the three federal bank regulatory authorities (Federal Deposit Insurance Corporation, Comptroller of the Currency, and the Federal Reserve) agreed to a common set of definitions regarding capital requirements.

Second, a uniform capital requirement was imposed on all insured banks. The 1985 reform set a minimum ratio of 5.5% of primary capital to average total assets and a 6% ratio for total capital to average total assets. Primary capital differs from other forms of capital in terms of permanence.

Third, in 1988 the Federal Reserve proposed (along with the FDIC and the OCC) and obtained agreement with 12 industrialized countries to adopt a common approach to measuring capital requirements, to raise capital requirements for all banks to 8% by 1992, and to adopt a risk-based weighing scheme for valuing assets. This represents a major change in capital requirements because for the first time, it explicitly relates the capital requirement to the measured risk of the institution. For example, mortgage loans have a higher risk index than do government securities in computing the capital ratio. In addition, the new capital requirements explicitly recognize the internationalization of banking and represent for the first time a major agreement among a number of countries on a common set of regulations.

Fourth, FIRREA raised the capital requirements of thrift institutions significantly, though they are still lower than those imposed on banks. In addition, FIRREA focused the capital requirements on tangible as opposed to nontangible (goodwill) capital.

Deposit Insurance

The establishment of federal deposit insurance in 1934 has been regarded as one of the most significant and stabilizing reforms enacted during the Great Depression. Deposit insurance greatly limits the contagion that might occur in the banking system when one or a few banks fail. Judged by the number of bank failures since the Great Depression, federal deposit insurance has been a major success.

In the 1980s however, deposit insurance no longer could be said to function so well, and by the end of the decade, major reforms were being proposed for federal deposit insurance. The FDIC's reserve fund as a percentage of insured deposits had declined, but more important, the Federal Savings and Loan Association Deposit Corporation (FSLIC) was insolvent by the mid-1980s since its reserve fund was insufficient to close the large number of insolvent thrift institutions. This situation sparked intense debate and a variety of proposals have been offered to reform federal deposit insurance.

The objective is to reduce the *moral hazard* of the current deposit insurance system. Moral hazard refers to the behavior that the existence of insurance generates, and in the case of deposit insurance, banks have a greater incentive to assume risk because they need not fear any discipline from the insured depositors. Thus, the federal insurers and ultimately taxpayers bear the cost of risk taking by the individual institution. Prior to deregulation, this was not a major problem because the limited opportunities to assume risk imposed by financial regulation constrained the amount of risk that banks and other depository institutions could assume. That is, the incentives to assume risk were constrained by the limited opportunities to assume risk prior to deregulation.

In the 1980s, depository institutions are now authorized to diversify asset and liability portfolios to a much greater extent, and financial innovation itself has increased opportunities to assume risk. Thus, the risk incentives provided by deposit insurance and the moral hazard of deposit insurance have become a major issue. The moral hazard problem could be reduced if deposit insurance premiums were risk based and adjusted according to the risk of the institutions; however, current deposit insurance is fixed-premium based. A number of observers of the deregulation process view the problems of deposit insurance as illustrating a fundamental flaw in the deregulation process. By providing enhanced opportunities to assume risk without addressing the moral hazard of deposit insurance, we have placed the cart before the horse and exposed the financial system to increased chance of failure.

A variety of proposals have been offered to reform deposit insurance and can be briefly summarized by the following points:

1. Many proposals argue that deposit insurance should be risk based and the premium adjusted to some measured risk of the institution. In addition, the insurance premium should be raised.

2. Proposals differ on the amount of deposits that should be insured. Some argue that all deposits should be insured while some suggest that the insurance limit be reduced from the current level of $100,000 in order to impose greater depositor discipline on depository institutions.

3. The FDIC does not have the power to declare an insured institution bankrupt independently of the OCC, and prior to 1989, the FSLIC also did not have the power to declare an insured institution bankrupt independently of the Federal Home Loan Bank Board. This sometimes creates conflicts because the regulatory agencies are directed to encourage the growth of banks and thrifts and may not fully consider the risk to the insurance fund of permitting troubled institutions to continue operations.

FIRREA introduced fundamental changes in the structure of deposit insurance. FSLIC has ceased to exist with its functions placed under the administration of the FDIC. The FDIC is now the major federal deposit insurer (credit unions still have a separate federal deposit insurer, however) and administers two funds: savings and bank insurance fund. Premium rates will initially be higher for thrifts; however, by the mid-1990s both thrifts and banks will pay the same premium. FIRREA also mandated a major study of deposit insurance, and as a result, major deposit insurance reforms are likely in the early 1990s.

Consumer Protectionist Issues

Consumer protectionist issues have played an important role in financial regulation in the past decade, and the current period of financial reform is no exception. In fact, the growing complexity of the financial system and the growth of electronic financial services has raised a number of concerns about consumer abuse. Two examples will illustrate this point.

Consumer groups had increasingly complained about the length of time depository institutions required before deposited funds could be accessed. Critics argued that the growing application of computers in the financial system and increases in the speed with which checks could be moved around the country were inconsistent with the requirement that depositors had to wait days and sometimes as much as three weeks before they could access deposited funds. In 1987, Congress passed the Expedited Funds Availability Act to limit how long financial institutions may delay access to deposited funds and require depository institutions to provide full disclo-

BOX 2   Expedited funds availability act of 1987

The 1987 act applies to all depository institutions whether the institution operates under a federal or state charter and whether or not the institution is federally insured. The act sets a maximum delay period that an institution can impose on funds deposited in a checking account (demand deposit, NOW, and share draft accounts) before they can be accessed by the customer.

The following schedule indicates the longest delay periods that can normally be imposed on deposited funds:

Table 1B   The longest times that institutions can delay use of deposited funds

Type of deposit	When the funds must be available to you
Cash The first $100 of any deposit of checks Government, cashier's, certified, or teller's checks Checks written on another account at the same institution Direct deposit and other electronic credits	The next business day after the day of deposit (certain conditions may apply—check with your institution)
Checks written on local institutions	The third business day after the day of deposit
Checks written on non-local institutions deposits made at an automated teller machine not belonging to your institution	The seventh business day after the day of deposit

The delay periods refer to business days, which include all days except Saturday, Sunday, and federal holidays.

The distinction between local and nonlocal institutions refers to the location of the receiving institution and the institution on which the check is drawn. A check is regarded as a local check if it is drawn on and deposited in institutions located in the same Federal Reserve check clearing region. There are presently 48 check-clearing regions in the United States

There are two important exceptions to the normal delay schedule. First, new accounts (less than 30 days) may be subject to longer delays, and second, certain conditions permit an institution to impose longer delays on established accounts—usually four additional business days. This will occur if you redeposit a check that has been returned unpaid, you have frequently overdrawn your account, you deposit checks totaling more than $5,000 in one day, or the institution has a reasonable basis to believe that the funds will not be available to cover the check you are depositing.

Consumer groups have strongly supported this type of regulation, and the Expedited Funds Availability Act certainly has a number of desirable features. At the same time, this type of legislation imposes costs as well as benefits. Depository institutions will be required to make adjustments that will add to their costs of operations, and in addition, the chance of losing funds to check-cashing fraud has increased to some extent. These costs will not be borne entirely by the depository institutions, but will be partly passed on to others in the form of higher checking account charges, higher loan rates, or lower returns on bank equities. There are no "free lunches" in the financial system!

Source: The majority of this material is drawn from "Making Deposits: When Will Your Money Be Available?" Board of Governors of the Federal Reserve System (August 1988)

sure to customers about availability of funds policies. Table 1B indicates the longest times that institutions can delay use of deposited funds as of September 1, 1988.

Consumer groups have also raised issues regarding less than full disclosure about deposit interest rates. Deregulation has permitted depository institutions to offer an almost endless number of deposits with varying conditions such as when interest is credited, minimum holding periods before interest is paid, minimum balances and how they are computed, "teaser" rates for opening a new account, and so on. At a minimum, this makes it difficult to determine the actual interest rate on a given deposit to compare against other deposit rates. Critics also charge that depository institutions have used this as an opportunity to mislead depositors. While several efforts to pass so-called Truth in Saving legislation in 1987 and 1988 were unsuccessful, Congress is likely in the future to pass some type of legislation requiring greater disclosure for depositors similar to the Truth in Lending Act passed in 1968.

Structure of Financial Regulation

The multiplicity of regulatory authorities at the federal level with overlapping responsibilities along with the existence of both federal and state regulatory authorities have frequently been criticized as generating uneven regulatory burdens for different financial institutions and at a minimum, adding to the cost of government. Even a cursory view of the development of financial regulation suggests that the bias is to create a new regulatory authority whenever there is a perceived need for greater regulation rather than to adapt an existing regulatory authority to the need.

Many studies have suggested proposals that would unify regulation, though none has seriously suggested an end to the dual system of regulation. Two early proposals—the 1949 Commission on Organization of the Executive Branch of Government or the Hoover Commission (1949) and the 1961 Commission on Money and Credit (1961)—recommended that the Federal Reserve assume a large number of regulatory powers then being handled by the OCC and the FDIC. Later proposals such as the 1971 Hunt Report took a somewhat different approach and recommended that the Federal Reserve concentrate on regulatory powers for which it was best suited and that other Federal Reserve responsibilities such as supervision of state member banks be transferred to other entities. The 1975 Financial Institutions and the Nation's Economy or FINE Study recommended a single "superagency" to combine all the regulatory and supervisory functions of the federal regulatory entities, including the Federal Reserve.

The structure of regulation has come under increased criticism in recent years because the deregulation process and financial innovation is blurring the distinctions between different depository institutions and the rationale of separate regulatory authorities is difficult to justify in the current environment. The multiplicity of regulators and the dual system of regulation also provides an environment where market participants may "shop" for the most favorable set of regulations. Many of the innovations of the past decade have utilized the unique structure of financial regulation in the United States. While one can make an argument for a multiplicity of regulators based on checks and balances, many observers regard the current structure as less than satisfactory in the more deregulated and competitive environment of the 1980s and the 1990s. In addition, a number of observers argue that the Federal Reserve should not play a major role in financial regulation but, rather, should devote all its attention to monetary policy issues.

The Task Group on Regulation of Financial Services (1984), chaired by then Vice President George Bush, provided the most recent set of proposals to restructure financial regulation. The Bush Report, however, offered relatively mild changes in the current regulatory structure and accepted the following four principals as the basis of their recommended regulatory structure: (1) the "dual banking system" and other elements of the check and balance system should be maintained in the reformed structure, (2) the day-to-day regulation of state-chartered banks should be handled by one entity rather than the FDIC and the Federal Reserve, (3) the entity that regulates the lead bank of the bank holding company should regulate the holding company, and (4) the Federal Reserve should play a meaningful rule in the reformed regulatory structure.

Despite these and other efforts, there has been little enthusiasm on the part of the regulatory entities or Congress to change the existing structure. FIRREA, however, has significantly changed the structure of thrift regulation. The Federal Home Loan Bank Board was renamed the Office of Thrift Supervision, reorganized, and made an office of the U.S. Treasury. Thus, it lost its independent status. FSLIC was brought into the FDIC. A new agency, the Federal Housing Board, was created to oversee the credit advance activities of the district Federal Home Loan Banks.

Social Contract to Support Housing

We have already discussed the role of housing in the United States and suggested that there exists a social contract between government, financial institutions that make mortgage loans, the housing industry, and purchasers of houses to encourage home ownership for every American. Tax policy, financial regulation, and government support of secondary mortgage markets all reflect the government's commitment to the contract. Thrift institutions, in particular, have been the major focus of the contract because they were regulated and provided with large tax incentives to allocate funds to residential mortgages.

Deregulation has weakened the social contract to some extent as depository institutions have increased the use of adjustable rate mortgages and thrifts have been provided with diversification powers to make consumer and business loans. At the same time, thrift institutions maintained large tax incentives to make mortgage loans during the first half of the 1980s. This seemed inconsistent with providing thrifts with greater portfolio flexibility; however, many of these tax incentives were removed in the 1986 Tax Reform Act. This action further reduced the government's commitment to the social contract to support housing, but the contract continues to play a major role in influencing government policy.

To illustrate, FIRREA actually increased the commitment of thrifts to support real estate. Previously thrifts were required to allocate 60% of assets to real estate–related loans. The requirement was raised to 70%. More significantly, the 1989 act is very clear that thrifts are to remain the nation's primary source of real estate credit.

Key Points

1. Starting October 1979 and ending October 1982, four major policy events dramatically transformed the structure of the financial system and the conduct of monetary policy.

2. The financial system was significantly changed by the 1980 Deregulation and Monetary Control Act and the 1982 Garn-St. Germain Depository Institutions Act. These reforms increased

portfolio flexibility, removed or relaxed interest rate ceilings, provided thrifts with enhanced portfolio flexibility, and increased the overall role of competition in the financial system. The 1982 act was passed in response to the deteriorating condition of the thrift industry and the disintermediation of funds from thrifts to MMMFs.

3. Monetary policy was influenced by the Federal Reserve October 1979 announcement and the February 1980 Federal Reserve redefinitions of the official money supply measures. These reforms were designed to enhance the Federal Reserve's control over the money supply.

4. Neither the 1980 nor 1982 act accomplished the goal of an efficient and stable financial system. In particular, a wide number of issues remained to be resolved and the thrift problem continued to increase in magnitude. In response, market and regulatory changes continued throughout the 1980s.

Key Terms

Automatic teller machines (ATMs)

Banks as opposed to bank affiliates or subsidiaries

Capital requirements

Cash management account (CMA)

Competitive Equality Banking Act of 1987

Deregulation and Monetary Control Act of March 1980

Electronic banking

Expedited Funds Availability Act of 1987

February 1980 redefinitions of the money supply

Financial innovation

Financial Institutions Reform, Recovery, and Enforcement Act of 1989 (FIRREA)

"Firewall" concept and Glass-Steagall

Garn-St. Germain Depository Institutions Act of October 1982

Glass-Steagall Act of 1932

Moral hazard of deposit insurance

Money market mutual funds (MMMFs)

Multiplicity of regulatory authorities

October 1979 announcement of the Federal Reserve

Phase-out of Regulation Q ceilings

Risk-based capital requirements

Risk-based deposit insurance premiums

Social contract to support housing and the thrift industry

Truth in saving

Questions

1. Explain how MMMFs intensified the disintermediation process in the late 1970s and early 1980s?

2. The problems in the financial system such as disintermediation had been recognized since the mid-1960s. Why did it take so long for major regulatory reforms to occur?

3. How did monetary policy contribute to the problem of disintermediation?

4. Describe the major features of the Deregulation and Monetary Control Act in terms of the structure of the financial system and the conduct of monetary policy.

5. Describe the major features of the Garn-St. Germain Act in terms of the structure of the financial system and the conduct of monetary policy.

6. How did both the 1980 and 1982 acts shift regulatory power from the state to the federal level?

7. How do the regulatory reforms of the 1980s differ from those during the Great Depression?

8. How did the Garn-St. Germain Act enable depository institutions to compete with MMMFs?

9. What is meant by the moral hazard of deposit insurance? Why has it become an important issue in the financial reform process?

10. Discuss several areas that have received regulatory attention since October 1982. What is the major focus of the 1987 Competitive Equality Bank Act and the 1989 FIRREA?

Suggested Readings

Chapter 14 presents an extensive suggested reading list.

An Assessment of Financial Reform and the Thrift Problem

Chapter Overview

This chapter completes the three-part discussion of the financial reform process by assessing the accomplishments and issues raised by the process as it evolved through the 1980s with special focus on the thrift problem.

 The chapter focuses on four areas. First, we assess the financial reforms from the perspective of achieving a more *efficient* and *competitive* financial environment. Second, we assess the reforms from the perspective of achieving a more *stable* and *sound* financial environment. Third, we provide an historical perspective of how the thrift or S&L problem emerged and how the Competitive Equality Banking Act (CEBA) of 1987 and the Financial Institutions Reform, Recovery and Enforcement Act (FIRREA) of August 1989 were designed to deal with the thrift problem. Fourth, we discuss the moral hazard of government deposit guarantees and how government deals with institutions that cannot remain viable in a more competitive environment. In many ways the magnitude of the thrift problem clearly illustrates the importance of these issues.

Reform of the Financial System: Efficiency Considerations

Portfolio constraints on depository institutions, especially deposit ceilings, seriously interfered with an efficient flow of funds between lenders and borrowers. Thus, a major objective of regulatory reform was to increase the efficiency of intermediation markets in general and depository institutions in particular.

The structure of intermediation markets was changed in five ways. First, depository institutions were authorized to issue new sources of funds such as NOW and MMDAs. Thrifts were permitted to offer demand deposits under limited circumstances. Second, interest rate ceilings (Regulation Q) on all deposit sources of funds, with the exception of demand deposits, were removed in a series of steps by March 31, 1986. Third, interest rate ceilings or usury limits imposed on various categories of loans were either removed or relaxed at the federal level and removed or relaxed at the state level via a federal override. Fourth, thrifts were authorized to diversify their asset portfolios with consumer and business loans and were permitted to offer credit card and fiduciary services. Fifth, the Federal Deposit Insurance Corporation (FDIC) along with other federal regulators, were provided with enhanced powers to deal with depository institutions that could not remain viable in the more competitive environment; for example, cross-industry and cross-state mergers were permitted under certain circumstances.

These changes provided depository institutions, especially thrifts, with increased portfolio flexibility and raised the overall degree of competition in the financial system. They were designed to provide depository institutions with greater ability to operate in an environment of high and uncertain interest rates, thereby enhancing the efficiency of the flow of funds. The intermediation market—thus, the entire financial system—is undoubtedly more competitive than it was previously. Expanded competition in markets for loans and transaction deposits has increased the choice set for the consumers of financial services, and the substitution of price for nonprice competition has improved the efficiency of the financial system.

These accomplishments are meaningful; however, the goal of an efficient financial system has not been achieved. Market innovations in the 1980s slowed their pace compared to the 1970s, but the spread of nonbank banks (until 1987), regional interstate banking agreements, and continuing pressure from banks and securities companies to expand their activities into each other's traditional market suggest that regulatory constraints still restrain competitive forces and limit profit opportunities. Market innovations and legal developments have brought the United States closer to interstate banking, but geographic constraints continue to limit entry and restrain competitive forces. Regulation still limits diversification of thrift loan portfolios. Banks still retain a virtual monopoly position as the major supplier of demand deposits, the only transaction deposit that can legally be held by profit-oriented entities. In addition, the zero interest rate ceiling on demand deposits remains in place, and although repurchase agreements circumvent the zero ceiling for large account holders, small businesses have no choice but to hold a noninterest-earning transaction deposit.

Thus, remaining constraints on the flow of funds continue to limit the efficiency of the financial system. Yet the changes in the structure of intermediation markets should not be underrated. The financial system is undoubtedly more competitive than previously, and the consumers of financial services are now presented with a more extensive set of choices that are more competitively priced.

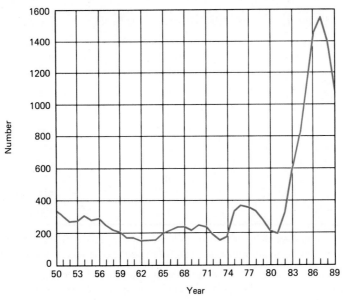

Souce: Federal Deposit Insurance Corporation.

FIGURE 14-1   **Number of banks on the problem list, 1950-1989**

Reform of the Financial System: Stability Considerations

The regulatory reforms started in 1979 were designed to enhance the stability and efficiency of intermediation finance, and hence the entire financial system. This was to be accomplished by three approaches: first, by increasing portfolio flexibility of depository institutions, especially thrifts; second, by removing Regulation Q ceilings and/or relaxing other interest rate constraints; and third, by enhancing the power of the regulatory authorities to deal with troubled institutions.

At the end of the 1980s, however, the evidence suggested that serious stability issues remained in the intermediation sector of the financial system despite major structural changes. First, the number of bank failures steadily increased after 1975 (Figure 11-1 C). Second, the number of banks placed on the "problem list" steadily increased after 1975 (Figure 14-1). The problem list is determined by ratings assigned by the FDIC and Comptroller of the Currency (see Box 2 in Chapter 11). Third, the failure of large institutions such as Continental Illinois Bank in 1984 and First Republic Bank Corporation in 1988 attracted considerable public attention as did the well-publicized problems of Bank-America Corporation in 1987, the perceived pillar of American banking. Fourth, a large number of thrift institutions, primarily S&Ls were either financially weak or insolvent but were still in operation at the end of the 1980s (Table 14-1). Fifth, the failure in 1985 of two state-sponsored thrift deposit insurance systems (Ohio and Maryland), and associated runs on thrift institutions in those two states rekindled memories of the banking collapse in the 1930s.

TABLE 14-1   FSLIC-insured thrift failures and insolvencies, 1980–1988

Year	Failed Institutions[1]	Insolvent Institutions	Newly Insolvent Institutions[2]
1980	11	43	20
1981	28	85	70
1982	63	237	215
1983	36	293	92
1984	22	445	174
1985	31	470	56
1986	46	471	47
1987	47	515	91
1988 June	43	496	24

[1] Equals the number of institutions liquidated or merged with FSLIC assistance.

[2] Equals the number of failed institutions plus the *change* in the number of insolvent thrifts.

Source: FSLIC and FDIC data, as reported in James R. Barth and Michael G. Bradley, "Thrift Deregulation and Federal Deposit Insurance," *Journal of Financial Services Research*, 2 (September 1989), p. 248.

These considerations indicated to many observers that the financial system was not as stable or sound as it could or should have been after almost a decade of financial reform. Two views have emerged to explain the growth in the number of troubled banks and thrifts. The first is called the *more deregulation* view that argues for a removal of additional constraints that limit portfolio flexibility, especially product line and geographic constraints. Both sets of constraints limit the flexibility of depository institutions and thus make it difficult to manage risk; for example, some have argued that the problems experienced by Continental Illinois Bank prior to its failure may have been averted if Illinois were not a unit banking state. The second is called the *less deregulation* view that argues that the signs of instability in the financial system are the result of too much deregulation and too much enhanced portfolio flexibility. Depository institutions have been given too much freedom to assume risk. Some advocates of the less deregulation view even suggest reimposing constraints on financial institutions, though most merely suggest a slowdown in the deregulation process.

Facts can be used to support elements of either view; however, the problems that remained in the intermediation sector of the financial system at the end of the 1980s are far too complex to be explained by simple views such as more or less deregulation.

There appear to be at least two aspects of the failure to achieve a stable and sound financial environment by the end of the 1980s: first, the thrift problem rather than a banking problem had become the major concern in intermediation finance, and second, the moral hazard of regulatory treatment of troubled institutions and government deposit guarantees provided strong incentives to assume risk. Let us first consider the evolution of the thrift problem.

The Problem with Thrifts or Equivalently, the Problem with S&Ls

S&Ls and savings banks are collectively called *thrifts*. The term derives from the traditional role of these institutions as a place where households held their savings; however, thrift institutions have come to rely heavily on transactions deposits, and time and savings deposits can no longer be regarded as long-term sources of funds. Despite the changed nature of the source of funds, however, the term has continued to be used. The reader should also keep in mind that S&Ls dominate the thrift industry in terms of numbers, growth, and total assets. Financial assets held by thrift institutions in 1988 were $1,640 billion, of which only 17.0% was held by savings banks.

To confuse things even more the term *savings institution* refers to S&Ls, savings banks, and credit unions. Occasionally, one will encounter the term savings institution as a reference to S&Ls and savings banks. Given that credit unions represent a very small percentage of total financial assets, it is obvious that S&Ls also dominate the savings industry. Thus, the thrift problem is primarily an S&L problem.

The thrift industry has been an important feature of the U.S. financial system and the focus of much of the deregulation effort of the past decade. To understand the current issues surrounding thrifts, we need to consider their role in supporting the *social contract for housing*, the emergence of *interest rate risk* and *disintermediation* in the 1970s, and the rapid growth of insolvent and financially weak thrifts in the 1980s. Finally, we review the Competitive Equality Banking Act of 1987 and the Financial Institutions Reform, Recovery, and Enforcement Act of 1989 as regulatory responses to the thrift problem. Let us consider each issue.

Thrifts and the Social Contract to Support Housing

The goal of providing home ownership to every American household is an important part of social policy in the United States. The Housing Act of 1949 declared a national housing policy to provide "a decent home and suitable living environment for every American family, thus contributing to the development and redevelopment of communities and to the advancement of the growth, wealth, and security of the Nation." There thus exists a social contract among the government, the housing industry, the purchasers of housing, and the institutions that provide mortgage funding designed to support housing in many different ways. Tax policy, financial regulation, and a wide variety of government programs play critical roles in this social contract, and in particular, thrifts have been a major part of this contract since they were and still are the single largest supplier of mortgage credit in the United States. At year-end 1975 before deregulation permitted thrifts to expand their nonmortgage lending, thrift institutions provided 53% of the home mortgages to the household sector.

Thrift Problem in the 1970s: Interest Rate Risk and Disintermediation

Favorable tax treatment and regulation encouraged thrifts to allocate as much as 85% of their assets to fixed rate, long-term (FRLT) residential mortgage loans. Even though this exposed thrifts to potential interest rate risks since the uses of funds had a longer maturity than did the sources of funds, the maturity imbalance did not create a problem for thrifts in the 1950s and early 1960s. Interest rates were low and stable compared to more recent times, and long-term rates were generally higher than short-term rates—the yield curve was upward sloping. As a result, the thrift industry was profitable through 1978, even though individual institutions were beginning to experience serious difficulties (Table 14-2). The condition of the thrift industry deteriorated rapidly after 1980. The deterioration of the thrift industry had its beginnings in the 1960s.

Problems first emerged in the thrift industry about 1965. In 1965 and 1966, interest rates rose significantly and exposed thrifts to new pressures. For the first time, thrifts found that their cost of funds rose faster than the return on their mortgage portfolio. Thrifts were not originally subject to Regulation Q deposit ceilings. Past loans had been made assuming an expected future cost of funds that turned out to be grossly underestimated. Even though new fixed rate mortgages might be made at market rates, the thrift had a backlog of low-yielding mortgages that dominated the return on the asset portfolio. Thrift sources of funds were more sensitive to market interest rates than were the uses of funds; that is, thrifts were making long-term fixed rate loans on the basis of short-term and market-sensitive funds.

The thrift industry convinced Congress that to maintain a steady flow of funds to support housing, Regulation Q ceilings needed to be extended to thrift institutions. The Interest Rate Adjustment Act of September 1966 did just that—after 1966, virtually all time and savings deposits at federally insured depository institutions were subject to Regulation Q ceilings. It was believed that government regulation could keep the cost of funds down for thrifts and thereby make it possible for thrifts to continue making FRLT mortgages at favorable interest rates.

This only changed the form of the problem facing thrifts. Instead of interest rate risk, thrifts now faced the risk of *disintermediation*. As interest rates rose in the open money and capital markets, thrifts experienced an outflow of funds at several points in time and, over time, experienced an overall slower growth in the sources of funds.

While banks increasingly innovated around the Regulation Q ceilings by relying on RPs, large CDs, and Eurodollar deposits, these options were not readily available to thrifts. Thrifts, instead, resorted to a variety of *implicit* interest payments to maintain and attract deposits. Institutions offered a wide variety of premiums— toasters, electric can openers, televisions, and so on as substitutes for *explicit* interest that they were prevented from offering by Regulation Q. Thrifts resorted to branching as a form of attracting deposits to an intensity more than any other depository institution. Even though the number of S&Ls declined steadily in the 1970s, the number of offices per association continued to increase at a faster rate than did offices per bank. In 1970 the numbers of offices per S&L and bank were 1.8 and 2.6, respectively; however, by 1980, the ratios were 5.2 and 3.7. Despite these efforts, disintermediation remained a serious problem for the thrift industry.

Federal regulators responded in three ways. First, they assisted in the contraction of the industry by arranging mergers between weak and strong thrifts. As a result, the number of thrifts declined from about 6,500 in 1970 to about 3,000 as of

TABLE 14-2 Alternating profitability ratios observed for federally insured savings institutions, 1960–1987

	FSLIC-insured savings institutions				FDIC-insured savings banks			
Year	Gross return on assets[1]	Profit margin[2]	Return on equity[3]	Return on average assets[4]	Gross return on assets[1]	Profit margin[2]	Return on equity[3]	Return on average assets[4]
1960	5.55%	15.55%	12.35%	0.86%	4.25%	11.50%	5.76%	0.49%
1965	5.72	11.63	9.83	0.67	4.93	9.33	5.83	0.46
1970	6.60	8.56	8.02	0.57	5.87	4.31	3.37	0.25
1971	6.93	10.24	10.51	0.71	6.15	7.59	6.56	0.47
1972	7.02	11.01	12.14	0.77	6.38	9.05	8.41	0.58
1973	7.34	10.31	12.15	0.76	6.68	7.88	7.64	0.53
1974	7.63	7.03	8.63	0.54	6.87	4.89	4.85	0.33
1975	7.73	6.06	7.82	0.47	7.06	5.08	5.30	0.36
1976	8.01	7.87	11.10	0.63	7.29	6.09	6.81	0.44
1977	8.23	9.32	13.94	0.77	7.43	7.23	8.39	0.54
1978	8.50	9.57	14.84	0.82	7.75	7.58	9.09	0.59
1979	9.08	7.37	12.06	0.67	8.24	5.42	6.79	0.45
1980	9.60	1.38	2.44	0.13	8.67	−1.58	−2.56	−0.17
1981	10.48	−6.96	−15.44	−0.73	9.47	−9.91	−16.21	−0.94
1982	11.27	−5.64	−16.13	−0.65	9.72	−8.21	−15.77	−0.80
1983	11.20	2.34	6.77	0.27	9.76	−1.07	−2.16	−0.10
1984	11.66	1.05	3.15	0.13	10.35	0.68	1.56	0.07
1985	11.49	3.27	9.14	0.39	10.61	7.11	14.49	0.75
1986	10.68	0.08	0.20	0.01	10.15	10.55	16.21	1.07
1987[5]	9.44	−6.00	−13.10	−0.56	NA	NA	NA	NA

Note: Beginning in 1982, average assets exclude certain contra-asset balances that had been reported as liabilities.

[1] Total income divided by average assets (net of loans in process or contra-assets).

[2] Net after-tax income divided by total income.

[3] Net after-tax income divided by average net worth.

[4] Net after-tax income divided by average assets (net of loans in process or contra-assets).

[5] Preliminary.

NA = not available.

Source: United States League of Savings Associations, 1988 Savings Institution Sourcebook, p. 53, as reported in Edward J. Kane, The S&L Insurance Mess: How Did It Happen? (Washington, D.C.: Urban Institute, 1989), pp. 14–15.

1988. In many cases, the federal regulators provided funding assistance to support the merger.

Second, in an effort to reduce disintermediation, regulators in 1978 created the money market certificate or MMC. The MMC was not subject to Regulation Q, had a six-month maturity, had a $10,000 minimum balance, and its interest rate was tied to the six-month Treasury bill rate. The MMC increased the ability of depository institutions in general and thrifts in particular, to retain funds that would have been disintermediated. Unfortunately, the MMC actually made the situation worse for thrifts. Since a major part of their loan portfolios consisted of FRLT mortgages, the increased interest-rate sensitivity of the sources of funds resulting from the MMC increased interest rate risk. At the same time, regulation and tax incentives prevented thrifts from diversifying away from FRLT mortgages. Third and most important, the regulators and others finally became convinced by the late 1970s that a fundamental restructuring of the financial system was in order. Thrifts in particular required increased diversification powers to better manage interest rate and disintermediation risk. Only in this way could thrifts remain important suppliers of mortgage credit. Thus, the start of the official financial reform process was an attempt to deal with the thrift problem of the 1970s. The Deregulation and Monetary Control Act of 1980 and the Garn-St. Germain Depository Institutions Act of 1982 were both focused on improving the viability of thrifts, though the reforms had implications for the entire financial system.

The 1980 and 1982 acts as well as a large number of other regulatory changes sought to increase the ability of thrifts to remain viable but at the same time remain primary mortgage lenders. The following represent some of the major changes:

1. Thrifts were permitted to offer new market-sensitive sources of funds such as NOW accounts, ATS accounts, and MMDAs.

2. Thrifts were permitted to diversify into nonmortgage loans so that by 1988, mortgages represented a little more than 50% of their financial assets compared to 85% in the 1970s. At the state level, thrifts were given even greater asset diversification powers, especially in California and Texas.

3. Thrifts were permitted to offer adjustable rate mortgages or ARMs to reduce interest rate risk.

4. The tax incentives to encourage thrift mortgage lending were essentially removed by the 1986 Tax Reform Act.

5. Regulators relaxed restrictions on interstate and interindustry acquisitions of troubled thrifts so that a bank or thrift in one state would be able to take over a troubled thrift in another state.

6. The Federal National Mortgage Association and the Government Mortgage Company intensified efforts to develop secondary markets for mortgages to permit thrifts to package mortgages for resale in the open market.

The Thrift Problem in the 1980s: Failure to Close Insolvent Thrifts or Decade of the Living Dead

Despite these major changes, the thrift problem continued to grow throughout the 1980s (Table 14-2). By 1985 the problem had become immense. A General Accounting Office study[1] noted that in mid-1985 there were 461 insolvent thrifts holding about 8.8% of thrift assets. To close these institutions, sell the assets, and use FSLIC

---

[1] *Thrift Industry Problems: Potential Demands on the FSLIC Insurance Fund.* Washington, D.C.: GAO, February 1986.

Source: North American Syndicate, Inc., 235 East 45th Street, New York, New York 10017.

FIGURE 14-2.   **Taxpayers bear the cost of the failure to close insolvent thrifts**

funds to pay off insured deposits in excess of the revenue obtained from selling the assets would cost the FSLIC about $16.9 billion. Year-end FSLIC reserves, however, were $4.56 billion. Thus, not only a major portion of the thrift industry was insolvent, but FSLIC was also insolvent. In addition to the insolvent thrifts, another 600 to 800 thrifts were operating with net worth of 3% or less of assets and, while not dead, could be classified as financially comatose. The GAO report indicated that together the insolvent and financially weak thrift represented 43% of the thrift assets.

Thus, the thrift industry was in serious trouble, and in a sense, the insolvent and financially weak thrift institutions became the living dead of the 1980s—not unlike the protagonist in the horror movie *Night of the Living Dead.*[2] The insolvent and financially weak thrifts should have been closed. Unfortunately, the delayed action permitted the thrift problem to reach massive proportions by the end of the 1980s that imposed a serious deadweight loss on the rest of the financial system and a burden that is being borne by the taxpayer (Figure 14-2)

The magnitude of the thrift problem by the end of the 1980s had become the focus of much public attention and the obvious question is how the problem reached

[2] This characterization is a variation of one found in Edward J. Kane's writings in which he frequently refers to insolvent thrifts as "zombie thrifts"; for example, see *The S&L Insurance Mess: How Did it Happen?* (Washington, D.C.: Urban Institute, 1989).

such proportions. The answer cannot rely on the view that the problem occurred so fast that no one saw it coming. On the contrary, the evidence of a thrift problem was readily available in the very first few years of the deregulation process. In the early 1980s, increasing numbers of thrift institutions were having difficulty adjusting to the new competitive environment; income was declining as was net worth.

Two interrelated considerations account for the magnitude of the thrift problem.

Flaws in the Regulatory Reform Process Thrift institutions were provided with new portfolio diversification powers, though many of the new powers involved real estate–related credit. Thrifts were permitted to invest in "junk" bonds—high-yielding but high-risk bonds—and make direct investments in real estate development projects. Thrift regulators in California and Texas gave even greater diversification powers to thrifts, and as it turned out, the majority of troubled thrifts have been located in these two states. This does not mean to say that deregulation is the source of the thrift problem. While some of the new diversification powers were not appropriate for any depository institution, the source of the thrift problem was a failure to restructure federal deposit insurance and other forms of government deposit guarantees to match the greater diversification powers of depository institutions.

The new asset diversification powers permitted thrifts to assume greater risk, while at the same time, federal deposit insurance provided incentives to assume risk. Federal deposit insurance premiums are not adjusted for the risk of an individual institution, and hence, the fixed premium structure subsidizes risk taking. Thus, part of the thrift problem reflects a general problem with deregulation in the United States. Deposit insurance has an adverse *moral hazard* in that it provides incentives to assume risk, while at the same time, financial innovation and regulatory reforms are increasing the opportunities to assume risk.

The importance of the adverse moral hazard is illustrated by the increasing asset quality problem of thrift institutions after 1985. While declining interest rates had reduced interest rate risk exposure, the troubled and insolvent thrift institutions in the late 1980s were mainly a reflection of poor asset quality.

Regulatory Treatment of Troubled Thrifts The willingness of the FHLBB and FSLIC to permit large numbers of troubled thrifts to continue operation contributed greatly to the magnitude of the problem. Financially dead or comatose thrifts assumed high levels of risk in such an environment since there was no penalty if risky loans and investments failed to pay off while, at the same time, there was some chance that a high-risk investment or loan would generate income to improve the thrift's position. This is no different from the gambler who plays with someone else's money. A study by the Federal Reserve Bank of Dallas presented in Table 14-3, for example, clearly shows that insolvent thrifts in Texas adopted riskier positions than solvent institutions. Table 14-3 shows that insolvent thrift assets grew faster in the early 1980s, insolvent thrifts paid higher deposit rates, and insolvent thrifts had a higher expected return on loans. This strategy did not work. Insolvent thrifts continued to lose money (Figure 14-3).

Thrift regulators failed in their public responsibility as did the administration and Congress. These groups were reluctant to disclose the magnitude of the problem since it would require an infusion of taxpayer funds. In addition, the role of thrifts in the social contract for housing placed them in a powerful political position to induce regulators to adopt strategies that were not costly from their perspective. Individual

TABLE 14-3 Management differences: solvent versus insolvent Texas thrifts

	Solvent	Insolvent	Difference
Average asset growth[1]			
1980-Q4 to 1984-Q4	23%	39%	16**
1984-Q4 to 1988-Q1	13%	5%	−8**
Average loan rate[2]	11.54%	12.30%	0.76**
Average Deposit rate[3]	10.60%	10.96%	0.36**

1. Figures are the averages of the annualized growth in assets at individual institutions. Growth from mergers is included.

2. Figures are the averages of annualized rates earned on mortgage loans and contracts at individual institutions in the fourth quarter of 1984.

3. Figures are the averages of annualized rates paid on deposits at individual institutions in the fourth quarter of 1984.

** Denotes that the difference is significant at the 99% level of significance.

Note: Information based on Federal Home Loan Bank Board Thrift Financial Report.

Source: Genie D. Short and Jeffery W. Gunther, "The Texas Thrift Situation: Implications for the Texas Financial Industry," Federal Reserve Bank of Dallas (September 1989).

and powerful members of Congress were more than willing on a number of occasions to intervene on the behalf of troubled thrift institutions.

As a result, regulators adopted a gradualist approach to dealing with the thrift problem based on a firm foundation of wishful thinking! Regulators adopted a series of short-run policies short of closing insolvent and financially weak institutions in the hope that they would "work their way out of the problem." Specifically, regulators relaxed capital requirements on thrifts and introduced "regulatory accounting practices" or RAP as an alternative to "generally accepted accounting practices" or GAAP. RAP permitted what might be termed "liberal" rules for valuing assets and capital. Thus, the problem of negative net worth could be dealt with by changing the defi-

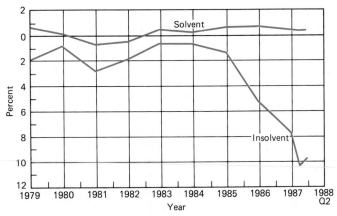

Source: James R. Barth and Michael G. Bradley, "Thrift Deregulation and Federal Deposit Insurance," *Journal of Financial Services Research*, 2 (September 1989), p. 244.

FIGURE 14-3 Net after-tax income of FSLIC-insured solvent and insolvent thrift institutions grouped according to GAAP, 1979–second quarter 1988

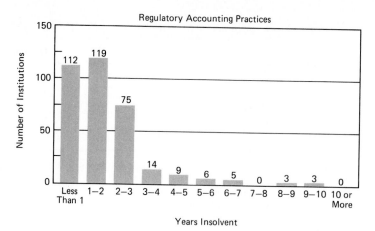

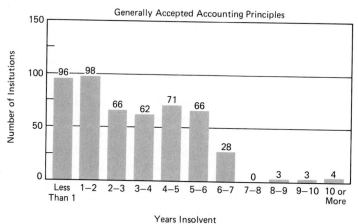

Source: James R. Barth and Michael G. Bradley, "Thrift Deregulation and Federal Deposit Insurance," *Journal of Financial Services Research*, 2 (September 1989), p. 249

FIGURE 14-4 FSLIC-insured insolvent thrift institutions—length of insolvency according to RAP and GAAP as of June 1988

nitions! Figure 14-4 shows how RAP minimized the problem. According to RAP, only 40 thrifts had been insolvent for more than three years, while according to GAAP, 237 thrifts had been insolvent for more than three years.

Like fixed premium deposit insurance, the treatment of insolvent and financially weak thrift institutions had an adverse moral hazard. It provided incentives to assume risk.

The inability of the thrift regulators to respond to the growing crisis was partly a failure of the deregulation process to recognize and plan for the new responsibilities that would be required of thrift regulators. The FHLBB and FSLIC gained their experience during a period when thrift institutions were relatively simple. They obtained funds from issuing savings and time deposits and made residential mortgages at fixed rates. Deregulation, however, dramatically increased their ability to obtain and use funds. This sudden increase in opportunities to assume risk was beyond the ability of the thrift regulators to monitor properly. According to George Kaufman:

"Some associations were not examined for three or four years and violations identified by field examiners frequently were not pursued by their supervisors and corrected. There was a major meltdown in surveillance, examination, and supervision. For example, in 1983 the Little Rock Federal Home Loan Bank, which was in the heart of the problem area, was moved to Dallas. Only 11 of the 48 members of the supervisory staff were willing to make the move. As a result, the annual number of examinations in this district declined from 261 in 1982–1983 to 183 in 1983–1984 and 173 in 1984–1985 before increasing again to 283 in 1985–1986."[3]

The lack of supervision and general unwillingness to deal with troubled institutions also provided an environment conducive to fraud at some institutions. Vernon Savings and Loan Association in Vernon, Texas is a classical example. When Vernon Savings was taken over in 1987, 96 percent of its loans were in default. The remaining 4 percent were mostly deferred interest loans, on which interest had not yet been paid.[4]

Competitive Equality Banking Act of 1987

The Competitive Equality Banking Act of 1987 was the first attempt by Congress to deal explicitly with the thrift problem. The 1987 act represents an interesting piece of financial reform legislation in many respects. The name is misleading and is derived from a provision of the act prohibiting nonbank banks. Most of the act deals with issues that would be hard to classify as competitive equality–related issues. What was even more underwhelming about the act is the Alice in Wonderland premise that a $10.8 billion recapitalization of the FSLIC would solve the thrift problem! Estimates of the cost of dealing with the thrift problem in 1987 even by the GAO greatly exceeded this amount. Outside observers were suggesting that as much as $50 billion would be needed to close the insolvent and financially weak thrift institutions and that further delay would add billions to the total cost. Lobbying pressure from the thrift industry resulted in relaxed regulatory treatment of troubled thrifts in Texas until their condition improved. The act did, however, make a positive contribution by making it easier for banks to acquire failed or failing thrifts.

The problem only increased in dimension after the 1987 act; however, with a presidential election in November 1988, there was little enthusiasm to take bold action. The Bush administration finally introduced a bill which was passed and signed into law August 9, 1989. FIRREA is a major effort to deal with the thrift problem and stands along with the 1980 and 1982 acts as a major piece of financial reform legislation.

[3] George G. Kaufmann, "The Savings and Loan Rescue of 1989: Causes and Perspective," Working Paper, Federal Reserve Bank of Chicago (November 1989), 6.

[4] George G. Kaufman, "The Savings and Loan Rescue of 1989: Causes and Perspective," Working Paper, Federal Reserve Bank of Chicago (November 1989), 10.

FIRREA

FIRREA represents a major policy event designed to deal with the thrift problem. The 1989 act is complex, consisting of many components. There are five stated objectives of the act: First, the act provides regulators with enhanced powers to deal with insolvent and weak thrifts; second, the act imposes portfolio constraints to reduce risk taken by thrifts, especially troubled thrifts; third, the act intends to strengthen the financial condition of the thrift industry by redefining and raising capital standards and to improve supervision over thrift activities; fourth, the act intends to strengthen the financial condition of the government deposit insurance fund by raising the fixed-premium for computing deposit insurance payments; and fifth, the act intends the thrift industry to remain an important part of the social contract to supply mortgage credit and additionally, to be a vehicle for promoting affordable housing financing.

The more important components of the act designed to deal with the thrift problem can be summarized by the following:

1. The act is a bailout for the thrift industry and an explicit statement by Congress that the full faith and credit of the U.S. government stands behind federal deposit insurance. All federally insured deposits of depository institutions, including thrift deposits, are covered up to the $100,000 limit.

2. The act abolished the FHLBB and FSLIC. Thrift regulation is now the responsibility of the Office of Thrift Supervision (OTS) under the general administration of the U.S. Treasury. FSLIC is reorganized and recapitalized as the Savings Association Insurance Fund (SAIF) under the general administration of the FDIC. A new agency, the Federal Housing Agency, is responsible for overseeing the credit advance activities of the Federal Home Loan District Banks.

3. Thrift asset powers are reduced. Specifically, direct investment powers and junk bond purchases are significantly reduced to limit risk taking. Thrifts are ordered to divest themselves of all junk bond holdings by July 1, 1994.

4. The requirement that thrifts invest 60% of their assets in real estate–related loans is raised to 70% to reaffirm the role of thrifts as suppliers of mortgage credit.

5. The act requires higher capital asset ratios in terms of tangible capital as opposed to intangible (goodwill) capital. Thrifts are required to meet a 1.5% ratio almost immediately and a 3.0% ratio by January 1995.

6. The act gives thrift regulators tough new powers to deal with thrifts that engage in risk or fraudulent activities that threaten the federal insurance fund.

7. The FDIC administers both insurance funds—bank and thrift. Premium rates are to be increased for both funds in a series of steps. Bank Insurance Fund rates, 8.3 cents for each $100 in deposits in 1989, increase to 12 cents in 1990 and 15 cents in 1991. Savings Association Insurance Fund rates, 20.8 cents per $100 deposits in 1989, increase to 23 cents in 1991 and decline back to 15 cents by 1998. The FDIC can increase rates for either fund up to a maximum of 32.5 cents per $100 of deposits after 1995. The objective of the rate in-

creases is to put both banks and thrifts on the same premium schedule and to achieve a 1.25% ($1.25 per $100 of insured deposits) reserve ratio for both the Bank Insurance Fund and Savings Association Insurance Fund.

8. The act established a bailout agency called the Resolution Trust Corporation to liquidate assets of failed thrifts. Another agency called the Resolution Funding Corporation is created to fund much of the bailout. An agency of the FDIC is created called the FSLIC Resolution Fund to assume the assets and liabilities of the defunct FSLIC except those transferred to the Resolution Trust Corporation.

9. The official cost of the bailout is $166 billion with interest expenditures on borrowed funds over a 10-year period and $300 billion over a 30-year period. Much of this will come directly or indirectly from taxpayers.

10. To help eliminate the insolvent thrifts, the act permits bank holding companies to purchase insolvent and *solvent* thrifts immediately.

The 1989 act is a major financial reform that introduces a number of important changes. At the same time, it would be premature to think that the act has solved the thrift problem. A great deal will depend on how fast regulators can close insolvent and financially weak thrifts before they add even more deadweight loss to the thrift industry. Simply in terms of numbers of institutions and human resources, the task is immense. The FDIC in late 1989 was planning to hire 500 to 600 lawyers and examiners in a short period of time to deal with the new responsibilities. More than human resources, the financial resources in the opinion of many are grossly understated. The cost estimate of dealing with the thrifts is not taken seriously by many observers because it is based on unrealistic assumptions about the economy, thrift deposit growth, and how fast regulators can close insolvent institutions. In the past, the government has had a poor record of estimating the cost of dealing with the thrift problem. Almost every cost estimate is significantly increased several months later. Only a few months after the 1989 act was signed into law, the FDIC announced that the bailout would likely cost an additional $50 billion because thrift losses in 1989 were larger than predicted. Thus, most observers of the scene argue that the ultimate cost of the bailout will be far above the official estimate at the time the act was signed. A number of cynics argue that the 1989 act is only "Part 1" of what will be several bailout efforts in the 1990s.

The 1989 act will sharply reduce the numbers of thrifts, and those that survive will be more conservatively managed and less risky. Whether the act will deal with the thrift problem once and for all remains to be seen.

Moral Hazard of Deposit Insurance: Fundamental Flaw in the Deregulation Process

Federal deposit insurance subsidizes risk taking because the premiums are not risk sensitive. Deregulation has expanded portfolio opportunities that permit financial institutions to assume risk yet has kept in place a deposit insurance framework that subsidizes risk taking. The cart has been placed before the horse—deregulation has increased the opportunities to assume risk while at the same time, the reforms have not adequately addressed the incentives to assume risk embedded in government deposit guarantees. The risk incentive feature of fixed rate deposit insurance was enhanced in 1980 when the Deregulation and Monetary Control Act raised the insured deposit limit from $40,000 to $100,000.

By 1990 there appeared to be greater recognition of this fundamental problem and a greater willingness to institute reforms to bring government deposit guarantees more in line with the enhanced ability of depository institutions to assume risk. FIRREA, for example, requires a complete overview of deposit insurance that may generate fundamental changes in how federal deposit insurance is administered and priced. Risk-based capital-asset requirements have been established for U.S. banks as an alternative approach. Deposit insurance premiums have been raised by FIRREA for both thrifts and banks, and the FDIC is given greater powers to raise deposit insurance rates in the future.

At the same time, it is difficult to be optimistic about meaningful reforms for two reasons: First, the risk-subsidizing element of federal deposit insurance has been well known for some time, and the 1982 Garn-St Germain act had earlier called for a major review of deposit insurance. Second, the thrift problem was not widely perceived as a crisis, and in the opinion of many regulators, the problem was solved with FIRREA.

What About the Banking System?

The banking system as a whole was in a much stronger financial position in the late 1980s than the thrift industry, and the FDIC was in a much stronger financial position than FSLIC with reserves in 1988 of $18 billion compared to FSLIC reserves of $4 billion. At the same time, concern was being raised about the financial soundness of the banking system and how regulatory authorities handled troubled banks.

The number of bank failures increased significantly in the 1980s compared to the 1970s. Among these failures were banks that were not closed but permitted to continue operating with new management and new capital such as Continental Illinois in 1984 and First Republic Bank Corporation in 1988. There are three approaches to dealing with a failing institution: (1) insured deposit transfers, (2) liquidation or payoffs, and (3) purchase and assumptions or P&As. In the case of insured deposit transfers, the FDIC transfers the insured deposits to another institution. In the case of payoffs, the FDIC pays off insured depositors. In the case of P&As, the FDIC arranges to sell the deposits (insured and uninsured) and all or a portion of the assets to another bank. P&As have become the preferred approach. In 1988, 164 of the 200 banks that failed during the year were handled by P&A while 30 were handled by insured deposit transfers, and 6 were handled by payoffs.

The procedure used by the FDIC is based on minimizing the cost to the insurance fund and generating the smallest impact on the community being served by the failed bank. At the same time, large depositors (above $100,000) benefit from a P&A,

---

BOX 1   A Gathering crisis in deposit insurance—a warning in 1985

Edward J. Kane's *A Gathering Crisis in Federal Deposit Insurance* published in 1985 by the MIT Press severely criticized the way in which deposit insurance has functioned in the United States. While some may disagree with Kane's arguments, there is widespread acceptance of the main thrust of the study—the structure and administration of federal deposit insurance has encouraged excessive risk taking by depository institutions and has greatly extended government guarantees to depository institutions that will ultimately be borne by the taxpayer. While there is little chance of a collapse of federal deposit insurance, Kane does not completely rule out such an event. The gathering crisis emanates from the moral hazard of deposit insurance, the failure to price deposit insurance correctly, the political sensitivity of the deposit insurance funds, and the reliance on nonmarket accounting conventions for calculating depository institution net worth that overstates performance.

The study does not reject the need for some type of federal deposit insurance to limit contagion and support public confidence in deposit money; however, the current system's apparent success through the late 1970s as measured by the small number of bank and thrift failures has provided a false sense of security.

Kane suggests a six-point reform of federal deposit insurance to minimize the risk incentives of the current system and the burden that is being placed on the taxpayer:

1. Regulatory practices have permitted depository institutions to carry assets at book value for those assets whose cash flows are current. Assets valued at book value irrespective of market developments misrepresents the economic condition of the institution, and as such, Kane recommends that loans and investments be valued according to market rather than book value.

2. At present, the FDIC cannot declare an institution insolvent without the cooperation of the Comptroller or the Office of Thrift Supervision. Insuring agencies should have more autonomy to deal with troubled institutions since the Comptroller, the Office of Thrift Supervision, and state agencies are more likely to adopt policies to delay reducing the number of depository institutions under their respective jurisdiction. Enhanced flexibility to the insuring agencies would permit them to better manage their own risk exposure.

3. Insurance coverage needs to be recalibrated in several ways; for example, the basic coverage per account should be lowered to protect the deposits of most households. Deposit insurance was never meant to cover all deposits as under the current system.

4. Deposit insurance premiums should be risk rated.

5. Opportunities should be enhanced for mixed private and governmental competition in providing deposit insurance.

6. The TBTF or "too big to fail" concept that is currently part of the regulatory approach to troubled institutions should be rejected. This concept was officially expressed in September 1984, when the Comptroller of the Currency made a reference to the fact that the federal government could not permit any of the nation's 11 largest banks to be liquidated. Statutory limits should be placed on the ability of regulatory authorities to bail out large insolvent institutions.

Kane's recommendations have been voiced by others. Deposit insurance reform is under consideration as of the writing of this book. While it was unlikely that Kane's recommendation would be adopted in whole, deposit insurance appears to be slowly moving in the direction of reducing the risk incentives embedded in the system.

---

whereas large depositors are subject to losses from insured deposit transfers or payoffs. This has raised two issues: (1) P&As provide an indirect form of government deposit guarantee for deposits above $100,000 and as a result, reduce the market discipline that large depositors might impose on a bank. (2) P&As are generally arranged for large banks and, hence, provide a disincentive for large depositors to place their funds in smaller banks since they may be more at risk.

The FDIC's increased reliance on P&As for dealing with troubled banks has come under increasing criticism since the explicit or implicit FDIC guarantees made to purchasing institutions conceal the true cost of the bank failure and may expose the FDIC to future claims. In addition, it provides another adverse moral hazard embedded in the government deposit guarantee and thus provides incentives to take risks.

The FDIC has also been criticized for its "Too Big to Fail" or TBTF, attitude. That is, the FDIC and other federal regulators pursue policies that maintain a large bank as a going concern while smaller banks are declared bankrupt. The most well-known example of this was the effort to keep Continental Illinois bank from failing in 1984. Fear of withdrawals of large CDs, especially by foreign depositors, motivated the FDIC and other federal regulators to declare that all deposits would be covered. In addition, the Federal Reserve provided almost $5 billion of discount funds in one week. Continental was the seventh largest bank in the United States at the time and as a result was regarded as TBTF. This does not imply that costs were not imposed on Continental. Shareholders lost as did management; however, many observers regard the decision to insure deposits over $100,000 as inappropriate.

FIRREA has transferred the responsibility of dealing with insolvent and financially weak thrifts to the FDIC. There is little reason to believe that the FDIC will depart from its reliance on P&As in this new responsibility and even perhaps adopt a TBTF attitude toward large thrifts.

Future Path of Regulatory Reform

The deregulation process in the United States has been plagued by increasing numbers of troubled institutions, especially thrifts. Many of these problems derive from the risk incentives provided by fixed premium deposit insurance, the unwillingness of the regulatory authorities to impose market discipline on institutions that are no longer viable, and the unwillingness of the administration and Congress to recognize the need for further reforms.

While the deregulation process has achieved major results in many areas, especially the end of Regulation Q ceilings, it has yet to deal with the conflict between enhanced opportunities to assume risk and the incentives to assume risk inherent in the entire set of government deposit guarantees. The deregulation process must resolve this conflict.

The magnitude of the thrift problem has made it clear that delayed reaction to closing troubled institutions merely makes the situation worse a few years down the line. The deposit insurance system, it is hoped, will be reformed to be more compatible with a competitive financial environment that provides increasing opportunities to assume risk. While FIRREA is a step in the right direction, it became obvious only a few months after the act was passed that additional reform would be required.

Less Than One Year After FIRREA—
Billions More and
Additional Reforms Needed

FIRREA did not end controversy over how to deal with the thrift problem. Both during the writing of the act and when it was passed August 1989 critics pointed out that it did not go far enough, fast enough, or initiate the regulatory changes that would be needed to contain the problem. The more important criticisms focused on two areas. First, FIRREA grossly underestimated the cost of closing insolvent and troubled thrifts and second, FIRREA failed to deal with fundamental causes of the thrift problem. In fact, an article published by Elijah Brewer III in the Federal Reserve Bank of Chicago's *Economic Perspectives*[5] referred to the act as a "half-measure cure" for a "full-blown crisis." Few observers disagreed with this assessment and as events unfolded after August 1989 through mid-1990, FIRREA was fast becoming even less than a half-measure cure.

How Much Is the Thrift Problem Going to Cost? There is considerable difference of opinion about the cost of the thrift problem. Part of the confusion arises from whether one is expressing the cost in *present value* terms or including the interest expenses incurred in selling bonds to obtain funding to deal with the problem. Most of the estimates mentioned in the news media focus on the amount of funds that need to be raised by the Resolution Funding Corporation plus the interest cost on the bonds issued to obtain the funds. The present value cost is the appropriate estimate of the cost because it represents today's resources that must be allocated to deal with the problem. Consider a simple illustration. Assume you have a problem to solve which will cost $100. If you spend $100 today to solve the problem, the present value cost is $100. If you borrow $100 at 5% interst for one year to deal with the problem, it will still represent a net cost of $100. This is because the $105 you will need to pay at the end of the year is offset by the interest (5%) you will earn on $100 that you did not have to spend because you borrowed the $100. The reader should keep this point in mind as we discuss the various cost estimates of the thrift bailout. In July 1989, the Office of Management and Budget (OMB) had estimated the cost of dealing with the thrift problem to be $257 billion over a 33 year period. This was the amount needed to pay off FSLIC's obligations, resolve the problems of thrifts awaiting resolution, pay interest on bonds issued by the Resolution Funding Corporation (REFCORP), and pay some administrative expenses. The estimate was based on specific assumptions regarding future interest rates, deposit growth at thrifts, and recoveries of troubled institutions. When FIRREA was passed in August 1989, the official cost was given at $166 over a 10 year period and double that amount over a 30 year period. The bulk of the funds would be provided directly or indirectly by taxpayers.

Critics pointed out that the underlying assumptions about the economy and the thrift industry were too optimistic and that delayed response—that is, dealing with the problem over a 10 or 30 year period—would greatly raise the cost far beyond the official estimates. Events were to prove the critics correct.

[5] Elijah Brewer III, "Full-Blown Crisis, Half Measure Cure," Federal Reserve Bank of Chicago, (November/December 1990), 2–16.

During the following months one encountered news item after news item that the cost of the thrift problem was higher than anticipated by the government. The RTC was having difficulty selling failed thrift assets, admitting after only several months in operation that additional funds would be required. Bond sales to finance a major part of the thrift bailout so as to keep the cost "off budget" found an unreceptive market and rates were higher than anticipated. It became obvious that the thrift problem had reached crisis proportions as larger numbers of thrifts became insolvent in response to continuing regional problems (southwest) and as the decline in "junk bond" prices in the first half of 1990 further deteriorated thrift assets (FIRREA required divestiture of junk bonds by July 1994). Real estate markets did not improve in the southwest and there was an indication that flat or declining real estate values in the northeast might cause further thrift problems. Finally, the involvement of prominent members of the Senate in the Lincoln Savings and Loan scandal further revealed the depth of the thrift crisis.

On April 6, 1990 the General Accounting Office in testimony before the Committee on Banking, Housing and Urban Affairs of the U.S. Senate,[6] officially indicated that the original cost of dealing with the thrift problem needed to be revised upward to the range of $325 to $500 billion over a 30 year period. The rationale for the new estimates included:

—value of thrift assets lower than originally estimated

—longer period of time required to sell thrift assets than originally estimated

—higher operating losses of insolvent and troubled thrifts than estimated

—higher administrative expenses for RTC than originally estimated

—higher interest cost on borrowed funds for RTC than anticipated

—use of 40 year rather than 30 year bonds to fund the RTC and greater difficulty in selling bonds than anticipated.

The GAO regarded the $325 billion estimated as a "least cost" estimate. In plain language this meant that there was about as much probability of snow in Hawaii during July that the $325 billion estimate was realistic. The GAO indicated that it was more likely that the correct figure was closer to $500 billion, in part because the $325 billion estimate was based on "optimistic" assumptions about the economy and thrift deposit growth contained in the earlier OMB estimate.

The April 1990 GAO testimony was only one more estimate of the cost that had the same element of consistency as the previous government estimates—it was higher than the last! No one knows what the total cost will be since it depends on so many factors and how long it takes to resolve the problem. The $325–$500 billion range was probably one of the more realistic estimates that has come out of the U.S. government which as late as July 1988 argued that only $15 billion would be required to deal with the thrift problem.

There is obviously great uncertainty about the cost because of the number of factors that will influence the ultimate cost of closing insolvent and troubled thrift institutions. In addition, the cost estimates coming from various sources, official or

[6] Testimony of Charles A. Bowsher, Comptroller General of the United States before the Committee on Banking, Housing and Urban Affairs U.S. Senate, April 6, 1990.

otherwise, are not consistently reported. Some cost estimates are in terms of present value dollars and others such as the GAO estimate are for a period of time such as 10 or 30 years. At the time of this writing in mid 1990, most observers would estimate the cost in present value dollars to be in the range of $125 to $200 billion. In all honesty, however, these are only educated guesses. The thrift problem has become a financial black hole.

Failure to Deal with Fundamental Problems Critics also emphasized the failure of FIRREA to deal with fundamental problems that were the cause of the problem. The most serious is the failure to deal with the risk incentives of federal deposit insurance. Fixed-premium deposit insurance (though the rates will be increased) continues to provide incentives to adopt risky loan and investment portfolios, but combined with a general unwillingness to require market value as opposed to book-value accounting, leaves unchanged a fundamental cause of the thrift problem. Failure to value assets at market value can easily overstate book-value net worth and thus eliminate some of the beneficial effects of higher and redefined asset capital ratios. Book-value accounting makes thrifts look better on paper than they appear to the market, increasing potential claims on the insurance fund (ultimately taxpayers). Again, this provides an incentive to take risk.

The failure to incorporate market-value accounting to determine net worth also increases the time lags of closing market-value insolvent institutions. As long as an institution can show positive book value net worth, the OTS and the FDIC despite their new powers will have difficulty closing the institution. During the time market-value insolvent institutions remain operating, they have an incentive to adopt risky loan and investment strategies and can finance these strategies by offering higher deposit rates on insured deposits. As a result, there is no depositor discipline on the institution.

FIRREA continues to permit forbearance even for book-value insolvent institutions. At the discretion of the OTS, institutions that fail to meet the new capital requirements can be granted an exception by submitting an acceptable capital plan. Since many thrifts have been unable to meet the new standards, the government continues to be in the business of granting forbearance.

Critics also point to another part of FIRREA that makes it difficult for thrifts to function and effectively deal with risk. The act requires thrifts to increase their assets in mortgage related loans from 60 to 70 percent. This is inconsistent with past reforms designed to increase thrift diversification to better manage risk. This aspect of the act reflects a view of some observers that the thrift problem was the result of too much diversification that induced thrifts to move away from traditional home mortgage lending. This is incorrect. The thrift problem is not the result of deregulation for at least three reasons. First, thrifts in the 1980s did shift away from home mortgages but many of these funds were allocated to activities directly and indirectly related to real estate; second, the risk-incentives of government deposit guarantees combined with limited supervision provided thrifts with incentives to assume risk; and third, the failure of thrift regulators and the government to respond to the growing thrift problem during the 1980s provided further incentives to assume risk and greatly contributed to the magnitude of the problem.

As a result of the magnitude of the thrift problem and the failure of FIRREA to effectively deal with the problem, major financial legislation is likely in the near future. In mid-1990 the U.S. Treasury announced that it was using the FIRREA mandated deposit insurance study as a vehicle for a comprehensive overhaul of the

U.S. financial system. The Treasury has specifically requested input from the Board of Governors of the Federal Reserve, the FDIC, and the Securities and Exchange Commission. It is difficult to forecast how the structure of the financial system will change in the next few years, but there is no doubt that major changes are forthcoming.

Key Points

1. Deregulation has made the financial system more competitive than previously. In many ways depository institutions are better suited to deal with uncertain interest rates and manage risk than in the past; however, additional reforms are needed to ensure the soundness of the financial system.

2. The thrift problem represents the most important reason why a sound financial environment has yet to be achieved.

3. Delayed regulatory response has permitted the thrift problem to reach a size that large taxpayer-supplied funding is the only option open to closing insolvent and financially weak thrifts. This has had an adverse moral hazard impact in the sense that it encourages risk taking. The CEBA and FIRREA represent recent efforts to deal with the thrift problem.

4. The deposit insurance framework in general has an adverse moral hazard since it encourages risk taking. This problem has been widely recognized. FIRREA calls for a major review of deposit insurance by 1991.

5. A fundamental problem with the deregulation process has been the conflict between a process that increases the opportunities to assume risk and regulations that encourage risk taking.

Key Terms

Bank failures

Competitive Equality Banking Act (CEBA) of 1987

Conflict between enhanced opportunities to assume risk and incentives to assume risk

Financial Institutions Reform, Recovery, and Enforcement Act (FIRREA) of 1989

Moral hazard of government deposit guarantees

Problem banks

Purchase and assumption (P&A)

Thrift problem

Too Big to Fail (TBTF)

Questions

1. Is the financial system more efficient than it was in the 1970s before the start of official deregulation?

2. What is moral hazard and how does fixed rate deposit insurance provide an adverse moral hazard problem in the financial system?

3. How does the TBTF attitude on the part of federal regulatory authorities provide incentives to take risk? If you were a small bank, how would you react to the TBTF attitude?

4. What is a P&A? What are the other two approaches to dealing with a failing bank? If you were a large depositor, which approach would you like the FDIC to adopt?

5. Compare the thrift problem of the 1970s with that of the 1980s.

6. What is moral hazard and how does risk adjusted deposit insurance influence the moral hazard of deposit insurance?

7. Why would insolvent thrifts permitted to continue operation have faster asset growth, higher deposit rates, and higher loan rates than solvent thrifts?

Suggested Readings

1. Jill Abramson and Paul Duke, Jr., "The Keating Five: Senators Who Helped Lincoln S&L Now Face Threat to Their Careers," *The Wall Street Journal* (December 13, 1989). Political aspects of how the thrift problem reached massive proportions with focus on Lincoln S&L in Southern California.

2. John F. Bovenzi and Arthur J. Murton, "Resolution Costs of Bank Failures," *FDIC Banking Review*, Federal Deposit Insurance Corporation, 1 (Fall 1988), 1–13. Provides an overview of FDIC procedures for dealing with bank failures in 1985 and 1986.

3. Mitchell Berlin, "Banking Reform: An Overview of the Restructuring Debate," *Business Review*, Federal Reserve Bank of Philadelphia (July/August 1988), 3–14. Good summary of restructuring the banking industry.

4. Elijah Brewer III, "Full-blown crisis, half-measure cure," *Economic Perspectives* (November/December 1989), 2–17. A critical summary of FIRREA.

5. Elijah Brewer, III, Diana Fortier, and Christine Pavel, "Bank risk from nonbank activities," *Economic Perspectives*, Federal Reserve Bank of Chicago (July/August 1989), 14–26. Discusses whether bank risk has increased as a result of expanded bank product lines.

6. Thomas F. Cargill and Gillian G. Garcia, *Financial Deregulation and Monetary Control* (1982) and *Financial Reform in the 1980s* (1985) (Stanford, Calif.: Hoover Institution Press). These two books focus on the Deregulation and Monetary Control Act of 1980, the Garn-St Germain Depository Institutions Act of 1982, and other related policy events.

7. Andrew S. Carron, "Banking on Change: The Reorganization of Financial Regulation," *Bookings Review*, 2 (Spring 1984), 12–21. Discusses the need for reform of the regulatory structure as part of the overall deregulation process.

8. Kerry Cooper and Donald R. Fraser, *Banking Deregulation and the New Competition in Financial Services* (Cambridge, Mass.: Ballinger, 1986). A good overview of the deregulation process.

9. Franklin R. Edwards, "Can Regulatory Reform Prevent the Impending Disaster in Financial Markets?" *Economic Review*, Federal Reserve Bank of Kansas City (January 1988), 29–39. A critical assessment of the failure of deregulation to achieve a stable and sound financial environment.

10. Federal Deposit Insurance Corporation, *Mandate for Change: Restructuring the Banking Industry* (Washington, D.C.: FDIC 1987). A general discussion of deposit insurance.

11. Federal Deposit Insurance Corporation, *Deposit Insurance in a Changing Environment* (Washington, D.C.: FDIC 1983). A general discussion of deposit insurance.

12. Federal Reserve Bank of Chicago, *Bank Structure and Competition*, 1987. This is a proceedings volume of a conference sponsored by the Federal Reserve Bank of Chicago and contains a number of papers on the thrift problem as well as other aspects of the deregulation process. The Federal Reserve Bank of Chicago also publishes *Economic Perspectives* and the September–October 1985 issue is devoted to deregulation in the 1980s.

13. George E. French, "Measuring the Interest-Rate

Exposure of Financial Intermediaries" *FDIC Banking Review*, Federal Deposit Insurance Corporation, 1 (Fall 1988), 14–27. An easy-to-read example of duration and gap measures of interest rate risk.

14. Thomas G. Fischer, William H. Gram, George G. Kaufman, and Larry R. Mote, 1984. "The Securities Activities of Commercial Banks: A Legal and Economic Analysis," *Tennessee Law Review*, 51 (1984), 467–518. Discusses the legal aspects of the 1933 Glass-Steagall Act on how the act has been interpreted by the courts.

15. John H. Fund, "The S&L Looters' Water-Boy," *The Wall Street Journal*, August 28, 1989, p. A8. Discusses how the Federal Home Loan Bank Board failed in its public responsibility to provide for the soundness of the thrift industry.

16. Gary G. Gilbert, "The Bush Committee Report: Implementation Problems and Prospects," in *Bank Structure and Competition*, Federal Reserve Bank of Chicago, 1984. Discusses the Bush Report's recommendation for changing the structure of government financial regulation.

17. R. Alton Gilbert, "A Comparison of Proposals to Restructure the U.S. Financial System," *Review*, Federal Reserve Bank of St. Louis (July–August 1988), 58–73.

18. Edward J. Kane, "Accelerating Inflation, Technological Innovation, and the Decreasing Effectiveness of Banking Regulation," *Journal of Finance* (May 1981), 355–367. A concise statement of how markets innovate and frustrate financial regulation.

19. Edward J. Kane, *The Gathering Crisis in Federal Deposit Insurance* (Cambridge, Mass.: MIT Press, 1985). A critical appraisal of federal deposit insurance.

20. Edward J. Kane, *The S&L Insurance Mess: How Did It Happen?* (Washington, D.C.: The Urban Institute, 1989). Critical appraisal of how the thrift problem had been handled through mid-1989.

21. George G. Kaufman, "The Federal Safety Net: Not for Banks Only," *Economic Perspectives*, Federal Reserve Bank of Chicago (November–December 1987), 19–29.

22. Paul M. Horvitz, "The Case Against Risk-Related Deposit Insurance Premiums," *Housing Finance Review*, 2 (July 1983), 253–263. A counterargument to risk-related insurance premium proposals.

23. Thomas A. Mayer, "Should Large Banks Be Allowed to Fail?" *Journal of Financial and Quantitative Analysis*, 10 (November 1975), 603–613. A discussion of the "too big to fail" view.

24. Charles McCoy and Paulette Thomas, "Hundreds of S&Ls Fall Hopelessly Short of New Capital Rules," *The Wall Street Journal* (December 7, 1989). Illustrates the difficulty of solving the thrift problem even only a few months after FIRREA was passed.

25. Arthur J. Murton, "Bank Intermediation, Runs, and Deposit Insurance," *FDIC Banking Review* (Spring/Summer 1989), 1–10. Discusses the role of deposit insurance.

26. Jonathan A. Neuberger, "FIRREA and Deposit Insurance Reform," *Weekly Letter*, Federal Reserve Bank of San Francisco (December 1, 1989). Discusses the need for deposit insurance reform.

27. Randall J. Pozdena, "Do Banks Need Securities Powers?" *Weekly Letter*, Federal Reserve Bank of San Francisco (December 29, 1989).

28. David H. Pyle, "Deregulation and Deposit Insurance Reform," *Economic Review*, Federal Reserve Bank of San Francisco (Spring 1984), 5–15. An overview of deposit insurance issues.

29. James Tobin, "A Case for Preserving Regulatory Distinctions," *Challenge* (November–December 1987), 10–17. Argues against the repeal of Glass-Steagall.

30. U.S. General Accounting Office, *Thrift Industry Problems: Potential Demands on the FSLIC Insurance Fund* (February 1986), and *Thrift Industry: Cost to FSLIC of Delaying Action on Insolvent Savings Institutions* (September 1986) (Washington, D.C.: U.S. Government Printing Office). These GAO reports were among the first official indications that a serious thrift problem existed.

31. U.S. General Accounting Office, *Issues Related to Repeal of the Glass-Steagall Act* (Washington, D.C.: U.S. Government Printing Office, January 1988). An excellent overview of the efforts and issues to repeal Glass-Steagall.

International Finance

CHAPTER 15

The International Environment, Statement of International Transactions, and Exchange Rates

Chapter Overview

The United States has never been an economic and financial island unto itself, though for several decades after the end of World War II, the rest of the world was far more dependent on the U.S. economy than the reverse. The situation has radically changed during the past two decades. The world is more economically integrated than at any time in its history, and specifically, the United States is more internationalized and dependent on other countries than at almost any time in its history. The signs of internationalization are everywhere.

This chapter outlines the international environment of the U.S. economy and focuses on five topics. First, we indicate how the international environment has changed in the past two decades from the perspective of the United States. Second, the balance of payments or the Statement of International Transactions is introduced as a way to summarize the trade and financial relationships between the United States and the rest of the world. Third, we then discuss the determinants of the exchange rate and show how the flows of goods, services, and financial assets are reflected in the *foreign exchange market*. The foreign exchange market is the foundation of international finance and the connecting link between all the trading countries of the world. Fourth, we examine the two basic approaches to managing a country's external relationship. These are the *fixed* and the *floating* or *flexible* exchange rate systems. Fifth, a brief historical review of the fixed and flexible exchange rate systems from 1944 through the late 1980s is provided.

The International Environment

We have come to accept as natural the large number of foreign-produced goods and services in the United States. Imports and exports of goods and services in 1988 represented 9.1% and 6.5% of U.S. GNP, respectively. More significantly, there has been a growing presence of foreign financial institutions in the United States. In California, for example, Japanese banks accounted for 11% of bank assets in 1982 while in 1989 they accounted for about 30%. Foreign countries are increasingly making direct investments in the United States. One cannot read the daily newspaper or listen to the news on television without hearing some reference to international trade issues and exchange rates.

The most significant change in world economic integration from the perspective of monetary economics has been a dramatic increase in world financial integration. The majority of industrialized and many developing economies are currently liberalizing their domestic financial systems and reducing restrictions on financial inflows and outflows. Thus, the individual financial systems and economies of the world are becoming more closely interrelated than ever before. The phrases *internationalization of finance* and *globalization of finance* are frequently used to describe the growing integration of world finance.

The United States is a major player in the world economy; however, the rapid growth of economic and financial integration has been associated with a shift in roles among the industrialized countries. Prior to the 1980s, the United States was clearly the dominant force in international trade and finance. Starting in the 1970s, however, and accelerating in the 1980s, a fundamental change occurred. While the United States remains the largest economy in terms of GNP and contributes the largest share of exports and imports to world exports and imports, Japan has moved into a strong second place. Japan has been literally the phoenix arisen from the ashes of World War II to become the world's second largest economic superpower with Germany holding a solid third place position.

The shift in roles in the 1980s was manifested by three changes. First, the United States in the 1980s experienced massive external trade deficits with the rest of the world, especially with Japan. The massive trade imbalances have been financed by borrowing from the rest of the world and, again, especially from Japan. As a result, in 1985 the United States became the largest debtor nation in the world with its liabilities to the rest of the world exceeding its claims on the rest of the world. Second, Japan became the world's largest creditor nation and Tokyo was rapidly becoming a major international financial market. Third, the Federal Reserve found that in the 1980s, it was increasingly required to take into account international conditions in deciding domestic monetary policy. There has been increased emphasis on monetary policy coordination among the major countries and meetings of their respective central banks have become common. U.S. stabilization policy must now adopt an international perspective to an extent not experienced in the past.

Despite the shift in relative roles between the United States, Japan, Germany, and other countries, the U.S. dollar continues to be the major *key currency* for world trade and finance. A key currency is similar to an internationally accepted medium of exchange. While a number of advantages come with being a key currency country, it also places burdens and in the 1980s the United States has encouraged other countries, especially Japan, to assume more responsibility for supporting the international financial system.

U.S. Statement of International Transactions

The balance of payments or Statement of International Transactions (SIT) is a flow of funds statement of receipts and payments from the point of view of the United States, which reflects the real and financial relationship between the United States and the rest of the world. Receipts occur whenever the United States sells goods, services, financial assets, or official reserve assets to the rest of the world. Payments occur whenever the United States purchases goods, services, financial assets, or official reserve assets from the rest of the world.

The SIT is based on double-entry bookkeeping, and thus total receipts must equal total payments. If the SIT always balances, how can we then talk of deficits or surpluses? The reference to a deficit or surplus refers to the relationship between receipts and payments for certain subdivisions of the total statement. A subbalance is in deficit if payments exceed receipts and it is in surplus if receipts exceed payments.

These and other aspects of the SIT can be illustrated by the 1988 statement in Table 15-1. The SIT is divided into two parts. The first part (items 1 through 10) represents *current account* transactions that reflect the flow of currently produced goods and services between the United States and the rest of the world. The second part (items 11 through 15) records transactions in financial assets or *capital flows* between the United States and the rest of the world.

Current Account Transactions   The current account records the flow of goods and services, most of which are conducted for profit and reflect basic economic differences between the United States and the rest of the world. Sales or exports of goods and services to the rest of the world represent a receipt, whereas purchases or imports of goods and services represent a payment. Sales of services include expenditures by foreign tourists visiting the United States, while purchases of services include expenditures by American tourists abroad. Receipts and payments of investment income are included in the current account because they represent the return on the current services of capital. Interest or dividends received by the United States are recorded as a receipt and investment income payments by the United States to foreigners are recorded as a payment. Private and official transfers, such as development grants or gifts to the rest of the world, are recorded as a payment while foreign transfers to the United States are recorded as a receipt.

The overall balance of the current account (item 10) indicates the payments exceeded receipts by $126.6 billion. The United States thus purchased more goods and services from the rest of the world than it sold. The balance on current account

TABLE 15-1   U.S. international transactions: (+) receipts, (−) payments, 1988

Receipts or Payments	Amount (billions)
Current Account	
1. Merchandise exports	+319.3
2. Merchandise imports	−446.5
3. *Trade balance* (1 + 2)	−127.2
4. Military transactions (net)	−4.6
5. Investment income (net)	+2.2
6. Other service transactions (net)	+17.7
7. *Balance on goods and services* (3 + 4 + 5 + 6)	−111.9
8. Remittances, pensions, and other transfers	−4.3
9. U.S. government grants (excluding military)	−10.4
10. *Balance on current account* (7 + 8 + 9)	−126.6
Capital account	
11. Change in U.S. assets in foreign countries	
11a. Private	−81.5
11b. U.S. government official reserve assets	−3.6
11c. U.S. government assets other than official	+3.0
12. Change in total U.S. assets in foreign countries (11a + 11b + 11c) or change in U.S. claims on the rest of the world	−82.1
13. Change in foreign assets in the United States	
13a. Foreign private assets	+180.4
13b. Foreign official reserve assets	+38.9
14. Change in total foreign assets in the United States (13a + 13b) or change in foreign claims on the United States	+219.3
15. *Balance on capital account official and nonofficial* (12 + 14)	+137.2
16. Statistical discrepancy	−10.6
17. *Balance on capital account (official, nonofficial, and statistical discrepancy)* (15 + 16)	+126.6

Source: Federal Reserve Bulletin (September 1989).

contains two useful subbalances. The *trade balance* (item 3) is the difference between exports and imports of merchandise items and is one of the oldest and most familiar measures of the state of the balance of payments. The *goods and services balance* (item 7) combines the merchandise and service account and is similar to the net foreign investment component of the GNP accounts discussed in Chapter 17. In Table 15-1, the trade balance and goods and services balance were in deficit by $127.2 billion and $111.9 billion, respectively.

The overall SIT must balance because it is based on double-entry bookkeeping; that is, total receipts must equal total payments. A deficit in the current account is offset by a net decrease in U.S. claims on the rest of the world. This occurs when the United States increases its liabilities to the rest of the world by issuing financial assets and/or by the rest of the world reducing its liabilities to the United States. A surplus in the current account is offset by a net increase in U.S. claims on the rest of the world. This occurs when the United States decreases its liabilities to the rest of the world and/or by the rest of the world increasing its liabilities to the United States by issuing financial assets.

Let's take a closer look at the capital account transactions to see how the 1988 current account deficit was financed.

Transactions in Financial Assets or Capital Flows   This component of the SIT represents changes in U.S. claims held against the rest of the world (U.S. assets) and changes in foreign claims held against the United States (U.S. liabilities). The majority of financial flows are private or nonofficial capital transactions; however, changes in official reserve assets play an important role in the capital account and reflect efforts on the part of central banks to influence the exchange rate.

An increase in foreign financial assets held by the United States is recorded as a payment $(-)$ because the United States uses funds to *import* financial assets. At the same time, the United States is *exporting* capital to the rest of the world and hence, U.S. financial assets abroad are also referred to as a *capital outflow or capital export.* According to the 1988 SIT, the United States increased its holdings of foreign financial assets on a nonofficial basis by $78.5 billion (item 11a + item 11c). If the United States decreased its holdings of foreign financial assets, the transaction would be recorded as a receipt or capital import.

The sale of U.S. financial assets to the rest of the world is recorded as a receipt $(+)$ because the United States is *exporting* financial assets and receiving funds in exchange. At the same time, this is a *capital inflow or capital import* to the United States. According to the 1988 SIT, the rest of the world increased its holdings of U.S. nonofficial financial assets by $180.4 billion (item 13a). If the rest of the world reduced its holdings of U.S. financial assets, the transaction would be recorded as a payment or capital export.

The difference between receipts and payments in the nonofficial capital account represents the net financial position of the United States with respect to the rest of the world on a nonofficial or private basis. In 1988, the nonofficial capital account was a surplus of $101.9 billion ($-$78.5 + $180.4). Nonofficial capital inflows (receipts) exceeded nonofficial capital outflows (payments).

Official reserve asset transactions occur when governments and central banks sell and purchase official reserve assets to achieve certain exchange rate objectives. U.S. official reserve assets are gold, Special Drawing Rights (or SDRs), reserve balances at the International Monetary Fund, and holdings of foreign exchange. An increase in U.S. official reserve assets is recorded as a payment or capital outflow because the United States is importing reserve assets or claims on the rest of the world. Should the United States reduce its holdings of reserve assets, the transaction will be recorded as a receipt or capital inflow. In 1988, the United States increased its stock of official reserve assets by $3.6 billion. When foreign governments increase (decrease) their holdings of official claims on the United States, the transaction is recorded as a receipt (payment) or capital inflow (outflow). Foreign official assets in the United States consist primarily of holdings of Treasury securities.

The capital account balance on an official basis is referred to as the *official reserve balance.* It is represented by the net change in U.S. official claims on the rest of the world and in 1988, the official reserve balance was a surplus of $35.3 billion (item 11b + item 13b).

Relationship Between the Current Account and Capital Account   The SIT must balance because it is based on double-entry bookkeeping so that every transaction is recorded twice. This is expressed by the following:

Receipts in current accounts + receipts in capital flow accounts (capital inflow) = payments in current account + payments in capital flow accounts (capital outflow)

or

Current account balance = capital outflow − capital inflow

Thus a surplus (deficit) in the current account must be offset by a deficit (surplus) in the capital flow transactions.

Let us consider how the capital flow transactions were used in Table 15-1 to offset the deficit in the current account of $126.6 billion. U.S. total claims on foreigners increased by $82.1 billion (item 12), which represents a payment or capital outflow from the point of view of the United States. Foreign claims on the United States increased by $219.3 billion (item 14), which represents a receipt or capital inflow from the point of view of the United States. The capital flows thus indicate a surplus since receipts (item 14) exceed payments (item 12) by $137.2 billion (item 15); however, this does not exactly offset the deficit in the current account. The reason has to do with measurement problems taken into account by the item statistical discrepancy (item 16). Theoretically, total receipts must equal total payments, but given the realities of data collection, the statistical discrepancy ensures that the current and capital flow transactions will offset each other. Thus, the current account deficit of $126.6 billion is offset by the capital flow surplus plus statistical discrepancy ($137.2 billion − 10.6 billion = 126.6 billion).

International Transactions and the Foreign Exchange Market

Each item in the SIT is reflected in the foreign exchange market, which is an international financial market that makes it possible to convert one country's currency into another country's currency. We can conceptualize the foreign exchange market in terms of the demand and supply for foreign exchange or the demand and supply for dollars. Let us consider the SIT from the perspective of demand and supply for dollars and let us simplify the analysis further, by assuming that Japan and the United States are the only trading countries in the world.

A U.S. citizen wishes to purchase a Honda automobile from Japan, but has only dollars to spend. The Japanese exporter ultimately wants to be paid in yen, the domestic currency in Japan. Thus, the U.S. import will be reflected by an increased supply of dollars in the foreign exchange market in order to acquire the yen to purchase the Japanese-produced car. In fact, any good, service, or yen-denominated financial asset purchase by the United States is reflected by an increased supply of dollars.

A Japanese citizen wishing to purchase a U.S.-produced good such as an IBM PC only has yen to spend. The U.S. exporter ultimately wants to be paid in dollars. Thus, the U.S. export (Japanese import) will be reflected by an increased demand for dollars in the foreign exchange market in order to purchase the U.S.-produced good. Any good, service, or dollar-denominated financial asset purchased by the Japanese is reflected by an increased demand for dollars.

The price of one country's currency in terms of another country's currency is called the *foreign exchange rate*. Table 15-2 presents how the foreign exchange rates are expressed in *The Wall Street Journal*. Rates are expressed as the number of dollars that can be purchased with one unit of foreign currency or equivalently as the number of units of foreign currency that can be purchased with one dollar. The yen-dollar exchange rate, for example, of 142.88 means that $1.00 would purchase ¥142.88 on October 31, 1989 or in terms of dollars per yen, ¥0.00699 (1/142.88) yen would purchase $1.00.

In the following discussion, we will focus on the rate expressed as the number yen per dollar. An *increase* in this exchange rate means that the dollar has *appreciated* in value since the dollar purchases more yen or the yen has *depreciated* because it takes more yen to purchase a dollar. A *decrease* in the exchange rate means that the dollar has *depreciated* in value since the dollar will purchase fewer yen or the yen has *appreciated* because it takes fewer yen to purchase a dollar.

Because all exchange rates in Table 15-2 are in terms of dollars, the exchange rate between any two foreign currencies can be easily determined. For example, given the yen-dollar rate of 142.88 and the mark-dollar rate of 1.8415, the yen-mark exchange rate would be

$$\frac{\text{Yen}}{\text{Mark}} = \frac{\left(\frac{\text{yen}}{\text{dollar}}\right)}{\left(\frac{\text{mark}}{\text{dollar}}\right)} = \frac{142.88}{1.8415} = 77.589$$

That is, ¥77.589 will purchase 1 mark.

Determinants of the Exchange Rate

The exchange rate, like any price, is determined by demand and supply, as illustrated in Figure 15-1. This could be in terms of either the demand and supply for yen or the demand and supply for dollars. We will focus on the latter, and hence, the exchange rate is expressed as the number of yen required to purchase one dollar. To understand equilibrium in the foreign exchange market, however, two aspects of the foreign exchange market require clarification. First, we need to explain why the demand and supply functions for dollars are downward and upward sloping, respectively. Second, we need to understand the major forces that shift the demand and supply functions.

EXCHANGE RATES
Tuesday, October 31, 1989

The New York foreign exchange selling rates below apply to trading among banks in amounts of $1 million and more, as quoted at 3 P.M. Eastern time by Bankers Trust Co. Retail transactions provide fewer units of foreign currency per dollar.

Country	U.S. $ Tues.	equiv. Mon.	Currency per U.S. $ Tues.	Mon.	Country	U.S. $ Tues.	equiv. Mon.	Currency per U.S. $ Tues.	Mon.
Argentina (Australi)	.001626	.001626	615.00	615.00	Kuwait (Dinar)	3.3681	3.3681	.29690	.29690
Australia (Dollar)	.7815	.7830	1.2795	1.2771	Lebanon (Pound)	.002227	.002227	449.00	449.00
Austria (Schilling)	.07725	.07742	12.41	12.91	Malaysia (Ringgit)	.3709	.3712	2.6960	2.6935
Bahrain (Dinar)	2.6521	2.6521	.3770	.3770	Malta (Lira)	2.8653	2.8653	.3490	.3490
Belgium (Franc)					Mexico (Peso)				
Commercial rate	.02589	.02595	38.61	38.52	Floating rate	.0003822	.0003822	2616.00	2616.00
Financial rate	.02583	.02590	38.70	38.29	Netherland (Guilder)	.4818	.4828	2.0755	2.0710
Brazil (Cruzado)	.19282	.19607	5.1860	5.1002	New Zealand (Dollar) ...	.5880	.5885	1.7006	1.6992
Britain (Pound)	1.5815	1.5815	.6323	.6323	Norway (Krone)	.1451	.1452	6.8900	6.8825
30-Day Forward	1.5726	1.5730	.6358	.6357	Pakistan (Rupee)	.04750	.04750	21.05	21.05
90-Day Forward	1.5564	1.5556	.6425	.6428	Peru (Inti)	.0001780	.0001780	5615.00	5615.00
180-Day Forward	1.5335	1.5328	.6521	.6524	Philippines (Peso)	.046728	.046728	21.40	21.40
Canada (Dollar)	.8514	.8521	1.1745	1.1735	Portugal (Escudo)	.006343	.006343	157.65	157.65
30-Day Forward	.8488	.8496	1.1780	1.1770	Saudi Arabia (Riyal)	.26680	.26680	3.7480	3.7480
90-Day Forward	.8440	.8445	1.1847	1.1840	Singapore (Dollar)	.5112	.5115	1.9560	1.9550
180-Day Forward	.8371	.8376	1.1946	1.1938	South Africa (Rand)				
Chile (Official rate)	.0036972	.0036972	270.47	270.47	Commercial rate	.3795	.3801	2.6348	2.6308
China (Yuan)	.268665	.268665	3.7221	3.7221	Financial rate	.2503	.2503	3.9950	3.9950
Colombia (Peso)	.002369	.002369	422.00	422.00	South Korea (Won)	.0014889	.0014889	671.60	671.60
Denmark (Krone)	.1399	.140242	7.1452	7.1305	Spain (Peseta)	.008574	.008561	116.63	116.80
Ecuador (Sucre)					Sweden (Krona)	.1560	.1561	6.4090	6.4035
Floating rate	.001597	.001597	625.80	625.80	Switzerland (Franc)	.6190	.6226	1.6155	1.6060
Finland (Markka)	.2353	.2354	4.2490	4.2470	30-Day Forward	.6195	.6232	1.6142	1.6046
France (Franc)	.1600	.1605	6.2485	6.2280	90-Day Forward	.6200	.6237	1.6129	1.6032
30-Day Forward	.1602	.1607	6.2400	6.2210	180-Day Forward	.6203	.6241	1.6121	1.6023
90-Day Forward	.1606	.1611	6.2255	6.2050	Taiwan (Dollar)	.038910	.038910	25.70	25.70
180-Day Forward	.1612	.1617	6.2010	6.1805	Thailand (Baht)	.038895	.038895	25.71	25.71
Greece (Drachma)	.006075	.006090	164.60	164.20	Turkey (Lira)	.0004401	.0004401	2272.00	2272.00
Hong Kong (Dollar)	.128040	.128073	7.8100	7.8080	United Arab (Dirham) ..	.2722	.2722	3.6725	3.6725
India (Rupee)	.0594530	.0594530	16.82	16.82	Uruguay (New Peso)				
Indonesia (Rupiah)	.0005599	.0005599	1786.00	1786.00	Financial	.001382	.001382	723.50	723.50
Ireland (Punt)	1.4435	1.4445	.69276	.69228	Venezuela (Bolivar)				
Israel (Shekel)	.5212	.5212	1.9186	1.9186	Floating rate	.0251572	.0251572	39.75	39.75
Italy (Lira)	.0007407	.0007423	1350.00	1347.00	W. Germany (Mark)	.5430	.5450	1.8415	1.8348
Japan (Yen)	.006998	.007047	142.88	141.90	30-Day Forward	.5433	.5452	1.8406	1.8339
30-Day Forward	.007014	.007061	142.56	141.61	90-Day Forward	.5434	.5456	1.8400	1.8328
90-Day Forward	.007037	.007086	142.09	141.12	180-Day Forward	.5440	.5457	1.8382	1.8325
180-Day Forward	.007065	.007114	141.54	140.56	SDR	1.27782	1.27857	0.782583	0.782126
Jordan (Dinar)	1.6249	1.6249	.6154	.6154	ECU	1.11697	1.11661	......	......

Special Drawing Rights (SDR) are based on exchange rates for the U.S., West German, British, French and Japanese currencies. Source: International Monetary Fund.

European Currency Unit (ECU) is based on a basket of community currencies. Source: European Community Commission.

Source: The Wall Street Journal, *November 1, 1989, p. c12.*

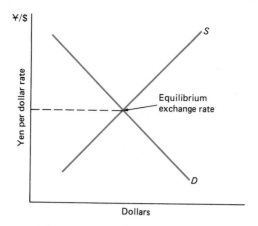

FIGURE 15-1   The foreign exchange market

Before discussing the demand and supply functions, however, we should clear up an important point. The foreign exchange market is discussed primarily in terms of a currency exchange market, and it might be tempting for the reader to visualize this market as a market where currencies such as dollar bills are exchanged for yen notes. Despite the reference to the foreign exchange market as a currency market, the market is actually a market for financial assets denominated in foreign currencies. The majority of transactions in the market involve the exchange of bank deposits denominated in different currencies at the exchange rate. The opportunity cost in terms of lost interest income provides strong incentives for the foreign exchange market to be conducted in financial assets rather than actual currency.

The Quantity of Dollars Demanded/Supplied and the Exchange Rate

The inverse relationship between the quantity of dollars demanded and the exchange rate can best be illustrated by considering the case of U.S. merchandise exports to Japan. Remember, the demand for dollars reflects Japanese demand for U.S. pro-duced goods, services, and dollar-denominated financial assets. The inverse relation-ship is based on the fact that the price of U.S. exports to Japan declines as the exchange rate declines, other things held constant. At ¥250 to the dollar, a U.S.-produced good that sells for $1,000 in the United States, will cost a Japanese im-porter ¥250,000. At a lower exchange rate of ¥200 to the dollar, the U.S.-produced good will now cost the Japanese importer ¥200,000 even though the U.S. price remains constant. Hence, the quantity of dollars demanded will increase (decrease) when the exchange rate decreases (increases). The exchange rate determines the price of U.S. exports paid by Japanese importers, other things held constant.

The positive relationship between the quantity of dollars supplied and the ex-change rate is based on the fact that the dollar price of Japanese goods, services, and yen-denominated financial assets paid by U.S. importers is determined by the ex-change rate, other things held constant. At ¥200 to the dollar, a Japanese-produced good that sells in Japan for ¥100,000 will cost the U.S. importer $500. At a higher exchange rate of ¥250 to the dollar, the Japanese-produced good will now cost the U.S. importer $400. Hence, as the exchange rate increases (decreases), the quantity of dollars supplied increases (decreases), other things held constant.

Shifts in the Demand and Supply Functions

In general, we need to distinguish between two types of transactions in the exchange market to understand fully what factors account for shifts in either the demand or supply function for dollars.

First, dollars are demanded and supplied to reflect the flows of goods and services between Japan and the United States. The transactions in the foreign exchange market are conducted to facilitate the flows of currently produced goods and services, and in this regard, the demand and supply functions respond to differences between the two countries in regard to income, productivity, preferences for foreign goods, tariffs and quotas, subsidies, the domestic price level, or other "economic fundamentals" that influence the flow of goods and services. Anything that changes U.S. demand for Japanese-produced goods and services will shift the supply of dollars, and anything that changes Japanese demand for U.S.-produced goods and services will shift the demand for dollars, though in practice a change in any element that shifts the demand (supply) function is likely to have secondary effects on the position of the supply (demand) function.

Second, transactions in the exchange market also reflect the flows of financial assets between Japan and the United States, and though the flows of financial assets are influenced by many of the same forces that influence the flow of currently produced goods and services, they require separate treatment in terms of their relationship to the exchange rate.

Flows of Currently Produced Goods and Services   The flows of goods and services between Japan and the United States depend on each country's income, productivity, preferences for foreign-produced goods and services, subsidies to export industries, tariffs and other government-imposed restrictions on trade, and the domestic price level in each country. Let us consider how each of these elements could increase Japanese demand for U.S.-produced goods and services and thus shift the demand function for dollars to the *right*, that is, increase the quantity of dollars demanded at any exchange rate. The effect of a rightward shift in demand holding supply constant is to increase the exchange rate thereby appreciating the dollar and depreciating the value of the yen.

1. An increase in Japan's real GNP will increase demand in Japan for both domestically and U.S.-produced goods and services and, hence, shift the demand for dollars to the right.
2. An increase in Japanese preferences for U.S.-produced goods and services because of perceived quality or status considerations will shift demand to the right.
3. An increase in U.S. productivity that permits U.S. exporters to charge lower prices on exports to Japan will induce a rightward shift in the demand for dollars.

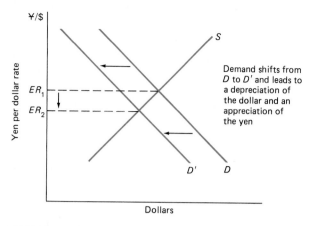

FIGURE 15-2 The effect of a decrease in Japan's GNP on the foreign exchange rate

4. A government subsidy to U.S. exporters that permits them to change lower prices on exports to Japan will induce a rightward demand shift.

5. A decline in Japanese tariffs or quotas on U.S.-produced goods and services or other actions that increase U.S. access to Japanese markets will shift the demand to the right.

6. A decrease in the U.S. domestic price level will shift demand to the right since this will reduce the price of U.S.-produced goods and services to Japanese importers.

Readers should convince themselves that an opposite change in items 1 through 6 will shift the demand function for dollars to the *left*, lowering the exchange rate. Figure 15-2 illustrates the effect of a decrease in Japan's real GNP on the foreign exchange market.

Now let us turn to see how the foregoing elements could increase U.S. demand for Japanese-produced goods and services and thus shift the supply function for dollars to the *right*. A rightward shift in supply will decrease the exchange rate holding demand constant; that is, the dollar will depreciate and the yen will appreciate.

1. An increase in U.S. real GNP will increase demand in the United States for both domestically and Japanese-produced goods and services and, hence, shift the supply of dollars to the right.

2. An increase in U.S. preferences for Japanese-produced goods and services because of perceived quality or status considerations will shift supply to the right.

3. An increase in Japanese productivity that permits Japanese exporters to charge lower prices on exports to the United States will induce a rightward shift in the supply of dollars.

4. A government subsidy to Japanese exporters that permits them to change lower prices on exports to the United States will induce a rightward supply shift.

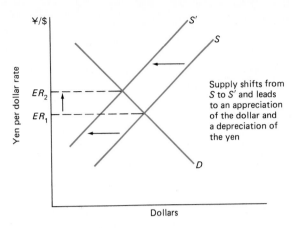

FIGURE 15-3   **The effect of an increase in Japan's domestic price level on the foreign exchange rate**

5. A decline in U.S. tariffs or quotas on Japanese-produced goods and services or other actions that increase Japan's access to U.S. markets will shift supply to the right.

6. A decrease in Japan's domestic price level will shift supply to the right since this will reduce the price of Japanese-produced goods and services to U.S. importers.

Again, readers should convince themselves that an opposite change in items 1 through 6 will shift the supply of dollars to the *left*. Figure 15-3 shows the effect of an increase in the Japanese price level; in this case, the dollar will appreciate and the yen will depreciate as illustrated.

Item 6 offers an opportunity to see how a changed economic situation can influence both functions. Consider a lower U.S. price level assuming the Japanese price level remains constant. A decrease in U.S. inflation shifts the demand for dollars to the right as U.S.-produced goods became cheaper to the Japanese. At the same time, U.S. citizens will also substitute less expensive domestically-produced goods for relatively more expensive imports from Japan. Hence, lower U.S. inflation not only shifts demand to the right, but will shift the supply of dollars to the left. Both shifts, however, will increase the exchange rate.

Flows of Financial Assets   Those elements that determine the flow of goods and services between countries are considered the long-run determinants of the exchange rate; however, flows of financial assets have come to play the most important role in determining short-run exchange rate movements. In addition, flows of financial assets are of a much larger volume at any given time than are flows of goods and services. The rapid growth of financial flows between countries has been the result of financial innovation, deregulation, and the shift to a floating exchange rate environment after 1973.

Short-run movements in the exchange rate in response to flows of financial assets are primarily the result of shifts in the demand for dollar-denominated assets rather

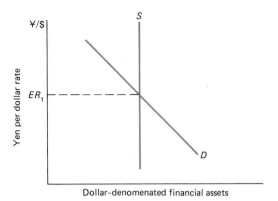

FIGURE 15-4 **Demand and supply for dollar-denominated financial assets in the foreign exchange market**

than shifts in supply. This is because the total supply of dollar-denominated financial assets is very large and largely insensitive to the exchange rate. Figure 15-4 illustrates the typical demand and supply function for dollar-denominated assets based on the assumption that quantity supplied is not sensitive to the exchange rate. Let us now consider the underlying determinants of the demand function for dollar-denominated financial assets.

The demand for dollar-denominated financial assets depends on the expected rate of return of holding these assets, which in turn depends on:

1. The real interest rate
2. Expected movements in the exchange rate over the maturity of the financial asset

Imagine yourself as a potential Japanese purchaser of U.S. Treasury bills. First, you are interested in the real rate of interest rather than the nominal interest rate, and second, you are concerned about the future exchange rate because when the asset matures, you will then need to convert dollars into yen. This latter point is important because it suggests that anything that influences expected future values of the exchange rate will influence the demand for dollar-denominated financial assets. This is a primary reason for the exchange rate volatility of the past decade.

Let us now consider how these elements will shift the demand function. The demand for dollar-denominated financial assets shifts to the *right* (*left*) if real interest rates in the United States are higher (lower) than in Japan, other things held constant. The most important "other things held constant," however, is the expected change in the exchange rate. At given real interest rates, an anticipated decrease in the exchange rate will shift the demand for dollars to the *left* while an anticipated increase in the exchange rate will shift the demand for dollars to the *right*. Anticipated movements in the exchange rates themselves are a function of anticipated changes in income, productivity, tariffs, quotas, subsidies, and inflation as well as anticipated movements in real interest rates in each country. For example, if Japan anticipated inflation in the United States, this would shift the demand for dollar

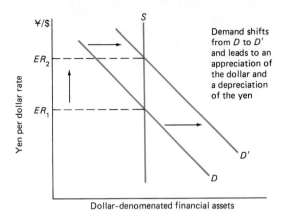

FIGURE 15-5   The effect on an increase in
the real rate of interest in the United States
on the foreign exchange rate

financial assets to the left because the expected rate of return is less at a given real
interest rate.

Figure 15-5 illustrates the case where the real rate of interest in the United
States increases relative to the real rate of interest in Japan, other things held
constant.

Central Bank Intervention: Flows of Financial Assets   Central banks frequently
intervene in the foreign exchange market to achieve specific exchange rate objectives. For example, in 1985 central banks attempted to depreciate the dollar and
appreciate the yen to reduce the trade imbalances between Japan and the United
States. In 1987, central banks became concerned that the dollar had depreciated too
much and intervened to prevent the dollar from falling further.

Central bank intervention in the foreign exchange market can influence either
the demand or supply function. If the United States purchases dollar-denominated
financial assets with its holdings of international reserve assets (gold, SDRs, or foreign exchange), this will shift the supply function to the left while selling dollar assets
in exchange for international reserves will shift the supply function to the right. If the
Bank of Japan intervenes in the foreign exchange market, this will be reflected by
shifts in the demand for dollar-denominated financial assets.

Putting it Together: What Determines
the Exchange Rate?

The exchange rate from the perspective of the United States is the price of dollars in
terms of yen and is influenced by factors that determine the flow of currently produced goods and services, flows of financial assets, and on occasion, intervention by
central banks. It is important to distinguish between the *nominal* and the *real*

exchange rate. This will help us understand how the exchange rate is determined, how it changes over time, and how it relates to the domestic interest rate.

The nominal exchange rate is the actual rate observed in the market and reported in such places as *The Wall Street Journal.* It is the price of U.S. dollars in terms of yen and is the real exchange rate adjusted for differences in price levels in the United States and Japan. The real exchange rate is determined by the basic elements that influence the flow of goods, services, and financial assets. It is essentially the price of U.S. goods, services, and financial assets in terms of Japanese goods, services, and financial assets.

Formally, the relationship between the nominal exchange rate (NER) and the real exchange rate (RER) for Japan and the United States is given by

$$\text{NER (¥/\$)} = \text{RER} \cdot \frac{\text{price level in Japan}}{\text{price level in United States}} \tag{1}$$

To illustrate the meaning of this expression, let us assume that wine is the only good traded between Japan and the United States. Given income levels, tastes, and other economic fundamentals but abstracting from the domestic price level in each country, U.S. wine is regarded as twice as valuable as Japanese wine. In this case, the real rate of exchange, RER, would be 2 to 1, which expresses the price of U.S. goods in terms of Japanese goods. If U.S. wine is twice as valuable, then its price in terms of Japanese wine should be twice as much.

The NER equals the RER adjusted for price level differences between the two countries. That is, if U.S. wine sells for $10 and Japanese wine for ¥2,500, then the NER will equal ¥500 to $1. At this rate, one U.S. bottle of wine will exchange for two bottles of Japanese wine; that is, U.S. wine is twice as valuable. Ten dollars would purchase ¥5,000, which in turn, would purchase two bottles of Japanese wine. Why must this be the case?

If the NER were different from ¥500 to $1, profit opportunities would exist that would ensure a return to the ¥500 to $1 rate. Assume that the rate were ¥250 to $1. In this case, one bottle of Japanese wine would be equal to one bottle of U.S. wine contrary to the real rate of exchange. A sum of ¥2,500 would purchase $10 in the foreign exchange market, which would then purchase one bottle of U.S. wine. At an exchange rate of ¥250 to $1, there would be increased demand for dollars to purchase U.S. wine which would raise the exchange rate until it equalled the rate indicated by expression (1), that is, ¥500 to $1.

External Equilibrium and the Foreign Exchange Market

We have introduced the SIT and discussed the basic determinants of the exchange rate and as already explained, items in the SIT are reflected in the demand and supply functions for dollars. It is now time to consider the concept of overall external equilibrium or balance-of-payments equilibrium. Unfortunately, this concept does not have a clear meaning and as a result, it is not easy to measure.

BOX 1 Exchange rates and interest rates—an example of exchange rate determination

Exchange rate movements are closely associated with movements in domestic interest rates. This is not surprising, since both are determined in interrelated financial markets and both respond to similar forces. Financial innovation and deregulation have relaxed barriers between domestic and international finance for many countries. As a result, one frequently encounters references to the relationship between interest rates and the value of the dollar in the financial press. We can utilize our understanding of the foreign exchange market discussed so far to review the relationship during the 1970s and 1980s.[1] This will help us understand the international environment of the United States.

Figure 1B illustrates the relationship between the nominal interest rate measured as the long-term Treasury security rate and the exchange rate expressed as an index. In the 1970s, the relationship was generally inverse; that is, the value of the dollar and the interest rate moved in opposite directions. In the 1980s, the relationship was generally positive; that is, the value of the dollar and the interest rate moved together.

The apparent change in the relationship, however, is not due to a change in the underlying relationship between exchange rates and interest rates, but is due to a change in the fundamental determinants of interest rates and exchange rates. To understand the two periods, we need to consider the differences between nominal and real interest rates and nominal and real exchange rates.

The nominal interest rate is equal to the real interest rate plus the anticipated inflation rate.

Nominal interest rate = real interest rate + anticipated inflation

This was fully discussed in Chapter 5. On page 339 in this chapter, we distinguished between the nominal and the real exchange rate.

Keeping these concepts in mind will help us to understand exchange rate and interest rate movements since 1973. The basic notion is that the nominal measure represents the combined impact of two sets of forces: fundamental real forces independent of inflation effects and inflation effects.

In the 1970s, the evidence strongly suggests that anticipated inflation was the fundamental determinant of the nominal interest rate rather than changes in the real rate of interest. That is, most of the variation in nominal interest rates was due to anticipated inflation rather than to changes in the real rate of interest.

The expression for the nominal exchange rate on page 339 indicates that changes in the nominal exchange rate are composed of changes in the real exchange rate and the U.S. inflation rate relative to other countries. If inflation in the United States is higher than in other countries, the value of the dollar will decline, holding the real exchange rate constant. We thus observe an inverse association between the nominal exchange rate and U.S. inflation. This turns out to be the case in the 1970s. During the 1974–1979 period according to Figure 2B, the exchange rate is inversely related to the differential inflation rate between the United States and the rest of the world (U.S. inflation minus rest of the world inflation). Thus, the variation in the exchange rate appears to be the result of variation in the U.S. inflation rate relative to inflation in other countries.

Considering that the sources of movements in interest rates and exchange rates in the 1970s are primarily the result of inflation suggests an *inverse* relationship between exchange rates and interest rates. This, in fact, was the case.

The relationship between interest rates and exchange rates changed in the 1980s because the source of variation in interest rates and exchange rates changed from inflationary impacts to real impacts. After the early 1980s, inflation was significantly reduced in the United States relative to inflation in other countries, and thus, inflation was no longer as important a determinant of interest rates and exchange rates as it was in the 1970s.

In the United States, changes in the real interest rate came to account for much of the movement in nominal interest rates. Real interest rates increased after 1980 because of the growth of federal budget deficits and reduced personal saving.

Real interest rates in the United States rose above real interest rates in other countries and thus increased the demand for dollar-denominated financial assets. As a result, this increased the real exchange rate and in turn, the nominal exchange rate. Figure 3B illustrates the real interest rate differential (U.S. real interest rates less real interest rates in other countries) and the exchange rate. The positive association as predicted is obvious.

Hence, in the 1980s both interest rates and exchange rates were responding to real forces, and as a result, both were likely to move in the same direction. This in fact was the case.

[1] This discussion is drawn from Craig S. Hakkio, "Interest Rates and Exchange Rates—What Is the Relationship?" *Economic Review*, Federal Reserve Bank of Kansas City (November 1986), 33–43.

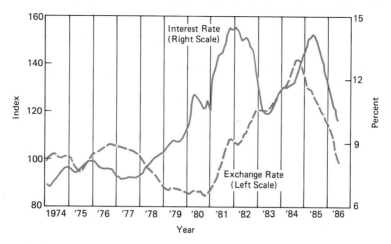

FIGURE 1B   Nominal exchange rates and nominal interest rates in the United States, 1970s and 1980s
Source: Craig S. Hakkio, "Interest Rates and Exchange Rates—What Is the Relationship?" *Economic Review,* Federal Reserve Bank of Kansas City (November 1986), 34–43.

Is there some aspect of the SIT that measures the overall balance or external equilibrium? Unfortunately, there are many subbalances that may reflect external balance or imbalance; however, there is no one measure that reflects the overall state of our economic relationship with the rest of the world. While we hear frequent references to the trade balance, the trade balance is only part of our relationship with the rest of the world. The same holds for the balance on goods and services and the current account balance. It is tempting to use the current account balance as a measure of overall equilibrium; however, that omits major financial flows that are

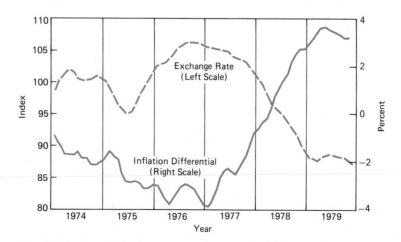

FIGURE 2B   Relationship between exchange rate and inflation differential between the United States and the rest of the world, 1974–1979
Source: Craig S. Hakkio, "Interest Rates and Exchange Rates—What Is the Relationship?" *Economic Review,* Federal Reserve Bank of Kansas City (November 1986), 34–43.

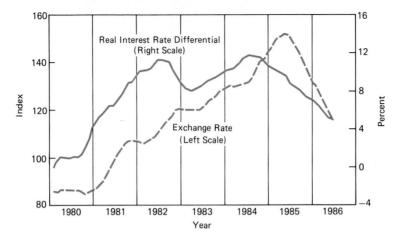

FIGURE 3B   Relationship between exchange rates and the
differential real interest rate between the United States and the rest
of the world, 1980–1986
Source: Craig S. Hakkio, "Interest Rates and Exchange Rates—What Is the Relationship?"
Economic Review, Federal Reserve Bank of Kansas City (November 1986), 34–43.

important to an economy's development. To illustrate, at certain stages of economic
development it may be optimal for a country to import large amounts of capital and
hence, operate with a current account deficit. This does not mean however, that a
country is fundamentally in external disequilibrium.

One approach to conceptualizing external equilibrium is to distinguish between
autonomous and *induced* transactions. Autonomous transactions refer to flows of
goods, services, and financial assets that reflect economic fundamentals among trading countries: income, preferences, tariffs, subsidies, quotas, productivity, inflation,
and real interest rates. Induced transactions, which are primarily financial, are not
the result of economic fundamentals and tend to be transitory in nature; for example,
government efforts to stabilize or influence exchange rates in a particular direction
are regarded as induced transactions.

There is little disagreement in principle about the difference between autonomous and induced; however, where does one "draw the line" between these transactions in the SIT? Even if a country has a deficit in autonomous transactions or "above
the line" transactions, does this imply external disequilibrium. Not necessarily. It depends on the country's stage of development and endowment of resources.

There is no easy way to clear up this ambiguity; however, using the concepts of
"above the line" and "below the line" transactions, we can use the demand and
supply functions for dollars to illustrate the concept of external or balance-of-
payments equilibrium. Regard the demand and supply functions in Figure 15-6 as
reflecting transactions based on economic fundamentals, that is, autonomous transactions. If these transactions result in equality between the quantity of dollars demanded and supplied at the existing exchange rate (Figure 15-6A), then external or
balance-of-payments equilibrium has been achieved, and no further adjustments will
be required. An external imbalance results when quantity demanded and supplied
are not equal at the existing exchange rate, which in turn will require further ad-

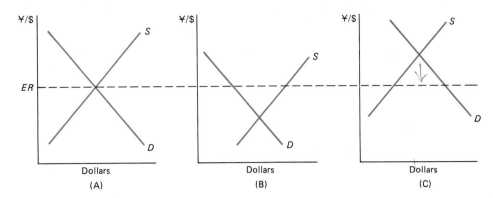

FIGURE 15-6 External or balance-of-payments equilibrium and the foreign exchange market

justment. Figure 15-6B illustrates the case of an external deficit where the quantity of dollars supplied exceeds the quantity demanded at the existing exchange rate. Figure 15-6C illustrates the case of an external surplus where the quantity of dollars demanded exceeds the quantity supplied at the existing exchange rate. Both conditions will require further adjustment to achieve external equilibrium. The nature of this adjustment will depend on whether the foreign exchange market is based on the fixed or the flexible exchange rate system.

The Balance-of-Payments Adjustment Process

Fixed Exchange Rate Standard

The fixed exchange rate standard establishes a fixed rate of exchange between the dollar and other foreign currencies. The central bank is then required to take actions to ensure that the established rate is maintained in the face of shifts in the demand and/or supply function for dollars. The gold standard is an example of how fixed exchange rates among foreign currencies are maintained. Gold is a homogeneous commodity. All countries agree on what an ounce of gold looks and feels like. If each country fixed the price of gold in terms of its own currency, a set of exchange rates would be established for all currencies as they are all valued in terms of a standard unit of measurement: an ounce of gold. For example, if the United States sets the dollar price of gold at $25 per ounce and Japan sets the yen price of gold at ¥10,000 per ounce, then the exchange rate between the dollar and yen will be ¥400 = $1 or ¥1 = 0.0025.

How are the exchange rates maintained at a fixed level over time? Each country must be willing to buy and sell gold at the official price in unlimited quantities. For example, if the official price of gold is $25, the U.S. government must use gold to purchase all dollars at the rate of $25 per ounce. Under a complete gold standard, all domestically and foreign-held currency is convertible into gold at the official rate; however, the international monetary system developed after World War II was a modified gold standard. Each country stood ready to exchange gold for currency held by foreigners but not for domestically held currency.

Fixed exchange rate standards do not have to be tied to gold because the central bank can use any widely acceptable international reserve to maintain a fixed exchange rate. International reserves consist of gold, foreign currencies, and any other medium that may be mutually agreed on by the participating countries.

The central bank can establish and maintain a fixed exchange rate as long as it is willing to use international reserves to maintain the official exchange rate. Let us see how this works in practice. In Figure 15-6, assume that the exchange rate, *ER*, in each of the three examples is the one established by the central bank. The market-determined rate is the rate determined by the intersection of the demand and supply functions for dollars. In panel A, no adjustment process is required because the market-determined exchange rate equals the official exchange rate. In this case, the balance of payments is in a state of equilibrium. In panel B, however, the market-determined exchange rate is lower than the official rate. According to the market, it takes less yen to purchase a dollar than the official rate. The official rate *overvalues* the dollar. At the official rate, the balance of payments is in deficit, or, what amounts to the same thing, at the fixed official rate, the quantity of dollars supplied to the foreign exchange market exceeds the quantity of dollars demanded. The excess supply of dollars is equivalent to saying that there is an excess demand for yen at the *official rate*. Since the dollar is overvalued at the official rate and the government desires to maintain the exchange rate at *ER*, the government, acting through the central bank, will intervene in the foreign exchange market to maintain the official rate of exchange. The central bank sells international reserves to absorb the excess supply of dollars or what amounts to the same thing to finance the excess demand for yen.

In the case of a surplus (in panel C), the official exchange rate *undervalues* the dollar in the foreign exchange market since there is an excess demand for dollars at *ER*. The central bank will then purchase international reserves with dollar-denominated financial assets to maintain the exchange rate at *ER*.

As long as the demand and supply functions remain as they are in panels B and C, the central bank must continually sell or buy international reserves to eliminate the excess supply or demand for dollars in the market, respectively. There are limits to how far this can continue. Especially in the case of the deficit, the United States has a finite amount of reserves with which to purchase the excess supply of dollars. In the case of a surplus, other countries have a finite supply of reserves that they can sell to eliminate the excess demand for dollars.

The use of international reserves is a temporary solution to eliminate the disequilibrium in the balance of payments; however, a more permanent solution may be required. This will involve shifts in the supply and/or demand functions for dollars. In the following sections, we will consider the adjustment process for the case of a deficit (panel B) for two reasons. First, large deficits have characterized U.S. balance of payments in recent years; second, countries are much more concerned about eliminating a deficit than they are about eliminating a surplus.

Restricting of Domestic Economic Activity

The traditional solution to a long-run balance-of-payments deficit under the fixed exchange rate standard is to contract economic activity. When the central bank is required to use international reserves to support the official exchange rate, it signals the need to initiate tight monetary policy. Tight monetary policy will lead to lower real GNP, lower prices, and higher interest rates relative to those of other countries. A tight monetary policy will then shift the demand and supply functions in such a way that they will intersect at the official exchange rate. The decline in GNP in the United States will shift the supply of dollars to the left as U.S. residents reduce their domestic and foreign demand for goods and services. The decline in U.S. prices reduces the prices of U.S.-produced goods and services relative to other countries', thereby increasing foreign demand for U.S. exports. This shifts the demand for dollars to the right. Higher interest rates relative to interest rates in other countries increase foreign demand for dollar-denominated financial assets and, hence, the demand for dollars shifts to the right. To achieve balance-of-payments equilibrium under a fixed exchange rate standard thus requires a forced slowdown in the rate of economic activity in the country with a deficit. There are additional policies that can be followed.

Tariffs, Subsidies, Quotas, and "Buy American"

A tariff on foreign-produced goods and services is tantamount to shifting the supply function for dollars to the left as it increases the cost of any foreign-produced good or service to a resident of the United States. Other things being equal, U.S. residents will then substitute domestically produced for foreign-produced goods and services. A subsidy paid to selected U.S. producers who sell in the international marketplace allows them to charge lower prices and leads to a rightward shift in the demand for dollars.

Quotas—either for exports or imports—establish limits on the number of units of the good traded. In the case of a deficit, an import quota will shift the supply function to the left, because fewer goods can be imported at any price.

"Buy American" campaigns attempt to serve the same function as a tariff (shift supply to the left) without increasing the actual cost of buying a foreign-produced good or service.

Devaluation

Devaluation is considered an extreme step to solve a balance-of-payments deficit. The basic problem is that the demand and supply functions intersect at a rate below the official rate (panel B in Figure 15-6). If attempts to use monetary policy, tariffs, quotas, and subsidies fail to shift the functions sufficiently to eliminate the deficit, the United States can officially change the price of the dollar. Lowering the official exchange rate is called *devaluation*. Under the gold standard, it is accomplished by increasing the dollar price of gold. For example, we saw that at $25 per ounce of gold, the exchange rate between dollars and yen was ¥400 = $1.00. If the United States doubled the price of gold to $50 per ounce and Japan did not change the yen price of gold (¥10,000 = 1 ounce of gold), the exchange rate would decline to ¥200 = $1.00.

Exchange Control

An extreme form of adjustment is referred to as exchange control. In a sense, tariffs, subsidies, and quotas represent a form of exchange control, but the term is usually reserved for direct governmental controls on the flow of foreign exchange. There are many types of exchange controls. The most common form is to require exporters receiving foreign exchange to turn it over to the government and then the government will release the foreign exchange to importers according to a priority ranking of transactions.

Adjustment Under Fixed Exchange Rates—Summary

In summary, then, a deficit in the balance of payments under a fixed exchange rate system is dealt with on two levels. First, a temporary and transient deficit can be accommodated by selling international reserves to eliminate the excess supply of dollars. Short-term borrowing from other countries can also be employed to fill the gap.

Second, if the deficit is more than temporary and due to fundamental demand and supply relationships, a more permanent solution is required. The deficit can be eliminated by restraining economic activity by monetary policy. Tariffs, subsidies, quotas, and "Buy American" policies can also be implemented. If the deficit persists, stronger action in the form of devaluation of the official exchange rate or even some type of exchange control may be undertaken.

A surplus in the balance of payments under the fixed exchange rate system is handled in the opposite manner. First, a temporary surplus can be accommodated by purchasing international reserves with dollar financial assets to eliminate the excess demand for dollars in the foreign exchange market. Second, if the surplus condition is more fundamental, then easy monetary policy, tariff reductions, reduced subsidies, or appreciation of the currency by lowering the price of gold can be employed to eliminate the surplus.

The Adjustment Process May Be Painful and Not Always Effective

A basic problem with the fixed exchange rate system eventually led to its abandonment in 1973. Persistent deficits require unpopular and sometimes ineffective corrective measures. The traditional approach to a deficit is to restrain economic activity in the domestic economy. This is not a popular corrective measure.

Other corrective measures do not impose the same type of political problem, but they raise additional issues. A number of years ago, one author described attempts such as tariffs, devaluations, and exchange controls as "beggar my neighbor" policies.[1] The action may well improve the country's external balance, but it may also lead to retaliation. Increasing tariffs, for example, may precipitate a trade war. If the United

---

[1] Joan Robinson, "Beggar-My-Neighbour Remedies for Unemployment," in *Readings in the Theory of International Trade*, Readings selected by a committee of the American Economic Association (Homewood, Ill.: Richard D. Irwin, 1949), pp. 393–407.

States increases tariffs and shifts the supply function to the left, other countries may also increase tariffs on U.S.-produced goods, thereby causing a leftward shift in the demand function. The end result leaves the market-determined exchange rate unchanged, and, hence, the deficit remains, but the value of trade is reduced.

Devaluations also create difficulties. A devaluation works only if other countries maintain the value of their currencies in terms of gold; if they also increase the price of gold in terms of their own currencies, the net effect of the original devaluation is zero.

Arguments For and Against the Fixed Exchange Rate Standard

Fixed exchange rate standards have been popular among central bankers and businesspeople engaged in exporting and importing for two reasons. First, fixed exchange rates remove a significant amount of uncertainty in international trade as they guarantee that profits will not be influenced by major shifts in the rate of exchange between currencies. In addition, fluctuating exchange rates may lead to destabilizing speculation.

Second, the fixed exchange rate system makes it more difficult for governments to engage in inflationary policy because this will eventually be reflected by balance-of-payments deficits and call attention to those actions responsible for inflation. To illustrate, consider the case in which the United States instituted easy monetary policy that resulted in inflationary pressures. This would cause the demand and supply functions for dollars to shift in such a way as to either increase any existing deficit or reduce any existing surplus. As prices increased in the United States relative to other countries, U.S.-produced goods became relatively more expensive. Foreigners shift demand from U.S.-produced goods and services to either other countries' or their own domestically produced goods, which would then cause the demand function for dollars to shift to the left. U.S. residents would substitute foreign-produced goods and services for the relatively more expensive U.S.-produced items, thereby leading to a rightward shift in the supply function for dollars. Any increase in income and employment induced by easy monetary policy would also shift the supply of dollars to the right as U.S. residents increase demand for domestically and foreign-produced goods and services. In addition, lower interest rates induced by easy monetary policy would shift the demand for dollars to the left.

Thus, expansionary monetary policy eventually induces shifts in the demand and supply functions for dollars that generate an external deficit and would call attention to the inflationary monetary policy. In this manner, the fixed exchange rate system imposes a constraint on the willingness of governments to engage in inflationary policies.

However, opponents of the fixed exchange rate system point out a number of problems with these arguments. First, the argument that fixed or stable exchange rates facilitate international trade is exaggerated in the sense that fluctuating exchange rates do not seriously hinder international trade. The uncertainty of future changes in the rates of exchange can be handled by futures markets in foreign currency. The foreign exchange market can be thought of as consisting of a spot and a forward market. The spot market refers to the demand and supply of foreign exchange for today's delivery; the forward market deals in contracts for delivery of foreign exchange at a stated price sometime in the future.

Let us consider the case of a U.S. importer and the way in which he can remove the uncertainty of fluctuating exchange rates by dealing in the forward market. The importer knows that he will require ¥10,000 in three months to purchase Japanese goods. To hedge against buying yen at an uncertain price three months from now, he purchases a futures contract to accept delivery of ¥10,000 three months from now at a stated price. The futures price is essentially the market's expectation of what the price of yen will be in three months. By purchasing the futures contract, the importer has eliminated the risk of fluctuating exchange rates.

Likewise, an exporter can also use the forward market to reduce risk. He will deliver goods to a Japanese importer in three months but wants to ensure against an uncertain exchange rate between the dollar and yen. He knows that he will receive a certain sum of yen in three months, so he sells a futures contract in the forward market to deliver ¥10,000 at a stated price.

Second, there is little evidence that fluctuating exchange rates encourage destabilizing speculation. The evidence to date is not consistent with the argument that flexible exchange rates are prone to destabilizing swings. In fact, it can be argued that, to the extent that speculators have interpreted correctly all the information, their actions are likely to keep exchange rates close to the equilibrium values, that is, the values determined by demand and supply.

Third, the possibilities of speculation are not removed under the fixed exchange rate system. In fact, the fixed exchange rate system can, under certain conditions, lead to greater instability than can a freely fluctuating system. To illustrate, consider the case of the United States in the late 1960s. The United States had been running large external deficits. There was considerable pressure from foreign governments to restrain economic activity and reduce the deficit; however, this was not done. The longer the United States delayed taking action, the more likely it became that the United States would devalue the dollar. Anticipation of devaluation caused individuals to speculate against the dollar by selling dollar assets. This made the situation worse and made it even more likely that the United States would devalue.

Fourth, fixed exchange rates do not impose effective constraints on government inflationary policies. Only if countries are willing to play the rules of the "fixed exchange rate game" will it provide a deterrent to expansionary policies. The basic assumption is that governments will be forced to restrain themselves because they know that eventual external deficits will have to be eliminated by policies that force a slowdown in the economy. When deficits do occur, however, few governments deliberately pursue policies to increase the rate of unemployment or lower the growth of real output to achieve balance-of-payments equilibrium. The temptation is greater to use one of the other methods of adjustment—tariffs, subsidies, devaluation, and even exchange controls. The tendency to resort to these other methods of adjustment increases the likelihood that other countries will retaliate. In the long run, the fixed exchange rate may actually hinder international trade.

Brief History of the Fixed Exchange Rate System: 1944–1973

At Bretton Woods, New Hampshire, in 1944, the international financial system that lasted until 1973 was set up and based on a fixed exchange rate standard. Fixed rates were regarded as necessary to revitalize world trade that had largely disappeared during the depression of the 1930s and the war years. It was felt at that time that any system of fluctuating rates would introduce too much uncertainty in international trade as well as lead to opportunities for speculation.

The system was based on a modified gold standard to be overseen by the International Monetary Fund. The IMF is an international organization of member countries that has functions similar to a central bank. At present, 151 counties belong to the IMF. The IMF was established to provide stable exchange rates and a temporary source of foreign exchange to countries needing to offset a deficit.

The IMF imposed stable, not fixed, rates of exchange. Once a country had established the value of its currency in terms of gold, the market-determined exchange rate was allowed to fluctuate within a narrow band around the official rate. Movements of the market rate, however, were not to be permitted outside the band. If the demand and supply functions intersected at a rate outside the band, the country was expected to use its international reserves to offset the deficit or surplus. If the deficit or surplus persisted, "appropriate" domestic policies were to be used. It was also recognized that devaluation of a country's currency might be needed in the case of persistent deficits. The IMF allowed countries to make small official price changes of their currency (within 10% of the official price). However, any significant price change required consultation and approval from the IMF. This led a number of commentators to refer to the system as the "adjustable peg" system. Foreign exchange rates were pegged at the official level, but they could be altered.

There was one problem with this system. International reserves played an important role in providing liquidity since they could be used to offset a deficit for a short period of time. International reserves consisted primarily of gold and certain *key currencies*.

Key currencies were those currencies used widely in international trade and had a sufficiently high confidence factor to be regarded as being as "good as gold." The U.S. dollar played the dominant role as a key currency. A key currency country is placed in an especially difficult position under a fixed exchange rate system, however.

Almost from the beginning, the United States experienced difficulties. During the 1950s, the U.S. balance of payments continually ran large deficits. There is some controversy as to the reasons for these deficits, but much had to do with the emergence of very competitive participants in international trade, especially West Germany and Japan. In addition, because the dollar was a key currency, the United States was required to run deficits to supply reserves to other countries. However, not all the excess supply of dollars in the foreign exchange market was held and used as international reserves. Much was returned for gold at $35 an ounce. By 1960, the United States did not possess enough gold to exchange for all the outstanding dollars in the foreign exchange market. The deficits started getting larger, and increased concern was expressed that the dollar was not "as good as gold."

In the late 1960s, inflation became a serious problem, and increasing pressure was being brought on the United States to restrain domestic economic activity to improve the balance of payments. Instead, other policies were pursued to improve the deficit. In 1964, a tax on the purchase of foreign securities was imposed to restrain U.S. investment abroad. In 1967, the Federal Reserve imposed the Voluntary Foreign Credit Restraint Program with the objective of restricting financial institutions from lending in foreign countries. In 1968, a two-tiered gold price system was established. The official price of gold was set at $35 per ounce, and the United States and other countries announced that no effort would be made to keep the free market price of gold in line with the official price. Events deteriorated rapidly until 1971, when the United States stated that it would no longer exchange gold for dollars even with other central banks and imposed a 10% surcharge (tariff) on imported goods.

Each of these steps only increased the speculation that the dollar would have to be devalued. Fears of devaluation led to widespread selling of dollars on the foreign exchange market. It became increasingly difficult to maintain the official exchange rate. Two further events rang the death knell for the fixed exchange rate system.

In late 1971, the Smithsonian Agreement was reached between the United States and nine other Western European nations. At that time, the United States agreed to remove the 10% surcharge on imports, the band around the official exchange rate was widened by the IMF, and a complete readjustment of official exchange rates was made. The dollar was devalued by increasing the price of gold from $35 to $38 an ounce. Several other revaluations were made by other countries, all with the objective of establishing exchange rates that were compatible with demand and supply functions of each country's currency. The basic intent of the Smithsonian Agreement, however, was to retain the fixed exchange rate system.

In 1973, renewed pressure on the dollar started by a run on the Italian lira, led the United States to announce another devaluation by raising the price of gold from $38 to $42.22 an ounce. In addition, for the first time in years, a large trade deficit was being reported.

These events, along with the rapid increase in the U.S. inflation rate, perpetrated a run on the dollar in anticipation of further devaluations. There was considerable fear among central banks that an international monetary collapse was fast approaching. In March 1973, the Brussels Agreement, for all practical purposes, ended the entire structure of exchange rates established at Bretton Woods in 1944. Major nations agreed to let their currencies "float," so that demand and supply in the foreign exchange market would be allowed to determine the exchange rate. Several years later, the floating or flexible exchange rate system was officially accepted by the IMF.

The flexible exchange rate system has worked relatively well since its inception in 1973. There are many who believe that the oil and energy crisis of 1973–74 would have led to a worldwide monetary collapse under the previous fixed exchange rate standard, whereas the flexible exchange rate system was able to absorb the huge price increases established by OPEC.

The present flexible exchange rate system is not completely flexible, as central banks still intervene by selling and purchasing official reserve assets to keep exchange rates from fluctuating too widely. In addition, not all countries allow their currencies to fluctuate independently of others' currencies. Most major countries have allowed their currencies to fluctuate independently, but many have chosen to peg their currencies to other currencies, chiefly to the dollar.

The Flexible Exchange Rate Standard

The flexible or floating exchange rate system allows for balance-of-payments adjustment by market-determined changes in the rate of exchange. In the case of a deficit, the excess supply of dollars leads to a decline in the exchange rate. As a result, the quantity of dollars supplied for imports declines and the quantity of dollars demanded for exports increases. The exchange rate moves downward until the quantity of dollars demanded is equal to the quantity supplied. Rather than depend on shifts in the demand or supply functions, the flexible exchange rate system achieves equilibrium by changes in the rate itself. It should be kept in mind, however, that even under a flexible rate system a deficit country may wish to sell international reserves and increase borrowing to slow down or smooth out the adjustment process. In the case of a surplus, the excess demand for dollars leads to an increase in the exchange rate. This eliminates the surplus in the balance of payments without the need to shift the demand and supply functions for dollars. However, international reserve purchases and increased lending activities may be used to slow down or smooth out the adjustment process.

We can use Figure 15-6 to illustrate the flexible exchange rate system. Regard *ER* as the existing rate of exchange (not the officially determined rate). In panel A, no adjustment in the exchange rate is required, since demand and supply intersect at the existing rate of exchange. In the case of a deficit (panel B), there is an excess supply of dollars at the existing rate and the rate will decline until the demand and supply for dollars are equal. In the case of a surplus (panel C), the excess demand for dollars will lead to an increase in the existing rate of exchange until the demand and supply for dollars are equal.

Arguments For Flexible Exchange Rates

Two arguments are offered in support of a flexible exchange rate system. First, market forces automatically determine equilibrium in the balance of payments. Government intervention is not needed, although governments can still intervene to prevent extreme exchange rate fluctuations.

Second, stabilization policy is not dictated by the state of the balance of payments to the same extent as they are under a fixed standard since under a flexible system, the exchange rate itself will adjust to eliminate a deficit. This is not to say that a country can pursue inflationary policies with no negative impacts on the balance of payments, however. Inflationary policies will increase domestic prices relative to foreign prices and lead to shifts in the demand and supply functions for dollars that will create a deficit and decline in the value of the dollar. Although the exchange rate will adjust to eliminate the deficit, the depreciation could increase domestic inflation as the domestic price of imports is increased. Increased prices of foreign imports is likely to lead to increased prices of domestically produced goods. Higher domestic inflation will then lead to further decline in the value of the dollar, and thus a "vicious circle" could ensue. The upshot of this is that, even under a floating system, stabilization policy cannot neglect the impacts that it will have on the balance of payments.

The Need for Further Reform

There is little argument that the Bretton Woods system of fixed exchange rates could not have been maintained after 1973. While the flexible exchange rate system has functioned reasonably well, controversy continues over the type of exchange rate system that will provide a stable environment for international trade and finance. The discussion focuses on three issues: (1) what specific type of flexible exchange rate system should be adopted, (2) the need to coordinate domestic monetary and fiscal policies among the major trading countries of the world, and (3) the continuing need for international reserves.

First, the choices of exchange rate systems fall into three classes: fixed exchange rate system, flexible exchange rate system, and some combination of fixed and flexible exchange rate systems. It is unlikely that the international community will return to the fixed exchange rate system. While exchange rates during the 1970s and 1980s fluctuated more than proponents of flexible rates had anticipated, the system worked reasonably well, and further reform will probably not be in the direction of fixed exchange rates.

Exchange rates have fluctuated far more than anticipated because flows of financial assets shift rapidly in response to differences in real interest rates among countries, but more important, because of anticipated changes in exchange rates. Changes in anticipated exchange rates in turn are dependent primarily on how the foreign exchange market views future monetary and fiscal policy in a given country. Returning to a fixed or semifixed exchange rate system will not eliminate the fundamental differences between countries that generate uncertainty over future exchange rates. This is one reason why more emphasis is being placed on international policy coordination than moving to a different exchange rate system.

Second, the need to coordinate monetary and fiscal policies among the major trading countries has become apparent under the flexible exchange rate system. Early arguments for flexible rates were often based on the view that domestic monetary and fiscal policies could then be administered independently of the balance of payments. Imbalances would be dealt with by fluctuations in the exchange rate rather than shifts in demand and supply for currency. While essentially correct, the past two decades have shown that countries cannot pursue policies independently of other countries. The United States, especially, found that expansionary fiscal policy combined with stable monetary growth in the first part of the 1980s produced high real interest rates. High interest rates relative to the rest of the world induced significant capital flows into the United States. As a result, the value of the dollar increased and resulted in unprecedented trade deficits.

The greater than anticipated exchange rate variability under the flexible system is due in part to uneven monetary and fiscal policies. As one investigator stated,

> Consequently, even if exchange rate volatility is still considered "excessive" the solution is not to eliminate a channel of adjustment but rather to eliminate the sources of

exchange rate . . . volatility. Although open economies cannot isolate themselves from many types of economic shocks, like a large rise in the price of an imported commodity (oil), such economies—sharing highly integrated capital markets—may want to better cooperate to prevent large policy divergencies that lead to excessive asset price volatility.[2]

The so-called excessive variation in exchange rates is now widely recognized as the result of uneven macroeconomic policies across countries and, over time, especially with regard to those government policies that generate inflation. The previous discussion of the determinants of the exchange rate pointed out that financial flows are important in determining short-run exchange rate movements and that the demand for dollar-denominated financial assets is sensitive to expected future movements in the exchange rate. Therefore, any uncertainty about future macroeconomic policies will be reflected by shifts in the demand for financial assets and, thus, generate frequent changes in the exchange rate.

The solution is, therefore, not to abandon the flexible exchange rate system, but for individual countries to pursue macroeconomic policies in coordination with the other major industrialized countries. Of course, this is no easy undertaking.

Third, even under a flexible exchange rate system, there is a need for international reserves to provide liquidity. There is an incomplete synchronization between receipts and payments for a country, just as there is for an individual, and a country needs liquidity to offset short-run deficits even if the exchange rate itself eventually eliminates the deficit.

One basic problem of international monetary reform concerns the creation of a form of international reserves acceptable to all trading parties. Gold has been the traditional reserve asset; however, the supply of gold is generally regarded as insufficient to meet the liquidity needs of current levels of world trade. In addition, the supply of gold is more an accident than a rational process. The fact that South Africa and Russia are main suppliers of gold also provides a political rationale for reducing the importance of gold in international trade, at least by Western countries.

Foreign currencies, primarily the dollar, have also served the role of international liquidity. A key currency country, however, is placed under considerable pressure, a burden that should be shared rightly by other trading countries. In this vein, the United States and Japan reached an agreement in 1984 to pursue actions that would internationalize the Japanese yen, and, it was hoped, the yen would then share greater responsibility as a key currency. There has also been discussion of expanding the role of the IMF and Special Drawing Rights as a source of international liquidity, much as the Federal Reserve provides liquidity to the domestic financial system. In 1970, the IMF introduced SDRs as a new form of international liquidity. Often referred to as "paper gold," they have been used by countries to meet their payments obligations. While successful, SDRs are not presently a major international reserve asset.

---

[2] Jeffrey H. Bergstrand, "Is Exchange Rate Volatility 'Excessive'?" *New England Economic Review*, Federal Reserve Bank of Boston (September–October 1983), p. 5

Key Points

1. The United States is becoming increasingly internationalized in terms of international trade and finance. In addition, the dominant role of the United States in the world economy has shifted with the emergence of Japan as a major economic superpower in terms of international trade and finance.

2. The SIT or balance of payments summarizes the entire set of real and financial transactions between the United States and the rest of the world. The SIT is composed of two parts: the current account focusing on flows of currently produced goods and services and the capital account focusing on flows of financial assets, both private and official.

3. Every item in the SIT can be related to the demand and supply for dollars in the foreign exchange market, which is the fundamental link between countries engaged in international trade and finance.

4. External or balance-of-payments equilibrium exists when the quantity of dollars demanded and supplied as determined by the basic economic fundamentals present in each country are equal at the existing exchange rate. External deficit (surplus) exists when the quantity of dollars supplied is greater (less) than the quantity of dollars demanded at the existing exchange rate.

5. Persistent external deficits or surpluses require adjustment, and the type of adjustment depends on whether countries follow a fixed or flexible exchange rate regime. A fixed exchange rate regime requires a shift in either demand or supply for dollars holding the rate constant while a flexible regime requires the rate itself to change without resorting to actions designed to shift demand and/or supply.

6. The world economy was on a fixed exchange rate regime from 1944 through 1973. Since 1973, the major industrialized countries have followed a flexible exchange rate system with frequent intervention by central banks to stabilize exchange rate movements. While there persists debate about further reforms, the world economy is likely to remain on some type of flexible exchange rate standard for the foreseeable future.

Key Terms

Appreciation of a currency

Balance of payments

Balance-of-payments deficit

Balance-of-payments surplus

Bretton Woods, New Hamphsire, 1944

Brussels Agreement, 1973

Capital account

Capital inflows

Capital outflows

Current account

Depreciation of a currency

Fixed exchange rate system

Flexible exchange rate system

Foreign exchange market

Foreign exchange rate

Gold standard

Key currency

Nominal versus real exchange rate

Statement of International Transactions (SIT)

Trade balance or merchandise trade balance

Questions

1. Explain the relationship between the current and capital account. Why does the balance of payments always balance as a whole?

2. Why is the demand and supply functions for dollars negatively and positively sloped, respectively?

3. How do expectations of changes in U.S. real GNP, inflation, and productivity influence the demand to hold dollar-denominated financial assets?

4. Explain how a higher inflation rate in the United States compared to Japan would influence the demand and supply for dollars in terms of both the flow of goods and the flow of financial assets.

5. How does the gold standard establish a fixed exchange rate system? How does a country deal with a persistent external deficit in the context of a fixed exchange rate system. Could a fixed exchange rate system ultimately be harmful to international trade even though its claimed advantage is to stimulate international trade?

6. How are external deficits dealt with in the context of a flexible exchange rate system? Are international reserves needed under a flexible exchange rate system?

7. Why are exchange rates likely to fluctuate by fairly large amounts over short periods of time in the context of a flexible exchange rate system? Does this mean the flexible system is not functioning properly?

8. A claimed advantage of flexible exchange rates is that they permit governments to pursue domestic policies without undue regard to the balance of payments since the exchange rate will always move to eliminate an excess supply or demand for dollars. Is this correct?

9. Explain the concept of nominal and real exchange rates and does it have any relationship to the Fisher effect discussed in Chapter 5.

10. What are the political implications of a devaluation (increasing the domestic price of gold) under the fixed exchange rate system? How would the expectation of a devaluation help to ensure that a country would be required actually to devalue its currency?

Suggested Readings

1. Jeffrey H. Bergstrand, "Selected Views of Exchange Rate Determination After a Decade of 'Floating,' " *New England Economic Review*, Federal Reserve Bank of Boston (May–June 1983), 14–29. A review of the flexible exchange rate system from 1973 through 1983.

2. Peter Bernholz, "Flexible Exchange Rates in Historical Perspective," *Princeton Studies in International Finance* (July 1982). More on the experience with flexible exchange rates.

3. Michael David Bordo, "The Classical Gold Standard: Some Lessons for Today," *Review*, Federal Reserve Bank of St. Louis (May 1981). An empirical study of the effectiveness of the fixed exchange rate standard as a constraint on inflationary policies.

4. K. Alec Chrystal, "A Guide to Foreign Exchange Markets," *Review*, Federal Reserve Bank of St. Louis (March 1984), 5–18. Discusses the determinants of exchange rates.

5. Milton Friedman, "The Case for Flexible Exchange Rates," in Milton Friedman (ed.), *Essays in Positive Economics* (Chicago: University of Chicago Press, 1953). A classic discussion of the merits of flexible over fixed exchange rates.

6. Craig S. Hakkio, "Interest Rates and Exchange

Rates—What Is the Relationship?" *Economic Review,* Federal Reserve Bank of Kansas City (November 1986), 33–43. An excellent discussion of the relationship between domestic interest rates and exchange rates in terms of real and nominal concepts.

7. Donald L. Kohn, "Interdependence, Exchange Rate Flexibility, and National Economies," *Economic Review,* Federal Reserve Bank of Kansas City (April 1975), 2–10. Discusses the role of differing macroeconomic policies in each country as a source of exchange rate variation.

8. Robert Solomon, *The International Monetary System, 1945–81* (New York: Basic Books, 1983). Discusses the rise and fall of the fixed exchange rate system.

CHAPTER 16

External Currency Markets, International Financial Institutions, U.S. Trade Imbalances, and LDC Debt

Chapter Overview

Chapter 15 discussed the basic elements of international finance—the Statement of International Transactions, the foreign exchange market, determinants of the exchange rate, and exchange rate regimes for dealing with external disequilibrium. This chapter continues the discussion of international issues by focusing on three selected topics: capital mobility and external currency markets, international financial institutions, and U.S. trade imbalances and Third World or Less Developed Country (LDC) debt. These have been selected because they bear important relationships with each other and, more important, because they have assumed major importance in the world economy as we enter the last decade of the century.

The increased movement of capital across national boundaries and the rapid development of external currency markets are another manifestation of the internationalization of domestic economies. This is a relatively recent development and reflects the growing trade and financial interdependence of increasing numbers of countries. Increased international capital mobility has served as both a cause and an effect of financial liberalization throughout the world. Internationalization of finance has significantly changed the nature of domestic financial systems and the way monetary policy is formulated and executed in each country.

The increased capital mobility has elevated the importance of those institutions and markets that serve as conduits to channel funds among countries. These consist of private institutions such as banks, insurance companies, and security dealers and governmental institutions such as central banks, the International Monetary Fund, Bank for International Settlements, and the World Bank.

The massive trade imbalances experienced by the United States in the 1980s has threaten the world free trading system that has been painstakingly encouraged since the end of World War II because there is a natural tendency to resort to "beggar my neighbor" policies such as tariffs. To prevent this, the United States and other industrialized countries have emphasized the need to coordinate macroeconomic policies as a more effective way of dealing with the trade imbalances. In a similar vein, the large amounts of outstanding debt owed by LDCs, much of it to U.S. banks, has forced greater cooperation among the major economies to ensure stability in the world economy.

Capital Mobility and Increased World Financial Integration

In discussing the Statement of International Transactions and the foreign exchange market, we emphasized the importance of flows of financial assets between the United States and the rest of the world. In terms of magnitude, financial flows are many times greater than flows of goods and services over any given period of time, and the sensitivity of financial flows to differences in interest rates and expected changes in exchange rates has been a major reason why exchange rates fluctuate on a short-term basis. The ability of funds to flow across national boundaries in response to interest rate differences and other economic fundamentals has forced governments to recognize that even under a flexible exchange rate system, domestic policies are frequently constrained by external considerations. That is, changes in domestic policies will influence a country's exchange rate impacting exports and imports of goods and services.

There are four issues needing attention to get a better handle on the rapid increase in capital mobility during the past decade. First, what is meant by the phrase *capital mobility* and how can it be measured over time? Second, why has the mobility of capital increased in the past decade? Third, how has increased capital mobility influenced interest rate differentials between countries? And fourth, how has increased capital mobility influenced the linkages between domestic interest rates and exchange rates? After we consider these issues, we will then turn our attention to the *external currency* markets in general and the *Eurocurrency* markets in particular because these markets are an important link in the flow of funds among different countries.

The Phrase "Capital Mobility"   Capital mobility refers to the flow of financial assets between countries in response to differences in expected rates of return to holding financial assets subject to constraints imposed by the specific types of financial markets and regulation of those countries involved in the exchange of financial assets. These financial assets may be short term, such as Treasury bills, commercial paper, or CDs, or long term, such as government bonds, corporate bonds, corporate equity, or direct investments in land, plant, and equipment.

TABLE 16-1 Foreign assets held at domestic banks, 1982 versus 1987 (billions of dollars)

	1982		1987	
	Amount	*Percent of total*	*Amount*	*Percent of total*
All	$2,359.3	NA	$4,736.9	NA
United States	401.5	20.4	548.7	19.2
Japan	90.9	8.3	576.8	17.5
France	150.6	27.4	266.4	29.0
Germany	81.7	7.3	232.0	10.1
Switzerland	162.4	55.7	332.0	54.4
United Kingdom	462.8	51.5	875.7	49.1
Luxembourg	109.7	NA	227.6	NA
Hong Kong	58.2	NA	266.1	NA
Singapore	81.3	NA	209.8	NA
Cayman Islands	126.0	NA	242.5	NA

NA—not available.
Source: Christine Pavel, "Globalization in the Financial Services Industry," Federal Reserve Bank of Chicago, Working Paper (October 1986). Based on data from International Monetary Fund, *International Financial Statistics,* and various central bank statistical releases.

International capital flows are subject to more constraints than are domestic capital flows because of differing economic and regulatory structures and the need to consider future movements in exchange rates in order to derive an expected rate of return. Despite the increased flow of financial assets among countries in recent years, many industrialized countries impose varying degrees of restrictions on the inflows and outflows of capital. In general, the industrialized countries impose few constraints on short-term capital flows, though somewhat more constraints on long-term flows, especially direct investment. Developing countries impose even more restrictions on almost all types of capital flows.

The magnitude of international capital flows is large and has exhibited rapid growth in the past decade; however, there is no one measure of the magnitude of the flows. Tables 16-1, 16-2, 16-3, and 16-4 provide an indication of their magnitude. Tables 16-1 and 16-2 report foreign assets and liabilities held by domestic banks in a number of countries, respectively, and indicates significant growth from 1982 to 1987. Table 16-3 reports the growth of the international bond market from 1982 to 1987. International bonds are issued outside of the issuer's home country; for example, bonds issued by a foreign entity in the United States denominated in dollars (foreign bonds) or denominated in dollars but issued outside of the United States (Eurobonds). The issuance of international equities has also increased significantly in the 1980s. Table 16-4 reports information on international securities trading. The U.S. markets are the center of international securities trading because U.S. direct markets are the most open, extensive, and broadest in the world. Table 16-4 shows that foreign participation in U.S. bond and equity markets has increased dramatically since 1982. U.S. participation in foreign bond and equities trading has also increased, but not to the same extent as reflected in Table 16-4.

TABLE 16-2   Foreign liabilities held at domestic banks, 1982 versus 1987 (billions of dollars)

	1982		1987	
	Amount	*Percent of total*	*Amount*	*Percent of total*
All	$2,375.1	NA	$4,881.7	NA
United States	254.5	12.9	572.6	20.0
Japan	100.0	9.1	592.0	18.0
France	151.8	27.7	271.4	29.6
Germany	64.7	5.7	131.4	5.4
Switzerland	141.2	NA	247.9	NA
United Kingdom	489.68	44.5	927.5	43.9
Luxembourg	102.2	NA	98.6	NA
Hong Kong	54.1	NA	229.4	NA
Singapore	82.8	NA	216.8	NA
Cayman Islands	82.8	NA	233.3	NA

NA—Not available
Source: Christine Pavel, "Globalization in the Financial Services Industry," Federal Reserve Bank of Chicago, Working Paper (October 1986). Based on data from International Monetary Fund, *International Financial Statistics,* and various central bank statistical releases.

Two interesting characteristics of the international bond market are evident: first, industrial countries represent the major issuers of bonds and second, bonds denominated in U.S. dollars continue to represent the single largest currency category; however, the role of the dollar has steadily declined with respect to other currencies during the 1980s.

Reasons for Increased Capital Mobility   Why has capital mobility increased in the past decade and why has the world financial system become more integrated? Five reasons account for the rapid growth of the flows of financial assets between countries.

First, deregulation and financial reform have been international phenomena.

TABLE 16-3   International bond issuance, 1982–1987 (billions of dollars)

	Eurobonds	*Foreign bonds*	*Total International*
1982	$ 51.2	$26.4	$ 77.6
1983	48.5	27.8	76.3
1984	79.5	28.0	107.5
1985	136.7	31.0	167.7
1986	188.7	39.4	228.1
1987	140.5	40.3	180.8

Source: Christine Pavel, "Globalization in the Financial Services Industry," Federal Reserve Bank of Chicago, working paper (October 1986). Based on data from J. P. Morgan & Company.

TABLE 16-4 International bond markets, 1982–1988 (billions of dollars)			
	Foreign transactions in U.S. securities in U.S. markets	*Foreign transactions in foreign securities U.S. markets*	*Total*
1982	$ 41.8	$ 61.0	$102.8
1983	47.1	75.0	122.1
1984	22.2	54.0	76.2
1985	129.1	166.4	295.5
1986	195.7	337.7	533.4
1987	184.0	405.8	589.8
1988	144.7	443.1	587.8

Source: Christine Pavel, "Globalization in the Financial Services Industry," Federal Reserve Bank of Chicago, Working Paper (October 1986). Based on data from the Board of Governors of the Federal Reserve System.

Chapter 12 emphasized the fact that the forces transforming the U.S. financial system toward a more flexible and competitive structure are not unique to the United States. The financial systems of many industrialized and developing countries are undergoing a similar transformation. Financial structures that were previously constrained by government regulation are gradually being liberalized by market and regulatory reforms, and as a result, competitive forces play a larger role in allocating credit than previously. As part of this transition, regulatory and market innovations have made domestic financial systems more open to international forces. Governments have eliminated or relaxed controls over the inflow and outflow of capital and made it easier to substitute domestic for foreign financial assets. Governments have made it easier for foreign banks to operate in the domestic financial systems and for domestic banks to expand their operations internationally. While movements of short-term and long-term capital are not completely free, the 1980s witnessed major efforts by governments to enhance capital mobility. A major change is scheduled to take place in 1992 when 12 European countries establish a unified banking and financial structure and allow liberal access for foreign institutions.

Second, the financial reform process in a number of countries has expanded the number of markets and financial assets that are conducive to international finance. Financial reform has made available to residents and foreigners assets that are similar to financial assets in other countries, especially money market instruments such as Treasury bills, CDs, bankers' acceptances, and commercial paper. Markets for these money market instruments and the increasing openness of these markets to outsiders increases the interaction between the domestic and the international financial system, and thus, enhances capital mobility.

Third, a variety of financial innovations such as futures markets for foreign exchange and interest rate swaps have made it easier to manage exchange rate and interest rate risk for portfolios that include domestic and foreign financial assets.

Fourth, the massive external imbalances experienced by the United States and several other industrialized countries in the 1980s contributed greatly to the increased flows of capital among countries. In 1985, the United States became the largest debtor nation while Japan has emerged as the world's largest creditor nation.

Fifth, the external debt owed by developing countries—the world debt problem—has required continued expansion of bank credit to keep individual countries from defaulting on loans made in the past. A series of "debt restructuring" schemes were implemented in the 1980s to give debtor countries more time to manage the large amount of outstanding debt. As a result, international lending has increased to support past lending actions.

The Impact of Increased Capital Mobility on Interest Rate Differentials Competition forces interest rates on similar financial assets to be the same, and therefore, one might expect interest rate differentials between countries to decline with the increased mobility of capital among different countries. This has not been the case, however. Nominal and real interest rate differentials have been large and variable over time, and show no definite downward trend over time. Figure 16-1 presents nominal and real interest rate differentials for the United States with respect to Germany, Japan, the United Kingdom, and Canada during the period from 1961 through 1985. These countries have had virtually no restrictions on the inflow and outflow of capital or have recently relaxed restrictions on capital flows (Japan). Interest rate differentials remain large and variable.

Does this mean that increased capital mobility is an illusion or are other factors needed to account for the persistence of interest rate differentials in the face of increased financial integration of the world economy?

In Chapter 5, we discussed factors that account for differences in various interest rates in a given country: maturity, default risk, tax considerations, and other factors such as the existence of secondary markets. These same factors help to explain interest rate differentials across national boundaries; however, additional factors unique to international capital flows need to be considered.

To understand why interest differentials persist among countries despite increased ease with which funds can move from country to country, we need to discuss further the relationship between interest rates and exchange rates introduced in Chapter 15.[1]

To simplify the discussion, assume that a U.S. and a Japanese financial asset have the same maturity and same degree of default risk and that funds can flow into and out of both countries with ease. In addition, let us focus on real interest rate differentials since market participants are concerned with real rates of return rather than nominal rates of return. Thus, the story starts with a market participant choosing between a U.S. and a Japanese financial asset.

Market forces should equalize the expected rates of return to holding financial assets in the United States and Japan; however, that does not mean that differences between real interest rates in each country will disappear. Consider the following relationship:

$$\text{U.S. real interest rate } + \text{ expected change in the real}$$
$$\text{exchange rate } = \text{ Japanese real interest rate} \tag{1}$$

The nominal or market exchange rate is the rate quoted in the financial press and expresses the value of the dollar in terms of yen per dollar. The real exchange rate

---

[1] The following discussion is drawn from Craig S. Hakkio, "Interest Rates and Exchange Rates—What Is the Relationship?" *Economic Review*, Federal Reserve Bank of Kansas City (November 1986), 33–43.

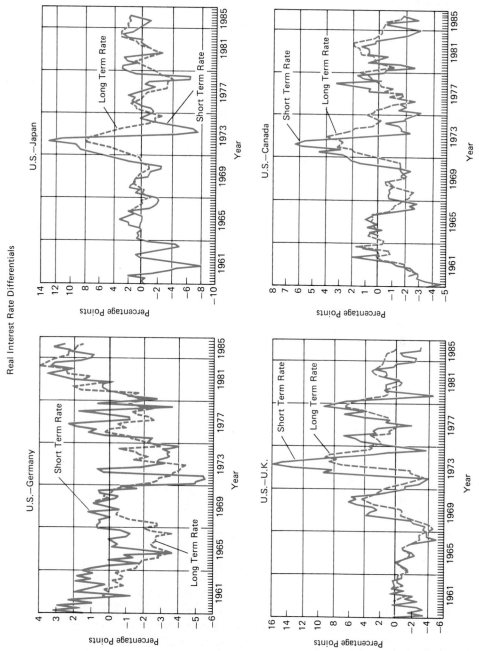

Source: Bruce Kasman and Charles Pigott, "An Examination of Interest Rate Divergences Among the Major Industrial Countries," in *International Integration of Financial Markets and U.S. Monetary Policy,* Federal Reserve Bank of New York (December 1987).

FIGURE 16-1 **Nominal and real interest rate differentials between the United States, Canada, Germany, Japan, and the United Kingdom, 1961–1985.**

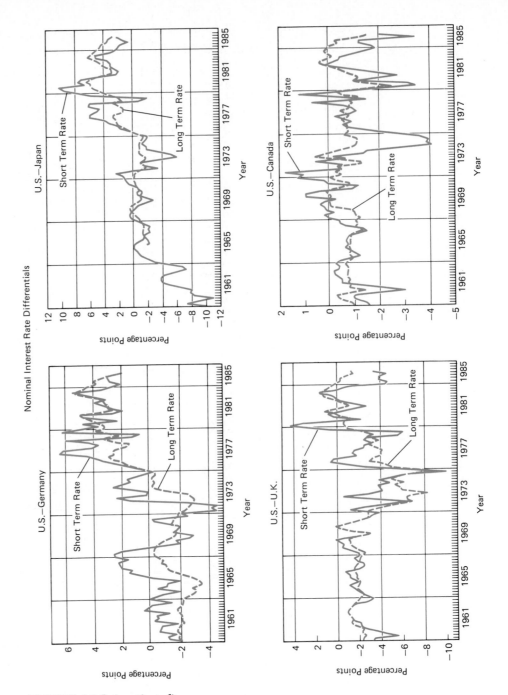

FIGURE 16-1 (continued)

is not directly observable. It is the price of U.S. goods in terms of Japanese goods often referred to as the "terms of trade between the United States and Japan."

Market forces imply that expression (1) should hold over time because capital flows will shift between the United States and Japan until rates of return are equalized. If real interest rates in the United States are higher than in Japan, this implies that market participants expect a decline in the real exchange rate (real dollar depreciation) in order for the total return of holding U.S. assets to be the same as holding Japanese assets.

The student might be confused with this and statements made in the previous chapter about the effect of changes in U.S. real interest rates on the exchange rate. In that discussion, we indicated that an increase in U.S. real interest rates relative to Japan would lead to a rightward shift in the demand for dollar-denominated financial assets and, hence, increase the exchange rate (dollar appreciation). Now we seem to be saying the opposite. Higher U.S. real interest rates are associated with expected declines in the exchange rate. There must be an answer and there is—in the previous case, we are talking about today's exchange rate and how it is determined by demand and supply for today's dollars, and in the current case, we are talking about expected values of the exchange rate relative to today's exchange rate.

To see that there is no contradiction, assume that the long-run real exchange rate is constant over time and that at this rate, the flow of goods and services between the United States and Japan are in balance. Next, assume that real interest rates increase in the United States because of increased government budget deficits and/or reduced saving. High real rates shift the demand for dollar assets to the right and increase the real exchange rate above the long-run level. Market participants then expect the exchange rate to decline at some point if real interest rates in the United States exceed those in Japan. Of course, this is not as simple in the real world as the example implies, though the mechanism does essentially work in this manner. Thus, anything that influences the expected exchange rate can generate an interest rate differential that persists over time despite increased capital mobility.

It is important to understand that expression (1) is a definition (or identity) and does not imply causation in the sense that interest rate differentials are determined by expected changes in exchange rates. Interest rates and exchange rates are both determined by other forces, and the expression only indicates the relationship that should persist over time between interest and exchange rates.

Despite the definitional character of expression (1), it does help us understand how increased capital mobility is consistent with differences in domestic real interest rates for Japan and the United States. There are two factors to consider. First, anything that influences expected real exchange rates over the holding period of the financial asset will permit interest rates to differ among countries. Expected changes in a country's income, productivity, tariffs, real interest rate, and so on will lead to expected changes in the supply and demand for dollars and hence, to expected changes in the exchange rate. Second, restrictions on the flow of capital between the United States and Japan can account for interest rate differences even if the market's expectation of a change in the exchange rate is zero. For example, Japan's financial system was once entirely closed to outsiders, and though it has become increasingly open since 1980, a variety of private and government restrictions limit the inflow and outflow of capital.

Capital Mobility and the Relationship Between Interest Rates and Exchange Rates

While increased mobility of capital will not eliminate or reduce interest rate differentials, there is growing evidence that increased capital mobility has increased the link between a country's domestic interest rate and its exchange rate. This has major implications for the conduct of monetary policy since it suggests that anything done by the monetary authority to influence the domestic economy will influence the exchange rate.

Capital Mobility and External Currency Markets

A U.S. market participant to the international financial system has three ways to hold an asset: (1) hold a home currency–denominated asset such as a dollar-denominated bond issued in the United States, (2) hold a foreign currency–denominated asset such as a yen-denominated bond issued in Japan, or (3) hold a Eurocurrency asset. The Eurocurrency asset is denominated in a currency other than the country in which the asset was issued; for example, a dollar-denominated bond issued in West Germany would be classified as a Eurodollar bond whereas a yen-denominated bond issued in West Germany would be classified as a Euroyen bond.

The external currency markets in bank deposit, loans, and bonds have grown rapidly and play an important role in linking different financial systems together and strengthening the relationship between interest rats and exchange rates. Thus, we need to consider these markets in greater detail.

External Currency Markets

External currency deposits are the foundation of the external currency markets. These are referred to as *Eurocurrency* deposits, or simply, *Eurocurrencies* because they first originated in banks located in Europe. The Eurocurrency market consists of foreign currency–denominated deposits of banks outside of the country that originally issued the currency. Banks in countries outside of the United States, including branches of U.S. banks, are permitted to accept deposits and make loans in currencies other than the country in which they are located. The Federal Reserve permitted U.S. banks as of 1990 to accept foreign currency deposits.

The most significant component of the Eurocurrency market is the *Eurodollar market*. The Eurodollar market consists of dollar-denominated deposits in banks located outside of the United States and has grown dramatically during the past three decades. Eurocurrency deposits other than Eurodollars such as Euromarks, Eurofrancs (Swiss), and recently, Euroyen represent about 35% of the total Eurocurrency market. While the terms Eurocurrencies and Eurodollars originated from activities of banks located in Europe, these external currency–denominated deposits are now issued by banks located throughout the world.

Eurocurrency deposits have grown rapidly in the 1980s (Table 16-5) and while the dollar continues to represent the most important currency of denomination, the

TABLE 16-5 Eurocurrency deposits, 1982–1987 (billions of dollars)

	Gross	*Net*	*%Eurodollar*
1982	$2,168	$1,285	80.3%
1983	2,278	1,382	81.0
1984	2,386	1,430	81.7
1985	2,846	1,676	75.4
1986	3,683	2,076	71.7
1987	4,509	2,587	66.0

Note: Net repress gross deposits less interbank deposits.

Source: Christine Pavel, "Globalization in the Financial Services Industry," Federal Reserve Bank of Chicago, working paper (October 1986). Based on data from J. P. Morgan & Co.

dollar's role has declined while the role of the Japanese yen and other currencies has increased.

Eurobanks primarily issue time deposits that range in maturity from overnight to several years. Overnight Eurodollars have demand deposit characteristics from the issuing bank's point of view since they are of such short duration. The time deposits are usually fixed rate instruments, although variable rate instruments are also offered. There is an active secondary market for Eurodollar deposits and, thus, they possess a high degree of liquidity.

Long-term debt obligations of enterprises and governments are also issued in the external currency market and have also grown rapidly in the 1980s (Table 16-3). *Eurobonds* are debt instruments denominated in a currency other than the currency of the country in which they are issued; for example, Eurobonds are often denominated in currencies like the dollar, mark, or other currency in which there is an active market. This provides the bonds with greater flexibility since they can be sold in several countries. Eurobonds are different from *foreign bonds*. Foreign bonds are denominated in the currency of the country where they are issued, but represent obligations of a foreign enterprise or government. For example, dollar-denominated bonds issued in the United States by foreigners are referred to as *Yankee bonds*. Foreign banks have recently expanded issuance of CDs (maturities of one year or less) in the United States and denominated in dollars. These are referred to as *Yankee CDs*.

Eurodollars in More Detail

Eurodollars constitute the bulk of the Eurocurrency market. The discussion of Eurodollars focuses on the following issues: (1) interest rates on Eurodollar deposits, (2) risk of holding Eurodollars, (3) Eurodollars and financial innovation, (4) Eurodollars and monetary control by the Federal Reserve and (5) Eurodollars in the official money supply measures.

Let us first consider an example of how a Eurodollar deposit is created. There are many ways in which Eurodollar deposits are established. They can be established as a result of trade between the United States and other countries; for example, a German exporter may sell goods to the United States and collect in dollars. The dollars can then be deposited in a German bank; hence, a Eurodollar deposit has been established. Much of the expansion in Eurodollar deposits, however, has been the result of depositors in the United States shifting domestic deposits or other financial assets into Eurodollars. In the 1970s this was done to avoid Regulation Q ceilings.

Individuals can convert demand deposits, other deposits, CDs, repurchase agreements, Treasury bills, or other money market assets into Eurodollars. Assume an individual decides to convert demand deposits into Eurodollars. This will be reflected by changes in the flow of funds for the individual, the U.S. bank, and the Eurobank.[2]

Individual		*U.S. Bank*		*Eurobank*	
Assets	Liabilities	Assets	Liabilities	Assets	Liabilities
Domestic demand deposit − $1 million			Domestic demand deposit − $1 million	Demand deposit in U.S. bank + $1 million	Eurodollar time deposit + $1 million
Eurodollar time deposit + $1 million			Demand deposit of Eurobank + $1 million		

The individual transfers by check $1 million to the Eurobank. The T-account shows that the individual has shifted assets from a demand deposit account at the U.S. bank to a Eurodollar time deposit at the Eurobank. The Eurobank's liabilities have increased by $1 million to the individual. At this point, the U.S. bank owes $1 million to the Eurobank. Let us assume that the Eurobank decides to maintain the reserve funds as a demand deposit at the U.S. bank. This will be reflected by an increase in deposits owed by the U.S. bank on the asset side of the account for the Eurobank. The U.S. bank shifts deposit liabilities from the individual account to the Eurobank account. This example assumes that the Eurobank maintains the reserve in the form of a demand deposit account at the U.S. bank. The Eurobank could also maintain the reserve in the form of an entry "due from" a United States bank on the asset side matched by an entry "due to" a foreign bank on the liability side of the United States bank. In this case, the account for the individual remains unchanged, but the accounts for the U.S. bank and Eurobank would now appear as

U.S. Bank		*Eurobank*	
Assets	Liabilities	Assets	Liabilities
	Domestic demand Deposit − $1 million	"Due from" U.S. bank + $1 million	Eurodollar time deposit + $1 million
	"Due to" Eurobank + $1 million		

[2] This and other examples are discussed in Anatol B. Balbach and David H. Resler, "Eurodollars and the U.S. Money Supply," *Review*, Federal Reserve Bank of St. Louis (June–July 1980), 2–12.

The example can be used to illustrate three aspects of Eurodollars. First, a large component (Table 16-5) of Eurodollars and Eurocurrencies are interbank liabilities. Second, Eurodollars provide a foundation for expanding credit worldwide. The Eurobank can use the reserves obtained as a result of the Eurodollar deposit to expand loans in dollars, or the U.S. bank can use the reserves freed up by the transfer of funds from the demand deposit to the Eurodeposit to expand loans and investments. Eurodollar deposits are now subject to a 3% reserve while transaction deposits are subject to a 12% reserve. The shift of funds from the demand deposit to the Eurodollar account provides the U.S. bank with additional reserves to expand lending and credit. Third, since Eurodollar deposits were not subject to interest rate ceilings in the 1970s, they were a financial innovation utilized by the market to circumvent interest rate ceilings.

Interest Rates on Eurodollar Deposits The Eurodollar interest rate is closely aligned with interest rates on close substitutes for Eurodollars. Interest rates on Federal funds (reserves traded between depository institutions in the United States), large CDs, and Eurodollars move very closely to each other over time.

Risk of Eurodollars Risk is relative to the country of residence for the holder of Eurodollars. Let us assume that risk is being considered from the point of view of a resident of the United States. There are two general types of risk associated with holding a financial asset. First, interest rate risk refers to the possible loss that can occur if the financial asset is sold before it matures. Since Eurodollar deposits have an active secondary market, Eurodollars are exposed to interest rate risk. Second, there are other types of risks that are unique to Eurodollars. (1) The Eurodollar deposit is held by a bank outside of the United States; thus, the government of that country may interfere with the transfer of funds. (2) Foreign banks may be riskier than U.S. banks, and determining the degree of riskiness will involve more resources on the part of the deposit holder. (3) Eurodollars are not insured and thus expose the deposit holder to default risk.

Despite these risks, the Eurodollar market has expanded greatly during the past three decades. The market has performed well; however, it is susceptible to problems if a number of large banks failed to meet their Eurodollar liabilities. In the 1980s, the international debt problem reached serious proportions, and some critics of the Eurodollar market claim that it provides a potential framework for collapse of the international financial system.

Eurodollars and Financial Innovation Two considerations about the origin of Eurodollars can be offered. The first is an ironic, but historically interesting, account of how they started. The second is the most important explanation of why they have grown so rapidly.

The Soviet Union is responsible for contributing to the initiation of the market. In the early 1950s, during the height of the cold war period, the Soviet Union wanted to hold dollar balances because the dollar was the major key currency for international trade; however, the Soviet Union did not want to hold these balances in U.S. banks. There was concern that the U.S. government might constrain the use of these funds, much like what happened with Iranian deposits in 1979. Thus, the Soviet Union arranged to have London banks hold dollar-denominated deposits.

While an interesting story of the beginning of the Eurodollar market, the real explanation for the growth and development of the market has to do with the binding constraints of financial regulation in the United States and the effort of private institutions and markets to shift activities to areas where the constraints were either non-existing or less binding. The process of financial innovation is a market-induced action designed to circumvent binding regulations that limit profit opportunities. There were and still are several constraints on U.S. banks that account for the growth of the Eurodollar market. (1) Banks outside the United States are generally less regulated and subject to more liberal tax treatment. This is why Eurodollar deposits are often located in places like Nassau and the Cayman Islands. (2) Eurodollar deposits are not subject to interest rate ceilings. In the 1970s, when Regulation Q was binding. Eurodollar deposits provided an important source of funds for U.S. banks. (3) Eurodollar deposits for a long time were not subject to reserve requirements; however, they are now subject to a 3% reserve when used as a source of funds for U.S. banks.

Eurodollars and Monetary Control   There has been some debate about the effect of Eurodollars on achieving effective monetary control. There is no doubt that Eurodollar deposits have some influence on the money supply, primarily by influencing the ratio of managed liabilities to transaction deposits (the *n* ratio) as illustrated in Chapter 10; however, their impact is small. An analysis of the impact of Eurodollars on monetary control found that over the period from 1973 to 1979 when Eurodollars grew rapidly, "Eurodollar flows were shown to have only minor effects on the U.S. money stock."[3]

Eurodollars and Money Supply Measures   Eurodollars are not transaction deposits and are excluded from the M1 measure of money; however, they are liquid and can influence spending decisions. Only part of the Eurodollar market is reflected in the broader money supply measures, however. Overnight Eurodollars issued to U.S. residents by foreign branches of U.S. banks worldwide are included in M2. In August 1988, overnight Eurodollars totaled about $16 billion, or about 0.5% of M2. Term Eurodollars are included in M3 and are defined as Eurodollar deposits longer than one day held by U.S. residents at foreign branches of U.S. banks worldwide and at all banking offices in the United Kingdom and Canada. In 1988 term Eurodollars totaled about $102 billion and represented about 3% of M3.

Institutions and the International Flow of Funds

Funds are transferred in the international financial system through private institutions, mainly banks in the Eurocurrency markets and private markets for Eurobonds and foreign bond issues. Official institutions also play a major role in the international financial system. The most important official institutions include the *International Monetary Fund* or the *IMF*, *International Bank for Reconstruction and Development* or the *World Bank*, *Bank for International Settlements*, and several affiliates of the World Bank.

---

[3] Anatol B. Balbach and David H. Resler, "Eurodollars and the U.S. Money Supply," *Review*, Federal Reserve Bank of St. Louis (June–July 1980), p. 11.

The Bank for International Settlements is located in Basel, Switzerland, and is a central banker's bank that encourages cooperation among countries to stabilize exchange rates, encourages international trade, provides a forum for the discussion of international financial issues, and collects and publishes data on international financial flows. The *International Development Association* and *International Finance Corporation* are specialized affiliates of the World Bank that function to transfer resources from the developed sector of the world economy to the developing sector.

The IMF and the World Bank are the most important official aspects of the international financial systems. These institutions, especially the IMF, have come to play a key role in the international debt problem of the 1980s.

International Monetary Fund

The IMF was an outcome of the Bretton Woods Agreement in 1944 to reestablish international trade on a fixed exchange rate basis. The IMF was originally designed by John Maynard Keynes to play a significant role in international finance by being a lender of last resort. The IMF would have the power to expand and contract world money supply in much the same fashion that the Federal Reserve expands and contracts domestic money supply. However, this was too bold a concept to consider in 1944 and is still not realistic today.

The purpose of the IMF was much more limited than that advocated by Keynes, but the IMF was still provided with a significant role in reestablishing world trade after 1944. The IMF was responsible for (1) promoting international monetary cooperation between countries; (2) expanding and encouraging international trade in a nonrestrictive environment; (3) encouraging exchange rate stability; (4) providing an environment for orderly and smooth changes in exchange rates if required; (5) encouraging balance of payments mechanisms that would allow a country to achieve external equilibrium without resorting to tariffs, quotas, exchange controls, and other methods that would interfere with free trade; and (6) providing loans and other assistance to countries that were experiencing balance-of-payments deficits.

The IMF is composed of member countries. Membership has expanded from 30 in 1945 to 151 in 1988 and includes China, Hungary, and Poland. Member countries contribute resources to the IMF on the basis of assigned quotas. The quotas are determined by the member country's level of economic activity and role in international trade. Quota contributions determine the member country's voting power and amount of funds that can be borrowed from the IMF. The quota contribution usually consists of gold (25%) and the member country's currency (75%). The contributions provide the basic lending resources available to the IMF. Thus, the IMF serves as an intermediary in international finance, collecting financial resources from one group of countries and distributing these resources to countries experiencing a need for liquidity.

Borrowing from the IMF

The ability to borrow from the IMF was important under the fixed exchange rate system prior to 1973; however, borrowing was not regarded as a long-term solution to balance-of-payment deficits but designed to provide a country with sufficient time to adjust its domestic economic performance without having to change the exchange rate and/or resort to tariffs, quotas, or other methods that would interfere with trade. Under the floating exchange rate system since 1973 however, borrowing from the IMF continues to be important. In fact, the international debt problem has made the IMF more important than ever in lending to member countries. There are two reasons why borrowing from the IMF remains important, aside from the current international debt problem. First, even under a floating exchange rate system, there is a need for liquidity to bridge the gap between receipts and expenditures. Over short periods of time, expenditures and receipts in a country's international transactions may not match, and borrowing from the IMF will prevent sharp changes in exchange rates. Second, despite the role of floating exchange rates, many countries either tie their exchange rate to a major currency such as the dollar or maintain fixed exchange rates. Developing countries, in particular, have more difficulty in operating under flexible than fixed exchange rates. Thus, for those countries on other than a floating exchange standard, the borrowing facility at the IMF is as important as it was prior to 1973.

Borrowing from the IMF is not without limitations. Member countries can borrow in excess of their quotas over time; however, the IMF imposes progressively more restrictive conditions on loans. The IMF can and does impose conditions that require a country to make fundamental changes in domestic policies to reduce imports and expand exports. IMF "austerity" conditions can be severe and must usually be accepted by a country in need of IMF resources. In addition, private and government lenders will not continue to provide funds to a country unless it has some continuing involvement with IMF and the country is following the recommendations of the IMF.

Special Drawing Rights

Special Drawing Rights or SDRs were introduced by the IMF in 1970. SDRs were designed a supplement existing international reserves such as gold and key currencies. They were distributed to member countries on the basis of each country's quota. SDRs can be used to meet payments obligations and have become an important international reserve asset. There are several features of SDRs worth noting. (1) They are a liability of the IMF and thus add to the world money supply. As we will see in Chapter 19, SDR allocations to the United States increase the monetary base, other things held constant. (2) There is a mechanism in place that requires deficit countries that use SDRs to pay interest to surplus countries that accept SDRs. The interest rate is based on short-term interest rates in the United States, the United Kingdom, Germany, France, and Japan. (3) The value of an SDR is determined by a weighted average of the value of the currencies of these five major countries.

The World Bank

The World Bank was established at the same time as the IMF to encourage world trade and economic development. Like the IMF, it is composed of member countries (151 in 1987), most of which are IMF members.

The World Bank functions as a financial intermediary and finances specific development projects. The sources of funds come primarily from I.O.U.s sold in developed economies such as the United States. The uses of funds represent loans to developing countries designed to establish an infrastructure in these countries to support economic growth. Loans can be made to either public or private groups within a country.

International Financial Problems in the 1990s

The international financial system has experienced much difficulty since the establishment of the Bretton Woods system in 1944. The previous chapter discussed a number of issues that led to abandonment of the fixed exchange system in favor of a floating exchange rate system. The floating system has worked reasonably well; however, the international financial system has still experienced problems since 1973.

Many concerns have been expressed about the flexible exchange rate system itself. We have already discussed the issue of short-term fluctuations in exchange rates in Chapter 15. Prior to establishing the flexible exchange rate system in 1973, many argued that exchange rates would smoothly and fairly quickly eliminate external imbalances between the demand and supply for dollars. This has not been the case. Exchange rates have fluctuated more than anticipated. More important, flexible exchanges rates in general and a major decline in the value of the dollar after 1985 in particular did not eliminate the large and persistent U.S. external imbalances in the 1980s.

The international or LDC debt problem has also been a major issue of concern regarding the international financial system. In the mid-1980s there was considerable fear that the huge amount of external debt of developing countries could generate a financial collapse because a major part of this debt was held by a small number of large U.S. banks. At the end of the 1980s, while the debt problem has not been resolved, there is considerably less concern that it possess serious problems for U.S. banks and the world financial system.

Let us take a close look at these two issues.

External Imbalances and the Domestic Economy

The flexible exchange rate system was intended to eliminate external deficits or surpluses quickly and smoothly; however, this has not been the case. The experience of the United States stands out in this regard. The United States has experienced persistent and large deficits in the trade balance, the balance on goods and services, and the overall current account since 1980 (Table 16-6). In fact, these reached unprecedented levels in the 1980s. During much of the 1980s, the external deficit

TABLE 16-6 U.S. International Transactions, 1970–1988 (dollars in millions)

Year	Trade Balance	Goods and Service Balance	Current Account Balance
1970	$ 2.6	$ 5.8	$ 2.3
1971	−2.3	2.4	−1.4
1972	−6.4	−1.7	−5.8
1973	0.9	11.2	7.1
1974	−5.5	9.4	2.0
1975	8.9	23.0	18.1
1976	−9.5	9.5	4.2
1977	−31.1	−9.5	−14.5
1978	−33.9	−9.9	−15.4
1979	−27.5	5.1	−1.0
1980	−25.5	9.5	1.9
1981	−28.0	14.3	6.9
1982	−36.4	0.3	−8.7
1983	−67.1	−36.8	−46.2
1984	−112.6	−95.0	−107.1
1985	−122.2	−100.1	−115.1
1986	−144.6	−123.5	−138.8
1987	−160.3	−140.5	−154.0
1988	−127.2	−137.0	−126.5

Source: Council of Economic Advisors, *Economic Report of the President, 1989; Federal Reserve Bulletin* (September 1989).

(measured by the balance on good and services) averaged about 2.5% of GNP—an unprecedented level in this century. According to the model of the foreign exchange market discussed in the previous chapter, such large external deficits should have induced offsetting exchange rate movements. But that has not been the case. In the first half of the 1980s, the value of the dollar increased as the external deficits increased, while after 1985, the value of the dollar declined, but the external deficits remained large and only began to show a downward trend in 1988. There are four issues that need explanation. First, why did the external deficit increase so rapidly after 1980 and reach unprecedented levels by 1985? Second, why has the external deficit persisted in the face of a major decline in the value of the dollar since 1985? Third, what is the relationship between internal and external balance? And fourth, what conditions in addition to flexible exchange rates are required for a more timely elimination of external imbalances than has been the case in the 1980s?

The U.S. External Imbalance: First Half of the 1980s   The trade balance and balance on goods and services were in deficit in 1980; however, the deficits were relatively small when compared to GNP. By 1985, the imbalances had reached massive proportions. Why? U.S. politicians and many others argued that the United States was the victim of unfair international competition, especially from Japan with which the United States experienced the largest deficits. While this explanation may have influenced some views and certainly brought about various U.S. proposals for Japan and other countries to adjust their trade and other policies to eliminate the imbalances, the cause of the massive imbalances lies with the macroeconomic policies of the United States. There is certainly some merit to the argument that other countries, especially Japan, have been less than enthusiastic about free world trade in terms of opening their markets to foreign competition; however, the rapid increase and magnitude of the U.S. trade imbalances simply cannot be explained by these factors.

The generally agreed-upon explanation goes something like this. In the early 1980s, real interest rates rose in the United States relative to other countries for a variety of reasons. From 1980 to 1982, the Federal Reserve imposed very tight monetary policy on the economy in order to break the upward trend of inflation and this required a sharp increase in real interest rates. After 1982, the rapid growth of the government budget deficit and the further downward trend in personal saving contributed to a high real interest rate. At the same time, foreigners were more optimistic about the willingness of the Federal Reserve to maintain price stability and, thus, did not anticipate a depreciation of the dollar.

High real interest rates and anticipations that the dollar would not likely fall in value combined to increase the expected rate of return to holding dollar-denominated financial assets. Thus, there was a rightward shift in the demand for dollars to purchase U.S. financial assets, and as a result, the dollar appreciated. This increased the price of U.S.-produced goods and services to the rest of the world and reduced the price of foreign-produced goods and services. Thus, the appreciation of the dollar induced a massive trade imbalance.

The U.S. External Imbalance: The Second Half of the 1980s   The dollar appreciated over 75% from 1980 to 1985, at which time, the dollar started to fall in value. The depreciation of the dollar was partly induced by central bank intervention in late 1985, especially by the Bank of Japan and the Bundesbank of Germany; however, market forces were the primary cause of the decline in the value of the dollar. The external deficits had reached massive levels and the dollar was responding to the excess supply of dollars in the foreign exchange market. Despite a major depreciation in the value of the dollar after 1985 however, the trade imbalances continued to increase and remained high. Why?

The explanation for the decline in the value of the dollar after 1985 and its failure to eliminate the external deficits can be illustrated in Figure 16-2. The demand and supply for dollars at the exchange rate ER_1 indicate an external deficit that induces a downward movement in the exchange rate. The exchange rate declines to ER_2, but at the same time, the demand and supply functions shift in such a manner that a deficit continues to persist at the lower value of the dollar. Figure 16-2 shows the supply function shifting to the right farther than the demand function. What might account for this?

This suggests that there is something fundamental about the U.S. or any economy that generates an external deficit or surplus irrespective of movements in the exchange rate. In fact, we have gradually come to recognize that external equilibrium requires more than merely adopting flexible exchange rates.

The Relationship Between Internal Balance and External Balance or Why Exchange Rate Movements Cannot Bear All of the Responsibility for Adjustment
The concept of internal balance refers to the relationship between private saving and

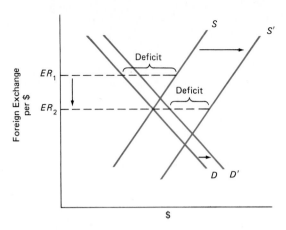

FIGURE 16-2   Falling exchange rate and
persistent deficits

investment (net private saving) and the relationship between government expenditures and receipts (budget deficit or surplus). The internal balance determines the
nature of the external balance.

A little national income accounting will help us understand the relationship
between the external and the internal balance. Expression (1) shows that GNP or
domestic output is equal to domestic consumption (C), domestic private investment
(I), domestic government spending (G), and the external balance (EB) measured as
the difference between exports of goods and services (X) and imports of goods and
services (M).

$$GNP = C + I + G + EB \qquad (1)$$

Expression (2) indicates there are only three things that can be done with national
output when it is considered as national income—it can be consumed (C), it can be
saved (S), and it can be taxed (T).

$$GNP = C + S + T \qquad (2)$$

Setting the right-hand side of each expression equal to each other and dropping C
yields the following expression:

$$(S - I) + (T - G) = EB = \text{capital flow} \quad (\text{capital outflow} - \text{capital inflow}) \qquad (3)$$

The internal balance consists of the sum of the private saving–investment balance
$(S - I)$ and the government balance $(T - G)$. If the internal balance is negative, EB
must be negative, and if EB is negative (imports exceed exports), there must be an
offsetting capital inflow to finance the external deficit. That is, if private saving is low
relative to investment and the government is running large deficits as has been the
case in the 1980s, EB must be negative. The United States must increase its liabilities
to the rest of the world to pay for the external deficit. In fact, the United States after
1985 had become the world's largest debtor.

It is important to realize that these expressions are accounting definitions that only illustrate relationships among the variables. They offer no evidence that government deficits and low private saving are the cause of the large external deficits. By the end of the 1980s, however, most observers came to accept that large government deficits accompanied by low private saving played a major role in the persistent external deficits despite substantial declines in the value of the dollar.

The relationship between internal and external balance can be viewed from another direction. If the United States has an internal deficit in the sense that the sum of $(S - I)$ and $(T - G)$ is less than zero, then this is equivalent to saying that domestic spending exceeds domestic output. Keep in mind that domestic spending $= C + I + G$ and that domestic output $= C + I + G + (X - M)$; therefore, for domestic spending to exceed domestic output, imports must exceed exports:

$$C + I + G > C + I + G + (X - M) \qquad (4)$$

Then

$$(X - M) < 0 \text{ or } EB < 0 \qquad (5)$$

Thus, the United States consumes more than it produces domestically and must import the difference.

The implication of this accounting exercise is fundamental and suggests that it may be difficult for the exchange rate to eliminate the external deficit as long as the United States continues to run large internal deficits in terms of the balance between saving and investment and the balance between government revenues and expenditures.

The Need for Greater International Policy Coordination The failure of the flexible exchange rate system to remove external imbalances smoothly and rapidly has brought increased recognition that additional requirements are needed to ensure a stable international financial environment that facilitates expanded world trade. Two important preconditions have been recognized.

First, central banks of each country need to conduct monetary policy so as to maintain steady and low inflation rates over the long run. Uncertain monetary policy and uncertainties over the future inflation rate induce frequent changes in the market's judgment of future changes in the exchange rate. Changes in expected future exchange rates change the expected return from holding financial assets denominated in another currency, and as the world financial system becomes more integrated and restrictions on capital mobility are relaxed, capital moves from country to country and induces frequent changes in the exchange rate. Thus, efforts of central banks in the major industrialized countries to stabilize prices and reduce inflationary expectations will go a long way toward stabilizing exchange rates.

Second, exchange rate movements will remain an important adjustment mechanism for dealing with external imbalances; however, the macroeconomic policies of a country with respect to saving, investment, and government budgets are critical to whether movements in the exchange rate can deal with external imbalances. As long as individual countries operate with different internal balances, exchange rate movements are not likely to remove external imbalances smoothly and quickly.

BOX 1   External debt of developing countries still a potential problem for U.S. banks

Barbara A. Bennett and Gary C. Zimmerman of the Federal Reserve Bank of San Francisco examined U.S. banks' exposure to external debt of developing or less developed countries (LDCs). Despite the decline in international lending exposure of U.S. banks either in terms of LDC debt as a percentage of assets or capital (Table 16-7), the external debt problem has not improved as much as these ratios suggest.

First, exposure to "troubled" LDCs has risen while loans to more creditworthy countries has fallen (Table 1B), and second, exposure to LDC debt has become concentrated in the largest U.S. banks (Table 2B).

They attribute the relative increase in exposure to more risky countries to three factors: involuntary lending, banks' relative advantage in working with troubled borrowers, and incentives provided by federal deposit insurance.

Involuntary lending occurs because the debtor country's threatened default on a bank loan places the bank on the horns of a dilemma. If the bank sells the loan, it will do so at a significant discount, and bank

profits will decline. If the bank declares the loan in default, losses will also occur since the collateral is generally insufficient to cover the loan, and again, bank profits will decline. Thus, the bank has an incentive to reschedule existing loans and even to extend new loans to provide funds to service existing loans.

Banks are very efficient in evaluation of creditworthiness. As the debt problem increased in the 1980s, debtor countries found bond markets less interested in financing their borrowing requests, and thus, banks assumed a more prominent role in international lending. This is one reason why loans to LDCs are concentrated in the large money center banks because they are the ones most actively involved in the international financial system.

Federal deposit insurance provides incentives to make risky loans since the fixed premium insurance rate imposes no penalty for assuming risk. This is the adverse moral hazard of the current structure of deposit insurance.

TABLE 1B   Shares of U.S. bank's international loans outstanding by country group, 1977–1986[1] (millions of dollars, percent of total)

Year	Total		G-10 and Switzerland		Non G-10 Developed		OPEC LDCs		Non-OPEC LDCs Non-Troubled		Non-OPEC LDCs Troubled		Baker 15[2]		Other	
1977	$194,571	100%	$83,610	43.0%	$16,114	8.3%	$15,945	8.2%	$14,479	7.4%	$50,699	26.1%	$40,992	21.1%	$13,723	7.1%
1978	217,337	100	92,044	42.4	17,172	7.9	21,342	9.8	17,337	8.0	54,117	24.9	47,485	21.8	15,324	7.1
1979	246,161	100	99,065	40.2	18,330	7.4	22,347	9.1	22,958	9.3	63,716	25.9	54,826	22.3	19,745	8.0
1980	286,527	100	118,503	41.4	20,997	7.3	23,319	8.1	29,935	10.4	74,739	26.1	66,846	23.3	19,034	6.6
1981	332,057	100	131,422	39.6	26,084	7.9	25,441	7.7	37,626	11.3	87,708	26.4	81,520	24.6	23,776	7.2
1982	352,293	100	139,824	39.7	29,742	8.4	27,760	7.9	42,424	12.0	92,033	26.1	91,084	25.9	21,509	6.1
1983	357,343	100	136,766	38.3	32,417	9.1	28,613	8.0	43,717	12.2	93,897	26.3	94,229	26.4	21,933	6.1
1984	323,324	100	113,400	35.1	30,529	9.4	26,164	8.1	39,019	12.1	93,819	29.0	95,375	29.5	20,393	6.3
1985	294,542	100	105,528	35.8	26,986	9.2	22,242	7.6	33,761	11.5	87,257	29.6	90,525	30.7	18,769	6.4
1986	275,639	100	104,017	37.7	22,728	8.2	19,550	7.1	31,676	11.5	81,112	29.4	86,176	31.3	16,556	6.0
Mean				39.3		8.3		8.2		10.6		27.0		25.7		6.7
Standard deviation				2.5		0.7		0.7		1.7		1.6		3.6		0.6

[1] Figures may not add due to rounding.
[2] In late 1985 U.S. Treasury Secretary Baker identified fifteen principal LDC debtors: Brazil, Mexico, Argentina, Venezuela, Philippines, Chile, Yugoslavia, Nigeria, Morocco, Colombia, Peru, Ecuador, Ivory Coast, Uruguay, Bolivia.
Source: Barbara A. Bennett and Gary C. Zimmerman, "U.S. Banks' Exposure to Developing Countries: An Examination of Recent Trends," *Economic Review*, Federal Reserve Bank of San Francisco (Spring 1988), p. 19.

TABLE 2B Shares of U.S. banks' exposure to troubled LDCs by size of bank, 1977–1986[1] (millions of dollars, percent of total)

Year	Total		Nine Money Center Banks		Next 14 Largest Banks		All Other Banks	
1977	$50,699.4	100%	$30,757.0	60.7%	$ 9,389.5	18.5%	$10,552.9	20.8%
1978	54,116.7	100	32,585.3	60.2	10,155.8	18.8	11,375.6	21.0
1979	63,715.7	100	39,482.7	62.0	11,320.3	17.8	12,912.7	20.3
1980	74,738.8	100	44,388.0	59.4	13,273.2	17.8	17,077.6	22.8
1981	87,707.8	100	50,099.5	57.1	16,565.1	18.9	21,043.2	24.0
1982	92,033.3	100	51,925.2	56.4	18,249.9	19.8	21,858.2	23.8
1983	93,896.8	100	53,571.3	57.1	18,594.1	19.8	21,731.4	23.1
1984	93,819.2	100	56,004.5	59.7	18,492.3	19.7	19,322.4	20.6
1985	87,257.0	100	54,084.3	62.0	15,496.7	17.8	17,676.0	20.3
1986	81,112.0	100	50,884.0	62.7	14,521.0	17.9	15,707.0	19.4
Mean				59.7		18.7		21.6
Standard deviation				2.1		0.8		1.6

[1] Figures may not add due to rounding.

The International Debt Problem

External debt has grown significantly since the late 1970s. In 1988 external debt was $1,248 billion, which represented a 134% increase from the amount of debt in 1979. The majority of external debt is concentrated in a small number of countries in the Western hemisphere. The largest debtors are Argentina, Bolivia, Brazil, Chile, Colombia, Mexico, Peru, Uruguay, and Venezuela. U.S. banks hold only about $120 billion of the external debt; however, the concern has been that much of this debt is held by a small number of large banks and much of it represented by loans to only a few countries.

Table 16-7 presents information on the risk exposure of U.S. banks over the period from 1977 through the first half of 1987. External claims on developing countries as a percentage of total assets have declined to some extent; however, the claims as a percentage of total capital have shown a declining trend over time. In the first half of 1987, the external claims were less than capital for the first time since 1977.

The ability of the developing countries to service and repay the outstanding debt has continually deteriorated in the 1980s. Countries have defaulted on past loans, numerous loan restructuring arrangements with private lenders have been negotiated, and international governmental organizations (IMF and World Bank) have taken a more active role in helping developing countries manage their external debt. Despite the various efforts to deal with the debt problem, few seriously believe that much of the debt will ever be repaid. The burden on the debtor countries has not decreased markedly nor have their economies improved significantly. Other considerations account for a reduced concern over the magnitude of the amount of external debt.

Two factors are important in this regard. First, the world economy has been stable

TABLE 16-7   Assets and capital of U.S. banks, 1977–first half 1987

	1977	1978	1979	1980	1981	1982	1983	1984	1985	1986	1987 First half
	(In billions of U.S. dollars)										
External claims on developing countries[1]	70.1	81.5	91.9	110.9	132.6	147.7	150.0	145.6	133.1	121.8	117.9
Total assets	717.1	823.6	941.3	1,066.3	1,164.5	1,261.0	1,336.0	1,413.0	1,529.0	1,613.0	1,593.0
Capital	40.9	45.5	49.7	56.9	62.7	70.6	79.3	92.2	105.4	116.1	124.4
	(In percent)										
Memorandum items											
Capital to total assets	5.7	5.5	5.3	5.3	5.4	5.6	5.9	6.5	6.9	7.2	7.8
External claims on developing countries to total assets	9.8	9.9	9.8	10.4	11.4	11.7	11.2	10.3	8.7	7.6	7.4
Capital to external claims on developing countries	58.4	55.8	54.1	51.3	47.3	47.8	52.9	63.3	79.2	95.3	105.5

The data presented in this table are on an exposure basis; that is, they are adjusted for guarantees and other risk transfers.
Source: Maxwell Watson, Donald Mathieson, Russell Kincaid, David Folkerts-Landau, Klaus Regling, and Caroline Atkinson. *International Capital Markets* (Washington, D.C.: International Monetary Fund, January 1988), p. 89.

and world demand for exports has expanded in general, and the U.S. economy in particular has lowered the inflation rate, and interest rates have declined from their historically high levels of the early 1980s. Interest rates are important for the external debt problem because many of the loans are flexible interest rate loans, and even small increases in U.S. interest rates can raise the servicing burden by billions of dollars.

Second, the large U.S. banks under pressure from regulators have increased their capital and thus reduced their risk exposure to some degree. More important, U.S. banks have been setting aside income in loan loss reserve accounts since 1987, thus, explicitly accepting what everyone already knew—most of the debts are not likely to be paid. These loan loss reserve accounts can absorb 20 to 30% of defaults on external debt.

Despite the actions of U.S. banks and the fact that the banking system has withstood several threats by some debtors to cease interest payments, the external debt problem continues to be a potentially serious problem for the international community and U.S. banks.

Key Points

1. Deregulation and financial reform have made it easier to exchange domestic for foreign financial assets, and as a result, short- and long-term capital has become more mobile in recent years. Differences in interest rates and changes in anticipated movements in exchange rates play an important role in the movement of capital from one country to another.

2. External currency markets consist of assets denominated in a currency other than the currency of the country in which the asset is issued.

Eurodeposits and bonds have grown significantly in the 1980s and play a major role in linking the domestic financial systems to each other.

3. Aside from banks and other financial institutions, government institutions play an important role in the international financial system. Central banks, IMF, World Bank, and Bank for International Settlements provide an infrastructure for world financial integration.

4. The international financial system has not functioned smoothly over the years despite the growth in internationalization and globalization of finance. In 1973 the fixed exchange rate system collapsed and was replaced with a flexible exchange rate system. Persistent external deficits by the United States in the face of a major decline in the value of the dollar suggest that considerations other than flexible exchange rates are important for achieving external equilibrium.

5. The large amount of external debt of developing countries has also put pressure on the international financial system. Most of this debt has been restructured several times, and it is difficult to be optimistic that the debtor countries can pay back even part of the principal. The risk exposure of a small number of large U.S. banks is high; however, it has declined in the last few years as U.S. banks have increased capital and set aside current income in loan loss reserve accounts.

Key Terms

Bank for International Settlements (BIS)

Capital mobility

Capital mobility and world interest rate differentials

Current versus anticipated exchange rate

Eurobond

Eurocurrency markets

Eurodollars

External and internal balance

External currency markets

Foreign bond

International debt problem

International Monetary Fund (IMF)

International policy coordination

Loan loss reserve accounts

Nominal and real exchange rate

Special Drawing Rights (SDRs)

World Bank (International Bank for Reconstruction and Development)

Questions

1. How did federal deposit insurance provide an incentive for U.S. banks to extend loans to developing countries?

2. Illustrate how a country's balance of saving, investment, taxes, and government spending influences its external balance.

3. Why haven't flexible exchange rates eliminated the large trade and current account deficits of the United States in the 1980s?

4. How does a decline in the value of the dollar, which can improve the trade balance, make the international debt problem worse?

5. Why have foreigners been more interested in trading in U.S. securities markets than U.S.

citizens are in trading in foreign securities markets?

6. Explain the concept of capital mobility and why it has increased in the 1980s. Are we moving to a global financial system as opposed to a collection of separate domestic financial systems?

7. Why will interest rate differentials between countries continue to exist even if capital is free to seek its highest return?

8. How did the U.S. trade deficit become so large in the 1980s?

Suggested Readings

1. Robert Aliber (ed.), *International Handbook of Financial Management* (Homewood, Ill.: Dow Jones–Irwin, 1989).

2. Anatol B. Balbach and David H. Resler, "Eurodollars and the U.S. Money Supply," *Review*, Federal Reserve Bank of St. Louis (June–July 1980), 2–12.

3. James R. Barth and Joseph Pelzman, *International Debt: Conflict and Resolution* (Fairfax, Va.: Department of Economics, George Mason University, January 1984). Overview of the debt problem.

4. Barbara A. Bennett and Gary C. Zimmerman, "U.S. Banks' Exposure to Developing Countries: An Examination of Recent Trends," *Economic Review*, Federal Reserve Bank of San Francisco (Spring 1988), 11–29. Recent discussion of U.S. bank exposure to external debt of developing countries.

5. Thomas F. Cargill, "A Perspective on Trade Imbalances and United States Policies Toward Japan," *Columbia Journal of World Business*, 22 (Winter 1987), 55–60. Instead of a Japan-bashing approach to the U.S. trade deficits in the 1980s, this paper takes a U.S.-bashing approach.

6. Hang-Sheng Cheng, "2 + 2 = 4," *Weekly Letter*, Federal Reserve Bank of San Francisco (March 27, 1987). Argues that the U.S. trade deficit reflects domestic conditions.

7. Rudiger Dornbusch, *Dollars, Debts, and Deficits* (Cambridge, Mass.: MIT Press, 1986). A collection of essays on exchange rates, international debt problem, and other issues discussed in this chapter.

8. Federal Reserve Bank of Minneapolis, *1986 Annual Report: The Unpleasant Arithmetic of Budget and Trade Deficits*. Same point as Hang-Sheng Cheng.

9. Martin Feldstein, "Correcting the Trade Deficit," *Foreign Affairs* (Spring 1987), 795–806. Discusses the reasons for the U.S. trade deficits in the 1980s.

10. Marvin Goodfriend, "Eurodollars," in Timothy Q. Cook and Bruce J. Summers (ed.), *Instruments of the Money Market*, Federal Reserve Bank of Richmond (1981), 123–133. Discusses Eurodollars.

11. Craig S. Hakkio, "Exchange Rate Volatility and Federal Reserve Policy," *Economic Review*, Federal Reserve Bank of Kansas City (July–August 1984), 18–31. Reviews reasons for exchange rate movements.

12. Ramon Moreno, "Saving, Investment, and the U.S. External Balance," *Economic Review*, Federal Reserve Bank of San Francisco (Fall 1988), 3–18. Shows how the U.S. external deficit in the 1980s is fundamentally a result of government deficits, saving, and investment.

13. Christine A. Pavel and John N. McElravey, "Globalization in the financial services industry," *Economic Perspectives*, Federal Reserve Bank of Chicago (May/June 1990), 3-18.

PART V

Introduction to Monetary Policy

CHAPTER 17

Introduction to Monetary Policy and Economic Stabilization

Chapter Overview

The previous chapters have provided the foundation for understanding the financial system both from a static and dynamic perspective. It is now time to build on this foundation and develop an understanding of the Federal Reserve, monetary policy, and how monetary policy is employed to achieve goals of economic stabilization.

Monetary policy is not the only method used by government to stabilize the economy; however, it has come to be recognized as *the* instrument of economic stabilization. This a relatively recent situation. A few decades ago, economists bitterly debated whether monetary policy was even capable of influencing spending with many arguing that monetary policy was less effective than fiscal or other types of government policy. That debate is over. Monetary policy is now recognized as a major determinant of economic activity while fiscal policy—the main alternative to monetary policy—is considered a less effective stabilization instrument.

This chapter introduces some basic considerations about the objectives of monetary policy as part of the overall effort of government to stabilize the economy. The issues discussed in this chapter provide an overview and historical perspective of monetary policy in the United States. With this in mind, the chapter accomplishes three tasks.

First, we will motivate the concept of monetary policy as an instrument of economic stabilization by illustrating its role in a schematic outline of general stabilization policy. We then turn our attention to the primary objectives of monetary policy in terms of desired performance characteristics of the economy.

Second, we review several basic measures of economic performance employed to determine whether the economy is or is not performing at desired levels that also serve as guideposts for monetary policy. The need for government stabilization via monetary policy, fiscal policy, or some other type of policy arises whenever there is a difference between desired and actual economic performance.

Third, we present an historical perspective of the evolution of stabilization policy in general and monetary policy in particular. Has stabilization policy always been a responsibility of government? If so, has the type of stabilization policy considered most appropriate changed over time? In this regard, we will emphasize the impact of the Great Depression of the 1930s on the evolution of government policy and views about how the market system functions in the absence of extensive government intervention. No other period in our history has so influenced views about these issues. On a much lesser note, we will review how events of the past two decades have also played a role in influencing our views of government policy and the market, though their impact is not anywhere nearly as dramatic as those brought about by the Great Depression.

Once these three issues are discussed we will be in a position to start a detailed study of the Federal Reserve and monetary policy.

Monetary Policy and Economic Stabilization

Figure 17-1 presents a schematic outline of general stabilization policy consisting of six parts. Part A represents the performance of the economy prior to any effort to stabilize the economy. Performance is measured by the unemployment rate, output, inflation, and other measures of macroeconomic performance. These are observed by the monetary and fiscal authorities in B—represented by the Federal Reserve and the Treasury, respectively. The two authorities control *policy instruments* that are used to influence the performance of the economy. In C, the money supply is the Federal Reserve's policy instrument, while the fiscal authority's policy instrument is the government budget (taxes and expenditures). The stabilization authorities possess a set of *policy targets* in D, that is, desired performance levels of the economy that satisfy the ultimate objectives of economic stabilization. In E, comparison of the policy targets with the actual performance of the economy in A provides the basis for the type of stabilization policy that will be enacted; for example, if the desired unemployment rate is 5% and the actual unemployment rate is 7%, the stabilization authorities will vary their policy instruments to stimulate the economy so as to lower the unemployment rate. Finally, F indicates that monetary and fiscal policy actions are based on a model of how economic activity is determined. Notwithstanding the fact that there are many competing models, any given model plays three roles in the conduct of stabilization policy:

1. It provides a "road map" to determine how to use the policy instruments to achieve the policy targets; that is, the model establishes the relationships between the policy instruments and the final policy targets.

2. It implies what type of monetary and fiscal policy is required, that is, whether activist or nonactivist approaches would contribute most effectively to overall economic stabilization.

3. It serves as a basis for constructing an econometric or statistical model of the economy that can be used to guide the policy instruments.

A. Economic performance prior to stabilization action measured by

   1. Unemployment rate.

   2. Output.

   3. Inflation.

   4. Other measures of economic performance.

B. Stabilization authorities

   1. Federal Reserve and monetary policy.

   2. Treasury and fiscal policy.

C. Policy instruments

   1. Money supply.

   2. Budget (taxes and government spending).

D. Policy targets: Desired performance of the economy in terms of

   1. Unemployment rate.

   2. Output.

   3. Inflation.

   4. Other measures of economic performance.

E. Performance of the economy in A is compared with policy targets in D to determine if the policy instruments in C will be utilized to stimulate or slow down the economy.

F. The conduct of monetary and fiscal policy is based on a model of the economy that describes how the final policy targets are related to the policy instruments.

FIGURE 17-1   Schematic outline of stabilization policy

The schematic outline is an oversimplification in that it omits a umber of complications, many of which will be discussed in the remainder of this book; however, it does reflect the current view of how stabilization policy is formulated and executed. Monetary policy has come to be the most important stabilization policy, and we now turn to the specific objectives of the monetary authority.

Stabilization Goals of Monetary Policy

Monetary policy is concerned with three general areas: (1) reducing fluctuations in domestic economic activity, full employment, price stability, and economic growth;

(2) ensuring a stable domestic financial system; and (3) ensuring that external equilibrium is achieved smoothly in a way consistent with expanding international trade and increased world financial integration.

Objectives Focused on the Domestic Economy

Reducing fluctuations in domestic economic activity can be conceptualized by considering the long-run or full-employment equilibrium of the economy over time. At full employment, the economy is producing goods and employing workers at a rate consistent with full utilization of available resources. The objective of stabilization policy then is to reduce fluctuations in unemployment and output around this long-run equilibrium level. In addition, stabilization policy should maintain a steady and low rate of inflation at the long-run equilibrium level.

Figure 17-2 shows how the actual level of output has fluctuated around the full-employment or potential level of output over the period from 1870 to 1988. The full-employment output level has risen over time because of the growth of the economy's resource base and technology.

Full employment does not imply that everyone is working; rather, full employment occurs when the economy is producing goods and services at a rate consistent with its resources base and even at this long-run equilibirum there will be some unemployment.

The level of unemployment coexisting with a full employment level of economic performance consists of *frictional* and *structural* unemployment both of which are unrelated to departures of the economy from its normal long-run equilibrium. Frictional unemployment results from the normal ebb and flow of economic activity, decisions of labor market participants to change jobs, and the time required for job search activities. Structural unemployment is closely related to frictional unemployment; however, it tends to be longer in duration. Structural unemployment results from structural characteristics of the labor force and labor market. Minimum wage legislation, affirmative action programs, noncompetitive rigidities such as labor unions, demographic makeup of the labor force in terms of male/female or young/old composition, mismatch between job requirements and educational makeup of the labor force, and other structural characteristics will ensure that a certain level of unemployment is consistent with full employment or the normal long-run growth path of the economy.

Economists have adopted the concept of the *natural unemployment rate* as the level of unemployment consistent with full utilization of the economy's resources given all the factors that influence frictional and structural unemployment. The natural unemployment rate is essentially the sum of the frictional and structural unemployment rate and is the full employment level of unemployment. A 6% unemployment rate in recent years has been regarded as a reasonable approximation of the natural unemployment rate; hence, anytime the actual unemployment rate is above 6%, the goal of full employment has not been achieved and indicates that the economy is performing below potential. In contrast, an unemployment rate lower than 6% generates inflationary pressures and indicates that the economy is attempting to perform above its potential.

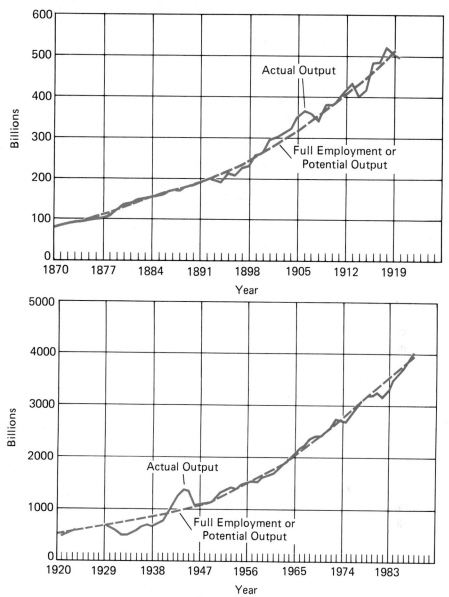

Source: Based on data provided by Robert J. Gordon which are reported in Robert J. Gordon, *Macroeconomics* (Glenview, Illinois: Scott, Foresman & Co., 1990).

FIGURE 17-2 **Actual and Full-Employment (Potential) Real GNP, 1870–1988.**

Thus, stabilization policy is concerned with reducing fluctuations of the unemployment rate around its natural level. Reducing fluctuations of unemployment around the natural level is closely related to reducing fluctuations in output around its full employment level. In fact, corresponding to the concept of natural unemployment, we define the concept of *potential output* to indicate the level of output produced when the economy is operating at full capacity—in other words, when the economy is operating at full employment.

Price stability technically means that, on the average, prices are constant from period to period. It does not imply that prices in individual markets remain constant since average prices can remain constant while there exists considerable price variation across markets. In actual practice, price stability is consistent with some positive inflation rate as long as the inflation rate is low, steady, and predictable, just as the full employment level of performance is associated with some unemployment.

The failure to achieve price stability has serious short and long effects on the economy, both from a domestic and international perspective. Inflation reduces economic efficiency and productivity, interferes with long-run capital accumulation, threatens the stability of the financial system, redistributes income, and reduces the economy's ability to compete in international trade. The severity of these problems varies directly with the degree to which the inflation rate is unpredictable. The more predictable the inflation rate, the more readily economic contracts can take inflation into account; however, this assumes that economic contracts have the flexibility to adjust to inflation. The obvious limits to contract flexibility dictate that if a positive inflation rate is consistent with price stability it should be low—perhaps in the one- to three-percentage-point range.

BOX 1   Output and unemployment: Okun's Law

There exists an inverse relationship between output and unemployment so that reducing fluctuations in one implies reducing fluctuations in the other. One way of expressing this relationship was developed by Arthur Okun and, of course, is now known as Okun's law.

To understand Okun's law we need to define the concept of *potential output*. Potential output is the output of goods and services that would be produced if everyone were working who wanted to work at the going wage rate, or what amounts to the same thing, potential output is the output that is produced when the unemployment rate is equal to the *natural unemployment rate*. In other terms, potential output is the output produced when the economy is at full employment and the natural unemployment rate is the unemployment rate when the economy is at full employment.

Okun's law in words states that for every percentage point unemployment is above the natural unemployment rate, output is three percentage points below the potential output. The percentage departure of actual output from potential output is thereby equal to the negative of the difference between the actual and natural unemployment rate, or in terms of symbols

$$\frac{(y - y^*)}{y^*} = -3(un - un^*) \qquad (1)$$

where y and un represent actual output and unemployment, respectively, and y^* and un^* represent potential output and the natural unemployment rate, respectively. Assume that un^* is 6%. If the actual unemployment rate is 7%, actual output will be less than potential output by three percentage points.

The percentage departure of actual output from potential output is referred to as the *output gap*. A positive output gap indicates that actual output is above potential output (actual unemployment is below natural unemployment), and a negative output gap indicates that actual output is below potential output (actual unemployment is above natural unemployment).

Figure 1B shows how actual output has varied around the potential output level over the period from 1890 to 1988 by calculating the left-hand side of expression (1) in the box. Figure 2B shows how the actual unemployment rate has varied around the natural unemployment rate over the same period. Notice that when actual output is below its potential level (such as in the 1930s), the actual unemployment rate is above its natural rate.

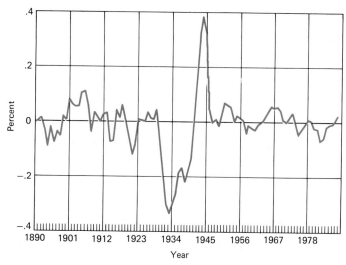

Source: Based on data provided by Robert J. Gordon which are reported in Robert J. Gordon, *Macroeconomics* (Glenview, Illinois: Scott Foresman & Co., 1990).

FIGURE 1B   **The output gap measured as the percentage departure of actual output from potential output, 1890–1988**

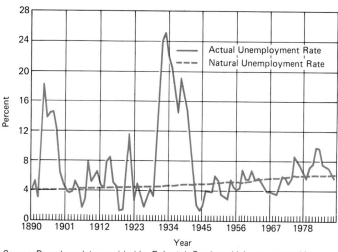

Source: Based on data provided by Robert J. Gordon which are reported in Robert J. Gordon, *Macroeconomics* (Glenview, Illinois: Scott, Foresman & Co., 1990).

FIGURE 2B   **Actual and natural unemployment rates, 1890–1988**

Full employment and price stability are considered important conditions for *economic growth*. Economic growth is the result of many complex economic and noneconomic forces; however, monetary policy can have a major impact on the economic growth path. Failure to achieve price stability and failure to limit fluctuations in employment and output around the full-employment level will have serious adverse effects on the economy's growth potential. Thus, success toward reducing fluctuations in domestic economic activity is an important contribution to enhancing economic growth.

Objectives Focused on the Domestic Financial System

Financial stability means that the financial system permits funds to flow from surplus to deficit units in a smooth and orderly fashion to support the spending, production, and consuming desires of the economy. Financial stability is consistent with fluctuations in interest rates and even the failure of individual institutions and markets. In contrast, the Great Depression of the 1930s provides a good example of the failure to achieve financial stability and the resulting impact on the overall level of economic performance. The collapse of the banking system seriously disrupted the flow of funds from surplus to deficit units and played a major role in reducing output and increasing unemployment.

Monetary policy contributes to financial stability in two important ways. First, the monetary authority is the *lender of last resort* because it can manufacture high-powered money. The failure of one or a small number of financial institutions could easily contaminate otherwise healthy institutions because modern financial systems operate on a fractional reserve basis. The monetary authority serves as a lender of last resort for those institutions experiencing deposit outflows. Funds provided by the Federal Reserve prevent institutions experiencing deposit outflows to remain viable and ensure public confidence in deposit money.

Second, the monetary authority contributes to financial stability by maintaining price stability. Fluctuations in the inflation rate will result in fluctuations in interest rates via the Fisher effect discussed in Chapter 5. Fluctuating interest rates create difficulties for market participants and may interfere with the flow of funds between institutions and markets. This was clearly the case in the 1970s when the failure to maintain price stability generated intense periods of disintermediation and a series of "credit crunches."

There is one difference between the goal of financial stability and the other two goals worth pointing out. While monetary and fiscal policy both share the goals of reducing fluctuations in domestic activity and both are concerned with external equilibrium, financial stability is largely the responsibility of the monetary authority. Fiscal policy may play some role, but financial stability is mainly the focus of monetary policy.

Objectives Focused on the International Economy

The external concerns of monetary policy arise from the fact that the United States is not an economic island unto itself. Flows of goods, services, and financial assets between the United States and the rest of the world require an external perspective for monetary policy. In this regard, monetary policy is concerned with preventing large exchange rate fluctuations that might interfere with trade and ensuring that exchange rates adjust in an orderly fashion to eliminate persistent imbalances between the demand and supply for dollars.

External equilibrium is achieved when the relationship between the United States and the rest of the world encourages domestic stability, a balance between flows of goods and services, and expanded international trade. How external equilibrium considerations influence policy depends importantly on the nature of the international financial system. Under the flexible exchange rate system operating since 1973, monetary policy has been concerned with reducing fluctuations in exchange rates. In addition, the Federal Reserve has increasingly recognized that policy actions designed to influence domestic activity have important effects on demand and supply for dollars, and thereby, monetary policy must increasingly consider the international effects of policy designed to influence domestic activity. Thus, just as the U.S. economy is not an economic island unto itself, monetary policy cannot operate in a domestic vacuum.

Indicators of Economic Performance

Indicators of economic performance are important for two reasons. First, they provide direct information on how well the economic system is performing in terms of the goals of stabilization. Second, the measures are important to those authorities responsible for the conduct of stabilization policy. Only by monitoring the economy's performance can the policymaker determine whether their actions are having the intended impact on the economy.

Indicators of economic performance fall into two categories. First, there is a collection of economic accounts, which focus on overall economic performance. These accounts provide information on individual components, but their major emphasis is on an overall measure of economic performance. The three major components to an accounting system for the United States consist of the gross national product (GNP) and national income (NY) accounts, the flow of funds accounts (FOF), and the balance of payments accounts or Statement of International Transactions (SIT). These provide a complete accounting system for the economy and render a fairly good overall impression of economic performance. The second category of indicators includes numerous measures that focus more on individual, yet important, aspects of the economy's performance such as employment, price behavior, production in specific sectors, credit, and money and capital markets.

Broad Indicators of Economic Performance

Gross National Product and Income Accounts

GNP and NY estimates, prepared on a quarterly and annual basis by the Department of Commerce, measure the final output of goods and services produced and the income earned by the factors of production in producing the output of goods and services. GNP provides information on investment spending for capital goods and NY provides information on the amount of saving during a given period.

GNP can be viewed either as the final output of goods and services or the total spending on these goods and services, the latter approach being the most convenient to use for measurement purposes. GNP is broken down into four components in terms of who does the spending on final output:

$$GNP = C + I_g + G + (X - M) \qquad (1)$$

C represents consumer or household spending for consumer nondurables, durables, and services. Housing expenditures are the only consumer expenditure not included in C. They are included as part of business investment spending on new equipment and buildings, as consumers' expenditures for houses have many characteristics in common with business investment. They are large in magnitude, involve long-term planning horizons, and use long-term financing, all of which are characteristic of business investment spending in plant and equipment. I_g represents the investment spending by the business sector, including that for replacement of worn-out capital goods and for new additions to capital goods. G represents total spending on goods and services by the three governmental units in the United States—local, state, and federal. $X - M$ is net foreign investment and represents the net spending of the rest of the world for United States output. Exports, X, are added because United States output sold to foreign countries is part of our final output, and not to include exports would understate the economy's performance. On the other hand, imports, M, are subtracted because of part C, I_g, and G includes purchases of foreign goods that do not represent U.S. production. Hence, imports are subtracted so as not to overstate the economy's performance.

I_g represents investment spending for new capital equipment and for replacement of worn-out capital equipment. There is no satisfactory measure of the amount of worn-out equipment during the year. The GNP accounts use the amount of reported depreciation as a measure of capital consumption, but this is not very satisfactory as the amount of depreciation at any point in time will be strongly influenced by existing tax laws. If the capital consumption allowance, D, is subtracted from I_g, we obtain net national product, NNP,

$$NNP = C + I + G + (X - M) \qquad (2)$$

The only difference between GNP and NNP is the capital consumption allowance. Table 17-1 presents the estimates of GNP and NNP for 1988.

GNP and NNP measure the output of the economy in terms of the sectors that purchased the final output: consumers or households, business firms, government, and the rest of the world. What about the factors of production that produced the current GNP? Can we determine how much income was earned by the factors of production in producing the GNP? Theoretically, the total output and the total income earned in producing the final output should be identical; however, in an economy with government, they are not exactly the same.

NY represents the income earned by the factors of production in producing the GNP. This income is represented by wages, salaries, interest income, rental income, and profits. The difference between GNP and NY are items included in GNP that are

TABLE 17-1   Gross and net national product, 1988 (billions of dollars)

Symbol	Item		Amount[1]
C	Personal consumption expenditures		$3,235.1
	Durable goods	$ 455.2	
	Nondurable goods	1,052.3	
	Services	1,727.6	
I_g	Gross private domestic investment		750.2
	Nonresidential fixed investment	487.2	
	Residential investment	232.4	
	Change in inventories	30.6	
G	Government purchases of goods and services		968.9
	Federal	381.3	
	State and local	587.6	
X − M	Net exports of goods and services		−73.6
	Exports	547.7	
	Imports	621.3	
GNP	Gross national product		4,880.6
D	Less: Capital consumption allowance		513.5
NNP	Net national product		$4,367.1

[1] Totals may not add due to rounding.
Source: U.S. Department of Commerce, *Survey of Current Business*, July 1989.

not regarded as part of earned income of factors of production: (1) capital consumption allowance, D, (2) indirect business taxes, IBT, and (3) statistical discrepancies, A.

$$NY = GNP - D - IBT - A \qquad (3)$$

Depreciation is not regarded as a payment to any factor of production for producing new goods and services. Indirect business taxes are primarily sales taxes on purchases, and, because these are included as part of the expenditures made by consumers, businesses, and the like, they are subtracted from GNP to obtain NY. Government is not regarded as a factor of production, and payments to government do not represent income payments. Statistical discrepancies represent an adjustment to equate the product and income sides of the national accounts. By definition, GNP less items that are not regarded as income to factors of production must equal national income; however, because GNP estimates are obtained from adding up all the expenditures made by consumers, government, and so on for final output and NY estimates are obtained by adding up all of the wages, salaries, interest income, rental income, and profits earned in producing the GNP, it would only be by accident that the two should be equal. Table 17-2 presents the NY estimates for 1988.

Another way in which to gain insight into GNP and NY can be obtained by considering the circular flow of economic activity introduced in Chapter 3 on page

TABLE 17-2 National income, 1988 (billions of dollars)			
Source	*Item*		*Amount*
GNP	Gross national product		$4,880.6
D	Less: Capital consumption allowance	$513.6	
IBT	Indirect business taxes and transfers	422.5	
A	Other adjustments plus statistical discrepancies	−28.1	
NY	National income		3,972.6
	Compensation of employees	2,907.6	
	Proprietors' income	327.8	
	Rental income	15.7	
	Corporate profits	328.6	
	Net interest income	392.9	

Source: U.S. Department of Commerce, *Survey of Current Business,* July 1989.

49. GNP is concerned with measuring the top portion of the circular flow, that is, the flow of expenditures in one direction and the flow of output in the other direction. The bottom portion of the figure is measured by NY and represents the flow of factor services in one direction and the flow of factor income in the other direction.

The NY accounts measure saving by factors of production as saving represents one of the uses of factor income. NY is the income earned in producing the GNP during the current year, not the total amount that households have available to spend or save. Income *earned* in a period is not the same as income *received* in the period.

The NY must be adjusted to determine the amount of funds available to households for spending and saving. Items that are earned in producing the GNP but are not paid out during the current period must be deducted from NY. Payments received by households during the current period that are not payments for productive effort in producing the GNP must be added to NY. These adjustments will then provide measures of personal and disposable income.

Table 17-3 illustrates the adjustment to NY. First, corporate profits are deducted. Corporate profits are composed of three parts: retained earnings, corporate profit income taxes, and dividends. Only dividends are paid out in the current period. Thus, corporate profits are deducted from NY and dividends are added to NY. Second, Social Security contributions, which are part of income but are not paid out to households during the current period, are deducted from NY. Third, interest paid by government represents interest paid on the national debt. These interest payments are not considered payment for current productive effort and are thus added to NY. Fourth, households receive various transfers from government and businesses that are not related to current productive effort. Government provides the largest part of these transfer payments in the form of Social Security payments, pensions, welfare payments, unemployment insurance, and so on.

The additions and deletions to NY will then provide an estimate of personal income. Personal income is not entirely available for spending or saving, as personal income taxes must be subtracted. When personal income taxes are deducted, we

TABLE 17-3 Relationship between national income and household consumption and saving, 1988 (billions of dollars)

Symbol	Item		Amount[1]
NY	National income		$3,972.6
	Less: Corporate profits	$ 328.6	
	Net interest	392.9	
	Social Security contributions	444.6	
	Plus: Government transfers	555.7	
	Interest paid by government and consumers	571.1	
	Dividend income	102.2	
	Business transfers	29.0	
	Personal income		4,064.5
	Less: Personal income taxes	586.6	
	Disposable income		3,477.8
	Consumption expenditures	3,235.1	
	Interest paid to business and transfers to foreigners (net)	98.0	
	Personal saving	144.7	

[1] Totals may not add due to rounding.

Source: U.S. Department of Commerce, *Survey of Current Business*, July 1989.

obtain disposable income, which can be allocated to consumption, interest payments, and saving. The part of disposable income that is consumed is identical to the consumption component of GNP in Table 17-1.

Distinction Between Nominal and Real Measures

It is important to distinguish between real and nominal measures of economic performance with regard to the national product accounts. GNP measured in current prices is referred to as current dollar or nominal GNP. Nominal GNP is the final output of goods and services valued at today's prices and is thus a price times quantity measure. GNP can also be measured in terms of constant prices, in which case we adjust for the price level to obtain a measure of the quantity of final output. GNP in constant dollars is referred to as constant dollar, or real, GNP.

The basic formula for converting nominal measures into real measures (or real into nominal measures) is

$$\text{Real measure} = \frac{\text{nominal measure}}{\text{price index}} \times 100 \tag{4}$$

This formula is general and can be used for any economic variable. To illustrate, 1988 nominal GNP is $4,880.6 billion and the 1988 GNP Deflator price index is 121.3 (1982 = 100). GNP valued in 1982 dollars or real GNP is equal to $4,023.6 billion ($4,880.6/121.3) × 100 or ($4,880.6/1.213).

Flow of Funds Accounts

The FOF accounts are based on the fundamental flow of funds equation developed in earlier chapters. This equation summarizes the investment, saving, lending, and borrowing decisions of any economic unit during a period of time. The FOF accounts essentially construct a basic flow of funds equation for selected sectors in the economy (e.g., households, nonfinancial businesses, and government). Intersector and intrasector flows are thus presented as are the total amount of funds advanced to the financial system, the flows through direct and indirect markets, and the total amount of funds raised or borrowed. The FOF accounts are reported on a quarterly and annual basis. The appendix to Chapter 3 presents a more complete description of these accounts and their interpretation. At this point, they are mentioned, only to underscore their importance in obtaining an overall view of the economy's performance.

Balance of Payments or Statement of International Transactions

The GNP and FOF accounts together provide a detailed description of economic activity during a period of time for the domestic economy. Both sets of accounts include some recognition of the relationship between the United States and the rest of the world. The GNP accounts include net foreign investment (exports less imports) as part of the final output of goods and services; the FOF accounts include a sector that summarizes the real and financial transactions of the United States with the rest of the world. There is a third set of accounts that focuses exclusively on the relationship between the United States and the rest of the world. The balance of payments or SIT was discussed in Chapter 15. It summarizes the real and financial relationship between the United States and other countries by recording these transactions on a flow of funds basis.

Specific Indicators of Economic Performance

The variety of specific indicators of economic performance is immense. To gain an appreciation of the number of indicators, thumb through recent issues of the *Federal Reserve Bulletin* published by the Board of Governors or the *Survey of Current Business* published by the U.S. Department of Commerce. The most important two specific indicators of economic activity in terms of goals of economic stabilization are the unemployment rate and the rate of inflation.

The Unemployment Rate

The unemployment rate is regarded as one of the most sensitive and important indicators of the economic well-being of the country. Measures of unemployment are based on the results of a monthly sample survey conducted by the Bureau of the Census. This survey provides a comprehensive employment status of individuals aged 16 years and over. The sample covers about 50,000 households. The unemployment rate is calculated by

$$\text{Rate of unemployment} = \frac{U}{E + U} \times 100 \qquad (5)$$

where E is the number of individuals in the labor force defined to be employed and U is the number of individuals in the labor force defined to be unemployed. The sum of E and U measures the total labor force.

The unemployment rate has two dimensions that serve as an indicator of the well-being of the country. First, there is an economic dimension that indicates the amount of excess supply of labor in the labor market. Those who are unemployed have lost income and experience a decline in their standard of living. The economy, in addition, has lost the results of their productive efforts. Second, there is a social aspect to the unemployment rate. Unemployment in a work-oriented society carries a social stigma, even when unemployment has nothing to do with the individuals' ability and efforts. In addition, when we consider the composition of the unemployment rate and notice that nonwhites and other minority groups typically have higher levels of unemployment at any point in time, high unemployment levels not only negatively affect the economy, they also heighten social unrest.

The unemployment rate is watched closely by economists, policymakers, and others to measure the results of stabilization policy; however, one must exercise considerable caution in interpreting the level and changes in the level of unemployment. First, the actual definition of the unemployment rate is partly social and does not always coincide with an economic definition of unemployment. For example, those persons in the survey are regarded as employed even if they "did not work but had a job or business from which they were temporarily absent because of vacation, illness, labor-management disputes, or bad weather or because they were taking time off for various other reasons." Thus, an individual on strike is regarded as employed even though no productive effort is being provided, whereas an individual looking for work is unemployed.

Second, the unemployment rate may not measure what you think is the obvious. We usually think of an unemployed individual as someone who has lost a job and must remain in an inactive pool of unemployed until the economy improves and new jobs are created. This traditional interpretation of the unemployment rate emerged during the 1930s. Then, it was essentially correct, but research has shown that this may now be a distorted view. One author has suggested that a high proportion (50%) of unemployeds are not job losers.[1] That is, a large proportion of the unemployed will return to their jobs. Although even temporary unemployment has significant negative implications for the individual and the economy, it does not carry the same implication as the traditional interpretation of the unemployed's situation.

[1] Martin S. Feldstein, "The Importance of Temporary Layoffs: An Empirical Analysis," *Brookings Papers on Economic Activity*, no. 3 (1975), pp. 725–744.

Third, the unemployment rate is the outcome of cyclical, frictional, and structural forces with the cyclical component directly related to the overall performance of the economy in terms of expansions and contractions. Frictional and structural unemployment represent the natural unemployment rate; however, this rate is neither easy to measure nor constant over time. Natural unemployment is a complex outcome of factors that influence job search activities, demographic factors, tax policy, structural characteristics of labor markets in terms of unionization, shifts in the industrial composition of the economy, affirmative action programs, and minimum wage legislation. Changes in the natural rate, which are unrelated to the performance of the economy, complicate the process of interpreting any change in the unemployment rate as the result of cyclical forces.

To illustrate how the unemployment rate changes over time because of changes in the natural rate, consider the results of a study of the unemployment rate[2] presented in Figure 17-3. The top part of Figure 17-3 shows the effect on the unemployment rate measured by fractions of a percentage point resulting from changes in the proportion of females, nonwhites, and young workers in the labor force over the period from 1955 through 1985. Increased participation of females and nonwhites increased the unemployment rate through the late 1970s because these groups had higher unemployment rates than average; however, even though the female participation rate has continued to increase, female unemployment rates have declined. Thus the female component in Figure 17-3 has lowered the unemployment rate in the 1980s. Nonwhites continue to have higher unemployment rates than average, however. The most dramatic effect on unemployment has been the age distribution of the labor force. The increasing proportion of younger workers (16- to 19- and 20- to 24-year-olds) increased the rate until 1975 because this group has a higher unemployment rate than average. However, this age group has declined significantly as a percentage of the labor force since the mid-1970s as a result of the aging of the World War II baby boomers.

Thus, changes in the unemployment rate not only reflect cyclical forces that are the primary concern of monetary policy, but, just as important, reflect all the forces that influence the natural unemployment rate. The bottom of Figure 17-3 presents one economist's estimate of the natural unemployment rate over a two-decade period and clearly shows that changes in the actual unemployment rate are not easy to interpret at any point in time.

The changing demographics of the labor force illustrated in the top part of Figure 17-3 have been one factor that has led economists to lower the value of the natural unemployment rate in the 1980s compared to the level in the 1970s.

Price Indexes

The rate of change of prices is measured by a price index. A price index is a weighted average of prices that is correlated with some base time period. The most widely used price indexes today are the consumer price index, the producer price index, and the GNP Deflator. The CPI, which is based on a wide variety of goods and services purchased by the typical consumer, is designed to measure the av-

[2] Ellen R. Rissman, "What Is the Natural Rate of Unemployment?" *Economic Perspectives*, Federal Reserve Bank of Chicago (September–October 1986), 3–17.

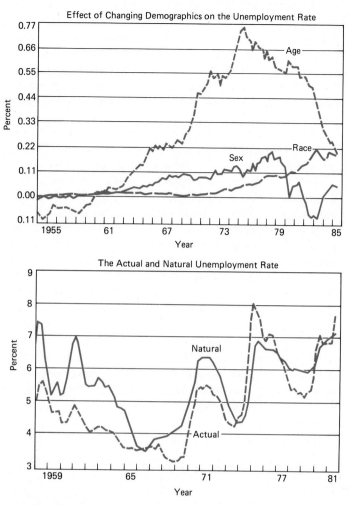

Source: Ellen R. Rissman, "What Is the natural rate of unemployment?" *Economic Perspectives,* Federal Reserve Bank of Chicago (September–October 1986), 5,15.

FIGURE 17-3 **Demographic changes, actual unemployment, and natural unemployment**

erage price paid by the typical household for consumer goods and services. The PPI (once referred to as the wholesale price index) is based on commodities that are not purchased directly by consumers. These include raw materials, intermediate products, and machinery used by businesses in the production of final goods and services. The GNP Deflator is an index derived as a by-product of constructing the national income and product accounts and represents the prices of all the items included in GNP. The GNP Deflator is by far the most comprehensive price index, as it includes the entire range of goods produced and consumed at any point in time. The CPI and PPI both represent a much narrower class of goods. All the price indexes are available in disaggregated form. For example, the CPI is broken down into price indexes for various types of services, consumer durables, nondurables, and so on.

Unfortunately, the GNP Deflator is only released on a quarterly basis and usually contains substantial revisions of previously released values. The CPI and PPI are released on a monthly basis and are thus more frequently available to indicate the extent of inflationary pressures in the economy.

Although the CPI, PPI, and GNP Deflator provide much information about inflation, they have two defects. First, it is difficult to incorporate quality changes into the price index, thus yielding a general upward bias in the index. The price of a visit to a doctor that was $10 in 1960 is now $40. Can we say that the price of the doctor's services has increased 300%? Probably not. The doctor visit today is a much different product from the visit in 1960. The doctor now has better training, more sophisticated diagnostic equipment, and a wider range of consultants. Thus, we are purchasing a better product, and it is difficult to determine how much of the $30 increase represents an improvement in the quality of the product and how much represents an increase in price. Some estimates indicate that the quality factor leads to as much as a 2%-per-year upward bias in the price indexes used to measure inflation.

Second, indexes are weighted averages of prices, and the weights are based on comprehensive surveys taken every several years. During periods of rapid price change in which relative prices also change, the use of weights determined several years in the past may introduce serious biases in the price index. For example, the rapid increase in the price of meat products reduces the importance of meat products in the household's basket of consumer goods, but the weights used in the CPI were derived before the rapid price increase. Thus, the CPI is biased upward because meat is valued at currently high prices but included at the earlier weight when meat prices were relatively low.

The Evolution of Stabilization Policy

There has always existed a required role for government in the private market. Adam Smith's *Wealth of Nations* in 1776, for example, made it clear that government had basic responsibilities to the private market. So what distinguishes the type of government policy practiced today from the past and what is responsible for the change?

The answer consists of distinguishing between *active* and *nonactive* stabilization policy and distinguishing between the pre- and post-Great Depression periods. Activist policy involves direct actions on the part of the government to influence private market decisions that vary in response to the state of the economy. In contrast, nonactivist policy involves a much more limited role for government and one that does not vary in response to the state of the economy. In a sense, the activist approach requires government to function as an "economic commander in chief" making decisions to influence the performance of the economy to achieve the goals of economic stabilization. The nonactivist approach requires government to be passive—limiting its actions to only a few areas while permitting the market to achieve its own equilibrium.

The nonactivist approach views the market as inherently stable and requiring little direction from government while the activist approach is predicated on the view that the market is inherently unstable or fails in some way to achieve the goals of economic stability in the absence of extensive government involvement.

The nonactivist approach dominated government policy prior to the Great Depression, at which time there occurred a major shift in the ideology of the market and the role that government should play in a market economy. Let us now turn our attention to a more detailed discussion of the pre- and post-Great Depression view of government and the private market.

Government Stabilization and the Market: Pre-Great Depression Period

The dominant view of the market system up to the depression of the 1930s was based on the notion that a competitive private economy would achieve socially desirable results with a minimum role for government. Briefly, the following assumptions were made about the market system:

1. Each individual, whether a consumer, worker, or producer, sought to maximize satisfaction or income to the highest degree possible within certain constraints.

2. Labor, capital, and land resources were mobile, so that resources could move in response to changes in economic opportunity.

3. Prices, including prices of factors of production, were flexible in both directions. Increases in demand led to price increases; decreases in demand led to price reductions.

4. Markets were essentially competitive in that no large business firms or labor unions were dominating the outcome of the market.

The market system was expected to achieve a level of economic activity at full employment once all the adjustments of resource movements from one sector of the economy to another were completed. It was recognized that short-run departures from full employment could occur, but given enough time for the forces of competition to function, the level of economic activity would equilibrate at full employment. Excess supply of labor (unemployment) in the labor market would lead to wage reductions until everyone who wanted to work at the going wage could find employment. The tendency to equilibrate at full employment, known as *Say's law of markets*, formed an important part of the *quantity theory of money*.

In addition to achieving full employment, the competitive market was regarded as providing the best environment in which to encourage innovation. The market rewarded the most productive and the most innovative individual and, hence, not only could full employment be counted on, but the level of economic activity would continually expand as a result of advances in technology.

The Role of Government

The economic goals of full employment and economic growth would be achieved automatically in a competitive market system. Was there any role for government?

Even the most ardent supporter of the market system did not rule out some type of government activity. There were essentially two roles for government.

First, government was needed to provide a legal framework in which economic contracts would be honored and to make certain types of expenditures that were not likely to be made by the private market, such as national defense and public projects such as highway and bridge construction. Second, government should provide for an adequate growth in the money supply to meet the growing needs of the economy, pursue policies to achieve external equilibrium, and ensure orderly and stable financial markets. The central bank was the primary governmental entity responsible for these functions.

Proper Monetary Growth   The government was responsible for ensuring that the money supply grew at a rate which satisfied the needs of trade while at the same time maintained price stability. The quantity theory provided the framework for determining the proper monetary growth rate,

$$MV = yP \tag{6}$$

where M is the money supply, V is velocity of money, y is real income or output as measured by real GNP, and P is the price level as measured by the GNP Deflator.

The concept of velocity can be made clearer by a numerical example. Velocity represents the turnover rate of the money stock and expresses how many times the money stock must circulate to support the current level of nominal income, yP. If yP is $100 billion and the money stock is $50 billion, then according to expression (6), the money stock will need to turn over two times during a given period to support the $100 billion amount of nominal income. If nominal income increases (decreases) and there is no change in the stock of money, velocity will have to increase (decrease). Before the student thinks that there is a definite mathematical relationship among M, V, y, and P, we should emphasize that expression (6) is a statement of the *equilibrium* relationship between the variables that regards some of the variables as being determined independently. In this regard, the money supply is determined by the central bank, y is determined by the basic resources and technology of the economy, V is determined by the institutional arrangements for making payments (frequency of receipts and expenditures, etc.), and P is passive in the sense that it depends on M, given the values of V and y.

Expression (6) is given in *static* terms, that is, without time subscripts; however, we can restate it in a form compatible with a growing economy:

$$\%\Delta M + \%\Delta V = \%\Delta y + \%\Delta P \tag{7}$$

Solving for the proper growth rate of the money supply based on equation (7) was simplified by two assumptions. First, the growth rate of real output would be along a full-employment path as a result of the competitive market economy. Say's law of markets indicated that, as a result of competitive forces in the labor market, full employment was the normal or long-run equilibrium condition. Second, the velocity of money was regarded as highly stable if not fixed over time. The velocity of money reflected the public's demand for money that was assumed to be a fixed proportion of the level of nominal output.

Combining a fixed velocity with the assumption that real income grew at the full-employment rate over time, the monetary authority's only responsibility was to ensure that M grew at a rate to meet the needs of the economy without significant price changes. Even if velocity changed over time, the solution of the proper amount of money in a competitive market setting was relatively simple as long as the rate of change in velocity was stable and predictable. For example, if V increased at a rate of 1% per year and y at 3% per year, then the money supply should be increased at a rate of 2% per year to maintain a stable price level ($\%\Delta P = 0$). In symbols, these assumptions imply that

$$\%\Delta V = 1\% \tag{8}$$

$$\%\Delta y = 3\%$$

Using (7) we want to solve for $\%\Delta M$ at which $\%\Delta P = 0$:

$$\%\Delta M + 1\% = 3\% + 0 \tag{9}$$

$$\%\Delta M = 3\% - 1\% = 2\%$$

.A constant level of velocity ($\%\Delta V = 0$) and y increasing at 3% per year would require M to increase at 3% per year to maintain a stable price level.

There was still a problem. Central banks did not have access to detailed statistics on the economy or ways to predict velocity, so they needed some set of rules, that if followed, would ensure that a noninflationary monetary growth rate would be achieved consistent with the quantity theory. This set of rules was provided by the *rule bills doctrine and the gold standard.*

Real Bills Doctrine

Prior to the Great Depression, central banks controlled the money supply by regulating loans made to private banks. Lending to banks—or the discount mechanism—was the primary instrument of monetary policy. Loans made to banks (called discounts) increased high-powered money while repayment of loans reduced high-powered money. The central bank regulated the amount of lending to banks by setting the discount rate and by adhering to a set of eligibility requirements that defined the type of loans that it would provide. These eligibility requirements were determined according to the real bills doctrine. To see how this worked, let us consider how a private bank would borrow from the central bank.

When a bank needed additional funds, it would present a commercial note to the central bank which represented an I.O.U. given by a business deficit unit to the bank and purchased at a discount by the bank. The bank, in turn, would give the note to the central bank, which would discount it again and transfer funds to the bank. Because the note was discounted twice, the mechanism was also referred to as the rediscount mechanism. When the bank had excess funds it was not lending, it would reduce its borrowings and pay off previously borrowed funds.

The eligibility requirements defined the type of notes or bills on which the central bank would loan funds, as *real bills*, bills that were backed by goods in process or some other security representing production activity. Bank loans made only for the short-term financing of current production were eligible for lending by the central bank. For example, notes issued to support an increase in the inventory of raw materials would be regarded as real bills. Formally, the 1913 Federal Reserve Act allowed the Federal Reserve to "discount notes, drafts, bills of exchange arising out of actual commercial transactions." Because the Federal Reserve made funds available only on the collateral of productive loans, each increase in credit and, hence, money supply would be matched by the needs of the production process. The entire mechanism was to be automatic.

To see more clearly how the real bills doctrine was expected to ensure the proper amount of money, consider the basic equation of the quantity theory in a slightly different form than expression (7). Instead of using real output (GNP), we can also express the equation in terms of total economic transactions in the economy, or

$$\%\Delta M \ + \ \%\Delta V \ = \ \%\Delta T \ + \ \%\Delta P_T \tag{10}$$

where T represents total real transactions taking place in the economy and P_T is the price level at which the transactions take place. T represents all economic transactions even if these transactions are not regarded as part of the final output of goods and services (GNP). For example, the purchase and sale of used goods would be included in T but not y (GNP). For some purposes, it does not make much difference whether you use (7) or (10), but the student should be aware of the difference.

The eligibility requirements were designed to ensure that increases in M over time would be matched by changes in T. Thus the real bills doctrine would ensure that only noninflationary changes in the money supply would occur.

External Equilibrium   The external relations with the rest of the world were regulated by adherence to another set of rules—the gold standard, which also helped insure a noninflationary monetary policy.

The gold standard existed in many versions; however, all versions had two characteristics in common: (1) the domestic money supply varied directly with the gold stock, and (2) as long as the price of gold was constant, rates of exchange between currencies were fixed.

The student may want to review the discussion of exchange rate systems in Chapter 15, which will help in following the discussion of how the gold standard was designed to work in the pre-1929 period. Assume that the United States has an external deficit; that is, at the fixed rate of exchange between the dollar and foreign currencies, the quantity of dollars supplied exceeds the quantity of dollars demanded. As long as the U.S. price of gold remains constant, the exchange rate will not decline and eliminate the excess supply of dollars. The adjustment according to the gold standard would involve (1) the United States sells gold to purchase the excess supply of dollars in the foreign exchange market; (2) the money supply declines as gold leaves the United States; (3) prices and income decline in the United States relative to the rest of the world as the money supply falls; and (4) the price and income declines in the United States shift the demand for dollars to the right and the supply of dollars to the left.

The decline in economic activity induced by the outflow of gold and decline in the money supply will continue for as long as there is a deficit. The adjustment process could be hastened by the central bank. By increasing the discount rate the money supply would decline at a faster rate and speed up the adjustment process. In addition, higher interest rates relative to the rest of the world would attract foreign exchange to purchase United States I.O.U.s, thus further reducing the deficit.

The adjustment process would work only if the government acted according to the rules of the gold standard. That is, to eliminate a deficit in the balance of payments, the government must allow and encourage the decline in money, prices, and economic activity to lower imports and increase exports.

Both the discount mechanism based on the real bills doctrine and the gold standard were designed to safeguard against an overexpansion of credit and money. The real bills doctrine ensured that every expansion of credit and money would be backed by productive activity. The gold standard provided another safeguard to overexpanding the money supply. Overexpansion of money and credit would increase the pace of economic activity, which in turn would shift the demand for dollars to the left (higher prices in the United States relative to other countries) and shift the supply for dollars to the right (higher domestic income and lower foreign prices relative to the United States). As a result, the monetary expansion would generate a balance-of-payments deficit, which in turn would automatically start to reduce the money supply.

Financial Stability Governments had a responsibility to ensure stable financial markets in a private market system because monetary systems naturally evolved from commodity based to fiat based. This has already been discussed in Chapter 11. The fiat based on fractional reserve banking systems of the past two centuries has the advantage of flexibility and minimal resource cost of producing money; however, it has the disadvantage of being subject to *contagion*. The failure of one or several banks could generate a widespread run on other institutions and generate a general financial collapse.

The private market found it difficult to deal with the contagion problem, and as a result, central banks assumed responsibility for limiting contagion. They did this by serving as a lender of last resort for institutions experiencing deposit withdrawals. Serving as a lender of last resort made it natural that central banks would also provide some supervision and regulation of banking; however, according to the ideology of the private market, supervision and regulation should be minimal.

What About Fiscal Policy?

The ideology of the market system required government involvement to provide a stable monetary framework to ensure a noninflationary money supply, external equilibrium, and financial stability. Beyond this, however, active monetary policy was not required. So far, nothing has been said about the role of fiscal policy in the pre-1929 ideology of the market system.

Fiscal policy involves the taxing and spending decisions of government. Because full employment would be achieved automatically by the competitive market system, there would be no need for active fiscal policy. Although governments were needed to provide national defense and other such services and a legal system to protect property and enforce economic contracts, these activities should be financed by balanced budgets; that is, tax revenue should equal spending.

There was an additional reason for balanced budgets. Even if a case could be made for stimulating the economy with a budget deficit, it would not increase real economic activity because of *crowding out.* That is, any increase in net government spending would be offset by an equivalent decrease in private spending. There were several ways to rationalize complete crowding out to be discussed later; however, crowding out was widely held in the pre-1929 view of government policy.

Government Stabilization and the Market: The Great Depression

Prior to the Great Depression government stabilization policy was characterized by the following points: (1) nonactivist and defined by rules such as the real bills doctrine and the gold standard, (2) confined to monetary policy actions, and (3) based on the view that the market was inherently stable.

This state of affairs changed radically during the Great Depression period. The start of the depression in August 1929 to the bottom in March 1933 is referred to as the Great Contraction because it represents the most dramatic decline in economic activity compared to any experienced before or after. Unemployment has been estimated to be 40% in 1933. Nominal and real GNP declined 46% and 31%, respectively, from 1929 to 1933. The banking and entire financial system collapse with almost 10,000 banks failing during the 1929–1933 period. President Roosevelt was required to call a national closing of banks to restore public confidence in the financial system. While the 1929–1933 decline was dramatic in terms of any measure and the low point of the depression was reached in March 1933, the entire decade of the 1930s was one of depression. Even in 1939, when the war preparation was stimulating the economy, the unemployment rate was still 17%!

Two important changes in attitudes emerged from the depressed conditions of the 1930s. First, the market system was no longer regarded as automatically producing socially acceptable levels of employment and economic growth. Even if the economy could eventually adjust to a state of full employment in the long run, as Keynes once remarked, "We are all dead in the long run." Second, Keynes introduced a new model of the economy in his *General Theory of Employment, Interest, and Money,* which was published in 1936. The Keynesian model quickly replaced the quantity theory of money as the model of macroeconomic activity. Essentially, the model was based on the idea that total spending in the economy determined the level of output and employment. There was no reason to believe that the private sector could generate enough spending to ensure a level of economic activity at full employment. If the private sector could not generate enough spending, then the only solution lay in government spending. Government could influence spending directly through the use of fiscal policy or indirectly through the use of monetary policy, although Keynes was interpreted to have emphasized fiscal policy. The apparent inability of the Federal Reserve to stimulate the economy through the early 1930s destroyed much of the previous faith in the potency and usefulness of monetary policy.

As a result, government assumed the right and the responsibility to ensure achievement of the major goals of stabilization with the goal of full employment considered the primary responsibility. This was given official recognition by Congress in 1946 with the passage of the Employment Act:

> The Congress hereby declares that it is the continuing policy of the Federal Government to use all practical means to . . . foster and promote free competitive enterprises and the general welfare, conditions under which there will be afforded useful employment opportunities, including self-employment, for those able, willing and seeking work and to promote maximum employment, production and purchasing power.

This was a sharp departure from the pre-1930s view. The Keynesian framework and the view that the market system was not self-equilibrating toward socially desired performance levels supported the activist approach to government stabilization policy. Prior to the Great Depression period, government played a nonactivist role. The activist approach, however, emphasized the need to vary the money supply, the government budget, or any other stabilization instrument to achieve full employment and economic growth. The activist approach has dominated government policymaking since the 1930s; however, it has come under increasing criticism since the mid-1970s.

Recent Questions About the Activist Approach

The 1960s and early 1970s were the heyday of the activist approach. A majority of economists and almost all policymakers accepted the view that the market system required active stabilization efforts and extensive government intervention in the market system to achieve the goals of economic stabilization. Since the mid-1970s, however, the nonactivist approach has regained some of the credibility lost during the Great Depression, and while most policymakers continue to hold the activist view, a number of economists have raised questions about the desirability of the activist approach. This partial shift in attitudes toward a less active role for government in the economy is traceable to the following factors: (1) reinterpretation of the causes of the Great Depression, (2) record of government stabilization policy, (3) developments in the theory of how the economy functions, and (4) developments in the theory of what motivates stabilization authorities. Let us briefly discuss each of these in turn.

Reinterpretation of the Great Depression　　The Great Depression was traditionally regarded as *the* example of market failure requiring the active involvement of government. The activist approach to fiscal and monetary policy as well as the extensive regulation of the financial system emerged from this view. This view was challenged in 1963 when Milton Friedman and Anna Jacobson Schwartz published *A Monetary History of the United States, 1867–1960*. They argued that the Great Depression was largely the outcome of inappropriate policies on the part of the Federal Reserve. They turned the activist argument on its head—in their view, it was government policy that was responsible for the depressed conditions rather than the depressed conditions rationalizing increased government stabilization.

Record of Government Stabilization   The 1970s and early 1980s represent one of the more economically unstable periods in the United States; at the same time that we had evolved an extensive set of stabilization instruments as well as developed impressive statistical models of the economy. High rates of inflation along with high levels of unemployment, declining productivity growth, and declining influence in the world economy were a disappointment to those advocating the activist approach and suggested that the record of activist policy was anything but reassuring.

Theoretical Developments in Understanding the Economy   The original Keynesian model rationalized activist policy on two grounds: instability in private demand generated fluctuations in unemployment, output, and inflation around the long-run full-employment growth path, or the economy would likely equilibrate with substantial amounts of unemployment if private demand was insufficient to generate full employment. Economists quickly recognized that long-run unemployment equilibrium could only occur if there existed wage or other price rigidities in the economy that, in turn, would be difficult to rationalize over long periods of time. Thus, by the 1960s economists regarded the classical and Keynesian models as essentially the same in regard to long-run equilibrium when one assumed away wage and other price rigidities. This did not destroy the case for activist policy, however. Activist policies now had to be rationalized on short-run wage and other price rigidities or instability in private demand.

   A number of economists raised issues about the effectiveness of active stabilization policy even if a case could be made for its utilization. Many suggested that activist policies were subject to lags and other information problems that rendered them destabilizing on balance. Lags in the effect of a given policy made it difficult to ensure that the effects of that policy occurred at the appropriate time.

   The emergence of the *rational expectations* approach in the late 1970s had profound implications for the activist approach. It has revolutionized macroeconomic modeling and raised a whole set of new issues for activist policy. These models suggest that efforts to influence economic performance systematically are part of the information set used by individuals to make decisions. As a result, anticipated changes in monetary policy have little or no effect on the real performance of the economy.

Motivation of Stabilization Authorities   The activist approach to stabilization policy assumes that government agencies function for the public good and concern themselves with achieving the goals of stabilization in the most direct manner possible. Experience and theoretical developments suggest otherwise. New theories of government decision making suggest that stabilization policy in a wide number of cases is strongly influenced by considerations different from those discussed at the beginning of this chapter. This can be illustrated by two examples.

   The last decade has witnessed increasing study of the *political business cycle hypothesis* that argues that there exists a relationship between an economy's macroeconomic performance and political institutions. Specifically, politicians influence the actions of the stabilization authorities to enhance the probability of remaining in power. Stabilization authorities are willing partners because they anticipate favorable legislative treatment.

   The last decade has also witnessed increased understanding of financial regulatory policy that raises issues about the ability of regulatory authorities to pursue policies for the general welfare. Financial regulation in the United States has been as concerned with protecting market shares of existing institutions and markets as it has been with ensuring overall financial stability.

Where Does This Leave Us?

These developments have raised a variety of issues about activist policies, many of which will be explored in more detail in the remainder of this book. While there is no doubt that activism continues to dominate U.S. stabilization policy despite the issues raised by economists in the past decade, few economists would advocate going back to the pre-Great Depression ideology of the market. Nonetheless, there has been some shift away from the activist approach of the Keynesian revolution, and economists in particular are less sanguine than they once were about the ability of government to influence the economy in a positive manner via activist policies.

Key Points

1. Stabilization policy involves using monetary and fiscal policy (or policy instruments) to influence the performance of the economy to achieve certain performance goals (policy targets).

2. The goals of monetary policy are full employment, price stability, economic growth, smoothly adjusting foreign exchange markets, and stable domestic financial markets. Monetary policy is the most important stabilization instrument in use today.

3. Measures of economic activity indicate to the policymaker whether the economy is performing at a satisfactory level and help the policymaker in varying the policy instruments. Economic measures can be either overall accounting systems or specifically focused on one part of the economy.

4. Government has always had an obligation to conduct some type of stabilization; however, the major distinction between the pre-and post-Great Depression concept of stabilization resides over how extensive and active the government effort. The pre-Great Depression role of government stabilization was confined to monetary policy, which in turn was governed by a set of rules. Specifically, the real bills doctrine and the gold standard were designed to limit discretionary or activist policy.

5. The activist approach has dominated policymaking since the 1930s; however, questions have been recently raised about the effectiveness of activist policies because of greater understanding of the Great Depression, the economy, and the motivations of policy makers.

Key Terms

Activist versus nonactivist stabilization policy

Employment Act of 1946

Frictional unemployment

Gold standard

Gross National Product (GNP)

Great Depression

Keynesian economics

Lender of last resort

National income (NY)

Natural unemployment rate

Okun's law

Policy instrument

Policy target

Potential output or potential real GNP

Quantity theory of money

Real bills doctrine

Say's law of markets

Stabilization authority

Structural unemployment

Questions

1. Assuming that there are conflicts between full employment and price stability, which goal receives more attention by the following: politicians, Treasury, and the Federal Reserve?

2. Which of the goals of monetary policy is emphasized by the Employment Act of 1946?

3. Real GNP per capita is often used to measure the standard of living over time and between countries. What are some of the problems with using real GNP per capita as an indicator of the standard of living?

4. If Japanese real GNP per capita valued in dollars exceeded that for the United States. Is Japan a wealthier country?

5. If inflation increased at the rate of 2 to 3% over a period of time, would you regard this as evidence of price stability?

6. List the various factors that can increase or decrease the unemployment rate independent of cyclical factors.

7. Despite the sophistication of techniques for collecting economic information, serious questions can be raised about the quality of the data, especially on a short-term basis such as a month. Comment on the emphasis by the news media on the latest statistical releases by the government.

8. Explain the difference between real and nominal GNP.

9. Using Okun's law in Box 1, calculate the GNP gap for 1988 using a natural unemployment rate of 6.0% and the actual 1988 unemployment rate of 5.5%. Explain the concept of potential real GNP and its relationship to the natural unemployment rate.

10. Is the quantity theory still a useful framework for monetary policy if velocity is not stable and predictable? If so, why not?

Suggested Reading

1. Milton Friedman, *A Program for Monetary Stability* (New York: Fordham University Press, 1959). A clear statement of the pre-Great Depression view of government stabilization.

2. Milton Friedman and Anna Jacobson Schwartz, *A Monetary History of the United States, 1867–1960* (Princeton, N.J.: Princeton University Press, 1963). History of monetary policy in the United States with special focus on the Great Depression period.

3. Keith M. Carlson, "Federal Fiscal Policy Since the Employment Act of 1946," *Review,* Federal Reserve Bank of St. Louis. (December 1987), 14–25. Focuses on the post-World War II record of fiscal policy as opposed to monetary policy.

4. Keith M. Carlson, "How Much Lower Can the Unemployment Rate Go?" *Review,* Federal Reserve Bank of St. Louis (July–August 1988), 44–57. Discusses what's behind movements in the unemployment rate.

5. William Greider, *Secrets of the Temple: How the Federal Reserve Runs the Country* (New York: Simon & Schuster, 1987).

6. Martin S. Feldstein, "The Importance of Temporary Layoffs: An Empirical Analysis," *Brookings Papers on Economic Activity,* no. 3 (1975), 725–744. Discusses difficulties in interpreting the unemployment rate.

7. Robert L. Heilbroner, *The Worldly Philosophers* (New York: Simon Schuster, 1961). An excellent overview of the evolution of economics and its contribution to government policy.

8. Oskar Morgenstern, *On the Accuracy of Economic Observations* (Princeton, N.J.: Princeton University Press, 1965). A classic study of the problems of using economic data that should be read by all concerned with stabilization policy.

9. Ellen R. Rissman, "What Is the Natural Rate of Unemployment?" *Economic Perspectives,* Federal Reserve Bank of Chicago (September–October 1986), 3–17. Discusses the distinction between actual and natural unemployment.

PART VI

The Federal Reserve System, Instruments of Monetary Policy, and How the Federal Reserve Controls the Money Supply

CHAPTER 18

The Structure of the Federal Reserve System

Chapter Overview

This chapter discusses the structure of the Federal Reserve System from the perspective of its current role and operation. The Federal Reserve System is a relatively recent institution established in 1913—a rather late date for an economy the size and complexity of the U.S. economy. Prior to 1913 the functions of a central bank were performed by various private and governmental institutions, frequently, in a less than satisfactory manner. In contrast, England and other European countries had established central banks at a much earlier date in their economic development.

The structure of the Federal Reserve is discussed from five perspectives. First, we focus on the pre- and post-Great Depression period of the Federal Reserve in terms of its responsibilities to the economy. The Federal Reserve was established at a time when central banks were not expected to play active roles in the economy; however, the Great Depression period radically changed the role of the central bank.

Second, we define the current organization of the Federal Reserve System in the broadest sense; that is, we review the various components that together constitute our central bank.

Third, we then review the basic responsibilities of the Federal Reserve, which can be categorized as those relating to monetary policy and those relating to nonmonetary policy concerns.

Fourth, we consider who is responsible for the various functions carried out by the Federal Reserve. In this regard, we compare the standard organization chart displayed in official Federal Reserve publications with the reality of who controls monetary policy. The current command structure is one that has evolved over time and one that differs radically from the original command structure established in 1913.

Fifth and finally, we discuss the so-called *independence* of the Federal Reserve System. News media comments on the Federal Reserve and monetary policy constantly emphasize independence, and Federal Reserve officials are quick to defend the Federal Reserve's independence. What does independence mean? Is the Federal Reserve independent? These are important issues that have implications for the conduct of monetary policy. As part of this discussion, we review some recent developments in the theory of bureaucracy and consider recent evidence regarding the politicalization of Federal Reserve policy.

The Federal Reserve Before the Great Depression

The original purpose of the Federal Reserve as the central bank was threefold: (1) to provide an elastic currency, (2) to provide facilities for discounting commercial notes, and (3) to improve the supervision of banking. These were regarded as basic central bank functions that, prior to 1913, had been performed by various institutions, but not in a satisfactory manner. In the late 1700s and early 1800s, the First and Second United States Banks were created as quasi-governmental institutions to perform some of these functions. The independent Treasury was established in 1840 and undertook certain central banking functions, and the National Bank Act of 1864 sought to unify the private banking industry. These half-hearted attempts to achieve objectives of a central bank met with little success.

The Federal Reserve was created to establish a stable monetary framework by providing an elastic currency, discounting facilities, bank supervision, and other functions. First, the country had no unified currency system that would allow currency to expand and contract with the changing needs of the economy. A wide range of currencies issued by the Treasury as well as numerous bank notes issued by private banks were in circulation. The Federal Reserve introduced a new type of currency called the *Federal Reserve note*, which has now become almost the only type of paper currency in circulation. In addition, the Federal Reserve established a mechanism whereby the banking system could obtain and return currency as the needs for currency in the economy changed.

Second, the discounting mechanism was set up to provide funds to individual banks and the banking system in an orderly and noninflationary manner. A bank could borrow from the Federal Reserve by selling commercial notes to the Federal Reserve at discount. Thus, a $1,000 note would be discounted at the *discount rate*, and the bank would receive less than $1,000. Since the note itself was purchased at discount when the bank originally made the loan to the business firm, the Federal Reserve's discount mechanism was also known as the rediscount mechanism. Specific rules were established that limited the type of notes discounted by the Federal Reserve to "notes, bills of exchange arising out of actual commercial transactions." Whenever the Federal Reserve purchased notes from the banking system, the monetary base was thereby increased, and, whenever the banks reduced their borrowing from the Federal Reserve, the monetary base was decreased. A noninflationary monetary and credit growth was achieved, as long as the real bills doctrine was adhered to in the sense that the Federal Reserve expanded credit to meet the real needs of the economy. The ability to borrow from the Federal Reserve in time of need also allowed the Federal Reserve to function as *lender of last resort*. The lender of last resort function is considered an important central bank function since central banks are the ultimate creators of money and liquidity.

The discount rate played an important part in the Federal Reserve's objectives of achieving a stable monetary framework. The United States was still on the gold standard, and the Federal Reserve was expected to take actions to ensure the stability of the exchange rate between the dollar and other currencies by maintaining the price of gold. Whenever a trade deficit occurred, gold would flow out of the economy. This would be a signal that the Federal Reserve should raise the discount rate to reduce borrowing and the money supply. Higher interest rates, reduced borrowing, and reduced monetary growth would bring the trade deficit into balance as the demand for imports declined and the demand for exports expanded. Likewise, in the face of a trade surplus, the Federal Reserve would lower the discount rate to stabilize the flow of gold and bring the trade surplus into balance.

The entire mechanism was essentially automatic. A stable monetary framework would result as long as the Federal Reserve provided funds according to the real bills doctrine, adhered to the gold standard, and used the discount rate to offset gold flows. In a sense, a set of rules defined the central bank functions.

The Federal Reserve contributed to a stable monetary framework in a third manner by increasing the degree of supervision over the banking industry. Along with the Comptroller of the Currency and state banking agencies, the Federal Reserve sought to prevent banks from activities inappropriate for institutions whose deposit liabilities constituted the major form of money.

Central banks, and in particular the Federal Reserve, were not expected to pursue active stabilization policies that we now take for granted. A stable monetary framework was considered achievable by adhering to the real bills doctrine and maintaining the gold standard. As long as a stable monetary framework was provided, competitive forces in the economy would ensure economic growth along the full employment path. This, of course, did not imply that full employment would be achieved at every point in time. It implied, rather, that the natural equilibrium position of the economy was along the full-employment path and that any departures from full employment (business cycles) would set up market adjustments in prices, wages, and interest rates that would automatically bring the economy back to the long-run growth path. Monetary policy could make the adjustment process less severe and shorter, but monetary policy, beyond maintaining a stable monetary framework, was not judged as necessary to ensure the inherent stability of the system.

The Federal Reserve after the Great Depression

The Great Depression radically changed the perceived role of the central bank. The attitude about the market system changed from one of faith in unregulated markets and the inherent stability of the economic system to the view that unregulated markets often produced socially undesirable outcomes and that the economy was inherently unstable. Full employment could no longer be expected to result from natural competitive forces, and even if full employment were achievable automatically in the long run, "We are all dead in the long run." The emergence of the Keynesian model rationalized these views and provided a framework for the active conduct of fiscal and monetary policy to stabilize the economy.

The Great Depression changed attitudes about the role of government stabilization policy and, at least at the abstract level, suggested that monetary policy must now take a more active role in the achievement of economic stability; however, monetary policy in the United States was placed on the back burner for almost three decades after the Great Depression. Many viewed the inability of the Federal Reserve to prevent or reverse the 1930s decline as evidence that monetary policy was a relatively impotent stabilization tool compared with fiscal policy. As a result, much of the emphasis on stabilization policy during the late 1940s through the mid-1960s was placed on expenditure and taxation policies. Monetary policy, however, came to be recognized as a powerful, if not the most powerful, stabilization force during the 1970s. The evolution of monetary policy is not yet complete. New debate has arisen regarding the entire concept of stabilization policy. Many policy makers argue that attempts by government to pursue the goals of stabilization actively via fiscal or monetary policy actually increase the degree of instability and that the economy would be served better if government operated with balanced budgets and the Federal Reserve returned to the less active role of providing a stable monetary framework.

These issues will be discussed later; however, at this time it is necessary to turn our attention to several aspects of the current day Federal Reserve.

Components of the Federal Reserve System

In the most general sense, the Federal Reserve is comprised of (1) the Board of Governors, (2) the Federal Open Market Committee, (3) the 12 regional Federal Reserve banks and their branches, (4) the Federal Advisory Council, and (5) the some 5,500 commercial banks that are official members of the system and, for all practical purposes, all depository institutions subject to Federal Reserve reserve requirements.

Board of Governors

The Board of Governors, located in Washington, D.C., is the top administrative division of the Federal Reserve System and the focal point of the formulation and conduct of monetary policy. The Board consists of seven members, each appointed for 14-year terms and staggered in such a way that one term expires every 2 years. An individual appointed to an unexpired term is eligible for reappointment to another term, but an individual serving a full term is not eligible for reappointment. Many Board members do not remain throughout the entire 14-year term. The average tenure of Board members has been approximately 6 years. Members of the Board are nominated formally by the president and nominations are subject to confirmation by the Senate. The president appoints the chair of the Board of Governors, who serves a 4-year chairmanship.

The lengthy and staggered terms reflect the desire to isolate the Federal Reserve from government as much as possible. The original objective of the Federal Reserve Act was to establish a central bank that would be independent of government. The framers of the Federal Reserve System viewed a dependent central bank as too much temptation for politicians to spend more than they receive in tax revenues.

The Board is required to (1) set the reserve requirements for transaction deposits and managed liabilities subject to reserve requirements (nonpersonal time deposits and Eurodollars), (2) "review and determine" the discount rate established by each of the 12 regional banks; the phrase "review and determine" has come to mean that the Board determines the discount rate for all practical purpose), (3) set the margin requirements on credit used to finance the purchase of equities or convertible bonds, (4) oversee certain operations of the regional Federal Reserve banks, approve the appointment of regional bank presidents, and appoint three of the nine members of the Board of Directors for each Federal Reserve bank, (5) evaluate applications and rule on mergers between banks and holding company acquisitions, and (6) establish bank examination procedures.

These responsibilities are certainly consistent with the notion that the Board is the top agency within the Federal Reserve System; however, the preceding list understates the Board's importance. The Board has one other responsibility—to serve as part of the Federal Open Market Committee (FOMC).

The Federal Open Market Committee

The FOMC, which consists of 12 members, holds eight scheduled meetings a year in Washington, D.C. The Board of Governors constitutes 7 of the 12 members. The chair of the Board of Governors is also the chair of the FOMC. The remaining members are the president of the Federal Reserve Bank of New York, a permanent member, and 4 Federal Reserve bank presidents of the remaining 11 regional banks chosen on a rotating basis.

The primary function of the FOMC is to formulate policies for the purchase and sale of government securities. These purchases and sales are referred to as open market operations and are the most flexible and effective general tool of monetary policy. Much more will be said later about open market operations and other instruments of monetary policy. The dominance of the Board on the FOMC and the other decision-making responsibilities wielded by the Board emphasize the important role of the Board in the formulation and conduct of monetary policy. In recent years, the chair of the Board has come to be the focal point of monetary policy, reflecting not only the structure of decision making within the Federal Reserve but, just as important, the personal qualities and forcefulness of the individual holding the chair.

Regional Federal Reserve Banks

The Federal Reserve Act divided the country into 12 regions and established a separate Federal Reserve bank in each region (see Figure 18-1). The official rationale for this regionalization of a central banking system argued that a large country such as the United States had different regional credit needs and that more than one central bank would be needed to administer the credit needs of the country. Although some regionalization may have been necessary, the primary reason for the 12 Federal Reserve

Source: Board of Governors of the Federal Reserve System, Federal Reserve Bulletin (June 1976), p. 487.

FIGURE 18-1 **The federal reserve system: boundaries of federal reserve districts and their branch territories**

banks is more a reflection of the fears of various groups of a true central bank and, in the West and Midwest, concern that a central bank would be dominated by the large Eastern banks. Also, many felt that a single central bank would more likely be dominated by the federal government than would 12 separate banks.

The 12 banks are officially "owned" by the member banks in each region under a provision of the Federal Reserve Act designed to allay fears that the central bank would be a mere agency of the federal government. Unfortunately, this provision has sometimes led to the argument that the Federal Reserve System and monetary policy are really controlled by private banks.

It would be incorrect to argue that private banks have no input into the formulation of monetary policy; however, the ownership provision of the Federal Reserve Act greatly overemphasizes the role of private banks in the operation of the Federal Reserve System. The ownership consists of the capital stock to which each member bank must subscribe upon entering the Federal Reserve System. Each bank is required to subscribe to 6% of its own capital and surplus and is entitled to a guaranteed 6% return on the paid-up stock. The stock ownership does not carry any of the usual rights of equity ownership, however. The stock is not marketable and must be redeemed at par if a bank leaves the Federal Reserve System. The only input into Federal Reserve operations provided by stock ownership is that the member banks are allowed to elect six of the nine members of the Board of Directors of each regional bank. The 6% return is the maximum that can be paid to member banks.

Each Federal Reserve bank has a nine-member Board of Directors that supervises the operation of the bank. Three members are appointed by the Board of Governors; the other six are elected by the banks in the region. Three elected members represent the banking community, three represent the general business community, and three, appointed by the Board, represent the general public. The Board of Directors elects a bank president subject to approval by the Board of Governors.

Federal Advisory Council

The Federal Advisory Council consists of 12 members representing each district. The members, selected annually by the Board of Directors in each region, are usually drawn from the banking community. The council meets at least four times a year in Washington, D.C., with the purpose of providing advice and recommendations on the conduct of monetary policy and other policy decisions being made by the Federal Reserve. The council is an attempt at public relations and has little meaningful input into the decision-making process of the Federal Reserve.

Official Member Banks and Other Depository Institutions

At present, less than half the commercial banks in the United States are official members of the Federal Reserve System, but they hold about 70% of total bank deposits. Thus, in terms of deposit size, membership in the system comprises the largest and most important banks in the United States.

Prior to passage of the 1980 Deregulation and Monetary Control Act, official membership involved a benefit-cost analysis for each bank. There were several important benefits to Federal Reserve membership, especially for larger banks. Members had access to discount facilities, use of the check-clearing process, and direct access to currency shipments and could share in a number of research programs conducted by the Federal Reserve. Federal Reserve membership provided some public relations advantages as well. Banks also obtained a direct financial return from membership since they received a 6% dividend on paid-up capital Federal Reserve stock. These benefits were offset by the costs of Federal Reserve membership, the most important being more restrictive regulations regarding reserve requirements compared with those set by a number of state banking agencies. The cost of Federal Reserve membership became increasingly higher throughout the 1970s as interest rates increased and thus raised the opportunity cost of Federal Reserve membership. Large numbers of banks were planning on leaving the System in late 1979.

The Deregulation and Monetary Control Act for all practical purposes eliminated the membership issue and most of the distinctions between member and nonmember institutions. All federally insured depository institutions (banks, S&Ls, savings banks, and credit unions) must meet Federal Reserve reserve requirements if they offer transaction deposits or other reservable deposits (nonpersonal time deposits or Eurodollar deposits). At the same time, institutions subject to reserve requirements have access to Federal Reserve services on a fee basis. These Federal Reserve services include almost all the same services that were provided to member banks; however, even member banks are now subject to the same fee schedule as other nonmember institutions.

The public relations advantage and the return on Federal Reserve stock are still benefits to official Federal Reserve membership; however, it is difficult to assess its advertising worth, and the 6% rate of return compares unfavorably with alternative rates of return. At this time, it is difficult to predict what will happen to the official membership base. In any event, the whole issue has become moot. All depository institutions, for practical purposes, are de facto members and subject to Federal Reserve influence. The act has provided the Federal Reserve with extensive new powers over all depository institutions, despite their official membership status.

What Does the Federal Reserve Do for a Living?

The Federal Reserve System has two basic responsibilities. First, it is responsible for the formulation and execution of monetary policy. Second, it is responsible for a wide range of nonmonetary policy actions. Indirectly these functions may involve questions of monetary policy, but their primary aim is to improve the flow of funds in the financial system and to regulate, supervise, and monitor the general condition of the financial system.

The first responsibility is of primary importance and will be the subject of much of the remainder of this book. The nonmonetary policy functions are important, but less spectacular, and seldom receive the attention given to monetary policy actions.

Nonmonetary Policy Functions of the Federal Reserve

The most important nonmonetary policy responsibilities of the Federal Reserve are (1) to provide for an efficient and flexible national payments mechanism, (2) to act as fiscal agent for the U.S. Treasury, (3) to supervise and regulate various aspects of bank operations, and (4) to provide financial and general economic information to the financial community and general public. It should be emphasized again that it is somewhat arbitrary to call these responsibilities nonmonetary, as almost anything that the Federal Reserve does will have some impact on the conduct of monetary policy; however, these responsibilities are generally carried out without reference to current monetary policy actions.

National Payments Mechanism

We use money and credit to conduct the majority of our economic transactions. Money and credit can be thought of as the "oil" that lubricates the economic machine. An important responsibility of the Federal Reserve is to ensure the flow of money and credit through the economic system so as to reflect the desires and needs of the population. In fact, a primary objective of the Federal Reserve Act of 1913 was to institute a more efficient and flexible national payments mechanism. Before the Federal Reserve was established, there was no simple and fast means of providing and absorbing currency from the economy. Nor was there a fast and efficient national check-clearing process. The lack of an efficient national payments mechanism led not only to long delays in carrying out economic transactions, but it contributed to frequent financial panics as well.

The Federal Reserve fulfills its national payments mechanism responsibility in two ways. First, it issues a special liability called a Federal Reserve note. Federal Reserve notes represent most of the paper currency in circulation. The Federal Reserve can increase the supply of Federal Reserve notes when there is increased demand for currency relative to the other components of the money supply such as occurs around holidays and vacation periods. The Federal Reserve also stands ready to absorb the excess supply of currency after holidays and vacation periods end. How does the Federal Reserve provide and absorb Federal Reserve notes?

Assume that a bank needs more currency in anticipation of the Christmas holidays. From past experience the bank knows that many individuals will be exchanging checks and savings accounts for currency and that stores will require more currency for the holiday shoppers. The bank can pay for these notes in one of several ways. The bank can issue an I.O.U. to the Federal Reserve, or it can reduce its reserve deposit at the Federal Reserve. In any event, the bank now has the additional currency needed to meet the increased demand for currency. After Christmas, the decreased public demand for currency will be reflected by the large deposits of currency being made to the bank. The bank will then return the Federal Reserve notes to the Federal Reserve and either increase its reserve deposit with the funds or use them to pay off the I.O.U.

The use of Federal Reserve notes and the role played by the Federal Reserve as either the provider or absorber of currency in response to the needs of the public contributes significantly to an efficient and flexible national payments mechanism. The changing demand for currency before the establishment of the Federal Reserve often led to serious problems because there was no simple, fast method to get currency into and out of the economy.

Second, the Federal Reserve provides for a national payments mechanism by establishing and administering a national check-clearing mechanism. This is extremely important to the national payments mechanism because checks are used in most economic transactions.

At any given time, an individual bank will receive a number of checks written on accounts in other banks, and other banks will likewise receive a number of checks written on the accounts of other banks. How are all these checks collected and paid for? Two methods can be used to clear a bank of all the checks it has outstanding and all the checks it holds that are payable by other banks. Checks can be cleared through a local clearing house arrangement among the banks in a given geographical area or via correspondent bank relationships. They can also be cleared through national check-clearing mechanism maintained and administered by the Federal Reserve System.

To illustrate the workings of a local clearing house, consider the information in Table 18-1. The local clearing house will collect all the checks written on accounts in the three banks and construct a matrix of who owes what to whom. For example, the left-hand side of the matrix lists the checks held by Banks A, B, and C that are payable by the other banks. Reading across each row we can see that Bank A, for example, holds $1,200 worth of checks written on accounts at Bank B and $300 worth

TABLE 18-1 Check-clearing process through a local clearing house

Checks Held by	*Checks Payable by* Bank A	Bank B	Bank C	Total
Bank A		$1,200	$300	$1,500
Bank B	$ 300		$100	$ 400
Bank C	$1,000	$ 200		$1,200
Total	$1,300	$1,400	$400	

Net clearing position:

Bank A	($1,500 − $1,300) =	+200
Bank B	($ 400 − $1,400) =	−1,000
Bank C	($1,200 − $ 400) =	+800

of checks written on accounts at Bank C. The top part of the matrix indicates the amount of outstanding checks payable by each bank. Bank B, for example, owes $1,200 to Bank A and $200 to Bank C. The clearing house will then compute the net clearing position of each bank and determine the final transfer of funds. In the example in Table 18-1, Banks A and C have a positive clearing position that is payable by Bank B.

A large number of checks in any given year are cleared through local clearing house arrangements; however, when a check must travel across a state boundary or several state boundaries, a national check-clearing mechanism is needed. The Federal Reserve System acts in the manner of a local clearing house to clear the large volume of checks flowing among banks that are separated by large distances.

To illustrate how checks clear through the national check-clearing process, consider the sequence of events when a $1,000 check is written on a bank in New York and is deposited in a bank in San Francisco. The T-accounts for both the Federal Reserve Bank of San Francisco (FRBSF) and New York (FRBNY) illustrate all the required transactions necessary to clear the check with each step indicated by the letters a, b, c, and d.

(a): The San Francisco bank sends the check to the FRBSF. The FRBSF does not immediately credit the depositing bank with the funds; rather, the FRBSF adds the amount of the check to the asset category cash items in process of collection (CIPC) and to the liability category deferred availability cash items (DACI). The FRBSF then sets up a schedule to indicate when the depositing bank will be allocated the funds, even if the check has not been cleared completely. The maximum waiting time is two business days.

FRBSF

Assets	*Liabilities*
CIPC	DACI
+$1,000 (a)	+$1,000 (a)
−$1,000 (b)	−$1,000 (b)
ISF	Reserve account of SF bank
+$1,000 (b)	+$1,000 (b)

FRBNY

Assets	*Liabilities*
CIPC	ISF
+$1,000 (c)	+$1,000 (c)
−$1,000 (d)	Reserve Account of NY bank
	−$1,000 (d)

(b): The check is then sent to the FRBNY. What happens from this point on depends on how much time lapses before the check is cleared completely. Assume that it takes more than two business days for the FRBNY to receive the check. After two days, even though the check has not cleared, the FRBSF will reduce CIPC and DACI and add the amount of the check to the reserve account of the San Francisco bank. The FRBSF will also increase an asset Interdistrict Settlement Fund (ISF) account by the amount of the check to indicate funds forthcoming from the FRBNY.

(c): When the FRBNY receives the check, the amount of the check will be added to CIPC and a liability ISF account[1] to indicate that it owes $1,000 in funds to the FRBSF. Notice that at this point there is still an amount of $1,000 in CIPC for the combined T-account of the FRBSF and FRBNY. This represents credit to the banking system provided by the check-clearing process and is called *Federal Reserve float*. Float is the difference between CIPC and DACI for the combined Federal Reserve balance sheet and can fluctuate by large amounts depending on the difficulty of transporting checks. In the present case, it represents the amount that has been added to the reserve account of the San Francisco bank but has not yet been deducted from the reserve account of the New York bank. Thus, the New York bank has temporary use of reserves that have already been provided to the bank in San Francisco. If the check had been cleared in New York at the same time that the funds were added to the reserve account of the depositing bank, then there would be no float.

(d): When the FRBNY receives the check, it is sent to the New York bank. After the check is declared valid by the bank, the FRBNY will reduce CIPC and deduct the funds from the reserve account of the New York bank. The ISF accounts at each Federal Reserve bank indicate the amount owed by each bank to the other banks in the System. These accounts are settled up at the end of the year.

Until passage of the Deregulation and Monetary Control Act, the check-clearing process was utilized primarily by member banks and nonmember banks through member correspondent banks. Now that depository institutions offer transaction deposits and thus have access to the check-clearing facilities of the Federal Reserve, the check-clearing process has increasingly come to service all depository institutions.

The Federal Reserve is constantly improving the check-clearing process, especially by the large-scale application of computer technology. The growth in the number of checks cleared through the national, as well as local, check-clearing arrangements has been phenomenal. The growth in paperwork has required the increasing use of computer technology and the search for substitutes for the paper check. Electronic funds transfer systems (EFTS) may ultimately record most financial transactions as magnetic marks on computer tapes, disks, and other devices without the actual transfer of paper. While a complete EFTS is in the distant future, the application of computer technology to financial transactions has been significant.

Fiscal Agent for the Treasury

The Federal Reserve system plays an important role in federal government financial operations by acting as the chief fiscal agent for the U.S. Treasury. The Federal

---

[1] Actually, the ISF account is an asset account to which a negative entry indicates "due to" other Federal Reserve banks and a positive entry indicates "due from" other Federal Reserve banks. There is no corresponding liability adjustment; however, the example is easier to follow if we regard the asset ISF as a "due from" and the liability ISF as a "due to" entry.

Reserve has a number of responsibilities as fiscal agent, the more important of which are as follows:

1. The Federal Reserve holds the primary working balances of the Treasury. All checks written by the Treasury are written on a deposit account held by the Federal Reserve. Additions to the working account are made periodically from tax and loan accounts maintained throughout the country in private commercial banks. The tax and loan accounts are the receiving accounts of the Treasury while the deposits held at the Federal Reserve are the paying accounts.

2. The Federal Reserve provides many services connected with the selling, redeeming, and general servicing of the government debt. However, this does not involve buying securities from the Treasury but only acting as an agent to service the federal debt.

3. The FRBNY is charged specifically with carrying out official gold and foreign exchange transactions with foreign governments and international institutions such as the International Monetary Fund.

Regulation and Supervision of Banking

The Federal Reserve is involved heavily in the regulation and supervision of banking in the United States. This responsibility includes examination of member banks, regulation of mergers and holding company acquisitions, and so on and are shared with other agencies such as the Comptroller of the Currency, the Federal Deposit Insurance Corporation, and various state banking commissions.

Economic Research

The Federal Reserve is active in collecting and analyzing economic data on both the regional and national level. Each of the 12 Federal Reserve banks has a research department, and the Board of Governors maintains a large research staff. These various research groups provide important inputs into regional and national policymaking, much of which are available to the public in published form. Each bank publishes a review periodically that contains the results of research by its staff on regional economic conditions as well as articles on monetary policy or other policy decisions by the Federal Reserve. In addition, a number of the regional banks also publish regional and national economic data.

The Board publishes the *Federal Reserve Bulletin* monthly. This publication is the best single source of information on actions taken by the Federal Reserve. The first half of the *Bulletin* contains articles, summaries of changes in Federal Reserve regulations, important legal developments affecting banks and the financial system, and summaries of previous meetings of the Federal Open Market Committee. The second half of the *Bulletin* contains statistical data on national and international economic variables.

Who Really Runs the Federal Reserve?

The Board and the FOMC have become the focal point of monetary policy, whereas the 12 Federal Reserve banks and their branches have become more concerned with the everyday operation such as lending to commercial banks, providing currency shipments, and so on. The Board and FOMC together control the most important instruments of monetary policy, and, as pointed out, the Board in practice dominates the FOMC.

This is a significant change from the original structure of the Federal Reserve in 1913, at which time there was considerable opposition to a central bank from various groups in the country; however, the need for a central bank to provide for a more efficient payments mechanism and to provide a lender of last resort service to the banking community was widely recognized. Thus, a compromise was reached. The Federal Reserve Act established a *decentralized* central bank. The system would have the responsibilities of a central bank, but the structure would be decentralized. The Board of Governors (then known as the Federal Reserve Board) was to be purely administrative without significant powers, whereas each of the 12 banks were to make the most important decisions regarding monetary policy and the operations of the system.

The weakness of 12 separate banks attempting to coordinate national policy became obvious as time passed, especially during the decline from 1929 to 1933. In 1935 the Federal Reserve System was reorganized along its present lines, and more power and significance were given to the Board of Governors. Since 1935, the role of the Board in monetary policy issues has steadily increased, whereas that of the 12 banks has steadily decreased. Aside from the regional bank membership on the FOMC, the regional banks have little impact on the actual formulation and execution of monetary policy.

Even more than the Board, the identification of monetary policy has come to be associated with the chair of the Board. Sherman J. Maisel, who served seven years on the Board summarized the sources of power of the chair as follows:

> The Chairman's power arises from five major extralegal sources: First, his appointment makes him the titular head of and the spokesman for the Federal Reserve system. . . . Second, the Chairman represents the System and he participates in many decisions which never come before the Board. . . . Third, any chairmanship carries certain inherent powers, such as the selection of the agenda and the leadership of meetings, which at times influence decisions. Fourth, the Federal Reserve Board has delegated much of its supervisory powers over the staff and the System to the Chairman. . . . And, finally, a less tangible strength is his ability, because of his powers, to attract extra votes at Board and FOMC meetings.[2]

Based on Maisel's impressions obtained during his tenure as a Board member, he assessed the relative power of the chair to be about 45% of the total when compared with the staff of the Board and FOMC, the other governors, and the Federal Reserve banks. Of course these impressions are debatable, but there is little debate over the dominance of the chair in running the Federal Reserve System.

---

[2] Sherman J. Maisel, *Managing the Dollar* (New York: W. W. Norton, 1975), pp. 123–124.

If anything, the role of the Chair may have increased in recent years if for no other reason than the news media devotes far more attention to monetary policy than it once did. As such, the news media's natural tendency is to identify an individual with a government agency. And who is a reasonable choice to identify with monetary policy—the Chair of the Board of Governors—who else? This was especially true during the period from 1979 through 1987 when Paul Volcker chaired the Board. If Maisel were making an assessment of Volcker's role, at least through 1985, the power rating would be significantly higher than 45%. As a further indication of Volcker's role at the Federal Reserve, William Greider's *Secrets of the Temple: How the Federal Reserve Controls the U.S. Economy,* which focused on the Volcker years, was a best-seller in 1987.

Thus, the Board clearly dominates monetary policy in terms of the major instruments used to control the money supply, and within the Board, even though the Chair's influence varies with the personality of the individual, Chairs have strongly influenced the direction of monetary policy in the past two decades.

Independence of the Federal Reserve

Central bank independence has a long history and the general view has been that central banks should be independent of the political process because of their ability to create money. This was certainly the view of the creators of the Federal Reserve. The 1913 legislation designed a central bank that was isolated from government, and even today, the Federal Reserve is considered one of the most formally independent central banks in the world.

Assessing the independence of the Federal Reserve raises many issues. What does independence really mean? What are the arguments for and against independence? Is the Federal Reserve independent?

Concept of Independence

The concept of independence must be tempered by two considerations. First, central bank independence from government is not to be taken in the literal sense. Few would argue that the central bank should have the right to conduct monetary policy in a vacuum separate from government institutions or the private institutions that are represented by government. Most observers regard the issue of independence as one of placing the monetary authority somewhere on a spectrum of independence bounded by two points: at one end is the central bank that must formulate and execute monetary policy in strict accordance with general government policy and at the other end is the central bank that can formulate and execute monetary policy without major consideration of government even if the effects of monetary policy conflict with general government policy. The distinction between different degrees of independence is necessarily vague since no one argues that the central bank should be, or could be, completely isolated from its institutional environment and no one has devised a meaningful index of independence that is time and country invariant. Thus, we can only meaningfully discuss different degrees of central bank independence either for a given economy over time or for different economies at the same point in time.

Second, discussions of central bank independence frequently focus on the formal relationship between the central bank and the government as defined by the laws and rules establishing the central bank. The formal relationship, however, can misrepresent the degree of central bank independence. Central banks that appear to have considerable formal independence may very well be more dependent on government than are central banks that have less formal independence.

With these two points in mind, let us define independence with respect to the Federal Reserve. The Federal Reserve operates within some constraints as Congress could always abolish the Federal Reserve by legislative act and independence is not a license to pursue arbitrary policies. What we mean by independence is an independent Federal Reserve that can pursue monetary policy according to its own reading of the evidence and with respect to its own view of the goals of stabilization. The question then is: Should the Federal Reserve be allowed to be independent in the sense of following a monetary policy that may be at variance with administrative and/or congressional desires?

Arguments for and against Independence

Thomas Mayer[3] has provided a concise summary of the arguments for and against independence.

The Case for More Independence   There are three meaningful arguments to support a more independent central bank and monetary policy. First, monetary policy should be isolated from the political process because the political process is inherently short run oriented and there exist short-run benefits to inflationary monetary policy even through the longer-run effects are harmful to the economy. Thus, a less independent central bank offers too many opportunities for the political process to influence monetary policy in ways that will be decidedly harmful to society in the long run.

Second, the decision to establish a less independent monetary authority still leaves unresolved the issue of which component of government to assign monetary policy responsibilities.

Third, an independent monetary authority permits the central bank to provide "outside" input on government policy questions. Those responsible for monetary policy possess an extensive overview of domestic and international economic activity and thus can offer meaningful input to government policy discussions. The opinions of a more independent central bank would be given greater weight in any such discussion.

The Case for Less Independence   There are three meaningful arguments to support less independence on the part of the central bank and monetary policy. First, the monetary authority has a major influence on the economy and monetary policy is a major responsibility of government. As such, the institutions responsible for the formulation and execution of monetary policy should not be based on a fundamentally different principle than other governmental institutions. Western concepts of government are based on the view that government needs to be responsive to the

---

[3] Thomas Mayer, "Structure and Operations of the Federal Reserve System," in *Compendium of Papers Prepared for the Financial Institutions and the Nation's Economy Study*, Book II, Committee on Banking, Currency and Housing, 94th Cong., 2d sess., 1976 (Washington, D.C.: GPO, 1976), pp. 669–723.

general public and at various times and in various ways subject itself to a vote of confidence by the general public. Why should the monetary authority be exempt? As rhetorically asked by a number of commentators, if presidents are elected on the basis of actual or proposed economic policies, why should the Federal Reserve be permitted to act independently of government? Or in other words, if we are willing to subject policies of different political parties that impact our lives to public vote, why should monetary policy be exempt from the political process?

Second, independently formulated and executed monetary policy may conflict with other government policies that have a higher weight in the economy's social welfare function. The government and the public may operate with a high discount rate and be fully willing to have the monetary authority increase employment in the short run even though inflation may be higher in the long run.

Third, even if there are no serious conflicts between the goals pursued by an independent monetary authority and the government, independence increases the difficulty of achieving coordination between monetary and other government policies. A less independent central bank increases the efficiency of government and improves overall government economic policy.

The arguments on both sides of the debate are substantial and cannot easily be dismissed. One's view of the independence issue hinges on at least three considerations: (1) the role that government is expected to play in the economy; (2) the ranking of the goals of economic stabilization, specifically, the ranking between employment and inflation, and (3) the actual contribution monetary policy can make to economic stability.

Is the Federal Reserve Independent?

There are many aspects to the formal relationship between the central bank and government; however, from almost any perspective the Federal Reserve is one of the more *formally* independent central banks in the world. Let us consider each of the important relationships between a central bank and the government to show that the Federal Reserve enjoys a considerable amount of formal independence.

Appointment Process   The Chair of the Board of Governors is selected by the president and serves as a Board member. Board members are appointed by the president subject to confirmation by the Senate. There is no specific requirement as to the members' background regarding previous government service and, once appointed, cannot be removed except in the most unusual of circumstances. The chair is appointed for a 4-year term while Board members serve 14-year appointments without the possibility of reappointment; however, an individual appointed to fill a partially completed 14-year term can be considered for reappointment. No other government agency is represented on the Board of Governors.

Thus, the makeup of the major policymaking entity within the Federal Reserve suggests considerable, though not complete, formal independence from the administration and Congress.

Legislated Independence from Government   The Federal Reserve Act incorporated a number of provisions to legislate an independent central bank. The 14-year Board

---

BOX 1   President Ronald Reagan and the Board of Governors

The staggered 14-year terms of Board members was designed to reduce the potential for politicalization of monetary policy by making it difficult for any president to stack a majority of the Board. This has not actually worked as anticipated. Some presidents serve two terms, and many Board members serve considerably less than 14 years. Thus, a given president may have an opportunity to nominate several Board members as well as select a Chair.

President Reagan (1980–1988), for example, was responsible for the appointment of all seven Board members at the end of his presidency in 1988. In addition, President Reagan was able to name Alan Greenspan as Chair to succeed Paul Volcker in 1987. Thus, President Reagan had far more direct influence on the Federal Reserve in terms of structuring the powerful Board of Governors than suggested by the formal structure of the Federal Reserve System.

Senator Proxmire (D. Wis.) who chaired the Senate Banking and Finance Committee responsible for confirming nominations to the Board was critical of President Reagan's last nomination during summer 1988 for this reason. Proxmire argued that while the letter of the law (Federal Reserve Act) was followed, the ability of President Reagan to play such an important role in structuring the Board was against the spirit of the law. In the end, President Reagan's nomination was approved.

---

appointments staggered in such a way that one comes vacant every 2 years strongly suggested that the creators of the Federal Reserve intended it to be legislatively independent from government, though this has not worked as intended. The Treasury was represented on the original Federal Reserve Board prior to its reorganization in 1935; however, the Board played a minor role in the conduct of monetary policy prior to 1935. The reorganized Board provided no representation for any other government entity.

The Power to Appropriate Funds   Even though an entity may be legislatively independent of the government, the power of the government to appropriate funds and approve budgets significantly reduces the independence of the entity. The Federal Reserve requires no explicit funding from the government since central banks generate large net revenue. The marginal cost of producing high-powered money is essentially zero compared to a positive marginal revenue of holding assets obtained by the high-powered money. In fact, the Federal Reserve transfers a large part of its net income back to the government (89% in 1988).

Government control could still be important via the budget supervision and approval process. In this regard, the Federal Reserve is largely free to formulate its own budgets and manage its own operations. The majority of operations are not even open for audits by the General Accounting Office.

Implementation of the Instruments of Monetary Policy   The Federal Reserve determines the general policy instruments independently of government. The Federal Reserve is formally required to confer with Congress on the behavior of the monetary aggregates and monetary policy twice yearly. This requirement resulted from the Concurrent Resolution 133 passed in 1975 and the 1978 Full Employment and Balanced Growth Act. While each of these actions was intended to increase congressional oversight over the Federal Reserve, the experience over the past decade has shown that the Federal Reserve still calls all the shots regarding monetary policy.

Independence—Form Versus Substance

Thus, by any reasonable standard, the Federal Reserve is formally independent of government. Does this mean that the Federal Reserve formulates and executes monetary policy independently of the political process. Research and experience during the past decade has convinced a increasing number of observers that the answer to this question is an emphatic No! Despite whatever independence the Federal Reserve has from a formal perspective, the Federal Reserve is not necessarily independent from a *substantive* perspective. There are at least two ways to consider the politicalization of monetary policy.

Attempts to Do Good But the Political Process Forces It to Do Otherwise   In this scenario, the Federal Reserve tries to pursue those goals that are most appropriate to a central bank which it believes will contribute to the general welfare such as long-run price stability and enhancing financial stability, but the political process in one way or another forces monetary policy to deviate from these legitimate responsibilities. This conflict could arise because the administration and/or Congress pressure the Federal Reserve to increase employment, maintain an expanding economy, or stabilize and keep interest rates low. The Federal Reserve may protest and argue that such policies are shortsighted and likely to generate inflationary pressures and make the job of controlling inflation even more difficult several years later. The administration and/or Congress may be unmoved by these arguments and pressure the Federal Reserve to accommodate their policies. This can be done in a variety of ways: for example, representatives of the administration and/or Congress can go on TV and tell everyone who will listen that the Federal Reserve will be responsible for any adverse economic problems because of its unwillingness to accommodate government policy, or a more serious pressure would be to reduce the Federal Reserve's independence legislatively.

This view recognizes that the Federal Reserve has a degree of independence to conduct monetary policy but that the political process imposes constraints that vary over time. Thus, the Federal Reserve is independent *within* government, but not *from* government. Maisel summed up this view in the following way:

> Monetary policy cannot run counter to national policy in either the domestic or the international sphere. . . . The Fed gradually came to understand that it could carry out its direct responsibilities for monetary policy better if it interacted more completely and at more different levels with the rest of the government.[4]

Thus, monetary policy can independently pursue price stability if it does not greatly interfere with employment or other important objectives of government or, in general, irritate the administration and/or Congress.

The Federal Reserve Is a Willing Partner in the Politicalization of Monetary Policy
According to this relationship between monetary policy and political institutions, the Federal Reserve may willingly use monetary policy in ways to further objectives that are more related to a set a bureaucratic motives that conflict with maintaining price stability and even financial stability. The Federal Reserve possesses a utility function

---

[4] Ibid., p. 146.

that may or may not conflict with the general responsibilities of a central bank to society. In addition to price stability, the Federal Reserve may also be concerned about enhancing its power, influence, and prestige as a monetary and financial regulatory authority. The administration and/or Congress do not have to pressure the Federal Reserve to accommodate their policies. The Federal Reserve utility function dictates that it may deviate from legitimate central bank responsibilities to maintain and enhance power. For example, the Federal Reserve may be so concerned with enhancing regulatory power or protecting its formal independence from government that it is willing to meet the political process behind the barn to cut a deal while out in front claiming the virtue of independence. This type of bureaucratic behavior suggests that the Federal Reserve will not only be responsive to the political process, but likely will be responsive to private groups whose interest it identifies with its own; for example, some observers have suggested that the Federal Reserve is more concerned with maintaining and enhancing the role of the banking industry than with broader issues of overall financial stability—in this respect, the Federal Reserve has been a strong advocate of the banking industry's desire to move into the securities business.

The differences between these two channels of the politicalization of monetary policy are subtle, the main difference being the attitude and the willingness of the Federal Reserve to accommodate the political process rather than pursue actions that are legitimate responsibilities to a central bank.

In a fundamental sense, no central bank is independent of government. The channels of political pressure are many and complex. Formal rules of independence have little meaning if the government really wants to influence monetary policy nor do formal rules of independence ensure responsible actions on the part of the central bank.

The real essence of independence is not a set of formal rules, but whether the government permits the central bank to pursue those policies for which it can make an effective and long-lasting contribution—price stability and on occasion, providing lender of last resort services to stabilize financial markets. This is the *substantive* meaning of independence and has little to do with formal rules of independence as illustrated by the accompanying comparison between the Bank of Japan and the Federal Reserve (in Box 2). Thus, the real essence of independence is whether the central bank can and is willing to pursue these goals unhampered by political considerations.

What's the Bottom Line?

Authors of textbooks (including this one) find it convenient to present monetary policy in the typical schematic outline as discussed in Chapter 17. In this outline, the Federal Reserve is a stabilization authority that pursues actions to achieve economic stability for the general welfare of society. In reality, the picture is far more complex. The Federal Reserve or for that matter, any central bank, is not independent of government influence irrespective of the formal rules that define the relationship between the Federal Reserve and the government. Unless there is a commitment by both the government and the Federal Reserve to pursue those objectives that are legitimate objectives for a central bank—price stability and financial stability—monetary policy will be influenced by political institutions that will ultimately be adverse to the general welfare.

BOX 2   The Federal Reserve and Bank of Japan—meaning of substantive independence

Formal independence does not guarantee either a non-inflationary monetary policy nor does it mean that a central bank is credible. The real issue is whether the central bank is able and willing to pursue price stability in a consistent fashion. While there are many debates as to what functions a central bank should perform, all regard price stability as a major, if not the most important, responsibility. There is little debate over the fact that long-run inflation can only be controlled if the central bank consciously pursues price stabilization policies with respect to the money supply.

Thus, to illustrate the difference between formal and substantive independence, let us consider the world's two most important central banks—the Federal Reserve and the Bank of Japan. The Federal Reserve is more formally independent while in contrast, the Bank of Japan is far more dependent on government. In terms of the appointment process, legislated role in the government, and other characteristics, the Bank of Japan is not formally independent of the Japanese government.[1]

How has this difference been reflected with respect to each bank's ability to control inflation and maintain credibility? Ironically, the Bank of Japan (BOJ) since 1975 has a more impressive record than the Federal Reserve on both counts. Michael Hutchison and John P. Judd of the Federal Reserve Bank of San Francisco[2] in 1989 stated: "The BOJ is among the world's most credible central banks. . . . Although initially it may not have been viewed as entirely credible, the BOJ demonstrated its resolve to fight inflation by quickly and decisively reacting to the first oil price shock. Money growth was lowered to 11% in 1974—less than half its rate in the previous year—and interest rates

were raised by almost ten percentage points, the largest increase among the major industrial powers. . . . Although the 1974–75 recession in Japan was very costly in terms of lost employment and output, by the middle of 1975 the inflation rate was below double digits and has continued falling since then."

In contrast, the Federal Reserve's policy in the 1970s was clearly inflationary. While the Federal Reserve's anti-inflation credibility improved in the 1980s, the experience of the 1970s suggests that formal independence is no guarantee that a central bank will pursue one of its most important goals—price stability.

At the same time, the lack of independence such as in the case of the Bank of Japan is also no guarantee that a central bank is more likely to pursue anti-inflation policies. While the Bank of Japan has achieved a successful anti-inflationary policy since 1975 despite its more formal dependence, Bank of Japan policy in the late 1960s and early 1970s was clearly inflationary.

The bottom line is that formal dependence or independence is not the crucial issue of whether monetary policy is inflationary or not. Central banks are necessarily part of government despite the status of their formal independence, and the real issue is whether the government in general and in particular, the central bank are concerned with controlling inflation.

[1] Thomas F. Cargill, *Central Bank Independence and Regulatory Responsibilities: The Bank of Japan and the Federal Reserve* (New York: Salomon Center for the Study of Financial Institutions, 1989).

[2] Michael M. Hutchison and John P. Judd, "What Makes a Central Bank Credible?" *Weekly Letter,* Federal Reserve Bank of San Francisco (July 14, 1989).

Key Points

1. The United States did not have a fully operational central bank until the passage of the Federal Reserve Act in 1913. The basic functions of the Federal Reserve in the pre-1929 ideology were to ensure a properly functioning financial system and to provide for adequate growth of money and credit. Only after the

1930s did active stabilization policy become the primary objective of the Federal Reserve.

2. There are five components to the Federal Reserve System: the Board of Governors, the FOMC, the 12 regional banks and their branches, the Federal Advisory Council, and

some 5,500 banks that are official members of the system as well as depository institutions now subject to Federal Reserve reserve requirements.

3. The Federal Reserve has two responsibilities: (a) nonmonetary policy functions that provide for a more efficient financial system, which include orderly changes in currency in circulation maintaining a national check-clearing mechanism, acting as fiscal agent for the Treasury, supervising and regulating banking, and providing financial and general information to the public, and (b) the formulation and execution of monetary policy to achieve economic stability.

4. The Board of Governors and more specifically the chair of the Board dominate the formulation of monetary policy. The Board dominates all the major instruments of monetary policy and is the focal point of decision making in the system.

5. The question of the proper degree of Federal Reserve independence from government has become an important issue. There are strong arguments for independence and dependence.

6. The Federal Reserve is one of the more formally independent central banks in the world in terms of appointments to major policymaking entities within the Federal Reserve, funding, reporting requirements to government, and control of the instruments of monetary policy. This does not mean the Federal Reserve is insensitive to political concerns.

Key Terms

Board of Governors

Chair of the Board of Governors

Check-clearing matrix

De facto versus official membership in the Federal Reserve System

Federal Open Market Committee (FOMC)

Federal Reserve banks

Federal Reserve float

Federal Reserve notes

Fiscal agent responsibilities

Independence—formal versus substantive

Lender of last resort

National payments mechanism

Questions

1. How would the absence of a national check-clearing process inhibit economic growth?

2. Many politicians would like to exercise strong influence over the formulation of monetary policy but do not want direct responsibility. Is this a rational position?

3. There have been several recommendations over the years to eliminate the private ownership provision in the Federal Reserve Act. Would you recommend such a change, and, if so, state your reasons?

4. Why would the Federal Reserve be motivated to argue that monetary factors had little to do with either causing the Great Depression in the 1930s or prolonging the depression?

5. Work out the net clearing positions of the matrix in Table 18-1, assuming the addition of Bank D, which holds $1,000 in checks payable by Bank A and C for $500 each.

6. Explain the difference between the Federal Reserve acting as a fiscal agent for the U.S.

Treasury by servicing the federal debt and the actions of the FOMC.

7. Is an independent central bank consistent with democracy? Present a general case against independence.

8. Paul Samuelson, a well-known Nobel prize winning economist, once remarked that the Federal Reserve is a "prisoner of its own independence." What did he mean by this statement? Do you agree?

9. Present an argument that formal independence from government as in the case of the Federal Reserve might actually provide an easier environment for government to influence monetary policy.

10. Present an argument that formal dependence on government as in the case of the Bank of Japan might actually provide a more difficult environment for government to adversely influence monetary policy.

Suggest Readings

1. Keith Acheson and John F. Chant, "Bureaucratic Theory and the Choice of Central Bank Goals," *Journal of Money Credit and Banking*, 5 (May 1973), 637–655. One of the early efforts to consider a central bank as a bureaucracy.

2. Board of Governors of the Federal Reserve System, *The Federal Reserve System, Purposes and Functions* (Washington, D.C.: GPO, 1984). The official overview of the Federal Reserve.

3. Arthur F. Burns, "The Independence of the Federal Reserve System," *Challenge* (July–August 1976), 21–24. Argument for independence.

4. Karl Brunner (ed.), "Congressional Supervision of Monetary Policy: A Symposium," *Journal of Monetary Economics*, 4 (April 1978), 325–388. Articles discuss the efforts of Congress to supervise monetary policy.

5. Thomas F. Cargill, *Central Bank Independence and Regulatory Responsibilities: The Bank of Japan and the Federal Reserve* (New York: Salomon Center for the Study of Financial Institutions, 1989). Concludes that the Bank of Japan has behaved in a more independent fashion than the Federal Reserve over the period from 1975 through 1986 in the sense of carrying out the legitimate responsibilities of a central bank.

6. Alex Cukierman, "Central Bank Behavior and Credibility: Some Recent Theoretical Developments," *Review*, Federal Reserve Bank of St. Louis (May 1986), 5–17. An overview of research on what motivates a central bank.

7. Milton Friedman, "The Case for Overhauling the Federal Reserve," *Challenge* (July–August 1985), 4–12. Argument for less independence.

8. Milton Friedman and Anna Jacobson Schwartz, *A Monetary History of the United States: 1867–1960* (Princeton, N.J.: Princeton University Press, 1963). An overview of the U.S. monetary system before and after the establishment of the Federal Reserve.

9. Edward J. Kane, "The Re-Politicization of the Federal Reserve," *Journal of Financial and Quantitative Analysis*, 9 (November 1974), 743–752.

10. Edward J. Kane, "External Pressure and the Operations of the Federal Reserve," in Raymond E. Lombra and Willard E. Witte, *Political Economics of International and Domestic Monetary Relations* (Ames: Iowa State University Press, 1982), pp. 611–632.

11. Thomas Mayer (ed.), *Political Economy of American Monetary Policy* (New York: Cambridge University Press, 1990). Collection of papers on the politicalization of monetary policy.

CHAPTER 19

Depository Institution Reserves, the Reserve Equation, and the Monetary Base

Chapter Overview

This and the next chapter provide all the elements needed to understand how the Federal Reserve controls the money supply. As discussed in Chapter 10, the money supply is determined by the joint interaction of depository institutions, the public, and the Federal Reserve. This interaction can be summarized in a money multiplier framework:

$$M = KM \cdot B \tag{1}$$

or

$$\Delta M = KM \cdot \Delta B \tag{2}$$

The money supply (M) is a multiple of the monetary base (B) at any point in time, and changes in the base (ΔB) lead to multiple changes in the money supply (ΔM); that is, KM is greater than one. The money multiplier can be derived for measures of the base other than the monetary base; however, the monetary base framework has found widespread acceptance as a framework for viewing the Federal Reserve's control over the money supply.

It is now time to complete our understanding of the forces that determine the money supply. We have a clear understanding of the mechanics of a change in the monetary base and the ultimate multiple change in the money supply as depicted by expression (1) or (2). Two other factors must be considered. First, this chapter develops a detailed view of what determines the monetary base and the degree of control the Federal Reserve can exercise over the base and, hence, the money supply. To understand the monetary base concept, we need to examine the balance sheet of the Federal Reserve, the depository institution reserve equation, total reserves available to depository institutions, and finally the monetary base concept itself. Second, in the next chapter we will take a close look at the *instruments of monetary policy*. These are methods used by the Federal Reserve to change the monetary base and, hence, the money supply.

Balance Sheet Statement of the Federal Reserve Banks

The combined balance sheet of the 12 Federal Reserve banks is the starting point for understanding the determinants of reserves and the monetary base. Table 19-1 presents the combined balance sheet released by the Board of Governors for January 31, 1989. A brief explanation of the major items is necessary to understand the factors determining the level of reserves available to depository institutions.

Asset Items

Gold Certificate Account   These represent Treasury obligations backed by gold. In a sense, they are warehouse receipts against the nation's gold stock. Gold certificates generally change when the Treasury's holdings of gold change. For example, if the Treasury acquired gold it may decide to issue gold certificates to the Federal Reserve in exchange for an equal amount added to its deposit account at the Federal Reserve. In this case, Federal Reserve assets and liabilities increase equally. Gold certificates are valued at the statutory price of gold ($42.22 per ounce). When the Treasury issues gold certificates to the Federal Reserve, the process is referred to as *monetizing* the gold stock.

Special Drawing Right Certificate Account   This account is closely related to Special Drawing Rights (SDRs) issued by the International Monetary Fund on agreed occasions to member countries. SDRs and the nation's gold stock are similar in that they are both international reserve assets that can be used to offset an imbalance between the demand and supply for dollars in the foreign exchange market. SDRs received by the U.S. government are held by the Treasury. At various times, the Treasury issues SDR certificates to the Federal Reserve in exchange for an equal amount added to the Treasury's deposit account at the Federal Reserve. When the Treasury issues SDR certificates to the Federal Reserve, the process is referred to as *monetizing* SDRs.

Coin   These are coins issued by the Treasury held by the Federal Reserve banks. When the Treasury issues coins to the Federal Reserve, the Federal Reserve increases its coin account and increases the Treasury deposit account by an equal

TABLE 19-1   Consolidated balance sheet of the Federal Reserve Banks, January 31, 1989

		Amount (millions)
Assets		
Gold certificate account		$11,057
Special drawing rights certificate account		5,018
Coin		480
Loans to depository institutions		863
Securities		239,752
Bought outright	$239,752	
Held under repurchase agreement	0	
Cash items in process of collection		9,959
Other assets		19,642
Bank premises	754	
Denominated in foreign currencies	9,823	
All other	9,065	
Total assets		$286,771
Liabilities		
Federal Reserve notes		221,619
Deposits		48,245
Depository institution reserve accounts	35,810	
U.S. Treasury account	11,766	
Other	669	
Deferred availability cash items		9,161
Other liabilities		3,079
Total liabilities		$282,104
Capital account		
Capital paid in		2,117
Surplus		2,112
Other capital accounts		438
Total liabilities and capital		$286,771

Source: Board of Governors of the Federal Reserve Ssytem, *Federal Reserve Bulletin* (May 1989), p. A10.

amount. The coin account also changes as depository institutions withdraw or deposit coin with the Federal Reserve.

The reader might notice that there is no provision in the assets side of the balance sheet for holdings of Federal Reserve notes. Any Federal Reserve note held as an asset by a Federal Reserve bank will be offset by the liability of the issuing Federal Reserve bank; hence, the combined balance sheet does not include Federal Reserve notes as part of assets.

Loans to Depository Institutions   As a result of the Deregulation and Monetary Control Act of 1980, all depository institutions subject to Federal Reserve reserve requirements can borrow from the Federal Reserve at the discount rate. Most of the loans to depository institutions represent loans to banks, however. Other depository institutions must first utilize their normal government sources of liquidity before turning to the Federal Reserve.

Securities   The Federal Reserve's security holdings change as a result of open market operations conducted by the Federal Open Market Committee. The security portfolio consists primarily of Treasury securities (bills, notes, and bonds). In addition, the Federal Reserve also holds small amounts of federal agency obligations and acceptances.

Most of the securities are purchased outright; however, repurchase agreements are also made in Treasury securities, agency issues, and acceptances. Repurchase arrangements are agreements whereby the seller agrees to repurchase the securities on a specified date (within 15 days) or earlier at the seller's or Federal Reserve's option.

Cash Items in Process of Collection   CIPC represents checks deposited with the Federal Reserve's check-clearing process that have not been collected from the institutions on which they were drawn. CIPC has a related entry on the liability side of the balance sheet called deferred availability cash items.

Other Assets   This category includes bank buildings, equipment, holdings of foreign exchange, and other assets.

Liability Items

Federal Reserve Notes   Federal Reserve notes are a liability of the Federal Reserve and represent the major form of paper currency. They are backed by the total assets of the Federal Reserve and have no specific gold reserve.

Deposits   The largest deposit account is the reserve balances of depository institutions. Reserve balances are used to satisfy reserve requirements and to facilitate the check-clearing process.

The Treasury also maintains a large working account at the Federal Reserve. The Treasury draws on this account to make payments and replenishes the account with transfers from tax and loan accounts at banks throughout the United States. The tax and loan accounts are receiving accounts for the Treasury and the account at the Federal Reserve is the paying account. The Treasury account reflects the importance of the Federal Reserve's nonmonetary policy function as fiscal agent for the Treasury.

There are several other deposit accounts for foreign central banks and governments, several federal agencies, and international organizations such as the World Bank, International Monetary Fund, and Bank for International Settlements.

Deferred Availability Cash Items   DACI is related to the CIPC account. When a check is deposited in the Federal Reserve's check-clearing process, the amount is not immediately added to the depositing institution's account. Rather, it is first added to

DACI and a schedule of payment is established depending on how far the check must travel to reach the institution on which it is drawn. DACI represents amounts owed by the Federal Reserve to depositing institutions.

Other Liabilities   This category includes a number of miscellaneous items such as accrued expenses, unearned discounts on securities and so on.

Capital Accounts

Capital Paid in   Paid-in capital represents the amount paid by member banks for Federal Reserve stock. Members must subscribe to stock in the Federal Reserve System equal to 6% of their own capital and surplus; however, only 3% must be paid and the remaining 3% is subject to call by the Board of Governors.

Surplus   The surplus account reflects the retained earnings. The Federal Reserve earns revenue from interest on securities, loans to depository institutions, and other activities. Part of the revenue is used to pay operating expenses, pay the 6% dividend on paid-in Federal Reserve stock, and a small portion is added to surplus. The majority of income earned (89% in 1988) is returned to the Treasury as intergovernmental transfer.

Reserves of Depository Institutions

Reserves held by depository institutions as a deposit at the Federal Reserve represent a liability to the Federal Reserve and an asset to the institutions. By adjusting the various accounts in the balance sheet, we can see that total reserves held as a deposit at the Federal Reserve can be expressed in terms of other balance sheet items:

$$\text{Federal Reserve assets} = \text{reserve deposits of depository institutions}$$
$$+ \text{ other Federal Reserve liabilities}$$
$$+ \text{ capital account}$$

or

$$\text{Reserve deposits of depository institutions}$$
$$= \text{Federal Reserve assets} - (\text{other Federal Reserve liabilities} + \text{capital account})$$

We can see that any increase (decrease) in Federal Reserve assets, other things held constant, will increase (decrease) reserve deposits. An increase (decrease) in other liabilities or capital will decrease (increase) reserve deposits, other things held constant.

The combined balance sheet provides a great deal of information on the factors influencing reserves held by depository institutions, but it does not provide a com-

plete picture. Certain monetary operations of the Treasury influence reserves that
are not reflected in the balance sheet, and we have made no mention of vault cash
held by depository institutions that can be used to satisfy the reserve requirement.

A complete statement of the factors determining the level of reserves is released
every week by the Board of Governors and is known as the *reserve equation*. This
statement is a combination of the Federal Reserve balance sheet and certain monetary operations of the Treasury. Specifically, the equation reflects the Treasury
holdings of gold, currency, and coin, as well as its issuance of currency and coin. It
is essentially a statement that views total reserves in the framework of a sources and
uses statement.

The Reserve Equation

The reserve equation summarizes all the forces determining reserves in terms of a
sources and uses statement. The sources side indicates factors creating reserve funds
available to depository institutions, whereas the uses side indicates the factors absorbing or using reserve funds, the basic framework of which is

$$\text{Total sources of reserve funds} = \text{total uses of reserve funds}$$

or

$$\text{Factors supplying reserves} = \text{factors absorbing reserves}$$

Separating out reserve balances at the Federal Reserve held by depository institutions, the sources and uses statement can be expressed as

Reserve deposits of depository institutions at Federal Reserve
$$= \text{total sources of reserve funds}$$
$$- \text{factors absorbing reserves other than reserve}$$
$$\text{deposits held by depository institutions}$$

The basic idea is to separate the uses of reserves by depository institutions from total
reserve funds supplied to the system arising from combined Federal Reserve-
Treasury activities and other influences. Table 19-2 presents the reserve equation for
January 31, 1989. We now turn to a discussion of each of the major items to determine how and why they influence reserves available to depository institutions.

Factors Supplying Reserves
to Depository Institutions

The most important factor supplying depository institutions is *Federal Reserve credit*
and is composed primarily of the Federal Reserve's holdings of securities, loans to
depository institutions, and float.

TABLE 19-2 Reserve equation for depository institutions, January 31, 1989		
		Amount January 31, 1989 (millions)
Factors supplying reserves		
Federal Reserve credit		$261,056
Securities	$239,752	
Loans	863	
Float (CIPC less DACI)	798	
Other Federal Reserve assets	19,643	
Gold stock		11,056
Special drawing night certificate account		5,018
Treasury currency outstanding		18,855
Total sources		$295,985
Factors absorbing reserves other than depository institution balances at Federal Reserve		
Currency in circulation		239,581
Treasury cash holdings		412
Treasury deposits at Federal Reserve		11,766
Foreign deposits at Federal Reserve		279
Service-related balances and adjustments		1,589
Other deposits not held by depository institutions		390
Other Federal Reserve liabilities and capital		7,746
Total uses other than reserve deposits of depository institutions		$261,763
Reserves on deposit at Federal Reserve		34,222
Vault cash[1]		28,376
Total reserves of depository institutions		$62,598
Required reserves[1]		61,498
Excess reserves		1,100

[1] Estimated by author

Source: Board of Governors of the Federal Reserve System, *Federal Reserve Bulletin* (May 1989), p. A4.

Securities   Holdings of securities are the single largest component of Federal Reserve credit. They represented 92% of Federal Reserve credit in January 1989. The overwhelming majority of security holdings are Treasury bills, notes, and bonds purchased on an outright basis (Table 19-3).

Increases (decreases) in the Federal Reserve's holdings of securities will increase (decrease) reserve funds on a dollar-for-dollar basis. It makes no difference from whom the Federal Reserve purchases or to whom it sells the obligations.

Consider a Federal Reserve purchase of a $1,000 bond from Joe Hickenlupper. The Federal Reserve obtains the bond and gives a check to Joe Hickenlupper, who then deposits the check in his depository institution, say, First National. First Na-

TABLE 19-3   Maturity distribution of loan and security holdings of the Federal Reserve

Type and maturity groupings	January 31, 1989 (millions)
1 Loans, total	$ 863
2 Within 15 days	854
3 16 days to 90 days	9
4 91 days to 1 year	0
5 Acceptances, total	0
6 Within 15 days	0
7 16 days to 90 days	0
8 91 days to 1 year	0
9 U.S. Treasury securities, total	232,933
10 Within 15 days	5,457
11 16 days to 90 days	58,957
12 91 days to 1 year	73,405
13 Over 1 year to 5 years	55,524
14 Over 5 years to 10 years	12,681
15 Over 10 years	26,909
16 Federal agency obligations, total	6,819
17 Within 15 days[1]	136
18 16 days to 90 days	835
19 91 days to 1 year	1,303
20 Over 1 year to 5 years	3,359
21 Over 5 years to 10 years	997
22 Over 10 years	189

[1]Holdings under repurchase agreements are classified as maturing within 15 days in accordance with maximum maturity of the agreements.
Source: Federal Reserve Bulletin (May 1989), p. A11.

tional presents the check to the Federal Reserve for payment. The Federal Reserve increases First National's reserve account. The T-accounts for the Federal Reserve and First National would appear as

	Federal Reserve			*First National*	
Assets		Liabilities		Assets	Liabilities
Bonds +$1,000		Reserve deposit of First National +$1,000		Reserve deposit at Federal Reserve +$1,000	Transaction deposit of J. H. +$1,000

The Federal Reserve now has $1,000 more in bonds, and depository institutions have $1,000 more in reserves. If the Federal Reserve had sold the bond to Joe Hickenlupper, the process would have been reversed, and institutions would have experienced a decline in reserves by the amount of $1,000 when Joe Hickenlupper wrote a check for $1,000 and gave it to the Federal Reserve in return for the $1,000 worth of bonds.

The effect of an increase in the bond purchase would be the same if the Federal Reserve had purchased the bond from any other seller. Increases (decreases) in holdings of securities will increase (decrease) reserves dollar for dollar.

Loans   All depository institutions have the privilege to request a loan form at the Federal Reserve since the passage of the Deregulation and Monetary Control Act. At present, almost all borrowing is done by banks. Nonbank institutions must first use their normal borrowing sources before coming to the Federal Reserve. S&Ls can borrow from the Federal Home Loan District banks and credit unions can borrow from the Central Liquidity Fund of the National Credit Union Administration. The rate of interest charged for borrowing from the Federal Reserve is known as the discount rate.

There are two methods of borrowing from the Federal Reserve. First and most important, institutions borrow on the basis of their own I.O.U. secured by holdings of Treasury securities or any other security deemed suitable by the Federal Reserve. This type of borrowing is called an *advance*. Second, institutions can rediscount commercial notes at the Federal Reserve. This type of borrowing is called a *discount*, even though it is really a rediscount of a note discounted originally for a business customer.

The lending facility of the Federal Reserve is not a source of continuous reserve funds; it is to be used only to help an institution over a particularly difficult period. Because borrowing from the Federal Reserve is temporary, the maturity on loans is short. The maximum maturity for most loans is 90 days (Table 19-3).

Any increase (decrease) in loans to depository institutions will increase (decrease) reserves dollar for dollar. For example, assume that First National borrows from the Federal Reserve on the basis of a promissory note in the amount of $1,000. The accounts for the Federal Reserve and First National would appear as

Federal Reserve		First National	
Assets	*Liabilities*	*Assets*	*Liabilities*
I.O.U. of First National +$1,000	Reserve deposit of First National +$1,000	Reserve deposit at Federal Reserve +$1,000	I.O.U. to Federal Reserve +$1,000

The Federal Reserve "creates" the funds to lend to First National simply by increasing the reserve account in the same way that it created the funds to pay for the bond in the previous example. Even though the increase in reserves is temporary— the loan will have to be repaid and reserves will be lowered at the time of repayment— the net impact of any increase in loans to any depository institution is to expand reserves at that time and in the same amount.

Float   Float is included as part of Federal Reserve credit. But, unlike holdings of security obligations and loans, the Federal Reserve has little or no control over the amount of float at any point in time. Float is a product of the time lags involved in the check-clearing process and is the difference between CIPC (an asset to the Federal Reserve) and DACI (a liability to the Federal Reserve). When a check enters the national check-clearing process, both the CIPC and DACI accounts are increased by the amount of the check. For example, assume that a check drawn on a bank in New York is deposited in a bank in San Francisco. When this check enters the Federal Reserve's check-clearing process, the account of the Federal Reserve will appear as

Federal Reserve

Assets	Liabilities
CIPC +$1,000 (amount to be collected from New York bank)	DACI +$1,000 (amount owed to depositing San Francisco bank)

The depositing San Francisco bank will not be credited immediately with the proceeds of the check. Instead, the Federal Reserve sets up a payment schedule depending on how far the check must travel to the bank on which it is drawn. The maximum time that the depositing institution can be made to wait before the credit, however, is two business days, no matter how long it takes for the check to be returned to the institution on which it is drawn. If the check has not been collected by the Federal Reserve at the end of two days, the DACI is reduced by the amount of the check, and the amount added to the account of the depositing institution.

Federal Reserve

Assets	Liabilities

CIPC +$1,000	DACI +$1,000
	            −$1,000
	
	Reserve
	deposit of
	San Francisco
	bank
	     +$1,000

The Federal Reserve still holds the check as a temporary asset (CIPC). The difference between CIPC and DACI represents extra reserves to depository institutions. The depositing institution has received reserves for the check, but the bank on which the check is drawn has not had its reserve account lowered. As a result of the Deregulation and Monetary Control Act, the Federal Reserve now imposes a charge on bank float.

Float can never be negative, but its magnitude fluctuates greatly over time. Float becomes large during the winter months because of delays in transporting of checks from one part of the country to another. In terms of the reserve equation, increases (decreases) in float will, dollar for dollar, increase (decrease) reserves.

Gold Stock and SDRs The gold stock and SDRs have a positive influence on reserve funds. If either gold stock and/or SDRs increase (decrease), bank reserves will increase (decrease) by the same amount. While the SDR item in Table 19-2 is the same as in Table 19-1, the gold stock item in Table 19-2 equals Treasury unmonetized gold holdings plus gold certificates held by the Federal Reserve. Because of accounting conventions, gold certificates were slightly in excess of gold stock.

SDRs are often referred to as "paper gold" because they were once defined as a certain weight of gold; however, SDRs are now valued by a currency basket. They were introduced in 1970 by the IMF as a method of supplying member countries with international reserves as the amount of gold held by several member countries (including the United States) was not sufficient to meet international monetary requirements.

The Treasury is no longer the sole legal purchaser and seller of gold within the United States, and gold does not normally flow between countries in the settlement of international trade deficits. Thus, the gold stock account of the reserve bank equation has changed little over the last several years.

Changes in either the stock of gold or SDRs have the same impact on reserves. To illustrate, consider an increase in the gold stock that results from the Treasury's purchase of $1,000 worth of gold from a private U.S. citizen. The Treasury will pay for the purchase with a check drawn on its account at the Federal Reserve. The $1,000 will be deposited in First National, which, in turn, will be sent to the Federal Reserve through the check-clearing process. The Federal Reserve will reduce the account of the Treasury by $1,000 and increase the account of First National by the $1,000.

Treasury			*Individual*	
Assets	*Liabilities*		*Assets*	*Liabilities*
Gold +$1,000			Gold −$1,000	
Deposit at Federal Reserve −$1,000			Deposit at First National +$1,000	

First National	
Assets	*Liabilities*
Reserve deposit at Federal Reserve +$1,000	Transaction deposit +$1,000

The Treasury, in turn, will issue gold certificates to the Federal Reserve to bring its account back to the previous level. Gold certificates are assets to the Federal Reserve and are backed 100% by the gold stock purchased by the Treasury. In the end, the Treasury holds the gold and the Federal Reserve holds the gold certificates. The transaction will appear as

Treasury			*Federal Reserve*	
Assets	*Liabilities*		*Assets*	*Liabilities*
Gold +$1,000	Gold certificates +$1,000		Gold certificates +$1,000	Reserve deposit of First National +$1,000
Deposit at Federal Reserve −$1,000 +$1,000				Treasury deposit −$1,000 +$1,000

This process is referred to as monetization of the gold stock. The net result of a Treasury purchase of $1,000 worth of gold or receiving an SDR allocation from the

IMF in the amount of $1,000 is to leave depository institutions with an increase in reserves of $1,000. A sale of $1,000 worth of gold by the Treasury or reduction in SDRs will reduce reserves by an equal amount.

Treasury Currency Outstanding Treasury currency outstanding consists of coin and currency that are direct obligations of the U.S. government. This item does not include Federal Reserve notes, which are obligations of the Federal Reserve. Treasury currency outstanding consists primarily of coin since Federal Reserve notes represent almost all the outstanding paper currency in circulation. At present, U.S. notes are the only currency authorized for issue other than Federal Reserve notes; however, there are other U.S. currencies still in circulation such as silver certificates. An increase (decrease) in Treasury currency outstanding leads to an equal increase (decrease) in reserve funds.

In sum, the major factors supplying reserves to depository institutions are Federal Reserve credit, the gold stock and SDRs, and Treasury currency outstanding. Changes in the levels of these factors can be either positive or negative. Positive changes will increase reserve balances held by depository institutions at the Federal Reserve; negative changes will decrease reserve balances held by depository institutions at the Federal Reserve. The published reserve equation reports the levels of these factors and changes in the levels of these factors from the preceding week and the preceding year.

The net sum of the factors supplying reserves to depository institutions represents the total amount of funds that potentially could end up as reserves; however, a number of other uses of these funds must be determined before reserves available to depository institutions can be derived.

Uses of Reserve Funds Other than Reserve Deposits of Depository Institutions

Currency in Circulation Currency in circulation is defined as the amount of coin and currency held outside of the Treasury and the Federal Reserve banks. The item consists primarily of Federal Reserve notes, the major type of paper currency in the United States today, and includes currency and coin held by the general public as well as the coin and currency held in the vaults of depository institutions. An increase (decrease) in currency in circulation will decrease (increase) reserves *on deposit* at the Federal Reserve, because it represents a use or absorbing factor of supplied reserves. Consider the following example. During the Christmas season, First National requires more currency and requests a currency shipment from the Federal Reserve. The transaction will appear as

Federal Reserve Assets	Federal Reserve Liabilities	First National Assets	First National Liabilities
	Federal Reserve notes +$1,000	Vault cash +$1,000	
	Reserve deposit of First National −$1,000	Reserve deposit at Federal Reserve −$1,000	

When the currency is returned to the Federal Reserve, the reserve account of First National will be increased, thus increasing the reserve balances held by depository institutions on deposit at the Federal Reserve.

Treasury Cash Holdings This item represents any currency and coin held by the Treasury in its own vaults and is a relatively inactive account consisting of Federal Reserve notes, Treasury coin and currency, and unmonetized gold. An increase (decrease) in Treasury cash holdings decreases (increases) reserve funds to depository institutions.

Treasury Deposits at the Federal Reserve The Federal Reserve acts as a fiscal agent for the Treasury by holding the working account of the Treasury. All checks written by the Treasury are drawn on this account; however, money received by the Treasury is not deposited directly into this working account. Rather, money received by the Treasury is deposited in special tax and loan accounts at commercial banks throughout the country. Transfer from the tax and loan accounts to the Federal Reserve is made on a prearranged schedule. An increase in the Treasury's deposit at the Federal Reserve follows a reduction in tax and loan deposits in the banking system. Assume that a transfer of $1,000 is scheduled to occur from the tax and loan account at First National to the Treasury's account at the Federal Reserve. The transfer will appear as follows on the accounts of the Treasury, First National, and the Federal Reserve:

Treasury		First National	
Assets	Liabilities	Assets	Liabilities
Tax and loan account at First National −$1,000		Reserve deposit at Federal Reserve −$1,000	Tax and loan account −$1,000
Deposit at Federal Reserve +$1,000			

Federal Reserve	
Assets	Liabilities
	Reserve deposit of First National −$1,000
	Treasury deposit +$1,000

The net result of the increase in the account at the Federal Reserve by $1,000 is to decrease reserve balances by $1,000. If the Treasury writes more checks than funds are being transferred to its account at the Federal Reserve, the Treasury's deposit account will decline, and reserve balances will increase.

Foreign and Other Deposits at the Federal Reserve Foreign central banks and governments maintain working accounts at the Federal Reserve, and changes in these accounts have the same impact on reserves as do Treasury deposits. There are also other deposits held primarily by governmental agencies and international organizations such as the World Bank that have the same impact on reserves as changes in the deposits of the Treasury.

In sum, the major uses of reserves supplied other than reserves held by depository institutions as a deposit at the Federal Reserve are currency in circulation, Treasury cash holdings, and Treasury and other deposits with the Federal Reserve banks. An increase in any item will decrease reserves on deposit at the Federal Reserve, any decrease in any item will increase reserves on deposit at the Federal Reserve.

The Reserve Equation for January 31, 1989

The only items that have not been discussed are "other Federal Reserve assets" and "other Federal Reserve liabilities and capital," which include such diverse items as buildings, fixtures, operating equipment, holdings of foreign currencies, accrued expenses, and so on. A detailed knowledge of how these accounts are altered is not necessary to understand their impact on reserves. "Other Federal Reserve assets" represent a source of reserves, and increases (decreases) in this account increase (decrease) reserves. Likewise, "other Federal Reserve liabilities and capital" represent a use of reserves, and increases (decreases) in this account decrease (increase) reserves. We ignore these two items and concentrate on the major factors supplying and absorbing reserves available to depository institutions.

Table 19-2 indicates that, on January 31, 1989, $296.0 billion of reserves were supplied to depository institutions. The Federal Reserve was the major source of reserves, chiefly through its holding of securities.

The factors absorbing or using the $296.0 billion of reserves are broken down into two categories. First are the factors absorbing reserves other than the reserve deposits maintained by depository institutions at the Federal Reserve. These consist of currency in circulation outside the Treasury and the Federal Reserve, Treasury cash holdings, Treasury deposits at the Federal Reserve, and foreign and other deposits at the Federal Reserve. These competing factors for reserves held at the Federal Reserve totaled $261.8 billion. Second are reserves held by depository institutions on deposit at the Federal Reserve, which represent the other major absorbing factor of the reserves supplied. Reserves held at the Federal Reserve totaled $34.2 billion. The reader may note that this amount is less than that reported on the Federal Reserve balance sheet in Table 19-1. The difference is due to the fact that the absorbing factor—service-related balances and adjustments—is reported as a separate item in the reserve equation while it is included in the value reported for reserves of depository institutions in the balance sheet.

The reserve equation can thus be written as

Total sources of reserve funds ($296.0 billion)

= total uses of reserve funds ($296.0 billion)

or

Reserve deposits of depository institutions at Federal Reserve

= total sources − (currency in circulation + Treasury cash holdings
+ Treasury deposits with Federal Reserve + foreign and other deposits with Federal Reserve
+ miscellaneous items)

$34.2 billion = $296.0 billion − 261.8 billion

It must be stressed, however, that reserves held on deposit at the Federal Reserve do not represent total reserves, because vault cash can be counted as reserves. Where is vault cash? Currency in circulation is listed as one factor absorbing or using reserves and represents currency in circulation outside the Treasury and the Federal Reserve but includes any currency held by depository institutions. Thus, a part of the $239.6 billion in currency in circulation is vault cash and must be added to the $34.2 billion to obtain an estimate of total reserves. Table 19-2 shows that depository institutions held $28.4 billion as vault cash to yield total reserves of $62.6 billion.

Table 19-2 presents the levels of the various items making up the reserve equation; however, for many uses the changes in the levels from the previous week or year provide more meaningful information on the direction of changes in the money supply.

The reserve equation can be expressed in terms of symbols.

S = Securities (Treasury securities, agency issues, and acceptances)
L = Loans to depository institutions
F = Float
G = Gold stock and SDRs
TCO = Treasury currency outstanding
CC = Currency in circulation outside the Federal Reserve and Treasury
C = Currency held by the public
VC = Vault cash held by depository institutions ($VC = CC − C$)
TCH = Treasury cash holdings
TD = Treasury deposits at the Federal Reserve
FD = Foreign and other deposits at the Federal Reserve
RD = Reserves held on deposit at the Federal Reserve by depository institutions
RT = Total reserves held by depository institutions

The level of reserves held on deposit at the Federal Reserve is given by

$$RD = (S + L + F + G + TCO) - (CC + TCH + TD + FD) \qquad (3)$$

and changes in the level of reserves held on deposit at the Federal Reserve is given by

$$\Delta RD = (\Delta S + \Delta L + \Delta F + \Delta G + \Delta TCO) - (\Delta CC + \Delta TCH + \Delta TD + \Delta FD) \quad (4)$$

Total reserves are determined by estimating the vault cash component of CC. Keeping in mind that $CC = C + VC$, we obtain the expression for the level of total reserves

$$RT = RD + VC = (S + L + F + G + TCO) - (C + TCH + TD + FD) \qquad (5)$$

or, in terms of changes,

$$\Delta RT = \Delta RD + \Delta VC$$
$$= (\Delta S + \Delta L + \Delta F + \Delta G + \Delta TCO) - (\Delta C + \Delta TCH + \Delta TD + \Delta FD) \quad (6)$$

Importance of Reserves and Various Reserve Measures

Reserves available to depository institutions as expressed in the reserve equation framework are an important indicator of movements in the money supply given the existence of fractional reserve requirements. Depository institutions can support several dollars of transaction deposits for every dollar of reserves. The relationship between reserves and the money supply is determined by the reserve requirement. The lower (higher) the reserve requirement, the higher (lower) the amount of deposits supportable by a given level of reserves.

There are several measures of reserves available to depository institutions, referred to as *reserve aggregates*. These are obtainable directly from the reserve equation and are monitored closely to determine movements in the money supply. The following measures have received the most attention in the formulation of monetary policy.

Total Reserves   This represents the reserve held by depository institutions at the Federal Reserve and the coin and currency held in their vaults.

Required Reserves   Required reserves are the amount of reserves legally required as a percentage of transaction deposits and other reservable deposits. Reserve requirements are administered by the Board of Governors.

Until recently, required reserves were based on deposit levels two weeks in the past. That is, current required reserves were computed by multiplying the reserve requirement ratio by deposit levels two weeks in the past. This is referred to as the *lagging reserve accounting system*. Introduced in 1968, it came under increasing criticism in the early 1980s. Lagged reserve accounting complicated the task of controlling the money supply since the Federal Reserve was often placed in the position of merely validating what depository institutions had done two weeks ago. In early 1984, the Federal Reserve introduced a new accounting system that is much closer to a *contemporaneous reserve accounting system* in which required reserves are based on current deposit levels.

Excess Reserves   The level of excess reserves is obtained by subtracting required reserves from total reserves. The term "excess" should be taken only as a legal definition as reserves in excess of required levels. There is no reason to regard legal excess reserves as undesirable from the point of view of a depository institution. Desired excess reserves depend on such variables as the discount rate, Federal funds rate, and other interest rates. The *e* ratio discussed in Chapter 10 is one way in which to express the desire to hold excess reserves on the part of depository institutions.

Free Reserves   Free reserves are calculated by subtracting from excess reserves the amount of borrowing from the Federal Reserve. The rationalization of the free reserve measure was to indicate the amount of reserves that depository institutions could regard as free with no strings attached—reserves that were not required as a

BOX 1   Where to get information on the reserve equation

There are several sources of information on the reserve equation as well as the Federal Reserve's balance sheet depending on the period of time one is most interested in. First, the *Federal Reserve Bulletin* presents information focused on the past year. Second, the Board of Governors' *Annual Statistics* published each year contains yearly information on the reserve equation and balance sheet covering many years. In addition, the Board's *Historical Chart Book* presents much of the historical information in chart form for easy identification of trends. Third, the most recent and up-to-date information is available from the Board's document H.4.1 released each Thursday to the public. This information is reported in *The Wall Street Journal* on Friday or Monday in a section titled "Federal Reserve Data."

The "Federal Reserve Data" section presents the bank reserve equation in terms of levels and changes. The level of reserves supplied on November 15, 1989 was $300.3 billion, and of this total, $261.2 billion was supplied by Federal Reserve credit (securities, loans, float, and other Federal Reserve assets). The nonreserve deposit uses of these reserves totaled $266.6 billion meaning that $33.7 billion were held by depository institutions as reserve balances at the Federal Reserve.

The statement also reports changes in the components of the reserve equation over the past week and past year; for example, the Federal Reserve's holdings of securities as of November 15 decreased $1.9 billion during the week and decreased $13.6 billion during the year.

		Chg fm	wk end
	Nov. 15, 1989	Nov. 8, 1989	Nov. 16, 1988
Reserve bank credit:			
U.S. Gov't securities:			
Bought outright	214,890	−1,861	−13,592
Held under repurch agreemt			−438
Federal agency issues:			
Bought outright	6,525		−577
Held under repurch agreemt			−127
Acceptances			
Borrowings from Fed:			
Adjustment credit	186	+160	−182
Seasonal borrowings	135	−24	−37
Extended credit	20	+1	−2,940
Float	1,206	−11	+37
Other Federal Reserve Assets	38,283	+278	+19,593
Total Reserve Bank Credit	261,245	−1,457	+1,737
Gold Stock	11,062		+1
SDR certificates	8,518		+3,500
Treasury currency outstanding	19,522	+14	+808
Total	300,347	−1,444	+6,045
Currency in circulation	251,338	+1,208	+10,712
Treasury cash holdings	449	+6	+45
Treasury dpts with F.R. Bnks	4,757	−604	−452
Foreign dpts with F.R. Bnks	213	−9	−20
Other dpts with F.R. Bnks	248	−81	57
Service related balances, adj	1,867	−103	−20
Other F.R. liabilities & capital	7,716	−362	−35
Total	266,590	+54	+10,175

Source: *The Wall Street Journal*, November 17, 1989, p. C13.

legal reserve behind deposit liabilities and reserves that would not have to be paid back to the Federal Reserve in the near future as a result of past borrowing.

In the 1950s and 1960s, the level of free reserves was regarded as an important indicator of monetary policy. High levels of free reserves indicated that monetary policy was easy; low or negative levels of free reserves indicated that monetary policy was tight. This interpretation has been pretty much discredited. Free reserves are a very difficult reserve measure to interpret in terms of whether monetary policy is tight or easy.

Nonborrowed Reserves   Nonborrowed reserves are calculated by subtracting borrowings from total reserves. Nonborrowed reserves played an important role in the

Federal Reserve's operating procedures from late 1979 through late 1982 when it focused attention on the monetary aggregates.

Borrowed Reserves   These are the same as loans made to depository institutions, and have played an important role in the Federal Reserve's operating procedures since October 1982 when it deemphasized monetary aggregates.

Reserve Measures and the Money Supply

Most reserve measures can be used in a money multiplier framework, although the multiplier formulas for a specific reserve measure differ depending on what particular reserve measure is used. In a money multiplier framework, you can show that an increase in total reserves and nonborrowed reserves will result in a multiple change in the money supply.

There is debate over which reserve measure should be emphasized. The issue can be illustrated with the following expressions:

$$M = f(R) + \epsilon \tag{7}$$

or

$$\Delta M = f(\Delta R) + \epsilon \tag{8}$$

The level or change in the level of the money supply is a function of the level or change in the level of reserves plus a random term ϵ; that is, the relationship between reserves and money is not exact because of erratic and unpredictable movements in the money supply that cannot be accounted for in the money supply framework. The issue of which reserve measure to emphasize depends on two considerations. First, how close is the relationship between M and the reserve measure, R? Other things being equal, we should use the reserve measure that best helps us determine the level and changes in the level of the money supply. This is satisfied by using reserve measures that have a close relationship with the money supply. Second, how much control does the Federal Reserve have over the reserve measure? Even if there is a close relationship between a given reserve measure and money, this will be of little help in controlling the money supply if the reserve measure is subject to influence from a variety of forces.

For example, total reserves in Table 19-2 is the product of many forces, only some of which are under the influence of the Federal Reserve. In fact, the Federal Reserve's holdings of securities are about the only item directly controllable because the Federal Reserve makes the decision to buy or sell securities. All other items range from being partly under the Federal Reserve's influence such as loans to depository institutions to being little influenced by the Federal Reserve such as float. The larger the number of non-Federal Reserve forces determining a particular reserve measure, the more difficult it is for the Federal Reserve to achieve a desired level of reserves.

TABLE 19-4   Sources and uses of the monetary base, January 31, 1989

	Amount (millions)
Sources of the base	
Federal Reserve credit	$ 261,056
Gold stock and SDRs	16,074
Treasury currency outstanding	18,855
Less: Treasury cash holding	−412
Treasury deposits at Federal Reserve	−11,766
Foreign and other deposits at Federal Reserve	−2,258
Other liabilities and capital accounts	−7,746
Monetary base (sum of the base sources)	$ 273,803
Uses of the base	
Depository institution balances at Federal Reserve Banks	34,222
Currency held by public and depository institutions	239,581
Monetary base (sum of the base uses)	$ 273,803

Source: Source and use items are taken from Table 19-2.

The Monetary Base

Most reserve measures address these two considerations to some extent; however, a number of economists have reduced the emphasis on the traditional reserve measures such as total reserves, excess reserves, free reserves, and nonborrowed reserves. Increased attention has been devoted to a reserve measure called the monetary base. There are two reasons for this shift of emphasis.

First, evidence indicates that the relationship between changes in the monetary base and money is closer than with other reserve measures. Second, of all the reserve measures, the Federal Reserve has the greatest control over the monetary base. The monetary base can be estimated from the information provided in the reserve equation. Table 19-4 presents an estimate of the monetary base in terms of a sources and uses statement. The source of the base emerges primarily from actions by the Federal Reserve and Treasury. There are three major uses of the base: (1) currency held by the public, other than depository institutions, (2) reserves held as a vault cash, and (3) reserves held as a deposit at the Federal Reserve. Any change in the base will lead to a multiple change in the money supply as indicated by the expressions developed in Chapter 10.

The uses and sources of the monetary base as of January 31, 1989 were $273.8 billion. The monetary base is reported in two versions: unadjusted and adjusted. The *unadjusted monetary base* is composed of depository institution balances at the Federal Reserve and currency in circulation, which consists of vault cash and currency held by the public. The unadjusted monetary base is an important determinant of the money supply, as reserves held by depository institutions influence directly the amount of credit and money they create, whereas currency held by the public is potentially available to support lending and investment activities. The unadjusted monetary base summarizes the net impact of direct Federal Reserve actions on the money stock. Federal Reserve holdings of securities are the largest single determinant of the source of the base. The unadjusted monetary base also summarizes the actions of the Federal Reserve with regard to loans made to depository institutions. However, the Federal Reserve can also change reserve requirements on transaction deposits or other reservable deposits, and the money multiplier framework developed earlier indicates that changes in the reserve requirement ratio, *rt* or *rn*, will change the value of the multiplier. A decrease (increase) in reserve requirements increases (decreases) the ability of depository institutions to expand the money supply with a given monetary base.

As a result of the importance of reserve requirement changes and the fact that the Board has changed requirements in the past, a reserve adjustment is added to the unadjusted monetary base to obtain the *adjusted monetary base*. The reserve adjustment calculation is complex. It incorporates not only changes in reserve requirements but also reserve requirement changes induced from shifts of deposits between transactions and nontransaction deposits subject to reserve requirements as well as deposit shifts between small and large depository institutions. The reserve requirement adjustment has almost always been positive, ranging from 5 to 10% of the unadjusted monetary base.

The Federal Reserve has greater control over the monetary base than, say, total reserves for two reasons. First, by examining the items in the sources of the base (Table 19-4), we see that Federal Reserve credit dominates movements in the monetary base. In the case of total reserves, Federal Reserve credit is still very important, but changes in currency in circulation also play a significant role in determining the level of reserves and changes in currency in circulation are large and difficult to forecast. Second, the items that make up the source of the base are readily available to the Federal Reserve, as they represent accounts at the Federal Reserve and Treasury. This provides a significant advantage in the control of the money supply. In the case of total reserves, the Federal Reserves would require estimates of currency in circulation that may be delayed or not very accurate on a short-run basis. By emphasizing the items that make up the source of the base, the Federal Reserve can obtain fairly accurate short-run estimates of the monetary base.

Key Points

1. The money supply can be expressed as a multiple of the monetary base at any point in time:

$$M = KM \cdot B$$

or

$$\Delta M = KM \cdot \Delta B$$

This provides a framework for monetary policy, as the Federal Reserve has some control over the money multiplier, *KM*, and much control over the monetary base, *B*.

2. There are several reserve measures consistent with the money multiplier framework. The best method of seeing how these reserve measures are computed is to examine the reserve equation published by the Board of Governors ev-

ery week. The equation summarizes all the factors supplying and absorbing reserves to depository institutions.

3. Federal Reserve credit is an important source of reserves to depository institutions and consists of the Federal Reserve's holdings of securities, loans made to depository institutions, and float. Because the holdings of securities are under the complete control of the Federal Reserve and represent a significant element of the factors supplying reserves, the Federal Reserve then has considerable influence over reserves available to depository institutions.

4. The reserve equation can be used to determine the level and changes in the level of reserves.

Based on this, we can calculate various reserve measures such as excess reserves, nonborrowed reserves, and the monetary base.

5. Considerable attention has been devoted to the monetary base measure of reserves, as it is directly controllable by the Federal Reserve and has a close relationship to the money supply.

6. Even though the money supply is closely related to the monetary base, there is still considerable random behavior in the money supply. The Federal Reserve can influence the level and changes in the level of the money supply within reasonable bounds, but it cannot achieve precise targets, especially over short periods of time.

Key Terms

Borrowed reserves

Contemporaneous reserve accounting

Currency in circulation

Excess reserves

Factors absorbing reserves

Factors supplying reserves

Federal Reserve credit

Float (CIPC – DACI)

Free reserves

Gold certificates

Lagged reserve accounting

Loans to depository institutions

Monetary base (adjusted and unadjusted)

Nonborrowed reserves

Reserve aggregates

Reserve deposits of depository institutions

Reserve equation

Securities held by the Federal Reserve

Special Drawing Rights (SDRs)

Total reserves

Treasury deposits

Value cash

Questions

1. If you were reading *The Wall Street Journal* on a particular day and noticed that total reserves increased 10% over those in the preceding week, would you regard this as evidence that monetary policy was becoming easy? Does this change indicate anything about monetary policy?

2. Why is it important to use a reserve measure that is controllable by the Federal Reserve?

3. What role do depository institutions play in determining the level of excess reserves?

4. We have stated several times that the Federal Reserve has considerable control over the

money supply based on its control over the monetary base. Looking at all of the various factors determining reserves and related measures, how can we say the Federal Reserve has considerable control over the monetary base?

5. The Deregulation and Monetary Control Act required the Federal Reserve to impose a charge for float starting in 1984. What effect did this action have on the magnitude of float in the reserve equation?

6. Can float ever be negative? Can float be zero? Explain how a zero value for float can occur.

7. The level of excess reserves reported for January 1989 in Table 19-2 totaled $1.1 billion. Recognizing that interest is not paid on reserve balances or vault cash, what does this level of excess reserves imply about the behavior of depository institutions?

8. Use a T-account framework to illustrate the effect on total reserves of depository institutions arising from the following: (a) Federal Reserve sells $1.0 billion in Treasury securities, (b) Federal Reserve sells $1.0 billion in acceptances, (c) depository institutions pay $2.0 billion to Federal Reserve for loans received in the past, (d) Treasury deposits at the Federal Reserve increases by $2.0 billion, and (e) the Federal Reserve increases reserve requirements.

9. Explain why the Federal Reserve has greater control over the monetary base than total reserves.

Suggested Readings

1. Anatol B. Balback and Albert E. Burger, "Derivation of the Monetary Base," *Review.* Federal Reserve Bank of St. Louis (November 1976), 2–8. Discusses the concept of the monetary base.

2. Alfred Broaddus, *A Primer on the Fed* (Richmond, Va.: Federal Reserve Bank of Richmond, 1988). Overview of Federal Reserve actions and how they impact reserves of depository institutions.

3. Albert E. Burger, "Alternative Measures of the Monetary Base," *Review,* Federal Reserve Bank of St. Louis (June 1979), 3–87. This article reviews estimates of the monetary base provided by the Federal Reserve Bank of St. Louis and the Board of Governors.

4. Board of Governors of the Federal Reserve System, *The Federal Reserve System: Purposes and Functions* (Washington, D.C.: Board of Governors, 1984). Succinct discussion of the Federal Reserve's balance sheet and reserve equation.

5. R. Alton Gilbert, "Revision of the St. Louis Federal Reserve's Adjusted Monetary Base," *Review,* Federal Reserve Bank of St. Louis (December 1980). This and the Tatom article deal with changes in measuring the monetary base required by the Deregulation and Monetary Control Act of 1980.

6. R. Alton Gilbert, "Two Measures of Reserves: Why Are They Different?" *Review,* Federal Reserve Bank of St. Louis (June–July 1983), 16–25. More on the differences between the St. Louis Fed's and Board's approach to measuring the monetary base.

7. John A. Tatom, "Issues in Measuring an Adjusted Monetary Base," *Review,* Federal Reserve Bank of St. Louis (December 1980).

CHAPTER 20

The Instruments of Monetary Policy

Chapter Overview

This chapter discusses the *policy instruments* available to the Federal Reserve to support its efforts to achieve economic stability. The most important policy instruments are those focused on controlling the money supply—referred to as *general instruments* of monetary policy. They are designed to influence the total amount of money and credit. There are three general instruments: open market operations, discount policy, and changes in reserve requirements. The chapter will discuss each in detail as well as indicate the relative roles of each instrument in the money supply framework developed in Chapter 10. As we will see, open market operations have become *the* major instrument for the conduct of monetary policy. Discount policy has become a distant second to general monetary control, but is recognized as of critical importance to the *lender of last resort* responsibility of the Federal Reserve. This was especially apparent during the October 1987 stock market crash. Changes in reserve requirements have become an inactive instrument for all practical purposes, though they are capable of inducing large changes in the money supply.

The Federal Reserve also has available and, in the past, has resorted to policy instruments focused on specific sectors of the financial system—these are referred to as *selective instruments* of monetary policy. They are designed to influence the amount of money and credit going into specific sectors of the economy, that is, selective instruments influence the allocation of credit and money rather than the total amount of credit and money. There has been considerable debate about these instruments, both in terms of technical and philosophical perspectives. In any event, selective instruments play a minor role in the conduct of monetary policy. In fact, the Federal Reserve currently has access to only one selective instrument—margin requirements—and this has been inactive since 1974.

Finally, the Federal Reserve has access to another instrument—moral suasion—a difficult to categorize instrument.

General Instruments of Monetary Policy

Open Market Operations

Open market operations are currently the most important instrument of monetary policy. What is amazing about the present role of open market operations is that this instrument was not even recognized in the legislation establishing the Federal Reserve in 1913. Open market operations did not become a major instrument of monetary policy until the 1930s, but, since then, they have been recognized as *the* instrument of monetary policy.

Open market operations involve the buying and selling of Treasury securities, federal agency obligations, and acceptances in the open market. The Federal Reserve does not purchase securities directly from the Treasury. The majority of open market operations are conducted in government securities at all maturity ranges, although short-term securities are generally considered the most important. Table 19-3 presents the maturity distribution of the government and other obligations held by the Federal Reserve on January 31, 1989. On this date, the Federal Reserve held only Treasury securities and agency obligations. Most of the Treasury portfolio had maturities of one year or less, whereas agency obligations were somewhat longer in maturity.

Open market operations are decided by the 12-member Federal Open Market Committee at each of its eight scheduled meetings a year. The FOMC formulates policies to purchase and sell government securities for the Open Market System Account in which all 12 Federal Reserve banks participate. The chair of the FOMC is the chair of the Board of Governors. In addition to the chair of the Board, the FOMC consists of the 6 other members of the Board, the president of the New York Federal Reserve Bank, and 4 presidents of the other 11 Federal Reserve banks chosen on a rotating basis. Given the rotating basis of 4 of the 12-member FOMC, the Board of Governors, and especially the chair of the Board, dominates the FOMC.

The FOMC meetings have become the center of monetary policy formulation for three reasons. First, open market operations are considered the most important general instrument of monetary policy for reasons discussed in the following paragraphs. Second, the other two general instruments of monetary policy—the discount mechanism and changes in reserve requirements—are either strongly influenced or are controlled by the Board. In addition, the Board also controls the only selective instruments currently available. Thus, the dominance of the Board on the FOMC brings together in one place the complete arsenal of monetary instruments available to the Federal Reserve. Third, the FOMC meetings are attended by all of the 12 Reserve Bank presidents—the 7 nonvoting presidents as well as the 5 voting presidents. Thus, the FOMC meetings bring together in one place and time key officials representing the entire System.

The FOMC's regular meetings take place in the boardroom of the Board of Governors in Washington, D.C. The meetings follow a fairly consistent set of steps:

BOX 1   Meeting of the Federal Open Market Committee

Meeting of the FOMC June 1988 when Alan Greenspan served as Chair of the Board and the FOMC. Seated around the table are the 7 governors, 12 Reserve bank presidents, secretary of the FOMC, senior advisors to the FOMC, and managers for foreign exchange and domestic operations. Other advisors (not shown) are seated around the sides of the room available to their principals if required.

Source: Provided by the Board of Governors of the Federal Reserve System. Photo by F. Harlan Hambright & Associates

1. Discussion of recent domestic and international conditions with special attention to interest rate and exchange rate movements.

2. Discussion of recent movements in the reserve and monetary aggregates, both in terms of their behavior compared to objectives set forth in the past FOMC meeting as well as in terms of future changes needed to meet goals set forth in two formal reports to Congress made in February and July.

3. The Board of Governors staff prepare three documents and circulate them to those who will attend the FOMC meeting and to others at each Federal Re-

serve bank who in turn will advise their presidents. These are described by the colors of their covers. The *green* book presents an appraisal of overall current economic conditions and forecasts future economic conditions usually based on the most recent monetary growth rate ranges adopted by the Federal Reserve. The *blue* book focuses on recent and prospective developments related to the behavior of money, credit, and interest rates. The *beige* book presents reports on regional economic conditions in each of the 12 Federal Reserve Districts.

4. Each of the 19 individuals present (12 official FOMC members and 7 nonvoting Reserve bank presidents) offers an opinion and conclusion as to the desired path of monetary policy. This is then followed by discussion of the directive that will be given to the account manager, who conducts the actual open market operations.

5. Conclusions of the FOMC are usually based on the chair's interpretation of the consensus.

6. At this point, the FOMC adopts an official policy directive to be issued to the Federal Reserve Bank of New York as the bank selected to carry out open market operations. This directive actually consists of four parts: (a) authorization for domestic open market operations, (b) domestic policy directive, (c) authorization for foreign exchange operations, and (d) a foreign currency directive.

7. A formal vote on the policy directive is taken and recorded.

The policy record for each FOMC meeting is released a few days following the next regularly scheduled FOMC meeting shortly followed by publication in the *Federal Reserve Bulletin*. In addition, the annual report of the Board of Governors contains a record of FOMC policy actions for the year.

Dynamic and Defensive Open Market Operations

The manager of the System Open Market Account conducts operations from the Trading Desk of the Federal Reserve Bank of New York according to the official directive of the FOMC. In the most general sense, the directive specifies desired levels of economic activity and money, credit, and interest rate conditions that will support the desired level of activity. This, or course, provides the manager with considerable discretionary power in terms of what operations are consistent with the directive as well as how to adjust operations for events not anticipated in the directive.

There are two general types of operations: *dynamic* and *defensive*. The difference between dynamic and defensive operations can be illustrated by the following example:

Assume the FOMC has directed the manager to increase total reserves by $10 billion each month for a three-month period. At the start of the three-month period the reserve base is $100 billion. If all the elements of the reserve equation illustrated in Table 19-2 remained constant, including the Federal Reserve's holdings of securities, the level of reserves at the end of each month would be

Month	Reserves (in billions)
1	$100
2	100
3	100

If elements other than security holdings remain constant, the manager should purchase $10 billion in securities each month. If this were accomplished, the level of reserves at the end of each month would be

Month	Reserves (in billions)
1	$110
2	120
3	130

We can think of these open market operations as dynamic since they are conducted in accordance with the directive. It is unlikely, however, that other things remain constant. The reserve equation includes many elements that impact reserves besides open market operations. For this reason, defensive operations are designed to offset anything that would cause reserves to deviate from the desired path. For example, assume that float increased by $15 billion in the first month. Instead of purchasing $10 billion in the first month, the manager would need to sell $5 billion in securities to defend the targeted base of $110 billion from the increase in float. If the manager had not adjusted operations to take float into account, the base would have increased to $125 billion in the first month.

Thus, actual open market operations include both a dynamic and defensive perspective. Defensive operations play a major role in changes in the Federal Reserve's holding of securities from week to week since many unexpected forces impact the reserve base. One should never expect to determine the direction of monetary policy by looking at open market operations at any point in time for this reason.

The concept of defensive operations also relates to the distinction between direct purchases and *repurchase agreements*. Most of the Federal Reserve's open market operations are direct purchases; however, the Federal Reserve also enters into repurchase agreements when it wants to inject reserves for a short period of time. The Federal Reserve purchases securities with the understanding that dealers will repurchase them back at a given date and given price. Repurchase agreements can range from 1 to 15 business days; however, most mature in 7 days. Premature withdrawals of repurchase agreements may also be arranged if the Federal Reserve desired to reduce reserves faster.

Impact of Open Market Operations

Open market operations have two impacts on the financial system. First, the immediate effect of a purchase (sale) of securities is to increase (decrease) the monetary base dollar for dollar. There is always someone who questions whether the Federal Reserve can buy or sell the amount of securities it desires. There is no problem, because the Federal Reserve does not conduct open market operations to make a profit and will simply bid up the price on securities to a high enough level to purchase the securities. Where does the Federal Reserve get the money? It simply "creates" the funds to purchase the securities by increasing the reserve accounts to the depository institutions involved in the transactions. Likewise, the Federal Reserve can sell any amount of securities it possesses, because it will continue to lower the price until the securities are purchased.

Second, the effect of the Federal Reserve as a net purchaser or seller of securities shifts the demand or supply function of securities in the open market and immediately affects security prices and interest rates. Once the interest rate on securities used for open market operations has been altered, the entire structure of interest rates in the financial system will be affected.

Why Are Open Market Operations So Important?

Open market operations are reflected in changes in the holdings of the Federal Reserve's securities in the reserve equation. Whether one emphasizes total reserves or the monetary base, the importance of the open market operations resides in the fact that they can be used to offset any other item influencing reserves to achieve a desired level of the reserve base within reasonable bounds. The ability to offset the movements in items not under the Federal Reserve's direct influence obviously depends on the ability to forecast the direction of movement in these items over time. In any event, the ability of the Federal Reserve to engage in open market operations gives it considerable influence over the reserve base and hence the money supply.

The Discount Mechanism

The discount mechanism is the oldest instrument of monetary policy and, at one time, was regarded as the primary instrument of monetary policy. The 1913 legislation establishing the Federal Reserve regarded the discount mechanism as the prime instrument of monetary policy. Since then, however, the role of the discount mechanism has changed significantly.

The discount mechanism involves two decisions on the part of the Federal Reserve. First, the discount rate is established by each of the 12 Federal Reserve banks and "reviewed and determined" by the Board of Governors. This means that in practice there is usually little variation among the 12 discount rates and that they are established by the Board, though the banks do have input in the process. The discount rate is the rate of interest that depository institutions must pay for borrowing from the Federal Reserve, in the form of advances or discounts. The discount rate is maintained at a level equal to or slightly above short-term rates of interest in the money market, usually Treasury bills, though this is not always easy to accomplish. The Federal Reserve can also impose a surcharge to the basic discount rate for large institutions who borrow frequently. Second, depository institutions that desire to borrow from the Federal Reserve must do so through their regional Federal Reserve bank. Borrowing is regarded as a *privilege* and not a right. Thus, the decision to say "yes" or "no" and the conditions of the loan represent the second aspect of the discount mechanism.

There are three types of borrowing from the Federal Reserve: adjustment credit, seasonal credit, and other extended credit. Adjustment credit represents about 50% of the borrowing and reflects the normal borrowing relationship between the Federal Reserve and the depository institution. According to the Federal Reserve, "appropriate reasons for adjustment borrowing include the coverage of sudden, unforeseen deposit outflows, the need to counter temporary and unexpected difficulty in obtaining funds from other sources, and, in some circumstances, the accommodation of unexpected increases in loan demand."[1]

Seasonal credit is made available to smaller institutions that can demonstrate a recurring pattern of movement in deposits and loans, such as institutions located in agricultural regions. Seasonal credit has ranged from 10 to 20% of total borrowing. Other extended credit, which increased in importance in the 1980s, is designed to meet two general types of needs: (1) institutions that are experiencing liquidity problems from circumstances unique to that institution and (2) institutions that are experiencing liquidity problems because of portfolios largely invested in long-term assets.

Impact of the Discount Mechanism

There are three aspects of the discount mechanism. First, the *cost effect* refers to the effect that changes in the discount rate have on the willingness of depository institutions to borrow from the Federal Reserve. Second, the *availability effect* refers to the decision of the regional Federal Reserve bank about the type of loan standards to apply to a borrowing institution. Increases (decreases) in the discount rate are usually associated with tighter (relaxed) loan standards. Third, changes in the discount rates are newsworthy and thus have an *announcement effect*. The announcement effect refers to the effect the announcement of a discount rate change itself has on lending, borrowing, and spending decisions.

In a tight monetary situation, the discount mechanism would involve an increase in the discount rate as well as a general tightening of the loan conditions imposed at each of the Federal Reserve banks. The increased discount rate would increase the cost of borrowing from the Federal Reserve, and the increased lending standards would reduce the availability of these funds. Both considerations would lower borrowing from the Federal Reserve and, hence, the money supply. In addition, the increase in the discount rate would be given wide news coverage signaling to the financial community and the general public that monetary policy was becoming more restrictive. If the Federal Reserve wanted to institute an easy monetary policy, the discount rate would be lowered, and standards would be relaxed, encouraging an expansion in reserves. In addition, the announcement effect would be a signal that monetary policy was becoming less restrictive.

---

[1] Board of Governors of the Federal Reserve System, *The Federal Reserve System: Purposes and Functions* (Washington, D.C.: Board of Governors, 1984), p. 60.

Selected Interest Rates

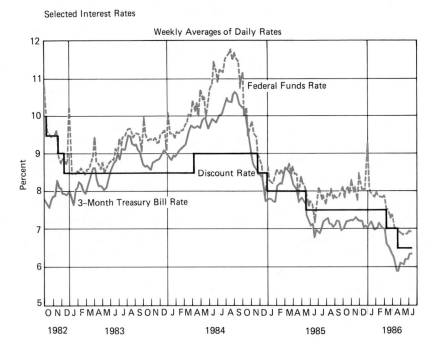

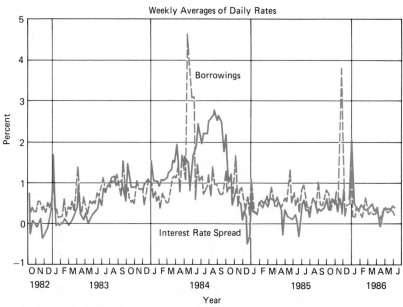

Source: Daniel L. Thornton, "The Discount Rate and Market Interest Rates: Theory and Evidence," *Review*, Federal Reserve Bank of St. Louis (August–September 1986), pp. 7, 11.

FIGURE 20-1   Interest Rates and borrowing from the Federal Reserve, October 1982–December 1985. Borrowings consist of adjustment plus seasonal borrowings.

The Discount Rate and Other Interest Rates

The traditional view of borrowing emphasized the reluctance of institutions to become indebted to the Federal Reserve; however, it is now recognized that borrowing from the Federal Reserve is regarded by depository institutions as a supplemental source of funds and is sensitive to the spread between money market interest rates and the discount rate. Figure 20-1 presents a comparison between selected interest rates and borrowings from the Federal Reserve for a recent period. As can be seen, borrowing tends to be associated positively with the spread between the Federal funds rate and the discount rate. There are restraints, however, on how much borrowing can occur. First, the Federal Reserve makes the final decision to grant a loan and changes the standards over time. In addition, repeat borrowers may be subject to a supplemental interest premium above the discount rate or have their loan application rejected. Second, depository institutions themselves may be reluctant to continue borrowing from the Federal Reserve since their large depositors may become alarmed or the depository institution anticipates an unfavorable reaction on the part of the Federal Reserve. This explains why the Federal funds rate will often rise significantly above the discount rate.

Thus, borrowing from the Federal Reserve depends on many factors, only one of which is the level of the discount rate. It is much more important to compare the discount rate with other short-term interest rates to determine the behavior of borrowing by depository institutions over time.

The reader should note the sharp increases in borrowing from the Federal Reserve for May–June 1984 and November 1985. The first spike is associated with the heavy borrowing by Continental Bank of Illinois when it was experiencing large CD withdrawals and the second spike is associated with large borrowings by the Bank of New York when it experienced a computer failure on November 21, 1985. Both episodes underlay the importance of the discount window as a lender of last resort.

Changes in Reserve Requirements

The Board has the authority to alter reserve requirements within a fairly wide range. Reserve requirements on transaction deposits are set at 3% for the first $41 million (in 1988) and can range between 8 and 14% for deposits in excess of $41 million. Requirements on transaction deposits have been set at 12%. The Board also can set requirements for nonpersonal time deposits and Eurodollars ranging from 0 to 9%. These requirements have been set at 3%. Reserve requirements imposed on transaction deposits, nonpersonal time deposits, and Eurodollars do not earn interest income.

Changes in reserve requirements shift the allocation of reserves between required and nonrequired reserves for depository institutions and thus influence their ability to expand and contract credit and the money supply. In addition to influencing the value of the money multiplier, reserve requirement changes also have an announcement effect.

Impact of the General Instruments on the Money Supply

Let us summarize the way in which each instrument functions in terms of the money multiplier framework developed in Chapter 10. Changes in the money supply depend on the value of the money multiplier, *KM*, and the change in the monetary base.

$$\Delta M = \frac{1 + k}{rt + k + rn \cdot n + e} \Delta B \tag{1}$$

Open market operations are reflected by changes in the Federal Reserve's holdings of securities. An increase in security holdings of $1 million (open market purchase) will increase the monetary base, *B*, by $1 million. A decrease in securities (open market sale) by $1 million will decrease the monetary base by $1 million. Changes in the monetary base in either case will change the money supply by a multiple amount of the change in the base.

Changes in the discount rate and/or changes in the lending policies of the Federal Reserve in making loans to depository institutions will also change the level of the base. An increase (decrease) in borrowing from the Federal Reserve will increase (decrease) the monetary base dollar for dollar.

Changes in the reserve requirement for transaction and/or other deposits will change the value of the money multiplier, *KM*. Reductions in *rt* and/or *rn* increase the value of *KM*, so that any given level of the monetary base leads to a larger money supply.

The three general instruments are used to influence total credit and money in the economy. Monetary policy is characterized as either tight or easy depending on whether policy is trying to restrain or stimulate the economy, respectively. Table 20-1 summarizes the way in which each of the general instruments would be used in tight and easy monetary policy actions.

TABLE 20-1   Use of the three general instruments in tight and easy monetary policy actions

	Monetary policy objective	
General instrument	*Tight policy*	*Easy policy*
1. Open market operations	Sell securities	Purchase securities
2. Discount mechanism	Increase discount rate; raise loan standards	Decrease discount rate; lower loan standards
3. Changes in reserve requirements	Increase reserve requirements	Decrease reserve requirements

Relative Advantages and Disadvantages
of the General Instruments

Open market operations, the discount mechanism, and changes in reserve requirements are the general instruments of monetary policy. All are capable of influencing the total amount of credit and money in the economy; however, they do not have equal efficiency as general tools of monetary policy.

Open market operations are considered the most important instrument of monetary policy and have a number of advantages unique to open market operations or shared with the other two instruments. In addition, they have none of the major disadvantages of the discount mechanism and changes in reserve requirements.

First, open market operations are under the complete control of the Federal Reserve. The initiative to buy or sell resides solely with the FOMC limited only by the amount of securities in the financial system or the amount of securities held in the Federal Reserve's portfolio. These are technical limits that have no practical bearing on the conduct of open market operations. Changes in reserve requirements are also under the control of the Federal Reserve, but the discount mechanism is only partly under the Federal Reserve's control. The Federal Reserve can change the discount rate and administer the lending policy at its own initiative, but it is up to depository institutions to make a decision to borrow from the Federal Reserve. The old saying "You can lead a horse to water, but you can't make it drink" restrains the usefulness of the discount mechanism.

Second, open market operations are flexible in that large purchases followed by large sales can be made within short periods of time. In addition, the existence of repurchase agreements allows considerable flexibility to change the monetary base for short periods of time on a regular basis. Frequent changes in the discount rate or reserve requirements would create confusion in the financial community and engender administrative problems for depository institutions.

Third, for all practical purposes open market operations possess no announcement effect. One would have to examine the reserve equation carefully over time to determine whether the Federal Reserve was making net purchases of sales of securities. Changes in the discount rate and reserve requirements have announcement effects that reduce their flexibility. For example, if the Federal Reserve errs in setting the discount rate or reserve requirement, it will be reluctant to reverse itself quickly. We must always remember that the Federal Reserve is a bureaucracy that does not want to be responsible for mistakes. If the Federal Reserve errs in open market operations, it can reverse itself quickly and without great fanfare.

The importance of no announcement effect for open market operations cannot be overemphasized. There are two major problems with announcement effects.

1. The financial community may misinterpret a technical adjustment in the discount rate or reserve requirement for a change in the stance of monetary policy. For example, the discount rate is generally maintained at a level equal to or slightly above short-term rates in the money market to discourage depository institutions from using the discount facility as a continuing source of funding; however, the discount rate is an administered rate, whereas short-

term rates are competitively determined. Short-term rates are more volatile, and it is not always possible to maintain the discount rate in the proper relationship to short-term rates. Thus, the discount rate may be adjusted from time to time to maintain the proper relationship, but, because the change is newsworthy, the financial community may interpret the change as representing a fundamental change in the stance of monetary policy.

2. Even if the announcement effect is interpreted properly by the financial community, it may have just the opposite of the desired effect. The claimed advantage of the announcement effect is to signal a change in monetary policy with the objective of encouraging spending decisions in the right direction. For example, when the Federal Reserve is moving toward tighter monetary policy, the announcement effects are intended to induce people to postpone spending decisions and create a more cautious lending environment among banks and other lending institutions. However, the announcement effect when interpreted properly could have just the opposite effect. If credit conditions are expected to tighten in the future, the decision to spend may very well move up closer in time to avoid the higher interest rates and reduced availability of credit. To this extent, the announcement has had just the opposite of the desired effect and would necessitate an even tighter monetary policy in the future.

These two problems are due to the vagueness of announcement effects in general. One economist has described the announcement effect of the discount mechanism this way:

> The truth is that changes in the discount rate constitute the crudest kind of sign language. Why this stone age form of communication should be regarded as superior to ordinary English is really quite difficult to understand. . . . There are surely other satisfactory means available, e.g., English, French, Latin, or Zulu.[2]

Fourth, in addition to the problems of the announcement effect, the discount mechanism suffers another disadvantage compared with either open market operations or changes in the reserve requirement. A given change in the discount rate, other things held constant, will lead to a change in the monetary base, but the magnitude of the relationship fluctuates over time and is not particularly large for the size of the changes usually made by the Federal Reserve. Thus the discount mechanism is probably the least powerful of the three general tools in terms of changing the base in a short period of time.

Fifth, changes in reserve requirements are very powerful, perhaps even too powerful. Even small changes in the reserve requirement have significant effects. For example, consider the value of the money multiplier based on $rt = 0.10$, $k = 0.20$, $rn = 0.03$, $n = 1.2$, and $e = 0.10$.

$$KM = \frac{1 + k}{rt + k + rn \cdot n + e} \tag{2}$$

$$= \frac{1 + 0.20}{0.10 + 0.20 + (0.03)(1.20) + 0.10} = 2.75$$

[2] Warren L. Smith, "The Instruments of General Monetary Control," *National Banking Review*, (September 1963), 47–76, especially pp. 60 and 64.

An increase in *rt* to 0.12 will cause *KM* to decline from 2.75 to 2.63, a 4.4% reduction in the money supply. In addition, frequent changes in the reserve requirement would create considerable difficulty for depository institutions, especially smaller institutions.

Current Status of the General Instruments

There is general recognition that open market operations possess a number of advantages not shared by the discount mechanism or changes in reserve requirements. Open market operations are regarded as not only being the most flexible, but they are directly controlled by the Federal Reserve, have no announcement effect, and represent a powerful instrument of monetary policy.

The discount mechanism is still regarded as a useful instrument of monetary policy. There are two views on the usefulness of the discount mechanism. One view places considerable emphasis on the discount mechanism as a method of influencing credit in the financial system. This view regards changes in the cost of credit (interest rates) and the availability of credit as an important part of the monetary policy. The view also underemphasizes the disadvantages of the announcement effect and argues that under certain conditions the change in the discount rate can be a useful supplement to general monetary policy. Another view regards the discount mechanism more as a *safety valve* or *lender of last resort* instrument than as an independent instrument of monetary policy. The existence of the borrowing facility allows depository institutions experiencing trouble to obtain funds. In this regard, the existence of the discount facility allows the Federal Reserve to be more aggressive in the use of open market operations. In the event that depository institutions experience heavy pressure from open market sales by the Federal Reserve, they can use the discount facility.

The discount mechanism has been the subject of much discussion and debate over the years. The majority of economists view the discount mechanism as playing an important safety valve function that provides an effective means for the Federal Reserve to function as a lender of last resort. At the same time, the discount mechanism is not nearly as effective as a general instrument compared with open market operations. Some economists have suggested that the discount rate be pegged slightly above a short-term interest rate such as the Treasury bill rate. In this manner, the discount mechanism could still serve as a safety valve while eliminating the problems created by announcement effects. This, of course, would preclude the Federal Reserve from actively setting the discount rate.

There is general agreement that changes in reserve requirements should not be used as a major instrument of monetary policy. They are simply too powerful, inflexible, and too blunt an instrument to employ on a continued basis. Among the suggestions for reform of the reserve requirement instrument, one group has argued that the inflexibility of reserve requirement changes prevent them from being an effective instrument of monetary policy, and, as such, they should be set at a uniform level for all depository institutions and fixed permanently. Reserve requirements of less than 100% provide the Federal Reserve with a fulcrum to control the money supply, whereas fixing them at a given level eliminates a cumbersome and inefficient instrument.

BOX 2   Federal reserve as lender of last resort—Continental Illinois National Bank and the stock market crash of October 1987

The discount mechanism is the primary way to provide lender of last resort services to the economy since it can be targeted to one or a small group of institutions. To minimize the impact of lender of last resort borrowing, the Federal Reserve can use open market operations to offset reserves provided at the discount window. Two recent examples will illustrate the importance of the discount mechanism as a critical part of being a lender of last resort.

Continental Illinois National Bank in mid-1984 was experiencing withdrawals of large CDs, especially from foreign depositors, because of growing rumors (firmly based in fact) that Continental's loan portfolio was in doubt. The FDIC arranged a bailout, which techni-

cally prevented Continental from failing. As part of this bailout, the Federal Reserve provided over $5 billion in funds at the discount window. These actions were designed to limit contagion.

The Federal Reserve responded to the stock market crash of October 1987 in a similar fashion, though the Federal Reserve's lender of last resort actions were directed toward a much larger group of institutions. On Monday, October 19, 1987, stock prices fell 22%. To allay fears of widespread financial panic, the Federal Reserve announced on Tuesday, October 20, 1987, that it stood ready to provide whatever liquidity was needed to maintain financial and economic stability.

A much smaller group led by Milton Friedman has called for the complete elimination of fractional reserves in the United States. That is, they recommend "100% banking." The argument for 100% banking is based on the view that because reserves are less than 100%, depository institutions have considerable influence over the amount of money that a given monetary base can support chiefly through their willingness to hold excess reserves. As a result, the changing values of the k ratio create considerable difficulty for the Federal Reserve in controlling the money supply. Although 100% banking has been advocated in the past, such a significant structural change in the financial system is not likely. In addition, available evidence indicates that even with the fractional reserve system, the Federal Reserve has considerable control over the money supply.

Selective Instruments of Monetary Policy

The general instruments are designed to affect the reserves or the money multiplier directly and, hence, the total amount of money and credit in the economy. The Federal Reserve on occasion has also resorted to various types of selective instruments. These are designed to influence the allocation of credit in specific sectors of the economy. Examples of selective instruments include interest rate ceilings on deposits (Regulation Q), margin requirements on the purchase of stocks or convertible bonds (Regulations T, U, G, and X), and consumer and real estate credit controls.

Each of these selective instruments has been used in the past; however, margin requirements are the only instrument currently available to the Federal Reserve. Deposit rate ceilings were phased-out as of March 31, 1986 as specified by the 1980 Deregulation and Monetary Control Act. Credit controls were last employed in 1980 under authority by the 1969 Credit Control Act; however, the Credit Control Act expired in 1982.

Margin requirements are set by the Board of Governors and specify in percentage terms the cash down payment required to purchase stocks, convertible bonds, and related instruments. Margin requirements apply to credit provided by brokers and dealers (Regulation T), banks (Regulation U), and other lenders (Regulation G) as well as to all U.S. persons who use securities credit (Regulation X). The margin requirement can vary from 0 to 100%; however, marginal requirements have been unchanged at 50% since 1974.

Margin requirements had their origin in the collapse of the financial system in the early part of the 1930s and were established by the Securities and Exchange Act of 1934.

At the time; it was believed that excessive bank credit had been used to support the speculative stock market in the late 1920s, which led subsequently to the stock market crash of 1929. The Federal Reserve argued that it was unable to restrict the amount of credit going into the stock market because it possessed only general instruments and the rest of the economy was performing at a satisfactory rate. If the Federal Reserve had introduced tight monetary policy and raised interest rates to reduce the flow of credit into the stock market, it would, at the same time, have restricted general economic activity when general restriction was not required. Hence, margin requirements were designed to give the Federal Reserve selective control over credit in the stock market.

Role of Selective Instruments

At one time the Federal Reserve placed considerable importance on selective policy instruments; however, their overall role in monetary policy has declined. Margin requirements have remained unchanged since 1974 suggesting that the Federal Reserve places a low priority on them. More importantly, the experience of the rather extensive consumer credit controls initiated March 14, 1980 and ended Summer 1980 illustrated the difficulty of selective controls.

An extensive set of controls were imposed by the Federal Reserve under the terms of the 1969 Credit Control Act to restrain the rapid growth of consumer credit that was fueling inflation. These included: "voluntary special credit restraints" to limit the growth of bank credit to 6–9%; 15% reserve requirement on increases in certain categories of consumer credit after March 14 applicable to a wide range of lenders; and other selective controls such as a special marginal reserve requirement on managed liabilities and the assets of money market mutual funds.

The impact of these extensive controls is debatable. Many observers argued that the subsequent decline in the growth of consumer credit would have occurred in the absence of the controls and in fact, the Federal Reserve dismantled the controls in June 1989 even before the administrative structure was even completely in place to implement the controls. By fall, the controls were removed. The experience highlights the basic two problems of selective controls.

First, any effort to control or restrain credit in any one sector of the financial system is likely to be circumvented by some type of financial innovation. Regulation

Q deposit rate ceilings at one time were regarded as a selective policy instrument; however, the disintermediation of the 1970s showed how easy rate ceilings could be circumvented. Trying to regulate the amount of credit going into equity markets by margin requirements is not likely to be successful because other forms of credit can be substituted for security loans. In fact, research has shown that during the period when margin requirements were changed on occasion (1934–1974), there is no relationship between margin requirement changes and stock market behavior. There is more than enough evidence to suggest that the 1980 consumer credit controls had little or no impact on the behavior of consumer credit in 1980.

Second, selective instruments require a considerable amount of administrative effort on the part of the Federal Reserve; for example, the 1980 consumer credit controls diverted a large number of Federal Reserve personnel to administer the program. By the time the administrative structure was almost complete the controls were being dismantled.

These two problems are technical in nature. There are also those who argue on more general grounds that a central bank has no business interfering with the allocation of credit. The Federal Reserve's responsibility is to control the overall growth of money and credit to maintain price stability and provide lender of last resort services on occasion. The market should determine the allocation of credit while the Federal Reserve should confine its attention to a noninflationary growth of money and credit.

Moral Suasion as an Instrument?

The Federal Reserve in the past has emphasized another instrument not mentioned so far. *Moral suasion* is a type of announcement policy designed to change the behavior of the financial community by a process of persuasion through speeches, congressional testimony, and news releases. Aside from the difficulty of classifying this as a general or selective instrument, moral suasion has all of the problems of announcement effects in general.

Key Points

1. Two sets of instruments are available to the Federal Reserve in the conduct of monetary policy. General instruments are designed to influence the money supply; selective instruments are concerned with influencing the flow of credit into certain sectors of the economy.

2. The three general instruments are open market operations, discount policy, and changes in reserve requirements. Open market operations and the discount mechanism change the monetary base directly and, hence, in a money multiplier framework, the money supply. Changes in reserve requirements change the value of the money multiplier itself.

3. Although all three instruments can change the money supply, open market operations are the only instrument over which the Federal Reserve has complete and flexible control. The

discount policy is only partly controlled by the Federal Reserve, as its effectiveness depends on the willingness of depository institutions to borrow from the Federal Reserve. Changes in reserve requirements are inflexible and limit the Federal Reserve's ability to use them as a tool of tight monetary policy given the wide range of institutions subject to reserve requirements.

4. Selective instruments have in the past included the setting of margin requirements, Regulation Q ceilings, and use of controls over consumer and real estate credit. There is considerable controversy about selective controls. Many regard them as simply unworkable because they are too easy to circumvent. Others regard them as an improper incursion of government on the allocation of credit in the economy. Margin requirements are the only selective instrument available to the Federal Reserve at this time.

5. The March 14, 1980 credit control program represents one of the few instances of the aggressive use of selective instruments.

6. Moral suasion is a form of an announcement policy with all of the problems of any announcement effect.

Key Terms

Announcement effect

Defensive open market operations

Direct open market purchases

Discount Policy

Dynamic open market operations

Federal Open Market Committee (FOMC)

General instruments of monetary policy

Lender of last resort

Margin requirements

Moral suasion

Open market operations

Policy instruments

Repurchase agreements

Reserve requirement changes

Selective instruments of monetary policy

Questions

1. Evaluate this statement: "The discount mechanism permits the Federal Reserve to be more aggressive with open market operations during periods of tight monetary policy."

2. How would pegging the discount rate to the Treasury bill rate remove announcement effects of discount rate changes?

3. Why does the Federal funds rate move above the discount rate when depository institutions have access to the discount window?

4. Does an increase in borrowing from the Federal Reserve indicate easy or tight monetary policy? Can increased borrowing be consistent with either type of policy?

5. Is the decision to borrow from the Federal Reserve a function of the level of the discount rate or the spread between the discount rate and other money market rates?

6. Explain how the discount mechanism serves the function of lender of last resort.

7. Is there any conflict between the lender of last resort function of the Federal Reserve and the goal of price stability?

8. Explain the difference between defensive and

dynamic open market operations. In what sense does the manager of the Open Market Account play a role in the conduct of monetary policy?

9. Does an increase in the discount rate signify a shift toward restrictive policy?

10. If the reserve equation in a given week indicated that the Federal Reserve's holdings of securities declined significantly over the week, would this indicate that monetary policy had become more restrictive?

Suggested Readings

1. Milton Friedman, *A Program for Monetary Stability* (New York: Fordham University Press, 1959). Discusses reforms of the instruments of monetary policy. Though dated, it is worthwhile reading since many of the arguments remain valid.

2. Gillian Garcia and Elizabeth Plautz, *The Federal Reserve: Lender of Last Resort* (Cambridge, Mass.: Ballinger, 1988). A comprehensive review of the lender of last resort responsibility of the Federal Reserve.

3. Marvin Goodfriend, "A Historical Assessment of the Rationales and Functions of Reserve Requirements," *Economic Review*, Federal Reserve Bank of Richmond (March–April 1983), 3–21.

4. David L. Mengle, "The Discount Window," *Economic Review*, Federal Reserve Bank of Richmond (May–June 1986), 2–10.

5. Robert V. Roosa, *Federal Reserve Operations in the Money and Government Securities Markets* (Federal Reserve Bank of New York, 1956). A classic discussion of the distinction between defensive and dynamic open market operations.

6. Howard L. Roth, "Federal Reserve Open Market Operations," Federal Reserve Bank of Kansas City, *Economic Review* (March 1986), 3–15.

7. Warren L. Smith, "The Instruments of General Monetary Control," *National Banking Review*, 1 (September 1963), 47–76. A dated but still useful review of the Federal Reserve's policy instrument.

8. Daniel L. Thornton, "The Discount Rate and Market Interest Rates: Theory and Evidence," *Review*, Federal Reserve Bank of St. Louis (August–September 1986), 5–19. Discusses the role of the discount rate as a determinant of market interest rates.

PART VII

Monetary Policy and Models of the Economy: Classical, Keynesian, and Extensions

CHAPTER 21

Framework for Stabilization Policy

Chapter Overview

It is now time to start a formal discussion of the conduct of monetary policy. First, this involves a review of several models of economic activity that help us to understand how monetary policy impacts the economy, and second, this involves a detailed review of the Federal Reserve's actual operating procedures and various problems facing the actual conduct of monetary policy.

This chapter introduces the concept of a macroeconomic model that, as illustrated in Figure 17-1, plays a part in the sequence of steps that describe the conduct of stabilization policy. This chapter has two objectives: first, to develop a clear notion of the purpose of an economic model and to elaborate on the role of an economic model in the overall sequence of stabilization policy introduced in Chapter 17 and, second, to briefly review the historical evolution of economic models and their implications for monetary policy. This overview will help the reader keep some perspective as we consider in detail the formal models in the following chapters.

Following this introduction, Chapters 22 through 26 focus on the various models of monetary policy. After reviewing the major models used to understand how monetary policy influences the economy and the type of monetary policy that will most effectively contribute to economic stabilization, we will then be in a position to consider the actual operating procedures of the Federal Reserve. In this regard, several important policy issues regarding the conduct of monetary policy can be discussed. These will be discussed in Chapters 27 through 29.

Concept of an Economic Model

An economic model is a collection of relationships among economic variables; however, models can also include noneconomic variables. These relationships summarize how the level of economic activity is determined as measured by output, employ-

481

ment, prices, interest rates, and so on. There are two important classifications of economic variables for understanding stabilization policy in general and monetary policy in particular. First, there are *endogenous variables*—variables whose numerical values the model is designed to explain and determine. Then, there are *exogenous variables*—variables whose numerical values are determined outside the model. These influence the outcome of the model but whose value we take as given. Exogenous variables that are under the influence of the stabilization authorities are called *policy instruments*. The policy instruments of the Federal Reserve include open market operations, the discount mechanism, and changes in reserve requirements that can be used to influence the money supply, credit, and interest rates. The instruments of fiscal policy include changes in taxes and government expenditures.

A model has three purposes. First, it indicates the equilibrium condition of the economy for a given value of the exogenous variables. Equilibrium is defined as a state of "no net tendency to change." That is, as long as the model is not disturbed (there are no changes in the exogenous variables), the endogenous variables remain constant. Why be so concerned about equilibrium, especially when the exogenous variables are always subject to change in the real world? Equilibrium is an important concept in economics because it indicates the direction in which the economy is moving at any point in time.

Second, an economic model is a system response mechanism that shows how the endogenous variables (measure of general economic activity) will respond to changes in the exogenous variables. Some of the exogenous variables are under the direct influence of the fiscal and monetary authorities. Thus, the model can indicate the relationship between the policy instruments and the level of economic activity.

Third, the model forms the basis for constructing an *econometric* model. An econometric model consists of statistical estimates of the model relationships. Once we have estimates of the model, they can be used for forecasting and simulation purposes under a variety of assumptions about the exogenous variables. Using econometric models for forecasting and simulation probably comes about as close as economics can get to laboratory-type experiments.

Economic Models for Stabilization Policy

There is considerable debate among economists and policymakers regarding the most appropriate model for monetary policy. Historically, views have ranged from models that emphasize market stability to views emphasizing market instability. Even among activist models, there has been debate over the relative importance of monetary and fiscal policy instruments. While we understand a great deal more about the economy than even a few decades ago and we are armed with sophisticated theoretical, mathematical, and statistical tools; no one model framework can be said to dominate current thinking. Thus, we are forced to consider different models with different implications for monetary policy.

There are two basic or foundation models to be considered: the *classical* or *quantity theory of money* and the *Keynesian* models. The classical model dominated economic and policy views prior to the Great Depression while the origin and widespread acceptance of the Keynesian model is rooted in the events of the Great Depression period.

While the past few decades have witnessed a number of new developments referred to as *monetarism, rational expectations, real business cycle theories, supply-side economics, information-based models,* and *micro-focused labor market models,* these and other similar developments share two common elements. First, each is essentially an extension of one of the foundation models in terms of underlying theory and methodology while, at the same time, retaining the same view of the market and the role of government stabilization policy. Second, most of the developments have focused on a well-known relationship between inflation and unemployment, referred to as the *Phillips curve* and, thus, will be discussed in that context (Chapter 26).

The classical and Keynesian models differ in three fundamental ways:

1. Each holds opposing views about the ability of market forces to return the economy to its natural or long-run growth path whenever the actual level of real output is pushed above or below potential real output. The classical view assumes that prices and wages are sufficiently flexible to keep the actual path of real output close to the potential or natural level. In contrast, the Keynesian view assumes that wage and price adjustments cannot be relied upon to return the economy to full employment. Either some prices are fixed, or more likely, price and wage adjustments are so sluggish that waiting for their effects to take place brings to mind Keynes's comment that "we are all dead in the long run."

2. Each holds opposing views about the stability of total spending. Keynesian models emphasize instability in various components of total spending, especially business investment, that generate economic fluctuations, while classical models emphasize stability in the components in total spending. Even if components of spending are unstable, classical models rely on flexible wage and price adjustments to prevent long-run departures from the potential level of output over time.

3. Each holds opposing views about the type of government stabilization policy most likely to contribute to economic stability. The classical view adopts a nonactivist approach, while in contrast, the Keynesian view adopts an activist approach.

Evolution of the Classical and Keynesian Views

The classical or quantity theory dominated economic thinking prior to the Great Depression. It emphasized the inherent stability of a market system. Wage and price adjustments would ensure that actual output would grow at the potential level determined by the economy's resource base and technology. Government policy should be nonactivist. Specifically, fiscal policy should operate with a balanced budget. Monetary policy should be concerned with a steady noninflationary monetary growth rate and with ensuring a stable financial environment via regulation and providing lender of last resort services.

The classical model did not, however, hold that the market system would achieve complete stability over time. Economic fluctuations were still possible. It did, however, emphasize the ability of wage and price adjustments to restore equilibrium smoothly once the economy had been pushed away from its normal growth path. Beyond stable monetary growth and balanced budgets, there was no need for government stabilization policy.

The classical model was rejected by economists as a result of events during the Great Depression. The classical emphasis on the inherent stability and smooth adjustment of the economy back to the natural growth path appeared grossly inconsistent with the prolonged collapse of the economy in the 1930s. The classical emphasis on a nonactivist stance for government policy also appeared unacceptable for dealing with the social and economic problems caused by the Great Depression. To paraphrase Keynes, we live in the short run and die in the long run—the type of unemployment experienced in the 1930s could not be tempered by informing unemployed workers that the economy will eventually equilibrate at full employment. The classical model, however, returned in the form of *monetarism* during the 1960s. In fact, the discussions that led to the reemergence of the classical view are referred to as the *monetarist-Keynesian* debate. The term "monetarism" was based on the key role assigned to money as a determinant of economic activity; nonetheless, it was a logical extension of classical economics.

The Keynesian model had already been in a development stage in the 1920s; however, the events of the Great Depression brought the framework into the forefront. The model seemed so consistent with the events and offered solutions that seemed so reasonable that the Keynesian model rapidly displaced the classical model. In fact, the displacement was so rapid that the acceptance of the model by economists in the 1940s and 1950s is referred to as the *Keynesian revolution*. The Keynesian model emphasized the inherent instability of the market, the possibility of permanent unemployment, and the need for government to take an activist role to achieve the goals of economic stabilization.

The early Keynesian model had two major characteristics. First, the model assumed the existence of various rigidities in the ability of wage and price adjustments to return the economy to full employment equilibrium as envisaged by the classical model. Specifically, the Keynesian model assumed that prices were flexible in both directions but that wages were fixed in a downward direction. No detailed explanation was offered to explain rigid wages; however, such an assumption generated a model much different than the classical model.

Second, the nature of key relationships in the model rendered fiscal policy the most effective activist instrument. Monetary policy was largely ineffective.

The Keynesian model has experienced modification in regard to these two characteristics partly as a result of the monetarism-Keynesian debate. First, economists now recognize that simply assuming wages fixed in a downward direction is not sufficient and generates models that are less than complete. Actually, recent years have shown that there does exist wage and price flexibility, though in the opinion of many, not to the degree assumed in the classical model. Emphasis has now shifted to explaining why wage and price adjustments might occur slowly over time and, thus, still provide a rationalization for activist policy.

Second, monetary policy has become the major instrument of activist policy within the Keynesian framework while fiscal policy is now regarded as relatively ineffective. As a leading Keynesian economist once said, "money is too important to be left to the monetarists!"

Despite the rethinking and extensions of the Keynesian model, the basic message of the original Keynesian model remains much the same as when it was originally introduced in the 1930s. A market economy is not likely to achieve the goals of economic stabilization on its own, and thus, government has the right and responsibility to use monetary or any other effective stabilization instrument to achieve these goals, though modern Keynesian-oriented models offer less of an activist role for monetary policy than was advocated several decades ago.

Political Models of Economic Activity

The classical and Keynesian views and their various extensions focus on the relationships between economic agents concerned with maximizing behavior and how these relationships generate an overall level of economic activity. Political institutions are generally held constant in these models reflecting the economists concern with "objective" issues.

The past decade has witnessed an alternative approach to modeling economic activity and the role that monetary policy plays that emphasizes the relationship between political institutions and macroeconomic performance. These models are referred to as *political business cycle* models. They adopt the same type of economic relationships common to the more "objective" models; however, they focus on political relationships between the administration and/or Congress and the agents of stabilization, especially the Federal Reserve. A common characteristic of these models is that the Federal Reserve becomes a willing partner to the wishes of the administration and/or Congress to manage the economy in order to maximize and solidify political power.

These models are still in a development stage and no consensus has evolved; however, they add an additional and important element to our understanding of the conduct of monetary policy.

Why So Many Models?

A natural question arises. Why so many models? Why haven't economists, armed with sophisticated mathematical and statistical tools, been able to develop a set of relationships that adequately describe the economy? The answer is far more complex than attributing the large variety of models to a sadistic desire to make life difficult for the student. In fact, life is difficult for the economist!

It is too early to even attempt an answer to this question. It is merely brought up at this introductory stage to warn the student that considerable debate exists among economists about the appropriate model of the economy. Perhaps the reader will try to answer the question as he or she works through the next several chapters. At the end of the discussion of the formal models, we will attempt to offer some explanation as to why there is so much difference of opinion.

Key Points

1. Economic models consist of relationships among exogenous and endogenous variables, determine the equilibrium level of economic activity, and can be used to understand how monetary policy and fiscal policy influence the economy. A subset of exogenous variables is under the control of the stabilization authorities and are referred to as policy instruments.

2. Economic models provide information on how monetary and fiscal policy influence the economy and, likewise, the proper type of policies required to achieve economic stabilization.

3. There are two foundation models: classical and Keynesian. Classical models emphasize the inherent stability of a market and the nonactivist responsibilities of government policy. In contrast, Keynesian models emphasize the inherent instability of a market and the resulting need for activist policies. A number of new and important modeling developments in recent years can be regarded as extensions of each of the two foundation models.

4. A relatively recent development departs from the traditional economic model by incorporating relationships between political institutions and economic performance that help to understand how the level of economic activity is determined and how monetary policy decisions are made. The political business cycle literature is new and not universally accepted, but appears to add some important insights into the conduct of monetary policy.

5. The variety of models forces us to explain why so much debate remains among economists despite the awesome array of analytical and computer tools. Discussion of this issue is postponed to Chapter 26 after we finish the review of the formal models for monetary policy.

Key Terms

Agents of stabilization

Economic model

Endogenous variables

Exogenous variables

Classical (quantity theory of money) model

Keynesian model

Monetarism

Policy instruments

Policy targets

Political business cycle model

Questions

1. Is it possible that economic models give us a false sense of precision concerning what we know about the economy?

2. Economic models are designed to indicate the equilibrium state of the endogenous variables given values of the exogenous variables. In reality, however, exogenous variables are constantly changing; thus, economic models are useless because equilibrium is never achieved. Comment on this statement.

3. Since economic models can be roughly categorized as to whether they advocate activist or

nonactivist approaches to government stabilization, is there a relationship between one's political values and choice of model?

4. The Keynesian model emerged from the events of the Great Depression. To what extent, if any, do current events influence one's choice of an economic model?

5. Along the same lines as question 4, do we vote for or against a model as an explanation of how the economy works? That is, does any model that captures the attention of economists and policymakers win by default?

Suggested Readings

The following chapters will provide extensive references on the material introduced in this chapter; therefore, only a few references are provided at this point.

1. Mark Blaug, *Economic Theory in Retrospect* (London: Cambridge University Press, 1985). A detailed discussion of the emergence and development of economic modeling from both a micro and macro perspective.

2. Robert L. Heilbroner, *The Worldly Philosophers* (New York: Simon & Schuster, 1972). An easy-to-read guide to the development of economic modeling. Does a good job of explaining how the activist approach to policy emerged.

3. Jan Tinbergen, *On the Theory of Economic Policy* (Amsterdam: North-Holland, 1952), and *Economic Policy: Principles and Design* (Amsterdam: North-Holland, 1967). Discusses the role of economic models in formulating economic policy.

CHAPTER 22

The Pre-Great Depression Classical or Quantity Theory View

Chapter Overview

This chapter commences our discussion of the formal models of monetary policy by considering the classical or quantity theory of money view as it existed prior to the Great Depression of the 1930s.

The classical model and the quantity theory of money are essentially one and the same, though each focuses on different aspects of market behavior. Thus, whenever we refer to either the classical or quantity theory model, the other model is implied.

This chapter presents the basic outline of the classical model and its implications for government stabilization policy prior to the Great Depression period. The discussion is divided into two parts based on the two sectors analyzed separately by the classical model: the money sector and the commodity or real sector. The economy is in overall equilibrium when the demand and supply for commodities are equal and at the same time, the demand and supply for money are equal.

The classical model employs the quantity theory of money to describe the money sector, how equilibrium between the supply and demand for money is achieved, and how the overall price level is determined. The commodity sector incorporates the market mechanism in the context of flexible prices and wages to determine the level of real output and how the economy equilibrates at full employment.

The chapter has four objectives.

The first is to describe the quantity theory of money from the perspective of what determines the public's desire to hold a given stock of money. In this regard, we discuss the two major versions of the quantity theory referred to as the *transactions* and the *Cambridge* version. The quantity theory will then be summarized in terms of the concept of *aggregate demand*—a modern concept that will help us to understand the classical view of the economy and the proper role for government stabilization.

The second objective is to turn our attention to the commodity side of the economy and show how flexible wages and prices generate a full-employment equilibrium. The commodity sector will be summarized in terms of the concept of *aggregate supply*.

Third, we bring together aggregate demand and supply to illustrate the implications of the classical model for stabilization policy in general and monetary policy in particular.

Fourth, we indicate how the events of the Great Depression led to the rejection of the classical model and its implications for government stabilization policy.

Monetary Side of the Economy

The classical model's view of the demand and supply of money is rooted in the development of the quantity theory of money, which experienced two major developments prior to the Great Depression. The transactions version emphasized the concept of *velocity* rather than the *demand for money* and, thus, limited our perspective of how the demand for money was determined. Economists at Cambridge University, chiefly Alfred Marshall, reformulated the quantity theory to consider money explicitly as something the public demanded to hold and provided a framework that made it possible to see the effects of the money supply in terms of the demand and supply concepts. Ironically, it was the Cambridge version of the quantity theory that provided an important building block for the Keynesian model.

Fisher's Transactions Version

Irving Fisher, one of America's most famous economists, is generally credited with the transactions version of the quantity theory of money, although one can find statements of the theory by Bodin in 1568, Henry Thornton in 1802, David Ricardo in 1821, and others. Fisher brought all the different elements of the quantity theory together and expressed them in a simple form.[1]

The quantity theory expresses the relationship between money, velocity, transactions or output, and the price level. The relationship among these variables can be expressed in terms of either an *identity* or *behavioral relationship*. An identity is true by definition while a behavioral relationship only holds true under certain conditions. Another way to state the same point is to say that an identity is always consistent with the facts while a behavioral relationship is only consistent with the facts under certain conditions. Early writers often failed to distinguish between the quantity theory as an identity and a behavioral or economic model and, as such, created much confusion in the literature.

The identity version of the quantity theory is referred to as the *equation of*

[1] Irving Fisher, *The Purchasing Power of Money* (New York: Augustus M. Kelley, 1963).

exchange, and to indicate the identity nature of the relationship, the symbol "≡" is employed.

$$MV \equiv TP_T \tag{1}$$

where

$$
\begin{aligned}
M &= \text{the money supply} \\
V &= \text{the transactions velocity of money} \\
T &= \text{total real transactions in the economy} \\
P_T &= \text{the price level at which the real transactions took place}
\end{aligned}
$$

Total transactions include all expenditures in the economy, whether they were made for final output of goods and services or for intermediate products or any other type of expenditure that might not be included in the real GNP. Thus, T would exceed real GNP by the amount of expenditures on activities that are not regarded as final output.

Expression (1) is an identity. A moment's thought will indicate why. The total amount of expenditures, T, times the price level at which the expenditures took place, P_T, must equal the amount of money, M, times the turnover rate or velocity of money, V. The equation of exchange must always hold no matter what the level of economic activity.

Many writers modified the equation of exchange by substituting the level of real output of final goods and services for T and the price level of final goods and services for P_T. Expression (1) is then

$$MV \equiv yP \tag{2}$$

where

$$
\begin{aligned}
M &= \text{the money supply} \\
V &= \text{the income velocity of money} \\
y &= \text{real GNP} \\
P &= \text{the GNP deflator}
\end{aligned}
$$

Expression (2) is also an identity. It expresses a relationship between important macroeconomic variables but does not imply causation from one variable to another and holds true under all conditions. For example, an increase in M by 10% must be accompanied by offsetting changes in V, y, or P. The 10% increase in M with a constant V could be associated with a 20% increase in y and a 10% decrease in P or some other combination of changes in V, y, or P. However, the equation as it stands offers no theory of how one variable influences the other variables.

The equation is transformed into a theory or behavioral relationship by imposing additional information on the variables. First, V and y in the long run are independent of changes in the money supply. Second, the change in the money supply causes a change in the price level. Third, V changes slowly over time and can be regarded as either stable or fixed in the long run. Fourth, the growth of capital, labor, and technology combined with flexible ways and prices increase the level of y over time along a full-employment or natural growth path. The competitive market ensures that the long-run equilibrium value of y is at full employment (Say's law of markets). Fifth, it is important to distinguish between the short and long run when analyzing the impact of changes in the money supply on the level of economic activity.

To emphasize the behavioral nature of the equation, the symbol "$\equiv$" is replaced by "$=$." Thus, the equation becomes a statement of the long-run equilibrium relationship between M, V, y, and P.

$$MV = yP \qquad (3)$$

The level of y is independent of M, V, and P in the long run, and flexible wages and prices will ensure that competition maintains output at the potential or full-employment level. It is important to keep in mind that the quantity theory is a theory about the long-run equilibrium relationship between key macroeconomic variables. While the theory has a short-run version (discussed later in the chapter), expression (3) needs to be first considered as a description of the long-run or normal performance level of the economy.

The level of M is determined by the type of monetary system. Under current institutional arrangements, the central bank controls the money supply.

Velocity of money, V, represents the rate of utilization of money, that is, how fast or how many times money changes hands during a period of time in carrying out transactions. (Velocity is defined by the relationship between the amount of money held by the public and income, $V = yP/M$ or $1/V = M/yP$.) Early quantity theorists regarded V as stable or even fixed because it was assumed to be dependent on institutional factors that changed little over time. The amount of money held by the public relative to income (velocity) depended basically on the payments system in the economy with regard to frequency, regularity, and correspondence between receipts and expenditures. Other factors such as the density of population and the development of the transportation system also influenced the amount of money held by the public. All these factors were regarded as slow to change.

The quantity theory at this stage of development did not associate velocity directly with the demand for money, even though the association was recognized on occasion. In Chapter 5, we developed this association and showed that velocity and money demand are two sides of the same coin. Increases (decreases) in velocity are reflected by decreases (increases) in the demand for money. While the relationship between velocity and demand for money became an important part of the Cambridge and modern approaches to the quantity theory, the early theory emphasized velocity almost exclusively. The early quantity theory viewed money primarily as a medium of exchange, and thus money had usefulness only in terms of bridging the gap between receipts and expenditures, and individuals held money only to satisfy transaction motives. Velocity (demand for money) was not so much a variable to be determined by economic behavior as it was a variable determined by society's money-using institutions. Thus, the early quantity theory was concerned only that the supply of money was sufficient, given velocity, to support economic activity.

The price level, P, was regarded as the passive variable that took on whatever value was required to satisfy expression (3) since the other variables were determined by forces independent of the price level in the long run. Velocity was determined by the institutions of the payments system, money was determined by the central bank, and output was determined by competition at the full employment level. To illustrate, assume $M = \$1,000$, $V = 5.0$, and $y = \$4,000$; then P would necessarily be 1.25, expressed as an index to some base period at which $P = 1.00$.

The quantity theory emphasized that the price level was dependent on the money supply in the long run since V and y were determined independently of P and M. The proportional relationship between prices and money was one of the most important conclusions of the quantity theory. The fact that changes in money only impacted the price level in the long run is referred to as the *neutrality of money* characteristic of the quantity theory. The neutrality of money was a long-run characteristic of the quantity theory that did not hold true in the short run. In the short run, changes in the money supply could influence V and y as well as P; however, the effects on V and y were transitory. Once the economy adjusted to the change in the money supply, only the price level, P, would be affected while V and y would return to their respective long-run values.

There is one final point we should consider before leaving the transactions version of the quantity theory. Expression (3) states the theory in static terms; that is, the variables are considered in levels rather than changes over time. We can restate the theory in dynamic terms:

$$\%\Delta M + \%\Delta V = \%\Delta y + \%\Delta P \tag{4}$$

Now, the theory implies that the percentage change in velocity and real output are independent of the percentage change in the money supply and price level. Thus, a 5% increase in the growth of money will eventually generate a 5% increase in the rate of price change or inflation.

Cambridge Version

The Fisher version viewed money primarily as a medium of exchange held to bridge the gap between receipts and expenditures. Velocity was then determined by institutional arrangements. The Cambridge version viewed money as an asset to be held for economic reasons and expressed the quantity theory in a form that highlighted the fact that people actually make an economic decision to hold more or less money in relationship to their income. This decision to hold money depended on economic variables as well as on institutions associated with using money. This version of the quantity theory is referred to as the Cambridge approach because it was developed by economists at Cambridge University, especially Alfred Marshall.[2]

The Cambridge version is algebraically identical to the Fisher version but much different in that the emphasis is placed on the concept of a demand for money. The Cambridge version expresses the demand for money as a proportion of nominal income.

$$DM = kyP \tag{5}$$

where $k = 1/V$.

[2] Alfred Marshall, *Money Credit and Commerce* (London: Macmillan, 1924).

The basic difference between expressions (5) and (3) resides in the expression of the demand for money as a fraction of the level of income. The Cambridge version makes use of traditional supply and demand analysis to understand how changes in money affect economic activity. According to the Cambridge version, the economy is in equilibrium when the supply of money is equal to the demand for money

$$MS = DM = kyP \tag{6}$$

whereas the Fisher version states that the economy is in equilibrium when

$$MV = yP \tag{7}$$

However, M is the money supply and in equilibrium will be the same as the demand and supply for money in the Cambridge version. We can replace M with MS in expression (7) and divide both sides by V and end up with the Cambridge version.

$$
\begin{aligned}
(MS)V &= yP \\
\frac{(MS)V}{V} &= \frac{yP}{V}, \text{ and letting } k = \frac{1}{V} \\
MS &= kyP \\
MS &= DM = kyP
\end{aligned}
\tag{8}
$$

The differences are more in methodology than in basic results, as the Cambridge version also used Say's law of markets to argue that y would be at the full-employment level in the long run and that k, the reciprocal of velocity, was stable (fixed) and independent of the money supply. In the long run, divergence between money demand and supply was eliminated by changes in the price level. To illustrate, the demand for money would be $100 billion, assuming a level of nominal income (yP) equal to $400 billion and a value of $k = 0.25$. There would be excess money demand if the money supply were $50 billion, and equilibrium would be achieved only when the price level declined so that nominal income was $200 billion. As long as k remained constant, the Cambridge version yielded the same proportional relationship between the money supply and the price level in the long run, since y would be at the full-employment level via flexible prices and wages. In the long run, changes in the money supply induced equal changes in the price level, while k and y remained at their long-run values. Thus, the neutrality of money result was also part of the Cambridge approach.

There are three significant differences between the Cambridge and Fisher versions of the quantity theory. (1) The Cambridge version emphasized the demand for money rather than submerging the demand for money in the velocity concept. (2) The Cambridge version expressed monetary theory in terms of demand and supply concepts so that changes in economic activity result from a divergence between the demand for and supply of money. (3) The Cambridge version expressed the demand for money as k times the level of income. Once the demand for money was expressed in this form, we start to move away from regarding the demand for money, k, as fixed. The parameter k itself could depend on economic variables. Changes in k could change the level of real economic activity in the short run independently of changes in the money supply as well as influence the relationship between money and prices in the long run. The proportional relationship between money and prices depended on the stability of velocity or k. The Cambridge version suggested that k as a behavioral variable may not be stable.

The Cambridge version promised significant improvement over the earlier transactions version of the quantity theory; however, it was expressed most often in terms of a fixed value of k. In this way, the Cambridge version merely became an alternative algebraic expression of the earlier view. It was left to Keynes, a student of Marshall, to extend the Cambridge version into a more complete theory of the demand for money. Ironically, the Keynesian demand for money in turn provided much of the foundation for the modern approach to the quantity theory of money.

Classical Quantity Theory of Money and Aggregate Demand

The Cambridge version represented the most advanced stage of development of the classical quantity theory. Thus, we will use this version to illustrate the concept of an *aggregate demand function* in the classical framework. The concept of aggregate demand is a modern device not available to the classical economists but one that will help us to understand more clearly the classical model as well as differences between it and the Keynesian model. The aggregate demand function expresses the relationship between the price level, P, and the demand for real output, y. Let us now see how the Cambridge equation can be utilized to derive the aggregate demand function.

Equilibrium in the money market exists when the supply of money equals the demand for money at a given level of real output. The level of real output is determined in the commodity market and, hence, taken as given in determining equilibrium in the money market. This means that the price level must adjust to equate the demand and supply for money. Figure 22-1 illustrates how the price level is determined by equilibrium in the money market. The Cambridge equation is expressed by line LL. At a given level of nominal income, $(Py)_o$, the demand for money is MD_o given the value of k. If the money supply is MS_o, then the money market is in equilibrium. Keep in mind that y is assumed constant since it is determined in the commodity market; hence the only way in which changes in nominal income can occur are through changes in the price level.

Assume that the money supply increases to MS_1. At the previous level of income, $(Py)_o$, there is now an excess supply of money. Individuals will spend the excess supply on commodities, which in turn will increase the price level. Remember that y is assumed constant; hence, nominal income increases because prices increase. When the price level increases in the same proportion as the money supply, nominal income will increase from $(Py)_o$ to $(Py)_1$. At this level of income, the demand for money increases from MD_o to MD_1 and the money market is back in equilibrium. Thus, the money market determines the price level at which demand and supply for money are equal, and there exists a direct relationship between money and prices.

Once the money market has achieved equilibrium and there are no changes in the supply of money or k, the level of nominal income and, hence, the price level

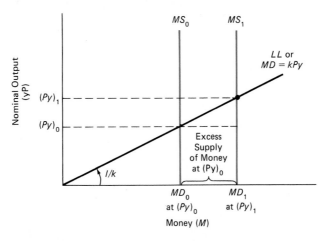

FIGURE 22-1   The money market in terms of the
Cambridge version of the quantity theory

are constant. Let us now consider what will happen if the level of output changes. Since (Py) is constant when the money market is in equilibrium, an increase (decrease) in y must be accompanied by a decrease (increase) in P. This can be illustrated by rewriting the Cambridge equation in the following way

$$P = \frac{M}{ky} \qquad (9)$$

where M represents the level of money at which $MS = MD$. As long as the money supply and k remain constant, there exists an inverse relationship between P and y. This relationship is the aggregate demand function (Figure 22-2) that shows an inverse relationship between the price level and real output. Or in terms of words, the quantity of real output demanded increases as the price level decreases.

Changes in M and/or k will shift the aggregate demand function. Figure 22-3 indicates the effect of an increase in the money supply or decrease in k. In both cases, at every level of y, a higher level of P will be required to maintain equilibrium in the money market.

Commodity Sector of the Classical Model

Implicit in both the transactions and Cambridge versions of the quantity theory is the view that the level of real output, y, will be at the full-employment level in the long run because of flexible wages and prices. It is now time to consider this point more closely, and in doing so, we can then construct the classical *aggregate supply function*. The aggregate supply function illustrates the relationship between the supply of real output and the price level.

The price level is determined in the money market; that is, the quantity theory of money provides the price level that would equate the demand and supply for

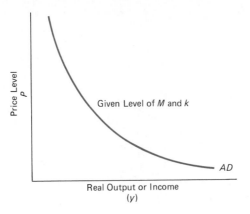

FIGURE 22-2   The quantity theory of money and aggregate demand

money. Equilibrium in the commodity market can be illustrated by taking this price level as a given. Assume that the price level determined in the money market with a money supply of MS_o is denoted by P_o. With this in mind, let us now see how employment and real output are determined. Figure 22-4 illustrates the classical view of the commodity market. In panel A, the demand and supply for labor depend on the real wage rate, that is, the nominal wage, W, divided by the price level, P. Decisions to demand labor are based on the real cost of labor as are decisions to supply labor effort; however, the actual bargaining between workers and employers is over the nominal wage because this is subject to negotiation while the overall price level is not. Nonetheless, it is the real wage rate that is of concern to both employers and workers. The labor market is in equilibrium when the quantity of labor demanded equals the quantity of labor supplied at the going wage rate, W_o. Given the price level P_o already determined in the money market, the equilibrium real wage rate is then $(W_o/P_o)_o$. Why? If nominal wages were higher than W_o, the real wage rate would be above $(W_o/P_o)_o$ and as a result there would be an excess supply of labor (unemployment above the natural level). Competition would bid down the nominal

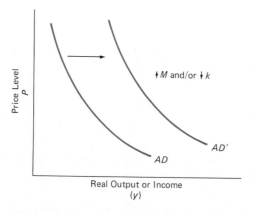

FIGURE 22-3   Shift in aggregate demand

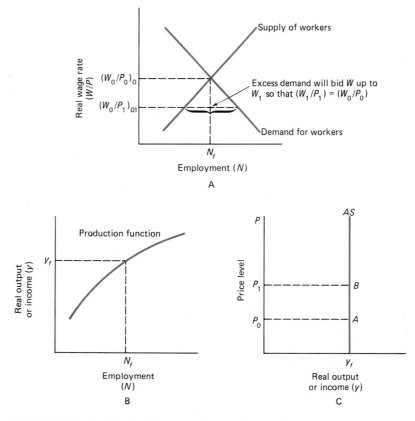

FIGURE 22-4 Classical commodity market and the aggregate supply function

wage rate until the excess supply of labor was eliminated. If nominal wages were lower than W_o, competition would force nominal wages up until the excess demand for labor was eliminated. At the real wage rate, $(W_o/P_o)_o$ then, the labor market is in equilibrium at employment level N_f. Keep in mind that full employment does not mean a zero unemployment rate, and while not reflected in Figure 22-4, the full-employment position actually means that actual unemployment equals the natural unemployment rate.

Panel B illustrates the production function for the economy, which shows how much real output can be produced with employment at N_f. The production function shows how the output of commodities varies as employment varies given the economy's capital stock, land resources, and technology. The function is drawn to incorporate diminishing returns to labor; that is, as additional amounts of labor are utilized, real output increases at a decreasing rate. Given the full-employment level of employment, N_f, determined in the labor market, the output of commodities is y_f. Again, we think of this level of output as the full employment, natural, or potential output of the economy.

We can now begin to construct the aggregate supply function in Panel C of Figure 22-4. We already have the equilibrium price level, P_o, and output, y_f. This provides us with one point on the supply function (point A). To get another point, we simply determine the equilibrium in the commodity market at a different price level.

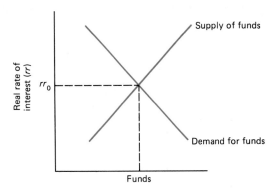

FIGURE 22-5   The financial system in the classical model

Assume a price level P_1 that exceeds P_0. As Panel A indicates, a higher price level will lower the real wage to $(W_0/P_1)_{o1}$ assuming money wages have not changed. There is now an excess demand for labor and competition will ensure that money wages are bid up. How much will money wages increase? They must increase in the same proportion as the price level to return the real wage rate to the equilibrium level. The higher money wage rate is denoted as W_1. When this occurs, the real wage rate will be the same as before but wages and prices will both be higher. Thus, the price level P_1 is associated with the same level of real output as before, which is indicated as point B in Panel C.

The classical aggregate supply function is thus a vertical line at the full-employment (natural unemployment or potential output) level of y. Competition and flexible wages and prices ensure that the full employment output is not influenced by the price level in the long run.

Saving, Investment, and the Financial System in the Classical Model

The classical model developed so far omits a financial system. It considers only one financial asset—money used to purchase commodities. However, the model can be easily extended to consider financial assets representing lending and borrowing activity. In this manner, we can recognize that output is produced for both consumption and investment.

Figure 22-5 illustrates one version of the financial system in the classical model that is essentially a *loanable funds* model of the interest rate discussed in Chapter 5. The demand for funds reflects desired investment activity and is inversely related to the real rate of interest. The supply of funds reflects desires to save that are positively related to the real rate of interest. In addition, the supply of funds can be influenced by changes in the money supply.

The real rate of interest is determined by the demand and supply for loadable funds. In equilibrium, the real rate determines the composition of total output between consumption and investment output, but not the level of output. Thus, the

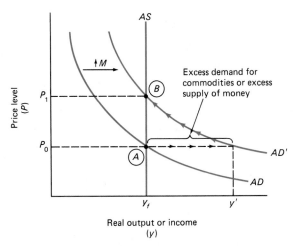

FIGURE 22-6   Effects of an increase in the money supply

existence of saving, investment, lending, and borrowing presents no problem in the classical model since the interest rate brought the financial system into equilibrium.

The real rate is not observed in the market; however, the real rate and the nominal rate will be the same in equilibrium if prices are constant. The following expresses the relationship between nominal and real interest rates

$$\text{Nominal interest rate} = \text{real interest rate} + \text{anticipated inflation} \qquad (10)$$

In the static equilibrium form of the classical model considered at this point, equilibrium requires a constant price level. As such, inflation and anticipations of inflation are zero, rendering the nominal and real rates of interest identical.

Impact of Changes in the Money Supply

We can employ the aggregate demand and supply functions to illustrate the effects of changes in the money supply in the classical model. In a sense, we have already done this in our discussion of the Fisher and Cambridge versions of the quantity theory. We saw that changes in the money supply only impacted the price level in the long run. We can use the demand and supply functions to illustrate this more clearly, however. In addition, we will also be in a position to differentiate between the short- and long-run effects of changes in the money supply.

Figure 22-6 illustrates the short- and long-run effects of an increase in the money supply. Assume the economy is initially in equilibrium at P_o and y_f (point A). An increase in the money supply shifts the aggregate demand function to the right. At the initial equilibrium price level, there is now excess demand for commodities that is matched by an excess supply of money in the money market. The excess supply of money and excess demand for commodities sets into motion a number of events that eventually will return the economy to a new equilibrium position indicated by the intersection of the new aggregate demand function (AD') and the aggregate supply function (point B). That is, once all the adjustments have been completed, the higher money supply will generate a higher price level, P_1; however, the level of real output will remain at the full employment level, N_f. What about money wages? Money wages will also increase in the same proportion as the price level in order to maintain equilibrium in the labor market at full employment; thus, the real wage rate will remain at the level that equates demand and supply for labor. What about interest rates? Once all adjustments are completed and the price level settles at the higher level, the absence of inflation means that the nominal and real interest rates will be identical and the real rate will be determined by supply and demand for funds. Thus, changes in money affect prices and other nominal values and not real output in the long run. This is the meaning of *neutrality of money* in the classical model.

What about the short-run effects of the increase in the money supply? How do we move from the initial equilibrium to the new equilibrium in Figure 22-6? The movement from one equilibrium to another is referred to as the *transmission* process, and in this process, the impact of changes in the money supply are quite different from the ultimate long-run impacts. The classical economists offered a number of views about the transmission process. We will consider a simple version to highlight the difference between short- and long-run effects of changes in the money supply. The short-run effects (indicated by the arrow marks in Figure 22-6) can be summarized by the following points:

1. The increase in money supply shifts aggregate demand to the right. Excess supply of money generates increased spending reflected by excess demand in the commodity market as illustrated in Figure 22-6.

2. Prices are bid upward. As a result, the real wage rate in the labor market is pushed below the level that equates the demand and supply for labor. Additional workers are hired, and output increases above its natural or full-employment level (from y_f to y') or in terms of unemployment concepts, the actual unemployment rate falls below the natural unemployment rate. Thus, the increase in the money supply has real effects in the short run.

3. The nominal interest rate equals the real rate of interest and anticipated inflation; however, since the price level was constant before the money supply increased, anticipated inflation was zero. Hence, the nominal and market interest rates were identical; however, because of their contractual nature, nominal interest rates are slow to adjust to anticipated inflation as prices begin to increase. This adds further to excess demand in the commodity market because higher prices generate a fall in the real rate of interest since nominal rates are lagging price increases.

4. Increasing prices, however, set into motion events that will reverse the short-run real effects of the money supply. The decline in real wages in the labor market and resulting excess demand for labor will generate higher money wages, thereby bringing the real wage rate back to its initial position. This will reduce employment back toward the full-employment level and reduce output back to the potential or natural level. This action will reduce the excess demand for commodities.

5. Increasing prices will eventually increase nominal interest rates as inflationary anticipations are incorporated into nominal rates. Higher nominal interest rates will bring the real rate back to its equilibrium level determined by the supply and demand for funds. This will further reduce excess demand for commodities.

6. The increased price level increases the level of nominal income, which in turn, increases the demand for money and reduces the excess supply of money.

7. These forces will eventually eliminate the excess supply of money and excess demand for commodities, and the economy will return to its long-run equilibrium position as indicated by point *B* in Figure 22-6. In the long run, money has only nominal effects; that is, an increase in the money supply will only increase prices, money wages, and nominal interest rates. The real performance of the economy in terms of the real wage rate, employment, output, and the real interest rate remain unchanged.

Role of Stabilization Policy in the Classical Model

The classical and quantity theory regarded the economy as inherently stable in two respects. First, the underlying relationships of the market system were stable over time in the sense that aggregate demand and supply changed slowly over time. Specifically, the demand for money and, hence, aggregate demand was stable. Second, the normal equilibrium position of the economy was one of full employment, and any departures from full employment would set into motion forces operating through flexible prices and wages to bring the economy back to full employment in a smooth and predictable fashion.

Government stabilization policy would necessarily play a nonactivist role in the classical model. Activist policy in general was not required and, in fact, could not improve upon the performance of the private economy. Monetary policy should be concerned only with maintaining a noninflationary growth of money to meet the growing needs of the economy. Additionally, the monetary authority should be a lender of last resort to limit contagion. The dynamic version of the quantity theory presented in expression (4) can illustrate the proper type of monetary policy in the classical model. Assume that the growth of full employment or potential real output is 5% and velocity is growing at 1%. Further, keep in mind that these growth rates are determined independently of monetary policy and price behavior in the long run. The monetary authority should then maintain a monetary growth rate consistent with either a very low or zero inflation rate. If the objective is to keep inflation at 2%, monetary growth should be set at 6%. The emphasis on stable monetary growth reflected a widely accepted view prior to the Great Depression that cyclical fluctuations in economic activity were most frequently associated with erratic changes in the growth of money from its long-run equilibrium level.

Clark Warburton, a forerunner of the modern-day monetarists, expressed best the commonly held view of money and the quantity theory of money.

The dominant conclusion suggested by the foregoing data is the primacy of variability in the quantity of money, relative to the expanding amount needed to accompany growth in population and increase in productivity, as the originating factor in business fluctuations, particularly with respect to violent fluctuations, such as the great depression of the 1930s.[3]

Both the long- and short-run view of the quantity theory are reflected in Warburton's statement. In the long run, money supply should grow to meet the basic needs of the economy as represented by the growing value of y, and deviations of M from this growth rate would induce either inflation or depression as the economy adjusts. The solution to business cycles was obvious. Keep the money supply growing at a stable rate to meet the growing real needs of the economy. Once a stable monetary growth was achieved, there was no further need of stabilization policy on the part of government other than for the central bank to be a lender of last resort on occasion.

What about fiscal policy? The classical model regarded changes in the government budget as subject to complete crowding out effects. That is, an increase in government spending over taxes would be offset by an equivalent decrease in private spending. Thus, fiscal policy had no lasting impact on the economy and, in any event, was not required since the economy was inherently stable. Government budgets should be balanced.

Downfall of the Classical Model in the 1930s

The Great Depression led to the rejection of the classical and quantity theory by the majority of economists and policymakers. Events during the 1930s appeared grossly inconsistent with the classical model's emphasis on the inherent stability of the economy and nonactivist role for government policy. As a result, economists and policymakers looked around for an alternative model of the economy more consistent with events. They turned to the Keynesian model that had radically different views of the economy and government stabilization policy. Let us briefly review the specific criticisms directed toward the classical and quantity theory that emerged from the Great Depression period.

Failure of the Federal Reserve to Prevent or Reduce the Severity of the Great Depression   Monetary policy could not change the real performance of the economy in the long run according to the classical model; however, in the face of such a dramatic decline, an easy monetary policy would have generated short-run beneficial effects. As lender of last resort, the monetary authority could also maintain stability of the financial system.

---

[3] Clark Warburton, "The Misplaced Emphasis in Contemporary Business Fluctuation Theory," in Clark Warburton (ed.), *Depression, Inflation, and Monetary Policy* (Baltimore: Johns Hopkins University Press, 1966), p. 81.

The Great Depression did much to destroy faith in the importance of money and monetary policy, since the Federal Reserve claimed throughout the depression that it did everything it could to reduce the severity of the decline. The view was widely held that the problems of the economy were nonmonetary in origin, and thus, easy monetary policy could do little to stimulate the economy.

The Keynesian model in its early version drove another nail in the coffin of monetary policy by showing that key relationships in the economy implied that monetary policy in general was not nearly as effective as fiscal policy.

Assumption of Full Employment   The Great Depression destroyed faith in any model that implied a smooth return to departures from full employment. The Keynesian model offered an explanation more consistent with the events of the 1930s. The Keynesian model in one version (fixed wages) argued that permanent unemployment equilibrium was possible, and even in the case of flexible wages and prices, the adjustment process would be so long and uncertain as to impose serious social and economic costs on society. Activist government stabilization policy was the only solution to return the economy to full employment and in this regard, fiscal policy was a more effective instrument than was monetary policy.

Assumption of Constant V or k   Quantity theorists assumed that V and k were independent of changes in the money supply. Keynes argued that velocity was not independent of changes in M and that an increase in M was likely to induce an offsetting movement in velocity; that is, any impact on income by an increase in M would be partially or even completely offset by a decrease in V (increase in the demand for money). In addition, the demand function for money was highly unstable even in the absence of changes in money. Thus, the quantity theory could not predict the effect on income of a change in money because of unstable velocity.

Assumed Stability of the Market System   The quantity theory emphasized the inherent stability of the market system. The Great Depression provided little comfort for any model emphasizing inherent stability.

Key Points

1. The classical model and the quantity theory of money were the most widely accepted views of how the economy functioned and the proper role for government stabilization policy prior to the Great Depression.

2. The classical model and quantity theory are for the most part interchangeable. The quantity theory focused on the public's demand for money and how the price level was deter-

mined. The transactions and Cambridge version generated the same results; however, the Cambridge version possessed a more appealing theoretical foundation of how money influenced the economy.

3. The classical model can be summarized by the concepts of aggregate demand and supply. In the long run, the economy equilibrated at full employment and changes in the money supply

had only nominal effects. Monetary policy in the long run cannot influence the real performance of the economy. In the short run, however, changes in the money supply did have real effects during the transition period.

4. The classical model viewed the economy as inherently stable and relied on competition in an institutional environment of flexible wages and prices to ensure that the economy would grow at its natural full-employment path.

5. Government stabilization policy should be non-active. Monetary policy should be concerned only with maintaining a stable noninflationary monetary growth rate and being a lender of last resort on occasion. Government budgets should be balanced over time.

6. The classical model along with the quantity theory were rejected by a major portion of the profession because their predictions appeared inconsistent with the events of the Great Depression period. The times called for a new approach to understanding the economy and a more activist role for government. The Keynesian model satisfied both these needs.

Key Terms

Aggregate demand function

Aggregate supply function

Behavioral relationship

Cambridge version of the quantity theory

Classical model

Demand for money

Equation of exchange

Fisher's transactions version of the quantity theory

Great Depression and the classical model

Identity relationship

Long-run effects of changes in money

Neutrality of money

Quantity theory of money

Short-run effects of changes in money

Velocity

Questions

1. Explain how the Fisher and Cambridge versions of the quantity theory both offer the same implications for the money market in the classical model.

2. Is the balance sheet relationship — assets = liabilities + net worth — an identity or behavioral relationship?

3. Fisher argued that velocity was institutionally determined. Explain how velocity might be influenced by the following institutional changes: increases in density of population, increases in efficiency of the transportation system, and advances in computer technology.

4. If nominal income is $5,000 and the money supply is $1,000, what is the velocity of money?

5. Explain why a fixed or stable V in the quantity theory is necessary to predict the effects of changes in the money supply. If the demand for money is unstable, how will this influence the aggregate demand function?

6. Explain the short- and long-run effects of a decline in the money supply.

7. Explain the short- and long-run effects of an increase in the money supply.

8. Why would the Federal Reserve have a vested interest in downplaying the importance of monetary policy during the Great Depression?

9. The classical model relies heavily on wage and price adjustments to achieve market stability. If wages were sluggish or even fixed over periods of time, how would this affect the classical model's implication for government stabilization policy?

10. In light of the rejection of the classical model by the events of the Great Depression and its replacement by the Keynesian model, evaluate the following statement: "We vote against rather than in favor of an economic model."

Suggested Readings

1. Gardner Ackley, *Macroeconomics* (New York: Macmillan, 1961). A detailed presentation of the classical model and quantity theory of money.

2. Irving Fisher, *The Purchasing Power of Money* (New York: Augustus M. Kelley, 1963). The classic statement of the short- and long-run transactions version of the quantity theory.

3. Milton Friedman, "Money: The Quantity Theory of Money," *International Encyclopedia of the Social Sciences* (1968). Discusses the quantity theory of money.

4. Byron Higgins, "Velocity: Money's Second Dimension," *Economic Review*, Federal Reserve Bank of Kansas City (June 1978), 15–31. Discusses the relationship between velocity and money.

5. Thomas M. Humphrey, "Evolution of the Concept of the Demand for Money," in Thomas M. Humphrey, *Essays on Inflation*, Federal Reserve Bank of Richmond (1984), 245–255. A nontechnical overview of the demand for money starting with the transactions version.

6. A. C. Pigou, "The Value of Money," *Quarterly Journal of Economics*, 32 (November 1917), 38–65. Compares the transactions and Cambridge versions.

7. Daniel Thornton, "Why Does Velocity Matter?" *Review*, Federal Reserve Bank of St. Louis (December 1983), 5–13. Discusses the importance of velocity in monetary theory and policy.

CHAPTER 23

The Basic Keynesian Model

Chapter Overview

The events of the Great Depression led to the wholesale rejection of the classical model and quantity theory of money. The *General Theory of Employment, Interest, and Money* by John Maynard Keynes published in 1936 initiated the Keynesian revolution that continued unabated until the 1960s, at which time, the classical model reemerged in the form of monetarism to challenge the Keynesian model.

The Keynesian model presented in the *General Theory* was in many respects based on work that had been in progress in the 1920s, and while Keynes was the primary intellectual force, other economists contributed to the foundation of the Keynesian model.

The Keynesian model is developed in two stages in this and the next chapter. This chapter focuses on the simplest version of the Keynesian model. Specifically, the model is developed in a *partial equilibrium* setting and assumes wages and prices are fixed. Thus, all variables are in real terms or what is the same thing, all nominal values are real values. The next chapter considers a *general equilibrium* approach and discusses the implications of departures from the fixed price and wage assumption.

Within the partial equilibrium and fixed price/wage setting, the Keynesian model in this chapter is discussed, first, with regard to the real sector and, second, with regard to the money sector. In each case, we consider the model without government and then consider the effects of government in the form of monetary and fiscal policy. The chapter also discusses the key relationships in the Keynesian model that influence their relative effectiveness.

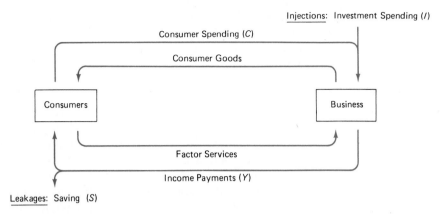

FIGURE 23-1   Circular flow of income and output

Meaning of the Partial Equilibrium Approach

The Keynesian model adopts the same sectoral approach as we used in the previous chapter in the sense that the economy is divided into two sectors: the real, or commodity, sector and the money, or financial, sector. The real sector is concerned with the level of spending, output, and employment, while the money sector is concerned with flows of financial assets associated with activities in the real sector.

The partial equilibrium approach means that we consider equilibrium in one sector while holding the other sector constant; for example, when we consider the real sector, the interest rate determined in the money sector will be taken as given. Likewise, when we consider the money sector, the level of income determined in the real sector will be taken as given.

Once we understand equilibrium in each sector holding the other sector constant, we are in a position to bring them together to determine the overall equilibrium of the econor y. This chapter accomplishes this task in an informal manner, while the next chapte. provides a more formal treatment of Keynesian general equilibrium.

The Real Sector

In the circular flow of economic activity illustrated in Figure 23-1, consuming units obtain income by selling factor services to producers. They either spend income on consumption goods or save their income. Producers receive funds from selling consumer goods but also add to the spending stream by purchasing investment goods from other producers. The equilibrium level of income or output is achieved when total spending for goods equals the total output of goods produced, or

$$TS = TO \tag{1}$$

TS represents the total spending for final output, consisting of consumption, *C*, and investment, *I*, spending. *TO* represents the total output of consumer and investment goods, and, because total output is paid to the various factors of production, it can also be regarded as total income earned by the factors of production in producing the output of goods and services.

To illustrate why expression (1) is a condition of equilibrium in the real sector, consider the sequence of events when spending is less than output. The level of income, output, and employment will decline because producers are unable to sell all they produce and will be forced to cut back on production. The level of income, output, and employment will expand when spending exceeds supply. Producers find themselves unable to produce all they can sell and will increase the level of production. Only when spending equals supply will the level of income and output remain in equilibrium; that is, there will be "no net tendency" for income and output to change.

Equilibrium can also be expressed in terms of the relationship between leakages from the income stream and injections to the spending stream. Saving is a leakage from the income stream not spent on consumption; investment is an injection to the spending stream on consumer goods. The level of income and output will be in equilibrium when saving equals investment or, what amounts to the same thing, leakages equal injections. The level of income and output will decline when saving exceeds investment because more will be withdrawn from the income-spending stream than is added back. Likewise, if investment exceeds saving, the level of income and output will expand because more is added to the spending stream than is taken out.

Algebra can be used to show the relationship between the two equilibrium conditions. The level of income and output (denoted as *Y*) is in equilibrium when spending equals output, or

$$Y = C + I \tag{2}$$

where *Y* = output (or income), *C* = consumption, and *I* = investment. Define the level of saving as income not spent on consumption.

$$S = Y - C \tag{3}$$

Combining (2) and (3), we express the equilibrium condition in terms of saving and investment.

$$Y - C = I \tag{4}$$

$$S = I$$

Thus, equilibrium is the level of income and output at which *TS* = *TO* and is equivalent to the condition *S* = *I*. In addition, when *TS* > *TO*, *I* > *S*, and, when *TO* > *TS*, *S* > *I*.

What happens when *TS* ≠ *TO* (or *S* ≠ *I*)? Disequilibrium in the real sector will set into motion a sequence of events that change the level of spending to bring *TS* back into equilibrium with *TO*. To understand how this is accomplished, we must take a closer look at the components of spending and how they interact together.

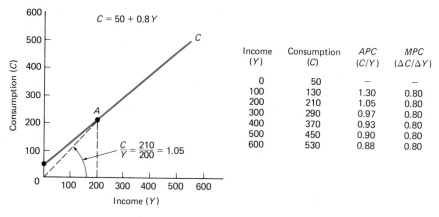

Income (Y)	Consumption (C)	APC (C/Y)	MPC (ΔC/ΔY)
0	50	—	—
100	130	1.30	0.80
200	210	1.05	0.80
300	290	0.97	0.80
400	370	0.93	0.80
500	450	0.90	0.80
600	530	0.88	0.80

FIGURE 23-2   A consumption function relationship

Consumption

Consumption depends on the level of income.

$$C = C(Y); \quad \frac{\Delta C}{\Delta Y} > 0 \tag{5}$$

Expression (5), known as the consumption function, expresses the positive relationship between the level of consumption, C, and the level of income, Y. We can write the expression as a linear functional form:

$$C = a + bY \tag{6}$$

The parameters of the expression, a and b, express the relationship between C and Y. The parameter a is the constant term that indicates the amount of consumption when income is zero, $C = a + b(0)$. Even if income is zero, consumption would still occur as measured by a. This makes perfect sense. If income declines even to zero, people still need to purchase the basic necessities of life such as food, apparel, and housing. The parameter b is the slope of the consumption function and indicates the change in consumption due to a change in income ($\Delta C = b \cdot \Delta Y$).

Figure 23-2 illustrates the consumption function for specific values of a and b. The consumption function is characterized by the average propensity to consume, *APC*, and the marginal propensity to consume, *MPC*. *APC* is the proportion of income consumed and defined as C/Y. The *APC* of the consumption function is indicated by the slope of a line from the origin of the diagram to a point on the consumption function. For example, at $Y = 200$, *APC* equals the slope of the line $0A$. Notice that, as income increases, the slope of a line from the origin to points along the consumption function declines, indicating that the *APC* declines as income increases. At higher levels of income, consumers spend a smaller proportion of their income on consumer goods and services.

The *MPC* is the change in consumption due to a change in income and defined as $\Delta C/\Delta Y$. The slope of the consumption function, b, indicates the *MPC*. The *MPC* is constant at all levels of income for a linear consumption function. *MPC* is less than one, meaning that, if income increased by \$100, consumption would increase by a lesser amount (at $b = 0.8$, C would increase by \$80). Extensive empirical research has shown that the *MPC* ranges from 0.6 to 0.9, depending on the definition of income and consumption.

Consumers do only two things with their income. They either spend income on consumption goods, C, or save income, S. Because we have not yet included government, consumers do not pay taxes. Saving is defined as the difference between income and consumption. In fact, there is a saving function for any given consumption function. The saving function is defined as

$$
\begin{aligned}
S &= Y - C \\
&= Y - a - bY \\
&= -a + (1 - b)Y
\end{aligned}
\tag{7}
$$

for the specific version of the consumption function, or

$$
S = S(Y); \qquad \frac{\Delta S}{\Delta Y} > 0
\tag{8}
$$

in general terms.

Figure 23-3 illustrates the relationship between the saving function and the consumption function. A 45° line has been drawn on the consumption function diagram to indicate a series of points at which income equals consumption. Notice that, at the point at which the consumption function crosses the 45° line, saving is zero (at $Y = 250$). At income levels below this point, where consumption exceeds income, saving is negative, and, at income levels above this point, where income exceeds consumption, saving is positive. Negative saving can result from selling off real and financial assets and/or borrowing.

The saving function is characterized by the average propensity to save, *APS*, and the marginal propensity to save, *MPS*. The *APS* is defined as the ratio of saving to income, S/Y, and increases as income increases. The *MPS* is defined as the change in saving due to a change in income, $\Delta S/\Delta Y$. Because consumers either spend or save their income, the following relationships exist between saving and consumption:

$$
APC + APS = 1
\tag{9}
$$
$$
MPC + MPS = 1
\tag{10}
$$

If consumers are spending \$80 out of \$100 on consumer goods, their *APC* is 0.8 and their *APS* is 0.2. If income increases by \$100 and consumption increases by \$75, *MPC* would be 0.75 and *MPS* would be 0.25.

Investment

Investment is a volatile component of total spending and, according to Keynesians, one of the primary factors creating instability over time and requiring active stabilization policy. Many factors determine the level of business investment; however,

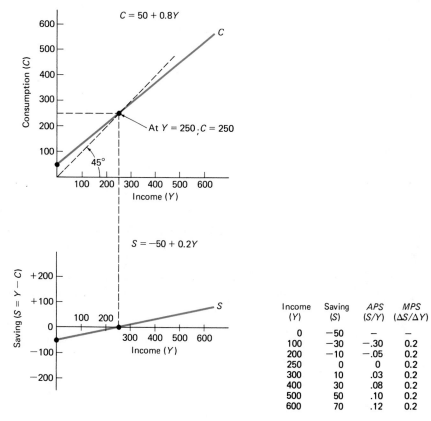

FIGURE 23-3   Relationship between consumption and saving functions

Income (Y)	Saving (S)	APS (S/Y)	MPS ($\Delta S/\Delta Y$)
0	−50	—	—
100	−30	−.30	0.2
200	−10	−.05	0.2
250	0	0	0.2
300	10	.03	0.2
400	30	.08	0.2
500	50	.10	0.2
600	70	.12	0.2

for the purposes of the basic model we regard investment as an inverse function of the rate of interest, r.

$$I = I(r); \qquad \frac{\Delta I}{\Delta r} < 0 \qquad\qquad (11)$$

This is an inverse function because an increase in the interest rate, which represents the cost of borrowing funds, will lead to a decline in the amount of investment. It is important to distinguish investment spending in expression (11) from financial investment activities. Financial investment represents lending or financial asset acquisition activities. Investment spending, on the other hand, represents the physical addition to the capital stock such as the purchase of new plant and equipment. Investment spending requires funds obtained either by borrowing in the financial system or using internally generated funds such as selling assets or using retained earnings. In either case, the interest rate represents the cost of funds used to finance investment spending.

The inverse relationship between investment and the rate of interest can be rationalized by thinking of a range of investment projects existing at any point in time. These projects have varying degrees of attractiveness to the businessperson as measured by some type of rate of return on the amount invested. Several methods

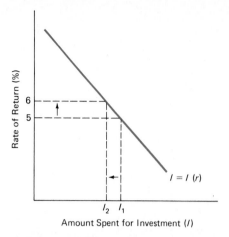

FIGURE 23-4 **Inverse relationship between investment and the rate of interest**

can be used to determine the rate of return on an investment project. One involves determining the rate of return that will equate the present value of the amount spent on the investment project to the present value of the stream of net revenue generated by the project. For example, the rate of return on, or, as it is sometimes called, marginal efficiency of investment, is determined from

$$C = \frac{R_1}{1 + rr} + \frac{R}{(1 + rr)^2} + \cdots + \frac{R_n}{(1 + rr)^n} \tag{12}$$

where

C = amount spent on the project in first period
R = net revenue generated by the project for each period over the life of the investment project
n = the life of the investment project
rr = rate (in percent) that equates the sum of the revenue stream to the amount spent on the project

The profitability of any given investment project can be determined by comparing the project's rate of return, rr, with the cost of obtaining funds to finance the investment spending. If the project's rate of return is 10% and the cost of funds is 8%, then the project is profitable. In terms of the projected revenue stream and the amount spent on the project, the rate of return is higher than the cost of obtaining the funds. On the other hand, the investment project is not profitable if the cost of funds exceeds the return of the project in terms of its projected revenue stream and cost.

Figure 23-4, illustrates the relationship between the rate of return and the amount spent on investment projects, and indicates that the rate of return is high when only a small amount is being spent on investment; that is, the most attractive investment projects are undertaken first. As the amount of investment expands, the rate of return declines. Assume that the going rate of interest determined in the financial market is 5%. Thus, all investment projects yielding a rate of return exceeding 5% will be undertaken and the amount of investment spending would be I_1. If the rate of interest increased to 6%, some investment projects would no

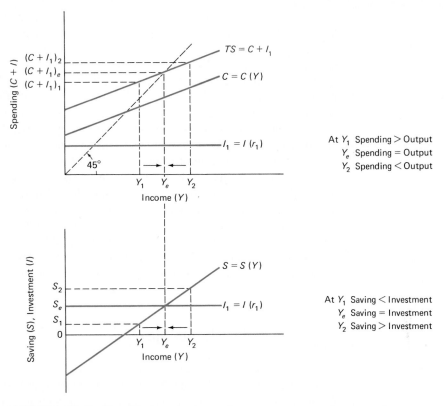

FIGURE 23-5   **Equilibrium in the real sector assuming the rate of interest is constant**

longer yield a positive return, and the amount of investment spending would decline to I_2.

Equilibrium in the Real Sector

We can now bring the consumption and investment elements together to determine the equilibrium level of income in the real sector. We define the equilibrium level of income when

$$Y = C + I \tag{13}$$

In the real sector we are concerned only with the level of income, output, and spending. When we solve for the equilibrium condition in the real sector, we hold the financial variables constant, in this case, the interest rate. Likewise, when we solve for the equilibrium solution in the money or financial sector, we hold the level of income constant.

Figure 23-5 illustrates how equilibrium income and output are determined in the real sector. The top part of the figure illustrates equilibrium in the real sector in terms of total spending and total output concepts; the bottom part illustrates the same process in terms of saving and investment.

The *TS* line is the vertical sum of the consumption function and the investment function. The investment function is drawn as a constant at all levels of income because it has been hypothesized to depend only on the rate of interest, which is held constant at r_1. The 45° line indicates all levels of income for which $C + I$ equal Y; that is, it traces out all possible points of equilibrium in the real sector. If the level of income or output is Y_1, the *TS* line indicates that total spending will be $(C + I_1)_1$, in which case spending exceeds output. If producers sell more than they are producing currently and experience unintended inventory reductions, they will increase output and demand for workers. Output and employment will increase. As long as total spending exceeds total output, income will continue to increase.

If the level of income is Y_2, the *TS* line indicates that total spending will be $(C + I_1)_2$, in which case output exceeds spending. Producers will be unable to sell all they produce and will experience unintended inventory accumulations, leading to production cuts, layoffs, lower output, and lower employment. As long as output exceeds spending and producers experience unintended inventory accumulation, income will continue to fall. The equilibrium level of income is indicated at Y_e, where the *TS* line crosses the 45° line because at this level of income spending will equal the level of income or output.

Autonomous Changes in Spending

The equilibrium level of income, Y_e, will remain constant as long as none of the spending functions shift. Changes in spending can either be *induced* or *autonomous*. Induced changes in spending occur as a result of a change in income. That is, they are induced by the change in income. Consumption depends on income, and, as income increases or decreases, we move along the consumption function.

Autonomous changes in spending result from changes in one or more exogenous variables or shifts in any one of the spending functions and thus lead to a new equilibrium level of income. Autonomous changes in spending are independent of the changes in the level of income. Investment spending has always been considered an unstable component of total spending. To determine how an autonomous change in spending affects income, assume that investment shifts from I_1 to I_2 (Figure 23-6). The higher investment function means that investment spending will be higher by ΔI at any level of income. The *TS* line will also shift up by ΔI. The new equilibrium level of income will be Y'_e. Notice, however, that the increase in income, ΔY, exceeds the autonomous increase in spending, ΔI. The change in investment has led to a multiple increase in income. This result illustrates the concept of the *income multiplier*. In fact, any autonomous change in spending will lead to a multiple change in income.

In Figure 23-6, the total change in income is made up of the autonomous change in investment plus a change in consumption induced by an increasing level of income.

$$\Delta Y = \Delta I + \Delta C \tag{14}$$

The change in consumption is equal to the *MPC* times the change in income or $b \cdot \Delta Y$ if we use the specific version of the consumption function. Substituting and making several adjustments

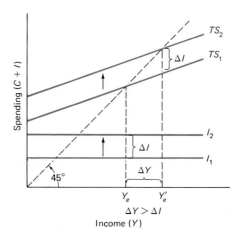

FIGURE 23-6   **Effect of autonomous increase in the investment function**

$$\Delta Y = \Delta I + b \cdot \Delta Y$$
$$\Delta Y - b \cdot \Delta Y = \Delta I$$
$$\Delta Y(1 - b) = \Delta I$$
$$\Delta Y = \frac{1}{1 - b} \cdot \Delta I \tag{15}$$

we end up with an expression that says the change in income will equal $1/1 - b$ times the change in investment. The expression $1/1 - b$ is the *income multiplier*, and because $b < 1$, $1/1 - b > 1$. If $b = 0.8$, the income multiplier will be $1/1 - 0.8$, or 5, indicating that an increase in investment by \$100 will increase income by \$500. The multiplier works just as well for autonomous declines in spending. If investment spending were to decline by \$100, eventually income would fall by \$500.

The concept of the income multiplier applies to any change in autonomous spending such as a shift in the consumption function or shift in any other component of spending we care to include in the model. The mathematics require that $1/1 - MPC > 1$ as long as $MPC < 1$.

What does the multiplier mean in words? Suppose that suddenly the auto companies retool to produce smaller and more-gas-efficient cars and spend an additional \$10 billion every year. We can regard this sudden increase as an autonomous increase in I. When the \$10 billion is paid out, it becomes income to others in the form of wages, rents, profits, and so on. As income increases, consumption will also increase, but this will lead to a further increase in income, which will lead to a further increase in consumption, and on and on. The sequence will appear as

Original \$10 billion autonomous
    increase in I⎯⎯⎯⎯⎯⎯⎯⎯⎯⎯→ΔY by \$10 million
Increase in C by $MPC \cdot$ \$10 billion→ ΔY by $MPC \cdot$ \$10 billion
Increase in C by $MPC^2 \cdot$ \$10 billion↙ ΔY by $MPC^2 \cdot$ \$10 billion
Increase in C by $MPC^3 \cdot$ \$10 billion↙ and on and on

Each round of spending leads to another increase in income, which in turn leads to an additional increase in spending. The result will be a series of additions to income equal to

$$\Delta Y = \$10 + MPC \cdot \$10 + MPC^2 \cdot \$10 + MPC^3 \cdot \$10 + \cdots$$
$$= \$10(1 + MPC + MPC^2 + MPC^3 + \cdots)$$
$$= \$10 \cdot \frac{1}{1 - MPC} \tag{16}$$

Thus the total increase in income, ΔY, will be the multiplier times the autonomous change in spending. If $MPC = 0.8$, then the multiplier is 5, and income will eventually increase by \$50 billion if there is an autonomous and sustained increase in investment spending by \$10 billion.

What Is the Nature of the Equilibrium Solution?

There are two characteristics of the equilibrium solution that differentiate the Keynesian model from the quantity theory of money. First, equilibrium is not necessarily a full-employment equilibrium. There is nothing particularly good or bad about the equilibrium solution of an economic model. It is simply the state of "no net tendency to change" and is determined by the functional relationships of the model. In the case of the real sector, the equilibrium level of income is determined by the intersection of the TS line with the 45° line and could occur at any one point along a range of income levels. The point of equilibrium depends on the total spending of the economy, and there is no inherent reason for the equilibrium level of income and output to correspond with full employment of the labor force. That is, there is no "unique" or specific equilibirium solution. Each value of Y on the horizontal axis in Figure 23-5 corresponds to a specific level of employment, and only one point would be defined as a full-employment level of output. Thus the Keynesian model implies that full employment is not an automatic result of the market system. The private market may simply not generate enough spending to maintain the level of economic activity at full employment.

Second, even if full-employment equilibrium were possible, the inherent instability of the investment function would constantly expose the economy to periods of recession followed by expansion. Thus, instability of investment and, hence total spending generate an unstable economy that would make it difficult to achieve equilibrium, even if it were a full-employment equilibrium.

Addition of Government: Fiscal Policy

The preceding discussion indicates that spending decisions by the public may be insufficient to generate income and output at a full-employment level. What was needed according to Keynes was government fiscal policy to increase total spending to increase the equilibrium level of income and output to the full employment level.

Government fiscal policy can be added to the analysis by expanding total spending to include government spending on goods and services, *G*, and define equilibrium as

$$Y = C + I + G \tag{17}$$

Changes in government spending are reflected by shifts in the *TS* line. The *TS* line will shift upward for increases in government spending and downward for decreases in government spending. Changes in government spending are regarded as autonomous and, hence, lead to a multiplier effect on the level of income.

Taxes also influence the real sector by shifting the *TS* line. They do this by shifting the consumption function. We saw earlier that the level of consumption was a function of the level of income.

$$C = a + bY \tag{18}$$

The level of income earned in producing the output of goods and services is the same as disposable income in an economy without taxation; however, when taxation is added, we need to distinguish between the total level of income and disposable income. Taxes paid to the government represent the difference between total income and disposable income. The consumption function will now be expressed as a relationship between consumption and disposable income,

$$\begin{aligned} C &= a + b(Y - T) \\ &= a + bY - bT \end{aligned} \tag{19}$$

where *T* is defined as the amount of taxes paid by consumers. Notice that an increase in taxes leads to a reduction in the level of consumption at any income level; however, the decline in consumption is less than the amount of the tax. If taxes increased by $100, consumption would decline by *b* times the increase in taxes. The parameter *b* is the *MPC*. Increases in *T* will shift the consumption function and, hence, the *TS* line downward, whereas decreases in *T* will shift the consumption function and, hence, the *TS* line upward.[1]

We can also expand the equilibrium condition in terms of leakages and injections to include government activity. In addition to saving, taxation represents a leakage from the income stream, and, in addition to investment, government spending is

---

[1] Expression (19) assumes that taxes are independent of the level of income. This is done for simplicity and does not invalidate any of the major results of the model. A more realistic tax structure would regard taxes as being composed of two parts: a lump-sum amount and taxes that are proportional to the level of income or $T = c + tY$, where *T* is the total amount of taxes, *c* is a constant or lump-sum amount of taxes independent of the level of income, and *tY* is the amount of taxes dependent on the level of income. The parameter, *t*, represents the marginal rate of taxation. Substitution of the tax function into the consumption function yields $C = (a - bc) + b(1 - t)Y$. Consumption is now influenced by the lump-sum portion of total taxes, *c*, and the marginal tax rate, *t*. A change in *c* will shift the consumption function while maintaining the same slope and a change in *t* will shift the consumption function by changing its slope.

regarded as an injection to the spending stream. Equilibrium is determined when the level of income is such that the leakages equal the injections, or

$$S + T = I + G \qquad (20)$$

This is equivalent to the condition $TS = TO$. In an economy with government, total income is consumed, saved, or taxed:

$$Y = C + S + T \qquad (21)$$

Combining (17) and (21),

$$Y = C + I + G$$
$$Y - C = I + G$$

and since $Y - C = S + T$,

$$S + T = I + G \qquad (22)$$

Fiscal policy thus involves changes in government spending, G, and/or taxes, T. Given the possibility of unemployment equilibrium and/or inherent instability in private spending, fiscal policy can take an activist role to improve economic performance.

Increases in government spending and/or reductions in taxes will increase total spending to shift the economy from an unemployment to a full-employment equilibrium. Government spending will directly increase total spending, while reduced taxes will increase disposable income, which in turn, will increase consumption.

Instability in private spending can be offset by opposite changes in government spending and/or taxes. A decline in private spending, for example, can be offset with an increase in government spending and/or reduction in taxes. This type of fiscal policy is referred to as *countercyclical* because it attempts to offset fluctuations in private spending that keep the economy from achieving its economic goals.

The Money Sector

The equilibrium level of income in Figure 23-5 depends on a constant rate of interest, r_1. If the rate of interest is different from r_1, the investment line and, hence, the TS line would either be lower (interest rate greater than r_1) or higher (interest rate lower than r_1). We must now look at the money sector of the economy to see how the rate of interest is determined.

The Keynesian view of the money or financial sector is based on a portfolio adjustment process. Each individual is assumed to have a desired portfolio of money and income-earning assets. The distribution of this portfolio reflects the individual's choice between money, which has perfect liquidity but yields no interest income, and other financial assets with varying degrees of liquidity and interest income. In

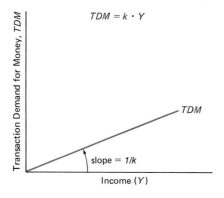

FIGURE 23-7   Relationship between transaction demand for money and the level of income

the basic version of the Keynesian system, we assume that individuals choose between holding money or bonds, with bonds representing all possible income-yielding financial assets.

Keynes originally expressed the demand for money as a function of three factors. First, there is a *transaction demand* for money to carry on daily transactions, as receipts and expenditures are not perfectly synchronized. The transaction demand, *TDM*, can be represented as a positive function of the level of Y. Second, there is a *precautionary demand, PDM*, for money against uncertain expenditures. The precautionary demand is a complex component, so, to keep life simple, we will combine it with the transaction demand and consider them together as a positive function of the level of income. Figure 23-7 illustrates how the transaction demand for money relates to the level of income. We usually express the transaction component of the demand for money as a proportional relationship to the level of income.

The third component of the demand for money is called the *speculative demand* for money, *SDM*. This component is viewed as being inversely related to the rate of interest. Figure 23-8 illustrates the inverse relationships between *SDM* and the rate of interest. The inverse relationship can be rationalized in several ways as already discussed in Chapter 5. First, we can think of the interest rate as the *opportunity cost* of holding money, which yields perfect liquidity but no interest income. As interest rates increase, the opportunity cost of holding money also increases, and individuals reduce their money balances. As interest rates decline, the opportunity cost of holding money declines, and individuals are willing to hold onto larger money balances.

Second, individuals have an expected or *normal* rate of interest that they believe will prevail in the future. This expected rate could derive from detailed analysis or just a "feeling" on the part of the individual. At high rates of interest, a large number of individuals are more than likely to expect lower rates of interest than are prevailing presently. If they follow through on their anticipations, they will hold bonds rather than money. Individuals expect interest rates to fall in the near future, which will increase the price of bonds leading to capital gains. At low rates of interest, a large number of individuals are more likely to expect higher rates of interest than is currently the case, and, if they act on their anticipations, they will hold fewer bonds and more money. When interest rates increase, bonds experience capital losses.

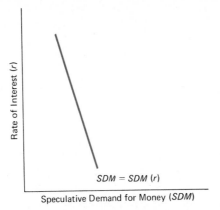

FIGURE 23-8   Relationship between the speculative demand for money and the rate of interest

Third, the interest rate is the reward for assuming risk. Bonds are riskier than money since the actual return from holding a bond may differ from the expected return because of changing market conditions while the expected return from holding money is known with certainty. Thus, if interest rates increase and assuming no change in perceived risk, individuals will shift their assets from money to bonds because they earn a higher expected return from holding a portfolio with more bonds and less money.

The total demand for money thus depends positively on the level of income (transactions and precautionary components) and inversely on the rate of interest (speculative component)

$$DM = DM(Y,\ r);\qquad \frac{\Delta DM}{\Delta Y} > 0,\qquad \frac{\Delta DM}{\Delta r} < 0 \qquad\qquad (23)$$

where $DM = TDM + SDM$.

Figure 23-9 illustrates how the total demand for money can be expressed as a function of the interest rate for a given level of income. At Y_1, transaction demand is TDM_1, and by adding this horizontally to the speculative demand, we obtain DM as a function of r for a given level of income, Y_1. A change in the level of income will shift the demand function for money.

Equilibrium in the Money Sector

Equilibrium in the money market is determined when the demand for money is equal to the supply of money.

$$DM = MS \qquad\qquad (24)$$

Recall that the supply of money is determined outside the model and is considered an exogenous variable. To determine equilibrium in the money market we need to assume that the level of income is constant. Figure 23-10 illustrates how equilibrium

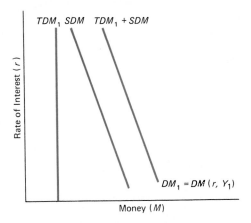

FIGURE 23-9 **Combining the transaction and speculative components into one total demand function for money**

is determined in the money market. If the rate of interest is r_1, the supply of money exceeds the demand for money. According the Keynesian view, individuals do not spend the excess money on goods and services; rather, they purchase bonds, which are close substitutes for money but yield an interest income. As the total demand for bonds increases, the price of bonds will also increase and lower the rate of interest toward the equilibrium rate, r_e. On the other hand, if the rate of interest is r_2, the demand for money will exceed the supply of money. To restore their money balances, individuals will sell off some of their bond holdings. The increased supply of bonds will lower price and increase the interest rate toward r_e. As long as there is a divergence between the demand and supply of money, bonds will either be bought or sold, and the interest rate will continue to change until the demand and supply for money are equal.

Notice that we have to hold the level of income constant to determine the

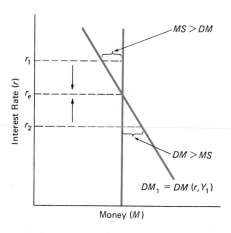

FIGURE 23-10 **Equilibrium in the money market, assuming a constant level of income**

equilibrium interest rate in the financial system. An increase (decrease) in the level of income will shift the demand function for money to the right (left) and change the equilibrium level of the rate of interest.

Addition of Monetary Policy

The money market analysis provides the basis for monetary policy in the Keynesian system. The central bank controls the money supply, which in turn, influences the interest rate. The interest rate determines investment spending, a component of total spending.

Thus, activist monetary policy can be used to shift the economy from unemployment to full-employment equilibrium or used to offset fluctuations in private spending.

Interrelationship between the Real and Money Sectors

We have developed each sector of the economy under the partial equilibrium approach. That is, equilibrium in the real sector was determined by holding the rate of interest constant. Equilibrium in the money sector was determined by holding the level of income constant. We had to make these assumptions to determine equilibrium in each market; however, the partial equilibrium approach ignores the significant feedback relationships that exist between the real and money markets in the Keynesian system. For example, a change in the money supply in the money market will change the level of interest. Changes in the interest rate will shift the investment line and, hence, the TS line in the real sector and alter the level of income. The change in the level of income will feed back on the money market and shift the demand function for money, as part of the demand for money depends on the level of income, and on and on.

In addition, separate treatment of each sector provides us with no easy insight into the nature of the overall or general equilibrium solution. To achieve overall equilibrium, we must determine an interest rate *and* level of income at which the real and money markets are *simultaneously* in equilibrium. Consider the following steps that need to be taken into account in determining overall equilibrium.

1. We determine equilibrium in the real sector by determining the level of income at which total spending equals total output. However, the investment component of total spending depends on the interest rate, which we held constant in determining equilibrium in the real sector.

2. Then, go to the financial sector and determine an equilibrium rate of interest given the level of income determined in step 1. Equilibrium in the financial sector is obtained when the demand for money equals the supply of money.

However, we hold the level of income constant to determine equilibrium in this market.

3. The equilibrium interest rate from step 2 will probably differ from the interest rate assumed constant in step 1, in which case we will need to redetermine equilibrium in the real sector. But, if we determine a different equilibrium level of income in the real sector, this will involve a redetermination of equilibrium in the financial sector, which will affect the equilibrium in the real sector, and on and on. By iterating back and forth between the two sectors, eventually we will reach a point where the real and money sectors will be in equilibrium simultaneously.

Because the partial equilibrium view of the Keynesian system fails to incorporate feedback and determine overall equilibrium adequately, the model is limited in determining the impacts of fiscal and monetary policy on the level of economic activity.

The primary motivation for developing the Keynesian model is to determine how monetary and fiscal policy function. We will deal with this issue in two steps. First, we will use the partial equilibrium framework developed to this stage and examine the impacts of monetary and fiscal policy. This analysis will be incomplete because it cannot incorporate easily the feedback relationship between the real and the money sectors; however, it will provide useful insight into how monetary and fiscal policy function in the Keynesian framework. Second, we will extend the Keynesian model in Chapter 24 to incorporate explicitly the feedback relationships between the two sectors, to determine general equilibrium and examine the final impacts of monetary and fiscal policy.

Impacts of Monetary and Fiscal Policy

Monetary Policy

In the Keynesian system, the real sector determines the level of output and employment. Fiscal policy operates directly on the real sector and was regarded by Keynes and his followers as a powerful stabilization tool. Monetary policy was viewed as another stabilization tool but, according to many past Keynesians, was not as effective as fiscal policy.

Monetary policy in this model is represented by changes in the money supply and influences the real sector *indirectly* by first changing the rate of interest in the money sector. Figure 23-11 illustrates the initial impact of expansionary monetary policy. An increase in the money supply shifts the supply function of money to the right. At the existing rate of interest, there is an excess supply of money. Individuals use the excess funds to purchase bonds. Bond prices increase and the interest rate declines. The rate of interest represents the cost and availability of credit. As the cost of credit declines and the availability of credit expands, investment spending will increase. An increase in investment spending will be reflected as an upward shift in the investment line and, hence, the *TS* line.

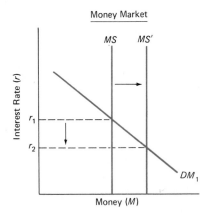

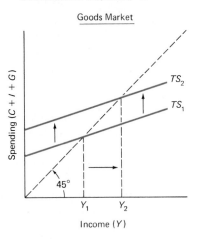

FIGURE 23-11   **Initial impact of expansionary monetary policy**

Figure 23-11 illustrates only the first-round effects of an easy monetary policy. Changes in the level of income in the real sector influence the money sector by shifting the demand function for money. Changes in the level of income change the transaction component of the demand for money and, hence, shift the total demand function, leading to a change in the rate of interest. The change in the rate of interest will then feed back on the real sector by changing the level of investment. Eventually, the process iterates to an equilibrium solution in which the final effects of the increase in the money supply will be lower rate of interest and a higher level of income.

Tight monetary policy directed at reducing the level of income is represented by a decrease in the money supply. A reduction in the money supply will increase the rate of interest and discourage investment spending in the real sector.

Fiscal Policy

Fiscal policy influences the real sector directly by shifting the *TS* line by changes in *G* and/or *T*. Figure 23-12 illustrates the initial impact of a fiscal action designed to increase the level of income; however, changes in the real sector will feed back on the money sector by shifting the demand for money and changing the rate of interest. In addition, before we can understand even the proximate impact of fiscal policy, we must consider the monetary implications of the fiscal action. The monetary aspect of fiscal policy is concerned with how a deficit ($G > T$) is to be financed or how a surplus ($G < T$) is to be distributed. Monetary aspects are important because fiscal policy is constrained by the fact that

$$G = T + \Delta D \tag{25}$$

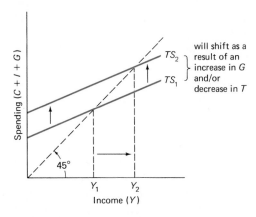

FIGURE 23-12   Initial impact of expansionary fiscal policy

where D represents government bonds or debt. This constraint means that, if $G > T$, government must sell bonds, $\Delta D > 0$, and, if $T > G$, the government can retire a part of the national debt, $\Delta D < 0$.

The change in outstanding bonds involves both the Treasury and the Federal Reserve. The Treasury determines the maturity distribution of the outstanding securities by either selling (retiring) short-, medium-, or long-term securities, whereas the Federal Reserve determines the impact that changes in securities will have on interest rates.

Deficits   There are two ways in which a deficit can be financed. First, the government sells I.O.U.s in the financial system to obtain the funds needed for spending beyond tax revenues and the money supply remains constant. As the Treasury sells bonds, their price will decline and interest rates will start to increase. In addition, as Y increases in the real sector of the economy, the financial sector will be influenced because the demand function for money will shift to the right as Y increases. As long as the money supply remains constant, the increasing demand for money will increase interest rates further. The increase in interest rates will decrease investment spending in the real sector and to some extent offset the original increase in the TS line, resulting from the government deficit. The overall impact, however, will lead to an increase in the level of income as well as an increase in the rate of interest.

Second, the monetary authority can increase the money supply to offset the pressure to increase interest rates. The increased money supply will offset the increased demand for money so that interest rates need not increase. A deficit financed by increases in the money supply will be more expansive than will a deficit with an unchanged supply of money because the tendency for interest rates to increase is offset by an increase in the money supply.

Deficits financed by increases in the money supply can be accomplished by the Federal Reserve's purchase of existing securities in the open market and increasing reserves. The expanded monetary base and, hence, money supply will provide the funds to purchase the new securities being offered by the Treasury to finance the deficit. The Federal Reserve has increased the money supply to finance the deficit or *monetized* the debt.

Surpluses   Treasury surpluses also have monetary effects that must be considered in determining even the proximate impact of fiscal policy. First, a surplus with a constant money supply in the hands of the public will lead to lower rates of interest. As the surplus shifts down the *TS* line and lowers *Y*, the demand for money shifts to the left and results in a lower equilibrium rate of interest. The lower interest rate increases investment spending and offsets to some extent the original downward shift in the *TS* line resulting from the surplus. A constant money supply in the hands of the public with a surplus will arise when the Treasury uses the funds to pay off some of the national debt.

Second, a surplus with a reduced money supply in the hands of the public will not necessarily lower the rate of interest. The surplus lowers *TS* and *Y* in the real sector and leads to a decline in the demand for money; however, if the money supply is also reduced, the level of interest in the money market may remain constant. The reduction in the demand for money is offset by a reduction in the money supply. The money supply held by the public would decline if the Treasury simply held onto the excess funds collected.

Monetary and Fiscal Policy Compared

Fiscal policy operates directly on the real sector of the economy. Both changes in *G* and *T* lead to multiple changes in income and output. The *direct* impact of fiscal policy can be represented as

ΔT — — →consumption function shifts ↘

$\qquad\qquad\qquad\qquad\qquad\qquad\qquad$ *TS* line shifts→ΔY

ΔG_ _ _ _ _ _ _ _ _ _ _ _ _ ↗

Monetary policy affects the level of economic activity only *indirectly* by operating first through the financial system. The indirect impacts of monetary policy can be represented as

$\qquad\qquad\Delta M$— — → Δr — — → ΔI— — → *TS* line shifts in real sector

Monetary and fiscal policy are both potentially important instruments of policy within the Keynesian model; however, their relative importance depends on the *interest elasticity of the demand function for money* and the *interest elasticity of the investment function*. Interest elasticity of money demand expresses the response of the quantity of money demanded to changes in the interest rate. Formally, money demand elasticity is defined as the ratio of the percentage change in the quantity of money demand to the percentage change in the interest rate. Interest elasticity of the investment function expresses the response of the quantity of investment to changes in the interest rate. Formally, investment elasticity is defined as the ratio of the percentage change in the quantity of investment to the percentage change in the interest rate.

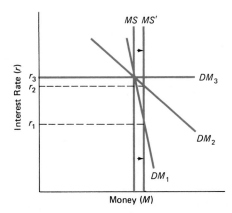

FIGURE 23-13   The response of the interest rate to changes in the money supply and the elasticity of the demand function for money

Interest elasticity of either money demand or investment is negative; however, it is easier to consider elasticity in terms of its absolute values over the range from 0 to ∞. The value of the elasticity ratio over this range determines whether the money demand or investment function is *completely inelastic, inelastic, unitary elastic, elastic,* or *completely* or *infinitely elastic.*

Value of elasticity	Type of elasticity
0	Completely inelastic
Greater than 0 and less than 1	Inelastic
1	Unitary elastic
Greater than 1 and less than ∞	Elastic
∞	Completely or infinitely elastic

Let us now consider the role that money demand and investment elasticity play in the Keynesian model.

Key Relationships for Monetary Policy

Money in the Keynesian model has an indirect rather than a direct impact on total spending. There are two key links in the transmission process. The interest elasticity of the demand for money function determines the response of the interest rate to a change in the money supply. And the interest elasticity of investment spending determines the response of investment spending to a change in the interest rate.

Interest Elasticity of the Demand for Money   The greater the interest elasticity of the demand for money, the greater the change in money supply needed to achieve a given change in the interest rate. Figure 23-13 illustrates three demand functions for money: an interest inelastic function (DM_1), an interest elastic function (DM_2), and a completely elastic demand function representing the Keynesian liquidity trap (DM_3). The liquidity trap is a special Keynesian case that might occur in a deep depression and would render expansionary monetary policy completely ineffective since any increase in the money supply would be held by the public and not used to purchase bonds and lower interest rates.

A given change in the money supply in Figure 23-13 will have differing effects on the interest rate depending on the elasticity of the demand function for money. The more interest elastic the demand function, the smaller the change in the interest rate. In the case of the completely elastic function, a change in the money supply has no impact on the rate of interest. What possible rationale could the liquidity trap have?

Keynes argued that at very low rates of interest, such as during depressed conditions in the economy in the 1930s, individuals expect interest rates to rise in the future. Rates are already so low that no one believes they could fall any farther. Rational individuals would not use the excess money to purchase securities because they expect interest rates will increase in the future and lower the price of bonds. Any bonds in their portfolio would experience significant capital losses.

Keynes referred to this extreme view of the demand function for money as the liquidity trap, and as one early commentator poetically put it, "against the rock of 'liquidity preference' the waves of monetary expansion will beat in vain."[2] No matter how much the Federal Reserve increased the money supply to stimulate the economy, velocity would fall (quantity of money demanded would increase) to offset completely the effects of the increased money supply. Monetary policy would be completely impotent.

Even Keynes, however, was skeptical about the reality of the liquidity trap, but more likely the demand for money was highly sensitive to the interest rate. A highly elastic demand function for money would require very large changes in the money supply to achieve even small changes in the interest rate.

The Keynesian demand function for money has been subjected to numerous empirical tests over the last three decades, and a fairly accepted consensus has emerged. The demand for money can be expressed as a positive function of the level of income (or some other proxy of aggregate economic activity) and an inverse function of the rate of interest. The interest rate elasticity ranges from -0.15 to -0.25. Not only do interest elasticity estimates rule out the extreme case of the liquidity trap, they also indicate that the demand function for money is basically interest inelastic so that moderate changes in the money supply can result in significant changes in the interest rate using the Keynesian model framework. Thus, the evidence indicates that one cannot argue the ineffectiveness of monetary policy on the basis of a highly elastic demand function for money.

Interest Elasticity of the Investment Function   Monetary policy could encounter another problem in the Keynesian model. Even if the Federal Reserve could lower interest rates with relatively small changes in the money supply, the impact of easy monetary policy would depend on just how sensitive investment or other types of spending are to the changes in the cost of credit.

Investment was regarded as the most important component of total spending that

---

[2] D. H. Robertson, *Essays in Monetary Theory* (London: King & Son, 1940), p. 150.

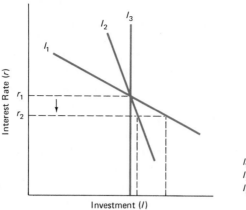

FIGURE 23-14 Relationship between interest elasticity of the investment function and changes in the rate of interest

could be sensitive to the rate of interest. Figure 23-14 illustrates three possible investment functions corresponding to different degrees of interest rate elasticity. The more interest elastic the investment schedule, the greater the increase in investment spending resulting from a decline in the rate of interest. The more interest inelastic the investment function, generally the steeper the function and the less investment will respond to a decline in the interest rate. Figure 23-14 illustrates that a decline in interest rates will have a large, moderate, or small impact on investment spending depending on the interest elasticity of the investment function.

Economists once believed that the investment function was extremely interest inelastic; in fact, many believed that changes in interest had little to do with the businessperson's decision to invest. This attitude was based on two considerations: First, interest rates were low during the 1930s, yet business investment was continually depressed. Second, a number of surveys in the late 1930s to the early 1950s indicated that businesspeople paid little or no attention to the prevailing level of interest in deciding on how much to invest.

Theoretical and empirical work started in the late 1950s on investment spending began to show that investment spending was much more sensitive to the rate of interest than previously thought. The presence of low interest rates and low rates of investment in the 1930s did not necessarily imply that no relationship existed. Low interest rates and investment were both influenced by the low level of economic activity during the 1930s. In addition, the radical shift in government policy initiated by the New Deal of the Roosevelt administration certainly had an adverse impact on the willingness to invest at any level of the interest rate. To reach any conclusion about the observed relationship between investment and the interest rate required a detailed statistical analysis of all the variables likely to influence the relationship. In addition, the surveys that had been used to support the lack of a relationship were shown to have a serious bias toward indicating the absence of a relationship.

A survey of empirical evidence on the relationship between investment in plant and equipment and the rate of interest indicates that investment spending is related significantly but inelastically to the rate of interest and that the full effect of a change in the rate of interest on investment takes considerable time to emerge—up to four years according to some estimates. Several well-known estimates[3] of the interest elasticity of the investment function have ranged from -0.12 to -0.32.

Not only is there evidence that business investment is related to the rate of interest, there is also evidence that other components of total spending may be more interest sensitive than was previously thought. Housing, state and local government, and consumption expenditures appear to be sensitive to the rate of interest. It is not surprising that housing and municipal expenditures are sensitive to interest rates. They involve large long-term expenditures that must be financed over long periods of time. Even small changes in the interest rate lead to large changes in the total interest cost.

Evidence has also indicated that consumption expenditures are sensitive to interest rate changes. The more sophisticated version of the consumption function includes a wealth variable in addition to income:

$$ C = C(Y, W); \qquad \frac{\Delta C}{\Delta Y} > 0, \quad \frac{\Delta C}{\Delta W} > 0 \qquad (26) $$

Wealth, W, is a stock, whereas income is a flow variable. There are many ways in which to measure wealth, but, to estimate consumption functions, we generally use the accumulated value of household holdings of financial assets.

The interest rate can influence the amount of consumption spending in two ways—directly or indirectly. Direct effects depend on the interest elasticity of demand for consumer credit and the role of consumer credit in purchasing consumer goods. Most evidence indicates, however, that the interest elasticity of demand for consumer credit is rather low and that the direct effect of changes on the rate of interest on consumption appears at most to be minor. Attention to possible indirect effects of changes in the rate of interest reveals financial wealth as an important component in the consumption function and that interest rate changes influence the amount of financial wealth. The following sequence indicates the indirect effects of the decrease in interest rates on consumption:

$$ \downarrow r \; \begin{array}{l} \nearrow \uparrow \text{ bond prices} \\ \searrow \uparrow \text{ stock prices} \end{array} \quad \rightarrow W \rightarrow C $$

The interest rate decrease will increase the value of bond holdings. In addition, interest rates in the bond market will bear a direct relationship to rates of return in the stock market adjusted by risk differences between the two markets. Bond interest rates and stock yields are all part of the structure of interest rates in the financial system. As bond rates decline, equities become more attractive and the demand for equities increases. As the demand for equities increases, their yield declines and their price (value) increases. Thus, as a result of the initial decline in interest rates, bond and stock prices will increase, thereby raising the value of wealth. There is ample evidence to suggest that changes in the value of wealth significantly affect consumer spending.

---

[3] Sherman J. Maisel, "The Effect of Monetary Policy on Expenditures in Specific Sectors of the Economy," in William E. Gibson and George G. Kaufman (eds.), *Monetary Economics: Readings on Current Issues* (New York: McGraw-Hill, 1971), p. 495.

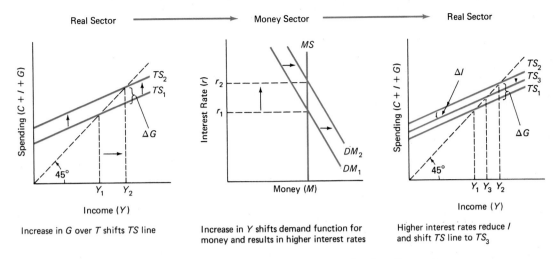

FIGURE 23-15 **Partial crowding out of an expansionary fiscal policy action**

Thus, the evidence suggests that major components of total spending are sensitive to the cost and availability of credit. Although it appears that these expenditures respond to changes in the interest rate, it also appears that there is a considerable lag in the time that some types of expenditure take to adjust; that is, a 100-basis-point change in the interest rate may not be fully felt on various types of spending for as long as up to four years.

Key Relationships for Fiscal Policy

There is an asymmetrical relationship between fiscal and monetary policy with respect to the interest elasticity of the demand function for money and the investment function. Values of interest elasticity that render monetary policy more (less) effective also render fiscal policy less (more) effective. At one time, economists argued that high interest elasticity of money demand and low interest elasticity of investment rendered monetary policy considerably less effective than fiscal policy. This is no longer accepted. Empirical evidence on the key relationships suggests that monetary policy is very important in the Keynesian model. In fact, the tables have been turned on fiscal policy. It is now regarded as subject to important *crowding-out effects*. Crowding out refers to the impact that deficit spending has on private spending. Complete or 100% crowding out occurs when an increased deficit of $1 billion causes a reduction in private spending by $1 billion. Partial crowding out occurs when the reduction in private spending is less than the increase in the deficit.

Let us first consider the effect of the elasticity of the money demand function on the outcome of deficit spending. Figure 23-15 indicates that total spending is shifted up by the amount of the increased G and the real sector of the economy is no longer in equilibrium at income Y_1. At income level Y_1 excess spending leads to an increase in income, output, and employment, to Y_2. However the increase in income influences the money market by shifting the demand function for money to the right, from

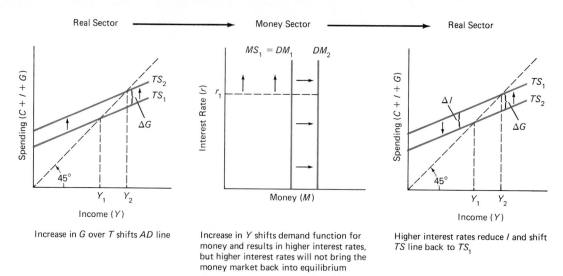

FIGURE 23-16   **Complete crowding out of an expansionary fiscal policy action**

DM_1 to DM_2. If the demand function for money is interest inelastic, the interest rate must increase by a large amount to bring the supply and demand for money back into equilibrium. The increase in the interest rate, however, offsets part of the original increase in G by decreasing the amount of investment spending. The TS line shifted originally to TS_2, but, as a result of the increase in r, the TS line shifts down to TS_3. As long as the demand for money is sensitive (even if highly interest inelastic) to the rate of interest, the net effect of the increase in G and subsequent decline in I will be positive. An increase in G with no change in MS increases economic activity. However, if the demand for money is completely interest inelastic and only a function of the level of income, the increase in G is offset completely by the decline in I.

Figure 23-16 illustrates a completely interest inelastic demand function for money. An increase in G leads to an increase in economic activity, shifting the demand function for money to the right and creating an excess demand for money. The money market diagram may look a little strange at first. At the initial state of equilibrium, Y_1, the demand function is vertical, because it is unaffected by changes in r; in equilibrium, the vertical demand for money will coincide with the vertical supply function for money at $MS_1 = DM_1$. The interest rate, r_1, is actually determined in the real sector by saving and investment. As Y expands, the vertical demand function shifts to the right, from DM_1 to DM_2, and creates an excess demand for money at the existing rate of interest. Because the demand for money is not sensitive to the rate of interest, the increase in the interest rate will not bring the money market back into equilibrium. It will continue to increase and cause investment to decline until the decline in investment spending completely offsets the increase in G and the level of economic activity returns to its original position. At Y_1, the demand function for money shifts to the left and becomes equal to the supply at the original level of income Y_1.

Thus the more interest inelastic the demand function for money, the greater the magnitude of the crowding-out effect, other things held constant. The elasticity of the investment function also influences the magnitude of crowding out. The more interest elastic the investment function, the greater the magnitude of the crowding-out effect. An interest elastic investment function means that a larger amount of investment spending will be reduced in response to any increase in the interest rate caused by the deficit.

Considerable empirical work has been done on the crowding-out hypothesis. This will be more fully discussed in Chapter 25; however, at this point we can summarize the three major conclusions. First, deficits do have significant crowding-out effects, though there is considerable debate over whether crowding out is 100%. Second, within the Keynesian model, the elasticity relationships in the real world do not lead to 100% crowding out. That is, the demand function for money is not completely inelastic nor is the investment function completely elastic. Evidence indicates that both the demand for money and investment functions are interest inelastic. Third, there are other important channels through which crowding out can occur in addition to the elasticity relationships in the Keynesian model.

Key Points

1. The basic Keynesian model holds prices and wages fixed so that changes in nominal values are changes in real values.

2. Equilibrium in the real sector is determined when the level of income (or output) is such that total spending for goods and services equals total output of goods and services. There is nothing particularly good about equilibrium income, as it may be associated with substantial amounts of unemployment.

3. Equilibrium in the money sector is determined when the interest rate is such that the demand for money is equal to the supply of money.

4. We adopt a partial equilibrium approach to the Keynesian system by first determining the conditions for equilibrium in the real sector, assuming that the interest rate is constant, and then determining the conditions for equilibrium in the money sector, assuming that the level of income is constant. Overall equilibrium will exist when both the real and money sectors are in equilibrium at the same time and at the same level of interest and income. The diagrams in this chapter cannot readily illustrate final equilibrium.

5. Monetary policy affects the real sector indirectly first by shifting the money supply line in the money sector and changing the interest rate. Once the interest rate has changed, the investment function and, hence, the *TS* line in the real sector will shift.

6. Fiscal policy affects the real sector directly by shifting the *TS* line by changing government expenditures and/or taxes. The final impact of a fiscal action requires consideration of the monetary aspects of the fiscal action.

7. The Keynesian model regards monetary policy as having an indirect effect on the real sector as compared with the direct effects of fiscal policy.

8. The impact of monetary and fiscal policy depends on the interest elasticity of the demand function for money and the investment function. At one time, Keynesians argued that a high interest elastic money demand and a low interest elastic investment function rendered fiscal policy as a more effective instrument than monetary policy. Evidence now indicates that monetary policy is more important than fiscal policy.

9. Fiscal policy is subject to crowding-out effects in that increased deficits reduce private investment spending because of higher interest rates and other causes; however, there is debate over the magnitude of the crowding-out effect.

Key Terms

Average propensity to consume

Consumption function

Countercyclical fiscal and monetary policy

Crowding-out effects of fiscal policy

Direct effects of fiscal policy

Fiscal policy

General equilibrium

Income multiplier

Indirect effects of monetary policy

Interest elasticity of investment

Interest elasticity of the demand for money

Investment function

Marginal propensity to consume

Monetary policy

Partial equilibrium

Precautionary demand for money

Speculative demand for money

Total spending

Transactions demand for money

Unemployment equilibrium

Questions

1. Taxes on consumption such as the general sales tax are often regarded as regressive since the tax burden declines as income increases. Does the consumption function imply anything about this issue?

2. Will a reduction in tax revenue by $1 billion have the same impact on spending as an increase in government expenditures by $1 billion?

3. We have assumed that there are two financial assets: money and bonds. Money is assumed to yield a zero interest return; however, various components of the U.S. money supply now earn explicit interest. How does the payment of interest on money change the money market analysis in the Keynesian model?

4. Is the value of the income multiplier on page 515 influenced by adding lump-sum taxes to the model? Is the value of the income multiplier influenced by adding a more sophisticated tax function such as explained in the footnote on page 517?

5. Does the interaction between the real and money sectors resulting from a government deficit help us understand the political conflicts that exist between Congress and/or the administration and the Federal Reserve?

6. Trace out several of the feedback effects of an expansionary monetary policy using diagrams.

7. Explain why a highly interest elastic demand function for money would suggest that monetary policy in a recession is like "pushing on a string."

8. Explain why the key relationships that make monetary policy an ineffective stabilization instrument in the Keynesian system render fiscal policy an effective instrument and vice versa.

9. The discussion of the multiplier held constant

the money market. Is the income multiplier independent of the money market, and if not, how is the multiplier influenced by the money market?

10. Trace out several of the feedback effects of an expansionary pure fiscal policy.

Suggested Readings

References are provided in Chapter 24.

The Extended Keynesian Model, General Equilibrium, and the *IS-LM* Framework

Chapter Overview

This chapter continues the Keynesian model by first developing it in terms of the *IS-LM* framework to consider more formally the general equilibrium nature of the model. Within the general equilibrium setting, we then consider the impact and effectiveness of monetary and fiscal policy. At this stage, however, we still retain the assumption of fixed prices and wages.

We then relax the fixed price and wage assumption thereby permitting us to restate the Keynesian model in terms of aggregate demand and supply previously employed in Chapter 23 to summarize the classical model. The chapter then considers the implications of two assumptions about wages and prices. The first—that prices and wages are flexible as in the classical model—and the second—that prices are flexible but wages are flexible only in an upward direction. The second assumption was the most widely adopted during the Keynesian revolution period.

The second assumption of rigid wages in a downward direction provides an Keynesian aggregate supply function that differs from the classical supply function with fundamentally different implications for the role of government policy. The Keynesian supply function implies the possibility of unemployment equilibrium and the need for activist government policy. As we will see, however, the same supply function would characterize the classical model if wages were assumed to be rigid in a downward direction in the classical setting.

On the other hand, flexible prices and wages for all practical purposes render the

Keynesian model a long-run full-employment equilibrium model in much the same vein as the classical model. In this case, the aggregate supply function in the Keynesian and classical models is identical in the long run.

Keynes and early Keynesian economists failed to explain why wages should be rigid in a downward direction. It became apparent to others that the assumption of rigid wages created a logical problem for the Keynesian model. At the same time, the assumption of flexible wages and prices rendered the Keynesian model essentially classical in nature in terms of its long-run equilibrium characteristics.

Thus, by the 1960s it was apparent that despite all the methodological differences between the Keynesian and classical models, the underlying rationale for activist policies depended on how much reliance could be placed on flexible prices and wages.

The Real Sector—*IS* Function

Equilibrium in the real sector can be expressed in terms of spending and output concepts. The equilibrium condition is given by

$$Y = C + I + G_0 \tag{1}$$

or, recognizing the behavioral relationships for consumption and investment.

$$Y = C(Y) + I(r) + G_0 \tag{2}$$

The level of government expenditures, G, is exogenously given at G_0. The equilibrium solution depends on finding a combination of Y and r that will lead to a level of income at which output equals total spending for goods. For a given r, there is some value of Y at which spending equals output. At a different r, then, there will be some other value of Y at which total spending equals output. In fact, there are a large number combinations of interest and income levels at which the real sector will be in equilibrium.

The level of investment is determined for a given rate of interest, and, combining this level of investment with the level of government expenditures and the consumption function, we obtain the total spending line. By changing the rate of interest, we obtain a new total spending line, as the level of investment will change even though the level of government expenditures and the consumption function remain unchanged.

In Figure 24-1, TS_1 is the total spending function, assuming an interest rate of r_1. The equilibrium level of income is then Y_1. At the lower interest rate of r_2, the TS line shifts upward to TS_2. The only difference between TS_1 and TS_2 is a higher level of investment as a result of a lower interest rate. The new total spending line determines a new level of equilibrium income at Y_2. We can plot the two equilibrium combinations of interest and income (r_1, Y_1) and (r_2, Y_2) in Figure 24-1 and construct the IS function. Only two points are needed as we are dealing with linear functions. The IS function indicates all possible Y and r combinations that yield equilibrium in the real sector.

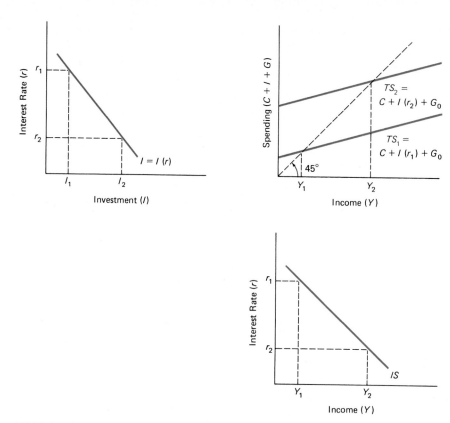

FIGURE 24-1   Construction of the *IS* function

Notice that the *IS* function has a negative slope. A high level of income is associated with a low interest rate to achieve equilibrium in the real sector. To see the reason for this negative slope of the *IS* function, we need to consider equilibrium in the real sector in terms of leakage and injections. The condition $TS = TO$ is the same as $(S + T_0) = (I + G_0)$. Remember that T and G are exogenous to the model and taken as given at fixed levels. At a high level of income, saving will be high, so the total leakage from income stream $(S + T_0)$ will be high. For equilibrium to occur, the level of injections must also be high, and given the level of G_0, the only way for injections to be high is when the level of investment is high. Investment will be high only at a low rate of interest. Thus, a high level of income requires a low interest rate to achieve equilibrium in the real sector.

Shift in the *IS* Function

The *IS* function is a summary statement of all the functional relationships that define the real sector. It is an easy way to see the various combinations of Y and r that determine equilibrium. The slopes of the underlining functions influence the slope of the *IS* line, whereas shifts in the functions shift the *IS* line.

Any autonomous shift in a spending function in the real sector will shift the *IS* function; however, we are concerned primarily with the effect on the *IS* function of

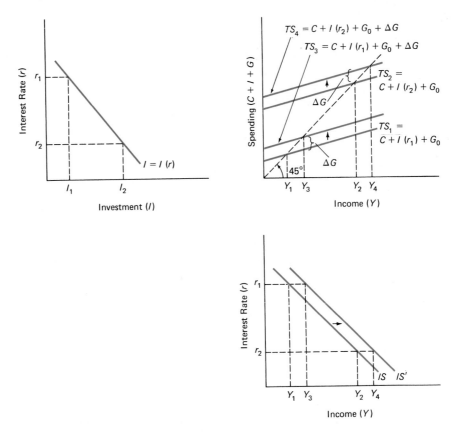

FIGURE 24-2   **Effect on *IS* function of an increase in government expenditures**

a change in G and/or T. An increase in G or a reduction in T will shift the IS line to the right, so at every level of the interest rate the equilibrium level of income will be higher. A decrease in G and/or increase in T will shift the IS line to the left, so at every level of the interest rate the equilibrium level of income will be lower.

Let us consider the effect of an increase in G and/or reduction in T. Either action will shift the TS line upward, although each operates through a slightly different route. Changes in G directly change the TS line, whereas changes in T change the TS line by inducing a change in the consumption function. Assume no change in the interest rate so the level of investment remains constant.

Figure 24-2 illustrates the effect of an increase in G on the IS function. TS_3 shows the aggregate demand line with a higher level of government expenditures as compared with TS_1. The only difference between TS_3 and TS_1 is the higher level G. The interest rate is constant at r_1, so the level of investment is the same, and there has been no change in the consumption function. Notice that TS_3 yields a higher level of equilibrium income, Y_3, than TS_1. The interest rate r_1 is now associated with a higher level of equilibrium income.

TS_4 shows the total spending line with the higher level of government expenditures as compared with TS_2. The only difference between TS_4 and TS_2 is the higher level of G. The interest rate is constant at r_2. Again, TS_4 yields a higher level of equilibrium income at the same rate of interest r_2 as compared with TS_2.

At the higher level of G, we now have two new combinations of interest and income that yield equilibrium in the real sector (r_1, Y_3) and (r_2, Y_4). Plotting these points in the bottom diagram indicates that the new *IS* function shifts to the right as a result of the increase in G. A reduction in taxes, *T*, would have the same effect on the *IS* function.

The relationship among government expenditures, taxes, and the *IS* function can be summarized by the following:

1. Increases in G shift the *IS* function to the right.
2. Decreases in G shift the *IS* function to the left.
3. Increases in T shift the *IS* function to the left.
4. Decreases in T shift the *IS* function to the right.

Note that a shift in the investment function (the relationship between investment and the rate of interest) will also shift the *IS* function. A rightward shift in the investment function (higher level of investment at every rate of interest) will shift the *IS* function to the right. Movements along a given investment function as a result of changes in *r* will not shift *IS* but will cause a movement along a given *IS* function.

Slope of the *IS* Function

The slopes of the various functions in the real sector influence the slope of the *IS* function; however, we are concerned primarily with the relationship between the slope of the investment function with respect to the rate of interest and the slope of the *IS* function.

The interest elasticity of the investment function expresses the relationship between the percentage change in the level of investment with respect to a percentage change in the rate of interest. An inelastic investment function has an elasticity coefficient of less than one in absolute value. An elastic investment function has an elasticity coefficient of greater than one in absolute value. For example, if the elasticity of investment with respect to the interest rate is 1.5, a reduction in the interest rate by 10% would lead to an increase in the level of investment by 15%. The elasticity coefficient is negative, indicating the inverse relationship between investment and the interest rate.

The interest elasticity of the investment function and the slope of the investment function are related in an approximate manner. The steeper the investment function, the more interest inelastic the investment function. The flatter the investment function, the more interest elastic the investment function.

Figure 24-3 illustrates the effect of a more inelastic investment function (steeper investment function) on the slope of the *IS* function. The investment function I' is drawn to represent a more interest inelastic investment function than the investment function used originally to construct the *IS* function. We have constructed the new investment function so at interest rate r_1 the two investment functions indicate the same level of investment, I_1. We can then regard TS_1 as representing the level of aggregate demand at the interest rate r_1 for either investment function. However, at the interest rate r_2, the new investment function indicates that the level of investment will be I_3. Using I_3 as the level of investment at r_2, the spending line is given

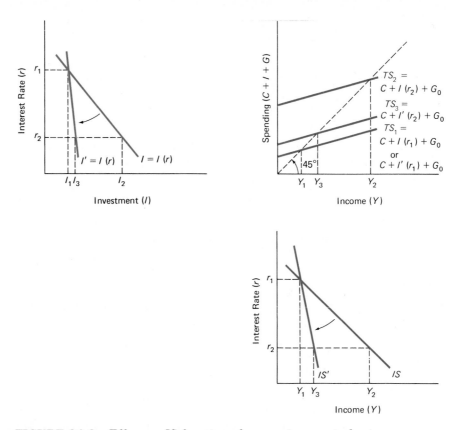

FIGURE 24-3   Effect on *IS* function of a more interest inelastic investment function

by TS_3. The only difference between TS_2 and TS_3 is the lower amount of investment at r_2. At the interest rate r_2, the equilibrium level of income is Y_3. TS_1 and TS_3 are the relevant spending functions at interest rates r_1 and r_2 respectively, and the equilibrium interest rate and income level indicate an *IS* function that is steeper than the original function.

The relationship between the interest elasticity of the investment function and the *IS* function can be summarized by the following:

1. The more inelastic (steeper) the investment function, the steeper the *IS* function.
2. The more elastic (flatter) the investment function, the flatter the *IS* function.

The Money Sector—*LM* Function

The money market is in equilibrium when the demand for money equals the supply of money. At a given level of income, the interest rate will equilibrate the demand

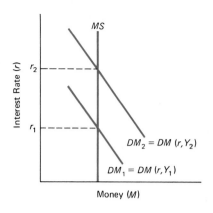 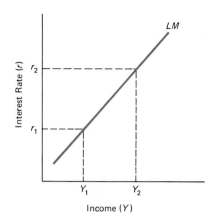

FIGURE 24-4   Construction of the *LM* function

and supply for money as individuals make portfolio adjustments between money and interest-yielding bonds. Formally, the money market is in equilibrium when

$$DM = MS \tag{3}$$

or, recognizing the behavioral relationships for the demand for money,

$$DM(r, Y) = MS \tag{4}$$

At a given level of Y, the interest rate will equilibrate the total demand and supply of money. At another income level, the equilibrium interest rate will change. Thus, from expression (4) we can see that a number of combinations of Y and r can determine equilibrium in the money market.

Figure 24-4 illustrates this point. The money supply is exogenous, and two demand functions for money are shown to correspond to two income levels. At Y_1, the demand for money is DM_1; at a higher level of income, Y_2, the demand for money shifts to the right, DM_2. At income Y_1, the equilibrium level of interest is r_1. At income Y_2, the equilibrium level of the interest rate is r_2. Plotting the two equilibrium points (r_1, Y_1) and (r_2, Y_2) on the adjacent diagram and connecting them constructs the *LM* function. The *LM* function indicates all combinations of interest and income that determine equilibrium in the money market.

The *LM* function's positive slope indicates that high levels of income are associated with high interest rates for equilibrium in the money market. To illustrate the positive relationship, consider the situation at a high level of income. At a high level of income, the transaction demand for money will be high, and, given the money supply, the speculative demand for money must be relatively low to achieve equilibrium. Speculative demand is relatively low only if the rate of interest is high. Thus, high levels of income are associated with high levels of the interest rate in the money market.

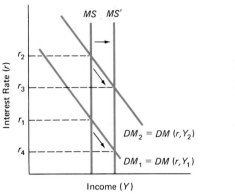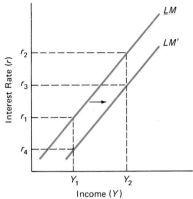

FIGURE 24-5   Effect on *LM* function of an increase in the money supply

Shift in the *LM* Function

Figure 24-5 illustrates the effect of an increase in the money supply by determining the new equilibrium interest rates when the money supply function shifts to the right. The original income levels of Y_1 and Y_2 are now associated with lower equilibrium interest rates, r_4 and r_3, respectively. Plotting the equilibrium combinations (r_4, Y_1) and (r_3, Y_2) on the right diagram indicates that an increase in the money supply shifts the *LM* function to the right.

The effect of a change in the money supply on the *LM* function can be summarized as

1. Increases in the money supply shift the *LM* function to the right.
2. Decreases in the money supply shift the *LM* function to the left.

Slope of the *LM* Function

The interest elasticity of the demand function for money influences the slope of the *LM* function. Figure 24-6 illustrates the effect of a more elastic demand function for money on the *LM* function. We assume that the response of the more elastic demand function, DM_3, to a change in income is the same as DM_1. That is, the horizontal distance between DM_3 and DM_4 is the same as that between DM_1 and DM_2. In both cases, the horizontal distance represents the response of the demand for money to an increase in the level of income from Y_1 to Y_2. We have drawn the more elastic DM_3 function corresponding to income Y_1 so that it determines the original equilibrium rate of interest, r_1. At a higher level of income, Y_2, the demand for money shifts to DM_4. The equilibrium rate of interest is r_4. Plotting the two new combinations of (r_1, Y_1) and (r_4, Y_2) that determine equilibrium in the money market on the adjacent diagram, we see that the *LM* function becomes flatter.

The relationship between the interest elasticity of the demand for money and the slope of the *LM* function can be summarized by

1. The more interest elastic (flatter) the demand function for money, the flatter the *LM* function.

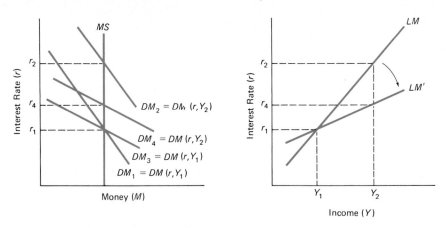

FIGURE 24-6   Effect on *LM* function of a more interest elastic demand for money function

2. The more interest inelastic (steeper) the demand function for money, the steeper the *LM* function.

Overall or General Equilibrium

The *IS* function defines all the combinations of *Y* and *r* that determine equilibrium in the real sector, and the *LM* function defines all the combinations of *Y* and *r* that determine equilibrium in the money sector. General equilibrium is determined when both money and real sectors are in equilibrium at the same *Y* and *r*. Figure 24-7 illustrates how the *IS* and *LM* functions define general equilibrium. Only at Y_e and r_e will both the money and real sector be in equilibrium at the same time.

Monetary Policy

Monetary policy has a direct effect on the money market. The Federal Reserve can alter the monetary base and, hence, the money supply. Changes in the money supply shift the *LM* function. Easy monetary policy is represented by a rightward shift in the *LM* function, and the new equilibrium is at a higher level of *Y* and lower *r*. Tight monetary policy is represented by a leftward shift in the *LM* function, and the new equilibrium is at a lower level of *Y* and higher level of *r*. Both types of monetary policy are illustrated in Figure 24-8.

One of the problems with *IS-LM* analysis is the temptation to use the diagrams in a mechanical fashion without understanding the "story" behind shifts and changes in the equilibrium level of interest and income. Let us make sure that we understand the story behind the impact of monetary policy by considering the sequence of events

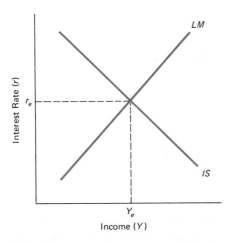

FIGURE 24-7   **General or overall equilibrium in the Keynesian model**

started by an increase in the money supply. The money and real sectors are in equilibrium before the increase in the money supply first impacts on the money market.

Money sector

1. $MS > DM$ as a result of increase in money supply.
2. Individuals make portfolio adjustments and use the excess supply of money to purchase bonds.
3. Increased demand for bonds leads to increased bond prices and a lower interest rate.
4. As interest rates decline (a) the declining interest rate increases the quantity of money demanded, as speculative demand is inversely related to the interest rate, and (b) the real sector will be affected by the declining interest rate.

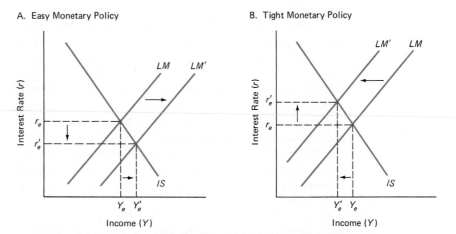

FIGURE 24-8   **Effects of monetary policy in an *IS-LM* framework**

Real sector

5. Investment increases in response to the decrease in the interest rate and shifts *TS* upward, leading to excess demand in the real sector at the original equilibrium level of output; that is, *TS* > *TO*.

6. Producers sell all they produce and experience unintended inventory reductions. They increase output and income payments. Total spending increases. And *Y* increases in the real sector.

7. As output increases, the excess demand in the real sector is thereby diminished.

Money sector

8. The increase in income in the real sector will feed back on the money sector by shifting the demand function for money to the right as transactions demand for money increases, leading to a further change in the interest rate that will feed back upon the real sector, and so on.

Eventually, both the money and real sectors will achieve a new interest rate and income at which both sectors are in equilibrium. The new equilibrium will have a higher level of income and a lower rate of interest than did the original equilibrium.

Effectiveness of Monetary Policy

Monetary policy operates by changing interest rates in the money market, which, in turn, influence the real sector. That is, monetary policy has an *indirect* impact on economic activity. The effectiveness of monetary policy depends on two relationships:

1. The interest elasticity of the demand for money
2. The interest elasticity of the investment function

Interest Elasticity of the Demand for Money   The more interest elastic the demand function for money, the flatter the *LM* function. Given the *IS* function, the flatter the *LM* function, the less effective monetary policy will be to change the equilibrium level of income. Figure 24-9 illustrates three *LM* functions corresponding to three demand functions for money. LM_1 is associated with an interest inelastic demand function. LM_2 is associated with an interest elastic function, whereas LM_3 is the liquidity trap case. When the demand function for money becomes horizontal at the existing interest rate (perfectly interest elastic), the corresponding *LM* function is also horizontal at the existing interest rate, indicating that no change in the money supply can alter the interest rate.

Figure 24-9 illustrates that the ability of easy monetary policy to increase the equilibrium level of *Y* is significantly affected by the slope of the *LM* function. In the extreme liquidity trap case, money supply has absolutely no impact on the equilibrium level of income.

Interest Elasticity of the Investment Function   The less elastic the investment function with respect to the rate of interest, the steeper the *IS* function. The steeper

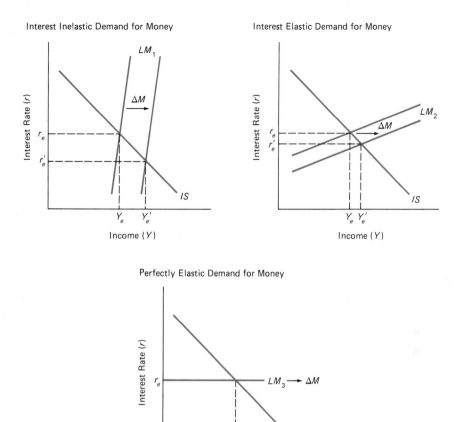

FIGURE 24-9   **Effectiveness of monetary policy and the interest elasticity of the demand function for money**

the *IS* function, the less effective monetary policy will be to change the equilibrium level of income. Figure 24-10 illustrates three *IS* functions corresponding to an interest elastic (IS_1), interest inelastic (IS_2), and completely interest inelastic (IS_3) investment function. The completely interest inelastic case is a special case in which no change in the rate of interest will influence the amount of investment. In this case, the *IS* function is a vertical line at the equilibrium level of income, indicating that changes in the rate of interest have no impact on the level of investment and, hence, the level of income.

Figure 24-10 indicates that the ability of easy monetary policy to increase the equilibrium level of income depends on the interest elasticity of the investment function. In the extreme case, any rightward shift in the *LM* function leads only to lower interest rates, with no change in the level of income. No matter how much the interest rate declines, investment spending is unchanged.

The Real World   The extensive empirical work already mentioned leads to the rejection of the extreme cases of either a horizontal *LM* function of a vertical *IS*

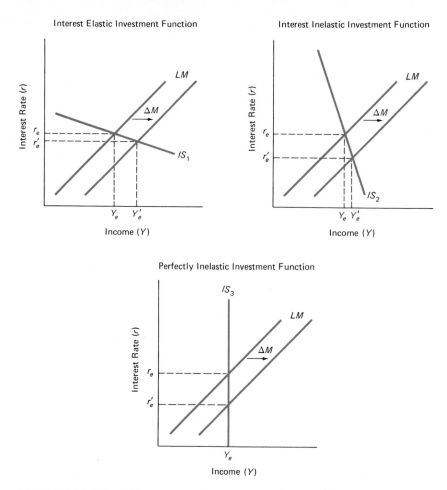

FIGURE 24-10 Effectiveness of monetary policy and the interest elasticity of the investment function

function. Rather, the evidence indicates that the *IS* function has a negative slope and the *LM* function a positive slope. In addition the position of the *LM* and *IS* functions is such that monetary policy can induce significant changes in the equilibrium level of income and output. The impact of monetary policy on income and the interest rate under different assumptions about the slopes of *IS* and *LM* are summarized in Table 24-1.

Fiscal Policy

Fiscal policy involves changes in *G* and/or *T* and directly affects the real sector first or, in terms of *IS-LM* analysis, directly affects the *IS* function.

TABLE 24-1 Summary of the effectiveness and impact of monetary and fiscal policy in the *IS-LM* framework

Policy	Which function is shifted?		Effectiveness of policy depends on the slope of the IS-LM function[1]				Final effects of policy
	IS	*LM*	*Flatter IS*	*Steeper IS*	*Flatter LM*	*Steeper LM*	
Monetary	No effect	Shift *LM*	More effective	Less effective	Less effective	More effective	Easy monetary policy: increase *Y* and decrease *r*
							Tight monetary policy: decrease *Y* and increase *r*
Fiscal	Shift *IS*	Depends on monetary aspects of fiscal action	Less effective	More effective	More effective	Less effective	Easy fiscal policy: increase *Y*; final effect on *r* depends on whether or not *LM* shifts
							Tight fiscal policy: decrease *Y*; final effect on *r* depends on whether or not *LM* shifts

[1] Effectiveness refers to the magnitude of the change in the level of income and output from an initial equilibrium position. Each of the four cases assumes that the other function has a normal slope.

Figure 24-11 illustrates the impact of a fiscal action designed to stimulate the economy. This can be accomplished by increasing *G* and/or decreasing *T* and will result in a deficit if the budget had been balanced before the fiscal action. The change in *G* and/or *T* will shift the *IS* function to the right; however, we must consider the monetary effects of this fiscal action before we can determine the new equilibrium levels of *Y* and *r*. A pure fiscal action (panel A) will involve increases in *G* and/or decreases in *T* without any change in the money supply. In this case, the government must borrow the funds in the money market to finance spending in excess of tax revenue. The *LM* function remains constant, and the new equilibrium will be at a higher level of *Y* and *r*.

If the Federal Reserve increased the money supply to accommodate the deficit spending (panel B), the *LM* function would also shift to the right. Income would be higher, but the final impact on the interest rate depends on the relative shifts in the *IS* and *LM* functions. In Figure 24-11 the *LM* function completely offsets the effect of the *IS* function on the interest rate.

Figure 24-12 illustrates the impact of a fiscal action designed to slow down the economy by increasing *T* and/or decreasing *G*. If the budget had been balanced originally, this fiscal action will lead to a surplus. The increase in *T* and/or decrease in *G* will shift the *IS* function to the left; however, we must consider the monetary effects of the fiscal action before the final equilibrium can be determined.

Panel A illustrates a surplus accompanied by a decrease in the public's money supply and, hence, shifts the *LM* function to the left. As the Treasury receives more than it spends and holds the funds, the money supply available to the public will

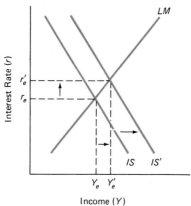

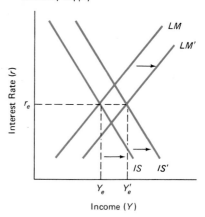

FIGURE 24-11 Expansionary fiscal policy in an *IS-LM* framework

decline and lead to a leftward shift in the *LM* function. The result of a leftward shift in the *IS* and *LM* functions will be a lower level of *Y*. The impact on *r* will depend on the relative shifts of *IS* and *LM*. On the other hand, if the Treasury uses the collected funds (panel B) to pay off some of the national debt, the money is then returned to the public and the *LM* function remains constant.

As in the case of monetary policy, we should investigate the story behind a fiscal policy action to see the sequence of events leading to a new equilibrium. Assume an increase in the level of government expenditures that will not be financed by an increase in the money supply. The real and money sectors were in equilibrium before the increase in government expenditures.

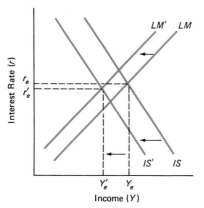

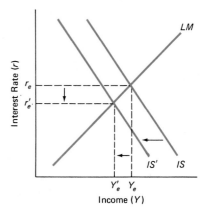

FIGURE 24-12 Tight fiscal policy in an *IS-LM* framework

Real sector

1. Increased *G* will lead to excess demand at the equilibrium level of income and output; that is, *TS* > *TO*.
2. Excess demand stimulates additional production and income. Output and spending increase and thereby reduce the excess demand.
3. The increased level of income at this point feeds back on the money sector.

Money sector

4. Increased income shifts the demand function for money to the right, thereby creating excess demand for money with a given money supply; that is, *DM* > *MS*.
5. In addition to the increased demand for money (for transactions), the government sells bonds to pay for the increased level of government spending. Both events increase the rate of interest in the money market.
6. The increase in the interest rate feeds back on the real sector.

Real sector

7. Increases in the interest rate lead to a decrease in investment and offset some of the impact of the original increase in the level of government expenditures.

Eventually, both the real and money sectors will achieve a new level of interest and income at which both are in equilibrium. The new equilibrium will have both a higher level of income and higher rate of interest as compared with the original equilibrium position.

The effectiveness of fiscal policy is also dependent on the slopes of the *IS* and *LM* functions as is the case with monetary policy. The impact of fiscal policy on income and the interest rate under different assumptions about the slopes are summarized in Table 24-1.

Crowding Out in an *IS-LM* Framework

The *IS-LM* framework can be used to illustrate partial and complete crowding out effects from government deficits. Consider first the *LM* function assuming a normally sloped *IS* function.

Figure 24-13 illustrates the case of partial crowding out. As long as the *LM* function has a positive slope (demand function for money has some interest elasticity), some crowding out will take place, although it is less than 100%. With an unchanged money supply, increased government expenditures lead to higher interest rates, which lead to a reduction in investment expenditures. As can be seen from Figure 24-13, the degree of crowding out varies directly with the steepness of the *LM* function. The steeper the *LM* function (less interest elastic the demand for money), the smaller the change in equilibrium income caused by a change in *G* and/or *T* and the greater the change in the interest rate.

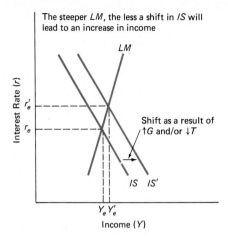

FIGURE 24-13   **Partial crowding out when the demand for money is highly interest inelastic**

Figure 24-14 illustrates the case of complete crowding out. The *LM* function is vertical at the equilibrium level of income, indicating that the demand function for money depends only on the level of income, not on the rate of interest. In this case, a shift is the *IS* function by increased *G*, and/or reduced *T* does not increase the level of equilibrium income; the only result is a higher interest rate that eventually decreases investment to offset completely the increased spending due to the government deficit.

The magnitude of the crowding-out effect also depends on the interest elasticity of the investment function and, hence, the slope of the *IS* function. Other things held constant, the flatter the *IS* function (more interest elastic the investment function), the greater the magnitude of crowding out.

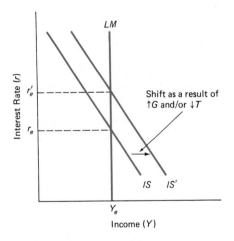

FIGURE 24-14   **Complete crowding out when the demand for money is completely interest inelastic**

Real and Nominal Changes in Economic Activity

So far we have avoided a complex issue. We have discussed the forces that determine the equilibrium level of income without indicating how the change in income or output is divided into changes in real and nominal magnitudes. By assuming a fixed price level, all changes in spending, income, and output have been real changes. As we did in the previous chapter on the classical model, we must now introduce more realistic assumptions about wage and price behavior and distinguish between real and nominal income.

Price and wage behavior is incorporated into the *IS-LM* framework in the following manner: (1) Prices are assumed to be flexible upward in response to excess demand and downward in response to excess supply. (2) Wages are assumed to be flexible upward (downward) in response to excess demand (supply). (3) Wages are assumed to be rigid downward in the face of excess supply while they respond in an upward direction to excess demand.

Thus, (1)-(2) and (1)-(3) provide two sets of price and wage assumptions. As we will demonstrate, the aggregate demand function is unaffected by which assumption we adopt. Whether we assume flexible or inflexible wages, the assumption of flexible prices permits us to derive an aggregate demand function with many characteristics in common with the classical demand function derived in Chapter 23. However, the aggregate supply function critically depends on which of the two assumptions we adopt.

Aggregate Demand and Aggregate Supply

The equilibrium relationship between the demand for real output and the price level is summarized by the aggregate demand function. Aggregate demand expresses the relationship between the level of real output *demanded* and the price level. Aggregate supply expresses the relationship between the level of real output *supplied* and the price level. Aggregate demand and supply allow us to determine the equilibrium price level and real income or output level given all of the relationships in the real and money sectors and the levels of government spending, taxation, money supply, and other variables summarized by the *IS-LM* framework. The product of the equilibrium price and real output level determines nominal output. We now discuss aggregate demand and supply in turn.

Aggregate Demand

The *IS* function in real terms has exactly the same properties as the *IS* function already developed. We now distinguish explicitly between nominal and real income

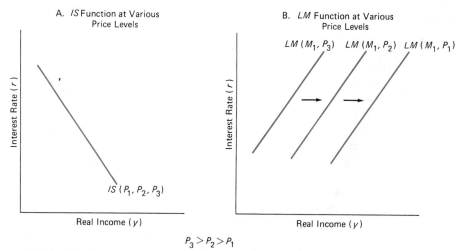

$$P_3 > P_2 > P_1$$

FIGURE 24-15   *IS* and *LM* in terms of real magnitudes

by defining the *IS* function as the combination of interest rates and *real* income (nominal income divided by the price index) that will equate demand and supply in the real or goods sector. Any change in the price level will induce a corresponding equal change in nominal spending, so that real spending remains constant.

Panel A in Figure 24-15 indicates that the *IS* function remains constant as the price level decreases from P_3 to P_2 to P_1. Note that we now measure explicitly real income or output on the horizontal axis; that is, $y = Y/P$. We will use y and Y as real and nominal income, respectively, whenever we are distinguishing explicitly between real and nominal magnitudes.

The position of the *LM* function, however, will be influenced by price changes. When prices were assumed constant, changes in the nominal money supply were equivalent to changes in the real money supply (M/P) and thus shifted the *LM* function. Changes in the price level can now change the real stock of money even though the nominal money stock remains constant and thus shift the *LM* function. In the case of the real sector, increased prices will only influence nominal spending and leave the relationship between real spending and real income unaffected. In the case of the money sector, however, a decrease in the price level will increase the real money stock, and, to induce people to hold a larger stock of real money balances, interest rates must decrease and real income must increase. Panel B in Figure 24-15 indicates that the *LM* function is shifted to the right (left) as the price level decreases (increases).

The aggregate demand for real output as a function of the price level that incorporates the *IS* and *LM* relationships and is derived in Figure 24-16. As the price level decreases, the *LM* function is shifted to the right and traces out a new equilibrium level of real income for each price level. Thus, for each price level, we have an equilibrium rate of interest and real income. The aggregate demand function is obtained by plotting the equilibrium level of output for each price level in a diagram measuring the price level on the vertical axis and real output on the horizontal axis. The aggregate demand function, *AD*, shows the combinations of the price level and real income that achieve overall equilibrium in the economy (intersections of the *IS* and *LM* functions). *AD* is downward sloping because lower price levels increase the

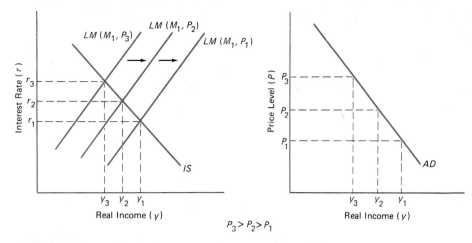

FIGURE 24-16   Derivation of the aggregate demand function

public's real money supply. To maintain equilibrium at lower price levels, real income must increase and interest rates must decrease to raise the public's demand for real money to the higher real supply of money.

The aggregate demand function is very similar to the aggregate demand concept already introduced in the context of the classical model.

Monetary Policy and Aggregate Demand

An increase in the nominal money supply will shift the aggregate demand, AD, to the right. This is illustrated in Figure 24-17. Assume that the price level is constant at P_1 and that the money supply increases from M_1 to M_2. The higher the level of the real money supply, the higher the level of equilibrium real income, even though the price level remains constant. In terms of aggregate demand, the AD line shifts to the right. If the money supply decreases and prices remain constant, the AD line shifts to the left.

The slopes of the LM and IS functions influence the responsiveness of the aggregate demand function to changes in the money supply. The steeper (flatter) the LM function for a given IS function, the greater (smaller) the shift in the AD function in response to a change in the money supply. The steeper (flatter) the IS function for a given LM function, the smaller (greater) the shift in the AD function in response to a change in the money supply.

Fiscal Policy and Aggregate Demand

An autonomous increase in spending (upward shift in consumption or investment function, decrease in taxes, or increase in government spending) will shift the AD function to the right. Assume that the price level remains constant in Figure 24-18 and that government spending is increased from G_1 to G_2. The higher levels of real income are associated with the same price level. Hence, the AD line shifts to the right. Decreases in autonomous spending will shift the AD function to the left.

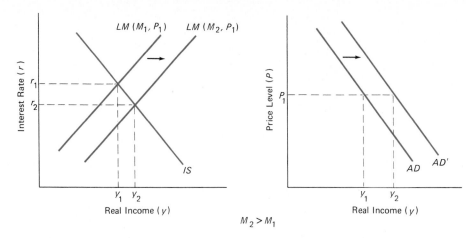

FIGURE 24-17   Impact of money supply increase on aggregate demand

The slopes of the *LM* and *IS* functions influence the impact of fiscal policy on the *AD* function. The steeper (flatter) the *LM* function with a given *IS* function, the smaller (greater) the response of aggregate demand to a fiscal policy action. The steeper (flatter) the *IS* function for a given *LM* function, the greater (smaller) the response of aggregate demand to a fiscal action.

Aggregate Supply

The aggregate supply function expresses the relationship between the amount of real output supplied and the price level. Its form depends critically on the type of wage and price behavior assumed in the model.

Figure 24-19 illustrates the Keynesian aggregate supply function assuming flex-

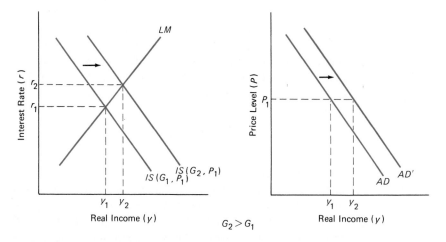

FIGURE 24-18   Impact of increased government spending on aggregate demand

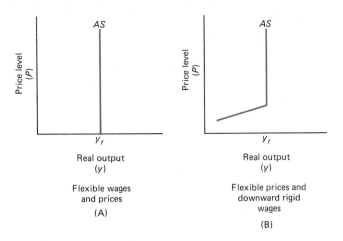

FIGURE 24-19   Keynesian aggregate supply function and wage behavior

ible and downward rigid wages in panels A and B, respectively. Both wage behavior assumptions regard prices as flexible in both directions. The supply function for flexible wages and prices is vertical at the full-employment level of output, y_f, while the function for downward rigid wages and flexible prices is "J" shaped. The "J"-shaped function indicates that real output supplied increases as the price level increases until the full-employment or potential level is reached, after which, real output does not respond to further price level increases.

Aggregate Supply with Flexible Wages   Let us review the classical aggregate supply function discussed on pages 495–498 to see why the Keynesian function would also be vertical at the full-employment level with flexible wages. The Keynesian labor market can be characterized in the same terms as the classical labor market. The demand for labor is an inverse function of the real wage rate and the supply of labor is a positive function of the real wage. Even though real wages are the main concern of employers and workers, they negotiate over the money wage rate. Thus, given the price level, competition will result in a money wage that generates a full-employment real wage rate.

Figure 24-20B illustrates the labor market at a given price level, P_o. The full-employment equilibrium real wage rate is denoted as (W_o/P_o), which equates the demand and supply of labor. This means that a negotiated money wage of W_o will generate the required real wage at the given price level. Remember that the subscript "o" for wages and prices does not mean that they have the same value. If the money wage is higher than W_o, say, at W_o', this will generate a real wage rate, (W_o'/P_o), at which the quantity of labor supplied exceeds the quantity demand. Wages will be bid downward in response to the excess supply of labor. If the money wage is lower than W_o, say, at W_o'', this will generate a real wage rate, (W_o''/P_o), at which the quantity of labor supplied is less than the quantity demanded. Wages will be bid upward in response to the excess demand of labor.

The same mechanism will occur whatever the price level taken as given. Figure 24-20A assumes a price level P_1, which is higher than P_o. In this case the money wage that clears the labor market is W_1. If money wages were higher, say, at W_1', the

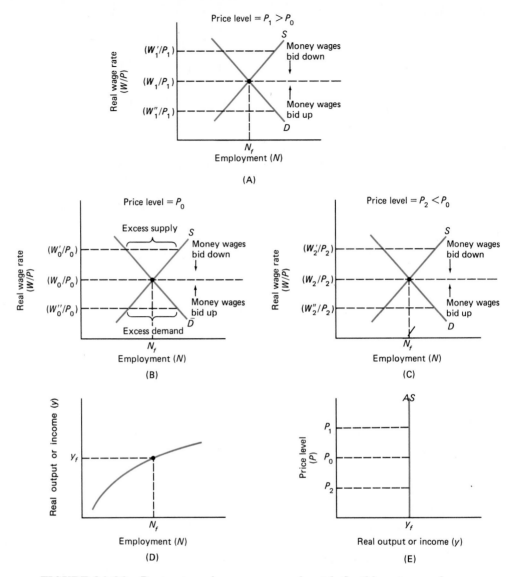

FIGURE 24-20   Derivation of aggregate supply with flexible prices and wages

resulting real wage rate would generate excess supply of labor, and money wages would be bid down. If money wages were lower, say, at W_1'', money wages would be bid upward in response to excess demand for labor. Panel C illustrates the same argument with a price level, P_2, which is assumed to be lower than P_0.

Thus, whatever the price level, money wages will move in response to competitive forces to establish a real wage rate that generates full employment, N_f. This, in turn, will ensure that real output supplied is at the full-employment or potential level no matter what the price level (D and E). Hence, the aggregate supply function is vertical at the full-employment level of real output. This is the same form as the classical supply function.

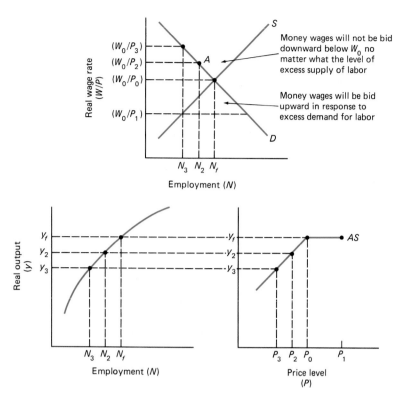

FIGURE 24-21 Derivation of aggregate supply with flexible prices and downward wage rigidity

Aggregate Supply with Downward Rigid Wages What happens if wage movements are restricted in any manner? Obviously the competitive mechanism cannot work as described in the preceding paragraphs. Figure 24-21 illustrates how the aggregate supply function is affected by downward wage rigidity.

Assume that wages are downward rigid at W_0. This means that money wages will not go below W_0 in response to excess labor supply; however, money wages will increase above W_0 in response to excess demand for labor. Assume that at a price level P_0, the full-employment equilibrium in the labor market is achieved when the money wage is W_0 because the resulting real wage (W_0/P_0) equates the demand and supply of labor. The impact of the downward rigid wage assumption on the shape of the aggregate supply function can be illustrated by changing the given price level.

Let us first see what happens when the assumed price level, P_1, is higher than P_0. In this case, the resulting real wage rate, (W_0/P_1), will generate an excess demand for labor. In this case, the market will bid wages upward until the full-employment equilibrium real wage rate is achieved. Now assume that the price level is P_2, which is lower than P_0. In this case, the resulting real wage rate, (W_0/P_2), will generate excess supply in the labor market. Since wages are rigid downward, money wages will not be bid downward, and the labor market will equilibrate at a point on the demand function (point A) with a resulting level of employment and output less than full employment indicated by N_2 and y_2, respectively. If we assume an even lower

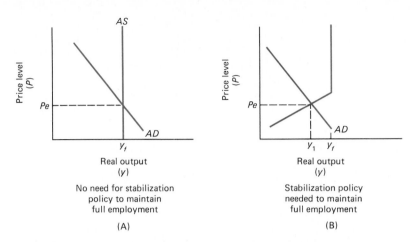

FIGURE 24-22   Stabilization policy and wage behavior

price level, P_3, so that $P_3 < P_2$, the resulting real wage rate (W_o/P_3) will generate an even lower level of employment, N_3, and real output, Y_3. Thus, the aggregate supply function is "J" shaped. At prices below a given price level, P_o, in this case, the supply of real output responds positively to increases in the price level. At prices above the given price level, the supply function becomes vertical at the full-employment or potential level of output.

Implications of Wage Behavior for Stabilization Policy

Figure 24-22 illustrates overall equilibrium under the two wage assumptions in terms of aggregate demand and supply. In panel A, the economy operates at the full-employment or potential level of output in the long run irrespective of the level of aggregate demand. Aggregate demand or total spending determines only the price level. This is essentially the classical result in that government stabilization policy is not required to maintain full employment. In panel B of Figure 24-22, the level of aggregate demand is critical to whether the economy achieves equilibrium at full employment. If as in the figure, aggregate demand is insufficient to maintain full employment, fiscal and/or monetary policy are needed to shift aggregate demand to the right until full employment is achieved. In this regard, Keynes emphasized the importance of *demand-oriented* or *demand-side* economics.

The assumed wage behavior is thus important for determining the long-run equilibrium characteristics of the economy. Flexible wages appear to suggest a non-activist approach while wage rigidities suggest an activist approach. This issue, however, is far more complicated. Specifically, we need to consider two things; (1) Can a case be made for activist policies even in the presence of flexible wages and prices? (2) How does one rationalize a particular type of wage or price rigidity?

Let us discuss each of these in turn.

Flexible Wages in the Keynesian Model: Full Employment?

The classical model implies a nonactivist approach to government stabilization because of the assumed flexibility of wages and prices. In the Keynesian framework also, flexible wages and prices generate a vertical supply function at full-employment output. While it is obvious that wage or other price rigidities interfere with the full-employment equilibrium of either the classical or Keynesian model, can a case still be made for activist policies in the presence of wage and price flexibility in the Keynesian model?

Keynes answered this with a resounding "yes."

First, private spending was inherently unstable, and as a result aggregate demand shifted back and forth over time in unpredictable ways. Even if the aggregate supply function were vertical in the long run, the economy would still experience fluctuations in output and employment. This would place even greater burden on flexible wages and prices to return the economy to full-employment equilibrium. Thus, there existed a case for *countercyclical* stabilization policy even in the presence of flexible wages and prices to smooth out fluctuations in output.

Second, the specific channels through which flexible wages and prices generated full employment in the Keynesian model suggested that such adjustments would be slow and painful, and even if they ultimately returned the economy to full employment, "we would all be dead in the long run." Let us spell out how flexible wages and prices worked in the Keynesian model to return the economy to full employment. Assume that real output is below full-employment output and that there exists an excess supply of labor in the labor market. Wage and corresponding price reductions would have the following sequence of effects:

1. Wage and price reductions would increase the real money supply given the nominal money supply, and since those factors that determine the demand for money had not yet changed, this would generate an excess supply of money in the money market.
2. The excess supply of money would be used to purchase bonds, which in turn, would lower interest rates.
3. Lower interest rates would increase investment spending and increase overall demand for goods and services.
4. Increased spending would increase employment and output.
5. Wage and price reductions would continue as long as output remained at less than full employment and repeat steps 1–4. Though not explained, this mechanism requires that wages decline more than prices or else wage and price reductions would be unable to eliminate excess supply in the labor market.

Figure 24-23 illustrates how this sequence of steps is reflected in the *LM-IS* framework. Assume that *LM* and *IS* intersect to generate a level of output, y_1, below full-employment output, y_f. Price and wage declines increase the real supply of money, thereby shifting the *LM* function to the right. It will continue to shift to the right until prices and wages stop falling, and this will only occur when the labor market is back to full employment. In terms of aggregate demand and supply, the same process is illustrated by the movement along the demand function from y_1 to y_f.

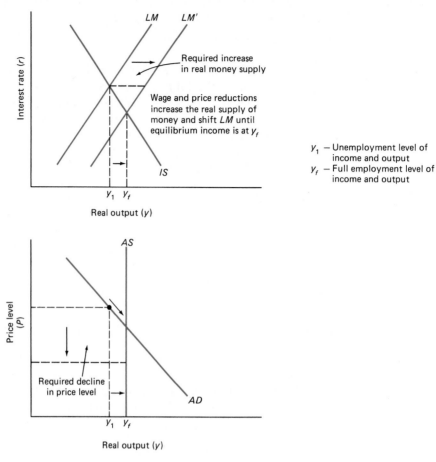

FIGURE 24-23   Full employment in the Keynesian
model with flexible wages and prices

There were two major obstacles suggested by Keynesians to this process: the
process would be slow and painful, or the process would never reach an equilibrium
at full employment. Let us consider each of these in turn.

The Process Would Be Slow and Painful   The channels through which wage and
price reductions generated full employment in the Keynesian model were likely to
encounter two problems according to Keynes. (1) In the foregoing sequence the increased real money supply reduces the interest rate; however, Keynesians regarded
the demand function for money as highly interest elastic. This would then require very
large price and wage reductions to induce even small declines in the interest rate. (2)
Even if the interest elasticity of the demand for money was not a problem, spending
would have to be sensitive to lower interest rates. Again, Keynesians argued that investment spending was highly interest inelastic and thus, very large reductions in interest rates would induce only a small increase in investment spending.

Both these problems meant that price and wage reductions would need to be
large and/or take considerable time to generate full employment. Figure 24-24 illus-

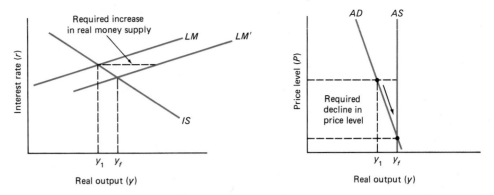

FIGURE 24-24   Highly interest elastic demand for money and flexible wages and prices

trates the case of a highly interest elastic demand for money in terms of *IS-LM* and aggregate demand and supply. The high interest elasticity of the demand for money makes the LM function very flat and the aggregate demand function very steep. This means that large reductions in the price level are required to generate full employment compared to the case where the demand for money is interest inelastic.

The Process May Not Even Work   Keynes suggested two reasons why flexible wages and prices might not even return the economy to full employment. These are extreme extensions of the two reasons why the process would be slow and painful. (1) The demand function for money might be *infinitely* interest elastic at a low interest rate because no one anticipates further interest rate declines. In this case, any increase in the real money supply would merely be held as a speculative balance rather than used to purchase bonds. This is the famous *liquidity trap*. (2) Even if the demand for money were not infinitely elastic, investors might be so pessimistic that even a zero interest rate could not generate enough investment spending to return the economy to full employment.

The liquidity trap case is illustrated in Figure 24-25. The *LM* function becomes horizontal at a low interest rate and the aggregate demand function becomes steep and does not intersect the aggregate supply function at full employment. A pessimistic investment function would generate the same result except that the *IS* function would become vertical at the less than full-employment level of output.

These two extreme cases not only indicate that flexible wages and prices would not return the economy to full employment but also render the final equilibrium of the model difficult to determine since prices and wages would not fall to zero in an economy with money as a medium of exchange and unit of value.

Why Wages Were Rigid in the Keynesian Model

Thus, even if one assumed flexible wages and prices in the Keynesian model, full employment equilibrium would not be reached anywhere nearly as quickly or as smoothly as depicted in the classical model, and in some cases, it might never be

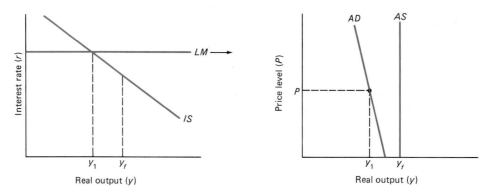

FIGURE 24-25   Infinitely elastic demand for money
and flexible wages and prices—the liquidity trap

reached. In any event, Keynes argued that wages (and other prices) should be
regarded as rigid during the time interval considered by any model of the economy.

Wage rigidity can arise for a variety of reasons, but Keynesians tended to emphasize either "institutional" or "money illusion" reasons.

Labor unions, labor contracts, and information imperfections provided institutional reasons why wages might be flexible upward but not downward. Money illusion refers to the confusion between nominal and real magnitudes that individuals
have in making economic decisions. Workers operating under money illusion are
more concerned about money wages than real wages and, hence, resist wage reductions even in the presence of price declines.

Was Keynes Correct
about Aggregate Supply?

The issue as to whether wages and prices are sufficiently flexible to provide a smooth
and rapid adjustment of the economy to full employment continues to be debated.
Before summarizing this discussion, however, let us take stock of those issues over
which a reasonable consensus can be found.

First, the proposition that flexible wages and prices will never return the economy to full employment either because of a liquidity trap and/or pessimistic investment function has little support on the basis of both theoretical and empirical
grounds. Theoretically, price reductions have effects in addition to increasing the
real money supply. The *Pigou or real balance* effect emphasizes the impact of price
reductions on the value of financial assets other than money, which in turn influence
total spending. Thus, price and wage reductions not only shift the *LM* function to the
right, but also shift the *IS* function to the right as increased asset values generate
increased spending. Empirically, there is virtually no support for a liquidity trap or
pessimistic investment function necessary to prevent full employment in the face of
price and wage reductions.

Second, Keynes argued that price and wage reductions would be slow and painful because of high interest elasticity of the demand for money and low interest elasticity of the investment function. Empirical work during the past few decades has shown however, that the demand for money is interest inelastic and that investment is sensitive to interest rate changes. Thus, the reasons emphasized by Keynes for a slow and painful adjustment process have not been borne out empirically.

Third, the original arguments used by Keynes and early Keynesian economists to support wage rigidities lacked theoretical foundation. Simply regarding money wages as institutionally determined is tantamount to saying that you have no explanation for an important macroeconomic variable and, in fact, creates logical problems for how the model behaves over time. For example, it might seem reasonable to say that during a period of time t, the wage rate, W_t, is fixed "institutionally" and proceed with determining aggregate demand and supply for time t. However, we live in a dynamic world that moves over time. To maintain wages at time $t + 1$ at the same level as t means that none of the economic values at time t plays any role in determining money wages in time $t + 1$, $t + 2$, $t + 3$, and so on. To argue that money wages are fixed because of money illusion conflicts with rational decision making. Individuals must ultimately be concerned with real and not nominal values. There is ample evidence to suggest that a model based on money illusion is unrealistic.

Thus, several of the early Keynesian arguments are no longer widely accepted. Does this mean that the Keynesian and classical model are the same with the same implications for stabilization policy? Absolutely not! The Keynesian model continues to hold the attention of many economists and policymakers.

Rather than fixed wages (or other prices), Keynesians now emphasize that wage and price adjustments are "sluggish" over time and fail to respond to excess demand or supply in a smooth and rapid fashion. Considerable theoretical effort has been devoted to explain why prices and wages might be sluggish. Whatever the reason, aggregate supply departs from the classical vertical position whenever wage rigidities are imposed. Keynesians continue to emphasize the inability of wage and price adjustments to generate full employment in a manner consistent with socially and politically accepted policy.

In addition to the view that wage and price adjustments are sluggish, Keynesians continue to emphasize the inherent instability of private spending and the fact that aggregate demand is likely to shift back and forth in unpredictable ways that require countercyclical policy.

Thus, even though the current Keynesian view differs from the model introduced in 1936, it continues to influence thinking about the economy and government policy. It continues to emphasize the inherent instability of a private market economy and the slowness of wage and price movements to reduce the amount and period of time the economy departs from its natural growth path. The persistence of departures from full employment despite the economy's eventual return to the natural growth path still provides a rationale for activist stabilization policy in the Keynesian view.

In contrast, the classical model has reemerged and regained recognition as an alternative view of the world. Like the Keynesian model, however, the modern version of the classical and quantity theory differs from the earlier statement in a number of important respects. The model still retains the essential classical message, though: the market system is inherently stable, wage and price adjustments smoothly and quickly return the economy to its potential growth path, and government policy should be nonactivist.

Thus, the debate continues.

Key Points

1. The *IS-LM* framework presents the Keynesian model more formally, showing how overall equilibrium is obtained as well as the complete effects of changes in fiscal and/or monetary policy.

2. The *IS* function indicates all combinations of income and the interest rate that will determine equilibrium in the real sector. The equilibrium condition is defined as the level of income and interest at which total spending equals total output or leakages equal injections.

3. The *LM* function indicates the combinations of income and the rate of interest that will determine equilibrium in the money market.

4. The intersection of the *IS* and *LM* functions indicates the level of income and interest rate at which both the real and money sectors are simultaneously in equilibrium.

5. The final impacts of fiscal and/or monetary policy depend on the nature of the *IS* and *LM*

functions. Table 24-1 presents a summary of the most important possibilities.

6. Differences between nominal and real magnitudes can be introduced into the Keynesian system in terms of the aggregate demand and supply functions.

7. The aggregate supply function in the long run is either vertical or "J" shaped, reflecting the specific assumption made about wage behavior. The nature of the aggregate supply function is a critical difference between classical and Keynesian models.

8. The Keynesian system has many variations, including one that yields full employment. However, the major point of the Keynesian model is the difficulty that a private enterprise economic system has in achieving a socially desirable level of economic activity without active government stabilization policy.

Key Terms

Aggregate demand
Aggregate supply
General equilibrium
IS function

Liquidity trap
LM function
Money illusion
Real balance or Pigou effect

Questions

1. Indicate how the *IS* function is influenced if the constant term in the consumption function increases. Is this an example of an autonomous change in spending?

2. What is the shape of the *LM* function if the demand function for money depends only on

income? Will this influence the shape of the aggregate demand function?

3. Explain why monetary and fiscal policy have different effects on the interest rate.

4. If the crowding out effects of fiscal policy are significant, how is this reflected by the posi-

tion of the *IS* function and the aggregate demand function?

5. According to the *IS-LM* framework, an increase in the money supply lowers the interest rate. Explain how the increase in the money supply first lowers the interest rate and then the feedback between the real and money sectors increases the interest rate to some extent.

6. In question 5, the combined interest rate movements net out to a decline in the interest rate in response to an increase in the money supply. If we consider the price anticipations effect on interest rates discussed in Chapter 5, can the ultimate effect of a monetary change on the interest rate be so easily identified?

7. Figures 24-24 and 24-25 illustrate the problems of achieving full employment even with flexible prices and wages in the case of a highly interest-elastic and infinitely interest-elastic demand function for money. Using similar figures, show how a highly interest-inelastic and completely inelastic investment function lead to the same implications.

8. Why does a decrease in the price level or an increase in the nominal money supply shift the *LM* function to the right, while only the increase in the nominal money supply shifts the aggregate demand function to the right?

9. Illustrate with diagrams how the interest elasticity of the demand for money and, hence, the *LM* function, influences the slope of the aggregate demand function.

10. Illustrate with diagrams how the interest elasticity of the investment function and, hence, the *IS* function, influences the slope of the aggregate demand function.

Suggested Readings

1. Rudiger Dornbusch and Stanley Fischer, *Macroeconomics* (New York: McGraw-Hill, 1987). Detailed discussion of the *IS*, *LM*, aggregate demand, and aggregate supply concepts.

2. John R. Hicks, "Mr. Keynes and the 'Classics': A Suggested Interpretation," *Econometrica*, 5 (April 1935), 147–159. Keynes did not invent *IS-LM* analysis, you have Hicks to thank.

3. John Maynard Keynes, *The General Theory of Employment, Interest, and Money* (New York: Harcourt Brace, 1964). The classic work of Keynes; however, this book is difficult going since Keynes made little use of the tools used in this and other textbooks.

4. Axel Leijonhufvud, *On Keynesian Economics and the Economics of Keynes* (New York: Oxford University Press, 1968). An attempt to focus on the real message of the Keynes model—the difficulty of relying on wage and price movements to generate full employment.

5. Don Patinkin, *Money, Interest, and Prices* (New York: Harper & Row, 1965). A classic study of the similarities of the Keynesian and classical model under the assumption of wage and price flexibility and the real balance effect.

6. Warren L. Smith, "A Graphical Exposition of the Complete Keynesian System," *Southern Economic Journal*, 23 (October 1956), 115–125. Probably one of the most concise and complete presentations of the Keynesian and classical models in *IS-LM* terms.

CHAPTER 25

Reemergence of the Classical Model: Monetarism and the Quantity Theory of Money

Chapter Overview

The initial enthusiasm for the Keynesian model began to wane by the 1960s as economists found that the model had its own theoretical problems, that the early antimonetary views of the Keynesian model could not be empirically substantiated, and that the model encountered increasing difficulty explaining the inflationary environment of the U.S. economy that began in the mid-1960s. At the same time, a number of economists were revising the classical and quantity theory approaches in ways that made that framework more appealing. This effort has been termed monetarism and led to the monetarist-Keynesian debate of the 1970s.

This chapter focuses on the monetarist view and its similarities and differences with the Keynesian view. The reader should be warned, however, that the terms "monetarism" and "Keynesian" imply more homogeneity within each group and heterogeneity between the two groups than one is likely to find in practice. They are terms used to categorize a variety of views, but economists cannot be placed so neatly in any one category in terms of their perspective of how the economy functions and the proper role for stabilization policy.

The chapter concerns three topics. First, we discuss those factors that led to the renewed interest in money and monetary policy within the Keynesian model and the renewed interest in the quantity theory of money. Second, we outline the major differences between the modern monetarist approach and the pre–Great Depression quantity theory. A simple monetarist model of the short- and long-run effects of changes in the money supply will help illustrate the modern monetarist view of the world. Third, we discuss the debate between the monetarist and Keynesian views. The debate started in the 1960s and reached a peak in the 1970s, and while consensus was reached on a number of issues, fundamental differences between the monetarist and Keynesian approaches persist.

The next chapter will focus on developments that emerged from the monetarist-Keynesian debate as economists attempted to develop explanations of economic behavior that improved on each of these approaches.

Changing Attitudes About Money

Until the early 1960s, economics and public policy were dominated by the Keynesian revolution. The experience of the Federal Reserve during the depression of the 1930s and the dominance of the Keynesian model overshadowed the quantity theory of money and faith in the ability of monetary policy to stimulate the economy. Starting in the early 1960s, however, professional attitudes began to change. By the 1970s, there was no longer doubt about the importance of money—all views recognized that money was an important determinant of economic activity. The reemergence of money and monetary policy also provided the foundation for the reemergence of the quantity theory in the form of monetarism and the monetarist-Keynesian debate.

Five factors account for the change in views about money and monetary policy:

1. Empirical evidence on key relationships within the Keynesian model.
2. Empirical evidence on the statistical association between money and economic activity.
3. Simple and complex econometric models that allocate an important role to money.
4. Reinterpretation of the role of monetary policy during the Great Depression.
5. Change in the nature of the economic problem facing the U.S. economy.

Key Relationships in the Keynesian Model The empirical evidence regarding the interest elasticity of the demand function for money and the investment function suggest that monetary policy is an effective instrument of stabilization even within the Keynesian model. This evidence was reviewed in Chapter 22.

Association Between Money and Economic Activity A large amount of empirical work has been directed toward investigating the relationship between changes in the money supply and changes in economic activity. These statistical associations are crude in that they are not based on a detailed theoretical model with a number of functional relationships. They are based on the hypothesis that, if changes in the money supply exert a significant and predictable impact on economic activity, we should be able to find a high degree of statistical association. In addition, changes in the money supply should precede the corresponding change in economic activity.

A strong statistical association between money and economic activity does not prove that money causes changes in economic activity; it is only consistent with the hypothesis. Likewise, if we observe that changes in the money supply precede a change in economic activity, this does not prove that the change in money caused the change in economic activity; it is only consistent with the hypothesis. Keeping these limitations in mind, we will summarize a well-known statistical study on the relationship between money and economic activity and a recent update of that study.

As part of their study of the role of money in the U.S. economy from 1867 through 1960, Friedman and Schwartz examined the statistical relationship between changes in the money supply and a general measure of economic activity.[1] Changes in the money supply were used to abstract from the strong trend component of money over the 100-year period. In fact, the 1930s were the only prolonged period over which the money supply declined in absolute terms. The measure of economic activity used were the turning points in general business activity established by the National Bureau of Economic Research (NBER).

Table 25-1 presents the peaks and troughs in general business established by the NBER. Each date represents the point in time when the economy moved from an expansion to a contraction in economic activity (peak) and the point in time the economy moved from a contraction to an expansion (trough).

Friedman and Schwartz compared the growth rate of the money supply with the change in economic activity represented by the business cycle turning points and reached the following conclusions. (1) The amplitude of changes in the money supply were closely associated with the magnitude of the business cycles. Minor fluctuations in economic activity were associated with minor fluctuations in the growth rate of the money supply, whereas major changes in activity were associated with major changes in the growth of money. (2) Changes in the money supply preceded the change in business for all the major economic fluctuations. The average lead of the change in money, or, as more commonly stated, the average lag in effect of the change in money, was 12 months for increases in the growth of money and 16 months for decreases in the growth of money. (3) Even though a consistent lag of changes in money was found, the individual lags fluctuated widely around the average values. (4) Detailed analysis of specific historical periods like the 1929–1933 period indicated that the change in money was not caused by the change in economic activity. That is, according to Friedman and Schwartz, it could not be claimed that the close association between money and economic activity was merely the result of changes in general economic activity causing changes in the money supply.

The Friedman and Schwartz study generated considerable debate and discussion; however, it has been one of the most important factors stimulating research into the role of money and monetary policy in determining economic activity. In an update of that study by Byron Higgins,[2] using a different method of comparing money and economic activity, similar conclusions were reached. The evidence over the period 1952–1979 indicated that recessions are preceded by decelerations in the money supply in most instances and suggested a definite relationship between monetary deceleration and a decline in economic activity.

---

[1] Milton Friedman and Anna Schwartz, "Money and Business Cycles," *Review of Economics and Statistics, Supplement,* 45 (February 1963), 32–78.

[2] Byron Higgins, "Monetary Growth and Business Cycles," *Economic Review,* Federal Reserve Bank of Kansas City (April 1979), 3–23.

TABLE 25-1   Business cycle expansions and contractions in the United States, 1854–1989

| Business Cycle Reference Dates | | Duration (months)[1] | | | |
| | | | | Cycle | |
Trough	Peak	Contraction (trough from previous peak)	Expansion (trough to peak)	Trough from Previous Trough	Peak from Previous Peak
December 1854	June 1857		30		
December 1858	October 1860	18	22	48	40
June 1861	April 1865	8	<u>46</u>	30	<u>54</u>
December 1867	June 1869	<u>32</u>	18	<u>78</u>	50
December 1870	October 1873	18	34	36	52
March 1879	March 1882	65	36	99	101
May 1885	March 1887	38	22	74	60
April 1888	July 1890	13	27	35	40
May 1891	January 1893	10	20	37	30
June 1894	December 1895	17	18	37	35
June 1897	June 1899	18	24	36	42
December 1900	September 1902	18	21	42	39
August 1904	May 1907	23	33	44	56
June 1908	January 1910	13	19	46	32
January 1912	January 1913	24	12	43	36
December 1914	August 1918	23	<u>44</u>	35	<u>67</u>
March 1919	January 1920	<u>7</u>	10	<u>51</u>	17
July 1921	May 1923	18	22	28	40
July 1924	October 1926	14	27	36	41
November 1927	August 1929	13	21	40	34
March 1933	May 1937	43	50	64	93
June 1938	February 1945	13	<u>80</u>	63	<u>93</u>
October 1945	November 1948	<u>8</u>	37	<u>88</u>	45
October 1949	July 1953	<u>11</u>	<u>45</u>	48	<u>56</u>
May 1954	August 1957	<u>10</u>	39	<u>55</u>	49
April 1958	April 1960	8	24	47	32
February 1961	December 1969	10	<u>106</u>	34	<u>116</u>
November 1970	November 1973	<u>11</u>	36	<u>117</u>	47
March 1975	January 1980	<u>16</u>	58	52	74
July 1980	July 1981	6	12	64	18
November 1982		16	—	28	—
Average, all cycles					
1854–1982 (30 cycles)		18	33	51	51[a]
1854–1919 (16 cycles)		22	27	48	49[b]
1919–1945 (6 cycles)		18	35	53	53
1945–1982 (8 cycles)		11	45	56	55[c]
Average, peacetime cycles					
1854–1982 (25 cycles)		19	27	46	46[c]
1854–1919 (14 cycles)		22	24	46	47[d]
1919–1945 (5 cycles)		20	26	46	45
1945–1982 (6 cycles)		11	34	46	44

[1] Underscored figures are the wartime expansions (Civil War, World Wars I and II, Korean war, and Vietnam war), the postwar contractions, and the full cycles that include the wartime expansions. As of mid-1990 the expansion that started November 1982 had not officially ended.

[a] 29 cycles.   [b] 15 cycles.   [c] 24 cycles.   [d] 13 cycles.

Source: U.S. Department of Commerce, *Business Conditions Digest* (Washington, D.C.: GPO, February 1984), p. 104.

Evidence from Econometric Models of the Economy   An econometric model is a statistical representation of a theoretical model and has three purposes. First, it can be used to test specific hypotheses about the nature of the economic system. Second, it can be used to simulate the values of the endogenous variables under alternative assumptions about the exogenous variables. Because some of the exogenous variables are the policy instruments of monetary and fiscal policy, we can use the econometric model to simulate how the economy responds to different policies. Third, it can be used to forecast the values of the endogenous variables once we make assumptions about the future values of the exogenous variables.

A wide range of econometric models have been built and estimated for the U.S. economy. These go by such names as the BEA (Bureau of Economic Analysis) model, Brookings model, MQEM (University of Michigan) model, DRI-74 (Data Resources, Inc.) model, MPS (M.I.T.-Pennsylvania-S.S.R.C.) model, St. Louis Federal Reserve model, and Wharton model among others. All these models indicate that changes in the money supply generate changes in economic activity. Thus money and monetary policy are important.

Reinterpretation of the Role of Monetary Policy in the Great Depression   The Great Depression, which started in 1929, was the most severe by any reasonable standard in U.S. history. Even though there were periods of expansion during the 1930s, the level of economic activity throughout the period never came close to the levels that had been reached in the late 1920s. Only our entrance into World War II brought an end to the depression. The depression of the 1930s actually evidenced three different periods.

1. *The Great Contraction.* The "Great Contraction" covered the period from August 1929 to March 1933, with August 1929 usually being regarded as the peak in economic activity. The rationale for referring to the decline over this four-year period as the Great Contraction reflects the magnitude of the decline compared with any other decline in U.S. history.

2. *Expansion from March 1933 to May 1937.* This period represents an expansion in economic activity, as most indicators of economic activity began to increase. But the term "expansion" is misleading and must be used in only a technical sense. At the peak of the expansion in May 1937, the level of unemployment was still 20%.

3. *Contraction from May 1937 to June 1938 and Ensuing Expansion into World War II.* The expansion from 1933 was interrupted by a sharp and short-lived contraction in 1937.

The magnitude and general features of the depression of the 1930s are fairly clear. The causes are not so clear. In fact, this is a real paradox. We have no completely adequate explanation for the greatest economic collapse in our own history. The causes of the depression are usually centered on the period of the Great Contraction, as this period strongly influenced the course of events through the decade until entry into World War II.

The Keynesian view of the decline from 1929 to 1933 emphasized the autonomous decline in investment spending, which turned a normal contraction in economic activity into a complete collapse of the system because of the structural defects that had built up during the previous decade. The economy was structurally weak when the downturn in 1929 occurred. By the end of the 1920s, there was growing evidence that investment opportunities had been exhausted, residential and commercial construction had been overextended, and banks had become too heavily involved in the stock market boom. The Great Contraction and subsequent depression were interpreted as a nonmonetary phenomenon. The inability of the Federal Reserve to reverse the decline was proof that monetary policy could not stimulate the economy.

The publication in 1963 of Friedman and Schwartz's *A Monetary History of the United States: 1867–1960* devoted several lengthy chapters to the period from 1929 through 1933 and rejected the then accepted interpretation. In their view, the experience of the 1930s demonstrated the extreme importance of monetary forces and that Federal Reserve policy contributed to the decline because monetary policy was tight and not easy. Friedman and Schwartz posed two questions: "What was the primary cause of the depressed conditions during the 1930s?" and "Was monetary policy easy?"

Friedman and Schwartz use the demand and supply of money framework to explain the decline in economic activity in terms of a decline in the supply of money initially caused by a decline in Federal Reserve credit. The initial decline in money was accompanied by a run on banks in 1930, when individuals tried to convert deposit accounts into currency. At this point, the decline in the money supply became self-reinforcing as individuals withdrew deposits from banks. Because banks held only a fractional reserve against deposit liabilities, many were forced to declare bankruptcy. The failure of some banks increased fears that other banks were financially unsound, so individuals converting their deposits into currency quickly transformed a financially strong bank into a weak one and ultimately brought about its bankruptcy, and so on and so on. Remember that FDIC insurance did not exist until 1933.

A sharp decline in the money supply along with a stable demand for money would necessarily result in a sharp decline in spending and general economic activity. Friedman and Schwartz argued that the decline in money was largely autonomous and caused the decline in spending and output as individuals adjusted to eliminate the excess demand for money to equal the lowered supply of money. The role of nonmonetary factors is not neglected in the analysis. In fact, Friedman and Schwartz suggest that nonmonetary factors may have started the initial decline in August 1929, but, once the decline started, monetary factors became paramount.

The response to the second question posed by Friedman and Schwartz was just as controversial as their interpretation of the causes of the Great Contraction. They argued that monetary policy was not easy in any realistic sense of the term; rather, the available evidence indicated that the Federal Reserve exercised a tight monetary policy stance with the exception of only one short period within the contraction. At any time during the contraction period from 1929 through 1933, the Federal Reserve could have used open market operations (purchased securities) to inject reserves into the banking system and reverse the money supply decline.

Keynesians had argued that monetary policy was easy during much of this period because interest rates were low by historical standards. Friedman and Schwartz dismissed this evidence as incorrect. Short-term rates were indeed low, but long-term rates were high and long-term rates are the most relevant in the Keynesian framework for investment spending. Even though the Federal Reserve's discount rate was low by historical standards, Friedman and Schwartz point out that it was actually high relative to other short-term rates of interest. Thus Friedman and Schwartz argue that interest rate behavior during the Great Depression provides a misleading picture of the stance of monetary policy.

The Friedman-Schwartz hypothesis can be summarized as follows:

1. The Great Contraction was due to a sharp decline in the money supply.

2. At any point during the Great Contraction, the Federal Reserve could have reversed the decline in the money supply and significantly reduced the severity of the decline in economic activity.

3. The Federal Reserve had imposed a tight rather than an easy monetary policy on the economy.

4. The Great Contraction cannot be used as evidence that monetary policy is impotent.

The hypothesis sparked a heated controversy; for example, Peter Temin attacked the Friedman-Schwartz view,[3] concluding that nonmonetary factors were the most significant. Temin's analysis has been criticized, however, and shown to contain a number of errors. Despite this, it still represents the only serious attack on the Friedman and Schwartz view since first appearing in 1963 and has raised some issues that will require further investigation, especially with respect to the behavior of interest rates during the first few years of the contraction phase. A collection of studies on the Great Depression published in 1981 summarizes much of the debate over the causes of the Great Depression. The paper by Robert J. Gordon and James A. Wilcox[4] perhaps best summarizes the current standing of the debate. They distinguish between four hypotheses about the causes of the Great Depression.

1. *Hard-line monetarism:* The 1929–1933 contraction was caused by the decline in the money supply and nonmonetary factors played essentially no role. This is not the Friedman and Schwartz view since they suggest that nonmonetary factors may have initiated the decline in 1929.

2. *Soft-line monetarism:* Monetary and/or nonmonetary forces caused the initial decline, but, once started, monetary factors became the primary force causing the Great Contraction. This is the Friedman and Schwartz view.

3. *Soft-line nonmonetarism or Keynesian:* The emphasis is placed on nonmonetary factors such as the autonomous decline in private spending as the cause of the decline, but monetary factors contributed to the severity of the decline. This is the new Keynesian position, which now recognizes the importance of money supply changes but still emphasizes nonmonetary factors to a greater extent.

4. *Hard-line nonmonetarism or Keynesian:* In this view, monetary factors were relatively important. This is the Temin view and the most popular Keynesian view during the 1940s, 1950s, and early 1960s.

[3] Peter Temin, *Did Monetary Forces Cause the Great Depression?* (New York: W. W. Norton, 1976).

[4] Robert J. Gordon and James A. Wilcox, "Monetarist Interpretations of the Great Depression: An Evaluation and Critique," in Karl Brunner (ed.), *The Great Depression Revisited* (Boston: Martinus Nijhoff, 1981), pp. 49–107.

The evidence to date rejects the two hard-line views; however, there is still debate over the two soft-line views. In many ways, the two soft-line views differ only in emphasis, and neither rejects the importance of money. This is a significant shift in professional attitude about the causes of the Great Depression. Before the 1950s, most economists simply rejected the notion that money played an important role in the 1930s decline.

Emergence of Inflation and Stagflation as Major Issues in the Late 1960s   Much of the Keynesian model before 1960 focused on the problem of unemployment and recession. The model was depression-born and thus emphasized an economy that operated at levels substantially below full employment. The Keynesian model was not well suited for explaining inflationary conditions and even less suitable for explaining stagflation conditions. As inflation came to be recognized as an important problem, economists found that nonmonetary explanations were inadequate. In the early 1970s, stagflation motivated economists to turn away from the Keynesian framework and focus on models that incorporated flexible wages and prices, inflationary expectations, and the money supply.

Summary of the Factors   These factors thus account for the reemergence of the view that money and monetary policy play an important role in the economy. No model, whether Keynesian or otherwise, could neglect to allocate an important role to money. This formed the foundation for the reformulation of the quantity theory.

Modern Quantity Theory or the Monetarist View

The revised quantity theory was related most closely to the Cambridge version—with one significant difference. Instead of regarding k as essentially fixed, k was assumed to be a stable function of a small number of economic variables. Modern-day monetarists emphasize that velocity does not have to be a fixed number for the essential elements of the quantity theory to hold. Instead, they regard velocity or the demand for money as a *stable function* of a small number of economic variables. As long as the demand for money is a stable function, changes in the money supply will have a significant and predictable impact on economic activity, even if there are some offsetting movements in velocity. Milton Friedman was the first to restate the quantity theory, and much of his analysis has been incorporated into the modern quantity theory approach.[5]

Friedman states that the quantity theory must be viewed as a theory of the demand for money and that the demand for money (or velocity) is related to economic variables in a stable and predictable manner. The demand for money is derived from the point of view of an individual utility maximizing economic unit for which total wealth can be held in many forms. We can think of each economic unit

---

[5] Milton Friedman, "A Restatement of the Quantity Theory of Money," in M. Friedman (ed.), *Studies in the Quantity Theory of Money* (Chicago: University of Chicago Press, 1956), pp. 3–21.

in terms of the fundamental flow of funds equation developed in the beginning of this book as attempting to achieve an equilibrium relationship between the items in the balance sheet. The equilibrium level of any asset item depends on the rate of return of that asset, the rates of return of holding other assets, the level of income and wealth, the level of prices, anticipated rates of price changes, and other variables. Each economic unit is attempting to achieve an overall equilibrium balance sheet given variables determined outside its sphere of activity. Money is one particular asset Friedman singles out for special attention.

The general form[6] of the demand for money can be expressed as

$$\frac{MD}{P} = f(y, W, r, \% \ \Delta P) \tag{1}$$

where

$$
\begin{aligned}
MD/P &= \text{demand for real money balances} \\
y &= \text{the level of real income} \\
W &= \text{the level of real wealth} \\
r &= \text{the rate of interest} \\
\%\Delta P &= \text{anticipated rate of change in the price level}
\end{aligned}
$$

The level of real income, y, and real wealth, W, have a positive effect on the demand for money. The interest rate, r, represents the opportunity cost of holding money and has an inverse effect on the demand for money. Anticipated inflation reduces the demand for money since the real value of money declines with inflation.

Expressing the demand for money in terms of the demand for real money balances (nominal money demanded divided by the price level) implies that any price level change, other things held constant, changes the demand to hold nominal money balances by the same amount in order to maintain a constant demand for real money balances.

Friedman's demand function for money looks very much like the Keynesian demand function for money. Both Friedman and Keynes agree on the basic elements in the demand for money; however, there are four significant differences.

First, Friedman views money as an asset that produces a large stream of services to the holder. The stream of services cannot be separated into components associated with precautionary, transaction, and speculative motives. Friedman claims that $1.00 of money balances serves all these functions as well as others and that any attempt to compartmentalize is artificial at best.

Second, opinions differ over the role of the rate of interest in the demand function for money. One Keynesian objection to the quantity theory was that changes in the money supply and velocity (demand for money) were not independent. A change in the money supply leads to a change in the quantity of money demanded as a result of changes in the rate of interest. Thus, changes in money were offset either partially or completely by opposite changes in velocity. Friedman and the monetarists in general downplay the role of the rate of interest and regard it as having only a small role in the demand function.

---

[6] This is a simplification of Friedman's demand function.

Third, both regard equality of the demand and supply for money as a necessary condition for equilibrium; however, they differ fundamentally over the determinants of output. Monetarists, in the tradition of the quantity theory, regard income and output as depending on the basic forces in the economy such as the level of population, capital stock, technology, and so on. In the long run, output will be the full-employment or natural unemployment level. Keynesians, on the other hand, are neither as willing to view output as passively determined, nor do they have faith that the economy will produce a level of output close to the full-employment level. Even if this were true in the long run, many Keynesians view the short run as the most important period for human welfare considerations.

Fourth, Keynesians and monetarists differ in how individuals react to a divergence between the demand and supply for money. For example, an increase in the money supply creates a condition of excess supply. The excess supply of money according to the monetarist will be spent on a wide range of financial and real assets. Not only will the excess funds be used to purchase bonds and other financial claims, but they will also be used to purchase goods and services directly. Keynesians view an excess supply of money as being entirely spent on financial assets that are close substitutes for money in the spectrum of liquidity. The range of assets involved in adjusting to either an excess supply or demand for money underlies much of the monetarist-Keynesian difference on how changes in the money supply influence the overall level of economic activity.

Importance of the Demand Function for Money

The demand function for money plays a critical role in models of the economy and how monetary policy influences economic activity. The monetarist reformulation of the classical demand for money was a critical step toward reestablishing the quantity theory of money as a legitimate approach. The Fisher version of the quantity theory of money did not focus on money as something that the public held for economic reasons. Velocity or money demand was institutionally determined by characteristics of the payments system and either changed slowly over time or remained constant. The Cambridge version was a significant theoretical improvement in the sense that it regarded money as something the public made a choice to hold relative to other things. The demand for money could be explicitly expressed as a proportion of nominal income, or by the Cambridge "k." Demand for money was no longer buried in the concept of velocity. Unfortunately, the Cambridge version tended to regard "k" as fixed or slow to change, which essentially rendered it as susceptible to criticism as the Fisher version.

Keynes significantly advanced the theory of the demand for money. The overall demand for money allowing prices to change was expressed as

$$\frac{MD}{P} = f(r, y) \qquad (2)$$

where *MD/P* represented the demand for real money balances, r represented the opportunity cost of holding money, and y represented real income.

While Friedman's demand function is more general than the Keynesian in the sense that it considers a broader number of different ways of holding wealth, the essential concept of Friedman's function is also represented by expression (2).

The early monetarists emphasized two issues that separated the quantity theory from the Keynesian model. First, Keynesians argued that the interest elasticity of the demand for money was so large that changes in the money supply would largely be offset by changes in velocity. In contrast, Friedman argued that the interest elasticity was low and, in fact, in the early stages of the monetarist approach, the interest rate was regarded as relatively unimportant compared to income in determining the demand for money. Second, despite the form of the demand function for money, Keynesians regarded the function itself as unstable and unpredictable. Friedman and other monetarists, in contrast, argued that the function was stable in the sense that the demand for money depended on a small set of economic variables in a stable and predictable manner.

Thus, the Friedman demand function was offered as a challenge to the Keynesians and the outcome of the debate over the demand for money would have critical importance for how the relationship between money and economic activity was viewed. In this regard, we need to consider three issues: (1) What is the relationship between the demand for money and velocity? (2) Why is the demand for money or velocity important for the conduct of monetary policy? and (3) What empirical conclusions have been reached by studies of the demand for money?

Relationship Between Demand for Money and Velocity

Theoretically, the demand for money is expressed by (2). This formulation assumes that it is the real quantity of money that is demanded even though the public can only determine the nominal quantity of money it holds. If prices increase by 10% while there is no change in r or y, expression (2) indicates that the demand for real money remains constant. This means that the demand for nominal money must increase by 10% to maintain the desired real money balance.

To show how expression (2) is related to velocity, remember that the Fisher equation can be written as

$$MV = Py \qquad (3)$$

or

$$V = \frac{Py}{M} \qquad (4)$$

In equilibrium, the demand and supply for nominal money must be equal; hence, expression (4) can be written as

$$V = \frac{Py}{MD} \qquad (5)$$

Using expression (2), we can derive the velocity function as

$$V = \frac{y}{f(r, y)} \tag{6}$$

Thus, the demand for money implies a velocity function that depends on the same factors and vice versa.

In expression (2), an increase (decrease) in r decreases (increases) the demand for money and from expression (6), an increase (decrease) in r increases (decreases) velocity. Thus, velocity and the demand for money move in opposite directions in response to a change in the interest rate.

The relationship between demand for money and velocity in response to a change in income depends on the income elasticity of the demand for money since y is in the numerator and the demand function for money is in the demoninator of expression (6). If the demand for money is elastic with respect to income, velocity will decline in response to an increase in income. To illustrate, assume a 10% increase in y and assume, further, that the income elasticity of the demand function is 1.25. This means that if y increases by 10%, the quantity of money demanded will increase by 12.5% and in terms of expression (6), the denominator will increase more than the numerator and hence, velocity will decrease. If the demand for money is income inelastic, velocity will increase in response to an increase in income.

Why Is the Demand for Money Important?

The demand for money is important because it influences the impact of money changes on the economy. In terms of the Fisher version in (3), a change in M will only have a predictable impact on income if velocity behaves in a stable manner.

Keynes argued that, first, the demand for money was highly interest elastic. In this case, an expansionary monetary policy would be offset by opposite movements in velocity. A highly interest elastic demand function for money means that even a small decline in the interest rate resulting from an increase in the money supply will generate a large increase in money demand. In expression (5) we see that a large increase in money demand will decrease velocity by a large amount if the demand function for money is highly interest elastic; hence, the increase in M is offset by an opposite movement in V. In the extreme liquidity trap case, the increase in M is completely offset by an opposite movement in V.

Friedman argued that a highly interest elastic demand for money was not consistent with the real world. In fact, Friedman argued that the interest rate played a very small role in the demand for money so that any change in M would have predictable effects on income.

Keynes also argued that despite the form of the demand function for money, it was unstable over time. That is, the relationship of the demand for money to r and y changed so much over time that given r and y, one could not even come close to determining the public's demand for money.

Friedman countered that the demand function for money was indeed stable and could be used to predict the direction that velocity would change in response to changes in r and/or y.

Obviously, these differences could only be settled by empirical verification.

Empirical Estimates of the Demand
Function for Money

At about the same time that Friedman and other monetarists launched their attack on the Keynesian model, computers became accessible to economists and enabled them to test predictions of each model. Theory can carry one only so far. Empirical verification, though difficult and sometimes misleading, is a necessary part of understanding how the economy works. In this regard, the demand function for money has received an extensive amount of empirical study.

The empirical study of the demand function for money has already been alluded to in Chapter 22. By the early 1970s, there was a fairly wide consensus that the demand for money could reasonably be expressed as a function of income and the interest rate. Moreover, there was overwhelming evidence that the function was interest inelastic in contrast to the earlier belief of the Keynesians. The function also had a high degree of stability from a statistical perspective and thus was not unstable as alleged by the early Keynesians.

Just at this time, however, when economists reached a consensus on the existence of a stable demand function for money, something happened.

Money demand functions that had performed well through the early 1970s began to seriously overpredict the demand for money (underpredict velocity) after 1974. This raised a number of questions as to whether the demand for money could continue to be regarded as stable. The situation worsened in the early 1980s when velocity departed significantly from past behavior. Figure 25-1 illustrates the actual value of M1 velocity over the period 1965 through 1988 and the predicted value of velocity from 1974 to 1978. The predicted value of velocity is based on a traditional money demand model that expresses the demand for real money balances as a function of real GNP and the short-term commercial paper rate. The underprediction of velocity from 1974 to 1978 and the departure of actual velocity from its historical upward trend after 1980 are clearly apparent.

The problems appeared related to the deregulation and financial innovation process that accelerated in the second half of the 1970s and continued throughout the 1980s. New forms of money and quasi-money were introduced that presented market participants with a much larger set of ways in which to hold wealth. In addition, major shifts in monetary policy and operating procedures in 1980 along with the imposition of credit controls in March 1980 may have disturbed traditional money demand functions. As a result, economists revised the demand for money to consider new measures of money and/or new variables that might be important in determining money demand.

By the end of the 1980s, however, economists were not so confident in a stable demand function for money as they were in 1973. The failure to predict velocity has led to a reduced interest in the monetarist approach on the part of many economists and policymakers. Others argue that stable demand functions for money exist; however, they are more difficult to identify since the financial system is in transition.

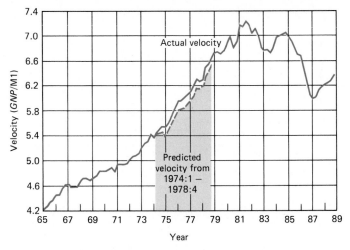

Source: Based on data provided by Citicorp Database Services.

FIGURE 25-1   Behavior of M1 velocity, first quarter 1965–fourth quarter 1988.

The dashed line represents predicted velocity based on an estimated money demand function. The money demand function expresses the demand for money as a function of real GNP, commercial paper rate, and lagged money. This is a well-known form of the demand for money and was estimated over the period from 1965:1 to 1973:4 and then used to predict the demand for money over the period from 1974:1 to 1978:4. Actual velocity is calculated as the ratio of income to actual money while predicted velocity is calculated as the ratio of income to predicted money demand.

Monetarist Framework

Monetarists argued that once the demand function for money was recast in terms of economic theory, the demand for money could be expressed as a stable function of a small number of variables. A stable demand for money function then implied that changes in the money supply would have predictable effects on the level of economic activity. At this point, the monetarist adopted the full-employment equilibrium view of the early classical model. Wages and prices could not be expected to react instantly to changes in aggregate demand induced by changes in the money supply; however, once these adjustments started, the economy would smoothly and quickly return to full employment.

Monetarists, like the earlier classical view, emphasized changes in the money supply as the primary force behind shifts in aggregate demand. While changes in money induced changes in prices and output in the short run, only prices responded to changes in money in the long run since potential output was determined by the economy's resource base.

We can illustrate the monetarist view in a series of diagrams presented in Figure 25-2.

These illustrate how a change in the growth of the money supply impacts the economy based on the following assumptions.

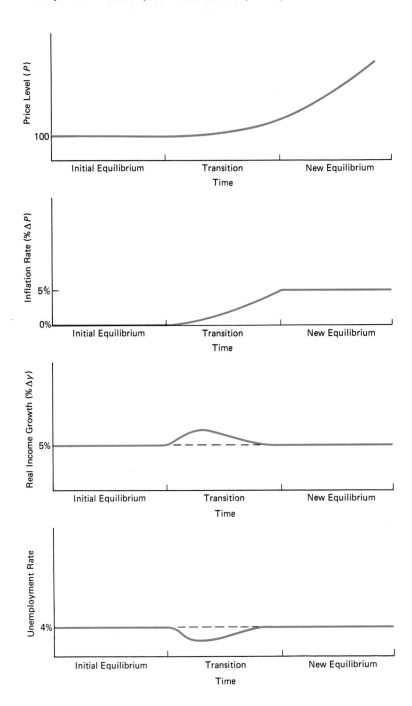

FIGURE 25-2   Adjustment of the economy to an increase in the growth rate of the money supply

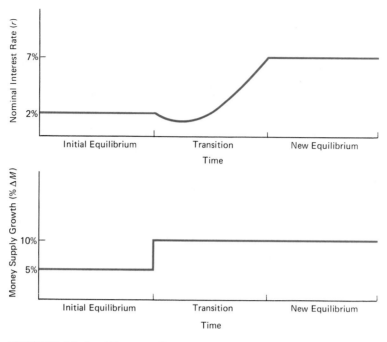

FIGURE 25-2 (Continued)

1. The economy is initially in a state of dynamic equilibrium in which the demand and supply for money are equal, money is growing at 5% per year, real output is growing at the natural or full-employment level at 5% per year, the unemployment rate is at the natural long-run level of 4%, the real rate of interest is 2%, and the price level is constant (set at a base of 100). These assumptions are illustrated in Figure 25-2 in the portion marked "Initial Equilibrium." According to the expression on page 492, the level of velocity is assumed to be constant, or $\%\Delta V = 0$.

2. The nominal rate of interest is equal to the real rate plus the anticipated rate of price change. The nominal rate of interest in the initial stage of equilibrium is 2%, since actual and anticipated price inflation are zero.

3. The Federal Reserve increases the growth rate of the money supply from 5 to 10% and maintains the higher growth rate.

Figure 25-2 traces out the response of the price level, rate of price change, real income, unemployment rate, and interest rate to the higher growth rate of the money supply. The higher growth rate of money initially creates an excess supply of money. We assume that individuals adjust to the excess supply by purchasing financial assets as well as increasing their spending on goods and services. The purchase of financial assets initially lowers the interest rate. The initial decline in the interest rate is referred to as the *liquidity effect* of a change in the growth rate of the money supply and results from the actions of market participants to reestablish equilibrium between the demand and supply for money. The purchase of goods and services increases the growth of real income above the long-run equilibrium level and lowers the unemployment rate below the long-run natural unemployment rate. The price level begins to increase and generates higher anticipated inflation rates. The increase in real income and anticipated inflation both operate to increase the interest rate. The increase in income increases the transactions demand for money and other things held constant, increases the interest rate. This is referred to as the *income effect* of a change in the growth rate of the money supply. High inflation generates high anticipated inflation and, as discussed in Chapter 5, is incorporated into market interest rates. This is referred to as the *price anticipation* or *Fisher effect* of the change in the growth rate of the money supply.

Why do real income and the unemployment rate initially increase and decrease, respectively, about the long-run growth path in response to the increased growth of money? One answer emphasizes the distinction between actual and anticipated inflation. Even if wage contracts incorporate all anticipated inflation, real wages are likely to decline initially in response to the monetary growth increase. Anticipated inflation depends on past inflation rates and is not likely to be adjusted immediately as a result of the increase in the money supply. There is a considerable lag in the response of prices to changes in monetary growth. The actual rate of inflation exceeds the anticipated rate of inflation thereby lowering real wages even if workers incorporate anticipated inflation into their wage contracts. Employers experience an unanticipated decline in the real wage rate while the anticipated inflation rate lags behind the actual inflation rate. Additional workers are hired and real income and output increase. The unemployment rate drops below the long-run equilibrium level. This process will not continue long, however. The price level accelerates more and approaches the new higher growth rate of the money supply. Anticipated inflation comes to incorporate more quickly actual price behavior, and thus wages increase more rapidly to equal the new higher inflation rate. The previous decline in real wages is now followed by an increase in real wages as wage contracts incorporate higher inflation rates. As a result, real output is reduced and the unemployment rate is increased.

The economy will return to equilibrium when everything has adjusted to the new higher growth of money. The level of real income and unemployment will return to their long-run growth paths determined by the economy's resources and technology. The price level will increase continually at 5% per year given that real output is growing at 5% and the money supply is growing at 10%. Nominal interest rates will increase to 7% as a result of the higher inflation rate; however, the real rate remains unchanged at 2%.

The modern quantity theory recognizes that changes in the money supply have significant and real impacts on economic activity in the short run or during the transition period; however, once the new equilibrium is reached, the level of real economic activity measured by real output and unemployment is unaffected. The primary impact of an increase in the money supply is to increase prices (and wages) and the nominal interest rate. These are the same results obtained by the earlier quantity theory, but the modern quantity theory is much richer in theoretical detail.

The foregoing sequence incorporates the notion that real economic activity is influenced by differences between anticipated and unanticipated events. The increased level of real output in response to higher prices occurs because the inflation rate exceeds the anticipated inflation rate and, thus, lowers real wages below anticipated real wages. The decrease in the nominal and hence the actual real interest rate occurs because inflation has exceeded anticipated inflation. This distinction between anticipated and unanticipated events has been an important contribution of the monetarist approach. This will be explored further in the next chapter, when we introduce the concept of the Phillips curve.

Monetarist-Keynesian Debate

The reemergence of the quantity theory of money in the form of monetarism in the 1960s generated a heated exchange between monetarists and Keynesians (or non-monetarists according to some writers). This section of the chapter summarizes the main outlines of that debate that reflect continuing and fundamental differences between the two groups.

Prior to discussing the differences, however, we first focus on the areas of agreement.

Similarities Between Monetarists and Keynesians

There is no disagreement between monetarists and Keynesians that money and monetary policy are important in determining the level of economic activity. Monetarists have always regarded changes in the money supply as the primary force behind changes in economic activity, and Keynesians now accept the importance of money and monetary policy within their own theoretical framework.

As one Keynesian-oriented discussion summarized, "Money is too important to be left to the Monetarists,"[7] reflecting more on the role of stabilization policy in a market system rather than on technical details of model formulation.

Issues That Separate Monetarists and Keynesians

The most important issues that separate monetarist and Keynesian approaches can be placed in one of two categories: First, there are issues that focus on the technical aspects of how money influences economic activity. Second, there are issues that focus on the broader aspects of the need for activist monetary policy. The distinction is based on their respective susceptibility to empirical investigation. Many of the technical aspects are more amenable to empirical investigation than the broader issues. In addition, the broader issues often involve fundamental value judgments

[7] Franco Modigliani and Lucas Papademos, "Monetary Policy for the Coming Quarters: The Conflicting Views," *New Economic Review*, Federal Reserve Bank of Boston (March–April 1976), 35.

about the role of government in society that are not likely to be decided by objective analysis.

Technical Aspects of Money and Economic Activity

The most important technical aspects of money that differentiate the monetarist from the Keynesian are the following:

1. The relative role of changes in the money supply and nonmonetary factors as the cause of changes in economic activity
2. The degree to which changes in the money supply can be regarded as exogenous
3. The nature of the transmission process between a change in the money supply and the change in economic activity
4. The relative roles of monetary and fiscal policy as instruments of economic stabilization
5. The use of monetary aggregates as an "indicator" of monetary policy
6. The use of large-scale structural models versus small reduced form models

Relative Importance of Monetary and Nonmonetary Factors

The monetarist regards changes in the money supply as the primary cause of changes in economic activity. Factors such as autonomous changes in spending can have an impact on economic activity, but, unless they are accompanied by a change in the money supply, their effect will be ephemeral. The importance of money as the basic cause of changes in economic activity is best stated by Friedman and Schwartz in their analysis of money in the United States from 1867 through 1960. They emphasized the conclusion that changes in the money supply were both a *sufficient* and *necessary* cause for major changes in economic activity.

Monetarists distinguish between the short-run and long-run effects of a change in the money supply in the same tradition of the early views of the quantity theory. In the short run, changes in the money supply influence both prices and real output. Velocity in the short run is also likely to change. In the long run, only the prices respond to changes in the money supply.

Keynesians have no difficulty in accepting the sufficient aspect of the monetarist position. Changes in the money supply in the Keynesian framework influence economic activity. In the short run, changes in the money supply influence both prices and real output; in the long run, real output is largely unaffected.

The necessary aspect of the monetarists' view is much more controversial. Monetarists believe that, unless there is a corresponding change in the money supply to accompany a change in spending, the net impact on real economic activity will essentially be zero. To see this more clearly, write the equation of exchange in the following way:

$$MV = yP = C + I + G \tag{7}$$

As long as the demand for money is stable and V does not change to support changes in C, I, or G, the only way in which a component of spending can change income is to be accompanied by a change in M. Keynesians are not willing to regard the demand for money as being as stable as the monetarists believe. That is, the Keynesians regard velocity as being much more flexible than the monetarists are willing to accept. Greater flexibility of velocity allows changes in spending to occur and influence income without corresponding changes in the money supply. Keynesians thus accept the sufficiency argument but reject the necessity argument.

Exogenous Versus Endogenous Money Supply Changes

Keynesians do not regard the money supply as an exogenous variable in contrast to monetarists who view significant changes in the money supply as being largely independent of current economic activity. Keynesians view changes in the money supply as being partially determined by current economic conditions. To see how this can occur, consider the determinants of the money supply developed in Chapter 10.

$$\Delta M = \frac{1 + k}{rt + k + rn \cdot n + e} \Delta B \tag{8}$$

The change in the money supply equals the change in the monetary base times the value of the money multiplier. The money supply can increase because of (1) an increase in the monetary base and/or (2) an increase in the value of the money multiplier. Keynesians argue that changes in the value of the money multiplier can occur as a result of changes in spending, thereby leading to changes in the money supply.

To illustrate, consider an autonomous rightward shift in aggregate demand. As a result, income, output, and employment expand in the real sector. This increases the precautionary and transaction demand for money and causes the total demand function for money to shift to the right. As a result, interest rates begin to increase in the money market. One of the determinants of the money multiplier is the e ratio, which expresses the relationship between desired excess reserves and transaction deposits. At higher rates of interest, the e ratio is likely to decline and thereby increase the value of the money multiplier. As the value of the money multiplier expands, the money supply will also increase, even if the monetary base remains constant. Thus, Keynesians argue that an increase in spending induces a change in the money supply.

Whether or not changes in the money supply can be treated as largely exogenous has an important bearing on the interpretation of historical relationships between changes in the money supply and changes in economic activity. Much effort has been devoted to comparing turning points in the money supply with turning points in general economic activity and estimating regression relationships between income and money. The results all demonstrate a highly significant relationship but do not prove that money causes changes in economic activity. They are also consistent with the reverse causation that changes in economic activity induce changes in the money supply if the money supply is essentially endogenous. The degree to which the money supply is endogenous has an important effect on the interpretation of the historical relationships between money and economic activity.

Transmission Process

The monetarists emphasize the direct relationship between changes in money and economic activity. As a result of a stable demand function for money, changes in the money supply create a divergence between demand and supply for money that are translated into adjustments in financial and real assets. Part of the effect of a change in the money supply does work through the financial system as described by Keynesians, but the primary impact operates directly on spending.

Keynesians emphasize the indirect effects of changes in the money supply that first change the cost and availability of credit in the financial system. This, in turn, will change the components of total spending that are sensitive to changes in the cost and availability of credit.

The Role of Fiscal Policy and the Crowding-Out Hypothesis

At one time, Keynesians regarded fiscal policy as the most effective instrument of stabilization. Deficits were capable of increasing aggregate demand and the potential for crowding out was minimized because of the view that the demand function for money was highly interest elastic and the investment function was highly interest inelastic. The monetarists argued that crowding-out effects from government deficits are large, at least equal 100%, and may exceed 100%. Let us first summarize the main arguments for crowding-out effects and then evaluate the evidence on the issue.

Completely Interest Inelastic Demand for Money   We have already discussed in Chapters 22 and 23 how the interest elasticity of the demand for money and investment function influence the magnitude of crowding-out effects from government deficits. Most of the debate has focused on the interest elasticity of money demand since the investment function is regarded as interest inelastic. Monetarists have argued that the demand for money is completely interest inelastic. In this case, crowding out in the Keynesian model is complete (100%). However, this argument is based on the view that the interest rate has no impact on the demand for money, which is not consistent with empirical evidence. There is general agreement that money demand is sensitive, but inelastic, with respect to the interest rate.

Expectations Effects   Monetarists also emphasize the expectations effects of changes in government spending on the private sector's decision to spend. In fact, they use arguments made by Keynes in the *General Theory* to criticize the effectiveness of fiscal policy. The expectations effect can operate through two channels. First, the "uncertainty and the confused psychology" that often accompanies government spending programs may increase the demand for liquidity (i.e., it will shift the demand function for money to the right independently of the level of income, thereby increasing the interest rate enough to decrease investment and offset the increase in government spending). Second, the "uncertainty and the confused psychology" could also cause the investment function to decline autonomously, thus offsetting the increase in aggregate demand caused by the initial increase in spending.

Direct Substitution Effects   The argument of direct substitution effects assumes that private and public debt are substitutable as far as the private economy is concerned. Whenever government increases the amount of outstanding debt (sells I.O.U.s in the financial markets), the public reduces their holdings of private debt issues. This is based on the assumption that households view the business and government sectors as extensions of themselves to the extent that government deficit spending and private investment spending both have the same implications for their future consumption benefits. A dollar of government deficit spending displaces exactly a dollar of private investment spending, as government bond issues displace private debt in the financial system. Reducing funds to support private investment hence reduces private spending.

Competition for Factors of Production Between the Public and Private Sector
Crowding-out effects can occur when government competes for resources with the private sector and increases their cost. This channel for crowding out depends on the composition of government spending and the opportunity cost of the resources in the private sector. Consider the case where government spending increases the demand for highly trained technical labor resources (engineers, mathematicians, computer programmers, and so on) that are already in high demand in the private sector. The increased demand for these resources will increase their wages. The resulting wage increases for these resources in both the public and private sectors will render some private investment projects unprofitable, reducing private investment spending.

Friedman Case: Initial Versus Subsequent Effects   Friedman and other monetarists have held a less inflexible position on crowding out in recent years than was the case when the argument was based on a completely inelastic demand function for money. Instead of arguing that deficits have no net effect in the short run, the argument now emphasizes the longer-run effects of a deficit. Government expenditures represent labor-intensive activities that ultimately lower the capital stock of the economy and its potential output. The initial effects of a deficit may be positive, but the negative effects on private spending and output will persist and eventually offset the initial increase in spending.

Empirical Evidence on the Crowding-Out Effect   The crowding-out effect has been the subject of much empirical work in the past. The most notable studies involve both monetarist- and Keynesian-oriented models of the economy. Despite the major differences in econometric methodology between the two approaches, estimates and simulations of various models suggest that changes in government deficits unaccompanied by changes in the money supply generate significant crowding-out effects. While there remains debate as to whether crowding-out is 100% or more and how long crowding-out effects take to accumulate, there is little disagreement that changes in government deficits have little long-lasting effect on real output and income. Some models even suggest that real income in the long run is actually reduced by government deficits. At the same time, the reader should keep in mind that changes in the money supply also have no long-run effects on real output.

The basic consensus can be stated as follows: monetary policy has predictable short-run effects on prices and output, while fiscal policy in the short run is likely to have large crowding-out effects that reduce its effectiveness to influence real income. Both monetary and fiscal policy in the long run have little impact on real income, and there is some evidence that fiscal policy may lower the growth of real income over time.

Monetary Policy Indicators

Indicators provide information about whether the Federal Reserve is following an easy or tight monetary policy and are important to understanding the impact that the Federal Reserve is exerting on the economy. Monetarists and Keynesians differ over the interpretation of the indicators of monetary policy, primarily as a reflection of their views of the transmission process. The monetarists emphasize the direct relationship between changes in the money supply and economic activity via a stable demand function for money. Thus, the best indicator of the net impact of Federal Reserve actions on the economy is the level and changes in the level of the money supply.

Keynesians emphasize the indirect effects of monetary policy that first operate through the financial system to change the cost and availability of credit before spending in the real section is affected. Although Keynesians do not disregard the money supply as an indicator of monetary policy, they place considerably more emphasis on such variables as bank reserves, the amount of credit outstanding, and interest rates as indicators of monetary policy.

Large-Scale Versus Small-Scale Models

Keynesians emphasize the need to construct large and detailed models of the economy to determine the impact of monetary policy. This reflects their view that monetary policy has an indirect impact on total spending and must first operate through the financial system. Large models are needed to spell out the specific channels through which monetary policy operates. Perhaps the best example of the bias toward large structural models of the economy is the Federal Reserve model. This very large model (several hundred equations) is based on a detailed view of how monetary policy works. The most widely known version is MPS (M.I.T.–University of Pennsylvania–Social Science Research Council). The model has over 400 equations and is referred to as a structural model because it develops detailed channels through which monetary and fiscal policy influence spending. Monetary policy is assumed to first influence the financial system and change the cost and availability of credit, which in turn, will change those spending components sensitive to the cost and availability of credit. The model emphasizes the Keynesian belief that monetary policy has an indirect rather than a direct impact on economic activity.

Monetarists, on the other hand, reject the need for large detailed models for two reasons. First, large models assume that we have a great deal more information about how the economy works than in fact we really have; the economic system is complex and our knowledge of its structure is not sufficient to develop large and realistic models of the Keynesian type. Second, changes in the money supply have direct as well as indirect effects on total spending. We simply do not have the information to spell out in detail how money affects the economy, and we are far better off using simple reduced form models such as the famous eight-equation monetarist model developed by the Federal Reserve Bank of St. Louis which is based on a direct relationship between GNP and the money supply.

Broader Issues of Stabilization Policy

Concern with the technical aspects of the monetarist-Keynesian debate can blur the basic distinction between the two groups. This distinction is fundamental and was best summarized by Franco Modigliani in his 1976 presidential address to the American Economic Association entitled "The Monetarist Controversy, or Should We Forsake Stabilization Policy?"

> In reality the distinguishing feature of the Monetarist school and the real issues of disagreement with non-Monetarists is not monetarism but rather the role that should probably be assigned to stabilization policies. Non-Monetarists accept what I regard to be the fundamental practical message of the *General Theory*: that a private enterprise economy using an intangible money *needs* to be stabilized, *can* be stabilized, and therefore *should* be stabilized by appropriate monetary and fiscal policies. Monetarists by contrast take the view that there is no serious need to stabilize the economy; that even if there were a need, it could not be done, for stabilization policies would be more likely to increase than to decrease instability; and, at least some Monetarists would go so far as to hold that, even in the unlikely event that stabilization policies could on balance prove beneficial, the government should not be trusted with the necessary power.[8]

Thus, the real distinction between monetarists and Keynesians or nonmonetarists, in Modigliani's terms, is between *activist* and *nonactivist* stabilization policy. There are several considerations to this basic point of difference.

Inherent Stability or Instability of the Market System Keynes's primary objective in the *General Theory* was to reject the automatic full-employment tendency of the economic system. Even if one could show that full employment would be achieved automatically by wage and price flexibility, Keynesians would argue that the system took too long to achieve full employment. In any event, the economy could not really be expected to stabilize at any level because it was always subject to changes in

[8] Franco Modigliani, "The Monetarist Controversy, or Should We Forsake Stabilization Policies?" *American Economic Review*, 67 (March 1977), 1.

autonomous spending, especially wide swings in business investment. Keynesians emphasize the inherent instability of the system primarily as a result of the autonomous changes in investment and other components of total spending that constantly require active government stabilization policy.

Monetarists emphasize the inherent stability of the market system and interpret much of the past economic instability to erratic changes in the money supply. The market economy over time will equilibrate at a *natural rate of unemployment*. In fact, there is very little that stabilization policy, including monetary policy, can do to change the long-run equilibrium output and employment level of the economy.

Stabilization Policy   Keynesians emphasize the need for discretionary fiscal and monetary policy to achieve the goals of economic stabilization in a market economy. By discretionary we mean that fiscal and monetary policy should be altered in reaction to economic activity and provide a countercyclical force. Fiscal and monetary policy can be used to "smooth out" the inherent fluctuations in economic activity. Keynesians now regard monetary policy as the most important policy instrument.

Monetarists oppose active stabilization policy. They reject fiscal policy because it is ineffective (complete crowding out) or because they are philosophically opposed to government intervention in the economy. Government should balance the budget rather than use the budget as an instrument of stabilization. Discretionary monetary policy is not necessary because the economic system is inherently stable. Monetary policy should be concerned with maintaining a close to constant growth rate of the money supply to meet the basic needs of the economy. Discretionary monetary policy can affect economic activity in the short run, but, because of the Federal Reserve's lack of information about the way in which the economy will react to a change in the money supply and the existence of a lag in the effect of monetary policy, there is doubt as to whether discretionary monetary policy will be stabilizing.

Causes of the Great Depression   During the Keynesian revolution, the Great Depression period provided ample support for the expanded role of government and the need for activist stabilization policy. The Keynesian view stressed the inherent instability in the private market as the cause of the depression and asserted that only extensive government regulation, supervision, and stabilization policy efforts would ensure achievement of socially desirable levels of activity.

The monetarists argue that the depressed conditions were more the result of inappropriate monetary policy than fundamental instability in the private market. Keynesians have accepted much of the argument that monetary policy contributed to the decline and the ultimate collapse of the banking system; however, they still emphasize the importance of nonmonetary factors and instability in private spending. Despite the common view that the Federal Reserve pursued inappropriate policies, monetarists and Keynesians still view the Great Depression period in fundamentally different terms.

At the same time, the period cannot easily be used to justify either view because the Federal Reserve allowed the money supply to decline so dramatically from 1929 through 1933. This is best summarized by Thomas Mayer:

> This leaves the third question, whether the Great Depression teaches us anything about the stability of the private sector. The answer to this question is a simple no. We know already that the system is unstable if we have a fractional reserve banking

system with no adequate provision for control of the quantity of money via a central bank that acts as lender of last resort. . . . The relevant question is whether the system is unstable if we *do* have a central bank that prevents large erratic shifts in the quantity of money. And there is little the Great Depression can tell us about this because the stock of money did decline drastically.[9]

[9] Thomas Mayer, "Money and the Great Depression: A Critique of Professor Temin's Thesis," *Explorations in Economic History*, 15 (April 1978), 143.

Key Points

1. Starting in the 1960s, the classical and quantity theory of money reemerged in the form of monetarism. The renewed interest in money and monetary policy in general and monetarism in particular was due to the following: empirical evidence on interest elasticity of key relationships in the Keynesian model, evidence of a statistical association between money and economic activity, reinterpretation of monetary policy during the Great Depression, and the emergence of inflation and stagflation as major policy concerns.

2. The basic element of the monetarist approach was to reformulate the demand function for money. Monetarists argued that the demand for money was stable and a function of a small number of economic variables. Thus, changes in the money supply had predictable effects on the economy. In the short run, changes in the money supply impacted both prices and output; however, in the tradition of the classical school, money was neutral in the long run.

3. The monetarist model of the economy is essentially the classical model warmed over with modern mathematics and statistics. It views the economy as inherently stable, departures from full employment occur largely as a result of erratic growth in the money supply, and that monetary policy should be nonactivist.

4. The reemergence of the quantity theory of money in the form of monetarism set the stage for a debate over economic models, role of money and monetary policy as determinants of economic activity, and the proper role of government stabilization policy. These and other related issues formed the monetarist-Keynesian debate that started in the mid-1960s and continued through the late 1970s.

5. Many aspects of the debate were technical in nature in the sense that careful statistical analysis could decide an issue one way or another; for example, there are no major differences between monetarists and Keynesians that crowding-out effects of fiscal policy are large or that significant changes in the money supply will induce significant changes in economic activity. In contrast, there are fundamental differences of opinion that continue to persist and are not amenable to objective analysis. These concern views about the inherent stability or instability of a market economy and the proper role for government in a market economy.

Key Terms

Business cycle turning points
Crowding-out effect of budget deficits

Demand for money as a stable function
Econometric models

Friedman-Schwartz hypothesis

Great Contraction

Great Depression

Hard monetarism

Hard nonmonetarism

Impact of money: short-run versus long-run effects

Indicators of monetary policy

Interest elasticity of the demand for money

Monetarist-Keynesian debate

Soft monetarism

Soft nonmonetarism

Stability of the demand for money

Transmission process

Velocity

Questions

1. List the reasons for the reemergence of the classical model in the form of monetarism.

2. How does the monetarist demand function for money differ from the Fisher and Cambridge demand functions for money?

3. What is the meaning of the phrase cited in the chapter on page 585, "Money is too important to be left to the monetarists."

4. Can the events of the Great Depression be used to support the view that a market economy is inherently unstable?

5. Trace the effects of a decrease in the growth rate of the money supply using the monetarist framework.

6. Show that a highly interest-elastic demand for money implies large offset movements in velocity. What is the relationship between the demand for money and velocity?

7. Why is a stable demand function for money important in the monetarist model?

Suggested Readings

1. Douglas Battenberge, Jared Enzler, and Arther Havenner, "MINNIE: A Small Version of the MIT-PENN-SSRC Econometric Model," *Federal Reserve Bulletin* (November 1975), 721–727. Discusses the early development stages of the Federal Reserve model maintained by the Board of Governors.

2. John T. Boorman, "A Survey of the Demand for Money: Theoretical Formulations and Pre-1973 Empirical Results," in Thomas M. Havrilesky and John T. Boorman (eds.), *Money Supply, Money Demand, and Macroeconomic Models* (Arlington Heights, Ill.: Harlan Davidson, 1982). A complete survey of pre-1973 empirical work on the demand for money.

3. Thomas F. Cooley and Stephen F. LeRoy, "Identification and Estimation of Money Demand," *American Economic Review*, 71 (December 1981), 825–844. A critical appraisal of all demand function for money studies.

4. William G. Dewald, "Monetarism Is Dead; Long Live the Quantity Theory," *Review*, Federal Reserve Bank of St. Louis (July–August 1988), 3–18. Focuses on the real meaning of monetarism rather than the version popularized in the press.

5. Federal Reserve Bank of St. Louis. The October 1986 issue of the *Review* is devoted to the St. Louis Federal Reserve monetarist model.

6. Milton Friedman (ed.), *Studies in the Quantity Theory of Money* (Chicago: University of Chicago Press, 1956). Many people view this as the start of the reemergence of the quantity theory of money.

7. Milton Friedman and Anna Jacobson Schwartz, *A Monetary History of the United States, 1867–1960*

(Princeton: N.J.: Princeton University Press, 1963). The source of the reinterpretation of the Federal Reserve's role in the Great Depression.

8. Emmanuel Goldenweiser, *American Monetary Policy* (New York: McGraw-Hill, 1951). The official Federal Reserve view of its actions during the Great Depression. Don't anticipate much criticism!

9. Robert J. Gordon (ed.), *Milton Friedman's Monetary Framework* (Chicago: University of Chicago Press, 1974). Survey of Friedman's framework.

10. Robert J. Gordon and James A. Wilcox, "Monetarist Interpretations of the Great Depression: An Evaluation and Critique," in Karl Brunner (ed.), *The Great Depression Revisited* (Boston: Martinus Nijhoff, 1981), pp. 49–107. Summarizes the debate over the Friedman-Schwartz hypothesis.

11. John P. Judd and John L. Scadding, "The Search for a Stable Money Demand Function: A Survey of the Post-1973 Literature," *Journal of Economic Literature,* 20 (September 1982), 993–1023. A complete survey of the post-1973 empirical work on the demand for money.

12. Thomas Mayer (ed.), *The Structure of Monetarism* (New York: W. W. Norton, 1978). A detailed statement of the monetarist view.

13. Thomas Mayer, "Money and the Great Depression: A Critique of Professor Temin's Thesis," *Explorations in Economic History,* 15 (April 1978), 127–145.

14. Franco Modigliani, "The Monetarist Controversy, or Should We Forsake Stabilization Policy?" *American Economic Review,* 67 (March 1977), 1–19. A clear statement of the essential difference between monetarist and Keynesian views of the world.

15. Jerome L. Stein (ed.), *Monetarism* (Amsterdam: North-Holland, 1976). General discussion of monetarist models.

16. Peter Temin, *Did Monetary Forces Cause the Great Depression?* (New York: W. W. Norton, 1976). Critique of the Friedman-Schwartz view.

17. Daniel L. Thornton, "Why Does Velocity Matter?" *Review,* Federal Reserve Bank of St. Louis (December 1983), 5–13.

18. Clark Warburton, *Depression, Inflation, and Monetary Policy* (Baltimore: Johns Hopkins University Press, 1966). Warburton was the first monetarist in the post-Keynesian period; however, his work was not appreciated at the time it was published in the late 1940s and early 1950s.

CHAPTER 26

Developments Beyond the Classical— Monetarist and Keynesian Models

Chapter Overview

Economists by the 1970s focused the majority of their attention on the two major approaches to modeling the economy: classical and Keynesian. The classical model in the post–World War II period had reemerged in the form of monetarism. Each implied sharply different views of how the economy worked and the proper role for stabilization policy. By the end of the monetarist-Keynesian debate in the late 1970s, there appeared to be a consensus of sorts characterized by the following:

First, macroeconomic models generally agreed that the long-run aggregate supply function was vertical at the full-employment or potential level of output. The potential level of output was not influenced by stabilization policy. The real problem was to explain fluctuations in economic activity around the potential level of output and what implications these explanations held for monetary policy.

Second, monetary policy rather than fiscal policy became increasingly recognized as the most important instrument of stabilization. Crowding-out effects of fiscal policy and the politicalization of government spending and taxing decisions reduced the earlier enthusiasm for fiscal policy as a flexible stabilization instrument.

Third, even though economists maintained the fundamental differences between the classical and Keynesian models, the activist approach became less activist in recognition that monetary policy could not change the potential level of output and that activist stabilization policy encountered a number of constraints that had not been fully appreciated during the Keynesian revolution or the monetarist-Keynesian debate.

This chapter begins with the basic issue faced by all macroeconomic models in that any model must be able to explain the fluctuations in output and prices that characterize the evolution of the economy over time.

The chapter adopts a three-part taxonomy of the newer model developments: (1) neoclassical, (2) neo-Keynesian, and (3) political economy. In addition, there is an approach referred to as supply-side economics that gained considerable popularity in the early 1980s. It is closely related to the classical view; however, its more recent manifestations are so eclectic that it is difficult to place in any one category and thus will be discussed in an appendix to this chapter.

The neoclassical or "new classical" models adopt the flexible wage and price assumption of the pre–Great Depression classical approach. The monetarist approach in Chapter 25 is essentially a neoclassical component; however, the term is usually used to describe models more firmly based on a microeconomic foundation. These include information-based approaches such as the *Lucas supply function* and *rational expectations* models and a relatively recent development, referred to as *real business cycle theories.*

The neo-Keynesian models in contrast argue that wage and prices are not nearly as flexible as maintained by the classical, monetarist, or neoclassical approaches; however, they reject the original Keynesian emphasis on fixed and rigid wages and/or prices. Rather, the neo-Keynesian efforts have been directed toward developing theoretically consistent explanations for why wages and/or prices might be "sluggish" or "sticky," thereby, making it difficult for the economy to return to its natural growth path. Even though wage and price adjustments will eventually return the economy to full employment, the adjustment process is long.

The political economy or political business cycle models adopt a perspective different from the neoclassical, supply-side, or Keynesian views. The emphasis here is to establish a relationship between the political institutions of the economy and its economic performance. Politicians use their influence over the policy instruments to manipulate the economy in such a manner as to maintain and enhance political power. In contrast, neoclassical and Keynesian models hold political institutions constant.

After reviewing these approaches, the chapter ends by offering some comments on a question that must be occurring to the reader at this point: "Why have economists been unable to develop a widely accepted model of the economy given the powerful mathematical, statistical, and computer tools available?"

The Problem—How to Explain the Persistence of Economic Fluctuations

There is no question that the economy has experienced fluctuations in real and nominal variables over time, and more important, these fluctuations have not disappeared in the post–World War II period despite the increased role of government stabilization policy. This is clearly reflected by Figure 26-1, which illustrates the deviations of real output from potential output, deviations of the actual unemployment rate from the natural unemployment rate, and the rate of inflation over the 1950–1988 period. When we consider the larger record of the U.S. economy over the past century as illustrated in Chapter 17, the economy has experienced considerable variation over time.

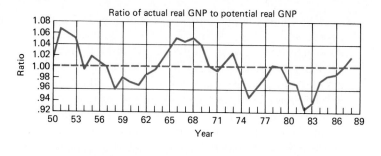

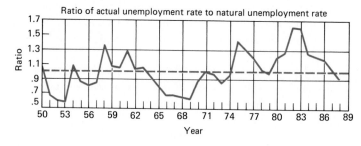

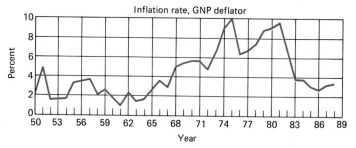

*Based on data provided by Robert J. Gordon which are reported in Robert J.
Gordon, Macroeconomics (Glenview, Illinois: Scott, Foresman, & Co., 1990).*

FIGURE 26-1   Economic fluctuations in the post–World War II period

Thus, any model must account for the persistence of fluctuations in the U.S.
economy. Increases in output and employment are associated with increasing inflation rates, while decreases in output and employment are associated with declining
inflation rates. We can state the problem facing a given model in terms of aggregate
demand and supply or, equivalently, in terms of a well-known relationship known as
the *Phillips curve.*

The top of Figure 26-2 (Panel A) illustrates the aggregate demand function while
two supply functions are shown. The vertical supply function labeled *LRAS* is the
long-run equilibrium of the economy at full employment or potential output. The
upward-sloping supply function labeled *SRAS* is a short-run supply function indicating that price and output are positively related in the short run. The fact that wage
and price adjustments do not occur immediately in the face of aggregate demand
changes implies that supply will respond positively to price increases in the short
run. The classical model, in fact, recognized that supply will respond to price changes
in the short run. The discussion of how money impacts the economy in the context

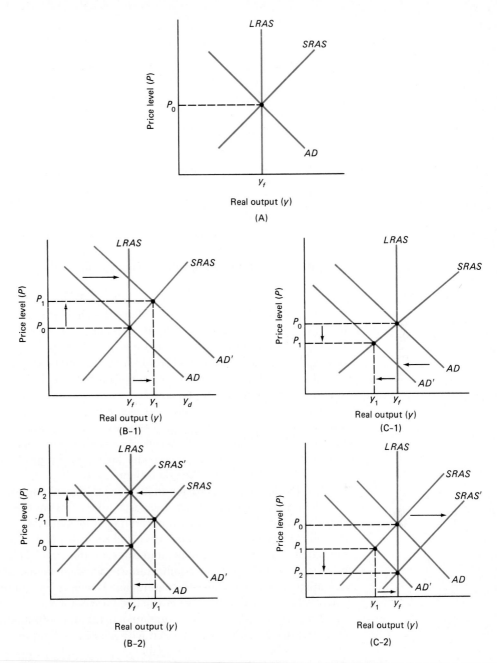

FIGURE 26-2   Aggregate demand/supply and economic fluctuations

of the classical. model on pages 499–501 provides one explanation for an upward-sloping aggregate supply function in the short run.

Assume that equilibrium is at price level P_o and potential output is y_f. If aggregate demand increases (Panel B-1) or decreases (Panel C-1), output and prices will increase or decrease, respectively. For example, an increase in aggregate demand from AD to AD' at the existing price level generates excess demand and output

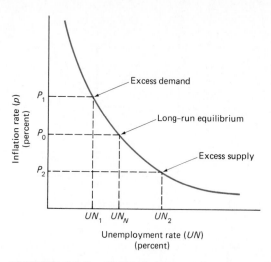

FIGURE 26-3   Phillips curve and economic fluctuations

increases above the potential level along the short-run aggregate supply function. Output of y_1 and price level of P_1 are temporary since the excess demand in commodity and labor markets will increase wages. Increasing wages will shift the short-run supply function upward (SRAS to SRAS′ in Panel B-2), and eventually, long-run equilibrium will involve no change in output but a higher price level at P_2 because of an increase in aggregate demand.

Virtually all models assume that eventually, the excess demand or supply will induce forces that will return the economy to its normal equilibrium. Figure 26-2 expresses the problem in static terms. As an alternative approach, the Phillips curve can be used to illustrate the same point; however, it permits us to express prices in terms of rates of change rather than their level.

The Phillips curve expresses an inverse relationship between the rate of inflation and the rate of unemployment. Increases (decreases) in the inflation rate are associated with decreases (increases) in the unemployment rate (or real output). Figure 26-3 illustrates a typical Phillips curve and indicates that at the rate of inflation, P_o, the actual and natural unemployment rates are the same. This equilibrium is similar in concept to the long-run equilibrium depicted in Figure 26-2. If the economy's unemployment rate is above the natural level (such as UN_2) or below the natural level (such as UN_2), the rate of inflation will decrease or increase, respectively. Since there is a direct relationship between unemployment and output, changes in the inflation rate tend to be positively associated with changes in output.

The problem, then, is to explain the persistence of fluctuations in output and prices around the long-run equilibrium or the inverse trade-off between inflation and employment in the short run. Economists in recent years found the pre–Great Depression classical model and the original Keynesian model wanting in this regard. The classical model's emphasis on flexible wages and prices implied too much stability in the economy and, as a result, required one to resort to various outside or exogenous forces to explain the fluctuations. In addition, the pre-1929 quantity theory of money was regarded as overly simplistic. The original Keynesian model, in contrast, implied too much instability. Once we had achieved a better understanding of the role of the Federal Reserve in the Great Depression, the Keynesian emphasis on unemployment equilibrium solutions and market failure could not be supported by the events of the 1930s. The economy has certainly experienced fluctuations, but there appeared to be an inherent ability of the economy to return to its potential growth path. In addition, the original Keynesian emphasis on wage and price rigidities appeared almost as simplistic as the early quantity theory views.

Thus, economists have been extending these models in new and exciting ways to explain economic fluctuations, and in this regard, let us turn to a review of these developments.

Neoclassical Explanations

Neoclassical models adopt the classical assumption of flexible wages and prices and the inherent stability of markets to adjust to excess supply and demand. These include various types of information-based approaches and the real business cycle theories. The monetarist approach should also be regarded as part of the neoclassical approach, though this is not a widely accepted convention.

Monetarism and Economic Fluctuations

We have already reviewed the monetarist approach in the previous chapter, and like the original classical model, monetarists emphasize changes in the money supply as the primary force behind shifts in aggregate demand. While changes in money induce changes in prices and output in the short run, only prices respond to changes in money in the long run since potential output is determined by the economy's resource base.

A monetarist framework was illustrated in Chapter 25. Embedded in that description of how money impacts the economy is a view of the Phillips curve and the importance of distinguishing between anticipated and unanticipated events. In that discussion, the real output effects of a higher monetary growth rate were induced by an actual inflation rate that exceeded anticipated inflation. As a result, real wages fell and induced a higher level of employment. This is what one would expect from the standard Phillips curve illustrated in Figure 26-3; however, once the market recognized the higher inflation rate and adjusted anticipations accordingly, wage contracts were adjusted to incorporate the higher inflation rate and the real effects of monetary growth disappeared. The economy returns to a long-run natural level of output.

The Phillips curve has come to play an important role in current discussions of economic fluctuations, and the monetarists made significant contributions to our current understanding of the relationship between inflation and employment.

The Original Phillips Curve

The Phillips curve was first developed in the tradition of the Keynesian model. As discussed earlier, the Keynesian assumption of rigid wages lacked a theoretical foun-

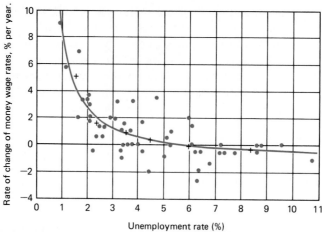

Source: A. W. Phillips, "The Relation Between Unemployment and the Rate of
Change of Money Wage Rates in the United Kingdom, 1861–1957,
Economica, 25 (August 1958), 285.

FIGURE 26-4   **The Phillips curve as originally estimated by
A. W. Phillips for the United Kingdom, 1861–1913**

dation, and in an effort to explain what determines the current wage level, the
Phillips curve was born. A. W. Phillips published his famous paper in 1958 and
argued that percentage changes in nominal wages responded inversely to the unemployment rate. He argued that the unemployment rate was a measure of excess
demand in the labor market and that the greater (lesser) the level of excess demand
the greater (lesser) pressure for money wages to increase; hence, Phillips argued that
the relationship was nonlinear. The Phillips curve was represented by

$$w = f(UN) \tag{1}$$

where w represents percentage changes in money wages, UN represented the unemployment rate, and the function, f, was taken as inverse.

Phillips estimated expression (1) to describe the relationship between wage
inflation and unemployment using annual data in Britain from 1861 to 1913 and found
a very close inverse relationship between percentage changes in the money wage and
the unemployment rate. Figure 26-4 reproduces Phillips's results. The dots are the
actual values of wage inflation and unemployment for each year, while the solid line
is the statistically estimated Phillips curve.

It is a straightforward matter to translate the Phillips curve into the more familiar
relationship between inflation and the unemployment rate by assuming that prices
are established by applying a fixed markup to labor costs, so that wage inflation
translates into price inflation, holding labor productivity constant.

The Phillips curve captured the interest of economists for a number of reasons:

1. It offered a way of making money wages rigid in one period by assuming that
   the current wage rate was related to unemployment in the past period. Thus,

fixed wages were not assumed to be independent of the pace of economic activity.

2. It focused on indicators of two important goals for stabilization policy: full employment and price stability.

3. It offered a way for policymakers to make choices between inflation and unemployment consistent with social welfare.

4. It was consistent with a variety of theories of inflation.

The Phillips curve was subjected to intense empirical study after 1958, and by the late 1960s, it had become firmly established as an analytical device. Just at the same time however, something began to happen to the Phillips curve relationship (Figure 26-5). Starting in the late 1960s and continuing in the 1970s, we began to experience *stagflation*—the simultaneous occurrence of high inflation and high unemployment. While proponents of the Phillips curve argued that this could be explained by rightward shifts in the curve over time, the occurrence of high inflation and high unemployment raised doubts about the stability of the Phillips curve. In fact, many of the new developments in monetary economics in particular and macroeconomics in general evolved from efforts to explain what had happened to the Phillips curve in the 1970s.

At this point, Milton Friedman and Edmund Phelps extended the Phillips curve in a way that yielded classical and monetarist results.

The Natural Unemployment Rate Hypothesis

Friedman and Phelps argued that the original Phillips curve was fundamentally flawed because it assumed that money wages were related to excess demand in the labor market. While money wages are the variable over which workers and employers bargain, it is the real wage rate that is of concern to workers and employers. Each could care less about the money wage. The concern is the real wage since that is what determines the real return from supplying labor and the real cost of employing labor. Their approach is referred to as the *natural unemployment rate hypothesis*.

They argued that the Phillips relationship in expression (1) should be redefined in the following steps. First, changes in real wages should replace changes in money wages on the left hand side of expression (1). The growth of real wages is defined as the growth of money wages less the inflation rate; that is, if money wages are growing at 5% and prices are growing at 4%, real wages are growing at 1%. Thus, expression (1) is changed to

$$w - p = f(UN) \tag{2}$$

where w and p represent wage and price inflation, respectively.

At the time of the wage bargain, however, workers and employers are concerned with anticipated real wages. That is, the current money wage relative to the antici-

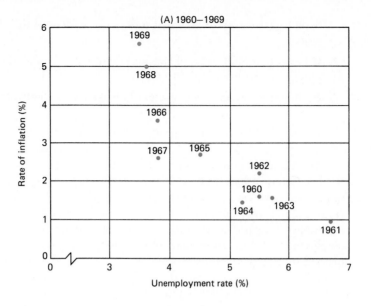

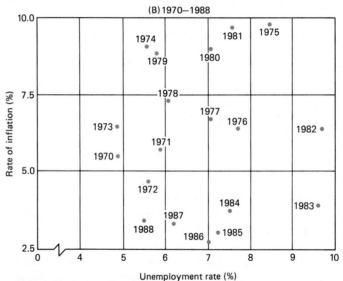

Source: Michelle R. Garfinkel, "What Is an 'Acceptable' Rate of Inflation?—A Review of the Issues." *Review,* Federal Reserve Bank of St. Louis (July–August 1989), 11–12.

FIGURE 26-5 Stable Phillips curve in the 1960s and disappearance of the Phillips curve in the 1970s

pated price level over the next period. Both workers and employers will bargain to set a real wage that incorporates anticipated inflation. Thus, expression (2) needs to be changed to

$$w = f(UN) + p_a \tag{3}$$

where p_a represents anticipated inflation.

Two other changes are required to derive the Friedman-Phelps model. The rate of inflation is used instead of the rate of money wages changes, and the difference between the actual and natural unemployment rate is used instead of the unemployment rate as a measure of excess demand in the labor market. Thus, expression (3) is changed to

$$p = f(UN - UN_n) + p_a \qquad (4)$$

where UN_n represents the natural unemployment rate.

Consider what expression (4) implies if anticipated and actual inflation are equal. This implies that the actual and natural unemployment rates are equal, and thus, the Phillips curve is vertical. There is no trade-off between inflation and unemployment. Friedman and Phelps argued that any observed trade-off was due to differences between anticipated and actual inflation. This is an important point so let us explore further how the Friedman-Phelps model works and its implications for stabilization policy.

It is important to distinguish between anticipated and unanticipated events to understand the short-run trade-off between inflation and unemployment. An unanticipated increase in the rate of inflation can indeed lower the rate of unemployment as the Phillips curve implies. Real wages will decline because workers have not adjusted their wage demands to the higher rate of inflation because it was not anticipated. As real wages fall, employers hire more workers and produce more output, leading to a decline in the level of unemployment. Likewise, an unanticipated decline in the rate of inflation increases real wages as employers fail to take into account the lower rate of inflation in setting wage bargains. The unemployment rate then increases as employment is cut back in response to the unanticipated decline in the rate of inflation.

Thus, changes in the rate of unanticipated inflation can produce a Phillips-type relationship in which there is an inverse relationship between the rate of unemployment and inflation. But can this Phillips curve relationship be used as the earlier Phillips curve proponents claimed? No! This relationship is only short run and is quite ephemeral. It pays for workers and employers to collect information in making economic decisions and unanticipated inflation, if continued, is surely to become anticipated inflation. Once the inflation rate is anticipated, it can have no meaningful impact on the level of unemployment. Anticipated inflation is incorporated into wage contracts, and the real wage will eventually return to the original level that determined the natural unemployment rate. There is no trade-off in the long run that can be used for stabilization purposes.

Figure 26-6 illustrates the basic idea of the natural unemployment rate hypothesis. Line *AA* represents a short-run Phillips curve relationship intersecting the vertical line at the natural unemployment rate, UN_n. Line *AA* as well as line *BB* is drawn assuming an anticipated rate of 3% and 6%, respectively. Start from point *C* where the actual rate of inflation is 3% and equal to the anticipated rate of inflation and the unemployment rate is at the natural level. Assume an increase in government spending or the money supply that increases the actual rate of inflation to 6%. The increased rate of inflation is unanticipated, and we move from *C* to *D* on line *AA*. The unanticipated inflation lowers real wages, increases output, and lowers the unemployment rate; however, as long as the 6% rate continues, it becomes completely anticipated. Ultimately, the short-run curve will shift to the one defined by

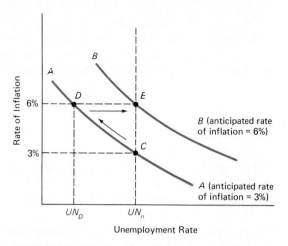

FIGURE 26-6   The Phillips curve and the natural unemployment rate hypothesis

a 6% anticipated rate of inflation (line *BB*), and unemployment will return to the natural level. The movement from *D* to *E* represents the incorporation of anticipated inflation into wage contracts and bargains, so the real wage rises to its original level. As the real wage increases, producers cut back on employment and eliminate the increased employment that resulted from the unanticipated price inflation.

Two important implications can be drawn from the analysis. First, fully anticipated inflation does not affect real economic behavior. It is important to understand the principle because it lies at the heart of much of the new approach to macroeconomic model building. Individuals are not subject to money illusion and can distinguish between real and nominal magnitudes. Economic activity depends not on absolute levels of wages, profits, assets, prices, but only on relative values. Consider the following examples. A producer's decision to hire more workers depends on a decline in the real wage rate, for only then has labor become relatively less expensive. The decision to increase real investment depends on a lower real rate, for only then has credit become relatively less expensive. A worker will not increase real consumption if both wages and prices increase by the same amount, since the worker realizes that he or she is not better off than before in real terms. An individual's decision to consume more butter and less margarine depends on a lower relative price of butter to margarine, but, if both prices fall or increase by the same amount, the relative price remains unchanged and the individual will not change relative expenditures on butter and margarine. Once inflation is anticipated fully and economic contracts and activities incorporate anticipated inflation, only absolute values will be affected without any change in relative values and real economic activity.

Second, there is no stable Phillips curve. There may appear to be a Phillips curve in the short run, but, in the long run, when actual rates of inflation are equal to anticipated rates of inflation, the Phillips curve is vertical.

The evidence to date tends to support a very steep Phillips curve in the long run. Whether it is vertical or not depends on whose evidence you read; however, the implication of the evidence is clear on one point. There appears to be no stable Phillips curve that can be estimated and used to make trade-off decisions between inflation and unemployment.

Fluctuations as Explained by the Monetarists

The monetarist regards the market system as inherently stable and argues that output and price fluctuations have been due to shifts in aggregate demand induced by changes in the money supply. Monetarists have long argued that the Federal Reserve is subject to many pressures, especially political pressures, that encourage unstable monetary growth rates. Monetarists argue that the overall record of monetary policy since the establishment of the Federal Reserve in 1913 has been unsatisfactory. Much of the economic instability experienced in the United States since that time can be directly traced to inappropriate monetary policy.

In addition, monetarists argue that even if a need for activist monetary policy could be demonstrated, technical problems would likely render monetary policy destabilizing. These technical problems arise from faulty operating procedures that generate monetary instability, lags in the effects of monetary policy, and other biases. These will be discussed in the last three chapters.

The failure of the Federal Reserve to achieve monetary stability underlines the monetarist argument that monetary policy should be conducted by a set of rules that relieve the Federal Reserve of almost all of its discretionary power to change the growth rate of the money supply. Friedman, for example, has long advocated that the Federal Reserve be limited to increasing the growth rate of the money supply by a constant amount year by year.

Information-Based Explanations

The original Phillips curve and the Friedman-Phelps version both attribute inflation-output correlations to differences between anticipated and unanticipated events. In the case of the natural unemployment rate hypothesis for example, wages are adjusted only after the market reaches a consensus about future rates of inflation.

In the 1970s Robert E. Lucas, Jr., developed an alternative perspective of the short-run Phillips curve based on correct and incorrect information about price changes at the individual decision making level. Lucas retained the classical flexible wage and price assumption, but based the Phillips curve relationship on *information mistakes*. The so-called Lucas supply function has had an important impact on modeling and has stimulated the study of how information influences decision making. In many respects, however, the Lucas approach is very similar to the monetarists in that in both, economic fluctuations occur because of mistakes in forecasting price changes.

The Lucas supply function can be explained in two steps. First, we consider how an individual supplier decides to change output after equilibrium has been attained, and second, we aggregate the individual supply decisions to obtain an economywide aggregate supply function.

Imagine yourself as a supplier of output. You know a great deal about the price you charge as well as about the prices charged by your competitors. You also have

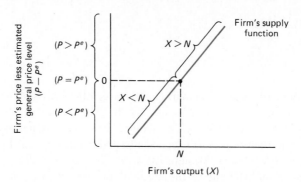

FIGURE 26-7   Lucas information-based supply function

information about prices of related products that might influence your market, though not to the same degree that you have about your own market. Beyond this, your knowledge of prices in other markets is not detailed and in many cases, nonexistent.

Assume further that you are faced with a change in the market price of your product. Is this because there has occurred a relative shift in demand toward your product and away from other products, or does this signify a general price increase? That is, you don't possess enough information to separate a *relative* from an *absolute* price change. The tendency will be to regard the change in the market price of your product as more of a relative than an absolute change, and as a result, an optimal decision might be to increase output but not as much as if you knew for certain that a relative shift in demand for your product had occurred.

This story can be represented for firm i by

$$X_i = N_i + a(P_i - P^e) \tag{5}$$

where X_i is the firm i's output, N_i is the normal or potential output for firm i, P_i is the price level for the firm's output, P^e is the firm's estimate of the overall price level for the economy, and a is a constant. If the price for firm i's output increases above the general price level, the firm will increase output. The constant a represents the response of the firm's output to any difference between the firm's price and the estimated general price level.

Figure 26-7 illustrates the Lucas supply function for an individual firm and shows that the firm will increase (decrease) output when the firm's output price is above (below) the estimated overall price level. By adding up similar supply functions for all producers, we obtain an upward-sloping aggregate supply function such as illustrated in Figure 26-2. This aggregate supply function is upward sloping because of imperfect information rather than because of slow wage and price adjustments.

Thus, shifts in aggregate demand induced by changes in the money supply are likely to induce changes in prices and output at least in the short run. An increase in the money supply increases the general price level; however, individual firms tend to interpret price increases for the product they produce and sell as evidence of a relative shift in demand toward their product. They respond by increasing output and employment; however, eventually it becomes clear that the general price level has increased. At this time, firms revise upward their estimated general price level and reduce output accordingly.

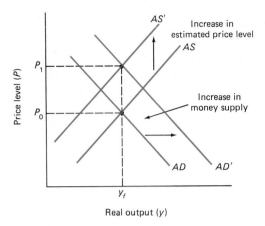

FIGURE 26-8 Policy ineffectiveness even in the short run

The impact of any shift in demand depends critically on whether price anticipations are adjusted. If the shift in demand induces a shift in price expectations, then prices will adjust and output will remain at the potential level. More likely, however, is that any factor that influences the price level will not be correctly perceived, and many producers will respond as if they were experiencing a relative increase in demand. Eventually, however, expectations will be adjusted upward, and long-run equilibrium will be attained and the aggregate supply function becomes vertical at the full-employment or potential output level.

One of the implications of the Lucas framework is the *policy ineffectiveness proposition.* Anticipated increase in the money supply will not impact real output even in the short run! Figure 26-8 illustrates policy ineffectiveness. The aggregate demand function shifts to the right as a result of an increase in the money supply. If individuals anticipate the increase in money supply and realize that the general price level will increase, suppliers will not increase supply. In this case, they will immediately adjust upward their estimate of the general price level as their own product prices are increasing. This is reflected in Figure 26-8 by an upward shift in aggregate supply that matches the rightward shift in demand. Hence, an increase in the money supply has no real effects on the economy, even in the short run.

This is an extreme view of the world and not accepted by most economists; however, it does illustrate just how important information can be in determining economic activity. The policy ineffectiveness proposition and the role of information are key elements of the rational expectations approach—an information based approach.

Rational Expectations

Rational expectations incorporates three assumptions:

1. Markets adjust and clear rapidly and smoothly. Wages and prices are flexible in both directions and move to eliminate excess demand or excess supply.

2. The economy grows at the natural rate over time determined by society's resource base and technology.

3. Individual economic units are *rational.* Rationality renders markets efficient collectors of information and ensures that individuals will not make *systematic* errors.

The first two assumptions are not the distinguishing characteristics of the rational expectations approach. The assumption of rational behavior, however, is unique. Rationality was implicitly part of the early quantity theory; however, the rational expectations approach has developed a rigorous view of what rationality means in a market context. When the assumption of rationality is combined with standard macro models, the approach yields results that are clearly unique and radical.

The basic foundation of this approach is the view that individuals are rational in their decision making. Individuals collect information about the economy in making their own individual plans in the future. This includes the anticipated effects of any systematic efforts to stabilize the economy by monetary or fiscal policy. This is not a particularly strong assumption to make in an economic setting, as it always pays to collect and use information that may influence the profit or loss of any economic activity, whether we are looking at the producer, the worker, or the consumer. At first glance, this appears to be a relatively simple proposition, but, when incorporated into macroeconomic models, it has significant implications for stabilization policy. At the outset, however, we should stress that rational expectations does not mean that individuals have perfect foresight or operate in a certain environment. Individuals will still make errors, but they will not make *systematic* errors, because any systematic error indicates that relevant information is not being incorporated correctly into individual decision making. Consider a classroom situation such as the course for which this book is being used. If the instructor is 5 minutes late the first day, most students will have arrived early, since the majority of students will have assumed that the instructor would arrive on time. If the instructor continues to be late for the next few days, students will begin to adjust their behavior and fewer and fewer students will arrive early. In fact, if the instructor is continually 5 minutes late, by the middle of the course most students will arrive a few minutes (less than 5) late for class.

A Simple Model of Rational Expectations

The model[1] consists of the following five relationships.

Aggregate Supply   The model assumes that aggregate supply is always tending toward the natural growth path as determined by the economy's resource base and technology. The actual growth of output (and employment) will be at the natural or

---

[1] The model is taken directly from Thomas M. Humphrey, "Some Recent Developments in Phillips Curve Analysis," *Economic Review,* Federal Reserve Bank of Richmond (January–February 1978), 15–23.

equilibrium level when actual wages and prices equal expected wages and prices. Expression (6) summarizes this equilibrium condition.

$$x = n + a(p - p^e) \tag{6}$$

where x is growth of output, n is natural growth of output, p is actual inflation, p^e is expected inflation, and a is a constant term. Expression (6) says that when actual and expected inflation are equal, at whatever level, the actual growth of output is equal to the natural growth rate. If actual inflation is greater (less) than expected inflation, then actual output growth will be above (below) the natural growth path. Neither one of these departures from equilibrium can persist. Market forces will ensure that actual output growth will equal the natural level. Let us illustrate how this can occur.

Assume an unexpected increase in the inflation rate. According to Lucas, producers have difficulty in separating out whether the price increases for their products are due to a relative shift in demand or are part of a general increase in prices. Since the increased inflation rate was unexpected, producers are mislead in the initial stages to view the unexpected price increases as an increase in the demand for their own products. They expand output and employment. Producers are also encouraged to expand output because labor becomes relatively less expensive. Employees had also not expected a general price increase and have not pushed for higher nominal wages to incorporate an inflation premium. Thus, actual real wages fall. In terms of expression (6), the unexpected inflation is represented by p exceeding p^e and, hence, causing actual output to exceed the natural level. Market forces will eventually come into play to increase the anticipated inflation rate. Producers will come to realize that they made an error in thinking that the higher prices represented a relative shift in demand for their products. They now realize that prices in general are increasing. Excess demand for labor will cause wages to increase, employees will become more aware of the general increase in higher nominal wages, and producers will be willing to grant higher nominal wages. These and other factors will cause economic units to reevaluate and revise p^e upward. When $p^e = p$, actual output growth will be at the natural rate, $x = n$.

Inflation Generating Mechanism   The actual inflation rate is based on a quantity theory of money equation

$$m + v = p + n \tag{7}$$

where m is money supply growth, v is velocity growth, p is inflation, and n is the natural growth rate of output. Assuming that v is zero and incorporating random or shock effects on prices, the inflation generating mechanism can then be expressed as

$$p = m - n + e \tag{8}$$

The actual inflation rate is thus determined by the growth of money relative to the natural growth of output plus a random term. The random term represents any influence on the inflation rate independent of money supply effects. Oil price shocks, labor disturbances, and so on are classified as random events.

Policy Reaction Function The policy reaction function indicates how the Federal Reserve changes monetary growth in response to changes in economic activity. The activist approach to policy, implicitly or explicitly, uses a reaction function to determine money supply growth. Expression (9) says that money supply growth is a function of actual output growth of the last period plus a random term that incorporates all influences on money supply growth independent of the last period's output.

$$m = f(x_{-1}) + u \tag{9}$$

The specific form of this reaction can vary; however, the specific form is not particularly important. What is important, however, is that the Federal Reserve changes the money supply in reaction to a change in actual performance of the economy. This is the heart of activist policy.

Price Expectations Formulation Individuals formulate price expectations rationally; that is, they understand the basic inflation generating mechanism and use this mechanism to establish price expectations. Expression (8) is the basic inflation generating mechanism, and, if expectations are rational, individuals understand this and use it to formulate price anticipations. Thus, the expected inflation rate is determined by the expected value of expression (8):

$$p^e = \text{expected value of } (m - n + e) \tag{10}$$

The expected value of the natural output growth rate is the natural rate itself, and the expected value of the random term is zero; hence, the expected inflation rate is equal to the expected money supply growth relative to natural output growth:

$$p^e = m^e - n \tag{11}$$

Expected Monetary Growth Formulation Rational expectations also explains how individuals formulate anticipations about future money supply growth. They understand the reaction function for monetary policy summarized by expression (9) and use this to formulate anticipated money growth. The expected value of expression (9) is the reaction function itself without the random term.

$$m^e = f(x_{-1}) \tag{12}$$

Expression (9) contains two parts. The first part, $f(x_{-1})$, is predictable its expected value is itself; the second part, u, is random, and its expected value is zero.

This five-equation model is uniquely rational because it assumes that individuals know and employ the basic relationships of the economy in formulating expected inflation and money supply growth. They are as knowledgeable as any government agency in this regard.

Implications for Activist Monetary Policy A basic premise of the Keynesian activist approach is that the Federal Reserve can use monetary policy to stimulate or slow down real economic activity. In this model, however, monetary policy actions that are anticipated have no effect on the growth of real output—even in the short run!

Formally, this can be seen by using expression (6) to derive the reduced form of the model. Expression (6) is the basic equilibrium condition. Substitute expression (9) into (8) and substitute the resultant into expression (6). Substitute (12) into (11) and substitute the resultant into expression (6):

$$x = n + a[f(x_{-1}) - n + u + e - f(x_{-1}) + n]$$ (13)

Cancellation of terms then yields the reduced form equation:

$$x = n + a(u + e)$$ (14)

Expression (14) indicates that deviations of the actual growth of real output from the natural path can be influenced only by random or shock events that are, by their nature, unanticipated. Thus, only an unexpected change in monetary policy, u, or a shock to price expectations mechanism, e, can influence actual output performance. There are two important implications.

First, anticipated policy will not influence real economic performance. Assume that the economy slows and, according to the policy reaction function, that the Federal Reserve will increase monetary growth. Individuals already know that any slowdown in output for whatever reason will induce future increases in money supply growth. They also know that increased monetary growth will increase the inflation rate, and, hence, they will revise upward their anticipated inflation. The end result is that attempts by the Federal Reserve to stimulate the economy via activist monetary policy are anticipated and offset by the private market.

Second, unanticipated monetary policy can influence output. That is, if the Federal Reserve changes money growth in some manner not anticipated and different from the known reaction function, unexpected money growth will induce unexpected price changes and, according to expression (6), induce output growth deviations from the natural growth path. Eventually individuals, however, will incorporate the new monetary policies if they persist and convert previously unexpected money supply changes into expected money supply changes. Thomas Sargent and Neil Wallace have summarized the dilemma facing activist policy:

> Finally, we want to take note of a very general implication of rationality that seems to present a dilemma. . . . Suppose an economy has been operating under one rule for a long time when secretly a new rule is adopted. It would seem that people would learn the new rule only gradually as they acquired data and that they would for some time make what from the viewpoint of the policy maker are forecastable prediction errors. During this time, a new rule could be effecting real variables.
>
> A telling objection to this line of argument is that new rules are not adopted in a vacuum. Something would cause the change—a change in administrations, new appointments, and so on. Moreover, if rational agents live in a world in which rules can be and are changed, their behavior should take into account such possibilities and should depend on the process generating the rule changes.[2]

[2] Thomas J. Sargent and Neil Wallace, "Rational Expectations and the Theory of Economic Policy," *Studies in Monetary Economics*, No. 2, Federal Reserve Bank of Minneapolis, (June 1975), 7.

Rational Expectations: Evaluation

The foregoing model of policy ineffectiveness of anticipated changes in the money supply has not been borne out by empirical analysis nor has it been accepted as a realistic model of the economy. The reasons are not hard to understand. The implied learning process for market participants is extreme to say the least, and the underlying foundation of rapidly adjusting prices and wages to clear markets is not realistic. At the same time, rational expectations as a concept has become an important part of macroeconomic models. First, it highlights the problems faced by discretionary monetary policy. Second, it can be used to show that traditional statistical models of the economy can provide misleading results if used to simulate different stabilization policies. Third, the idea that market participants formulate expectations in a rational manner has been incorporated in many models, including neo-Keynesian, that are capable of policy effectiveness in the short run. Anticipated money can influence the real performance of the economy even in the short run in the context of rational expectations by assuming sluggish wage and price adjustments, information asymmetries between different sectors of the economy, and other rigidities in the economy.

Real Business Cycle Theories

A common element of the monetarist and information-based approaches is that monetary changes play a key role in determining the level of aggregate demand. Aggregate supply is relatively stable and, hence, shifts in demand induce changes in output and prices. To the extent that a monetary change is unanticipated, output and price both respond since prices behave differently than anticipated. The extreme view of these information-based models assuming flexible wages and prices implies the policy ineffectiveness proposition. Anticipated changes in the money supply have no real effects on the economy.

In the late 1980s a new class of neoclassical models emerged referred to as *real business cycle theories.* They are called real theories because they focus on nonmonetary causes of economic fluctuations. Their development was initiated by concern over how the economy responded to the oil price shocks of the 1970s. In some sense they could just as well be regarded as neo-Keynesian given their nonmonetary character; however, these models adopt the classical assumption of flexible wages and prices. Hence, they are classified as neoclassical.

These models argue that the source of economic fluctuations comes from the supply side. Technological "shocks" shift the short- and long-run aggregate supply functions. Technological shocks induce shifts in the potential output of the economy over time, and even if aggregate demand did not change, we would observe fluctuations in prices and output as the economy was adjusting to technological shocks.

To illustrate, consider what might happen if there occurs a temporary decline in

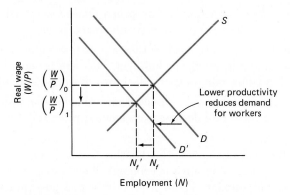

FIGURE 26-9 An example of real business cycle approach to economic fluctuations

the productivity in one sector of the economy. The lower productivity induces employers to reduce demand for workers at the given wage rate; hence, overall demand for labor shifts to the left (Figure 26-9). Because wages and prices are flexible, the real wage rate will decline to bring the labor market back into equilibrium at a lower employment and, hence, lower output level than before. A temporary increase in productivity will have the opposite effect.

How do real business cycle theories explain the observed correlation between money and economic activity? They argue that the causation does not run from money to the economy but rather the other way. Money is endogenous so that shifts in the supply function induce changes in the money supply.

Real business cycle theories have attracted considerable interest as of the time of this writing; however, no consensus has yet been reached. The theories have been developed to a high level of theoretical rigor but lack a similar effort to establish them empirically. For example, real business cycle theories have not provided convincing measures of technological shocks nor have they demonstrated a convincing argument that money is an endogenous and passive variable.

Monetarists were often criticized for measurement without theory and with some justification; however, the real business cycle theories can at least be equally criticized for theory without measurement.

Implications of Neoclassical Approaches
for Stabilization Policy

The monetarist and information-based models are nonactivist. The basic message that emerges from these models can be summarized as follows:

1. Monetary policy cannot change the long-run real performance of the economy since it is determined by the economy's resource base.

2. Output and price fluctuations are primarily due to monetary changes that cause actual prices to depart from anticipated prices.

3. Monetary changes, especially if they are unanticipated, will generate short-run price and output effects; however, once the economy adjusts to the changed inflation rate, output will return to the potential level.

4. Monetary policy should be directed toward achieving a steady and predictable monetary growth rate designed to maintain price stability.

While the real business cycle theories focus on supply shifts rather than on monetary changes as the source of economic fluctuations, the implications for stabilization policy are similar. There is very little that government can do to prevent price and output fluctuations over time and attempts by the monetary authority to offset these changes are likely to generate more instability. Again, the best monetary policy is one that aims at a steady and predictable monetary growth rate designed to achieve a steady long-run inflation rate.

Neo-Keynesian Approaches

The neoclassical models adopt the flexible wage and price assumption of the classical model. The original Keynesian model in contrast adopted fixed wages to explain output and price fluctuations. Recently, a number of economists have devoted considerable effort to explain why wages and prices might ultimately be flexible over time but, nonetheless, are sluggish and adjust very slowly to excess demand and supply at any point in time. Thus, wage and price sluggishness ensures a positively sloped short-run supply function or nonvertical Phillips curve even though the long-run functions might be vertical.

John B. Taylor, Stanley Fischer, and Jo Anna Gray in particular have developed models to explain sluggish or sticky wages. These models are not simple; however, they are based on three straightforward considerations. First, wages are contractually set; second, wage contracts remain constant over some period of time because of the costs of frequent adjustment; and third, wage contracts are staggered. These considerations do not require extensive unionization activities; in fact, they are applicable to a nonunion labor environment. In addition, the fact that no wage contract can take into account all contingencies and the desire to limit contract complexity means that indexing will not eliminate the need for wage contracts to remain in force over a period of time.

The lack of synchronized wage setting and the contractual nature of the wage contract (explicit or implicit) ensures that wages at any point in time represent an average of contracted wages established in the past that cannot be altered and contracted wages currently under negotiation. Thus, the money wage rate at any point in time is only partly flexible and induces a sluggishness or stickiness in the over all money wage rate.

The same considerations have also been made to explain sluggish and sticky prices. Firms typically employ markup pricing schemes that set price as a fixed markup over cost. Since wages represent a major part of total cost, sluggish and sticky wages induce sluggish and sticky prices.

Models that emphasize sluggish wage and price adjustments imply that any departure from full employment induced by shifts in demand will persist for a considerable period of time. Activist policy could potentially play a role in such an environment.

Neoclassical and Neo-Keynesian Views: Evaluation

The preceding extensions of the classical and Keynesian models have significantly extended our theoretical and empirical understanding of the economy and the impact of monetary policy. At the same time, the fundamental difference that separated the classical and the Keynesian views from each other persists in these modern extensions.

Those models that rely on the flexible wage and price adjustment mechanism of the classical model are inherently nonactivist in orientation. They regard the economy as inherently stable, and in any event, there is little that macroeconomic stabilization policy can contribute toward eliminating economic fluctuations. Government budgets should be balanced over time, and most important, the Federal Reserve should have a credible policy of price stability. That is, the Federal Reserve should maintain a noninflationary monetary growth rate over time. In addition, the Federal Reserve should stand ready to be a lender of last resort on occasion.

In contrast, models that rely on sluggish and sticky wage and/or price adjustments are inherently activist oriented. These models suggest a meaningful role for active monetary policy, though even these models have stepped back from the high degree of activism advocated by early Keynesians. In the 1960s, for example, one often heard the phrase of "fine tuning" the economy to describe the capabilities of stabilization policy. Few Keynesians now advocate such an activist approach, though they suggest that monetary policy and perhaps fiscal policy can play a more meaningful role in stabilizing the economy than suggested by the classical and neoclassical views.

Political Economy Approach

The foregoing models are intrinsically "economic" in that they employ economic relationships to explain fluctuations in prices and output while holding constant a wide variety of noneconomic elements. A number of economists have questioned the wisdom of this approach. While no model must account for every force that determines the level of economic activity, the omission of some noneconomic considerations might be a serious error.

Specifically, a number of economists have begun to investigate the interaction between economic relationships and political institutions to account for price and output fluctuations. These efforts agree on three points: (1) a consistent and logical theoretical model of political-macroeconomic interactions can be established even in a world of rational expectations, (2) empirical evidence appears consistent with some type of political-economic activity interaction for the United States as well as other industrial countries, and (3) the channels of interaction are complex and tend to change over time.

The literature on the political business cycle has proceeded in three steps. First, William Nordhaus in 1975 provided a theoretical foundation for the political business cycle model based on the assumption that politicians are only "office motivated," politicians can manipulate the policy instruments, there exists an exploitable short-run Phillips curve, and voters are not rational and have no preference as to which party is in power. Thus, politicians overstimulate the economy before an election and then reduce inflation with a recession shortly after the election. Second, D. Hibbs introduced the "partisan" perspective and the view that parties were ideologically motivated to pursue specific economic objectives; hence, Democrats tended to pursue employment goals more than Republicans while Republicans tended to pursue price stability goals more than Democrats. Thus, performance of the economy depended on who was in power and for how long. Third and most recently, models using rational expectations and asymmetric information between politicians and voters have been developed and tested.

The more recent models are fairly complex and would take us far afield of the subject. Even though the original Nordhaus model is subject to a number of problems, we can use it as an illustration of how political institutions may be responsible for some of the variation in prices and output.

Nordhaus Model of Political Business Cycles

Figure 26-10 illustrates the Nordhaus model. We have drawn a long-run vertical Phillips curve and assume the economy is in equilibrium at inflation rate, 5%, and unemployment rate equal to the natural rate of 6% (point *A*). A short-run Phillips curve is drawn through point *A* on the assumption that the anticipated rate of inflation is 5%. We have also drawn a series of lines concave and moving away from the original labeled D_1, D_2, D_3, and so on. These are *social disutility* curves. Each curve represents combinations of inflation and employment that generate the same level of disutility from society's point of view. As the disutility curves move away from the origin, the level of disutility increases. That is, society would rather be on curves closer to the origin than farther away.

We now have enough information to construct a political business cycle model. We start at point *A*. As an election is approached, policymakers pressure the Federal Reserve or use fiscal instruments to stimulate the economy by increasing aggregate demand. The stimulation shifts the economy from point *A* to point *B*, which necessarily touches a disutility curve closer to the origin than point *A*.

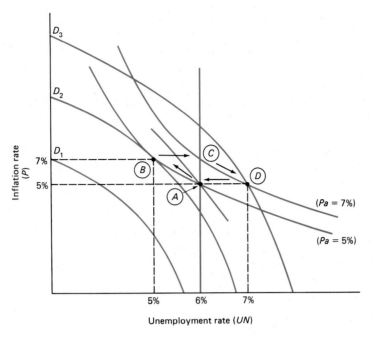

FIGURE 26-10 An example of a political business cycle model

Eventually anticipated inflation will be adjusted upward to recognize that the actual inflation rate has increased to 7%. The short-run Phillips curve will then shift upward to point C and reflect a higher anticipated inflation rate so that the unemployment rate will increase from 5% back to the natural level of 6%. By the time voters realize that the increased employment was purchased at a higher rate of inflation, the election is over and the incumbent political power remains in power.

After the election, the politicians must now deal with inflation. They restrict aggregate demand and move the economy from point C to point D. The actual inflation rate is brought down to 5%, and until anticipations of inflation are adjusted downward, unemployment will exceed the natural rate. Eventually, anticipations will be adjusted to the lower inflation rate, and the short-run Phillips curve will return to the original position, and the economy will be at original equilibrium at point A.

In the end, voters are no better off than before. They have been manipulated by politicians concerned more with holding office than pursuing goals of economic stabilization.

This model is very simplistic, but it does get the basic message of the political economy view across.

Problems with the Nordhaus Model

The Nordhaus model was subject to two major problems. First, it assumed voters were not rational since they failed to learn how they had been manipulated in the past. The rational expectations approach was especially critical of this type of model, since it explicitly assumed voters made *systematic* errors over time. Second, it assumed voters had no preference for one party over another and that political parties themselves were not ideologically motivated to pursue different economic policies.

Both problems have been dealt with in current political business cycle models. Even in a rational expectations world with rational voters, there exists a relationship among political parties, elections, and economic performance that might contribute to explain fluctuations in prices and output.

The empirical evidence has been suggestive to date but it is not definitive. There appears to be some relationship between politics and economic performance once partisan considerations are taken into account and a growing awareness that political institutions cannot be taken as given in modeling the economy. Alberto Alesina, after a careful review of the political economy approach in 1988, concluded:

> In summary, this paper suggests that positive models of economic policy cannot and should not ignore the political arena. Economists cannot ignore the political system and political scientists cannot ignore economic forces; a closer interaction between the two disciplines would be extremely fruitful.[3]

Why So Many Models?

The reader is understandably confused at this point and, by now, has achieved a deep understanding and appreciation of an often-repeated view of economists: "All of the economists in the world lined up end to end will not reach a conclusion." In response, we should attempt to offer some comments on the lack of consensus among economists about the proper model.

The basic problem is one of empirical verification rather than theoretical construction. Models must be evaluated first in terms of theoretical consistency and logic; however, once the model is consistently and logically constructed, it requires empirical verification to determine whether it offers meaningful insights. The models considered in this book meet the standards of consistency given their underlying assumptions though they differ considerably in the degree of theoretical rigor. For example, the real business cycle theories have been developed to a high level of rigor, whereas in contrast, the monetarist model has not received the same level of theoretical treatment. Economists, however, have not been willing to use the level of theoretical rigor as the separating standard once a given model has achieved a consistent and logical structure. To be very honest about it, even the most abstract and detailed theoretical models of monetary policy fail to capture the actual decision-making process. This is not a critical problem, however, since useful modes can be constructed that are only approximations of how markets function. The real issue is whether the model is consistent with how the economy actually behaves over time. Hence, model evaluation, and comparison with other models, requires empirical effort.

---

[3] "Macroeconomics and Politics," in Stanley Fischer, *NBER Macroeconomics Annual 1988* (Cambridge, Mass.: MIT Press, 1988), p. 47.

One would think that armed with the sophisticated mathematical, statistical, and computer tools of the late twentieth century and the availability of extensive data bases, that economists would be clever enough to devise tests to differentiate empirically between models. If judges at the Miss America contest can reach a consensus, why can't economists?

Several considerations come to mind:

1. Statistics can establish correlation and timing relationships but cannot establish causation among economic variables.

2. Historical events are unique in the sense that each event takes place within a framework that is likely to change by the time the next event occurs.

3. Economic models usually specify a set of variables as exogenous in empirical verification efforts; however, few variables are exogenous.

4. Quality of data limits statistical precision.

5. As a result of items (1)–(4), some fundamental differences between models cannot be empirically verified.

Let us consider each.

Causation in Statistics   Every student in his or her first statistics course learns that statistics, no matter how sophisticated, cannot prove that changes in one variable cause another variable to change. High correlation does not prove causation; it only suggests that two variables are meaningfully related to one another. Even timing relationships among variables does not prove causation. The fact that changes in money precede changes in economic activity does not prove that money causes changes in the economy, but is only suggestive of such causation.

In an effort to establish statistical tests that are more suggestive of causation, economists have resorted to sophisticated time series tests that determine whether one variable "statistically" causes another variable. The most famous of such tests is the Granger causality test. If one is trying to establish whether money causes income or income causes money, the Granger test involves two "distributed lag" equations:

$$Y_t = f(Y_{t-1}, Y_{t-2}, Y_{t-3}, M_{t-1}, M_{t-2}, M_{t-3}) \qquad (15)$$

and

$$M_t = f(Y_{t-1}, Y_{t-2}, Y_{t-3}, M_{t-1}, M_{t-2}, M_{t-3}) \qquad (16)$$

Expression (15) says that income is determined by its own lagged values and lagged values of money. Expression (16) says that money is determined by its own lagged values and lagged values of income. Estimates of these equations might help to establish causation; for example, if money is found to be important in (15) but income is not important in (16), then money "causes" income in terms of Granger causality.

These tests are interesting, but they have failed to settle the issue of which model is the most appropriate. Most important, statistical causality in the sense that money is more important than other variables in predicting income does not mean that money causes income. Additionally, tests such as Granger's possess a host of statistical problems that render their interpretation difficult at best.

Thus, despite the considerable sophistication of statistics, statistical tests alone cannot decide which model is best. While statistics has settled a large number of issues that once separated models, the fact that no one model has emerged reflects the inability of statistics to be the deciding factor.

Historical Events Are Unique   The economic changes associated with one historical event such as the Great Depression, the inflation of the 1970s, or any given business cycle take place within an economic and noneconomic framework that will likely change by the time another event takes place. Thus, economists have a serious sample problem in trying to empirically verify a model. Unlike the laboratory where the researcher can repeat a given event and carefully control the framework in which that event takes place, the economist is much less fortunate. The economist cannot repeat a historical event for closer study and the fact that events over time evolve within a changing framework means that the economist is frequently looking at a series of dissimilar events because of different environments.

"Exogenous" Variables Are Seldom Exogenous   Aside from the inability of statistics to establish causation, the application of statistics faces another problem. To verify a model empirically, some variables must be taken as exogenous in a statistical sense. Unfortunately, few economic variables are truly exogenous. Consider the money supply, for example. To the extent the Federal Reserve uses current and past levels of economic activity to determine future growth rates of money, money is not exogenous. Since policy instruments, whether monetary or fiscal, are set in regard to the current and past levels of economic activity, these instruments cannot be considered exogenous.

Quality of Data   The advent of PCs along with the availability of extensive data bases provides a false sense of precision regarding empirical verification. While data are of higher quality than ever, the majority of economists recognize that our economic data are frequently only an approximation of the variables of interest. While interest rate data tend to be fairly reliable even for short periods of time, data designed to measure money, employment, output, and prices are considered less reliable.

The problems of data quality and measurement have become an even more serious issue for empirical verification since the advent of new approaches that emphasize a difference between anticipated and actual values of a variable. While the concept of an anticipated variable is easy enough to establish, trying to measure anticipated variables for empirical verification is immensely difficult.

Persistence of Fundamental Differences   The reader should not get the notion that the above difficulties have prevented economists from reaching consensus on a number of important empirical issues. Many of these have been mentioned throughout this book; however, the fundamental difference between classical and Keynesian models and their extensions has not been easy to test.

Classical models view the economy as inherently stable and, hence, requiring a nonactivist role for government. Keynesian models view the economy as inherently

BOX 1 An example of why economists can't agree—has the postwar economy been more stable or not?

To illustrate why differences of opinion persist over which is the most appropriate model consider the issue of data quality summarized by Carl E. Walsh in a publication of the Federal Reserve Bank of San Francisco "Postwar Stability: Fact or Fiction?" The available statistical measures of GNP, unemployment, and industrial production show the post–World War II economy as being more stable than the prewar economy. According to Walsh,

> All conventional measures indicate that U.S. business cycles in the post–World War II period have been much less severe than were earlier cycles. For example, the peak-to-trough decline in detrended real GNP (that is, GNP that has been adjusted to remove secular growth trends) averaged 8 percent from 1893 to 1927, but only 4.4 percent since 1951. This disparity would be even greater if the Great Depression of the 1930s were included in the prewar measure. Likewise, the peak-to-trough rise in the unemployment rate for the pre-Depression period was 5 percentage points, compared to only 1.9 percentage points in the postwar period.

Much of this postwar stability has been attributed to the more active role of monetary and fiscal policy to stabilize the economy.

This result, however, has been recently questioned. Christina D. Romer,[1] for example, argues that the statistical stability of the U.S. economy compared to the past is more the result of improvements made in measuring economic activity than to some underlying change in the way the economy functions. Romer's analysis covers estimates of GNP, unemployment, and industrial production. In each case, once an effort is made to place the entire historical record on the same data foundation, there are virtually no differences between the prewar and postwar records of economic activity.

Romer is not the only economist to question the data used in estimating models and making judgments about the economy. Walsh concludes the following:

> Is the apparent reduction in economic instability during the postwar period in the U.S. fact or fiction? Although more research is needed before a definitive answer will be available, it appears that the old view of greater postwar stability may be weakened but not overturned. In any event, the debate serves to remind us that the way we see the economy depends importantly on the quality of our economic statistics.

[1] "Is the Stabilization of the Postwar Economy a Figment of the Data?" *American Economic Review*, 76 (June 1986), 314–334.

Carl E. Walsh, "Postwar Stability: Fact or Fiction?" *Weekly Letter*, Federal Reserve Bank of San Francisco (October 13, 1989).

unstable and, hence, in need of activist policy. This fundamental difference was well stated by Modigliani (Chapter 25, p. 591) when he was comparing the difference between monetarist (or classical) and nonmonetarist (or Keynesian) views.

Why can't the issue of inherent stability be put to an empirical test? The problems just discussed are certainly part of the answer, but there is another aspect. Many of the examples of inherent instability in U.S. economic history are difficult to interpret. This is especially the case with the Great Depression period. At one time Keynesians argued that the Great Depression was strong evidence of inherent instability. We now have a better understanding of this period because of the work by Friedman and Schwartz. We now realize that the Federal Reserve failed to be a lender of last resort and, as a consequence, permitted the money supply to decline by almost 25% from 1929 to 1933. As a result, the Great Depression provides little information about the inherent stability or instability of the market system. Even in the classical model, a major decline in the money supply will generate output and employment declines. This point was well summarized by Thomas Mayer on pages 592–593.

Other major changes in economic activity such as the panic of 1893 or 1908–09 have similar problems of interpretation and thus make it difficult to judge the issue of inherent stability or instability.

Thus, while statistics has settled a number of issues between different models, we have still found it necessary to develop a variety of extensions of the classical and Keynesian views. Our statistical tools are simply too crude to determine whether any particular classical (Keynesian) model is better than another classical (Keynesian) model, and more important, we have not been able to test adequately the fundamental difference between the classical and Keynesian views.

Key Points

1. Models must be able to account for the persistence of fluctuations of economic activity around the potential or long-run growth path.

2. The pre–Great Depression classical model was rejected because its inherent stability view of the market and nonactivist role for government stabilization appeared grossly inconsistent with what took place during the 1930s. The original Keynesian model seemed more consistent with the events of the 1930s, with its emphasis on inherent instability, wage and price rigidities, long-run unemployment equilibrium, and activist's role for government stabilization policy.

3. The classical model reemerged in the 1950s in the form of monetarism and gradually gained acceptance as a legitimate approach to modeling the economy. Monetarism set in motion a renewed interest in classical economics; hence, we classify monetarism and other recent extensions of the classical approach as "neo" or "new" classical economics. In addition to monetarism, neoclassical models include information-based approaches (Lucas supply function and rational expectations) and real business cycle theories.

4. Neoclassical models attribute fluctuations to unstable monetary growth rates that shift the aggregate demand function or in the case of real business cycle models, to technology shocks that shift aggregate supply. These models are inherently nonactivist.

5. Neo-Keynesian models retain the market instability notion of the original model, but provide theoretically sounder explanations for the slow adjustment process of wages and prices. Neo-Keynesian models are inherently activist, though not nearly as activist as in the past.

6. Both neoclassical and neo-Keynesian models hold political institutions constant. The political economy approach explicitly considers the interaction between political institutions and the performance of the economy. This view attributes fluctuations in prices and output to manipulative behavior by politicians in their endeavor to hold and enhance power. The political economy approach is the most recent and the least developed at this stage. Initial theoretical and empirical work, however, suggest that economic fluctuations may very well contain a political business cycle element. The political business cycle approach cannot be easily classified as activist or nonactivist; however, the implication of the approach is that political and institutional reforms may be an important part of achieving the goals of economic stabilization.

7. The existence of so many approaches and the failure to reach a consensus on whether the economy is inherently stable or unstable is due to many factors. Several important ones are the following: statistics cannot establish causation, historical events are unique, "exogenous" variables are seldom exogenous, and limited quality of economic data.

Key Terms

Anticipated versus unanticipated events

Lucas supply function

Natural unemployment rate hypothesis

Neoclassical

Neo-Keynesian

Phillips curve (long- and short-run version)

Policy ineffectiveness proposition

Political business cycles

Random forecast errors

Real business cycle theories

Systematic forecast errors

Wage contracts

Questions

1. Explain why the Great Depression cannot support either the classical or Keynesian view about inherent stability.

2. Using the monetarist framework on pages 581–585, explain how the economy will react to a decrease in the growth rate of the money supply from 5% to 3%.

3. Explain how a rational expectationist would answer question 2 assuming that the decreased growth of the money supply was completely anticipated.

4. Why does the natural unemployment rate view of the Phillips curve support a constant growth rate of money rule for monetary policy?

5. In illustrating the natural unemployment rate hypothesis, we assumed aggregate demand increased. Use the diagram on page 606 to show what would happen if aggregate demand declined.

6. Figure 26-10 employed the concept of a dis-

utility function for unemployment and inflation. How would the functions change if the public became more concerned about inflation than employment? If they became more concerned about employment than inflation?

7. Why does the Nordhaus model of the political business cycle assume nonrational voters and how does this conflict with the existence of rational expectations?

8. Explain the difference between systematic and random forecast errors.

9. Is the existence of an independent Federal Reserve consistent with political business cycle theories?

10. During the eighteenth and nineteenth centuries the topics in this chapter and book were referred to as *political* economy. Starting at the beginning of the twentieth century, we adopted the term economics and dropped the reference to political. Which do you prefer and why?

Suggested Readings

1. Alberto Alesina, "Macroeconomics and Politics," in Stanley Fischer (ed.), *NBER Macroeconomics Annual 1988* (Cambridge, Mass.: MIT Press, 1988), pp. 14–52. Summarizes the rational expectations approach to the political business cycle.

2. Milton Friedman, "The Role of Monetary Policy," *American Economic Review,* 58 (March 1968), 1–17. Statement of the natural unemployment rate hypothesis.

3. Stanley Fischer, "Long-Term Contracts, Rational Expectations, and the Optimal Money Supply Rule," *Journal of Political Economy,* 85 (February 1977), 191–205. Role of sluggish wages in macro models.

4. Thomas M. Humphrey, "The Evolution and Policy Implications of the Phillips Curve Analysis," *Economic Review,* Federal Reserve Bank of Richmond (March–April 1985), 3–22.

5. Robert Lucas, Jr., "Some International Evidence on Output-Inflation Tradeoffs," *American Economic Review,* 63 (June 1973), 326–334. The Lucas supply function.

6. Thomas Mayer, *The Political Economy of Monetary Policy* (New York: Cambridge University Press, 1990).

7. William Nordhaus, "The Political Business Cycle," *Review of Economic Studies,* 42 (April 1975), 169–190.

8. Edmund S. Phelps, "Phillips Curves, Expectations of Inflation, and Optimal Unemployment over Time," *Economica,* 34 (August 1967), 254–281. The natural unemployment rate hypothesis.

9. A. W. Phillips, "The Relation Between Unemployment and the Rate of Change of Money Wage Rates in the United Kingdom, 1861–1957," *Economica,* 25 (August 1958), 283–300.

10. Charles I. Plosser, "Understanding Real Business Cycles," *Journal of Economic Perspectives,* 3 (Summer 1989), 51–78. A readable discussion of real business cycle models and their motivation.

11. John B. Taylor, "Aggregate Demand and Staggered Contracts," *Journal of Political Economy,* 88 (February 1980), 1–23. Sluggish wages in macro models.

12. Thomas D. Willett (ed.), *Political Business Cycles* (Durham, N.C.: Duke University Press, 1988).

A P P E N D I X

Supply-Side Economics

In the 1980s supply-side economics received a great deal of attention, and though the earlier enthusiasm for the approach has waned in recent years, supply-side economics continues to receive attention. We place the discussion of supply-side economics in an appendix for three reasons. First, the approach is more concerned with economic growth and efficiency than with explaining economic fluctuations; second, the approach has not been formalized nearly as extensively as the other models; and third, the approach is not well-defined and is rather eclectic.

Supply-side economics is concerned with establishing a framework that will allow the economy to produce the greatest amount of goods and services with given resources and technology and will provide incentives for the economy to advance technology and productivity over time. Supply-side economics is thus concerned with economic growth and the efficiency with which the economy uses its resources. There are several important considerations to supply-side economics that require emphasis.

First, supply-side economics is neither new nor novel. The best known statement of the principles was made by Adam Smith in 1776 in his *Inquiry into the*

Nature and Causes of the Wealth of Nations. The focus in the *Wealth of Nations* was on establishing an environment that would enhance the output of goods and services. This environment was one that minimized the role of government regulation and allowed market forces more latitude to allocate society's resources. This environment was in direct contrast to the heavily regulated environment of mercantilism, which dominated government policy between 1500 and 1750. In many ways, modern-day supply-siders are reacting to the heavily government involved economic system of the post–Great Depression period in the same vein that Adam Smith was reacting to mercantilism.

Second, supply-side economics has not been well developed in a model framework as compared with monetarist, Keynesian, or rational expectations approaches. As such, it is difficult to evaluate, let alone define. Supply-side economics can be usefully thought of as a term used to describe two aspects of economic growth during the past two decades in the United States. (1) Supply-side economics places emphasis on the adverse effects of government involvement that have been responsible for slow growth, reduced efficiency, and inflation. (2) Supply-side economics advocates policies that minimize the adverse impact of government on economic growth. Supply-side economics ranges from the ad hoc concept of the Laffer curve to substantial issues that are concerned with the impact of government on economic growth.

Third, supply-side economics is critical of the Keynesian activist approach to stabilization policy. The supply-side approach often advocates a less activist approach; however, some care must be taken in categorizing the supply-side approach as nonactivist. There is no doubt that supply-side economics is close to the nonactivist view with regard to monetary and fiscal policy; however, some of the policy proposals of this approach can be activist when they are designed to encourage specific sectors in the economy that are judged to play an important role in the growth process.

What Is Supply-Side Economics?

The easiest way to understand supply-side economics is to start with a simple economy that produces two goods: A and B. At any point in time, this economy can devote all available resources and technology to producing A or B. Or this economy can use its resources and technology to produce different combinations of A and B. Figure A-1 illustrates the *production possibilities boundary* for the economy. The curve is concave from below because resources are not perfectly substitutable in producing A and B. Figure A-1 should appear familiar since it is widely used in introductory economics. First, at any point in time, the economy's resources and technology define combinations of A and B that can be produced. Second, the economy has attainable and unattainable production possibilities given the resource base and technology. Any point on the boundary $A_1 B_1 0$ or within the boundary is attainable with the given resource base and technology. Third, economic efficiency is achieved at points along the boundary $A_1 B_1$. It is inefficient to produce within the boundary even though it is attainable. Fourth, economic growth occurs when the resource base expands and/or technology allows more output from a given resource base. That is, economic growth is represented by an outward shift in the production possibility boundary.

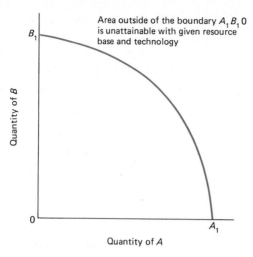

FIGURE A-1 Production possibility boundary
for an economy producing two goods

Supply-side economics is concerned with an economic environment that allows
production at some point on the curve and provides incentives to expand the curve
outward over time. This approach is critical of the activist demand management
policies that emerged in the Great Depression and were supported by the Keynesian
model. Some of the issues raised are similar to those raised by the monetarist and
rational expectations approaches; other issues are unique. Supply-side economics can
be summarized by considering two sets of issues. First are the factors used to account
for slow economic growth, slow productivity growth, and inflation; second are the
appropriate government policies that would encourage efficiency and economic
growth.

Factors that constrain the economy to operate within the production possibility
boundary and constrain the boundary from moving outward over time at a more
rapid rate Supply-side economics emphasizes four factors that account for slow
economic growth and inflation. First, unstable and excessive monetary growth has
generated inflation and high interest rates and has interfered with the flow of funds
between surplus units and deficit units by increasing the degree of uncertainty about
the future value of money. Adherence to activist monetary policies by the Federal
Reserve is partly responsible for excessive monetary growth. Second, extensive government regulation and supervision have interfered with the efficiency of resources.
Environmental regulations, safety regulations, and other regulations designed to
protect specific labor and product markets have seriously interfered with the allocation of resources. Third, government deficits have crowded out private investment
spending by raising interest rates, absorbing private saving, and competing for resources in the marketplace. Deficits have also contributed to excessive monetary
growth by imposing political pressures on the Federal Reserve to monetize the
federal debt. Fourth, the tax structure is overly progressive and complicated, it
rewards consumption at the expense of saving, and it provides incentives for society

to allocate a significant portion of saving to housing rather than capital accumulation and improved technology.

Appropriate Government Policies   Supply-side economics advocates a variety of policies to deal with the adverse impacts of these factors on the economic performance of the economy. First, excessive monetary growth should cease. Proposals range from having the Federal Reserve focus more on monetary aggregates and stable growth rates over periods such as a year to proposals that would replace the Federal Reserve with an exponential function. Some supply-siders have advocated a return to the gold standard as a method of taking discretionary monetary control away from the Federal Reserve. Second, government should more seriously consider the impact that regulation and supervision have on efficiency and economic growth and, in general, should allow more latitude for market forces to allocate resources. Supply-siders favor deregulation of the economy. Third, deficits should be eliminated, and some supply-siders advocate balanced budget amendments or other similar types of constraints on the discretion of government to spend in excess of revenues. Reduced expenditures, reduced tax rates, and restructuring of taxes should all be used to reduce and eliminate government deficits. Fourth, the tax structure should be modified to encourage investment and work effort and discourage consumption.

Supply-Side Economics and the Activist Approach

Supply-side economics focuses on the adverse impacts that government policies—supervision, regulation, monetary and fiscal policies—have on the supply of goods and services at a point in time and over time. The approach is critical of past policies based on the activist Keynesian framework. Rather than being concerned with off-setting every shift in private spending and regulating economic activity, government policy should take the long-run view toward improving economic efficiency and growth. This often requires a less activist role in general, a more stable monetary growth, and a balanced budget.

False Promise of Supply-Side Economics: The Laffer Curve

Considerable public discussion about supply-side economics in the early 1980s focused on the alleged effects that would result from major reductions in tax rates. The discussion concerned the *Laffer curve.* One version of the curve, illustrated in Figure A-2, expresses tax revenue as a function of the tax rate. At a tax rate of zero, tax revenue is zero. As the tax rate increases, tax revenue increases; however, at some point, the tax rate interferes with work effort and incentives. At this point,

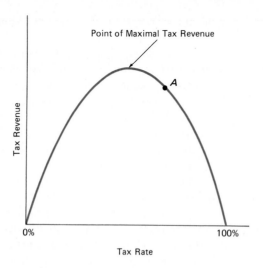

FIGURE A-2   Illustration of the Laffer curve

individuals reduce work effort, and, despite the higher tax rate, tax revenue declines. At a tax rate of 100%, work effort is zero and tax revenue is zero. According to some observers, the U.S. economy in the 1970s was somewhere to the right of the maximal tax revenue point, say, point A. An obvious implication of the Laffer curve would then be to reduce the tax rate. A lower tax rate would provide incentives for increased work effort and would actually increase tax revenue.

The Laffer curve and the argument that the U.S. economy was to the right of the maximal point were both based on ad hoc reasoning. The Laffer curve is far too simple to represent the tax structure or the effect that tax rates have on economic activity. In addition, the evidence that lower tax rates would have dramatic effects on work effort was nonexistent. The Laffer curve was interesting and expressed in a simple form ideas that had been stated previously; however, it was an inappropriate framework on which to base public policy. Unfortunately, it supported exaggerated claims of the benefits that would be derived from major tax cuts. The Reagan administration used the framework to justify large tax rate reductions in 1981. It is no wonder that politicians found the Laffer curve so appealing. What politician would argue against cutting tax rates, that would in turn increase economic activity and tax revenue, that could then be used to balance the budget or even support additional government expenditures? This is a clear case of belief in a free lunch.

The Laffer curve illustrated in Figure A-2 is a theoretical possibility; however, the evidence to support it is nonexistent. The curve should not be considered a realistic model of the effects of tax rate cuts or increases. The Reagan tax rate cuts of 1981 did not generate additional tax revenues as predicted nor will future tax rate cuts. There may be valid reasons to lower tax rates, but the Laffer curve cannot be used to support them.

It should be stressed that few economists believed in the Laffer curve, and it is now totally dismissed; however, its importance for our discussion is based on two considerations. First, it was part of the public discussion on supply-side economics and certainly one of the most frequently mentioned benefits of lower taxes by some.

Second, it is an interesting example of how economics can be misused by the political establishment.

The most serious impact of the Laffer curve has been the cloud that it has placed over the supply-side approach, which is concerned with issues that are valid and have considerable merit. Careful consideration of the supply-side impacts of government policies is a necessary component to sustained noninflationary growth.

Suggested Reading

1. Michael W. Keran, "The Supply-Side Miracle— Thank OPEC, not Laffer," *Journal of Portfolio Management* (Summer 1989).

2. John A. Tatom, "We Are All Supply-Siders Now!" *Review*, Federal Reserve Bank of St. Louis (May 1981), 18–30.

PART VIII

Federal Reserve Procedures, Interest Rates, Money, and Inflation

CHAPTER 27

Interest Rates, Monetary Aggregates, and Federal Reserve Procedures

Chapter Overview

In Chapter 17 we introduced a schematic outline of how monetary policy was used to achieve goals of economic stabilization as part of our introductory remarks about stabilization policy. In a sense, the chapters of this book have been filling in the details of that outline. It is now time to complete the schematic outline and provide a more detailed examination of how the Federal Reserve actually conducts monetary policy along with several important issues regarding the conduct of monetary policy.

First, we define those terms that are commonly used to describe monetary policy. These terms are frequently mentioned in the news media, official publications of the Federal Reserve, and especially the professional literature on monetary policy. Some terms we have already encountered, but we want to review all the relevant concepts in one place to gain an understanding of the actual operating framework used by the Federal Reserve. In this framework, *intermediate targets* also known as *indicators* of monetary policy play a critical role.

Second, we discuss the two intermediate targets available to the Federal Reserve: interest rates and monetary aggregates. We define a set of standards for an "ideal" intermediate target and then proceed to evaluate interest rates and monetary aggregates in light of the ideal.

Third, we provide a brief history of Federal Reserve operating procedures with special focus on events since the mid-1970s. These have experienced a number of changes and have been the subject of intense criticism of Federal Reserve policy in recent years.

Fourth, we focus on major changes in the financial and monetary environment brought about by deregulation, financial innovation, and world financial integration that have significantly changed the operating environment of Federal Reserve policy.

The Terminology of Monetary Policy

Discussions of monetary policy have adopted a set of terms that are frequently used.

Policy Instruments   Policy instruments are the methods used by the Federal Reserve to influence money and credit. General policy instruments include open market operations, the discount mechanism, and changes in reserve requirements. In the money multiplier framework, these policy instruments influence the total money supply by their impact on the monetary base and/or the money multiplier. There are also selective policy instruments designed to influence the allocation of credit; however, margin requirements for stock purchases are currently the only selective instrument used by the Federal Reserve.

Policy Targets   Policy targets refer to the ultimate objectives of monetary policy and represent the desired levels of unemployment, inflation, economic growth, and exchange rates that the Federal Reserve would like to see realized. Policy targets are thus the desired values of major indicators of economic performance that measure the performance of the economy with respect to the goals of economic stabilization.

Monetary Policy   Monetary policy is defined as the use of the policy instruments to achieve the policy targets, the link between the policy instruments and the policy targets being the transmission process. The transmission process describes the response of the economy to changes in monetary policy beginning with the change in the policy instruments and ending when the economy has adjusted fully to the change in monetary policy.

Intermediate Targets   Intermediate targets, as the term suggests, fall somewhere between the ultimate policy targets and the actions of the Federal Reserve to change the policy instruments. Intermediate targets are variables closely associated with the policy targets such as inflation, output, and employment. There are three intermediate targets: interest rates, monetary aggregates, and of lessor importance, credit aggregates or measures of credit advanced to nonfinancial sectors. Unlike policy instruments, the intermediate targets are not controlled directly by the Federal Reserve, but they are more controllable and closer to Federal Reserve actions than are the ultimate policy targets. Intermediate targets serve two important roles in the conduct of monetary policy given their role in the transmission process. First, they provide the Federal Reserve with feedback information to determine whether or not the policy instruments are having the desired impact on economic activity. Second, they determine whether the overall impact of monetary policy actions (changes in policy instruments) have been in the direction of stimulating the economy (easy monetary policy) or slowing the economy (tight monetary policy).

    The rationale of using intermediate targets is based on the fact that intermediate targets are associated closely with the policy targets, whereas policy instruments are

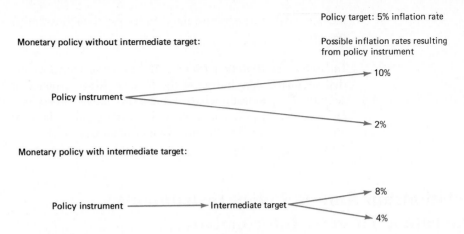

FIGURE 27-1   **The role of an intermediate
target in the conduct of monetary policy**

associated much less with the policy targets. Since the relationship between instruments and policy targets is more uncertain and subject to change, there is more chance of error in the impact of monetary policy without the use of intermediate targets. Given that policy instruments are associated closely with intermediate targets and intermediate targets are associated closely with the ultimate policy targets, the Federal Reserve is more likely to achieve its ultimate goals by using an intermediate target. This point is illustrated in Figure 27-1. Given the greater "distance" between the policy instrument and the ultimate policy target, monetary policy in the absence of an intermediate target is less certain of achieving the ultimate goal. For example, a change in the policy instrument designed to achieve a 5% inflation rate may result in inflation rates ranging from 2% to 10%. In the situation with intermediate targets, monetary policy is more likely to come closer to the ultimate target reflected by a range of outcomes from 4% to 8%.

This discussion suggests three desirable features of an intermediate target: (1) it must be an important variable in the transmission process, connecting changes in the policy instrument with changes in the ultimate policy target; (2) it should provide frequent and accurate readings so that it can be monitored easily; and (3) the Federal Reserve should be able to exert significant influence on the value of the intermediate target, and at the same time, the intermediate target should not be significantly influenced by non-Federal Reserve factors. While credit is sometimes regarded as an intermediate target, interest rates and monetary aggregates are the major intermediate targets used by the Federal Reserve.

Operating Targets   Operating targets play an important role in the day-to-day conduct of monetary policy. These variables are closely associated with the intermediate targets and policy instruments and fall in between the policy instruments and intermediate targets. By altering the policy instruments, the Federal Reserve has significant influence over the operating variables, which, in turn, are linked closely to the intermediate targets. Operating targets fall into two classifications: short-term interest rates such as the Federal funds rate, and reserve aggregates. Reserve aggregates include total reserves, the monetary base, nonborrowed reserves, and borrowed reserves.

Indicators of Monetary Policy   Indicators of monetary policy are those variables that summarize the impact of the Federal Reserve policy on the level of economic activity. They indicate whether monetary policy is easy or tight. The intermediate targets are the primary indicators of monetary policy; however, the operating targets are also used to judge the direction of monetary policy.

Relationship Among Policy Instruments, Operating Targets, Intermediate Targets, and Policy Targets

The various definitions are brought together to illustrate the operating procedure of monetary policy in Figure 27-2. First, the Federal Reserve formulates policy targets based on actual and forecasted economic performance and desired levels of performance. The policy targets might be expressed as either a point value or range of values of inflation, unemployment, growth, and so on; for example, if the current inflation rate were 10%, the policy target for inflation over the coming year could be expressed as lowering the inflation rate to a range of 5 to 7%. Second, once the policy targets are formulated, the Federal Reserve then uses the policy instruments to either stimulate or restrain the economy. The policy instruments first impact on the operational variables, which, in turn, impact on the intermediate variables. Since there is a close association between intermediate and policy target variables, the Federal Reserve is then able to use monetary policy to achieve the specific policy targets.

There are four important types of an operating-intermediate target relationship that can be employed. The first uses the Federal funds rate as the operational variable. Changes in the Federal funds rate then influence other interest rates, which are regarded as the intermediate variables. Economic activity is then influenced by both changes in short- and long-term interest rates. The second scheme uses the Federal funds rate as the operational variable to influence the monetary aggregates, which are regarded as the intermediate variable. The monetary aggregates, along with interest rates, in turn, influence overall economic activity. The third scheme uses reserve aggregates as the operational variable to influence the monetary aggre-

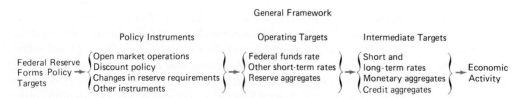

FIGURE 27-2   The framework of monetary policy

gates, which are regarded as the intermediate variable. Changes in monetary aggregates then impact on economic activity. The fourth scheme uses the Federal funds rate or reserves to influence credit, which in turn, influences economic activity. Credit, however, has not played as important a role as either interest rates or monetary aggregates.

The Federal Reserve relied on the first two sequences since the 1950s up until October 1979. Despite the appearance of monetary aggregates in the second sequence, both the first and second scheme place primary importance on interest rates as the method by which monetary policy influences economic activity. The third sequence, which emphasizes reserve and monetary aggregates, had been advocated by many Fed-watchers; however, the Federal Reserve resisted any operating procedure that would shift emphasis away from focusing monetary policy on interest rates. The Federal Reserve did adopt a reserve—monetary aggregate operating strategy from October 1979 to late 1982; however, since then it has returned to an interest rate–focused strategy not too different from that followed in the 1970s.

The framework for monetary policy illustrated in Figure 27-2 will provide a point of reference for much of the discussion to follow; however, it is a simplification of a fairly complex policymaking process and glosses over some difficult issues, especially with respect to the formulation of policy targets. The various goals of economic stabilization are not always compatible with each other, and sometimes trade-offs must be made between certain goals such as trying to control inflation and stimulating economic growth and employment. Aside from the issue of conflicts, each goal is not weighted equally by the Federal Reserve. Despite the public announcements by the Federal Reserve that it conducts monetary policy to achieve price stability, full employment, economic growth, and exchange rate stability altogether, the Federal Reserve attaches different weights to each goal. There is evidence that the Federal Reserve places more weight on the price stability goal than government in general and, what is more, has an additional goal of maintaining stable and orderly financial markets. Stable and orderly financial markets are usually interpreted to mean that interest rates should not fluctuate greatly, especially in an upward direction. This, however, can frequently conflict with the price stabilization goal.

Before discussing the actual operating procedures used by the Federal Reserve we will review the major issues regarding the use of interest rates and monetary aggregates as intermediate targets and indicators of monetary policy.

Interest Rates and Monetary Aggregates

The Federal Reserve attempts to achieve an interest rate or monetary aggregate target consistent with a desired policy target such as the level of income. If the Federal Reserve attempts to achieve an interest rate target consistent with an income target, it essentially loses control over the money supply because the money supply must be maintained at a level consistent with the interest rate target. If the Federal Reserve attempts to achieve a monetary aggregate target consistent with an income target, it essentially loses control over the interest rate because the interest rate must be allowed to reach a level consistent with the monetary aggregate target.

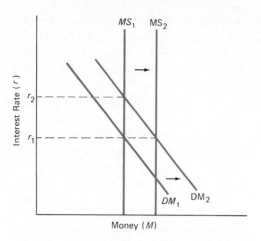

FIGURE 27-3   **Maintaining an interest rate target**

Figure 27-3 illustrates the difficulty of trying to control both the interest rate and the money supply simultaneously. The equilibrium rate of interest, r_1, is determined by the intersection of the demand, DM_1, and supply, MS_1, for money.

The Federal Reserve's attempt to maintain the interest rate at r_1 requires changes in the money supply to offset shifts in the demand function for money. Assume that there is an increase in government spending financed by issuing debt. The increase in aggregate demand leads to increased spending and income, which in turn, will increase the demand for money (shift the function to the right). The interest rate will increase to r_2 as long as the supply function for money remains at MS_1. The Federal Reserve would need to increase the money supply from MS_1 to MS_2 to offset the shift in money demand and maintain an interest rate of r_1. To maintain an interest rate target thus results in a loss of control over the money supply in the presence of shifts in the demand for money.

To maintain a money supply target, the Federal Reserve would have to give up control over the interest rate. Figure 27-4 illustrates the Federal Reserve's attempt to maintain the money supply at MS_1. However, shifts in the demand function for money will change the equilibrium interest rate from r_1. As long as the Federal Reserve wishes to maintain the money supply at MS_1, it cannot at the same time maintain the rate of interest at r_1. Thus, the Federal Reserve cannot achieve explicit interest rate and money supply targets at the same time but must emphasize one variable over the other.

Interest Rates as Indicators

The Keynesian view emphasizes interest rates as the primary operational and indicator variable because changes in the cost and availability of credit provide the main channel through which monetary policy influences economic activity. Keynesians do not reject monetary aggregates or various reserve measures out of hand. These can often provide important feedback information in the conduct of monetary policy, but the ultimate effect of monetary policy actions will be through the cost and availability of credit.

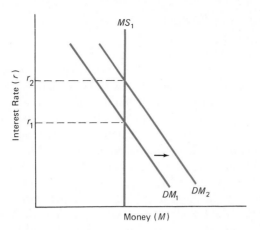

FIGURE 27-4   Maintaining a money supply target

The Federal Reserve has historically emphasized interest rate variables over monetary aggregates for two reasons. First, to the extent that the Federal Reserve has a theory of how monetary policy influences economic activity, it tends to be Keynesian. The Federal Reserve-M.I.T. econometric model is probably the best support for this statement. This model was developed primarily by economists at the Board and is used as a basis in formulating monetary policy by the Board and the FOMC. The model is Keynesian oriented and regards monetary policy as first changing the cost and availability of credit, which in turn will change various components of total spending sensitive to changes in the cost and availability of credit.

Second, the Federal Reserve has had a traditional objective to maintain orderly financial markets. The phrase "orderly financial markets" implies policies that reduce fluctuations in interest rates, especially in an upward direction. The Federal Reserve and many members of the financial community believe that fluctuating interest rates interfere with the flow of saving and investment.

The first and second reasons for emphasizing interest rates are not necessarily compatible. For example, one can emphasize interest rates as the proper operating target and indicator and argue that the Federal Reserve should pursue policies to change interest rates regularly to offset autonomous changes in private spending. During periods of expansion, when prices are increasing at a rapid rate, the Federal Reserve should use policy instruments to increase interest rates and slow down the rate of spending. During periods of decline, the Federal Reserve should reverse itself and stimulate the economy by pursuing policies to lower interest rates. However, this type of policy could very well conflict with the desire to maintain orderly financial markets. Likewise, attempts to keep interest rates from changing too much may very well interfere with the objective of stabilizing the economy.

The use of interest rates as the target and indicator of monetary policy has been criticized in recent years. There are two types of criticism that are often confused: the criticism of the objective of maintaining orderly financial markets, which is not necessarily a criticism of using interest rates as operating targets and indicators of monetary policy, and the criticism of using interest rates as legitimate intermediate targets and indicators.

Interest Rates and Orderly Financial Markets

There are several criticisms of the Federal Reserve's pursuit of orderly financial markets. First, the objective interferes with the economic function of interest rates in the economy. As a price for funds, interest rates serve to allocate loanable funds to the most productive use. Second, the attempt to maintain stable interest rates leads to large changes in the money supply that many regard as a more important variable determining the level of economic activity. Third, the Federal Reserve's attention to stable interest rates focuses on only one sector of the economic system; the central bank must have a broad perspective of the economy and be concerned with the impact of its actions on the entire economy and not only one sector. The most severe critics of the Federal Reserve's concern with day-to-day money market conditions and maintaining orderly financial markets had the following to say:

> the day-to-day operations that often dominate System Policy introduce a large amount of variation in the monetary base. As a result, such operations add to the variation of the money stock, weaken or reduce the "degree of control" over the money supply, and introduce substantial changes in the monthly rate of change in the money stock.[1]

This comment was made almost three decades ago; however, many economists regard it as an accurate description of current Federal Reserve actions.

Interest Rates Versus Monetary Aggregates

The controversy over interest rates or monetary aggregates as the intermediate targets or indicators depends on (1) the closeness of interest rates and monetary aggregates to the ideal standards of an operational target and indicator and (2) the relative stability of the interest rate–spending relationships in the real sector versus the demand function for money in the monetary sector. By stability, we mean the extent to which the respective function is predictable.

Three Standards

There are three reasonable standards for a variable to be a reliable indicator of the direction of monetary policy actions. (1) The availability of accurate and frequent readings on the variable. If one had to wait six months before the government statisticians could provide an accurate reading on some variable, it would be of very little use to measure the effects of monetary policy and provide feedback information to the Federal Reserve. (2) The variable must play an important part in the transmission mechanism between a change in the policy instrument and the ultimate

---

[1] Karl Brunner and Allan H. Meltzer, *An Alternative Approach to the Monetary Mechanism,* House of Representatives, Subcommittee on Domestic Finance Committee on Banking and Currency, 88th Cong., 2d sess., 1964, p. 79

effect on economic activity. (3) The variable should be influenced directly by the Federal Reserve in a clear and concise manner and should not be influenced significantly by non-Federal Reserve forces.

These are fairly strict standards, and it is doubtful that any economic variable could meet them entirely. However, we can use these standards to judge the suitability of interest rates and monetary aggregates as indicators of monetary policy.

Accurate and Frequent Information   There is detailed and accurate information available on interest rates on a day-to-day basis. The Federal funds rate can be read on an hour-by-hour basis. Accurate and timely monetary aggregate information, on the other hand, is more difficult to obtain. Although monetary aggregate estimates are made weekly, these estimates contain a significant degree of error. Even monthly and, to some extent, quarterly figures contain sizable measurement error.

Role in the Transmission Process   Interest rates play an important part in the transmission mechanism. Even monetarists admit the importance of interest rates in the conduct of monetary policy. The Keynesian approach emphasizes the indirect effects of monetary policy operating through interest rates. They point to simple and complex econometric models of the economy that support the indirect effects of monetary policy. The monetarists, on the other hand, argue that interest rates only tell part of the story of how monetary policy influences economic activity. Changes in monetary aggregates are a more reliable indicator of how economic activity will respond to changes in Federal Reserve policy. They emphasize the direct relationship between changes in the money supply and changes in economic activity. The monetarists also cite empirical evidence to support a direct relationship between changes in the money supply and changes in economic activity.

Federal Reserve and Non-Federal Reserve Influences   Interest rates and monetary aggregates are influenced directly by the Federal Reserve. Interest rates are determined by the supply and demand for money, and the Federal Reserve has considerable influence over the supply of money. There is no doubt the Federal Reserve can alter the interest rate significantly in either direction in a short period of time given its influence over the monetary base and money supply. As long as the money multiplier is not too sensitive to the rate of interest, the Federal Reserve can influence monetary aggregates in a fairly short period of time. Empirical evidence has shown that the money multiplier is not overly sensitive to the rate of interest, so the Federal Reserve can exercise considerable influence over the money supply and other monetary aggregates.

Non-Federal Reserve actions that influence the interest rate at any point in time are many. The interest rate is determined by the interaction of the demand and supply for money, which in turn interact with the real sector of the economy. At any one time, the level of the interest rate is the result of a number of factors, only one of which is the Federal Reserve. Critics of using interest rates as monetary policy indicators point out the difficulty of attributing any movement in interest rates to some action on the part of the Federal Reserve given the number of factors that determine interest rates.

The interest rate has another problem that becomes important during periods of changing anticipations about future inflation. The market or nominal rate of interest has two components: the real rate of interest and anticipated inflation. In terms of economic activity, it is the real interest rate that influences real spending decisions; yet the Federal Reserve can only influence directly the nominal or market interest rate.

In addition, the distinction between real and nominal interest rates raises another issue with regard to interest rates as intermediate targets and indicators. The response of the interest rate over time to a change in the money supply depends on the combined effect of three factors. Depending on the point in time considered, current interest rates can provide misleading information on the direction of monetary policy. The response of the nominal interest rate to a monetary change is composed of three phases: the *liquidity effect*, the *income effect*, and the *price anticipations effect*. These effects were discussed in Chapter 5. Figure 5.13 illustrated how an increase in the growth of money could be associated with falling or increasing interest rates depending how much time had elapsed from the time money growth increased.

The Federal Reserve is not the only determinant of monetary aggregates. As we saw in Chapters 10 and 19, many forces, such as float and changes in Treasury deposits, combine to determine the monetary base. In addition, the money multiplier is subject to variation outside of Federal Reserve actions due to the variation in the k, n, and e ratios. Thus, other factors besides the Federal Reserve can influence monetary aggregates, and some monetary aggregates are more influenced by outside factors than others.

The role of non-Fed influence on the monetary aggregates has probably increased in the 1980s as a result of regulatory changes and financial innovations. New forms of money and financial services in the opinion of some observers have weakened the Federal Reserve's control over the monetary aggregates and thereby reduced their usefulness as an intermediate target. Others argue that these are transitory changes and that the Federal Reserve retains considerable control over the monetary aggregates.

Summary of the Standards   How do we rank interest rates and monetary aggregates according to the three standards?

1. Interest rates have a decided advantage over monetary aggregates in terms of frequent and accurate measurement. Day-to-day data are readily available on interest rate movements, whereas measurement errors make it difficult to measure monetary aggregates accurately on a short-term basis.

2. Interest rates and monetary aggregates play an important part in the link between changes in the policy instruments and the policy targets. Theoretical and empirical evidence supports the importance of both but offers no real conclusion as to which is the more important.

3. The Federal Reserve has considerable control over longer-run monetary aggregates; however, the Federal Reserve has little control over week-to-week movements in the aggregates and some control over month-to-month movements. Evidence shows that the Federal Reserve is capable of achieving reasonable control over the money supply on a quarter-to-quarter basis and especially for periods longer than a quarter. The Federal Reserve's control over interest rates has been seriously questioned. There is little debate that the Federal Reserve can influence the interest rate over short periods of time; however, once income and price anticipations effects are considered, the Fed-

eral Reserve has difficulty in controlling interest rates over longer periods of time. The Federal Reserve may be able to lower interest rates in the short run via the liquidity effect, but increased monetary growth will eventually increase the rate of inflation and, hence, raise interest rates. If the Federal Reserve further attempted to lower interest rates as they rose in response to higher anticipated inflation, they may again decline somewhat, but they would soon increase to even higher levels as the increased monetary growth eventually increased the rate of inflation and anticipated inflation. Thus, if the Federal Reserve attempted to maintain a low interest rate target over a period of time inconsistent with price stability, changes in the money supply would induce liquidity, income, and price anticipation effects that would make it difficult, if not impossible, to maintain interest rates over the long run at that targeted level.

This last consideration became evident in the 1970s when a number of studies suggested that changes in the money supply had a *positive* rather than *negative* effect on interest rates. That is, once inflation became an ongoing process, the liquidity effect became very small or disappeared. Why? Because in the 1970s the public increasingly anticipated inflation and increasingly paid more attention to the growth of money as a leading indicator of future inflation rates. Financial markets incorporated these inflationary anticipations into market interest rates; hence, an increase in the money supply generated higher rather than lower interest rates.

This is consistent with the rational expectations argument that the public learns from the past that monetary growth is an important determinant of inflation.

On balance, monetary aggregates are probably the preferable intermediate target or indicator of monetary policy, especially during periods when anticipated inflation is likely to be significant.

Another View of the Indicator Problem: Relative Stability of the Real and Money Sectors of the Economy

The three standards represent one basis of comparing interest rates and monetary aggregates; however, the issue can be approached from another viewpoint.

The Keynesian model can be used to show that the choice between interest rates and monetary aggregates depends on the relative stability of the interest rate–expenditure relationship in the real sector compared with the demand function for money in the monetary sector.[2] The investment function is the primary interest-sensitive component of total spending. There are two possibilities:

1. The investment function is more stable than the demand function for money.
2. The demand function for money is more stable than the investment function.

---

[2] The implications of the relative stability of the money and real sectors of the economy are due to William Poole, "Optimal Choice of Monetary Policy Instruments in a Simple Stochastic Macro Model," *Quarterly Journal of Economics*, 84 (May 1970), 197–216, and Board of Governors of the Federal Reserve System, "Rules-of-Thumb for Guiding Monetary Policy," *Open Market Policies and Operating Procedures—Staff Studies* (July 1971), 135–189.

BOX 1:   Vanishing liquidity effect during high inflation

Yash Mehra of the Federal Reserve Bank of Richmond[1] conducted a detailed study of the relationship between monetary growth and interest rates to determine the relative roles of the liquidity effect, income effect, and inflationary expectations effect on interest rate movements. Mehra constructed and estimated a fairly complex model of interest rates and examined data over the period from 1952 to 1983. This interval of time included periods of very low inflation (1950s and early 1960s), moderate inflation (rest of the 1960s), and moderate to high rates of inflation (1970s and early 1980s). Mehra's study employed the Livingston survey of expected inflation discussed in Box 2 of Chapter 5.

The study reached two conclusions and from them, drew important implications for Federal Reserve policy.[2] According to Mehia:

> First, there did exist a statistically significant liquidity effect in the '50s and the early '60s when the average inflation rate was very low. This liquidity effect, however, has now almost vanished. The coefficient on the money growth variable in the nominal interest rate regression is negative, large, and statistically significant when this equation is estimated over the subperiod beginning in the '50s and ending in the mid-'60s or the early '70s, but it is not significant when the same equation is estimated over the subperiod beginning in the mid-'60s or the '70s but ending in 1979 or 1983.
>
> The second conclusion is that if the behavior of the Livingston survey participants is considered as representative of the behavior of other economic agents in the economy, this vanishing of the liquidity effect in the '70s is probably the result of increased responsiveness of inflationary expectations to higher money growth. An empirical analysis of the factors determining the Livingston survey inflation measure implies that these economic agents have over time paid more attention to money growth in forming their expectations of long-term inflation. This factor tends to reduce directly the magnitude of the liquidity effect associated with a given acceleration in money growth.
>
> The results presented here have important impli-

cations for monetary theory and policy. An important issue in discussion of the transmission mechanism of monetary policy is the time pattern of the effects of higher money growth on nominal interest rates. The Keynesian view is that one would initially observe lower nominal and real interest rates following an acceleration in the money growth rate. The policy implication of this view is that the Federal Reserve could bring down interest rates and hold them there in the short run (at least for six to nine months) by accelerating the money growth rate. The results here, however, imply that the Keynesian view may now have to be modified. While nominal interest rates may still decline immediately following an acceleration in the money growth rate, this lowering of interest rates is shorter lived and less exploitable for policy purposes. In the '50s and the '60s, the Federal Reserve could induce falling nominal and real interest rates at least for six months by increasing the growth rate of the money supply. It now appears that its ability to do so has declined, mainly due to the increased responsiveness of inflationary expectations to higher money growth.

Finally, it should be pointed out that the public's perception of the way the Federal Reserve formulates and executes its monetary policy has considerable influence on the responsiveness of inflationary expectations to higher money growth. The upward drift in the growth rate of money which occurred in the '70s probably contributed to the higher inflation rate observed during that period. More recently, however, the United States has had considerable success in curbing inflation, and public confidence in monetary policy as a means of controlling inflationary expectations may have risen as a result. If so, we may observe yet another change in the response of inflationary expectations and nominal interest rates to higher money growth. To the extent such a change is already under way, the empirical results for the sample period ending in the year 1983 must be viewed with caution.

[1] Yash Mehra, "Inflationary Expectations, Money Growth, and the Vanishing Liquidity Effect of Money on Interest: A Further Investigation," *Economic Review,* Federal Reserve Bank of Richmond (March/April 1985), 23–35.

[2] Ibid., p. 35.

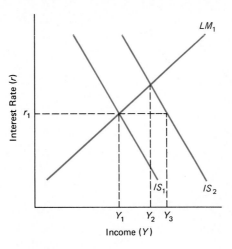

FIGURE 27-5   Stable *LM* function and unstable *IS* function

By the term "stable," we mean whether a given function is constantly shifting over a wide range or narrow range independent of the variables in the model.

To illustrate the importance of the relative stability of the investment function and demand function for money regarding the choice of indicators, we will consider two simple cases. First, we assume that the investment function is perfectly stable and that the demand function for money shifts within a range of possible values. Second, we assume that the demand function for money is perfectly stable, whereas the investment function shifts within a range of possible values. In practice, both functions shift, but it is the relative comparison between the two that is important for the issue.

The two polar cases are illustrated in Figures 27-5 and 27-6. In Figure 27-5, the *LM* function is assumed constant for a given supply of money, whereas the *IS* function shifts between IS_1 and IS_2 because of instability in the investment function or any other component of private spending. The *LM* function is stable for á given level of money at LM_1. A money supply target will be consistent with changes in income between Y_1 and Y_2; however, if we set the interest rate at r_1 by increasing or decreasing the money supply wherever necessary, then the swings in income would be from Y_1 to Y_3. Thus, a money supply target will provide greater stability in the level of income than will an interest rate target. This result depends on the spending functions that make up the *IS* function being relatively more unstable than the demand function for money.

Figure 27-6 illustrates a stable *IS* function and the *LM* function shifting between LM_1 to LM_2 with a constant money supply. A money supply target will thus cause income to move between Y_1 and Y_2, whereas an interest rate target would provide a stable level of income at Y_1. Thus, an interest rate target will lead to smaller fluctuations in income than will a money supply target when the demand function for money is relatively more unstable than the investment function or any other spending function in the real sector.

Monetarists regard the demand for money as relatively more stable than components of total spending (Figure 27-5) and thus emphasize the money supply as the most important target of monetary policy. Keynesians emphasize the interest rate as

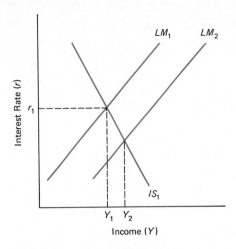

FIGURE 27-6   Stable *IS* function and unstable *LM* function

the most important because they regard the components of total spending as relatively more stable than the demand function for money (Figure 27-6).

What Is the Federal Reserve's Operating Strategy?

The operating procedure of the Federal Reserve has undergone significant change during the past several decades. To understand the actual procedure, the reader should keep in mind that the Federal Open Market Committee (FOMC) is the focal point of monetary policy formulation and execution for reasons explained in Chapter 18. The FOMC meets eight times yearly and formulates policy. The decisions of the FOMC are expressed in a directive to the Federal Open Market Trading Desk at the New York Federal Reserve Bank that instructs the Desk on how to conduct open market operations during the time to the next FOMC meeting.

The actual operating procedures and use of intermediate targets as well as the form of the directive have changed significantly since the 1950s. Until the early 1970s, the FOMC did not use intermediate targets in the sense of targets that would extend beyond one or more formal FOMC meetings. Instead, a set of short-term *money market* targets was established in each meeting and expressed in terms of free bank reserves, the Federal funds rate, and other short-term interest rates that represented the "feel and tone" of the financial markets. These money market targets were deemed suitable for achieving desired levels of economic activity. The money market targets were likely to be readjusted at each meeting. This short-run approach to monetary policy came under severe criticism by the mid-1960s. Critics argued that the procedure was too myopic, resulted in both short-run and long-run instability in the money supply, and prevented the Federal Reserve as well as outsiders from evaluating fully the success or failure of monetary policy since longer-term intermediate targets were never specified.

In the early 1970s, the FOMC began to formulate money market targets in terms of desired monetary aggregate targets. The FOMC still emphasized the achievement of short-term interest rates or other money market targets; however, it added the *proviso clause* that specified that monetary aggregates should not change by more than some indicated amount. Failure to achieve the longer-term monetary aggregate targets would then be a basis for readjusting the policy instruments. The early 1970s operating procedures represented an improvement in two ways over the meeting-by-meeting approach that focused only on money market conditions. First, longer-term intermediate targets in the sense of targets that might be maintained beyond one FOMC meeting came into use. Second, failure to achieve the longer-term targets would be the basis for a reevaluation of policy.

Despite the improvement, the Federal Reserve in practice still focused on short-term interest rates and other money market conditions as the primary target. The Federal Reserve was much more likely to alter policy instruments when desired money market conditions were not achieved than when desired monetary aggregate conditions were not achieved. The Federal Reserve came again under increased criticism, and the passage of Concurrent Resolution 133 in 1975, as will be discussed more fully in the next chapter, required the Federal Reserve to specify monetary aggregate intermediate targets and report quarterly to Congress on these targets and explain differences between actual and target behavior of the monetary aggregates. Rather than report a single target growth rate, ranges were specified.

There was considerable criticism regarding the manner in which the Federal Reserve established and reported the targeted growth rates of the monetary aggregates. Each quarter, the Federal Reserve adopted one-year growth ranges and reported these to Congress. The period covered by the growth ranges began with the base quarter and ended in the same quarter in the following year. For example, during the April 1978 FOMC meeting, the target growth ranges were based on the period from the first quarter of 1978 to the first quarter of 1979. During the July 1978 meeting, the ranges were based on the period from the second quarter 1978 to the second quarter of 1979. Thus, the base period for computing the growth ranges changed from quarter to quarter and resulted in *base drift*. Many argued that base drift provided a *forgiveness factor* to Federal Reserve failure to achieve indicated monetary targets.

For example, assume that the Federal Reserve set a 4% growth target for money using the first quarter of 1978 as the base; however, the money supply grew from $100.0 billion to $101.5 billion during the first quarter or at an annual rate[3] of 6%. The Federal Reserve could maintain the target growth rate of 4% at the next meeting, yet apply the 4% target to the second quarter money level of $101.5 billion. Assume that money supply grew during the second quarter by 4%, that is, from $101.5 billion to $102.5 billion. At first glance, the Federal Reserve appears to have kept monetary policy unchanged since the same 4% growth target was used during the two quarters; however, the money supply actually grew 5% on an annual basis during the two quarters. Also, by shifting the base, the Federal Reserve's failure to achieve the growth target in the first quarter was "forgiven," since the Federal Reserve "achieved" the target in the second quarter by the base shift.

In 1978, the Full Employment and Balanced Growth Act of 1978 or Humphrey-Hawkins Act altered the Federal Reserve's operating procedures. The act required the FOMC to establish calendar year growth ranges for monetary aggregates in

[3] In this and later numerical examples, compounding is ignored.

February of each year. These ranges covered the period from the fourth quarter of the previous year to the fourth quarter of the current year in which the ranges were set. Base drift was eliminated, at least within the calendar year, since the Federal Reserve now uses the fourth quarter in the previous year as the base to compute money growth rates for the current year. In addition, the FOMC was required to report to Congress twice yearly instead of four times a year.

Operating Procedure Prior to October 1979: The Federal Funds Approach

The operating procedure used in the late 1970s reflected the emphasis on interest rates as opposed to monetary aggregates. The Federal Reserve's procedure involved a complex process of short- and long-term target formulation for monetary aggregates and interest rates. The procedures were formalized along the lines of the framework presented in Figure 27-2.

First, the Federal Reserve undertook a detailed analysis of the economy to forecast economic performance under given conditions that then provided background information for each meeting of the FOMC. These forecasts were typically for one year ahead. Policy targets based on these forecasts and desired performance were formulated. Second, judgments were made as to the required growth in monetary aggregates consistent with achieving the policy targets. Third, the Federal Reserve then established a set of long-run or one-year growth rate intermediate targets for various monetary aggregates. Short-run (two-month) monetary growth targets were then established at each FOMC meeting consistent with the long-run target. To illustrate, assume that the Federal Reserve in February 1978 established a targeted 12-month monetary growth of 5% using the fourth quarter of 1977 as the base. If monetary growth during the first several months of 1978 exceeded 5%, the Federal Reserve would then establish a series of short-run targets lower than 5% that would bring the short-run monetary growth in line with the 12-month targeted growth. Thus the short-run monetary growth targets were designed to ensure that the longer-run target would be achieved. The short-run targets were also presented as a range rather than as a point target. Fourth, the Federal Reserve then adopted a procedure that would ensure short-run monetary growth. The Federal funds rate enters at this point as a pivotal operational variable in the Federal Reserve's pre–October 1979 procedures. The Federal funds rate was used to achieve the short-run and, hence, long-run monetary growth rate targets. How was the targeted Federal funds rate derived? Let us assume that the FOMC is meeting in February.

The Federal funds rate target was determined and achieved in two steps. (1) A short-run demand function for money was forecasted for March, and, given the desired increase in the money supply from February to March (short-run money supply target), equality of the demand and supply for money would determine the targeted Federal funds rate. (2) Open market operations were the chief policy instrument used to keep the Federal funds rate on target.

Figure 27-7 indicates that the Federal funds rate was 3% for January, given the money supply of $100 billion and the demand function for money. By March, the demand function for money is forecasted to shift rightward from MD_1 to MD_2 as a result

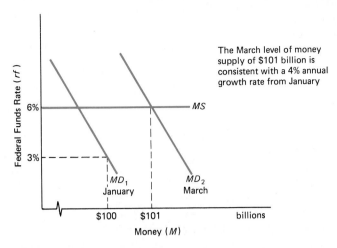

The March level of money supply of $101 billion is consistent with a 4% annual growth rate from January

FIGURE 27-7 Supply function for money becomes horizontal at targeted federal funds rate

of changes in income and other factors. Assume that the Federal Reserve wants the money supply to increase over the short run from January to March at an annual rate of 4%, which means that the desired level of money supply for March is $101 billion. This implies a Federal funds rate of 6%. Given the forecasted demand function for money in March, a Federal funds rate higher than 6% would result in a monetary growth less than 4% and a rate below 6% would result in monetary growth more than 4%. In economic terms, by setting the Federal funds rate at 6% for March, the Federal Reserve allows the demand for money to determine the supply for money. The supply of money essentially becomes horizontal at the 6% Federal funds rate.

The second step of the procedure involves determining the derived demand for reserves based on the public's demand for money. Reserves are required to support the expansion in transaction balances and reflect the shift in the demand for money. Figure 27-8 illustrates the forecasted demand for reserves for March based on the public's demand function for money. Given the discount rate and reserve requirements, the demand for reserves varies inversely with the Federal funds rate. As long as the Federal funds rate stays at 6%, the Federal Reserve will continue to supply reserves to the banking system, which, in turn, will increase the money supply. If the Federal funds rate increases above 6%, the Federal Reserve will supply more reserves, and, if the rate falls below 6%, the Federal Reserve will reduce the supply of reserves. The supply of reserves (RS) thus becomes horizontal at the targeted Federal funds rate. The supply of reserves and money are thus determined by the demand for reserves and money by the public. As long as the Federal funds rate remains at the target level of 6%, the Federal Reserve will continue to accommodate the economy with increased reserves and money.

The Federal funds rate was not only the operating target of monetary policy but also provided the necessary feedback information to ensure that short- and long-run monetary growth targets were being achieved. This can be summarized by the following:

Change in targeted Federal funds rate
$$= f(\text{actual money supply} - \text{targeted money supply}) \qquad (1)$$

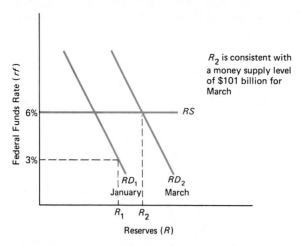

FIGURE 27-8   Supply function for reserves becomes horizontal at targeted federal funds rate

Change in reserves supplied
$$= f(\text{actual Federal funds rate} - \text{targeted Federal funds rate}) \qquad (2)$$

If the money supply is growing faster (slower) than desired, the Federal Reserve would increase (decrease) the targeted Federal funds rate according to expression (1). Open market sales (purchases) then would be used to reduce (increase) the level of reserves according to expression (2).

Problems with the Federal Funds Approach

Despite the appearance that monetary aggregates played an important role in the procedure just described, the Federal funds rate and other short-term interest rates were the primary focal point of monetary policy. There were several reasons for this bias toward interest rates. First, the long-standing objective of maintaining stable financial markets has been interpreted by the Federal Reserve as keeping interest rates from rising too rapidly. The Federal Reserve viewed short-run movements in the money supply as much less harmful to the economy. Why would achievement of the Federal funds target often result in large short-run movements in the money supply? As long as the functions moved as predicted, both the funds rate and money growth target could be achieved; however, the world is uncertain and the functions shifted unexpectedly. If the demand function for money expanded more than expected and the Federal Reserve achieved the desired money growth target, this could only be accomplished by allowing the Federal funds to increase above the funds target. The Federal Reserve was more likely to meet the funds target and allow the money supply target to be missed. Second, Federal funds and other short-term interest rates provided fast and accurate signals on the performance of the economy. This gave the Federal Reserve opportunity to reevaluate and change policy on a short-term basis. Third, the Federal Reserve regarded the relationship between reserves and the money supply as uncertain, so that, rather than set a reserve target

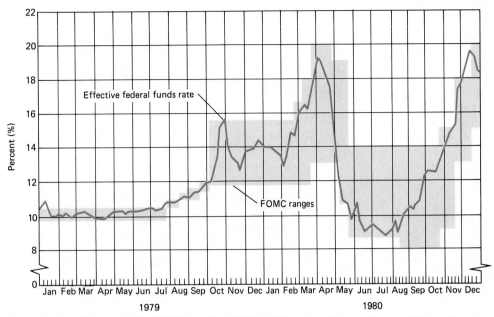

Source: R. Alton Gilbert and Michael E. Tribing, "The FOMC in 1980; A Year of Reserve Targeting," *Review,* Federal Reserve Bank of St. Louis (August–September 1981), p. 9

FIGURE 27-9 FOMC ranges for the federal funds rate of interest, January 1979–December 1980

and let the market determine the Federal funds rate, it would more likely achieve long-run monetary growth objectives by setting a Federal funds target.

The Federal funds approach was very successful in one regard. The Federal Reserve almost always achieved the Federal funds target; that is, the Federal funds rate was almost always within the tolerance ranges set up each month. On the other hand, the monetary growth targets were not always achieved, and the Federal Reserve often allowed the money supply to grow at rates faster than targeted. Figures 27-9 and 27-10 illustrate the Federal funds and monetary growth target success for 1979, respectively. The Federal Reserve appeared more concerned in 1979 about interest rate targets than monetary targets. Table 27-1 presents the Federal Reserve's record of monetary targeting since targets were first established in 1975.

There are many areas of criticism of the Federal funds approach; however, the most severe problem was that it tended to allow the money supply to grow *procyclically* and thus increase economic instability. During a downturn in economic activity, the demand function for money would shift to the left as smaller transactions balances were required by the public; however, the Federal Reserve was often slow to recognize that the demand for money had declined. With a given Federal funds target, a decrease in the demand for money and hence, a decrease in the demand for reserves, would decrease the money supply. Likewise, during an upturn in economic activity, the Federal Reserve would often fail to recognize the increasing demand for money and thus allow the money supply to grow more rapidly in an effort to meet the Federal funds target. In fact, the rapid increase in the money supply throughout much of the 1970s is attributed to the failure of the Federal Reserve to fully adjust

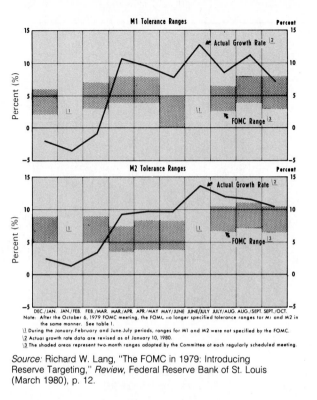

Source: Richard W. Lang, "The FOMC in 1979: Introducing Reserve Targeting," *Review,* Federal Reserve Bank of St. Louis (March 1980), p. 12.

FIGURE 27-10   **FOMC short-run ranges for monetary aggregates, 1979**
Note: M-1 and M-2 are pre-February 1980 measures of the money supply.

upward the forecasted demand function of money as the economy expanded from previous excessive increases in the money supply. To meet the Federal funds target, the Federal Reserve allowed the money supply to grow at rates greater than those targeted. This would stimulate the economy more and shift the money demand farther to the right. Even if the Federal Reserve raised the Federal funds target, it almost always acted with a lag and failed to adjust it high enough.

In addition to imparting a procyclical bias in monetary growth, the Federal funds approach faced another related problem. Traditional demand functions for money were becoming increasingly difficult to estimate and forecast by the mid-1970s. The first serious reflection of this problem occurred in 1975 when the Federal Reserve overpredicted the demand for money by a large magnitude. Actual money demand was much lower and actual velocity was much higher than the Federal Reserve had anticipated. Such difficulties raised fundamental questions about the viability of the Federal funds approach that placed considerable importance on being able to predict the demand function for money. Since 1975, the traditional money demand functions have continued to perform poorly, and there is a lively controversy over the reasons for their lack of performance. Many argue that the innovations in financial transactions and new money substitutes have made traditional money demand functions unstable and will continue to make it difficult, if not impossible, to forecast money demand with any degree of accuracy. Others argue that more detailed work on the

TABLE 27-1 Money growth targets and outcomes, 1975–1989						
	M1		M2		M3	
Year	Target[1]	Out-come[1]	Target	Out-come	Target	Out-come
1975	5.0–7.5	5.3	8.5–10.5	9.7	10.0–12.0	12.3
1976	4.5–7.5	5.8	7.5–10.5	10.9	9.0–12.0	12.7
1977	4.5–6.5	7.9	7.0–10.0	3.8	8.5–11.5	11.7
1978	4.0–6.5	7.2	6.5–9.0	8.7	7.5–10.0	9.5
1979	3.0–6.0	5.5	5.0–8.0	8.3	6.0–9.0	8.1
1980	4.0–6.5	7.4	6.0–9.0	8.9	6.5–9.5	9.5
1981	3.5–6.0	2.5[2]	6.0–9.0	9.3	6.5–9.5	12.3
1982	2.5–5.5	8.8	6.0–9.0	9.1	6.5–9.5	9.9
1983[3]	4.0–8.0	10.4	7.0–10.0	12.2	6.5–9.5	9.8
1984	4.0–8.0	5.4	6.0–9.0	7.9	6.0–9.0	10.6
1985[3]	4.0–7.0	12.0	6.0–9.0	8.9	6.0–9.5	7.8
1986	3.0–8.0	15.5	6.0–9.0	9.3	6.0–9.0	9.1
1987		6.3	5.5–8.5	4.3	5.5–8.5	5.8
1988		4.3	4.0–8.0	5.2	4.0–8.0	6.3
1989		0.6	3.0–7.0	4.6	3.5–7.5	3.3

[1] Data for targets and outcomes are for then current definitions.

[2] Both the target and reported outcome for M1 are for M1 adjusted for shifts into NOW accounts.

[3] These are target ranges announced at the start of the year. Targets were rebased in midyear.

Source: Data through 1985 are from Peter Isard and Lilliana Rojas-Suarez, "Velocity of Money and the Practice of Monetary Targeting: Experience, Theory, and the Policy Debate," *Staff Studies for the World Economic Outlook*, July 1986 (Washington, D.C.: International Monetary Fund, 1986). The table has been updated through 1989 with information provided in "1990 Monetary Policy Objectives: Summary Report of the Federal Reserve Board," February 20, 1990.

equations and proper measure of the money supply will allow us to again forecast money demand within reasonable ranges. The debate continues.

The Federal Reserve's use of the Federal funds rate came under increasing criticism by late 1979. The close association between inflation and excessive monetary growth and the tendency for monetary growth to exceed targets forced the Federal Reserve to reevaluate its entire operating procedure.

The October 1979 Announcement, The February 1980 Redefinitions of the Money Supply, and The 1980 Deregulation and Monetary Control Act

In late 1979, a crisis situation was developing in the financial system and the economy: inflation was increasing at rates of close to 20%, interest rates were increasing rapidly, disintermediation was again becoming serious, consumer credit was growing rapidly as the public purchased durables in anticipation of higher prices, the price of gold and silver on speculative markets reached levels that few had forecasted, and we were getting ready to "celebrate" the fiftieth anniversary of the Great Depression. On foreign exchange markets, the value of the dollar was falling, and there was growing concern that the Federal Reserve and U.S. government did not have the ability or the willingness to deal effectively with inflation.

The Federal Reserve had to achieve greater control over the money supply to bring inflation down to acceptable levels. The failure of interest rates as the major operating-intermediate target became apparent to almost everyone. Several major policy events occurred in reaction to the economic situation in late 1979 and early 1980. All should be considered together as a package in terms of understanding the new monetary control procedures of the Federal Reserve.

The October 1979 Announcement   On October 6, 1979, the Federal Reserve announced a series of actions to "assure better control over the expansion of money and bank credit, help curb speculative excesses in financial, foreign exchange, and commodity markets, and thereby serve to dampen inflationary forces."[4] The Federal Reserve introduced marginal reserve requirements on certain types of managed liabilities and raised the discount rate; however, the most important policy action was a change in the operating procedure of the FOMC:

> This action involves placing greater emphasis on day-to-day operations on the supply of bank reserves and less emphasis on confining short-term fluctuations in the federal funds rate.[5]

The new operating procedure consisted of the following steps. (1) The FOMC determines the desired short- and long-run target growth rates for the monetary aggregates. (2) Reserve paths are then determined that will result in the desired monetary growth paths. A family of reserve measures were available such as total reserves, the monetary base, and nonborrowed reserves; however, the Federal Reserve focused on *nonborrowed reserves*. That is, total reserves less borrowing at the discount window. (3) The policy instruments are then used to achieve the reserve and, hence, money supply targets.

Figure 27-11 illustrates the difference between the two procedures. In panel A, the Federal funds target requires the reserve supply function to be a horizontal line at the targeted Federal funds rate, rf^*. Thus the demand for reserves determines the supply of reserves and only if the reserve demand function is RD_1 will the desired reserve level, R^*, be achieved. In panel B, the reserve target approach requires the Federal Reserve to supply reserves equal to R^* and allows the Federal funds rate to range from rf_1 to rf_2 in response to any shifts in reserve demand. The Federal funds rate is allowed to fluctuate within a range of 600 or more basis points, whereas before October 1979 the funds rate was allowed to fluctuate within a range of 50 to 100 basis points.

February 1980 Redefinitions of the Money Supply   Given the new emphasis on monetary aggregates, and given the evolving nature of money, new measures of the

---

[4] Board of Governors of the Federal Reserve System, *Federal Reserve Bulletin* (October 1979), p. 830.
[5] *ibid.* p. 830.

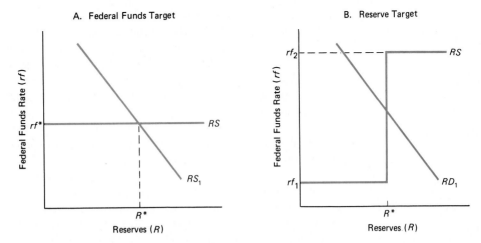

FIGURE 27-11   Basic difference between targeting the
Federal funds rate and the level of reserves

money supply were introduced by the Federal Reserve to reflect the growing importance of NOW accounts, ATS accounts, and credit union share drafts. This action is consistent with the shift in emphasis toward monetary aggregates announced in October 1979.

Deregulation and Monetary Control Act of 1980   The monetary control features of this act again are consistent with the Federal Reserve's desire to achieve more effective monetary control. The deregulation aspects of the act are also consistent with the shift in emphasis. Targeting reserves and monetary aggregates necessitated greater movements in short-term interest rates than previously; however, high and fluctuating interest rates in the context of Regulation Q ceilings and other constraints on competitive behavior resulted in disintermediation and threats of the viability of depository institutions. Thus, removal of Regulation Q ceilings and other deregulation features are again consistent with new emphasis on monetary aggregates.

Federal Reserve's Operating Procedure: October 1979–September 1982

The new operating procedure introduced in late 1979 was not in place for long. By late 1982 the Federal Reserve changed operating procedures again; in fact, the new operating procedure has the same characteristics as the Federal funds targeting procedure of the 1970s in terms of its focus on interest rates! Why was the October 1979 policy so short lived?

On the surface it appears the reserve–monetary control procedure was a failure. A notable feature of the 1979–1982 period was the increased variability of the money supply and the failure to meet annual monetary aggregate targets (Table 27-1). The

Federal funds rate did fluctuate more as anticipated; however, the growth of money became even more unstable than prior to October 1979.

The Federal Reserve argued this clearly illustrated the difficulty of focusing monetary policy on monetary aggregate targets. The Federal Reserve also claimed that the demand for money and hence velocity, had become so difficult to predict that any operating procedure focused on the monetary aggregates was likely to generate unpredictable effects on the economy. Velocity did depart from its historical trend pattern after 1980 as reflected in Figure 25-1 in Chapter 25. The Federal Reserve asserted that it had made a serious effort to conduct monetary policy by focusing on reserves and the monetary aggregates during the 1979–1982 period, but the "experiment" was unsuccessful. The deregulation process and the financial innovations rendered monetary aggregate targeting no longer feasible. The demand function for money (velocity) had become unstable and statistical measures of the money supply no longer accurately represented those financial assets/services used as money in the economy.

Some economists, however, questioned this view.

Technical Problems with the Federal Reserve's Interpretation of the Money-Focused Policy from October 1979 to September 1982

There are four technical issues that can account for the increased variability of the money supply after 1980.

First, reserve requirements imposed by the Federal Reserve were based on a *lagged reserve accounting* (LRA) system that complicated monetary targeting. LRA had been introduced in 1968 to make it easier for banks to compute and meet reserve requirements on settlement days. Under this system, reserve requirements were based on deposit levels two weeks in the past. Unfortunately, such a system forced the Federal Reserve frequently to choose between two alternatives; first, to validate decisions made by depository institutions two weeks in the past by supplying reserves to meet current requirements or, second, not to validate the past actions and allow sharp fluctuations in the Federal funds rate. The Federal Reserve was reluctant to follow the second alternative, and depository institutions were also aware of the Federal Reserve's reluctance. This made it difficult to achieve monetary growth targets if they were inconsistent with the combined actions of depository institutions.

To illustrate, assume that banks had expanded loans and deposits that generated a monetary growth rate higher than targeted but under LRA, however, reserves for these deposits would not be required until two weeks in the future. After two weeks, the Federal Reserve would be forced to permit the Federal funds rate to increase to high levels as banks scrambled for funds to meet the reserve requirement, or what was more likely, the Federal Reserve would provide the reserves and essentially validate the actions of the banks. After a time, the banks collectively knew large fluctuations in the Federal funds rate would not be permitted and acted accordingly. Under *contemporaneous reserve accounting* (CRA), however, banks would be required to match deposit increases with reserves immediately and not force a choice between validating what the banks had already done or allowing the funds rate to increase.

The importance of the reserve requirement accounting system was pointed out at numerous times. The Federal Reserve did finally modify the system in early 1984; however, on balance the new system was more a semi-CRA system and more complicated than the system it replaced. In any event, the Federal Reserve abandoned monetary targeting by this time, and the accounting system was less critical for an interest rate–focused policy.

Aside from the LRA problem, the Deregulation and Monetary Control Act of 1980 had introduced a new reserve requirement system that would extend to almost all depository institutions. While the new system was designed to be phased in over a long period, the transition to the new system compounded the problems of targeting reserves and hence the money supply.

Second, the events of the period from late 1979 through late 1982 were not very conducive to implementing a new monetary control procedure, and under the best of circumstances, the new operating procedure would encounter difficulties. Credit controls had been imposed in March 1980 and were being dismantled six months later. The economy experienced the sharpest recession since the Great Depression. Deregulation and financial innovation were making major changes in the structure of the financial system and the type and availability of financial assets held by the public. Disruptive disintermediation continued during this period as funds were withdrawn from depository institutions and placed in the rapidly growing money market mutual funds. Thrifts in particular were hard hit by disintermediation. Overall, it was a period of extreme economic and financial variability and one that would make it difficult to implement any new procedure successfully.

Third, the Federal Reserve has focused on interest rates from its inception. The "feel and tone" of the money market procedures of the 1950s and 1960s were essentially designed to reduce interest rate fluctuations. The Federal funds approach in the 1970s, despite its alleged focus on targeting the monetary aggregates, was operated to reduce interest rate fluctuations. Hence, it would be unrealistic for the Federal Reserve to expect success in a new operating strategy even in normal times, much less than the unstable times of the early 1980s. The Federal Reserve required a learning period to adopt its procedures to the new strategy.

Fourth, the unusual behavior of velocity after 1980 had many interpretations; for example, it could have reflected the unstable events of the early 1980s, or it could have reflected the market's adjustment to a new Federal Reserve operating procedure. Major changes were taking place in the financial system during the first half of the 1980s. New financial assets and services would have disrupted established relationships; however, once the pace of change slowed, velocity might return to a more stable pattern.

Thus, several technical factors suggest that targeting the monetary aggregates during the 1979–1982 period was bound to encounter problems. The fact that monetary growth rate variation actually increased should have been no surprise given the financial and institutional environment and, on balance, did not offer a strong argument to abandon monetary targeting. A number of observers also pointed out that many of the problems faced by the Federal Reserve as it attempted to focus on money such as the innovation process were the direct result of its failure to maintain noninflationary monetary growth rates in the 1970s. This is a fact the Federal Reserve frequently overlooked as it cited one piece of evidence after another that monetary targeting was no longer feasible. One could say that the Federal Reserve was the victim of its own failure to achieve noninflationary monetary growth in the 1970s. In any event, the Federal Reserve abandoned the emphasis on monetary aggregates in late 1982.

Federal Reserve's Operating Procedure: October 1982 to Present

In October 1982 the Federal Reserve returned to an interest rate–focused policy that was designed to reduce interest rate fluctuations and deemphasize monetary targeting. The abandonment of monetary targeting was made official when M1 targets were not specified for 1987 (see Table 27-1) though the Federal Reserve continues to set targets for M2 and M3 as well as debt.

The procedure introduced in October 1982 replaced nonborrowed reserves with *borrowed reserves* as the operating target. Borrowed reserves are the reserves obtained by depository institutions at the discount window. The borrowed reserve target is not an appropriate strategy if monetary control is the objective; however, it is essentially a strategy for targeting the Federal funds rate.

Figure 27-12A describes equilibrium in the reserve market under a borrowings procedure. The demand for total reserves by depository institutions (DTR) is a derived demand function from the demand for money. Any shift in the demand for money by the public will be reflected by the same directional shift in the demand for reserves by depository institutions. The supply of *nonborrowed reserves* is determined by the Federal Reserve and independent of the Federal funds rate. Nonborrowed reserves are increased (decreased) by open market purchases (sales). The total reserve supply function (STR) is obtained by adding to the nonborrowed reserve line (vertical line at NBR_1) the supply of borrowed reserves. The STR is drawn as upward sloping at point A because increasing levels of the Federal funds rate renders borrowing from the Federal Reserve more attractive given the discount rate which is assumed to be equal to the Federal funds rate, rf_o. The supply of borrowed reserves starts at point A because below this point, depository institutions will not borrow at the discount window assuming the discount rate equals rf_o.

Equilibrium in the reserve market occurs at funds rate rf_1. At this rate the quantity of total reserves demanded equals the quantity of reserves supplied by the Federal Reserve, TR_1. The quantity of reserves supplied consists of two parts: the amount of nonborrowed reserves, NBR_1, and the amount of borrowed reserves, BR_1. Borrowed reserves are equal to $(TR_1 - NBR_1)$. To understand the procedure, let us assume that the level of borrowed reserves in Panel A is also the targeted level of borrowed reserves.

Assume income increases and shifts the demand for money to the right, which in turn, will shift the demand for total reserves to the right (Panel B). Without any change in nonborrowed reserves, total reserves would increase to TR_2 and the Federal funds rate would increase to rf_2. The actual level of borrowed reserves, BR_2 or $(TR_2 - NBR_1)$, would now exceed the targeted level, BR_1.

The Federal Reserve would then need to increase NBR_1 to NBR_2 by open market purchases to hit the borrowed reserve target and, as a result, return the

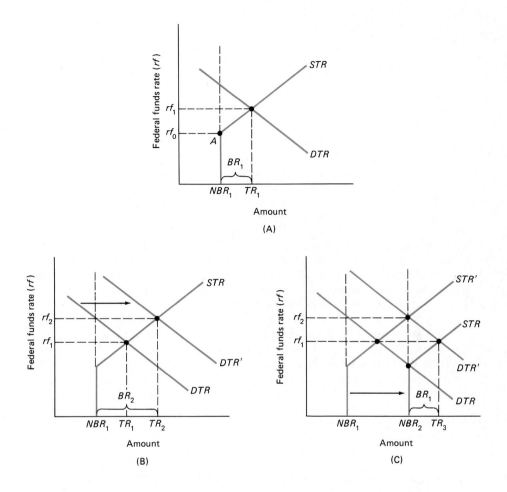

FIGURE 27-12 Effect of an increase in demand for total reserves under a borrowed reserve target procedure.

See paper by Daniel L. Thornton in reference list for more detail.

Federal funds rate to rf_1. In Panel C, the Federal Reserve increases total reserves by open market purchases so that the equilibrium level of borrowed reserves is back to BR_1. In the process, however, the Federal Reserve has permitted the money supply to expand as the economy is expanding. If the economy slowed down and shifted the demand for money and reserves to the left, the money supply would decline.

It is obvious from Figure 27-12 that the borrowed reserve strategy does a nice job if one is interested in targeting the Federal funds rate. This has led most observers to conclude that after 1982, the Federal Reserve returned to an interest rate–focused policy not much different than the one used in the 1970s.

It appears that in 1987 the Federal Reserve has made another change in operating strategy. While the borrowed reserve target continues to be discussed by the Federal Reserve, there is evidence that the Federal Reserve has returned to a more

---

BOX 2: Does an interest rate–focused policy mean inflationary monetary growth? Lessons from Japan

It is important to understand that there is a difference between operating targets and intermediate targets. There is general agreement that monetary aggregates provide a more reliable intermediate target or indicator of monetary policy in terms of how monetary policy influences economic activity. At the same time, targeting monetary growth as the key intermediate target does not mean that interest rates cannot be used as an operating target.

In this regard, the Federal Reserve in the 1970s could have employed the Federal funds procedure to achieve lower monetary growth rates if it had been willing to raise the targeted Federal funds rate and deemphasized its emphasis on reducing interest rate fluctuations. There was nothing inherently wrong with the Federal funds procedure, only with the way the Federal Reserve reacted to increases in the Federal funds rate.

The Bank of Japan provides an important lesson in this regard. The Bank of Japan approaches monetary control in much the same way the Federal Reserve did in the 1970s. That is, the Bank of Japan focuses on the "interbank loan rate" as a short-run operating variable that is similar to the Federal funds rate as the key operating target. However, the outcome in terms of monetary growth rates has been much different. Figure 27-13 shows the growth of money, prices, and income in Japan from 1954 to 1987. Starting in 1974, the Bank of Japan decided to focus on a noninflationary monetary growth rate. As is evident, the money supply was more stable after 1974 and inflation was gradually reduced. Since 1975 Japan has experienced little or no inflation. This noninflationary monetary growth rate has been achieved with an operating procedure focused on interest rates.

Michael Dotsey compared the operating procedures of the Bank of Japan and the Federal Reserve and concluded: "that although there are some interesting differences, the two central banks' daily operating procedures are very similar. Both monetary authorities basically use the interbank market interest rate as their policy instrument. Therefore, the reasons for the differences in macroeconomic performance attributed to the Bank of Japan and the Federal Reserve System of the United States will be found elsewhere."[1]

[1] Michael Dotsey, "Japanese Monetary Policy, a Comparative Analysis," *Monetary and Economic Studies*, The Bank of Japan (October 1986), 105.

---

explicit Federal funds target framework. Thus, the Federal Reserve appears to have come full circle in a ten year period—starting from the Federal funds target strategy back to the Federal funds target strategy.

The New Operating Environment of Monetary Policy: The 1990s

Despite the changes in operating procedures during the 1980s, the deemphasis on monetary aggregates, and a renewed focus on short-term interest rates, the Federal Reserve has done a reasonably good job of maintaining price stability after 1982. Despite the criticisms of the borrowed reserve and most recently, the return to a Federal funds target strategy, monetary growth has been reasonably noninflationary through 1986; however, in 1987 and until the writing of this book, the inflation rate had begun to creep into the 5% range. Whether this means a return to inflationary monetary policy remains to be seen.

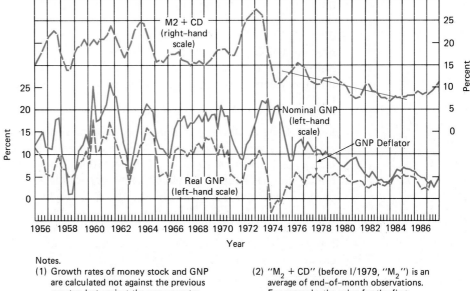

Notes.
(1) Growth rates of money stock and GNP are calculated not against the previous quarter, but against the same quarter in the previous year.

(2) "M₂ + CD" (before I/1979, "M₂") is an average of end-of-month observations. For example, the value for the first quarter is an average of the values at the end of January, February, and March. CD represents large CDs.

Source: Bank of Japan

FIGURE 27-13   Money Stock and GNP in Japan

What is certain, however, is that there are a number of major changes in the domestic and international operating environment that have complicated monetary policy. Let us consider several of the more important elements of this new environment.

Domestic Changes in the Federal Reserve's Operating Environment

Deregulation and Financial Innovation   The 1982 velocity decline raised considerable debate between those who argued that it was an atypical event when the unique factors of 1982 were taken into account and those who argued that such unexpected changes in velocity would be the rule rather than the exception. One factor mentioned by those who argued the second point was that the demand function for money would continue to be unstable in an environment of deregulation and financial innovation.

Deregulation and financial innovation introduce new financial services and assets, many of which make previous measures of the money supply obsolete. Thus, not only does the introduction of new financial services render the demand for money unstable, but they also make it likely that the Federal Reserve will be targeting some measure of the money supply that is no longer relevant.

There is no doubt that the implications of deregulation and financial innovation are serious and make monetary control more difficult; however, their degree of importance depends on whether they are transitory or longer lasting. All agree that the new financial assets such as NOW accounts and MMDAs have increased the difficulty of monetary control during the period in which the public adjusts to the new portfolio choices. Evidence indicates, however, that the adjustment period is rather short. The real issue is whether there will be a continual introduction of new financial assets either as a result of legislation or, more likely, financial innovation from the private sector.

One might be tempted to argue that new financial assets pose no real problem for the Federal Reserve because the Federal Reserve merely needs to keep account of the new innovations and redefine the money supply on occasion and perhaps extend its influence over new institutions on occasion. This solution appeals to one who has faith in the effectiveness of controls over the financial system; however, a number of economists have suggested that financial innovation may present a problem for the Federal Reserve to try to control anything called "money." The basic issue is that over time, the distinction between "money" and other financial assets is becoming less clear. Computer technology will make it continually easier to invent new and less regulated forms of money. Every time the Federal Reserve extends control to these new forms of money, the market will introduce even newer nonregulated forms of money. Thus the Federal Reserve will find in the future that attempts to achieve stabilization objectives by control of the money supply will be unsuccessful. New forms of monetary policy will need to be developed.

The potential problems resulting from deregulation and, more important, financial innovation are long-run concerns. At the time of this writing, it is difficult to assess how important the issue is in the 1990s.

Federal Deficits and Monetary Control   No one has yet devised a way to have noninflationary monetary growth, large federal deficits, *and* stable and low interest rates. The large federal deficits pose serious issues for the monetary authority, aside from the potential crowding-out effects on private spending. The Federal Reserve is faced with two choices. First, refuse to give into the pressure to monetize the deficits by expanding monetary growth. As long as deficits remain large and compete with the private sector, real interest rates and, hence, nominal interest rates are likely to remain high. Crowding-out effects will also operate through other channels and reduce economic growth. Second, the Federal Reserve could give into the pressures and expand monetary growth. Financial markets, however, now realize that expanded monetary growth will generate inflation. Anticipated inflation will be quickly incorporated into nominal interest rates with the result that interest rates will increase rather than decline.

Thus, there is little that the Federal Reserve can do to establish a stable financial and monetary environment for the economy in the presence of large federal deficits. Either significant crowding-out effects will occur as the deficit absorbs larger and larger shares of the net saving of the private sector, or expanded monetary growth will render financial markets unstable. The problem is made more difficult because of developments regarding the stability of depository institutions.

Bank Failures, the Thrift Problem, and Stability of the Financial System   Deregulation has raised concerns for the Federal Reserve and others regarding the stability of depository institutions and hence, the financial system. The 1980 and 1982 acts were designed to remove a number of key constraints on competitive behavior on depository institutions in order to improve the efficiency of the flow of funds, stimulate saving, end periods of disintermediation, improve monetary control, and improve the stability of the financial system in an environment of high and fluctuating interest rates.

The 1980 and 1981 acts combined with other financial reforms have improved the stability of the financial system compared to what it was in the late 1970s; however, the second half of the 1980s witnessed a significant increase in the number of bank failures and related difficulties that have serious implications for monetary control and further efforts to deregulate intermediation finance.

Let us summarize the reasons for renewed concern about the stability of the financial system and what it implies for monetary policy. First, several large bank failures (Penn Square National Bank in 1982, Seafirst Bank of Seattle in 1983, and Continental Illinois Bank of Chicago in 1984) attracted widespread attention. Continental Illinois was an especially serious bank problem because it was one of the largest banks in the United States (in the top ten) and required an unprecedented effort on the part of the federal government to maintain bank operations that amounted to the nationalization of the bank. Second, the number of bank failures significantly increased after 1980. In 1988, 229 banks failed, the highest number in any year since the Great Depression. Failure rates for other depository institutions have also increased. Third, the Comptroller of the Currency has sharply increased the number of banks included on the "problem list," that is, banks that require special supervision because their future viability is not certain. In 1980, the list included 212 banks. As of year-end 1988, the list included 1,394 banks.

Fourth, the October 1987 stock market crash was noteworthy on any reasonable basis. The Federal Reserve reacted by publicly stating that it stood ready to provide the financial system whatever liquidity was needed to prevent the market collapse from adversely affecting other markets. The 1987 crash ended up being the major "nonevent" of 1987 since it did not adversely affect the financial system or the general economy. The market by 1989 had regained most of its lost ground however, the crash and the Federal Reserve's reaction certainly reinforced concern about the stability of the financial system.

Fifth, the thrift problem attracted considerable attention in the late 1980s. Congress passed the Financial Institutions Reform, Recovery, and Enforcement Act in August 1989 and established a $166 billion bailout effort to close or merge with stronger institutions about 450 insolvent and at least as many financially weak thrift institutions. As part of this effort, the Federal Reserve established a liquidity support program to be jointly administered with thrift regulators for troubled thrifts during the transition period. Few observers believed at that time the 1989 act would be sufficient to deal with the thrift problem, and thrift institutions are likely to remain a serious consideration about the stability of the financial system.

These five considerations suggest that the Federal Reserve is far more concerned about financial stability than it has been at other times during the post–World War II period. In this regard, the lender of last resort responsibility of the Federal Reserve has taken on new meaning.

International Changes in the Federal Reserve's Operating Environment

International considerations have become more prominent in the formulation and conduct of monetary policy in the 1980s. Large U.S. external imbalances reflected by current account and trade deficits, risk exposure of U.S. banks to Third World debt, and the constant increase in world financial integration or globalization of finance. These issues weigh more heavily on Federal Reserve decision making than ever before. Monetary policy must increasingly concern itself with the international implications of any policies pursued for domestic objectives and increasingly, the Federal Reserve is called upon by the U.S. Treasury to intervene in the foreign exchange market to achieve external objectives. The Federal Reserve, for example, must now consider the effect any changes in domestic interest rates will have on the value of the dollar because interest rate differentials between countries can induce a major shift in capital flows and hence, influence exchange rates.

Key Points

1. The framework for the conduct of monetary is illustrated by the following sequence:

   policy instruments→operating targets→intermediate targets→economic activity/policy targets

2. Intermediate targets and indicators play an important role in the conduct of monetary policy. They provide a close target at which Federal Reserve actions can be directed and provide feedback information on the direction and magnitude of monetary policy.

3. The Federal Reserve cannot set and achieve explicit goals for interest rates and monetary aggregates at the same time and attempt to achieve a given level of income and employment. Attempts to achieve a target interest rate imply loss of control over monetary aggregates, whereas attempts to achieve a monetary aggregate target imply loss of control over the interest rate.

4. The choice between interest rates and monetary aggregates depends on how closely each conforms to a reasonable set of standards. On balance, monetary aggregates meet the standards to a higher degree.

5. Additional evidence on the interest rate–monetary aggregate controversy can be provided by considering the relative stability of the money and real sector of the economy. It can be shown that a money supply target is preferable in terms of a smaller variation in income and employment if the demand function for money is relatively more stable than the spending function in the real sector. The interest rate target is preferable if the spending function is more stable than the demand function for money in the money sector.

6. Traditionally the Federal Reserve emphasized interest rates and often failed to achieve monetary growth targets as the cost of obtaining interest rate targets. The Federal Reserve's operating procedures were criticized increasingly for contributing to excessive monetary growth and inflation during the 1970s. The October 1979 announcement represented a significant shift in policy away from interest rates and toward monetary aggregates.

7. The Federal Reserve adopted a nonborrowed reserve target as a method of targeting the money supply. The Federal Reserve's money-focused policy did not last for long, however.

By October 1982, the Federal Reserve had shifted to a borrowed reserve target that generates essentially the same outcome as the Federal funds procedure of the 1970s—reducing interest rate fluctuations. In 1987, the Federal Reserve ceased establishing M1 targets and has officially deemphasized a money-focused policy. Most recently, a more explicit Federal funds target appears to have replaced the borrowed reserve target.

Key Terms

Base drift

Borrowed reserve targeting procedure

Contemporaneous reserve accounting (CRA)

Deregulation and Monetary Control Act of 1980

February 1980 redefinitions of the money supply

Federal funds targeting procedure

Forgiveness factor

Income effect

Indicators of monetary policy

Intermediate targets

Lagged reserve accounting (LRA)

Liquidity effect

Monetary aggregate targets

Money market conditions

Nonborrowed reserve target procedure

October 1979 announcement

Operating targets

Policy instruments

Policy targets

Price anticipations effect

Procyclical basis of interest rate–focused procedures

Standards of an ideal intermediate target

Questions

1. We have used the terms interest rate and monetary aggregate as if they have clear definitions. List the various measures in each group.

2. Explain how increasing interest rates can be consistent with easy monetary policy.

3. If the money supply increased 4% during the year, would you regard this as easy monetary policy?

4. If interest rates increased during the year and the money supply grew at least by 4%, would you regard this as an indication that monetary policy had been tight?

5. If the e ratio in the money multiplier is highly sensitive to changes in the rate of interest, how would this affect the desirability of the money supply as an indicator?

6. Whenever we talk of changes in monetary policy in regard to monetary aggregates, we speak of changes in the rate of growth of the money supply rather than the level of the money supply. Why do we emphasize changes in the rate of growth rather than levels?

7. Evaluate the statement: "The Federal Reserve was never serious about monetary control in 1980, but used the monetary control issue to achieve other objectives."

8. Evaluate the statement: "The Federal Reserve made a serious effort to achieve monetary control in the early 1980s, but a variety of factors forced it to reintroduce an interest rate–focused policy."

9. Can the lender of last resort responsibility interfere with monetary control?

10. Use demand and supply functions for money

to show that one cannot target both interest rates and the money supply at a given level of income.

Suggested Reading

1. Board of Governors of the Federal Reserve System, *New Monetary Control Procedures*, Vols. I and II (Federal Reserve Staff Study, February 1981). Official discussion of the 1979–1982 operating procedure.

2. John F. Chant and Keith Acheson, "Mythology and Central Banking," *Kyklos*, 26 (1973 Fasc. 2), 362–3. Offers an explanation why central banks are reluctant to reveal their operating procedures.

3. Alex Cukierman, "Central Bank Behavior and Credibility: Some Recent Theoretical Developments," *Review*, Federal Reserve Bank of St. Louis (May 1989), 5–17. Discussion of central bank behavior that induces an inflationary bias to monetary policy.

4. Michael Dotsey, "Japanese Monetary Policy, A Comparative Analysis," *Monthly Review*, Federal Reserve Bank of Richmond (November/December 1986), 12–24. Shows that Federal Reserve operating procedure in the 1970s and Bank of Japan operating procedures are very similar.

5. Milton Friedman, "Has the Fed Changed Course?" *Newsweek*, October 22, 1979, p. 39. Skeptical discussion of the Federal Reserve's conversion to monetary targeting.

6. Milton Friedman, "Monetarism in Rhetoric and in Practice," in Albert Ando; Hidekaza Eguchi; Roger Farmer; and Yoshio Suzuki (eds.), *Monetary Policy in Our Times* (Cambridge, Mass.: MIT Press, 1985), pp. 15–28. Compares Bank of Japan and Federal Reserve performance.

7. Milton Friedman, "Monetary Variability: United States and Japan," *Journal of Money, Credit and Banking*, 15 (August 1983b), 339–343. Criticism of Federal Reserve's argument that it had achieved monetary stability in the early 1980s.

8. Milton Friedman, "The Fed's Monetarism Was Never Anything But Rhetoric," *The Wall Street Journal*, (December 18, 1985).

9. R. W. Hafer and Joseph H. Haslag, "The FOMC in 1987: The Effects of a Falling Dollar and the Stock Market Collapse," *Review*, Federal Reserve Bank of St. Louis (March–April 1988), 3–16. Good discussion of the increasing concern of the Federal Reserve with international and domestic financial stability issues.

10. Edward J. Kane, "External Pressure and the Operation of the Fed," in R. E. Lombra and W. E. Witte, *Political Economy of International and Domestic Monetary Relations* (Ames: Iowa State University Press, 1982), pp. 211–232.

11. Edward J. Kane, "Politics and Fed Policymaking: The More Things Change the More They Remain the Same," *Journal of Monetary Economics* (April 1980), 199–212.

12. Richard W. Lang, "The FOMC in 1979: Introducing Reserve Targeting," *Review*, Federal Reserve Bank of St. Louis (March 1980), 2–25.

13. Ann-Marie Meulendyke, *U.S. Monetary Policy and Financial Markets*, Federal Reserve Bank of New York, 1989.

14. William Poole, "Interest Rate Stability as a Monetary Policy Goal," *New England Economic Review*, Federal Reserve Bank of Boston (May–June 1976), 30–37.

15. Ronald L. Teigen, "The Choice of Short-Run Targets for Monetary Policy," *Economic Review*, Federal Reserve Bank of Kansas City (April 1981), 3–16.

16. Daniel L. Thornton, "The Borrowed-Reserves Operating Procedure: Theory and Evidence," *Review*, Federal Reserve Bank of St. Louis (January–February 1988), 30–54.

17. Vance V. Roley, "Market Perceptions of U.S. Monetary Policy Since 1982," *Economic Review*, Federal Reserve Bank of Kansas City (May 1986), 27–40.

18. Henry C. Wallich, "Recent Techniques of Monetary Policy," *Economic Review*, Federal Reserve Bank of Kansas City (May 1984), 21–30.

CHAPTER 28

Lags in the Effect of Monetary Policy, Rules Versus Authorities, and the Time Inconsistency Problem

Chapter Overview

There is little disagreement among the theoretical models of monetary policy that changes in the money supply will have significant effects on prices and output in the short run while price effects dominate in the long run. Classical-oriented models emphasize price effects more than output effects in the short run as market participants quickly incorporate the anticipated effects of monetary policy into wage and price contracts. While a few variations of the classical approach suggest the policy ineffectiveness proposition in the short run, this is not regarded as a realistic description of how money impacts the economy in the real world. Keynesian-oriented models emphasize short-run output effects more than price effects because of sluggish wages and prices. Even though they accept the economy's eventual return to the natural growth path, the time it takes for these market solutions to work is not socially acceptable. In addition, the economy is constantly subject to shocks of one form or another that make it difficult for the long-run equilibrium process to function properly.

The classical and Keynesian models imply differing roles for monetary policy—the classical view emphasizes a nonactivist approach while the Keynesians emphasize an activist approach. Much of the debate about activist and nonactivist policies revolves around which model is the most realistic; however, there exists another debate about whether the monetary authority should be conducted according to *rules* or *authorities*. The issues raised in this regard are essentially independent of the activist versus nonactivist debate discussed in previous chapters.

There is no question that monetary policy has the ability to influence economic activity; that is, monetary policy is a *powerful* instrument of stabilization. However, this is only a *necessary* and not a *sufficient* condition for monetary policy to make a positive contribution to the economy. Are there inherent characteristics about the implementation of monetary policy that might render it destabilizing over time? That is, even if a case can be made for activist policies from a model perspective, does this mean that an active monetary policy is beneficial? What do we mean by active monetary policy? To clarify these issues, economists have found it convenient to characterize monetary policy as either controlled by a set of rules or conducted by authorities in a discretionary manner.

We will review this issue in several steps. We will first define the rules versus authorities debate and then turn to consider the arguments supporting a rules approach and those supporting an authorities or discretionary approach. In this regard, we discuss issues related to the *lag in the effect of monetary policy,* the *time inconsistency problem,* and the role of the central bank as seen from the *central banker's perspective.* We will also review some of the efforts to establish a more rules-oriented approach to Federal Reserve policy and the success that past efforts in this regard have achieved.

Rules Versus Authorities

The rules versus authorities debate was first clearly defined by Henry Simons in 1936, and while it was originally associated with the monetarist approach, it is now recognized as independent of activist or nonactivist views of the world. What do we mean by the phrase "rules versus authorities?"

According to a rules-oriented monetary policy, the rule defines how the Federal Reserve will react to a given situation and leaves little or no room for discretionary action. According to an authority- or discretionary-oriented monetary policy, the Federal Reserve conducts policy on the basis of its own reading of the evidence and reacts in ways that are not predetermined.

Let us consider more formally what we mean by a rules-oriented policy. Expressions (1) and (2) illustrate two versions of the rules approach:

$$\text{Growth of money} = 4\% \text{ per year} \qquad (1)$$

$$\text{Growth of money} = 4\% \text{ per year} + 1.0*(UN - 6.0) \qquad (2)$$

Expression (1) is the rule advocated by a nonactivist and frequently associated with the monetarist model. A constant monetary growth rule is based on the assumption of a stable growth of velocity and small deviations of output from the natural growth path. The actual monetary growth rate is chosen to maintain a low and steady inflation rate. This is the simplest of rules and essentially suggests that the Federal Reserve should be replaced by a computer program. Expression (2) is also a rule, but one that is consistent with an activist orientation. Instead of a constant monetary growth rate of, say, 4%, expression (2) says that the money supply should grow at 4% per year as long as the actual unemployment rate equals 6%. Monetary growth should increase (decrease), however, if the unemployment rate rises above (falls below) the natural unemployment rate of 6%.

Both expressions are rules that leave no room for Federal Reserve discretion and clearly show that a rule is consistent with either a nonactivist or activist model. In contrast, monetary growth is not deterministic according to a discretionary approach. Monetary growth at any time will be determined by the Federal Reserve's reading of the evidence and new developments in the economy. While the Federal Reserve may be guided by general policy targets such as full employment or price stability, the way it conducts policy to achieve these targets is not constrained by a rule of any type.

In the following sections we will consider two problems with monetary policy: lags in the effect of monetary policy and the time inconsistency problem. Both problems lend support to a rules approach irrespective of activist or nonactivist models of how the economy functions. After considering arguments that support some type of rules approach, we then consider the counterarguments that support monetary policy according to authorities or discretion. After this, we will return to the rules versus authorities debate and summarize the arguments as well as recent efforts to impose rules on the Federal Reserve.

Lags in the Effect of Monetary Policy

Clark Warburton and Milton Friedman emphasized the lag in effect of monetary policy over four decades ago, though Friedman was the first to point out the potential problem it created for monetary policy. We approach the subject of lags in several steps. First, we define the meaning of the lag in effect of monetary policy; second, we indicate how lags can render any stabilization policy *destabilizing* on balance; and third, we review the empirical evidence on the existence of lags in the conduct of monetary policy.

What is the Lag in the Effect of Monetary Policy?

There are several components of the lag in the effect of monetary policy. Figure 28-1 illustrates the components of the total lag. The *recognition lag* covers the period from t_0 to t_1 and represents the time it takes for the Federal Reserve to collect economic data and interpret a change in economic activity calling for a change in monetary policy. At t_0, the level of economic activity has changed; for example, the unemployment rate increases significantly, but it takes a few months to obtain accurate readings on the unemployment rate and other relevant variables before the Federal Reserve will consider a change in monetary policy as necessary.

The *administrative lag* represents the time between the recognition of the need to change monetary policy, t_1, and the time that the Federal Reserve actually changes

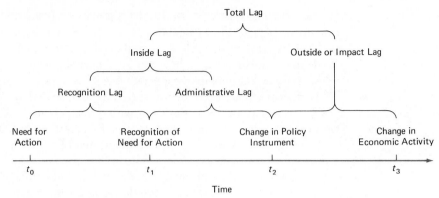

Source: Adapted from Mark H. Wallis, "Lags in Monetary and Fiscal Policy," *Business Review,* Federal Reserve Bank of Philadelphia (March 1968), 3.

FIGURE 28-1   Components of the total lag effect of monetary policy

one or more of the instruments of monetary policy, t_2. The sum of the recognition and administrative lags is referred to as the *inside lag*— that is, the total time between a change in economic activity calling for a change in monetary policy and a change in the policy instruments.

The *impact lag* measures the time between the change in the policy instrument, t_2, and when the major impact on economic activity is achieved, t_3. The impact lag measures the length of the transmission process connecting changes in the policy instrument to changes in the level of economic activity and is often referred to as the *outside lag* of monetary policy.

The sum of all the lags (recognition, administrative, and impact) represents the total lag in the effect of monetary policy. These lag components also exist for fiscal policy actions involving changes in government expenditures and/or taxes.

The Problem of Lags

In 1951 Friedman published a well-known paper that illustrated the problem created by lags in the effect of any attempt to stabilize the economy.[1] Lags in the effect of stabilization policy could easily turn attempts at stabilization into actions that intensified economic fluctuations.

The problem created by lags in the effect of stabilization policy can be illustrated by Figure 28-2. The line *AA* represents the behavior of real GNP over time without active stabilization policy. Real GNP is shown to fluctuate around potential real GNP, which is drawn as increasing over time. The level of actual GNP is shown to go through the typical business cycle pattern: expansion, peak, contraction, and trough. Although business cycles or fluctuations show up in most economic series,

---

[1] Milton Friedman, "The Effects of a Full-Employment Policy on Economic Stability: A Formal Analysis," in Milton Friedman (ed.), *Essays in Positive Economics* (Chicago: University of Chicago Press, 1953).

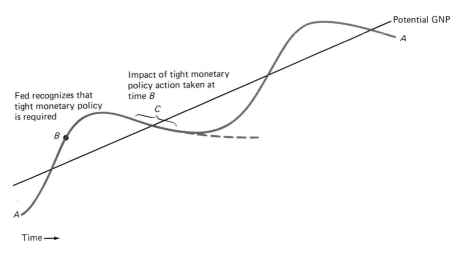

FIGURE 28-2   **Destabilizing monetary policy**

Figure 28-2 is an obvious simplification because it pictures GNP as having a well-defined periodicity above and below potential output. Although business cycles do not exhibit such well-defined periodicity and potential output does not exhibit a straight-line growth path, Figure 28-2 adequately reflects the problem encountered by stabilization policy when significant lags are apparent.

The problem with a lag in the effect of monetary policy can be illustrated by considering a tight monetary policy initiated at point *B*—as the economy enters the upper stages of an expansion with corresponding inflation. But, because it takes some time for the tight monetary policy to have an appreciable impact on economic activity, the economy continues to expand. The expansion reaches a peak and then begins the decline phase of the business cycle. At this time, however, the tight monetary policy initiated in the past begins to have its major impact, say, in the range indicated by *C*. The tight monetary policy is having an impact at just the wrong time. It will cause GNP to fall farther than it would have without monetary policy, for example, along the dashed line in Figure 28-2. The economy now needs an easy monetary policy. Thus, monetary policy designed to stabilize the economy may, on balance, actually lead to more instability.

The long lag itself creates difficulties for stabilization policy, but there is a way around the problem. If we have detailed knowledge of how the economy functions and ability to forecast several years into the future, then the long lags are not too troublesome. To illustrate, take another look at Figure 28-2. If we knew the pattern of GNP without government stabilization policy over a period of time, we could implement monetary policy at the required point in time, making allowances for the length of time required for the full impact of monetary policy to occur. For example, if the goal is to slow down the expansion around point B, we would tighten monetary policy well before this point, taking the lag into account.

Unfortunately, long lags have easier theoretical solutions than practical ones. The longer the lag, the greater the need to forecast with accuracy the direction of economic activity with and without stabilization actions. We simply do not have the necessary knowledge about the economic system to make forecasts beyond a few quarters, and even these amount to educated guesses. Many economists would regard the existence of a long lag as a real problem for the active use of stabilization policy.

The long lags actually encourage overreaction on the part of monetary policy that further compounds the problem. As the economy is entering an expansionary period with rapidly increasing prices, the Federal Reserve begins to move toward a tight monetary policy. However, the lag is such that the first few months of the tight monetary policy seem to have no effect on economic activity, so the Federal Reserve tightens just a little more. The tight monetary policy begins to show an effect, but some argue that it should be tightened just a little more to make sure the inflationary pressures will be slowed down. But, by this time, the initial tight monetary policy begins to have an impact as well as the additional tightenings. The Federal Reserve now realizes that it pushed too hard and tries to reverse itself. But, again, the easy monetary policy does not have an impact immediately, and pressure mounts to push even harder in the direction of an easier monetary policy. By the time the easy monetary policy begins to affect the economy, it becomes obvious that the Federal Reserve has pushed too hard in the direction of ease.

This type of sequence has been described in the following terms:

> The Federal Reserve's actions in pursuit of business cycle stability have been like the action of passengers on a ship who become worried about a temporary roll of the ship to starboard, and run to the port side of the ship in an effort to stabilize it. Slowly the ship responds to the extra weight on its port side, and recovers from its roll to starboard but then the motion continues and the ship rolls to the port side. The passengers now worry about the roll to port, and run to the starboard side in an effort to stabilize the ship once more. The ship responds slowly to the extra weight on its starboard side, straightens up, and then rolls to starboard again, perhaps more than before. Of course the passengers are only making things worse by their action. The proper thing for them to do is to run neither to the right nor to the left, but to position themselves so that their center of gravity is in the center of the ship, so that they do not aggravate and perpetuate its rolling motion.[2]

Friedman pointed out another and more serious problem with the lag in the effect of monetary policy. The lags are not only long, they are highly variable. The lag in the effect of monetary policy may be only a few quarters at one point in time but several years in length at another point in time. What complicates the situation further, according to Friedman, is that we have no sure way of knowing whether the lag will be short or long.

Thus, the long lag in the effect of monetary policy and the variability of this long lag make it technically difficult to achieve economic stabilization with monetary policy. Attempts to stabilize the economy with monetary policy may actually increase instability.

The Empirical Evidence

Friedman's argument that monetary policy on balance may be destabilizing because of long and variable lags led to numerous attempts to measure the timing relationship between monetary policy and changes in economic activity.

[2] Testimony by Carl Christ, *First Report on the Conduct of Monetary Policy*, U.S. Senate, 94th Cong., 1st sess., Committee on Banking, Housing and Urban Affairs, 1975, p. 9.

BOX 1   Friedman's formal analysis of the potential destabilization of stabilization policy

Friedman's formal analysis is based on the concept that stabilization policy is directed toward reducing the variation of income without any specific regard to the level of employment. Let $X(t)$ represent the level of GNP at time t with no stabilization policy. The objective of stabilization policy can be thought of as either adding to $X(t)$ if actual GNP is below the full-employment level or subtracting from $X(t)$ if actual GNP is above the full-employment level. The amount of income added to or subtracted from $X(t)$ by monetary and/or fiscal policy is given by $Y(t)$. Thus the actual level of the GNP that includes the effects of stabilization policy can be represented as the sum of $X(t)$ and $Y(t)$.

$$Z(t) = X(t) + Y(t) \qquad (1)$$

Friedman emphasizes that $Y(t)$ does not represent the effects of stabilization actions taken at time t but, rather, the effects of stabilization action taken at some time in the past.

The objective of stabilization policy is to reduce the variation of $Z(t)$ over time. Fluctuations in $X(t)$ due to autonomous shifts in investment or any other factor can be offset by opposite and like movements in $Y(t)$ induced by monetary and/or fiscal policy actions. Thus the objective of stabilization policy can be thought of as reducing the fluctuations in $Z(t)$. Whether this objective is met or not depends on the relative variances of $Z(t)$ and $X(t)$. There are three logical possibilities:

1. VAR(X) exceeds VAR(Z): Stabilization policy is successful, because the variance of GNP *without* stabi-

lization policy action is larger than the variance of GNP *with* stabilization actions.
2. VAR(Z) exceeds VAR(X): Stabilization policy is not successful. Stabilization policy actions have *increased* the variance of GNP. The variance of $Z(t)$ would have been less had there been no stabilization policy, that is, $Y(t) = 0$.
3. VAR(X) = VAR(Z): Stabilization policy is neutral in the sense that the variance of GNP with and without stabilization policy action is the same.

Friedman argues that only case 1 represents effective stabilization policy. He then investigates the conditions that are needed to achieve case 1. This depends on two considerations. First, the magnitude of the change in $Y(t)$ must be the same as the magnitude of the change in $X(t)$. That is, there must be a consistent and predictable relationship between the policy instruments and the level of GNP, and the change in income induced by the policy instruments must be equal to the autonomous change. Second, the timing relationship should be such that the change in GNP induced by stabilization policy actions must occur at the time needed to offset undesirable movements in $X(t)$. To highlight the importance of the timing relationship, we will assume that there is a consistent relationship between $X(t)$ and $Y(t)$ and that the magnitude of $Y(t)$ induced by stabilization policy is exactly the same as $X(t)$. There is then no problem with the stabilization policy being too strong or not strong enough. The only problem can come in the timing of the effects of stabilization policy.

(box continued)

Most attempts to measure the lag have been confined to measurement of the outside or impact lag, as this is where most of the controversy has focused. There has been little disagreement over the lengths of the recognition or administrative lags for monetary policy or fiscal policy.

The Length of the Outside or Impact Lag

There are three types of evidence on the lag in the effect of monetary policy. First, as part of their *Monetary History of the United States* study published in 1963,

BOX 1   Continued

There is a well-known equation for the variance of two items, so we can express the variance of $Z(t)$ as

$$VAR(Z) = VAR(X) + VAR(Y) \\ + 2R_{xy}\sqrt{VAR(X)}\sqrt{VAR(Y)} \qquad (2)$$

The symbol R_{xy} is the correlation coefficient between X and Y and measures the degree of the association between X and Y. The value of R_{xy} ranges from minus one to plus one. A perfectly timed stabilization policy would always have the change in income occur at the point in time needed to offset the undesired change in income. The correlation between X and Y would then be minus one. If X increased by \$5 billion, Y would decline by \$5 billion. A perverse stabilization policy would result if R_{xy} were plus one. Whenever X changes by \$5 billion, Y would also change by \$5 billion in the same direction, thus increasing the variation in total income over what it would have been without the stabilization policy action.

The assumption that the magnitude of stabilization policy is exactly correct is the same as saying that the variation of GNP without stabilization policy is equal to the variation of GNP added to or subtracted from by stabilization policy actions. That is, $VAR(X) = VAR(Y)$. Keeping this in mind, we can divide expression (2) by $VAR(X)$ and obtain

$$\frac{VAR(Z)}{VAR(X)} = 1 + \frac{VAR(Y)}{VAR(X)} + 2R_{xy}\frac{\sqrt{VAR(Y)}}{\sqrt{VAR(X)}} \qquad (3)$$

$$\frac{\text{Variance of income with stabilization policy}}{\text{Variation of income without stabilization policy}} = $$
$$\frac{VAR(Z)}{VAR(X)} = 2 + 2R_{xy}$$

This expresses the ratio of the variation of GNP with stabilization policy to the variation of GNP with no stabilization policy in terms of the correlation coefficient which summarizes the timing relationship.

For this ratio to be less than one, so that policy reduces the variation in GNP over what it would have been without stabilization policy, the value of R_{xy} must be between -0.5 and -1.0. That is, the impact of stabilization policy must occur at the right time at least 50% of the time or stabilization policy will actually increase the fluctuations in GNP. In fact, it must be in the right direction more than 50% of the time. A value of R_{xy} of -0.5 indicates that the ratio in (3) is 1.0. The variation in GNP is the same with and without stabilization policy, and, because stabilization policy requires human and material resources, the economy would be better off without stabilization policy.

Milton Friedman, "The Effects of a Full-Employment Policy on Economic Stability: A Formal Analysis," in Milton Friedman (ed.), *Essays in Positive Economics* (Chicago: University of Chicago Press, 1953).

Friedman and Schwartz estimated the average lag between changes in the money supply and turning points in general business. Second, studies have estimated distributed lag equations to estimate the length of the lag. Third, simulations of large econometric models have been used to determine how economic activity responds over time to a change in monetary policy. Each type of evidence will be taken up in turn.

Friedman and Schwartz Evidence   Friedman and Schwartz compared the turning points in percentage changes in the money supply with the turning points in general business activity estimated by the National Bureau of Economic Research. Percentage changes in the money supply were used to eliminate the strong upward trend in the money supply that reflects the growing size of the economy. Friedman and Schwartz were concerned with estimating the timing relationship between *changes* in the money supply and *changes* in economic activity measured by the business cycle turning points. They found that the changes in the money supply preceded the business cycle turning points and that the lag was long and variable.

They reached the following conclusions. (1) The peak in the rate of change of the money supply preceded the peak in general business on average by 16 months. (2) The trough in the rate of change of the money supply preceded the trough in general business on average by 12 months. (3) The leads (or lag in the effect of the money supply) varied from 4 months to 22 months.

The Friedman and Schwartz results set off a heated controversy and were a key element in the monetarist-Keynesian debate. They showed not only that changes in the money supply were highly correlated with changes in economic activity but that the lagged effects of changes in the money supply were so long and variable as to render active monetary policy a dangerous tool.

The implications of these findings for active monetary policy cannot be understated. In the large body of literature that has emerged since the publication of these results in 1963, some economists have simply rejected the results as inconsistent with the high degree of post–World War II stability compared with that in earlier years. The comparative stability of postwar years is often regarded as the result of active stabilization policy (See Box 1 in Chapter 26). Others have been critical of their methodology. Thus, an extensive empirical effort was made to measure lags in the effect of policy.

Regression Results   Numerous attempts were made to estimate relationships between a measure of monetary policy and a measure of economic activity that incorporated a lag. Most of these estimates require considerable sophistication in econometrics to discuss adequately. However, a widely known estimate of the lag by the St. Louis Federal Reserve Bank research staff can be used to illustrate the type of evidence offered by the regression studies.

The basic spending equation of the St. Louis model expresses the relationship between the growth rate of income and the growth rate of monetary and fiscal policy variables as a distributed lag model:

$$Y_t = f(M_t, M_{t-1}, M_{t-2}, \ldots, M_{t-n}, E_t, E_{t-1}, E_{t-2}, \ldots, E_{t-n}) \tag{3}$$

where

$$Y_t = \text{growth rate of nominal GNP in quarter } t$$
$$M_{t-i} = \text{growth rate of the money supply in quarter } t - i$$
$$E_{t-i} = \text{growth rate of the fiscal policy variable in quarter } t - i$$

Expression (3) is a distributed lag relationship because the current income growth (at time t) is a function of the current growth of the money supply (at time t), the previous quarter's growth of the money supply ($t - 1$), and so on out to n quarters. The growth of income is also expressed as a distributed lag of growth of the fiscal policy variable. The best fit was obtained with distributed lags of four quarters, and the results indicate that a change in the growth rate of money takes about one year to have its complete impact on income. The results also support the monetarists' claim that the cumulative impact of a change in fiscal policy is close to zero.

Measurements of the lag in effect of monetary policy with regression equations such as (3) are subject to serious problems. First, there is the problem of deciding on what variable to use as the measure of changes in monetary policy. Even if one accepts that the money supply is the proper indicator, there is still a problem of choosing between the various measures of the money supply. Second, the majority of regression estimates of the lag in effect of monetary policy are based on reduced form relationships between monetary variables and income. A reduced form model does not specify the channels through which monetary and fiscal policy impact economic activity, but only measures the direct relationship between income and the policy variable. This has been referred to as the "black box" view of how monetary and fiscal policy influence the economy.

Simulation Results   Large econometric models are designed to capture the transmission process between changes in monetary policy and economic activity. Simulation results meet some of the problems encountered by regression estimates of the lag; however, they are far from problem free. In 1975, Gary Fromm and Lawrence R. Klein reported the results of an extensive number of simulations of well-known econometric models. The results revealed two implications for monetary policy. First, the impact on nominal and real GNP of a monetary policy action (measured as a change in nonborrowed reserves) built up slowly over time with larger impacts occurring several quarters after the initial change in monetary policy. Second, the impact on nominal and real GNP persisted even after as much as two years elapsed from the initial change in monetary policy.

By the mid-1970s researchers had accumulated a considerable body of empirical evidence that lags in the effect of monetary policy (and fiscal policy) did exist. Table 28-1 presents one researcher's impression of the range of estimates for monetary policy and fiscal policy. The outside lag in the effect of monetary policy ranges from a low of 1 month to a high of 20 months. Most economists would regard estimates of the outside lag of less than one year to be too low and most would place the lag at least one year in length. Combined with the two components of the inside lag, the total lag in the effect of monetary policy may very well be long enough to create real difficulties for active countercyclical stabilization policy.

Monetary and Fiscal Policy Lags Compared

Table 28-1 presents an interesting comparison between the monetary and fiscal policy lags. The recognition lag for the two is generally regarded as relatively short and equal. The Federal Reserve and the Treasury hire the same economists from the best schools, use the same computers, use the same data bases, and have access to the same type of information necessary to forecast the direction of economic activity. It would be surprising if the recognition lags between monetary and fiscal policy differed by a significant magnitude.

The administrative component of the inside lag, however, differs significantly between monetary and fiscal policy. Monetary policy is formulated by the FOMC, which meets at frequent intervals and whose members otherwise are in constant communication. Thus, changes in monetary policy can be made within a very short period of time. On the other hand, fiscal policy involves the spending and taxing

TABLE 28-1   Range of Estimates of Monetary and Fiscal Policy Lags

	Inside Lag (months)		Outside (impact) Lag (months)	Total Lag (months)
	Recognition	Administrative		
Monetary policy	3	0	1–20	4–23
Fiscal policy	3	1–15	1– 3	5–21

Source: Mark H. Wallis, "Lags in Monetary and Fiscal Policy," *Business Review,* Federal Reserve Bank of Philadelphia (March 1968), p. 7.

actions of the federal government and, thus, involves congressional approval of major changes in these items. This can sometimes be rapid or, as is most often the case, slow. Fiscal policy is far more politicized than is monetary policy and thus makes the administrative lag uncertain at any point in time.

Many economists regard the impact lag of monetary policy as exceeding the fiscal policy impact lag because the financial system represents a major channel through which changes in monetary policy impact the economy. Even monetarist models regard monetary policy's impact on the cost of credit an important channel through which monetary policy influences spending. Fiscal policy in contrast has a more direct effect on spending decisions.

Why Do Lags Exist?

Lags in the effect of monetary or fiscal policy exist for basically two reasons. First, there are costs of adjustment to any change in stabilization policy. It takes time to adjust contracts to incorporate new monetary policy. It takes time to shift from one type of financial asset to another. It takes time to adjust spending to changes in the cost and availability of credit. Second, economic decisions are importantly influenced by expectations of what monetary and fiscal policy will be. Many of the new approaches to modeling the economy focus on how expectations influence decisions to spend, save, and so on. If there is a difference between actual and expected policy, individuals will require more time to determine whether the difference signifies a new policy, and hence reason to adjust expectations and economic decisions, or merely a random departure from what was expected.

Variability of Lags Over Time

There is little disagreement that the lag in effect of monetary policy is probably at least one year, and some economists believe that the lag may be much longer. Few estimates of the lag in the effect of monetary policy address the question of the variability of the lag, however. Long lags with high variability make monetary policy unsuitable for countercyclical stabilization policy. The chances of having the impact of monetary policy occur at the wrong time are so great that the economy would be better off with a nonactive monetary policy. Long lags with little variability also create significant problems but at least do not automatically rule out active stabilization policy, though, when one considers the low development of our ability to forecast the future course of the economy, the practical effect of long lags with little variability may also be to rule out active stabilization policy. Shorter lags with high variability also make it less likely that active monetary policy will be stabilizing. Short lags of little variability provide the only strong case in which active monetary policy could achieve an effective countercyclical policy.

Econometric methods are not as well suited for measuring the variability of the lag in effect of monetary policy as they have been for providing evidence that lags exist. The limited amount of information suggests, however, that not only are the lags long but they appear to be variable as well.

Time Inconsistency

Many of the concepts stressed by Friedman in his work on lags and the rules versus discretion debate were extended and formalized in a famous paper written by Finn E. Kydland and Edward C. Prescott in 1977.[3]

This paper has had an important influence on revealing inherent problems in a discretionary as opposed to a rules approach to monetary policy. The issues raised by Kydland and Prescott are different from those raised by the existence of lags, but the general implication is the same. They emphasize the different and less desirable outcome one is likely to get when monetary policy decisions are made period by period (discretionary policy) compared to the situation when policy is decided period by period according to a rule that is constant over time.

Time inconsistency basically means that what is optimal from the long run perspective is not optimal from the short run perspective. The Federal Reserve conducting policy in a discretionary manner is likely to take actions that may seem optimal at the time the decision is made even if the long run consequences are not optimal. If the Federal Reserve were, instead, constrained by a rule that was tied to a long run objective no such time inconsistency would occur because every policy action would be rooted in the long run objective.

The time inconsistency argument can be illustrated by an analogy suggested by the course for which this book is being used. The long-term goal of the instructor is to achieve some specific level of understanding of the course material. Assume that this goal can reasonably be achieved by requiring each student to submit an assignment every week at a specific time and achieve at least a C level of performance.

Adherence to the rule, assuming it is realistically constructed, will achieve the intended result—the greatest number of students will comprehend the course material. Let us assume that discretion is permitted to enter at some point and see what

---

[3] "Rules Rather than Discretion: The Inconsistency of Optimal Plans," *Journal of Political Economy*, 85 (June 1977), 473–491.

might occur. At the beginning of the class students anticipate that an assignment will be required at the end of each week and that they must achieve at least a C grade; however, assume that after a few weeks of following the rule the students complain that the next week's assignment is too difficult and they need the weekend to complete the assignment. The instructor makes a discretionary decision and permits the extension, at the same time insisting that the following assignment will definitely be due at the end of the week. Obviously, the instructor's discretion raised the utility of the students and even the instructor—the students now think he or she is flexible and willing to adjust to new events and information. Unfortunately, this sets the stage for students to take the subsequent assignments less seriously no matter how strongly the instructor insists to the contrary. If the instructor makes a further discretionary decision to depart from the rule to increase utility in the short run, it will further contribute to a less serious attitude on the part of the students for subsequent assignments.

Thus, adherence to the rule ensures that the course objective is more likely to be achieved than if the instructor allows discretion at each period to permit actual performance to deviate from the rule (an assignment each week due on Friday).

The Kydland and Prescott paper formalized this type of problem in the context of monetary policy and argued that discretionary monetary policy is generally inferior to a rules policy because of time inconsistency, that is, the Federal Reserve will take actions each period under a discretionary approach that enhances welfare in the short run even though social welfare would be higher in the long run under a rules approach. Chapter 29 will present a simple version of this model to show how discretionary policy can have an inflation bias even though social welfare would be higher in the long run with a zero inflation rate.

It should be emphasized at this point, however, that the Kydland and Prescott model and its several extensions are formalized statements of a view offered by Friedman some years ago.

In a paper discussing the relative merits of a rules versus discretionary policy, Friedman emphasized the problems of a period-by-period approach to monetary policy:

> If each case is considered on its merits, the wrong decision is likely to be made in a large fraction of cases because the decision-makers are examining only a limited area and are not taking into account the cumulative consequences of the policy as a whole. On the other hand, if a general rule is adopted for a group of cases as a bundle, the existence of that rule has favorable effects on people's attitudes and beliefs and expectations that would not follow even from the discretionary adoption of precisely the same policy on a series of separate occasions.[4]

Other Considerations in Favor of a Rule

Aside from lags and time inconsistency, other considerations have been offered to support a rules approach to monetary policy. A number of advocates of the rules

---

[4] "Should There Be an Independent Monetary Authority?" in L. B. Yeager (ed.), *In Search of a Monetary Constitution* (Cambridge, Mass.: Harvard University Press, 1962), p. 241.

approach have an underlying distrust of government intervention. While they recognize the need for government intervention in the monetary system, such as the need for a central bank to provide lender of last resort services and to maintain price stability over the long run, they believe this necessary government intervention can best be provided by a rule.

Government extension beyond its basic responsibilities is regarded as undesirable, leading ultimately to a loss of freedom and liberty. If government is not defined clearly by a set of easy-to-understand rules, there is no way to hold government responsible for its actions, as it can always justify past acts by redefining the objectives at that point in time. The Federal Reserve's unwillingness to specify its mode of operation and its intermediate and ultimate goals permits sufficient ambiguity to preclude its being held responsible for past actions. Once government activity cannot be monitored readily, it becomes easy for government to extend its influence to areas beyond its original responsibility. To the extent that government must be involved in the economic system, it should be accomplished with a set of rules that are easy to understand.

Another variation of this same point is that a central bank is motivated like any self-interest seeking entity and as a result will engage in activities that enhance its power and prestige. These may very well conflict with the goal of price stability.

What Form Does the Rule Take and Will Rules Eliminate Economic Fluctuations?

Let us deal with the second question first. Advocates of the rules approach emphasize that monetary policy cannot influence the real performance of the economy in the long run but can only determine the inflation rate. In fact, this proposition is generally accepted by many economists today. Adherence to a rule designed to achieve long-run price stability does not mean the end of economic fluctuations. The economy is dynamic and subject to shocks over time that generate upward and downward movements in actual output around the long-run full-employment path. If a rule will not eliminate the fluctuations of output and employment around their long-run natural levels, why can't discretionary monetary policy improve on the rule by reducing or perhaps even eliminating the fluctuations?

Advocates of the rules approach argue that discretionary monetary policy will not outperform the rule—the choice is between some fluctuations versus even greater fluctuations because of inherent problems with discretionary policy. First, lags in the effect of monetary policy are likely to increase the variability of income and output. To suggest that the Federal Reserve is capable of offsetting shocks without adverse effects assumes that we know far more about how the economy functions than is in fact the case. Second, the focus on period-by-period outcomes ensures an inflationary bias to monetary policy without any long-term employment gains.

Thus, advocates of the rules approach do not suggest that a rule will eliminate economic fluctuations; however, they do argue that discretionary policy cannot improve on the rule, and in fact, it is likely to generate more instability and reduced social welfare in the long run.

BOX 2   Monetary policy for self-interest?

William Greider's *Secrets of the Temple* provides a number of examples of how the secrecy surrounding the formulation of Federal Reserve policy permitted an environment that on some occasions generated adverse effects on the economy. Arthur Burns, chair of the Board of Governors from 1968 through 1978, is alleged to have initiated easy monetary policy after the 1976 presidential election of Jimmy Carter to enhance his chance of being reappointed chair of the Board.

According to Greider;

"The word 'sordid' is probably too strong," a former aide to the chairman reflected, "but what Burns did immediately after Jimmy Carter's election in terms of monetary policy can be documented. There was a rapid shift in monetary policy and it was designed to ingratiate Burns with Carter so he would be reappointed chairman."

The records did indicate that shortly after the election of 1976 the Federal Reserve eased. The Discount rate was cut and money growth accelerated smartly. In fairness to Burns, the same evidence demonstrated that he did not play political games to help re-elect Gerald Ford. The recovery that began in 1975 was frustratingly slow, but as the economy gradually gathered momentum, Ford's prospects steadily improved. He lost narrowly in the end—without the extra monetary stimulus that might have put him over the top.

Burns was a Republican, appointed by a Republican President. According to one Fed associate, he "wanted desperately to be reappointed by a Democrat and go down in history like Bill Martin as a bipartisan chairman." Like Martin, Burns had one more year to serve before the new Democratic President could appoint a chairman to a new four-year term. During that year, Burns discreetly courted key members of the Carter Administration, hoping to win their friendship and approval.

A memorandum from one staff aide advised the Federal Reserve chairman in November 1977:

Carter can be seduced. . . reappointment would make Carter out to be a high-minded statesman, would reassure the national and international financial and business communities, would rally financial markets, etc. . . .

Carter will have to be reassured that, if you are reappointed, you will not continue to publicly criticize everything that is near and dear to him. . . . Any seduction program would have to reassure the President that you won't criticize him publicly every six months.

The courtship failed. Carter and the liberals in his White House, particularly Vice President Walter Mondale, distrusted Burns on several levels. They were not about to take the risk of letting him control money and interest rates during their term in office. In early 1978, Carter appointed G. William Miller, chief executive of Textron, as Burns's successor.

The Burns campaign for reappointment had ironic consequences for the Carter Presidency, though Carter himself seemed oblivious to them. The easy-money policy begun by the Federal Reserve in late 1976 and extended through 1977 laid the groundwork for the inflationary run-up that would engulf President Carter a year later. The double-digit price inflation that would ultimately help defeat Carter was widely attributed to inept management by G. William Miller. In hindsight, many officials at the Federal Reserve privately conceded that Arthur Burns himself deserved a larger share of the blame.

The evidence does seem consistent with Greider's interpretation. Incidents like this, claim the advocates of the rule approach, are likely when monetary policy is formulated and executed by discretion rather than rules.

William Greider, *Secrets of the Temple: How the Federal Reserve Runs the Country* (New York: Simon & Schuster, 1987), pp. 346–347.

What is the form of the rule? It is important to recognize that rules can be *activist* as well as *nonactivist* oriented. While the most well-known rule of a constant monetary growth rate has been suggested by a nonactivist, there is no inherent reason why an activist rule cannot be imposed on the Federal Reserve. Expression (2) is an example of an activist rule—one that requires the monetary growth rate to vary with the state of the economy. Expression (1) and (2) both rule out discretionary action.

In Defense of Discretion

One does not have to be a genius to realize that the Federal Reserve, as well as other central banks, is less than enthusiastic about any type of rules approach. Who is anxious to have their discretionary power replaced by a rule! According to Sherman J. Maisel, a former member of the Board of Governors:

> The Fed has always resisted being too specific about its methods and its goals, clothing its operation in a kind of mystique that left more freedom for maneuver. It took the position that the complexities and psychological factors inherent in the financial system were best dealt with by use of intuitive judgment. Experience and discretion were needed rather than reliance on formal theories and stated targets for performance.[5]

The arguments against a rules approach, however, are substantial and reflect more than merely wanting to maintain discretionary power for self-interest reasons.

The Federal Reserve and others take a dim view of the rules approach for several reasons. First, the extreme lack of knowledge about the economy prevents any simple rule from outperforming discretionary policy over the long run. For example, the deregulation and financial innovation process makes it unreasonable to believe that any type of monetary growth rule would work over long periods of time. How does one define money? Even if one came up with a reasonable money supply definition, wouldn't it have to be changed over time? How would one decide when to change the money supply definition? If one adopts a rule but allows for changes in the rule at given points in time, doesn't this essentially represent discretionary policy?

Second, the Federal Reserve acknowledges mistakes of past discretionary policy such as failure to act as an effective lender of last resort in the early 1930s and failing to contain inflation in the 1970s. The Federal Reserve, however, has learned from these mistakes and is unlikely to repeat them in the future.

Franco Modigliani and Sherman J. Maisel both summarize this point of view clearly. According to Modigliani, who argues that the need for stabilization policy in a market economy is the fundamental message of the *General Theory*,

> We must, therefore, categorically reject the Monetarist appeal to turn back the clock 40 years by discarding the basic message of the *General Theory*. We should instead concentrate our efforts in an endeavor to make stabilization policies even more effective in the future than they have been in the past.[6]

According to Maisel,

> Good monetary policy depends upon admitting how much we do not know, but at the same time recognizing that the dollar must be inevitably managed. Furthermore, by using the knowledge and judgment we have, we can do better than by following a rigid rule. It follows that we must expend more effort on improving knowledge so as to raise the level of our accomplishments.[7]

---

[5] Sherman J. Maisel, *Managing the Dollar* (New York: W. W. Norton, 1973), p. 26.

[6] Franco Modigliani, "The Monetarist Controversy, or Should We Forsake Stabilization Policies?" *American Economic Review*, 67 (March 1977), 1.

[7] Maisel, *Managing the Dollar*, p. 4.

Third, the Federal Reserve recognizes the problem of lags but argues that these do not rule out discretionary policy. They merely require it to conduct policy more carefully and make a greater effort to take the lags into account in formulating policy.

Fourth, the time inconsistency problem and the resulting inflationary bias are well-recognized problems; however, a central bank's concern for its credibility will generate the same long-run price stability as a rule but leave it with sufficient discretion to deal with unforeseen events. For example, the West German Bundesbank and the Bank of Japan are two examples of central banks that are not constrained by a rule of any type, but have achieved a price stability record during the past 15 years that is impressive by any standard. Thus, if a central bank places heavy weight on price stability as do the Bundesbank and the Bank of Japan, concern for its credibility and reputation can be as effective as a rule. In this respect, the Federal Reserve has achieved a high level of credibility in the early 1980s for bringing inflation under control. It has maintained that credibility throughout most of the 1980s because of the relatively low inflation rate achieved in the 1980s compared to the 1970s.

Fifth, the Federal Reserve rejects the notion that it misuses power or violates its public responsibility. It argues that its actions are constantly under public scrutiny and while monetary policy actions are not made in an open and public forum, the Federal Reserve's actions can easily be examined by the large amount of financial data available—most of it available from the Federal Reserve itself. In addition, the Federal Reserve is required to appear before Congress at least twice a year. Even in those cases where a serious error has been made, such as the inflationary monetary policy of the late 1970s, public scrutiny, especially by economists, provides a meaningful constraint. Thus, the Federal Reserve argues that there are many checks and balances despite its formal independence to limit a misuse of discretionary power.

Efforts to Impose a Rules-Oriented Monetary Policy

At one time those who advocated a rules approach to monetary policy were in a minority and were largely disregarded. This is no longer the case. While few economists would advocate restricting the Federal Reserve to a fixed and permanent rule of how it should perform, the rules versus authorities has raised a number of troublesome issues that cannot be ignored. Lags in the effect of monetary policy do in fact exist and limit the ability of monetary policy to offset shocks. The time inconsistency problem is real. There are many instances where the Federal Reserve has focused on the period-by-period outcomes and sacrificed long-run price stability in the process. And there is evidence that the Federal Reserve on occasion has pursued policies for its own self-interest at the cost of increased instability and inflation.

Thus, there is reason to require the Federal Reserve to be more accountable for pursuing actions consistent with its feasible long-term goals of price stability and ensuring financial stability by providing lender of last resort services. This explains the effort in the past to make the Federal Reserve more accountable. In this regard, there are two events worth noting.

Concurrent Resolution 133 in 1975

In 1975, the Senate Banking Committee conducted hearings on monetary policy. The chair, Senator William Proxmire (D., Wisc.), was strongly influenced by the monetarist arguments against the Federal Reserve's conduct of monetary policy. These were (1) that Federal Reserve policy had more of a destabilizing than stabilizing impact on the economy; (2) that the Federal Reserve was too concerned with interest rate movements and orderly financial markets; and (3) that the Federal Reserve was far too secretive about the future course of monetary policy, so there was no way to hold it accountable for past actions.

The outcome of these hearings was Concurrent Resolution 133, which required the Board to consult with congressional committees on a quarterly basis about monetary policy objectives and plans regarding the growth of monetary aggregates over the coming 12 months. Concurrent Resolution 133 was a significant step forward in requiring the Federal Reserve to be more open about its objectives and operations as well as elevating the importance of monetary aggregates. However, the results were considerably less than expected. Monetary policy can be a complex subject, especially with regard to understanding short-term operations, and few members of Congress can appropriately question the various spokespersons for the Federal Reserve. Most important, however, Concurrent Resolution 133 failed to provide a satisfactory basis for evaluating the Federal Reserve's performance because of the unique manner in which the monetary growth targets were established each quarter.

Humphrey-Hawkins Act or the Full Employment and Balanced Economic Growth Act of 1978

The manner in which the monetary growth targets were reported was improved by the Humphrey-Hawkins Act of 1978 or the Full Employment and Balanced Growth Act. The act restated the basic goals of economic stabilization: full employment (defined by the act as a maximum 4% unemployment rate), price stability (defined as a maximum rate of 3%), economic growth, and balance-of-payments equilibrium. As part of the pursuit of these and other goals stated in the act, the Federal Reserve was required to establish calendar year growth ranges for the monetary aggregates in February of each year. The Federal Reserve chose to use the fourth quarter of the preceding year as the base and cannot change the base period within the calendar year. The act thus eliminated base drift within the year resulting from changing the base each quarter, although base drift and the forgiveness factor are still relevant when the Federal Reserve establishes new targets in successive calendar years.

The 1978 act established a twice yearly meeting between the Federal Reserve and Congress. The July meeting is designed to be a preliminary outline of monetary policy actions and concerns for the coming year. At this meeting preliminary target ranges are announced for M2, M3, and debt. In February of the new year, final target ranges are set for the year.

Evaluation   Both the 1975 and 1978 policy events were designed to require more accountability from the Federal Reserve by requiring it to announce monetary aggregate targets and report to Congress. Just the opposite occurred. Monetary growth and inflation accelerated in the second half of the 1970s, and while the October 1979 announcement and February 1980 redefinitions of the money supply appeared to suggest that the Federal Reserve was finally going to take the monetary aggregates seriously, the Federal Reserve in the 1980s made it clear that it was not willing to be tied down by any type of rule. In fact, when one looks at almost a decade of monetary aggregate targeting (Table 27-1), the performance suggests that either the Federal Reserve does not have good control over the money supply or else the Federal Reserve is less than enthusiastic about monetary aggregate targets and the rules type of behavior they impose.

The operating procedure introduced in late 1982 began a process of deemphasizing monetary aggregate targeting that became official in 1987. Since 1987 the Federal Reserve no longer announces M1 targets and has deemphasized monetary aggregate targeting in general. The Federal Reserve argues that deregulation and innovation have both rendered monetary aggregate targets less reliable than in the past. Monetary policy is now conducted in much the same way it was in the 1970s. It focuses on reducing interest rate fluctuations and has deemphasized the importance of any explicit monetary aggregate targets.

The failure to impose rules on the Federal Reserve, however, has not led to inflation, and the most successful central banks in terms of price stability are not constrained by rules. Even though there is a potential inflationary bias to discretionary policy, this can be overcome by a central bank's concern for its reputation to avoid inflationary monetary policy. The Federal Reserve, for example, has achieved considerable credibility in the 1980s by maintaining a fairly effective price stabilization policy in spite of its deemphasis on monetary aggregate targeting and a return to a short-term interest rate–focused policy.

Again, we should emphasize the experiences of the Bundesbank and the Bank of Japan in this regard. Both central banks have excellent records for price stability, and yet, neither one of them is constrained by a set of rules. In fact, both central banks conduct monetary policy on a period-by-period approach and with a good deal of discretion, but their actions are constrained by their long-term goal of maintaining a reputation for price stability.

This then suggests an interesting question: Why are some central banks more inclined to generate inflationary monetary policy than others? We will take up this and other questions related to the inflationary process in the next and last chapter of this book.

Key Points

1. The fact that monetary policy can influence the level of economic activity is a necessary but not sufficient reason for monetary policy to make a positive contribution to economic stabilization.

2. Two polar types of monetary policy have been debated: the rules and discretionary approach.

The rules approach is consistent with either the activist or nonactivist models; however, nonactivists such as Milton Friedman have been the most vocal advocates of the rules approach. The rules approach specifies how the Federal Reserve will react in a situation and removes or greatly limits departures from the rule. Discretion means that the Federal Reserve is not constrained by a rule and may not always react in the same manner to similar situations.

3. The rules approach is justified by those who emphasize the following: (a) lags in the effect of monetary policy, (b) the time inconsistency problem, (c) philosophical concerns about allowing government too much flexibility, and (d) concerns that the Federal Reserve has its own self-interest agenda and will not always do what is best for the economy. The discretionary approach is justified by those who emphasize the following: (a) limited knowledge about the economy that prevents constructing a feasible rule, (b) conflicts between a constant rule and the changing nature of the economic system over time, (c) the fact that shocks do impact the economy and create real hardships that government has a responsibility to make some effort to offset, (d) lags are important but only mean that monetary policy should be more carefully formulated and executed; (e) time in-

consistency is important, but the central bank's concern for its reputation as a price stabilizer can offset the time inconsistency problem; and (f) there exist many checks and balances to prevent misuses of power.

4. Despite the theoretical issues, the Federal Reserve's performance in the 1980s and the performance of the Bundesbank and the Bank of Japan suggest that if a central bank is concerned about controlling inflation, then discretionary policy can produce price stability.

5. The rules versus authorities debate, however, has generated much interest in making the Federal Reserve more accountable in some type of rules framework. The Concurrent Resolution 133 of 1975 and the Humphrey-Hawkins Act of 1978 represent recent efforts to impose a rule; however, the effort has been a failure. The Federal Reserve has deemphasized monetary aggregate targeting and has returned to an operating strategy similar to the one in place in the 1970s.

Key Terms

Activist rules

Administrative lag

Concurrent Resolution 133

Humphrey-Hawkins Act of 1978

Impact Lag

Lag in effect of stabilization policy

Nonactivist rules

Recognition lag

Rules versus discretion debate

Time inconsistency problem

Variability of the lag in effect of policy

Questions

1. Explain why a lag in effect of monetary policy exists.

2. Why is a rules approach consistent with either the activist or nonactivist model?

3. Why are the recognition lags similar between monetary and fiscal policy? Why are the impact lags dissimilar?

4. What would be wrong with forcing the Federal Reserve to adhere to some rule for a period of five years to see whether a rule is superior to discretion? Would this be a valid test?

5. Even if the Federal Reserve were convinced from a technical point of view that a constant monetary growth rule could outperform discre-

tionary policy, why would the Federal Reserve oppose the imposition of such a rule?

6. Review the evolution of efforts to impose a monetary target rule on the Federal Reserve from 1975 through 1986. Is this evolution consistent with the saying: "The more things change, the more they remain the same"?

7. Is it fair to argue that the Federal Reserve should be confined by a rule because of mis-

takes made in the past with discretionary policy?

8. To what extent do fundamental views about freedom, liberty, and the role of the government influence one's position on the rules versus discretion debate?

9. List the arguments in favor of a constant monetary growth rule and list the arguments against such a rule.

Suggested Readings

1. Finn E. Kydland and Edward C. Prescott, "Rules Rather than Discretion: The Inconsistency of Optimal Plans," *Journal of Political Economy*, 85 (June 1977), 473–491. The source of the formal statement of the time inconsistency problem; however, this is extremely difficult reading.

2. Stanley Fischer, "Monetary Policy and Performance in the U.S., Japan, and Europe, 1973–86," in Yoshio Suzuki and Mitsuaki Okabe (eds.), *Toward a World of Economic Stability: Optimal Monetary Framework and Policy* (Tokyo: Tokyo University Press, 1988).

3. Milton Friedman, "Should There Be an Independent Monetary Authority?" in L. B. Yeager (ed.), *In Search of a Monetary Constitution* (Cambridge, Mass.: Harvard University Press, 1962), 219–243. An argument for the constant money growth rule.

4. Milton Friedman, *A Program for Monetary Stability* (New York: Fordham University Press, 1959). An overall plan to reform monetary policy in terms of rules.

5. Milton Friedman, "The Effects of a Full-Employment Policy on Economic Stabilization," in Milton Friedman, *Essays in Positive Economics* (Chicago: University of Chicago Press, 1953), 117–132.

6. Gary Fromm and Lawrence R. Klein, "The NBER/NSF Model Comparison Seminar: An Analysis of

Results," *Annals of Economic and Social Measurement*, 5 (Winter 1976).

7. Michael J. Hamburger, "The Lag in the Effect of Monetary Policy: A Survey of Recent Literature," *Review*, Federal Reserve Bank of New York (December 1971), 289–297. A survey of early efforts to establish that a lag in the effect of monetary policy did exist.

8. Bennett T. McCallum, *Monetary Economics* (New York: Macmillan, 1989), Chap. 12. A readable but still technical discussion of the time inconsistency problem.

9. Henry Simons, "Rules Versus Authorities in Monetary Policy," *Journal of Political Economy*, 44 (February 1936), 1–30. The classic statement of the rules versus discretion debate. Well worth reading.

10. Herb Taylor, "Time Inconsistency: A Potential Problem for Policymakers," *Business Review*, Federal Reserve Bank of Philadelphia (March–April 1985), 3–12. A very readable discussion of the time inconsistency problem.

11. Clark Warburton, "Monetary Disturbances and Business Fluctuations in Two Centuries of American History," in L. B. Yeager (ed.), *In Search of a Monetary Constitution* (Cambridge, Mass.: Harvard University Press, 1962), 61–93. One of the first economists to emphasize the existence of a lag in effect of monetary policy that predates Friedman.

CHAPTER 29

Inflation, Money, and Monetary Policy

Chapter Overview

Inflation is an important topic in monetary economics for several reasons: (1) Inflation imposes hardships on the economy and while theoretical models can be constructed to demonstrate that a steady inflation rate has no real effects on the economy, the necessary conditions to achieve this result simply do not exist in the real world. Inflation hurts and imposes costs on society. (2) Long-run or core inflation is closely associated with the monetary growth rate and, hence, largely under the control of the central bank. Therefore, periods of sustained inflation reflect the failure of the central bank to fulfill its obligations to economic stabilization. (3) The historical record suggests that the Federal Reserve has an inflation bias in the way it formulates and conducts monetary policy. It is thus important to try and understand why the Federal Reserve, as well as other central banks, has an inflation bias and what solutions might exist to reduce this bias. (4) Given that a low and steady inflation rate is a desirable policy target, what procedures must central banks adopt to achieve this target? In this regard, central bank credibility plays a critical role in how well they can maintain stable prices.

These issues are explored in the following steps. First, we define inflation and review the inflation record for the United States, focusing on the period since the establishment of the Federal Reserve in 1913. Second, we address the effects inflation has on the economy and why a low and steady inflation rate is a desirable policy target. Third, the relationship between inflation and the money supply is reviewed and consideration is given to nonmonetary factors that might generate inflationary monetary policy. Fourth, we discuss the reasons why monetary policy is likely to have an inflation bias and how the Federal Reserve can overcome this bias. In this regard, the role of central bank credibility in controlling inflation is emphasized.

The Meaning of Inflation

Inflation is defined as a continuous increase in the price level, measured as an annual percentage change in a price index like the CPI, PPI, or the GNP Deflator. While each price index at any point in time will register a different inflation rate, they all tend to move together over time. The most comprehensive index—the GNP Deflator—is perhaps the best measure of long-run inflation. Figure 29-1 il-

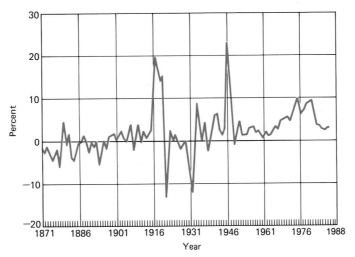

Source: Based on data provided by Robert J. Gordon which are reported in Robert J. Gordon, *Macroeconomics* (Glenview, Illinois: Scott, Foresman, & Co., 1990).

FIGURE 29-1 **Inflation rate measured by percentage changes in the GNP deflator, 1871–1988**

lustrates the behavior of the inflation rate measured as annual percentage changes in the GNP Deflator for the period 1870 to 1988. Inflation has fluctuated considerably over time; however, the behavior of the inflation rate in the post–World War II period has differed from its prewar pattern. Prior to 1950, the inflation rate both increased and decreased with no discernible trend; however, after 1950 the inflation rate exhibits a general upward trend. This is why a number of observers argue that Federal Reserve policy has an inflation bias. This, of course, assumes that inflation is a monetary phenomenon over the long run, an assumption that is widely accepted. Figure 29-2 shows the GNP Deflator price index over the 1870–1988 period and clearly indicates that the major increases in the price level have occurred in the past four decades! The GNP Deflator index rose in value 144% from 1870 to 1950; however, the index rose in value 408% over the 39-period from 1950 to 1988.

In the 1970s inflation was a major problem imposing a number of hardships on the economy. We have already discussed how inflation generated high nominal interest rates in the open money and capital markets. As open markets rose above the

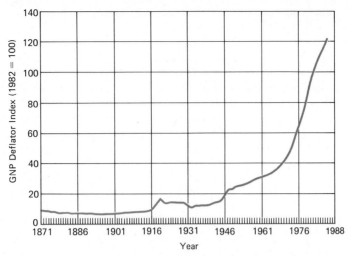

Source: Based on data provided by Robert J. Gordon which are reported in Robert J. Gordon, *Macroeconomics* (Glenview, Illinois: Scott, Foresman, & Co., 1990).

FIGURE 29-2   **Price level measured by the GNP deflator (1982 = 100), 1871–1988**

Regulation Q deposit rate ceilings imposed on depository institutions, funds were disintermediated out of financial institutions to the direct markets. This caused significant dislocations and threatened the viability of depository institutions and ultimately led to a major restructuring of the financial system.

To bring inflation under control in 1979 and 1980, the Federal Reserve imposed a restrictive monetary policy. The policy induced the sharpest recession experienced since the Great Depression associated with unemployment above 10%. The reduced output and employment represented the cost of disinflating the economy, and the fact that inflation has been kept at a low rate throughout the remainder of the 1980s represents a major achievement for Federal Reserve policy.

Even though inflation was reduced after 1983, the adverse effects of the inflationary period continued in the form of the thrift problem. The thrift problem had its origin in the inflationary environment of the late 1970s and early 1980s. During this time, thrift institutions experienced major disintermediation of funds and once they were permitted to offer market-sensitive deposits (money market certificates in 1978 and Super-NOWs in late 1982), they found that the cost of the sources of funds rose faster than the overall return from their loan portfolio. Much of the loan portfolio consisted of fixed rate mortgages made at relatively low rates in the past.

Thus, inflation has been a major characteristic of the U.S. economy in the post–World War II period in sharp contrast to earlier periods, and even a superficial review suggests that it has had a major adverse impact on the real performance of the economy. This suggests a number of questions. Why is inflation a problem? What causes inflation? Why does the post–World War II record of inflation differ from earlier periods? Is there an inflation bias to monetary policy? If so, how can monetary policy be rendered less inflationary?

BOX 1   Examples of hyperinflation

Hyperinflation is the most serious form of inflation. The United States has experienced only a very few brief periods of hyperinflation. These occurred at the time of the Revolutionary War and in some of the southern states at the time of the Civil War. The well-known examples of hyperinflation have occurred in other countries, the most notable examples being Germany during the early 1920s and Hungary in the 1920s and 1940s. Table 1B reports some examples of price increases that took place during hyperinflation. Notice that the average inflation rates are computed for a *month*!

TABLE 1B   Examples of hyperinflation

Country	Dates	Average Inflation Rate (percent per month)
Austria	Oct. 1921–Aug. 1922	47.1%
Germany	Aug. 1922–Nov. 1923	322.0
Greece	Nov. 1943–Nov. 1944	365.0
Hungary	Mar. 1923–Feb. 1924	46.0
Hungary	Aug. 1945–July 1946	19,800.0
Poland	Jan. 1923–Jan. 1924	81.1
Russia	Dec. 1921–Jan. 1924	57.0

Source: Phillip Cagan, "The Monetary Dynamics of Hyperinflation," in Milton Friedman (ed.), *Studies in the Quantity Theory of Money* (Chicago: University of Chicago Press, 1956).

Hyperinflation not only has major adverse economic impacts, but even more significantly, it can generate political movements that are even more harmful to the country and the world. The German hyperinflation and its impact on the German economy in the 1920s provided the environment for the rise of Adolf Hitler and the Nazi party.

Recent examples of inflation that approach hyperinflation proportions can still be found; for example, Brazil in the 1980s has experienced rapid price increases as reflected in Table 2B, although Brazil's inflation rate is far less than those reported in Table 1B. Keep in mind that the inflation rates in Table 2B are calculated as percentage increases in prices *per year*.

TABLE 2B   Consumer prices and inflation in Brazil, 1980–1988

	Consumer Prices (1980 = 100)	Inflation Rate
1980	100	—
1981	206	106.0%
1982	407	97.6
1983	984	141.8
1984	2924	197.2
1985	9556	226.8
1986	23436	145.2
1987	77258	229.7

Source: International Financial Statistics Yearbook, 1988 (Washington, D.C.: 1988) International Monetary Fund.

Types of Inflation: Hyperinflation Versus the Household Variety

Hyperinflation exists when the price level is expanding at a very rapid and self-sustaining rate. While there is no specific rate of price increase that separates hyperinflation from the more ordinary inflationary experiences, hyperinflation is associated with price increases exceeding 25 to 50% *per month*. Hyperinflation usually exists during major social and economic upheavals as during revolutions and wars though there are exceptions such as in some Latin American countries in recent years. (Box 1 illustrates some notable examples of hyperinflation.)

The consequences of hyperinflation can lead to a complete breakdown of the monetary and financial system if money loses value so rapidly that it ceases to function as a medium of exchange. Economic activity reverts back to a barter stage with an associated dramatic decline in economic activity and the standard of living.

Fortunately, hyperinflation is relatively rare, and there have been only a few short periods in U.S. history when inflation approached hyperinflation proportions. The most common type of inflation experienced by the United States and other countries is the common household variety of inflation. As such, we focus primarily on this type of inflation in which prices increase in the range of 5 to 20% *per year.* Despite the absence of a specific standard that separates this type of inflation from the far more serious hyperinflation, it is straightforward to distinguish it from hyperinflation. In the case of the household variety of inflation, the rate of price increase is considerably smaller, it can be controlled by monetary policy without major social and economic disruptions, and it does not have a self-sustaining quality that rapidly destroys the medium of exchange function of the nation's money supply.

The consequences of the more frequently experienced forms of inflation are related to whether inflation is anticipated or unanticipated and the variability of the inflation rate associated with unanticipated inflation.

Effects of Unanticipated Inflation and Inflation Uncertainty

The effects of unanticipated inflation holding constant inflation uncertainty can be illustrated by considering an increase in the inflation rate above the anticipated rate. Assume everyone anticipated inflation would be 5% for the coming year; however, the actual inflation rate turns out to be 15%. Assume, further, that at the end of the year the inflation rate returns to the anticipated level of 5%. What are the consequences of the unanticipated inflation of 10% for the one-year period?

Unanticipated inflation distorts the allocation of resources chiefly by changing the distribution of wealth among different sectors of the economy. Contracts that specify a fixed nominal cash flow over the year or adjust slowly to inflation will be adversely impacted by unanticipated inflation because they lose purchasing power.

In this regard, there are three costs of unanticipated inflation: (1) Anyone receiving a fixed nominal income over the year will experience a decline in welfare directly related to the rate of inflation. Workers whose nominal wage remains constant during the year will be hurt by inflation, while those who purchase their services benefit from inflation because the real cost of these services declines. While inflation-escalation clauses may mitigate some of the negative effects of unanticipated inflation, these adjustments occur only at discrete points in time and do not cover the majority of economic contracts. (2) The most important type of contract fixed in nominal terms are debt contracts. In this regard unanticipated inflation hurts creditors and benefits debtors. To the extent that nominal interest rates fail to incorporate unanticipated inflation, inflation lowers the real return to the lender and lowers the real cost to the borrower. (3) Inflation increases nominal income of any sector capable of adjusting their prices and/or contracts in response to unanticipated inflation. In this regard, there occurs a transfer of wealth from the private sector to the government sector if the income tax parameters are held constant. This is frequently referred to as *tax bracket creep.* In fact, inflation has been regarded as a form of taxation by government.

The effects of unanticipated inflation are compounded when we consider the fact that any unanticipated inflation will generate uncertainty as to further inflation rates. In the preceding discussion, it is not realistic for market participants to assume that the inflation rate in the next year will return to the anticipated rate. What is more likely is that market participants will be uncertain as to what to expect in the coming year because their inflation anticipations were not realized in the current year. Thus, uncertainty about future inflation is a separate cost of unanticipated inflation.

The impact of uncertainty is difficult to judge, but it would surely have negative effects on the willingness to invest and save with long-run consequences for economic growth. In addition, the uncertainty of inflation negatively affects the allocation of resources. It would encourage more speculative investment ventures, such as in gold and real estate, at the expense of more productive investment ventures. Firms would tend to hold higher than optimal inventories. In general, resources in the economy would be devoted to hedging against the uncertainties created by unanticipated inflation.

Models of the economy highlight the cost of inflation uncertainty. For example, the neoclassical models suggest that the positive association between output and prices in the short run is based on misconceptions at the micro level as to whether a price change represents an increase in demand for the firm's product or part of a general price level increase. The uncertainty generates output responses that eventually must be reversed and, hence, distorts the allocation of resources.

Effects of Anticipated Inflation

In the case of anticipated inflation, many of the adverse effects of unanticipated inflation are not present since contracts can be designed to take anticipated or future inflation into account. These efforts will reduce or eliminate the wealth transfers that take place in the context of unanticipated inflation. Workers can demand nominal wages that incorporate anticipated inflation that will be granted by employers because they, in turn, anticipate increases in the prices of the products they sell equal to the anticipated inflation. Lenders will demand an inflation premium be added to the real return equal to the anticipated inflation rate, while borrowers will grant the inflation premium because this will not influence the real rate of interest.

Anticipated inflation, however, still imposes a cost on society in four ways: (1) anticipated inflation imposes a tax on holding any form of money that does not earn a market rate of interest; (2) anticipated inflation imposes a transactions costs every time contracts are adjusted; (3) economic contracts cannot be adjusted continuously in practice while inflation is a continuous process; and (4) to the extent tax parameters are not fully adjusted, anticipated inflation can continue to transfer wealth from the private to the public sector.

The demand to hold money is inversely related to the rate of inflation because some forms of money earn no interest. The only forms of money that earn no interest in the United States are currency, traveler's checks, and demand deposits and together, these represent about half of the M1 money supply. Thus, any given money balance will lose purchasing power over time even if inflation is completely anticipated. This provides an incentive to economize on holding money, and as a result, the public devotes resources that have an opportunity cost to economize on their money balances. The resource costs are manifested by an increased number of trips to the bank, ATM, and so on and often referred to as "shoe leather costs." This tax on money balances has been a less serious problem since the 1980 Deregulation and Monetary Control Act permitted depository institutions to pay market-determined interest rates on checking accounts with the exception of demand deposit accounts; however, given that 25% of M1 is held in the form of coin, currency, and traveler's checks, which earn no interest, and 30% of M1 is held in the form of demand deposits, which by law are prohibited from earning interest, the tax on money balances caused by inflation remains a meaningful cost of anticipated inflation.

Even if contracts can be written to incorporate anticipated inflation, the fact that resources need to be devoted to this endeavor imposes a cost on society. In addition, contracts are not adjusted continuously, but rather at discrete points in time. Imagine the number of menus a chain restaurant must print every time it needs to adjust prices in response to changes in anticipated inflation. These types of costs are often referred to as "menu costs," and because contracts cannot be continuously revised in most cases, even anticipated inflation imposes wealth transfers among different groups.

Tax reforms introduced in 1985 have significantly mitigated the tax bracket creep problem. This was accomplished by indexing the federal tax brackets and deductions to the inflation rate; however, this has not completely eliminated tax bracket creep even in the context of anticipated inflation. The tax brackets are indexed to past inflation and not anticipated inflation, and in addition, some deductions are not completely indexed because they have nominal dollar limits.

Has Inflation Been Anticipated or Unanticipated?

Measuring actual inflation is not without problems; however, getting a handle on anticipated inflation is far more complex. Economists are interested in measuring anticipated inflation for two reasons: first, the costs of anticipated inflation are generally smaller than those of unanticipated inflation, and second, anticipated inflation and differences between it and actual inflation play a major role in modern models of the economy.

Of the various approaches available to measuring anticipated inflation, two have been heavily investigated: (1) a class of statistical models referred to as *autoregressive models* used to predict anticipated inflation from current and past actual inflation rates and (2) survey methods designed to measure directly the market's anticipated inflation rate.

Let us briefly consider each approach and how each approach decomposes recent inflation rate into anticipated and unanticipated components.

Autoregressive Models These models are based on a concept central to the Friedman-Phelps version of the Phillips curve. According to this view of the Phillips curve, the market adjusts its anticipated inflation to errors made in forecasting past inflation. This is called the *adaptive expectations hypothesis* because current anticipated inflation is adapted to recent inflation forecast errors. According to this hypothesis, the market adjusts anticipated inflation in the following way,

$$pa\ (t) - pa\ (t - 1) = \gamma[(p(t) - pa\ (t - 1)] \tag{1}$$

where *pa* stands for anticipated inflation at a given time, *p* stands for actual inflation at a given time, and γ is a constant measuring the "speed" with which anticipations respond to forecast errors. Expression (1) says that if the actual inflation rate at time *t* equals the anticipated inflation rate formulated at time $t - 1$, the market will not adjust its anticipated inflation upward or downward. For example, if at the end of 1990 the market anticipated inflation of 5% for 1991 and the actual inflation rate in 1991 was 5%, then the right-hand side of the expression would be zero. The market would continue to anticipate a 5% inflation rate for 1992.

Assume that the actual inflation rate for 1991, however, was 8% instead of the anticipated 5%. In this case, the market would have underpredicted inflation by 3 percentage points. In this case, the right-hand side of the expression would be 0.50 × (8.00–5.00), or 1.5, assuming that γ equals 0.50. This means anticipated inflation would increase from 5% to 6.5% in 1992. If the actual inflation rate continued to be 8%, then the right-hand side of the expression would be 0.50 (8.00–6.00) or 1.0 in 1992. Thus, anticipated inflation would be increased for 1993 from 6.5% to 7.5%. As you can see, the market adjusts or adapts anticipated inflation to the difference between the actual and anticipated inflation rate in the past. The coefficient "γ" represents the speed of adjustment. A higher (lower) value of γ means that anticipations are adjusted more rapidly (slowly).

The adaptive expectations hypothesis (with some mathematical manipulation) can be used to develop a variety of estimates of anticipated inflation all of which suggest that anticipated inflation for the next period depends on a weighted average of the current and past actual inflation rate; hence, the term autoregressive.

Survey Methods Survey methods might provide a more accurate estimate of anticipated inflation than simple statistical models. Two surveys of anticipated inflation are publicly available. One is the so-called Livingston survey, named after Joseph Livingston, a financial writer who began collecting and publishing anticipated inflation estimates in the late 1940s. This survey is maintained by the Federal Reserve Bank of Philadelphia and represents the market's anticipated inflation rate in terms of the CPI index for a given forecast horizon. The NBER-ASA survey is published periodically by the Survey Research Center of the University of Michigan. Unlike the Livingston survey, the NBER-ASA survey provides estimates of anticipated inflation in terms of the GNP Deflator for a given forecast horizon.

Figure 29-3 presents the actual inflation rate in terms of the GNP Deflator over the period from 1958 through 1986 and two alternative measures of anticipated

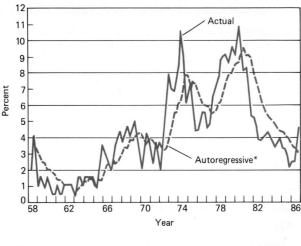

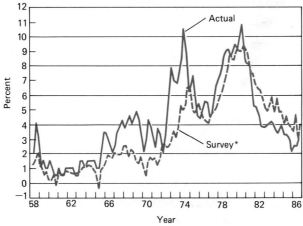

*Anticipated two quarters ahead

Source: Adrian W. Throop, "An Evaluation of Alternative Measures of Expected Inflation," *Economic Review*, Federal Reserve Bank of San Francisco (Summer 1988), 30.

FIGURE 29-3   **Actual GNP inflation and two measures of anticipated inflation, 1958–1986**

inflation. The estimates of anticipated inflation are for a period of six months into the future; that is, the anticipated inflation rate as of the first quarter 1985 represents the anticipated rate of inflation for the second and third quarter of 1985.

The first method (top of figure 29-3) estimates anticipated inflation by a simple autoregressive or statistical model, while the second method (NBER-ASA survey, bottom of figure 29-3) estimates anticipated inflation from survey responses of businesspersons, government officials, and so on.

Both approaches suggest that the market has difficulty forecasting inflation. There appears to be a significant difference between anticipated and actual inflation at any time. In the first and last part of the 1970s, inflation was underforecasted, while in the first half of the 1980s, inflation was overforecasted. Thus, the evidence suggests that there is a meaningful unanticipated component to the actual inflation rate.

What Causes Inflation?

There has been little debate over the years about the causes of hyperinflation. The hyperinflation process consists of three basic elements that interact to generate extremely rapid and destructive price increases over a short-period of time. First, normal or household variety inflation is transformed into hyperinflation when monetary growth is accelerated sharply and far beyond the productive capacity of the economy. This usually occurs during periods of social upheaval and/or war as governments use an expanding money supply to claim resources in the private sector. Second, as the money supply and inflation continue to expand, market participants anticipate further inflation and the cost of holding money increases in turn. Individuals make every effort to reduce money balances in exchange for goods and in so doing increase velocity. Velocity adds to the inflationary pressures of the increasing money supply. Third, the government is forced to expand the money supply even more as prices increase to even maintain their previous claim on resources.

The interaction of these elements can be illustrated with the equation of exchange:

$$\%\Delta M + \%\Delta V = \%\Delta y + \%\Delta P \tag{2}$$

As the rate of growth of M is accelerated far beyond the productive capacity of the system (represented by $\%\Delta y$), the rate of inflation accelerates. As individuals anticipate further increases in the money supply and prices, they reduce their money holdings (represented by an increase in $\%\Delta V$), which adds to the inflationary process. Finally, the inflation itself generates further increases in the money supply as governments try to maintain their command on resources, generating, further increases in velocity as the public anticipates further declines in the value of money. At this point, the entire process becomes self-generating and may bring about the collapse of the monetary and financial system.

The more common forms of inflation—the household variety—have been subject to more debate regarding causes than has hyperinflation. In the past, economists distinguished between *demand-pull*, *cost-push*, and *mixed* inflation.

Demand-pull inflation resulted from increases in aggregate demand generated by increased government spending and/or increased money supply. Increasing demand "pulled up" prices.

Cost-push inflation resulted from aggressive wage and/or price increases by noncompetitive labor market elements in the form of labor unions or noncompetitive product market elements in the form of oligopolistic market structures. The concentrated market power of these groups gave them the ability to increase prices even in the absence of increase in demand. Cost-push inflation was also referred to as either wage-push or profit-push depending on the source of aggressive price increases.

Mixed inflation resulted from a combination of demand-pull and cost-push elements; for example, demand increases may initiate an inflationary process that provides an incentive for labor or capital to further increase prices.

While there was little debate about the causes of hyperinflation—all agreed that hyperinflation was a monetary phenomenon—there was at one time considerable debate about the causes of the more frequently experienced forms of inflation. In fact, the three-part taxonomy suggests a wide difference of opinion about the causes of inflation. A key element of the monetarist-Keynesian debate of the 1970s was to what extent inflation was a monetary phenomenon. At that time, there were a number of inflation models that devoted relatively little or even no attention to the money supply as a cause of inflation.

Where Is the Money Supply?

A number of economists, primarily the monetarists, regarded the concepts of demand-pull and cost-push inflation as missing the point. There can be no sustained inflation unless the money supply is also increased. Likewise, without an increase in the money supply, no amount of demand-pull or cost-push can sustain inflation. Inflation is a monetary phenomenon. Because inflation means increasing prices of goods and services, the money supply or turnover rate of money (velocity) must increase to support higher prices. To see this more clearly, consider the following definitional relationship:

$$C + I + G = \text{GNP} = \text{NY} = MV \qquad (3)$$

This simple relationship says that total output of goods and services equals total income earned in producing the goods and services, which also equals total money multiplied by the number of times that money changes hands. Any change in aggregate demand (C, I, or G) or any increase in income claims must be accompanied by an increase in V and/or M.

In the Keynesian system, increases in the aggregate demand function increase income and prices even without an increase in the money supply. Increased aggregate demand leads to a greater transaction demand for money represented by a rightward shift in the demand function for money illustrated in Figure 29-4. The interest rate increases, bringing the money market back into equilibrium. Velocity increases as the quantity of money demanded declines along the new function, DM_2. Velocity is defined as the ratio of income-to-money supply, and, because an unchanged supply of money will support a higher level of income as a result of the increase in aggregate demand, velocity is thereby higher. But there is a limit to how much velocity can increase to accommodate an expanding aggregate demand function. Remember that demand for money includes transaction, precautionary, and speculative demand for money. Only the speculative demand is related to the interest rate. Thus, as total spending expands, the speculative component of the demand for money will eventually reach zero, and it will become increasingly difficult for velocity to continue to increase since the transaction and precautionary demand for money cannot easily be lowered. So, even in the Keynesian system, inflation cannot persist for long periods without an increase in the money supply.

What about cost-push elements? Unless cost-push increases in the price level are accompanied by an increase in total spending, it is difficult to see how cost-push elements can sustain inflation. Aggressive increases in wages beyond productivity

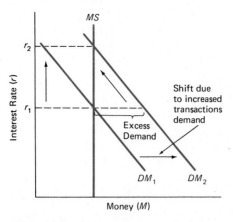

FIGURE 29-4 **Effect of increase in aggregate demand on the demand function for money**

gains and price increases to raise profit margins will produce unemployment if total spending is not increased. When total spending increases to sustain the aggressive wage and price increases, we refer to it as *validated cost-push inflation.* Here, again, increased spending must be accompanied by an increased M and/or V, and there are limits to the increase in V.

Let us summarize the causes of inflation:

1. Demand-pull elements can lead to inflation without an increase in M as long as V increases.

2. Cost-push elements can lead to inflation especially if aggressive wage and/or price increases are validated by increased government spending. However, V must increase without an increase in M.

3. There are limits to how much V can increase and ultimately M must increase to support continued inflation.

4. Increases in M lead to inflation. This can be demonstrated by almost any model.

Thus, sustained inflation over the long run must be accompanied by growth of the money supply. While this conclusion was debated extensively during the monetarist-Keynesian debate, the view that long-run inflation is a monetary phenomenon is widely accepted. Robert J. Gordon in 1975 summarized the professional view of the relationship between inflation and money:

Economic research on the causes of inflation has been primarily devoted to the theoretical and empirical study of the links between government policy variables and the rate of inflation. While debate continues on the process of short-run adjustment, most economists are prepared to agree that in the long-run "inflation is always and everywhere a monetary phenomenon." Abundant empirical evidence has confirmed that the major historical accelerations and decelerations of inflation—not only during wars and

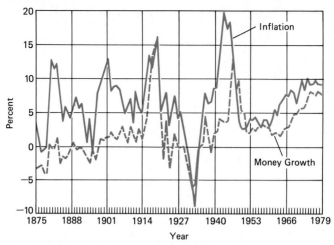

Source: Based on data provided by Robert J. Gordon which are reported in Robert J. Gordon, *Macroeconomics* (Glenview, Illinois: Scott, Foresman, & Co., 1990).

FIGURE 29-5   Trend Inflation and Trend Money Growth, 1875–1979. (Trend inflation (GNP Deflator) and money growth represented as a three-year moving average of annual growth rates. Old M2 (currency, demand deposits, savings and time deposits) measure of money used.)

hyperinflations but also during peacetime—have been accompanied by accelerations and decelerations in the rate growth of the supply of money.[1]

Figures 29-5 and 29-6 illustrate the relationship between trend inflation and trend money growth in the United States over two periods: first, over a long historical period from 1875 to 1979 using annual data and, second, over the more recent period from 1962 through mid-1989 using quarterly data. The figures reveal two implications.

First, the year-to-year relationship between inflation and money is not particularly close, so it appears that significant inflation can occur over short periods of time without matching increases in the money supply. Second, taking longer periods into account, there is a close association between inflation and the money supply. It would be difficult to argue that the inflation experience in the United States could have existed without a corresponding increase in the money supply.

Is Inflation Only a Monetary Phenomenon?

Milton Friedman's statement "inflation is always and everywhere a monetary phenomenon" would appear to be less than completely supported by the evidence presented in Figures 29-5 and 29-6. There does exist a long-run association between

[1] Robert J. Gordon, "The Demand for and Supply of Inflation," *Journal of Law and Economics*, 18 (December 1975), 807.

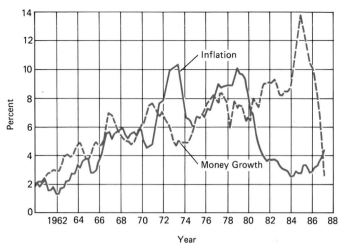

Source: Based on data by Robert J. Gordon which are reported in Robert J.
Gordon, *Macroeconomics* (Glenview, Illinois: Scott, Foresman, & Co., 1990).

FIGURE 29-6   **Trend Inflation (GNP Deflator) and Trend Money Growth (M1),
Second Quarter 1962–Second Quarter 1989. (Trend inflation represented as a
five-quarter moving average of annual inflation rate and trend money growth
represented as a nine-quarter moving average of the annual rates of money
growth.)**

inflation and monetary growth; however, it is certainly less than one to one. Even
though, theoretically, inflation is a monetary phenomenon, why is there a less than
one-to-one relationship between money and inflation?

There is no problem between the monetary interpretation of inflation and the
historical record illustrated in the figures once we take three considerations into
account.

Lags in the Effect of Monetary Growth on Inflation   Evidence suggests that
changes in the money supply induce changes in the inflation rate only after a considerable lag—as much as two years elapse before a higher monetary growth rate is
completely reflected by a higher inflation rate. Prior to that, higher monetary growth
is affecting both inflation and real output growth. Only after the economy has adjusted to the higher monetary growth rate will real output return to its long-run path
and the full effects of higher monetary growth on inflation be manifested. If the
monetary growth rate is changed before the long-run response is completed, it is
obvious that we will observe a less than one-to-one relationship between monetary
growth and inflation.

Nonmonetary Shocks That Influence the Inflation Rate   Inflation is a continuous
increase in the price level and thus can only be explained by some force that also
changes continuously. In the past a variety of nonmonetary "shocks" have been held
responsible for inflation—oil price increases and government budget deficits to name
two nonmonetary forces frequently mentioned. Do these explain inflation?

Let us first consider the influence of oil price shocks since we have experienced
four major such shocks: three oil price increases in 1974–75, 1979–80, and 1990 and

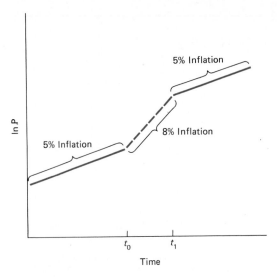

FIGURE 29-7   Impact of an oil price
increase on the inflation rate

one oil price decrease in 1986–87. Since they occur at discrete points in time, they can account only for a short-run acceleration or deceleration in the inflation rate, but once the economy adjusts to higher or lower oil prices, the inflation rate will return to its long-run trend determined by the monetary growth rate.

Figure 29-7 illustrates this basic point for an oil price increase that plots the natural logarithm of the price level against time. A constant slope of the price line in such a diagram means that the price level is increasing at a constant rate, and the steeper the slope of the price line, the higher the inflation rate. Assume the inflation rate determined by the monetary growth rate is 5% and at time t_o, oil prices suddenly increase as they did in 1973–74. In terms of aggregate demand and supply analysis, the oil price increase shifts the supply function to the left so that, at every level of real output, the price level will be higher. This is because higher oil prices reduce the productivity of capital previously dependent on low oil prices. As the economy adjusts to the higher oil prices the inflation rate temporarily accelerates to, say, 8% over the period from t_o to t_1; however, once the oil price increase has been absorbed, prices stop increasing and the inflation rate returns to its long-run path determined by monetary forces.

This helps to explain why the inflation rate moved above the monetary growth rate in the mid- and late 1970s. It also partly helps to explain why inflation and monetary growth have diverged in the 1980s. There is a close association between monetary growth and inflation in the early 1980s as the Federal Reserve dramatically reduced monetary growth as part of its price stabilization policy; however, after 1985, the inflation rate continued to decline while monetary growth remained high. The rapid decline in oil prices after 1985 helps to explain this period.

The same interpretation exists for a sudden increase in the government deficit. In terms of aggregate demand and supply, an increase in the deficit shifts the demand function to the right and raises prices. This does not explain inflation, except for the short period during which the economy is adjusting to the higher deficit.

The only way these types of nonmonetary shocks can explain inflation over the long run is if they occur continuously over time. In this case, the continuous increase in oil prices or government deficits could only support inflation if either the velocity of money or the money supply expanded. As we have already discussed, there are limits to how far velocity can support inflation, and ultimately, inflation can only exist in the long run if it is supported by monetary growth. Thus, long-run inflation is a monetary phenomenon.

New Forms of Money, Deregulation, and Financial Innovation The evidence offered for the monetary interpretation of inflation is based on statistical measures of the money supply and price level. Regarding the money supply measures, deregulation and financial innovation have made it more difficult to define and measure money. In addition, the new forms of money in themselves may represent shocks to the financial system and require time for market participants to incorporate them into their portfolio decisions. As a result, traditional measures of money may not be the best way in which to establish the monetary interpretation of inflation either because they don't adequately measure "money" in some fundamental sense, or the constant introduction of new forms of money generates an adjustment process that has yet to be completed. These factors may also explain the difference between the monetary growth rate and the inflation rate in the 1980s.

Why Do Central Banks Permit Inflationary Monetary Growth?

Inflation is a monetary phenomenon, and since the Federal Reserve controls the long-run growth of the money supply, why has the Federal Reserve in the past permitted inflationary monetary growth? The same question can be asked for other central banks that fail to achieve price stability. The response of the Federal Reserve is to argue that (1) nonmonetary forces play an important role in determining the inflation rate, (2) deregulation and financial innovation have altered the traditional relationship between money and inflation, and (3) effective control over the money supply exists only in textbooks, not the real world of monetary policy.

The argument that nonmonetary forces play an important role in determining long-run inflation is fairly well rejected by the evidence. Few economists seriously argue that long-run inflation can exist without a corresponding expansion in the money supply.

The deregulation and financial innovation argument has some merit for the 1980s; however, it is too early to tell whether the economy is still adjusting to the changes in regulatory parameters and new financial assets and services. More important, this argument does not explain why the Federal Reserve had an inflationary bias starting in the mid-1960s since it was only in the late 1970s that financial innovations such as money market mutual funds had a significant impact on the flow of funds. Official deregulation also did not commence until the late 1970s.

The argument that the Federal Reserve does not control the money supply as well as described in textbooks is not convincing. There is no doubt that short-run monetary control is difficult to achieve; however, there exists a well-established relationship between the growth of the monetary base and any one of several monetary aggregates over a long period of time.

Thus, accepting the premise that inflation is a monetary phenomenon and the Federal Reserve controls the monetary growth rate over the long run, why does inflationary monetary growth occur? There are several possible explanations:

1. Accommodation of federal deficits and debt
2. Focus on low and stable interest rates or orderly financial markets
3. Goals other than price stability
4. Political business cycle elements
5. Time inconsistency

This section will focus on points 1–4 while we will devote a separate section to time inconsistency because it is a major explanation of inflationary bias as well as a serious problem facing central bank policy.

Federal Deficits and Debt   There is no direct causal relationship between growth of government debt and monetary growth in the sense that growth of debt must induce monetary growth; however, the growth of debt could indirectly influence expansionary monetary policy. The growth of federal deficits and debt in the past two decades has been large enough to impact the financial system. When the government becomes a deficit unit, like any deficit unit, it must sell I.O.U.s in the financial system to secure funds needed to support spending above tax revenues. The increased demand for loanable funds, in turn, increases interest rates. Interest rates increases are politically unpopular and draw attention to the government's deficit spending. Thus, government pressure on the Federal Reserve to expand the supply of loanable funds and thus keep interest rates from rising, might account for inflationary monetary growth.

The relationship between monetary growth and growth of federal debt (Figure 29-8) suggests a positive correlation; however, there are a number of occasions when monetary and debt growth diverge.

Orderly Financial Markets   The Federal Reserve may focus on reducing interest rate fluctuations and maintaining interest rates at a level inconsistent with price stability for reasons other than pressures generated by government deficits. During the 1970s the Federal Reserve's Federal funds operating strategy was designed to stabilize interest rates, and because the Federal Reserve was slow to adjust the Federal funds targets upward when conditions warranted, inflationary monetary growth occurred. The Federal Reserve's reluctance to raise Federal fund rate targets reflected its desire to prevent disintermediation and hence curb criticism that it had contributed to worsening the condition of thrift institutions. In the end, this policy was frustrated because inflation generated inflationary anticipations, which in turn, raised nominal rates above the Regulation Q ceilings. Disintermediation, in fact, occurred as a result of the Federal Reserve's focus on stable and low interest rates.

The Federal Reserve has returned to an interest rate–focused policy that has similar implications for interest rate movements as the Federal funds operating procedure; however, the Federal Reserve has not made the same mistake in the past of trying to keep interest rates at levels inconsistent with low inflation. The Federal

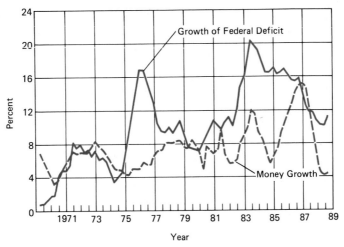

Source: Based on data from Citicorp Dataline Service

FIGURE 29-8 Trend money growth and trend growth in Federal debt, first quarter 1975–fourth quarter 1988. (Trend money growth and debt growth represented by a five-quarter moving average of annual growth rates.)

Reserve has maintained a low inflation rate in the 1980s despite its return in 1982 to an interest rate–focused operating strategy.

Policy Targets Other than Price Stability At one time there was widespread belief that there existed a stable Phillips curve trade-off between inflation and unemployment. If such a trade-off existed, then the Federal Reserve might choose to accept a higher inflation rate in exchange for a lower unemployment rate. In fact, it was widely believed in the 1960s and early 1970s that the underlying determinants of the Phillips curve dictated a socially and politically unacceptable level of unemployment that would be required to achieve an inflation rate of, say, 3% or 4%. Thus, the Federal Reserve was more likely to sacrifice some control over inflation to achieve full employment.

This situation, however, is no longer a relevant choice for monetary policy. The stable Phillips curve in the 1970s came under empirical and theoretical criticism. Economists reached a consensus that short-run trade-offs between inflation and employment were possible, but that the long-run Phillips curve was either vertical or very steep. The effects of unanticipated inflation, misconceptions about absolute and relative price changes, and nonsynchronized wage contracts all supported a positively sloped aggregate supply function in the short run, while long-run equilibrium was characterized by a vertical aggregate supply function. In this context, expansionary monetary policy could not permanently maintain the unemployment rate lower than the natural unemployment rate or, what amounts to the same, maintain output growth permanently above its natural level.

The general acceptance that expansionary monetary policy cannot maintain a level of output above its potential level over the long run has reduced the Federal Reserve's willingness to use monetary policy for employment objectives. Thus, belief in the Phillips curve may account for past inflation bias; however, it is not as important as it once was given our understanding of the short- and long-run trade-off between inflation and employment. At the same time, there are reasons why the Federal Reserve might want to exploit even a short-run trade-off between inflation and employment.

Political Business Cycle Phenomenon   The literature on the political business cycle may also offer some insight into the inflationary bias of monetary policy. According to this view, the Federal Reserve is induced to expand the economy prior to an election. Even though the long-run Phillips curve is vertical, the Federal Reserve can generate a short-run employment increase. If the politically induced monetary expansion is timed correctly, the market will not adjust inflationary anticipations upward and return employment back to the natural level until after the election. At this time, the Federal Reserve might have an incentive to reduce the inflation rate by inducing an increase in unemployment. The increase in unemployment above the natural rate occurs because the economy had anticipated a higher rate of inflation. When the economy adjusts inflationary anticipations downward, unemployment declines back to the natural level.

It is more likely, however, that the Federal Reserve's willingness in the political business cycle framework to reduce inflation after the election is not as intense as its willingness to expand the economy prior to the election. Hence, over time one would observe a general acceleration in the inflation rate.

Time Inconsistency and Central Bank Inflation Bias

A more general explanation of why the Federal Reserve as well as other central banks have an inflation bias can be traced to the time inconsistency problem. This explanation can incorporate many of the specific rationales of why the Federal Reserve has an inflation bias. Milton Friedman in the 1950s argued that discretionary policy was likely to generate greater instability than a simple monetary growth rate rule for at least two reasons:

1. Lags in the effect of monetary policy ensured that the impact of monetary policy would frequently occur at the wrong time.
2. The Federal Reserve would be influenced by special circumstances at each point in time that monetary policy was formulated.

The second point is the essence of the time inconsistency problem which was developed in a formal framework by Kydland and Prescott in 1977. The concept was further extended in 1983 by Robert J. Barro and David B. Gordon and has attracted considerable attention in the past few years. The argument is mathematically complex; however, a verbal example can illustrate the elements.[2]

First, assume the economy is characterized by a vertical long-run Phillips curve

---

[2] This and the next section draws from Alex Cukierman. "Central Bank Behavior and Credibility: Some Recent Theoretical Developments," *Review*, Federal Reserve Bank of St. Louis (May 1986), 5–17.

in which deviations in the unemployment rate from its natural level depend on unanticipated inflation.

Second, the Federal Reserve's utility function assigns negative weight to inflation and positive weight to employment, which also reflects society's attitude about inflation and unemployment. The Federal Reserve chooses a monetary growth rate which determines the inflation rate in such a way so as to maximize social welfare.

Third, the public understands how monetary policy is formulated and the incentives facing the Federal Reserve.

These three conditions suggest that the best or optimal monetary policy is to generate a zero inflation rate over the long run. In this manner, inflationary anticipations and the actual zero inflation rate are identical, and the unemployment rate is at the natural level (output is at its natural or potential level). The following expression will help us understand this point.

$$W = -m + 2(y - y_n) \qquad (4)$$

where W represents social welfare, m is the monetary growth rate, y is actual output growth, and y_n is the natural long-run equilibrium growth of output. This expression could also be stated in terms of actual and natural unemployment rates with no loss in meaning. Keeping in mind that the monetary growth rate determines the inflation rate, we can rewrite (4) as

$$W = -p^2 + 2(y - y_n) \qquad (5)$$

where we have substituted the rate of inflation, p, for the monetary growth rate. The monetary growth rate and inflation rate are raised to the second power because the public's dislike for inflation increases more than in proportion to an increase in the inflation rate. It also indicates that deflation ($p < 0$) lowers social welfare.

The negative sign for p^2 (or m in expression (4)) indicates that social welfare is reduced as monetary growth and inflation increase, while the positive sign for ($y - y_n$) indicates that social welfare increases when output rises above the natural level (unemployment falls below its natural level). The coefficient whose value is given as "2" in front of the output component indicates that output and employment have higher weight in the utility function than has inflation. That is, the public dislikes unemployment more than inflation, other things held constant.

Social welfare or W is at the highest level over the long run when p (and m) = 0 and actual output grows at its natural rate, so that ($y - y_n$) = 0. Numerically, the highest level of W in the case of expression (5) is zero.

The expression indicates that social welfare could be increased above zero if a trade-off existed between inflation and output. Start from the case when $W = 0$, that is $m = p = 0$ and ($y - y_n$) = 0. In addition, assume that the natural growth path is taken at the value of 5. Now increase the monetary growth to 1 ($p = 1$), which generates an output growth of 6 compared to the natural rate of 5. This occurs because the market did not anticipate the higher inflation rate, or there were misconceptions about whether relative prices or the general price level has increased, or wages adjusted in a sluggish manner because of the contractual nature of wages. In this case, the value of the welfare function is

$$W = -(1)^2 + 2(6 - 5) = 1 \qquad (6)$$

The negative effects of inflation are offset by the benefits of higher output and employment. However, this situation is only temporary since there are no long-run trade-offs between inflation and employment; that is, the long-run Phillips curve is vertical. Eventually the higher inflation rate comes to be anticipated and output returns to its natural level: however, the economy now has an inflation rate of 1. The new value for the social welfare function is

$$W = -(1)^2 + 2(5 - 5) = -1 \qquad (7)$$

Prisoners' Dilemma or What Is Optimal in the Long Run Is Less Optimal in the Short Run

The time inconsistency problem occurs because the Federal Reserve and the public are in a Prisoners' Dilemma "game" to determine the inflation and unemployment rate. Like the prisoners' dilemma, each acting in its own interest will generate an overall solution that is less optimal than from each side's perspective. The Prisoners' Dilemma originally arose in the context of two individuals arrested in the act of a crime. They are separated by the police before they can agree on a common story and the essence of each prisoner's dilemma is that each does not know what the other one will say when questioned by the police. The paradox is that if each seeks his most preferred outcome given the choices available, the overall outcome is less preferable for each prisoner.

Let us see how this works in regard to the outcome of monetary policy. At the beginning of the period, the public formulates anticipations of monetary policy and hence inflation. Assume there are two choices: (1) zero monetary growth, $m = 0$, and (2) inflationary monetary growth, $m = 1$. The choice will influence whether the public's contracts incorporate a zero or inflation rate of one.

The Federal Reserve then establishes a payoff matrix illustrated in Table 29-1 in terms of the social welfare function in deciding monetary policy at any point in time:

The payoff matrix has four elements:

TABLE 29-1   Payoff or outcome matrix: illustration of time inconsistency

		Public Anticipates	
		$m = p = 0$	$m = p = 1$
Federal Reserve Chooses	$m = p = 0$	$W = 0$ $y = y_n$	$W = -2$ $y < y_n$
	$m = p = 1$	$W = 1$ $y > y_n$	$W = -1$ $y = y_n$

Source: Adapted from Allex Cukierman, "Central Bank Behavior and Credibility: Some Recent Theoretical Developments," *Review,* Federal Reserve Bank of St. Louis (May 1986), p. 7.

1. Public anticipates $m = p = 0$, and Federal Reserve chooses $m = p = 0$. Plugging these values into the social welfare function generates a value for W of 0. The outcome will be zero inflation and output at the natural level.

2. Public anticipates $m = p = 0$, and Federal Reserve chooses $m = p = 1$. Plugging these values into the social welfare function generates a value for W of 1. The outcome will be inflation of 1 and output above the natural level.

3. Public anticipates $m = p = 1$, and Federal Reserve chooses $m = p = 0$. Plugging these values into the social welfare function generates a value for W of -2. The outcome will be zero inflation and output below the natural level.

4. Public anticipates $m = p = 1$, and Federal Reserve chooses $m = p = 1$. Plugging these values into the social welfare function generates a value for W of -1. The outcome will be inflation of 1 and output at the natural level.

The payoff matrix indicates that the Federal Reserve will choose the positive monetary growth because no matter what the public expects, social welfare will be higher than if it had chosen a zero monetary growth rate. Thus, the Federal Reserve has an incentive to inflate irrespective of public anticipations regarding monetary growth and inflation.

The public is also part of this game and doesn't like to be fooled into structuring contracts that assume zero inflation when, in fact, the Federal Reserve has an incentive to inflate. Therefore, the public comes to learn about the incentives facing the Federal Reserve and consistently anticipates a monetary growth of 1. The public learns from the past that to assume $m = p = 0$ results in contracts understating inflation and output first raising above then falling back to the natural level.

Over the long run the monetary growth of 1 generates an inflation rate of 1 while the actual output rate is equal to its natural rate. In terms of the payoff matrix, social welfare ends up being -1 (right-hand bottom-corner solution), whereas social welfare is clearly maximized at 0 (left-hand upper corner) when the Federal Reserve achieves price stability. Yet, the incentives facing the Federal Reserve and the public generate a level of social welfare less than if the Federal Reserve had achieved zero inflation.

Thus, in the long run the Federal Reserve has an inherent bias toward inflation even though it clearly recognizes that price stability is the optimal policy in the long run. The Federal Reserve's actions at each period are not time consistent with respect to achieving price stability. Even though society is better off when $m = p = 0$, the game character of monetary policy at each period ensures that positive inflation will occur.

Time Inconsistency and Central Bank Credibility

The prisoners' dilemma nature of the game between the Federal Reserve and the public with the resulting inflationary bias of monetary policy has had a dramatic impact on the thinking of economists and policymakers about the best way to conduct

---

BOX 2   What it takes to earn credibility—the Bank of Japan

The Federal Reserve achieved a reasonable degree of credibility by the mid-1980s because of its willingness to bring inflation under control even if it involved adverse effects on the economy. However, it is not regarded as the most credible central bank among the industrialized countries even at this time. That distinction belongs to the Bundesbank and the Bank of Japan, both of which have earned a reputation for focusing on long-run price stability.

The Bank of Japan in particular shows how a central bank earns credibility. Figure 27-13 in Chapter 27 illustrated real output growth, inflation, and monetary growth in Japan from 1956 through 1987.

In the late 1960s and early 1970s the Bank of Japan expanded the money supply under pressure from the government to maintain a high growth rate of real output. Instead of increased output growth, however, expansionary monetary policy generated inflation that reached almost 30% in 1973. The Bank of Japan and the government recognized the failure of expansionary monetary policy to stimulate the economy and recognized that a lower monetary growth rate would be required to bring inflation down to acceptable levels. A tight monetary policy was imposed on the economy which happened to coincide with the first oil price increases and by 1975, inflation had been significantly reduced.

The Bank of Japan has continued to maintain a non-inflationary monetary growth rate, at least through the end of the 1980s, and has made it clear that price stability is the ultimate goal of central bank policy. More important, these announcements are followed by actions designed to maintain a steady and low inflation rate. As a result, Japan has had one of the most stable and lowest inflation rates in the world. To illustrate the commitment to price stability consider what happened during the second oil price shock of 1979–80. The Bank of Japan *raised* the discount rate from 3.5% in the first quarter of 1979 to a high of 9.0% in the second quarter of 1980 to restrain inflationary pressures. This was done partly to convince the public that the Bank of Japan was not going to try and offset the adverse effects of the oil price shock and depart from its long-run goal of price stability.

The price stabilization policy of the Bank of Japan has been an important precondition for the impressive real performance of the Japanese economy. The sustained output growth with only small fluctuations has made Japan the envy of industrial economies. Only West Germany has achieved a similar performance, and part of its success is also related to the successful price stabilization policy of the central bank.

---

monetary policy. Is there a way out of the time inconsistency problem so that monetary institutions can focus on price stability?

There is a solution. It revolves around establishing up-front central bank credibility and a reputation for price stability. Once this is done and the Federal Reserve adheres to such a policy period by period, the public will come to anticipate price stability in formulating economic contracts. In this way, the economy will achieve an equilibrium at a welfare level indicated in the upper left-hand corner of the payoff matrix. How does one establish credibility for price stability? This can be accomplished only by adhering to the goal of price stability at each decision state and not giving in to "special circumstances" of the decision period to deviate from the long-run goal of price stability.

An extreme solution would be to impose serious penalties on the central bank for failing to achieve price stability; for example, the members of the Board of Governors and Federal Reserve Open Market Committee would have their salaries reduced by one percentage point for every percentage point the inflation rate was above zero. Such a penalty approach would generate a zero inflation rate; however, it is difficult to imagine government subjecting itself to such penalties. In addition, the inflation rate is not determined solely by the monetary growth rate at any point in time.

Another extreme approach would be to constrain Federal Reserve actions by a rule that ensured price stability in the long run. Many economists have argued that the Federal Reserve should be required to establish a constant growth rate for the monetary base or some monetary aggregate and forget about discretionary monetary policy. In essence, the Federal Reserve would be replaced by a computer program. In the present state of knowledge about the economy and the need for the Federal Reserve to function frequently as a lender of last resort, the strict rules approach has won few advocates, although in late 1989, Congress did consider a bill to require the Federal Reserve to achieve a zero inflation rate over a specified period of time.

Short of intense penalties or inflexible rules, the Federal Reserve can overcome much of the time inconsistency problem by establishing a credible policy of price stability. This means that it must announce ahead of time that it will stick to noninflationary monetary growth no matter what shocks impact the economy. More important, the Federal Reserve follows upon the announced anti-inflationary policy even if it imposes adverse effects on the economy. If the Federal Reserve deviates from price stability policies because of special circumstances, the public comes to regard the Federal Reserve as lacking in credibility and reputation for price stability.

The Bottom Line: Has the Federal Reserve Become a Credible Central Bank?

The Federal Reserve's credibility for controlling inflation was at an all-time low in the late 1970s. Few were convinced by Federal Reserve arguments frequently made in the 1970s that it had lost control over the monetary aggregates because of financial innovation or that inflation was being caused by a series of nonmonetary shocks. The situation reached a crisis stage in late 1979 when inflation was in the high double-digit levels and the economy was on the verge of a serious breakdown. President Carter appointed Paul Volcker as the new chair of the Board of Governors in late 1979. At this point, the Federal Reserve announced a new price stabilization policy and even went so far as to accept responsibility for the past inflationary monetary growth. This was followed by an extremely tight monetary policy that induced the most severe recession on the U.S. economy since the Great Depression. That, more than any announcements of the Federal Reserve, convinced the public that the Federal Reserve was serious about controlling inflation. By the mid-1980s the Federal Reserve had earned back some of the credibility it had previously lost, and the new Chair of the Board as of 1988, Alan Greenspan, has continued to emphasize the importance of noninflationary monetary policy.

As of 1990 the Federal Reserve has done a credible job of controlling inflation. At the same time, doubts persist as to whether this will continue. The time inconsistency problem is real, and the longer the economy experiences price stability, the more it and the Federal Reserve forget the costs of bringing past inflation down. As time goes on, it becomes more likely that the Federal Reserve and the economy will be willing to accept a higher inflation rate. This is an open question for which there is no easy answer.

Key Points

1. Inflation is a continuous increase in the price level measured by a specific price index.

2. The inflation record of the United States in the post–World War II periods differs from that of the earlier period. Most of the price increases have occurred since 1950, suggesting that the Federal Reserve has an inflationary bias.

3. The effects of inflation depend on the degree to which prices are increasing and the degree to which inflation is anticipated. Hyperinflation is the most destructive form of inflation; however, the more common household variety of inflation also imposes costs on society. Even if inflation is anticipated and contracts are adjusted for inflation, inflation still imposes costs on society. Thus, price stability or a low inflation rate is a desirable goal for central bank policy.

4. Anticipated inflation has been estimated by statistical methods such as autoregressive models or by survey methods. These estimates suggest that a meaningful part of the actual inflation rate is unanticipated by the public, again a further reason why price stability or a low inflation rate is a desirable central bank goal.

5. Inflation is a monetary phenomenon in the sense that inflation can exist over the long run only if supported by an expanding money supply. This does not imply that there exists a one-to-one relationship between money and inflation. Lags in the effect of monetary policy on the inflation rate, nonmonetary shocks to the inflation rate, and changing definitions of the money supply all account for departures of the money growth rate and inflation at any point in time.

6. The Federal Reserve, as well as many other central banks, has an inflation bias for the following reasons: (a) accommodation of federal deficits and debt, (b) concern with orderly financial markets, (c) belief in a stable trade-off between inflation and unemployment, (d) susceptibility to political considerations, and (e) time inconsistency.

7. The time inconsistency problem offers a reasonable and generally accepted rationale for why central banks have an inflation bias. This has generated a lively debate over how best to structure the central bank and monetary policy to ensure that price stability is maintained.

8. In the 1980s the Federal Reserve earned credibility because of its efforts to bring inflation under control in the early 1980s and its continued focus on price stability. The Bank of Japan and the Bundesbank are probably the two most credible central banks in the world in terms of their commitment to price stability.

Key Terms

Adaptive anticipations hypothesis

Anticipated versus unanticipated inflation

Central bank credibility

Hyperinflation

Inflation

Inflation as a tax on money balances

Inflation bias of monetary policy

Measures of anticipated inflation

Money and inflation

Nonmonetary shocks and the inflation rate

Phillips curve

Prisoners' dilemma

Resource costs of adjusting to inflation

Social welfare function

Tax bracket creep

Time inconsistency

Questions

1. Explain why an oil price increase such as took place in 1974–75, 1979–80, and 1990 can increase the inflation rate in the short run but not in the long run.

2. Why does the acceptance that inflation in the long run is a monetary phenomenon explain only part of the reason for the existence of inflation in the post–World War II period?

3. The Bank of Japan has had an excellent record of price stability over the period from 1975 through 1990, and yet, it is far more dependent on the government than is the Federal Reserve. Is formal independence a necessary or sufficient condition for a noninflationary monetary policy?

4. Explain the concept of time inconsistency and why it suggests an inflationary bias to monetary policy.

5. Is the time inconsistency problem unique to monetary policy, or is it a problem applicable to a wide range of government policies?

6. Explain the differences between anticipated and unanticipated inflation. How does each affect the economy?

Suggested Readings

1. Armen A. Alchian and Benjamin Klein, "On a Correct Measure of Inflation," Part 1, *Journal of Money, Credit and Banking* (February 1973), 173–181. Problems of measuring the true inflation rate.

2. Alex Cukierman, "Central Bank Behavior and Credibility: Some Recent Theoretical Developments," *Review* (May 1986), 5–17. An excellent survey of the time inconsistency problem and central bank credibility. Read this together with Mullineaux and Taylor for a good overview of time inconsistency.

3. Michelle R. Garfinkel, "What Is an 'Acceptable' Rate of Inflation?—A Review of the Issues," *Review*, Federal Reserve Bank of St. Louis (July–August 1989), 3–15. Reviews the effects of inflation, Phillips curve, and costs of anti-inflation policy.

4. Frank D. Graham, *Exchange, Prices, and Production in Hyperinflation: Germany, 1920–1923* (New York: Russell & Russell, 1967). Originally published by Princeton University Press, 1930. A classic study of the German hyperinflation after World War I.

5. R. W. Hafer, "Does Dollar Depreciation Cause Inflation?" *Review*, Federal Reserve Bank of St. Louis (July–August 1989), 16–28. Demonstrates that the declining value of the dollar is like any other price shock in that it only temporarily changes the inflation rate.

6. Dennis W. Jansen, "Does Inflation Uncertainty Affect Output Growth? Further Evidence," *Review*, Federal Reserve Bank of St. Louis (July–August 1989), 43–54. Measures the impact of inflation uncertainty and contains an extensive reference list on the subject.

7. Donald J. Mullineaux, "Monetary Rules and Contracts: Why Theory Loses to Practice," *Business Review*, Federal Reserve Bank of Philadelphia (March–April 1985), 13–19. An overview of the arguments against imposing simple rules on a central bank to ensure price stability. Read this together with Cukierman and Taylor for a good overview of time inconsistency.

8. Anna J. Schwartz, "Secular Price Change in Historical Perspective," *Journal of Money, Credit and Banking*, 5 (February 1973), 243–269. An overview of the inflation process in the United States.

9. Zalman F. Shiffer, "Adjusting to High Inflation: The Israeli Experience," *Review*, Federal Reserve Bank of St. Louis (May 1986), 18–29. Israel has experienced very high inflation rates since the early 1970s. This article discusses how the economy has tried to control and adapt to high inflation.

10. John A. Tatom, "Federal Income Tax Reform in 1985: Indexation," *Review*, Federal Reserve Bank of St. Louis (February 1985), 5–12. Discusses the partial elimination of tax bracket creep.

11. Herb Taylor, "Time Inconsistency: A Potential Problem for Policymakers," *Business Review* (March–April 1985), 3–12. Readable version of time inconsistency. Read this in combination with Cukierman and Mullineaux and you gain a good overview of the subject.

12. Adrian W. Throop, "An Evaluation of Alternative Measures of Expected Inflation," *Economic Review*, Federal Reserve Bank of San Francisco (Summer 1988), 27–43.

13. Jai-Hoon Yang, "The Case for and Against Indexation: An Attempt at Perspective," *Review*, Federal Reserve Bank of St. Louis (October 1974), 2–11.

INDEX